# Letters of H. P. Lovecraft

## VOLUME 7

### LETTERS TO ROBERT BLOCH AND OTHERS

*Robert Bloch*

# H. P. LOVECRAFT

## LETTERS TO ROBERT BLOCH AND OTHERS

### EDITED BY DAVID E. SCHULTZ AND S. T. JOSHI

Hippocampus Press

New York

# Contents

Introduction .......................................................................................................... 7
**Letters**
   *To Robert Bloch* ................................................................................................ *19*
   *To Natalie H. Wooley* ..................................................................................... *186*
   *To Robert and Mrs. Elmer Nelson* ................................................................. *215*
   *To William F. Anger* ....................................................................................... *223*
   *To Kenneth Sterling* ........................................................................................ *247*
   *To Donald A. Wollheim* .................................................................................. *302*
   *To Wilson Shepherd* ........................................................................................ *345*
   *To Willis Conover, Jr.* ...................................................................................... *374*
**Appendix** ...................................................................................................... **423**
   *Robert Bloch* .................................................................................................... *423*
      A Visit with H. P. Lovecraft ......................................................................... 423
      Lilies .............................................................................................................. 425
      The Black Lotus ............................................................................................ 427
      How I Get My Inspiration ............................................................................ 432
      Milwaukee Youth Writes Horror Tales, Sells 'Em ...................................... 432
   *Natalie H. Wooley* ........................................................................................... *435*
      Admonition ................................................................................................... 435
      Dream Fantasy .............................................................................................. 435
      Antares .......................................................................................................... 435
      Avatar ............................................................................................................ 435
      The Alien ...................................................................................................... 436
      Flight ............................................................................................................. 436
      A Heavenly Tragedy ..................................................................................... 437
      Lines to Cleopatra ........................................................................................ 437
      Coward .......................................................................................................... 437
      Sailor's Child ................................................................................................. 438
      Western Night ............................................................................................... 438
      Mountain Trail .............................................................................................. 438
      End of the Trail ............................................................................................ 439
      Mountain Pool .............................................................................................. 440
      Sanctuary ....................................................................................................... 440
      Dream Tryst .................................................................................................. 440
      The Adventure Story .................................................................................... 440
      Is Criticism Necessary? ................................................................................. 441
      Have You a Hobby? ...................................................................................... 442
      "Tillicum" ...................................................................................................... 443
      The Dance ..................................................................................................... 444
      Reminiscense ................................................................................................. 445
      Spurs of Death .............................................................................................. 446

*Robert Nelson* .................................................................................................. *449*
   Night of Unrest ............................................................................................ 449
   Fragment ..................................................................................................... 449
   The Unremembered Realm ........................................................................... 449
   Below the Phosphor ..................................................................................... 449
   Dream-Stair ................................................................................................ 450
   Jorgas ......................................................................................................... 451
   Sable Revelry .............................................................................................. 452
   Under the Tomb .......................................................................................... 453
   Lost Excerpts .............................................................................................. 454
   Trilogy of Death .......................................................................................... 455
   The Weird Tale (A Dialogue) ....................................................................... 455
*William F. Anger* ............................................................................................. *456*
   Fantastic Bread & Butter; or, the Mystery of the Missing Authors .................. 456
   An Interview with E. Hoffmann Price ........................................................... 459
*Donald A. Wollheim* ........................................................................................ *463*
   Review of THE NECRONOMICON ............................................................ 464
   Allalieor ...................................................................................................... 463
   Umbriel ...................................................................................................... 464
   Pure Fantasy ............................................................................................... 465
   Howard Phillips Lovecraft ............................................................................ 467
   Editor's Preface [to "The Shadow out of Time"] ........................................... 467
   The Future of Publishing ............................................................................. 468
*Kenneth Sterling* ............................................................................................. *471*
   The Horror Element in Poe .......................................................................... 471
*Wilson Shepherd* ............................................................................................. *485*
   Death .......................................................................................................... 485
*Willis Conover, Jr.* ........................................................................................... *486*
   Observations and Otherwise ......................................................................... 486
   The Lost Chord ........................................................................................... 487
   The Spirits Mourn ....................................................................................... 488

**Chronology** ................................................................................................. **489**

**Glossary of Frequently Mentioned Names** ................................................. **495**

**Bibliography** ................................................................................................ **501**

**Index** ........................................................................................................... **533**

# Introduction

As we know, H. P. Lovecraft wrote many letters daily. His admirers and indeed the world at large are well aware of his enormous correspondence. The effort Lovecraft made to respond to each correspondent surely was considerable. One sees that an offhand comment, an idle, almost rhetorical, inquiry, or even a terse challenge often resulted in a long discursive reply from Lovecraft that must have taken hours to compose and possibly a fair amount of research on his part. Consider Willis Conover's awed response to a simple inquiry that he made: "My jaw was hanging open. Can you imagine asking a simple question like 'Where can I get a copy of the *Necronomicon?*' and then—at fifteen—being hit with all this?"[1] *This* being several lengthy explanatory paragraphs on all manner of ancient books. Compound a response such as that which Conover describes with the fact that Lovecraft asked every budding writer of weird fiction to see his or her work for comment and advice, and one can see that idle letter writing was not merely a lark for this man of letters but in fact hard work. Each story that he read—depending on the skill of the author—received suggestions for improvement, sometimes as general advice contained within a letter, sometimes as heavy rewriting under his pen. The published text of Robert Bloch's "Satan's Servants" with Lovecraft's comments and a facsimile reproduction of just one page of R. H. Barlow's "'Till A' the Seas'" show that Lovecraft labored over the apprentice work of his young constituents, to improve all the elements that make for good story-writing.

About the scope of his correspondence, Lovecraft wrote "I have some 51 or 52 regular correspondents, & perhaps 75 counting long-term occasionals. The list keeps growing, & only a very few drop off. Some are of 20 years' standing. If I ever adopt a more intensive working programme—as I may have to do—I shall have to train myself to write more briefly . . . . . although there is scarcely any correspondent whom I'd wish to drop. With me correspondence largely takes the place of conversation. I've found very few congenial persons in my own town, hence seldom do much conversing except when on visits."[2] Indeed, his "[List of Correspondents to Whom Postcards Have Been Sent]" contains seventy names. In his last few months, dying of cancer, Lovecraft observed: "I find my list has grown to 97 now—which surely calls for some pruning. It goes without saying that I appreciate your remarks on my overcrowded list—but how the hell can one get out of epistolary obligations without becoming snobbish & uncivil? But damn some of these kids that the

---

1. *LAL* 31.
2. HPL to Duane W. Rimel, 12 September 1934 (ms., JHL).

'fan mags' drag in!"[3] Lovecraft certainly enjoyed hearing from and assisting "the kids," but the task of replying to the ever-increasing number of fans must have been increasingly difficult given the state of his health.

Each young correspondent may have thought that he or she was the only person privileged to benefit from Lovecraft's editorial ministrations, yet in fact Lovecraft must have received many stories for his evaluation—and not merely from youngsters, as represented by the few in this book, but also from seasoned professionals, such as Clark Ashton Smith, August Derleth, and others. Lovecraft initially did not consider his correspondence with youth to be burdensome, as he explained to young R. H. Barlow:

> I enjoy seeing a new generation spring up & blossom out & repeat—with variations—the things which my generation did 25 or 30 years ago. In watching the spectacle one has a welcome momentary feeling of the renewal of one's own youth. My correspondents are of all ages—from 96 down to 16. One gains a certain pleasant cosmic sense of timelessness by being in touch with persons of every age—both older & younger—instead of merely with those of one's own age.[4]

But around the time that Lovecraft told Duane Rimel he had fifty regular correspondents, the Big Bang of science fiction fandom occurred, and innumerable youngsters soon fancied themselves fictioneers, poets, artists, and publishers. When they found Lovecraft to be an easy touch, he was assailed from all sides for letters or for contributions to their little magazines. One writer suggested that perhaps Lovecraft should welcome more correspondents, to which he replied: "As for *trying* to increase my list of correspondents—hell! I wish you'd tell me how to trim it down & keep it under control! The reason I always try to encourage young editors is that I think they need such encouragement at the outset. A very little help means a good deal to them at that age, & it doesn't cost very much to give it."[5]

There is no doubt that Lovecraft enjoyed writing and receiving letters, even as his list of correspondents grew. This volume bears out Lovecraft's sentiment as expressed above, for it comprises primarily letters to youths, all aspiring writers, poets, or publishers. Some approached Lovecraft because of their fondness for "weird" fiction. Many were newly active in the science fiction fandom of the day; others were amateur writers. In time, some abandoned their youthful hobby, but others turned hobbies into professional careers.

This volume of Lovecraft's *Collected Letters* comprises relatively small batches of letters written late in life to eight young individuals, from 1933 until his death less than four years later. It contains 160 letters and postcards.

---

3. HPL to R. H. Barlow, 3 January 193[7]; *O Fortunate Floridian* 393.
4. HPL to R. H. Barlow, 13 July 1933; *O Fortunate Floridian* 69.
5. HPL to DAW, 30 August 1936, p. 346.

Many of us would find it inconceivable to write by hand that many lengthy letters of substance, and not merely short, chatty emails, outside our daily jobs over a four-year period. (Lovecraft wrote nearly 100 letters to August Derleth *alone* during the same period, to say nothing of numerous other letters to some six dozen or so other correspondents.) The Chronology gives a sense of how often Lovecraft was writing to just these eight individuals week by week. When one recognizes that they are only a small fraction of his overall correspondence, one recognizes the sheer volume of letters that flowed from Lovecraft's pen to be staggering.

Robert Bloch (1917–1994) is probably the best known of the correspondents represented herein. He first encountered Lovecraft's work in *Weird Tales* in 1927, when he was only ten, but did not look up Lovecraft until 1933 when he was a student in high school at age sixteen with dreams of becoming a writer and a comedian. Bloch's early work was, as one can well imagine, somewhat florid and imitative of Lovecraft's; but with Lovecraft's guidance and encouragement, he eventually developed his own voice and before long became a professional writer of horror, suspense, detective, and science fiction. Lovecraft mentions seeing more than forty stories and poems from Bloch. Lovecraft's sincere effort to help his pupil develop a critical eye and ear for his own writing is apparent. Bloch matured rapidly under Lovecraft's tutelage. In time, he invented an analogue to Lovecraft's *Necronomicon*—Ludvig Prinn's *Mysteries of the Worm*—in "The Secret in the Tomb" (*WT*, May 1935), but it was Lovecraft who coined the Latin title, *De Vermis Mysteriis*. Bloch also created *The Cabala of Saboth*, the *Black Rites* of the mad priest Luveh-Keraph, and *Cultes des Goules* (often misattributed to August Derleth because its *fictional* author is the "Comte d'Erlette"). He wrote a playful "trilogy" with Lovecraft, comprising Bloch's "The Shambler from the Stars" (*WT*, September 1935), Lovecraft's "The Haunter of the Dark" (written November 1935; *WT*, December 1936), and Bloch's "The Shadow from the Steeple" (*WT*, September 1950). Lovecraft advised Bloch on his early tale "Satan's Servants" (written in early 1935; first published in *Something about Cats*), but does not appear to have written any prose in the story. Most of Bloch's Lovecraftian tales are collected in *Mysteries of the Worm* (1981; rev. ed. 1993). Bloch later turned to the genres of mystery and suspense, writing such notable novels as *The Scarf* (1947), *Psycho* (1959), *The Dead Beat* (1960), and many others. *Strange Eons* (1978) is a Lovecraftian pastiche. His autobiography, *Once Around the Bloch* (1993), discusses his early (and later) writing career and Lovecraft's profound effect on it.

Females were scarce in the horror crowd in the early 1930s. Well-fêted as Bloch may be, Natalie Hartley Wooley (11 November 1904–1973) of Rosedale, Kansas, is antipodally obscure. Kenneth W. Faig, Jr., has pointed out that "In the 1925 KS state census, Natalie Wooley, age 20, born KS, was recorded in the Kansas City KS household of her husband George H. Wooley, age 24, born MO, a sheep driver in the stockyards. In the 1930 U.S. census, their household was recorded in Kansas City MO on 8 April 1930."[6] Mrs. Wooley was about twenty-seven when she began corresponding with Lovecraft, and therefore the oldest of the correspondents in this group. Although she contacted Lovecraft through *Weird Tales*, her own verses and fiction are not primarily weird, as was the case with most of the other young writers who approached him. The following is the only scant nugget about her that the editors could find through cursory examination of publications in which she appeared:

> NATALIE HARTLEY WOOLEY, Kansas, is a member of both the National and United Amateur Press Associations and has contributed to *Kansas City Star, Kansas City Journal-Post, Marvel Tales, The Fantasy Fan,* and to The Christian Board of Publication periodicals. She wrote the lyrics for "Querida, a Spanish Serenade," a song which may be heard on the radio.[7]

Wooley professed to have "an intense love of outdoors, a sort of carryover from a childhood spent in the Pacific Northwest." Lovecraft says that Wooley was among his many recruits to the National Amateur Press Association (NAPA), which he reentered in the 1930s as a critic. Wooley published briefly in amateur journals in the 1930s, as the Bibliography attests, beginning around the time she first approached Lovecraft. Although Lovecraft coined jocular names for most of his young correspondents, he addressed her courteously in every letter as "Mrs. Wooley."

Lovecraft wrote often, and favorably, of her verses in various amateur journals, as in this early notice:

> A new voice in the National is that of Mrs. Natalie Hartley Wooley, whose brief, wistful lyrics strike one's fancy with singular sharpness through certain faint overtones subtly suggesting magical vistas and dim regions beyond the confines of daylight reality. "Western Night", in the Summer *Goldenrod,* has great charm and power; while "Flight", in the October *Sea Gull,* unites with its general elfin quality a poignant human pathos.[8]

Besides poetry, she also wrote short fiction and nonfiction. She was, with Maurice W. Moe, John Adams, and Lovecraft, a member of a round-robin correspondence circle, the Coryciani, devoted mainly to the criticism of poetry, although a surviving fragmentary letter from the group mentions in particular her essay, "Intimations—The Hand in the Dark." She seems to have ceased writing, or at least publishing, c. the mid-1930s. Two poems by her appeared in the 1950s—in a little magazine to which she had contributed twenty years previously. Mrs. Wooley had one son and four grandchildren. She married a second time, to Bill Ashburn. And that is all we know of Natalie Hartley Wooley.

---

6. "Lovecraft's 1937 Diary," *Lovecraft Annual* No. 6 (2012): 176.
7. Under "Who's New," *Kaleidograph,* 6, No. 9 (December 1934): 15.
8. "Bureau of Critics," *National Amateur* 56, No. 4 (June 1934). In *CE* 1.375.

Robert Nelson (1912–1935) lived only long enough to make a brief mark in the field. His verses and short fiction began to appear first in the *Fantasy Fan,* then in *Weird Tales.* But it was not long before Lovecraft wrote to Bloch, "You'll be sorry to hear of the death on July 22 of young Robert Nelson—author of sundry verses in W T & of 'Lost Excerpts' in the F F—after an illness of 17 days." The young poet died a day shy of his twenty-third birthday.[9]

Likewise, little is known of William F. Anger (1921–1982), who went by the name "Fred" and was a mere thirteen years of age when he began corresponding with Lovecraft. In a single offhanded reference in *The Immortal Storm,* Sam Moskowitz calls Anger "an important fan." Harry Warner, Jr., refers to Anger not at all in *All Our Yesterdays,* but both historians make brief mention of Anger's colleague Louis C. Smith. The scant bits we have been able to learn about Anger come primarily from Lovecraft's pen. When Anger corresponded with Lovecraft he lived in Berkeley, California, and he became acquainted with Lovecraft because of a shared interest in weird fiction. Lovecraft put Anger in touch with E. Hoffmann Price, and the two once visited fellow-Californian Clark Ashton Smith. Anger and Louis Smith published a short piece on Price in the *Fantasy Fan* (December 1934), but their contemplated edition of Lovecraft's *Fungi from Yuggoth* and an "index" to *Weird Tales* never got off the ground. Anger himself wrote "Phantastic Bread & Butter; or, the Mystery of the Missing Authors."[10] Anger's modest correspondence with Lovecraft yields little about him and his fan activities, and he dropped from sight shortly after Lovecraft's death. Presumably his association with Price accounts for why Lovecraft's letters to both of them (Price's only as photocopies) can be found at the same repository, the University of Minnesota.

Lovecraft's letters to Anger are in some ways typical because they discuss primarily the merits of current stories in *Weird Tales.* (A chain letter is an amusing exception to this.) They also show Lovecraft's willingness to ac-

---

9. Nelson's work has been gathered in *Sable Revelry: Poems, Sketches, Letters,* ed. Douglas A. Anderson (Marcellus, MI: Nodens Books, 2012).

10. HPL to Duane W. Rimel, 20 December 1936 (ms., JHL): "I noted Anger's 'muckraking' article in the recent issue [of the *Phantagraph*]. This article exaggerates considerably, although it does point to certain actual financial conditions which have alienated many writers. Of course, if these writers were primarily interested in weird fiction for its own sake, they would not be so easily led away by better economic arrangements in other fields—but as it happens, they are not essentially weirdists. Quinn never professed any aim save to make money, & Long, Price, Wandrei, & others are becoming increasingly like him. They go where the cash comes quickest—& that is not in W T. Of course Anger makes a mistake in attributing all decreased productivity to W T's financial policy. Actually, other reasons have slowed down many old-timers, including myself. As you probably read elsewhere in the same issue, Wright will have a personal reply to Anger in the next issue. The real truth will probably lie about half way betwixt what he will say & what Anger has said."

commodate young publishers in their ventures, and hint at the growing frustration toward the end of his life at seeing his work rejected or published in shoddy, error-riddled form.

In early 1935, Kenneth Sterling (1920–1995), who had been born in Baltimore, moved with his family to Providence, where he attended Classical High School. A fan of the science fiction pulps and a member of the Science Fiction League, the fourteen-year-old was already a published author. (His "The Brain-Eaters of Pluto" appeared in *Wonder Stories* for March 1934.) In early March, Sterling boldly called on Lovecraft at home and introduced himself, as Lovecraft recounts:

> But behold! One of the ambitious savants of Leedle Shoolie's [Julius Schwartz's] science-fiction gang has just been transferred to the ancient soil of Providence! One night last week I was reading the paper in my study when my aunt entered to announce (with a somewhat amused air) a caller by the name of Mr. Kenneth Sterling. Close on her heels the important visitor appeared . . . . in the person of a little Jew boy about as high as my waist, with unchanged childish treble & swarthy cheeks innocent of the Gillette's harsh strokes. He *did* have long trousers—which somehow looked grotesque upon so tender an infant. It appears that he is one of the endless kid followers of *Wonder, Astounding,* F M, &c.—who had seen some of my stuff & learned my address from Hornig. A typical N.Y. Yid—but his papa (a Harvard graduate, & evidently quite a brilliant scion of Moses' line) has just been made manager of a local fur store—so Leedle Kenneth iss ah Providentian now, & a star pupil by der Classical High School. And oy, vhat ah shild! Vhat ah shild! If they all come as precocious as this, I don't wonder that Hitler is afraid they'll juggle the shirts off the German people! Damme if the little imp didn't talk like a man of 30—correcting all the mistakes in the current science yarns, reeling off facts & figures a mile a minute, & displaying the taste & judgment of a veteran. He's already sold a story to *Wonder* (& *collected* from Hugo the Rat!), & is bubbling over with ideas. Two of his story plots are really splendid. Others in his family have reviewed books for the N.Y. *Herald Tribune* & written for various "slicks". And now he is prepared to conquer ancient Providentium! He vants he should organise ah branch by der Science Fiction League here, &c. &c. I gave him some duplicate F F's & other items, & he says he's going to call again. Hope he won't prove a nuisance—but I wouldn't for the world discourage him in his endeavours. He really does seem like an astonishingly promising brat—& means to become a research biologist.[11]

Lovecraft repeated this chronicle in several other letters. It seems unkind—perhaps because he was taken aback by the youth who so brazenly showed up on his doorstep, in an area where Lovecraft had said there were very few fam-

---

11. HPL to R. H. Barlow, [16 March 1935], *O Fortunate Floridian* 216–17. See Sterling's own charming account of his visit in "Cavern's Measureless to Man."

ilies not of original New England Yankee stock. But even so, Lovecraft was much impressed with the boy's precocity and cheerfully continued the association. In fact, Sterling's father called on Lovecraft at home several times.

In January 1936, Sterling produced a draft of "In the Walls of Eryx" in 6,000 to 8,000 words. He had adopted the idea of the invisible maze from Edmond Hamilton's story, "The Monster-God of Mamurth" (*WT*, August 1926), one of few Hamilton stories that Lovecraft liked, concerning an invisible building in the Sahara Desert. Lovecraft rewrote the story ("in very short order," Sterling declares), lengthening it considerably.[12] Sterling's account suggests that the extant version is entirely Lovecraft's prose, but Lovecraft surely tried to preserve as much of Sterling's writing, and certainly his ideas, as possible. Sterling submitted the story to *Weird Tales* shortly after it was written, but it was rejected as being too long. Apparently he then submitted it to *Astounding Stories, Blue Book, Argosy, Wonder Stories,* and perhaps *Amazing Stories* (all these names, except the last, are crossed out on a sheet prefacing the typescript). Sterling resubmitted the story to *Weird Tales* following Lovecraft's death, and it was published in October 1939 as (at Lovecraft's insistence) "By Kenneth Sterling and H. P. Lovecraft." Sterling was paid $120, half of which he gave to Lovecraft's surviving aunt, Annie E. P. Gamwell. In Lovecraft's surviving correspondence, there is but a single mention of the story, and even then, not by name: "Young Sterling was here last month, & I helped him with a story laid in Venus—involving a maze of invisible crystal. The kid grows cleverer as time passes!"[13] In the tale, the authors made amusing in-jokes regarding certain mutual colleagues: the initials of the name Kenton J. Stanfield, narrator of the tale, are Sterling's own; sificlighs = Science Fiction League, to which Sterling belonged; farnoth-flies = editor Farnsworth Wright of *Weird Tales;* ugrats = Hugo the Rat, Lovecraft's sobriquet for editor Hugo Gernsback of *Wonder Stories;* effjay weeds and wriggling akmans = Forrest J Ackerman; tuckahs = Bob Tucker; darohs = Jack Darrow, these latter three being well-known fans. Some jokes surely are Lovecraft's, as they resemble the outlandish character names he devised for "The Battle That Ended the Century" (1934).

Sterling wrote little other fiction. His "The Bipeds of Bjhulhu" (*Wonder Stories,* February 1936) won second place in a contest based on the cover of the July 1935 *Wonder Stories.* The title presumably is a nod to Lovecraft's Cthulhu, but Lovecraft makes no note of this in his correspondence. Sterling had hoped to revive the defunct *Fantasy Fan* but demurred when learning of the expense incurred in publishing the late fanzine.

Sterling began attendance at Harvard in the fall of 1936, graduated from there in 1940, received a medical degree at Johns Hopkins, and later became a clinical professor of medicine at the Columbia University College of Physi-

---

12. Kenneth Sterling, "Caverns Measureless to Man" [1976]; in *LR* 375–78.
13. HPL to August Derleth, 11 February 1936; *Essential Solitude* 725.

cians and Surgeons, and also a specialist in thyroid diseases. His research advanced knowledge of how thyroid hormones affect human metabolism. He wrote a brief memoir of Lovecraft, "Lovecraft and Science," then the more substantial "Caverns Measureless to Man," in which he urged that Lovecraft be "remembered as a scholar and thinker as well as an author."

Donald A[llen] Wollheim (1914–1990), science fiction fan, was twenty-one when he first wrote Lovecraft. His first story, "The Man from Ariel," appeared in the *Wonder Stories* (January 1934) when he was nineteen. He was but one of dozens of editors of the burgeoning crop of fan magazines, and the only correspondent represented herein (aside from Kenneth Sterling, who lived briefly in Providence), who met Lovecraft in person. In 1935, Wollheim took over the *Bulletin* of the Terrestrial Fantascience Guild, previously edited by Wilson Shepherd, and renamed it the *Phantagraph*. It is something of a surprise when Wollheim informs us "*The Phantagraph* was always edited with him [Lovecraft] in mind. When selecting material for an issue, I always thought 'would HPL approve of this?'" Lovecraft contributed to it a handful of sonnets from *Fungi from Yuggoth* and the essays "Robert Ervin Howard: 1906–1936" (August 1936) and "The Weird Work of William Hope Hodgson" (February 1937). A letter Lovecraft had written to Duane W. Rimel (28 September 1935) appeared anonymously as "What's the Trouble with Weird Fiction?" (February 1937). Wollheim also coedited, with Shepherd, the sole issue of *Fanciful Tales* (Fall 1936), containing Lovecraft's "The Nameless City." Wollheim continued to publish Lovecraft's work in the *Phantagraph* after his death. He also published a Lovecraft sonnet in the *Science Fiction Bard*.

Unlike many of the budding fan publishers, Wollheim, the founder of the Futurians and the Fantasy Amateur Press Association, made a career of publishing science fiction. He became a distinguished science fiction and fantasy editor (*The Pocket Book of Science-Fiction* [1943]; *The Portable Novels of Science* [1945]; *Avon Fantasy Reader* [1947–52; 18 volumes]; *Terror in the Modern Vein* [1955]), was author of numerous science fiction tales for young adults, a long-time editor of Ace's science fiction line (1952–71), editor of the long-running *World's Best Science Fiction* annual anthologies, and founder and editor of DAW Books (1972–85). His "unauthorized" publication of J. R. R. Tolkein's *Lord of the Rings* trilogy in paperback launched the modern fantasy publication movement.

Wollheim may be second only to August Derleth in championing Lovecraft's work. Between 1947 and 1952 he published a Lovecraft story in eight different issues of *The Avon Fantasy Reader*. In 1947, he issued eleven stories from Avon in *The Lurking Fear*, which went through several printings in the U.S., Canada, and England (as *Cry Horror!*) through 1960. He also included Lovecraft stories in his anthologies *Terror in the Modern Vein* (1955) and *The Macabre Reader* (1959). But most significant perhaps was Wollheim's recognition that Lovecraft was primarily a science fiction writer and his inclusion of

"The Shadow out of Time" in *The Viking Portable Novels of Science* a scant eight years after Lovecraft's death.

The Viking Portable Library was intended to give readers—primarily soldiers serving in the war—not merely a book by an author, but a broad overview, or library, of an author's work. It also had the goal of presenting "a considerable quantity of widely popular reading in a volume so small that it can conveniently be carried and read in places where a book of ordinary format would be a hindrance." The first title was *As You Were: A Portable Library of American Prose and Poetry Assembled for Members of the Armed Forces and the Merchant Marines*, published in March 1943. Other titles swiftly followed, primarily of American authors, in time including work from around the world. Astonishingly, in the first year of the line, it published *Six Novels of the Supernatural* (1944) edited by Edward Wagenknecht. Perhaps the appearance of this title inspired Wollheim to bring to Viking his *Portable Novels of Science*, fifteenth in the series. (The book was preceded by volumes of Steinbeck, Dorothy Parker, Hemingway, Shakespeare, Whitman, Poe, and Fitzgerald.) The book does not contain the usual fare from the science fiction pulp magazines of the day, but such now classic items from the mainstream as *The First Men in the Moon* (H. G. Wells), *Before the Dawn* (John Taine), and *Odd John* (Olaf Stapledon). It does not appear that Lovecraft ever read Taine, but he had high regard for the work of Stapledon and Wells, and would have been pleased to be in such august company. Lovecraft's story technically *is* from a pulp magazine but not the likes of *Wonder Stories* and its ilk; and his science fiction was unlike the works typically published in so humble an arena as the pulp magazines. Readers' letters to the editor of *Astounding* howled in complaint that Lovecraft's atmospheric pieces were not at all like the action-packed fare to which they were accustomed.

In 1945, when Edmund Wilson callously dismissed Lovecraft and his work,[14] Wollheim boldly published "The Shadow out of Time" shoulder to shoulder, not with the pulpmeisters of the day, but with the titans of literary science fiction. These were not pulp hacks like Edmond Hamilton, Ray Cummings, and E. E. "Doc" Smith, but established literary figures. In other words, to be included in the Viking book was a very big deal—posthumously, of course, but a big deal none the less.

Wollheim's associate Wilson Shepherd (1917–1985) was a printer and publisher in Oakman, Alabama. Lovecraft had first heard of Shepherd (then age fifteen) in 1932 from R. H. Barlow, who claimed Shepherd was trying to bamboozle him in an exchange of some pulp magazines. Lovecraft's somewhat comical summation of the situation, "Correspondence between R. H. Barlow and Wilson Shepherd," attempts to unsnarl the misunderstanding. In 1936, Lovecraft himself heard directly from Shepherd, who was now assisting

14. "Tales of the Marvellous and the Ridiculous." *New Yorker* 21, No. 41 (24 November 1945): 100, 103–4, 106.

Donald A. Wollheim in publishing the *Phantagraph*. The two also conceived of a semi-professional magazine, *Fanciful Tales* (Fall 1936), which contained a severely misprinted version of Lovecraft's "The Nameless City." Shepherd was also attempting to write poetry. Lovecraft slightly touched up an apparently unpublished poem called "Death," and more exhaustively revised a poem called "Wanderer's Return," published in the *Literary Quarterly* (Winter 1937). Wollheim and Shepherd printed Lovecraft's sonnet "Background" (*Fungi from Yuggoth* XXX) as a broadside for his forty-sixth birthday (it purports to be Volume 47, No. 1 of *The Lovecrafter*). After Lovecraft's death Shepherd printed *A History of the Necronomicon* under the imprint of the Rebel Press (1937) for circulation through the American Amateur Press Association.

Willis Conover, Jr. (1920–1996), who corresponded with Lovecraft for a scant eight months, may well have been the last person Lovecraft wrote to, even if only three brief sentences and a few notes scrawled on a postcard received from Conover. (Those lines may be the most heartbreaking Lovecraft ever wrote.) Like so many of Lovecraft's younger correspondents, Conover was a weird fiction fan, a lad of only fifteen, who hoped to publish his own fanzine. His was to be the *Science-Fantasy Correspondent*, for which Lovecraft provided "Homecoming" (a sonnet from *Fungi from Yuggoth*), which appeared in the first issue (November–December 1936). Lovecraft's poem "In a Sequester'd Providence Churchyard Where Once Poe Walk'd" appeared in the March–April 1937 issue. Conover himself wrote and published a few brief items in the magazine. Late in 1936, Conover expressed his intention to resume the serialization of "Supernatural Horror in Literature" from the point at which it had ceased in the *Fantasy Fan;* accordingly, Lovecraft prepared a synopsis of the earlier segments. But Conover never got as far as publishing "Supernatural Horror in Literature," nor the synopsis, nor the celebrated portrait of Lovecraft as an eighteenth-century gentleman, which he commissioned from Virgil Finlay. The latter appeared on the cover of the May–June 1937 issue of *Amateur Correspondent*, Corwin F. Stickney's successor to *Science-Fantasy Correspondent*. In part as a result of Lovecraft's death, Conover lost his interest in weird fiction for many years.

It was Conover who sent Lovecraft a rather macabre Christmas gift—a skull taken from an Indian mound not far from Conover's home. Had Conover known that Lovecraft would be dead in three months from the cancer he suffered from, Conover might have thought better of sending his grim present. One can only wonder what Lovecraft himself thought, but he described the gift with fanciful gusto (see p. 183) in letters to correspondents.

For much of his career, Conover worked as a broadcaster with the Voice of America. It was not until 1974 that he finally published the condensed initial part of Lovecraft's essay as a booklet, *Supernatural Horror in Literature as Revised in 1936*. Then in 1975 he published his exquisitely designed memoir, *Lovecraft at Last,* containing extracts of his letters from Lovecraft cast not chronologically but in a conversational mode, and much other interesting matter. The effect of Lovecraft's death on Conover is conveyed poignantly in both words and images—in what is said, and in what is not. Conover recommenced the *Science-Fantasy Correspondent* in a much more ambitious format in 1975, but it saw only one large issue that contained Kenneth Sterling's fine memoir, "Caverns Measureless to Man," along with extracts from a letter by Lovecraft to Clark Ashton Smith.

*Lovecraft at Last* appeared the same year as L. Sprague de Camp's *Lovecraft: A Biography*. Although *Lovecraft at Last* covered only the last eight months of Lovecraft's life, and then in a somewhat artificial way (because of the conversational tone that Conover wished to evoke), it rings far truer as an accurate portrait of H. P. Lovecraft and the profound effect he had on others, achieved only through the mails. We do not have many accounts of the influence Lovecraft had on his youthful disciples, but perhaps Willis Conover speaks for them all when he states: "I have long regretted that all Lovecraft ever knew of me was unawakened and immature. Neither reality nor dreams had qualified me for discourse with him. I cannot imagine why he gave me his time. I wish he could have known how his words to me would shape my life."[15]

—DAVID E. SCHULTZ
S. T. JOSHI

## *A Note on the Texts*

This edition consolidates the contents of *H. P. Lovecraft: Letters to Robert Bloch* (August 1993) and *H. P. Lovecraft: Letters to Robert Bloch—Supplement* (October 1993). The reader is referred to Bloch's autobiography *Once Around the Bloch* (1993) for additional information about his correspondence with Lovecraft.

The letters and postcards to Robert Bloch, Wilson Shepherd, Donald A. Wollheim, and William F. Anger derive virtually entirely from autograph manuscripts. Letters 2, 4, 8, 10, 12, 17, 43, 48, 53–55, 61–63, 65, and 67 to Robert Bloch are held at the John Hay Library, Brown University, as are the letters to Wilson Shepherd. The letters to William F. Anger are among the Howard Phillips Lovecraft Correspondence (Mss 46), University of Minnesota Libraries, Minneapolis MN. The letters to Robert Nelson derive from images posted on the Internet. The letters to Donald A. Wollheim are owned by Betsy Wollheim and are printed with her permission. Copies of Lovecraft's letters and postcards to Willis Conover, Jr., and a photo of Conover, were obtained from the University of North Texas Music Library, the repository holding Conover's papers. The letters to Natalie H. Wooley and Kenneth J. Sterling derive primarily from the Arkham House transcripts.

Except for notes obviously pertaining to type of manuscript, postmarks, postscripts, enclosures, and a few corrections, square brackets within the text of

---

15. *LAL* xxv.

Lovecraft's letters are his own. The letters are presented with as little alteration as possible, and the editors have retained Lovecraft's idiosyncrasies of usage and spelling. No omission has knowingly been made in the text. The ellipses in the letters to the letters to Kenneth Sterling are those of the original transcriber.

The writings of Lovecraft's correspondents included in the Appendix are meant to be representative, not exhaustive. The same can be said for items cited in the bibliography.

*Acknowledgments*

The editors wish to thank Gregory Belt, Robert Bloch, Leslie Crabtree, Sean Donnelly, Alistair Durie, Stefan Dziemianowicz, Kenneth W. Faig, Jr., Maristella Feustle, Music Special Collections Librarian of the University of North Texas, Christopher Geissler of the John Hay Library, Brown University, Donovan K. Loucks, Charles Lovecraft, Eileen McNamara, Steve Miller, Christopher O'Brien, Robert M. Price, Peter Ruber, Sara A Stilley, University of California–Riverside Library, and James Woodruff. We are particularly grateful to Paul La Farge for providing scans and a transcript of the letters to Donald A. Wollheim.

*Abbreviations*

| | |
|---|---|
| AHT | Arkham House transcripts |
| ALS | autograph letter, signed |
| A.Ms. | autograph manuscript |
| ANS | autograph note (postcard), signed |
| CAS | Clark Ashton Smith |
| *CE* | *Collected Essays* (2004–06; 5 vols.) |
| *CF* | *Collected Fiction* (2014; 3 vols.) |
| DAW | Donald A. Wollheim |
| *FF* | *Fantasy Fan* |
| *FM* | *Fantasy Magazine* |
| HPL | H. P. Lovecraft |
| JHL | John Hay Library, Brown University |
| *LAL* | H. P. Lovecraft and Willis Conover, *Lovecraft at Last* (1975) |
| *LL* | S. T. Joshi, *Lovecraft's Library: A Catalogue* (2002; rev. ed. 2012) |
| NAPA | National Amateur Press Association |
| NHW | Natalie H. Wooley |
| RB | Robert Bloch |
| *SFC* | *Science-Fantasy Correspondent* |
| *SL* | *Selected Letters: 1911–1937* (1965–76; 5 vols.) |
| TLS | typed letter, signed |
| T.Ms. | typed manuscript |
| WC | Willis Conover, Jr. |
| WFA | William F. Anger |
| *WT* | *Weird Tales* |

# Letters to Robert Bloch

[1]    [ALS]

April 22, 1933

Dear Mr. Bloch:—

    Your very flattering note has just been forwarded to me by *Weird Tales*, & I am indeed pleased to learn of your favourable opinion of my work. Possibly you will be glad to know that a new tale of mine, "The Dreams in the Witch-House", is scheduled for the July W.T., & that my "Festival" will also be reprinted soon. I have just finished a long sequel to "The Silver Key" in collaboration with E. Hoffmann Price—but it has not yet been submitted to the magazine.[1]

    Now regarding copies of my tales—if it is *permanent* copies which you are seeking, I regret to say that I can't be of any help, since my only duplicates are constantly used lending-copies almost on the point of disintegration. When some of these wear out I shall have no duplicates at all\*—though others have been copied for me by kindly persons to whom they have been lent.

    However—if the *loan* of any of my old tales would do you any good, I'll be glad to send along tattered copies without any obligation of especial haste in returning. I can supply in this temporary way all but a few of my efforts. Enclosed is a list on which you can check off, in pencil, any stories which you would like me to lend. I don't quite gather from your letter whether the stories which you say you "know I have written" are ones which you *have read & would like to own,* or ones which you *have not read at all.* If the latter is the case, I can supply the primary deficiency in short order by means of a loan.

    As for permanent copies—a few of my things have been printed in anthologies, hence *may* be obtainable if one is willing to lay out the price of a whole book for each story. "Erich Zann" is in Dashiell Hammett's "Creeps by Night", published by the John Day Co. ("Cthulhu" is in Harré's "Beware After Dark", but you say you have that tale.) "The Rats in the Walls" is in "Switch on the Light" (one of the Selwyn & Blount "Not at Night" series published in London & probably obtainable for a dollar each through the Argus Book Shop of Chicago). Other tales of mine in Selwyn & Blount anthologies are "The Horror at Red Hook" in "You'll Need a Night Light", & "Pickman's Model" in "By Daylight Only". It is possible that "The Picture in the House" may appear in an anthology, for E. Hoffmann Price & W. Kirk Mashburn have included it in one they are trying to get published. However,

---

\*I hate typing so bitterly that I simply can't bring myself to make copies of my things.

the latest news from this venture is a rejection from the Thomas Y. Crowell Co. Another possibility is the issuance of my "Shunned House" as a small brochure by itself.[2]

I see by your citations that you have done some pretty classic weird reading. Do you know the work of M. R. James, the few weird tales by Walter de la Mare, the early fantastic writings (so different from his later stuff!) of Robert W. Chambers, & the dreamlike & varicoloured weavings of Lord Dunsany? If not, you have something ahead of you. Also—are you familiar with the so-called "Gothic" novels of the later 18th & early 19th centuries—Mrs. Radcliffe's "Udolpho", Lewis's "Monk", Maturin's "Melmoth", &c? Some years ago I wrote an article on the history of the weird tale, mentioning the titles of things which had particularly impressed me.[3] If you'd like to see this as a guide to weird reading I might be able to dig up a duplicate to lend you. I could also lend some of the books themselves if you can't get them at libraries—I have a few weird books, although my library isn't as strong in that line as I wish it could be. The best library of weird stuff which I know of is that of H. Warner Munn, Route 1, Athol, Mass.

By the way—you seem to have so much knowledge of me (that I live in Providence, what my full name is, & that Long is a friend of mine) that I am led to wonder whether you are a pupil of my good old friend Maurice W. Moe in the English department of West Division High School. If so, give him my regards when you see him! Wisconsin—& adjacent parts of the Northwest—form a rather fertile soil for weird writers. Possibly you know that August W. Derleth lives at Sauk City, while Donald Wandrei (though now in N.Y. for a time) lives in St. Paul, Minn.

Incidentally—have you attempted any weird writing of your own? If so, I'd like to see a specimen some day. I wrote a good deal at your age, though my stuff was not as good as that of other sixteen-year-olds whom I have since noticed. Years later I destroyed almost everything which I wrote in my teens.

Again regretting that I cannot supply *permanent* copies of my stuff, but assuring you of my pleased readiness to *lend* any story which you may wish to see, I am,

> With best wishes,
> Yrs most cordially & sincerely—
> H P Lovecraft

P.S. Don't let this address sink too deeply into your mind, for I fear that financial circumstances will compel me to change it within a month

[T.Ms.⁴]

## Tales by H. P. Lovecraft
### (dates are of writing, not publication)

The Tomb (1917)
Dagon (1917)
Psychopompos (in verse—1917–1918)
Polaris (1918)
Beyond the Wall of Sleep (1919)
The White Ship (1919)
The Doom that came to Sarnath (1919)
The Statement of Randolph Carter (1919)
The Terrible Old Man (1920)
The Tree (1920)
The Cats of Ulthar (1920)
The Temple (1920)
Arthur Jermyn (1920)
Celephaïs (1920)
From Beyond (1920)
~~Nyarlathotep (1920)~~
The Picture in the House (1920)
The Nameless City (1921)
The Moon-Bog (1921)
The Quest of Iranon (1921)
Herbert West—Reanimator (1921–1922)  X
The Outsider (1921)
The Other Gods (1921)
The Music of Erich Zann (1921)  X
Hypnos (1922)  X
The Hound (1922)
The Lurking Fear (1922)
The Rats in the Walls (1923)
The Unnamable (1923)
The Festival (1923)
The Shunned House (1924)
The Horror at Red Hook (1925)
He (1925)
In the Vault (1925)
Cool Air (1926)
The Call of Cthulhu (1926)
Pickman's Model (1926)
The Silver Key (1926)

The Strange High House in the Mist (1926)
The Dream-Quest of Unknown Kadath (1926–27)  #
The Case of Charles Dexter Ward (1927)  #
The Colour out of Space (1927)
The Dunwich Horror (1928)
The Whisperer in Darkness (1930)
At the Mountains of Madness (1931)
The Shadow over Innsmouth (1931)
The Dreams in the Witch House (1932)
Thru the Gates of the Silver Key (1933)

#—these are short novels—never typed, & therefore not in lending shape at present.

X—no lendable copies just now.

> Check off the ones you want to see & return this list. I'll gradually send you all those which are in mailable shape.

*Notes*

1. "Through the Gates of the Silver Key."
2. For the story of *The Shunned House* see RB 2, n. 8.
3. All authors mentioned are discussed in "Supernatural Horror in Literature" (1925–27).
4. This list may have been typed by R. H. Barlow. The last two titles have been written in by hand.

[2]     [ALS]

> 10 Barnes St.,
> Providence, R.I.,
> April 27, 1933

My dear Mr. Bloch:—

Your letter of the 24th proved highly interesting, & I was very glad to learn more about yourself & your activities. Judging by your school activities, & by the variety of your other interests, you have great reason to be proud of the abilities which sixteen brief years have brought you; & I trust that your future progress may be commensurate. Wisconsin seems to be very favourable soil for precocious brilliancy, since at least two other Sons of the Badger whom I know began as infant wonders—young Derleth, who began contributing to W.T. at seventeen, & my now older friend Alfred Galpin of Appleton (once a pupil of my Milwaukee friend Moe), who at 16 or 17 was a living encyclopaedia of literature & philosophy, & who now (at 31) holds a French instructorship at Lawrence College besides being a musical composer of no mean attainments (a pupil of the late Vincent d'Indy[1] & others in Paris). Incidentally, I think you'll like Moe if you meet him. He lives at 1034 N. 23d St, & has two brilliant sons of collegiate age. He is a native of Milwaukee & a graduate of the U. of Wis. in 1904.

So it was from O'Brien that you heard about me.[2] It is so long since he has listed me that I had almost forgotten about his annual. Yes—I've heard that the current O. Henry mentions my "Strange High House",[3] although I haven't seen a copy. Long is a very brilliant young man of 31, whom I have known since he was your age. He lives with his parents at 230 W. 97th St., New York City, & I usually visit him once or twice a year. Glad you appreciate Clark Ashton Smith, who lives in Auburn, California, & is one of my best correspondents, although I've never met him personally. He is a fantastic poet & pictorial artist as well as story-writer, & was a protege of the late George Sterling. Just now he is issuing a booklet of 6 splendid short stories which W.T. has rejected as too fantastic.[4] You really ought to have this—it is obtainable from the author at a price of 25¢. Address Box 385. Auburn is a small village in the picturesque country between Sacramento & the Nevada line—within sight of some delightful mountains. Smith—whose age is 40—lives in a cottage outside the compact part of the village with his aged parents. Wandrei is a bright young fellow of 24—lately an instructor in the U. of Minn. but now seeking his literary fortune in N.Y. He has several times visited me. Price is a brilliant chap of 35—a West Pointer & ex army officer, also with business experience, who comes from Chicago but now lives in New Orleans. I saw a good deal of him a year ago, when I spent over a fortnight in N.O. Seabury Quinn is 46 years old, & although a lawyer is now the editor of an undertaker's trade journal—quite an occupation for a weird writer! He lives in Brooklyn, N.Y., where I met him a couple of years ago. Robert E. Howard is a most unusual character—the son of a physician in the wild & woolly, rip-roaring West Texas country, which is actually much *more* like the sanguinary West of cheap fiction than we commonly realise. Howard is 27, & is probably the greatest living authority on the history & traditions of the Southwest, & the lives of America's noted outlaws. He is a burly, athletic chap fonder of fighting than of literature, & possessed of the curious belief that primitive barbarism is a more desirable sort of social organisation than civilisation. His letters have a greater literary value than his tales. Hugh B. Cave is a Rhode Islander—living in Pawtucket, just north of Providence—although I don't know him beyond the exchange of a few notes. The late Henry S. Whitehead was toward the close of his life one of my best friends. In 1931 I paid him a three-weeks' visit in Dunedin. He was one of the most fascinating, versatile, & altogether admirable persons I have ever known.

You will find M. R. James a revelation. He starts out in a familiar, homely, commonplace style—& then springs something! There is a new one-volume edition of his collected tales on the market.[5] Of his work I like best

"The Treasure of Abbot Thomas" & "Count Magnus." Weird writing is only an avocation with him—he is provost of Eton College, & an antiquary of wide fame. Rather like James is H. R. Wakefield, whose book of short tales, "They Return at Evening" is worth reading. And for weird *novels*, don't miss "Witch Wood" by John Buchan & "The Place Called Dagon" by Herbert Gorman. Later on—when I get settled after the hellish moving orgy which looms ahead—I'll send you a list of the weird volumes in my library,[6] & will be glad to lend by mail any items unobtainable in Milwaukee. Also, I'll send a copy of that sketch of mine on the history of horror-fiction. The best published treatise on supernatural fiction—or parts of it—are Birkhead's "The Tale of Terror", Railo's "The Haunted Castle", & Scarborough's "Supernatural in Modern English Fiction."[7]

As for loans of my own stuff—here are the first few on your list, with the exception of "The Shunned House", which is just now lent to Derleth. If this latter tale appears in booklet form (the vicissitudes of its possible publication form a story in themselves)[8] I shall certainly see that you have a permanent copy. Of the tales enclosed, "He" is without doubt the poorest. "The Picture in the House" is the first tale in which I used the imaginary town of Arkham, Mass. In a way, "Arkham" may be considered as a sort of modified version of *Salem,* while "Kingsport" roughly corresponds to *Marblehead.* I find the lore & colour of my native soil a very powerful & fascinating influence, hence tend to give my tales an emphatic geographical background. I am by nature an antiquarian of lifelong enthusiasm, with a curious sense of kinship with the 18th century. My chief hobby is colonial architecture, & my chief pastime is visiting various ancient towns where strong traces of the past linger in the houses & streets. Providence itself is very quaint—the steep hill on which I live having kept one section free from commercial exploitation—& I dare say its colonial doorways & steeples had much to do with the formation of my tastes. I have chosen as the design for my bookplate a typical Old Providence doorway—as the enclosed specimen illustrates.[9] However, certain smaller towns are still more redolent of antiquity—Quebec (a French walled town with ancient houses & silvered belfries which utterly repudiates the present), Portsmouth, N.H., Newburyport, Salem, Marblehead, & Plymouth, Mass., Newport, Bristol, Warren, & Wickford, R.I., Farmington & Guilford, Conn., Kingston, N.Y., Germantown, Pa., Annapolis, Md., Fredericksburg, Williamsburg, & Yorktown, Va., Charleston, S.C. (with suggestions of subtropical influence in its tiled, stuccoed, & veranda'd houses), & Natchez, Miss., being veritable living pages from bygone centuries. And the charm of St. Augustine, Fla.—with houses as old as 1571, 1580, & 1591—is past description. For me no pleasure is half so keen as the absorption of this kind of archaic atmosphere—& I dare say a goodly amount of this predilection crops out in my fictional attempts. I have never had the good luck to live in one of the ancient houses I so greatly love to dream & write about, although there is a possibility that my coming move will take me into one. If so, half the pangs of moving will be assuaged by the eminent appropriateness of the new setting.

What you say of my stories pleases me exceedingly—though I grow more & more conscious of the shortcomings of my attempts. They do not reach the really accomplished level I would like to attain, & I rather doubt whether they ever will. I fear that cheap magazines like W.T. have influenced my style more than I used to realise—though I have always striven against such influences. In 1931 the house of Putnam asked to see a number of my stories with a view to possible book publication, but the final decision was adverse.[10] I now greatly doubt whether I shall ever have a published book to my credit. Of all my tales I like best "The Colour Out of Space", with "The Music of Erich Zann" as a second choice. Since 1927 I have been trying to experiment with improvements in style, though relapses have been frequent.

It was with the keenest interest & pleasure that I read your two brief horror-sketches; whose rhythm & atmospheric colouring convey a very genuine air of unholy immanence & nameless menace, & which strike me as promising in the very highest degree. I think you have managed to create a dark tension & apprehension of a sort all too seldom encountered in weird fiction, & believe that your gift for this atmosphere-weaving will serve you in good stead when you attempt longer & more intricately plotted pieces. That you have a gift for plot seems indisputable in view of the extremely clever climactic revelation in "The Gallows." Of course, these productions are not free from the earmarks of youth. A critic might complain that the colouring is laid on too thickly—too much *overt inculcation* of horror as opposed to the *subtle, gradual suggestion of concealed horror* which actually raises fear to its highest pitch. In later work you will probably be less disposed to pile on great numbers of horrific words (an early & scarcely-conquered habit of my own), but will seek rather to select a *few* words—whose precise position in the text, & whose deep associative power, will make them in effect more terrible than any barrage of monstrous adjectives, malign nouns, & unhallowed verbs. To effect such an economy without sacrificing the intangible element of menace & hideous expectancy is the perennial problem of the horror-writer—a problem whose solution I fear I shall never completely master. By the way—in the opening of "The Gallows" the order of sentences seems to imply the falling of darkness & use of a torch *before* sunset—a point which I have ventured to modify through a suggestion of rearrangement.

Well—I hope the enclosed tales will not disappoint you. There's no need of bothering about the postage—& no need of haste in returning, so long as they *do* get back sooner or later. I fear they're too long to make copying easy. As I said, I haven't the energy to make the copies which I need myself, to replace those which are wearing out.

With every good wish, & congratulating you on the force & vividness of your two prose-poems, I remain

Yrs most cordially & sincerely,

H P Lovecraft

*Notes*

1. Vincent d'Indy (1851–1931), French composer, pupil of César Franck, founder of the Schola Cantorum, Paris (1911–31).

2. Edward J. O'Brien (1890–1941), ed. *The Best Short Stories . . . and the Yearbook of the American Short Story* (1915–32). HPL's "The Picture in the House" and "The Silver Key" were given one-star ratings (1924, 1929); "The Colour out of Space" and "The Dunwich Horror" were given three-star ratings and placed on the Roll of Honor (1928, 1929). It was presumably from the "Biographical Notice" in the 1928 volume that RB learned most of the biographical details about HPL alluded to in RB 1.

3. *O. Henry Memorial Award Prize Stories,* ed. Blanche Colton Williams (Garden City, NY: Doubleday, 1932). Previously "The Strange High House in the Mist" had been ranked first (1932), "The Silver Key" and "In the Vault" second (1929, 1932), and "Pickman's Model" third (1928).

4. *The Double Shadow and Other Fantasies.*

5. *The Collected Ghost Stories of M. R. James.*

6. See the enclosure to RB 5, and cf. "Weird Items in Library of H. P. Lovecraft" (an appendix to *LL*).

7. HPL read Scarborough's book in late March 1932, when J. Vernon Shea lent it to him (HPL to J. V. Shea, 22 and 31 March 1932; mss., JHL).

8. *The Shunned House* was set in type and printed in 1928 by W. Paul Cook of the Recluse Press, but the sheets were not bound. In 1933, Walter J. Coates of the Driftwind Press was going to bind the sheets but never did so. R. H. Barlow acquired 115 copies in 1934 and 150 more in 1935, but bound only a few copies. The sheets Barlow obtained eventually were bound and distributed by Arkham House in the 1960s.

9. The bookplate, designed by Wilfred Blanch Talman, is reprinted in Talman's *The Normal Lovecraft* (Saddle River, NJ: Gerry de la Ree, 1973), 11.

10. See *SL* 3.395–96.

[3]     [ALS]

Address after May 15          10 Barnes St.,

—66 COLLEGE ST.          Providence, R.I.,

May 9, 1933

Dear Mr. Bloch:—

I am very glad that you found the first batch of stories interesting, & hope the second lot—enclosed & under separate cover—will average as high in your estimation. You are like E. Hoffmann Price in having an especial liking for "Pickman's Model"—the setting of which is quite realistic in its architectural details. As late as 1926 the crooked court (Foster St.) forming the scene of the denouement actually existed, though I was gravely disappointed the very next year when I tried to show it to young Wandrei during his first trip east. The intervening months had witnessed its complete demolition—the whole labyrinth of old houses for a block on either side being razed to the ground. Only the paved zigzag line of the vanished alley, winding among cellar walls laid open to the sun, remained to hint of the dismal picturesqueness of the former scene. Old tunnels of unexplained use have actually been found beneath houses in this sinister section—their real purpose being probably connected with pre-revolutionary smuggling. Last year two incredibly fantastic old houses—built respectively in 1695 & 1698—were torn down near there, though even now a great deal of 18th century material is left. However, with the passing of these houses the Paul Revere house in North Square (1676) remains the only known 17th century edifice in Boston. Salem, however, has plenty of 17th century houses—some going back to the 1640's. The oldest house in New England is the Fairbanks farmhouse in Dedham (between Boston & Providence), built in 1636. It is indeed the oldest *private dwelling* of English origin on this continent—only St. Luke's Church in Isle of Wight County, Virginia (1632) surpassing it in age.[1]

Of the new material you will probably like "The Colour Out of Space" best. The long novelette "At the Mountains of Madness", however, represents one of my most persistent imaginative conceptions—the ineffable mystery & potential horror of the vast, aeon-dead *antarctic* having haunted my fancy ever since I was 11 or 12 years old. Wright rejected this for W.T. "Innsmouth" reflects a sort of exaggeration of ancient Newburyport, Mass., whose increasing quiescence & depopulation are getting to be almost spectral. "Red Hook" exploits the suggestion of lurking horror in an actual decaying section of Brooklyn. I lived in Brooklyn 2 years—from March 1924 to April 1926. "The White Ship" is one of my poorest pieces of junk—a mawkish piece of Dunsanian imitation perpetrated in 1919 when the charm of a first reading of Dunsany was fresh & hypnotically powerful. For years after that I found the Dunsany influence hard to escape, even though this style is not at all well suited to me. "The Strange High House"—written in 1926—is perhaps the last (& least mawkish) of my pseudo-Dunsaniana. Take your time about reading & returning these items—& perhaps you'd better send them to my new address, *66 College St.,* which will probably be effective after May 15.

Glad you saw Moe—who has been a delightful correspondent of mine since 1914, & whom I met in person in 1923, when he visited the East. I must notify him of my changing address. Since he mentioned that dream-story of mine, I'll enclose that ahead of your prescribed order with the present batch. The following of my dream of late December, 1919, is quite literal except for the names.[2] In the dream I was "Randolph Carter", while "Harley Warren" was my friend Samuel Loveman (then of Cleveland, Ohio, now of Brooklyn, N.Y.)—a poet of fantastic imaginative power, whose reading recommendations had done much toward opening up the field of weird literature to me. Incidentally, I am enclosing printed matter pertaining to the institution of "amateur journalism" which first placed Moe, Loveman, & me in touch with one another. While many phases of its activities are rather elementary & quasi-juvenile, it has maturer aspects which no one can afford to scorn. Through it I have encountered many highly interesting correspondents. In case you would like to join, I enclose an application blank with data corrected to date. For one thing, amateur journalism would provide you with an instant avenue to *print*—if representation in the small amateur papers of the members means anything to you. I myself found it an extremely helpful & encouraging influence. Which reminds me—let me see "The Grave" when you finish it. Your work is undoubtedly better than the stuff I turned out at a similar age—the bulk of which, as I probably mentioned, I destroyed in 1908.

You are right in saying that Clark Ashton Smith produces too much. That is the tragedy of economic necessity—he knows that much of his stuff is hack junk, yet has to keep grinding it out for the sake of the cash. I've tried such hack writing myself, but simply can't do it. My disgust for popular conventional hokum is such that it virtually paralyses my pen when I try to dabble in it. Instead, I try to do *revisory* work—doctoring up the MSS. of half-baked or technically inadequate writers. It is all devilishly unremunerative, as my alarming & increasing poverty attests! You are also right in assuming that Robert E. Howard has never been to Britain. So far as I know, he has never been east of New Orleans—but his imagination is limitless, & he closely identifies himself with his Celtic & Norse ancestors. As for his incessant swordplay—which Clark Ashton Smith calls "monotonous manslaughter"—that is undoubtedly an outgrowth of the same frontier psychology which makes him so fond of barbaric life. It is a part of his personality, & I don't suppose it could be eradicated without upsetting the whole emotional arrangement which makes him a literary creator. He has a very vivid sense of *incredible antiquity*, & finely suggests the existence of unhallowed elder worlds & forgotten reaches of time. Quinn, also, has frankly sold his soul to Mammon—but he could turn out magnificent stuff if he would. His best piece was "The Phantom Farmhouse", in an early issue of W.T. Wandrei's most cosmic things have never been published—in fact, of his best lot only "The Red Brain" has appeared.[3] If you can find the "Creeps by Night" anthology in any local library, you can read "The Red Brain." Maurice Level, of course, is a well-known French author, whose tales W.T. probably gets through a literary agency.[4] A very promising youngster is Carl Jacobi of Minneapolis—a friend of Wandrei & Derleth—whose vampire tale you have doubtless noticed.[5] He will be worth watching. By the way—did I tell you last time that Smith is issuing 6 of his best (& rejected) tales as a 25¢ booklet? That will be worth getting when it appears.

As to the validity, if any, of the weird assumptions underlying my tales—I may assure you most thoroughly that there isn't any. So far as I can see, all non-materialistic interpretations of the cosmos are pure mythology—though the very natural & age-long holding of supernatural beliefs by the majority gives them an emotional & aesthetic value independent of their actual baselessness. Supernatural assumptions in art—though known to be false—afford a convenient mode of emotional escape for those who feel oppressed by the rigid limitations of time, space, & natural law. By the way—there is no "Necronomicon of the mad Arab Abdul Alhazred". That hellish & forbidden volume is an imaginative conception of mine, which others of the W.T. group have also used as a background of allusion. Other wholly fictitious terror-books are my "Pnakotic Manuscripts", Smith's "Book of Eibon", & Howard's "Black Book of von Junzt".[6] The whole mythology of Yog-Sothoth & Cthulhu is a creation of my own—a sort of dark counterpart of Dunsany's synthetic pantheon of "Pegāna". "Tsathoggua" is a creation of Smith's.

As for my love of old-time architecture—at last, for the first time in my life, I am about to move into one of the venerable Georgian houses which I have admired for 40 years! This place—whose upper part I shall inhabit jointly with my only surviving aunt[7]—is a yellow wooden house on the crest of Providence's ancient hill about half a mile south of Barnes St. It lies in a quaint grassy court off precipitous College St.—behind & next to the marble John Hay Library of Brown University. The fine colonial doorway is much like my bookplate—which I herewith enclose, after forgetting to do so last time. In the rear is a picturesque, village-like garden. My quarters—a large study & a small bedroom—will be on the south side, with my working table under a west window affording a splendid view of the lower town's outspread roofs & of the mystical sunsets that flame behind them. The interior is as fascinating as the exterior—with colonial fireplaces, mantels, & chimney cupboards, curving Georgian staircase, wide floor-boards, old-fashioned latches, small-paned windows, six-panel doors, rear wing with floor at a different level (3 steps down), quaint attic, &c—just like the old houses open as museums. After admiring such all my life, there is something magical & dreamlike in the idea of *actually living in one.*[8] And yet the move is really an economy measure. Moving is such a devastating ordeal that I'd never undertake it voluntarily—unless, perhaps, I had the cash to recover my beloved birthplace.

With every good wish, & hoping you will like some of the accompanying tales, I remain

Yrs most cordially,
H P Lovecraft

*Notes*

1. See HPL's "An Account of a Trip to the Antient Fairbanks House, in Dedham, and to the Red Horse Tavern in Sudbury, in the Province of the Massachusetts-Bay" (1929; *CE* 4.62–66).
2. See *SL* 1.94–97.

3. Seabury Quinn, "The Phantom Farmhouse" (*WT,* October 1923; rpt. March 1929); Donald Wandrei, "The Red Brain" (*WT,* October 1927; rpt. May 1936).

4. Maurice Level (1875–1926) had three stories in *WT* in 1932–33.

5. "Revelations in Black" (*WT,* April 1933).

6. Robert E. Howard's invented book was *Unaussprechlichen Kulten* (*Nameless Cults*). In "The Black Stone" (*WT,* November 1931), Howard refers to von Junzt's "Nameless Cults in the original edition, the so-called Black Book."

7. Annie E. P. Gamwell. HPL's other aunt, Lillian D. Clark, had died in 1932.

8. The Samuel Mumford House (c. 1825), now standing at 65 Prospect Street. Cf. HPL's description of the house in "The Haunter of the Dark" (November 1935):

> It was a cosy and fascinating place, in a little garden oasis of village-like antiquity where huge, friendly cats sunned themselves atop a convenient shed. The square Georgian house had a monitor roof, classic doorway with fan carving, small-paned windows, and all the other earmarks of early nineteenth-century workmanship. Inside were six-panelled doors, wide floor-boards, a curving colonial staircase, white Adam-period mantels, and a rear set of rooms three steps below the general level.
>
> Blake's study, a large southwest chamber, overlooked the front garden on one side, while its west windows—before one of which he had his desk—faced off from the brow of the hill and commanded a splendid view of the lower town's outspread roofs and of the mystical sunsets that flamed behind them. On the far horizon were the open countryside's purple slopes. Against these, some two miles away, rose the spectral hump of Federal Hill, bristling with huddled roofs and steeples whose remote outlines wavered mysteriously, taking fantastic forms as the smoke of the city swirled up and enmeshed them. Blake had a curious sense that he was looking upon some unknown, ethereal world which might or might not vanish in dream if ever he tried to seek it out and enter it in person.

[4]     [ALS]

H. P. LOVECRAFT

~~10 BARNES ST~~     66 College Street

PROVIDENCE, R.I.

[late May 1933]

My dear Bloch:—

Yes, I am moved, but the worst part is yet to come. I refer to the sorting & placing of my 2000 books, which are now piled in the vacant room which will be my aunt's living-room when she moves in on June 1st. In the intervening week I must get that room clear—a fearful job, since the proper arrangement of my shelves is always a very slow process. I have bought 4 small extra bookcases, which will be needed to take care of the books that occupied built-in shelves at 10 Barnes. This place is certainly splendid, & my furniture makes it ineffably homelike. Having 2 rooms all my own, & having an attic to overflow into, I shall not be forced to crowd my quarters as I did at #10, where I had only one room & alcove. The accompanying sketch gives a rough idea of the house—whose location in a court beside the John Hay Library I think I described to you. The more I see of it, the more fascinating it seems—& I can hardly believe that I am actually *living* here. It is so much like like [*sic*] the old houses open as museums that I keep wondering whether a guard will appear & kick me out at 5 o'clock closing time. The views from the various windows are delightful. My bedroom commands an ancient steeple, while the desk over-

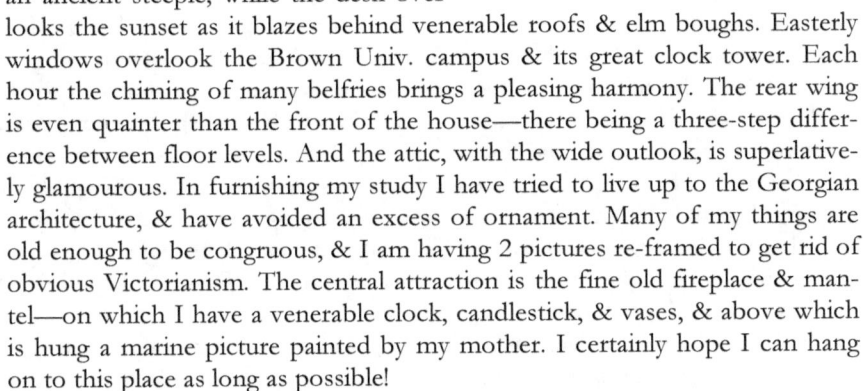

looks the sunset as it blazes behind venerable roofs & elm boughs. Easterly windows overlook the Brown Univ. campus & its great clock tower. Each hour the chiming of many belfries brings a pleasing harmony. The rear wing is even quainter than the front of the house—there being a three-step difference between floor levels. And the attic, with the wide outlook, is superlatively glamourous. In furnishing my study I have tried to live up to the Georgian architecture, & have avoided an excess of ornament. Many of my things are old enough to be congruous, & I am having 2 pictures re-framed to get rid of obvious Victorianism. The central attraction is the fine old fireplace & mantel—on which I have a venerable clock, candlestick, & vases, & above which is hung a marine picture painted by my mother. I certainly hope I can hang on to this place as long as possible!

I think you'll find the N.A.P.A.[1] a very enjoyable & encouraging organisation when you join it. I expect to attend its convention in N.Y. next July. Glad to hear that your minstrel activities are prospering, & certainly hope you will be able to extract some financial profit (a rare thing in these days!) from the enterprise. The tawdry atmosphere of cabarets would be well worth enduring for the sake of anything like a regular job!

Glad you survived the stories. Here are all the rest of those on your list, except "The Shunned House", of which I have no copy at the moment.

Of this batch, the worst items are probably the naive & melodramatic "Tree" & the ineffably mawkish "Quest of Iranon"—though some of the others are pretty bad indeed. All this stuff is about a decade or more old—except "Cool Air", which dates from '25 or '26. I note with interest your opinion of the previous batch of tales, & am sorry that "Randolph Carter" cuts the ground from under the feet of your new story. But let me see "The Grave" none the less. Often several stories can successfully revolve around the same subject-matter—differences in mood & treatment giving to each an adequate individuality. As for the synthetic myth-cycle—I suppose I got the idea from Poe's allusions to fabulous lands of his own dreaming, from Dunsany's artificial pantheon, & from Machen's portentous references to "Aklo letters", "Voorish domes", &c. "Nyarlathotep" is a horrible messenger of the evil gods to earth, who usually appears in human form. "Kadath" is a lofty & terrible mountain in an unknown cold waste, atop which inconceivable secret things brood. "Leng" is a cold & horrible plateau inhabited by a nameless race of priests who dwell in windowless stone towers & traffick with Outside powers. Human beings who seek out Leng never return.

"Innsmouth", as I possibly mentioned last time, is an exaggeration of Newburyport, Mass. Yes—there is to me something evilly fascinating in the decadent types which evolve in ancient & neglected backwaters. Reversion to primitive forms always inspires terror, & the terror is double when the stock concerned is close at hand & related to one's own civilisation. *Decadence* always holds a horror which mere *primitiveness* does not. An African tribe may be *repulsive,* but it is not *horrible*—but an American community lapsing from civilisation to a state like that of an African tribe *is* infinitely horrible.

During the upheaval of moving I discovered at last a duplicate of my "Supernatural Horror in Literature", & am herewith sending it under separate cover. Return it some time, but no hurry. Parts of it may seem verbose & boresome, & if I were to re-write it today the style would be considerably different. I would also perhaps revise some of my judgments at least slightly. Also, I would have to add mention of a great many excellent things which have appeared since 1926, when I wrote this sketch. But possibly the thing will give you a few helpful reading suggestions.

Well—the sunset deepens, & I must get to work at my book-sorting. For the first time I am assembling all my weird volumes in one place, & they certain cover an astonishing amount of shelf footage. I didn't buy any too many extra cases!

With best wishes—

Yrs most cordially—

H P L

## Notes

1. The National Amateur Press Association, one of two major surviving amateur press associations (the other being the United Amateur Press Association of America, led by J. F. Roy Erford) following the demise of HPL's faction of the United Amateur Press Association c. 1926.

[5]    [ALS]

66 College St.,
Providence, R.I.,
June 1, 1933

Dear Bloch:—

Sorry to hear that your minstrel show is in peril, & hope exceedingly that you can make the necessary replacements in time to carry out the contemplated programme. Certainly, the world is full of unexpected & disheartening obstacles!

Glad you found the historical sketch of interest, & hope you'll be able to get hold of most of the items mentioned in the course of time. Since the appearance of this article in 1927 I've jotted down other important weird items which ought to be cited in any second edition—some that I'd overlooked, & others that have appeared subsequently to the article.[1] I'll transcribe that list here (I can lend items marked *):

### Novels
H. B. Drake—The Shadowy Thing (1928)
John Buchan—Witch Wood (1927)
*Leonard Cline—The Dark Chamber (1927)
Herbert S. Gorman—The Place Called Dagon (1927)
Arthur Ransome—The Elixir of Life (1915)
Leland Hall—Sinister House (1919)

### Short Stories in Anthologies & Collections
*Joseph Lewis French—Ghosts, Grim & Gentle (1926)*
H. G. Wells—The Ghost of Fear
Ralph Adams Cram—The Dead Valley
de Maupassant—On the River
*Cynthia Asquith—The Ghost Book (1927)*
Algernon Blackwood—Chemical
Hugh Walpole—Mrs. Lunt
L. P. Hartley—A Visitor from Down Under
Walter de la Mare—A Recluse
*H. R. Wakefield—They Return At Evening (1928)*
He Cometh & He Passeth By
The Red Lodge
The Seventeenth Hole at Duncaster
And He Shall Sing
*H. R. Wakefield—Others Who Returned (1929)*
The Cairn
Look Up There!
Blind Man's Buff

*\*John Buchan—The Runagates' Club (1928)*
    The Green Wildebeest
    The Wind in the Portico
    Skule Skerry
*E. F. Benson—Spook Stories*
    The Face
*Mrs. H. D. Everett—Short Stories*[2]

Speaking of weird books—I'll enclose a rather chaotic list of those in my library, which you can keep for reference. I'll be glad to lend any that you may care to borrow. Hope you can decipher the thing—which is a rough set of names used as the first stage in making a catalogue. This weird department, as now arranged in my study, covers over 17 feet of shelfage.

Enclosed are the three tales you want to see. "The Festival" (1923) is indisputably the least rotten of these—& will, by the way, be reprinted in W.T. before long. "Celephaïs" (1920) is one of my mawkish pseudo-Dunsaniana, & "From Beyond" (1920) is a dull & commonplace piece of junk. Wright rejected both of these latter two, for which I don't blame him. I was interested in your reactions to the previous batch. "Cool Air" was a favourite of mine, but Wright didn't like it. I later sold it to an ephemeral Philadelphia magazine for only $17.50.[3] "The Tree" doesn't seem like much to me. Obvious or not, "Arthur Jermyn" is one of my favourites. "The Nameless City" was never accepted. Glad you like "The Tomb" (written about the time you were born!), for that marks the very beginning of my present series of tales. I had scribbled weird junk between the ages of 7 & 18, but in 1908 decided I had not the gift, & destroyed all but two of my stories. Later, when I entered "amateur journalism" (of which I sent you circulars), I submitted one of these two as a credential—& when it was published W. Paul Cook began encouraging me to write some more.[4] For a while I held off, but in the summer of 1917 produced "The Tomb" & "Dagon" as an experiment—after 9 solid years of fictional silence. I didn't know how well they'd be received, but the response was so favourable that I've kept scribbling weird stuff off & on ever since. "Polaris" is interesting in its indication of how ready I was to fall for Dunsany on first acquaintance—for when I wrote it I had never read a line of D.! As you see, the atmosphere & language shew a marked inclination toward the Dunsanian mood. However, that was not the style that fitted me best.

Glad you liked Wandrei's poem in the *Recluse*.[5] He has published two small volumes of verse which include a great deal of charnel & macabre material—"Ecstasy" & "Dark Odyssey." If you feel like investing in these (I forget the price, but it can't be much over a dollar each) you might write to the author, whose present semi-permanent address is 84 Horatio St., New York City. Klarkash-Ton, High Priest of Tsathoggua, reported hearing from you. Too bad his booklet has been further delayed—did he send you a copy of the new descriptive circular? And by the way—it looks as if my "Shunned House" were to be published at last. Cook has found the unbound edition, & Walter J. Coates (editor of *Driftwind*) plans to bind & issue it. I'll see that you get a copy. It has a preface by Frank B. Long Jr.

By all means write Derleth—he'll be glad to hear from you. His weird work does not represent his serious side at all, for he is primarily a delicately reminiscent realist in the tradition of Marcel Proust. He places his serious work in the high-grade smaller magazines like *Story, The Midland, Pagany, Frontier*, &c., & is steadily building up a literary reputation. O'Brien is 3-starring him for the second consecutive year.[6] If you want to get an idea of the real Derleth, ask him to lend you the MS. of his "Evening in Spring."

As for a rough attempt at self-portraiture—I'm not much at pictorial art, but there's no harm in emulating Clark Ashton Smith, whose drawings of hideous monsters are as famous among his friends as his tales & verse. So here goes for Grandpa Cthulhu, or, the Nameless Blasphemy . . . . . one of those Shapes which Lucian Grey[7] might have sketched in one of his darker moments. The most salient feature of the awful being is its nose—behind which is a more or less negligible carcass. It is 5 ft 11 in. tall, & weighs about 150 lbs—with brown fur getting greyish & thin on top, & with shoulders having a sadly non-athletic stoop. Second to its nose, its chin is the longest thing about it. Since such horrors are really beyond the power of the unskilled pen to portray, I will enclose the ruthless record of the camera in the

*The Hellish Nether Entity*

matter—a record of 2 years ago, though the progress of senecence has not caused much external change since them. Kindly return the print, since I haven't the negative. For good measure, & to mitigate the horror with a wholesome human form, I have chosen a view which includes my young friend Frank Belknap Long, Jun. Incidentally, I wouldn't mind seeing a sketch or snap of you whenever you happen to have such a thing handy.

I read Rohmer's "Day the World Ended" about a year ago, & thought it very fair of its kind. The best thing Rohmer ever did, though, is "Brood of The Witch Queen." That is what I call a story! I want to pick up a copy of my own some day.[8]

I have examined your stories with the keenest interest, & congratulate you upon some very vivid & effective writing. You manage to get a tense & brooding atmosphere every time—the style admirably suiting the theme. As before noted, the main fault is what one might call *overcolouring*—laying the emotions on too thick. That is my own fault, also. Time will tend to modify it, hence at present it need not be regarded as a major defect. "The Grave" is a good story, & I need pick only a few points to pieces. One thing I'd advise you to clarify somewhat is the matter of *motivation*. Ancient graveyards are not the normal prey of the body-snatcher, since their specimens are never in good condition. Skeletons quickly begin to crumble, & I doubt if anything of any use could be extracted from an 80 year old grave. Certainly, no such grave would be opened at random by a professional ghoul. Right here, too, I'll mention another point. Skeletons are never found in an *articulated* state after the flesh is gone. Even the most perfect skeleton is merely a collection of separate bones which must be gathered one by one—except, of course, where chance creates some adhesion at a joint. The perfect skeletonic shapes we commonly see are the result of careful wiring. Thus the idea of caching an exhumed skeleton in a tree & returning with a wagon is a bit strained. In reality, the robber of an old grave would merely bring a large sack—into which he would carefully deposit every bone found, & which he could readily carry away by hand. The articulation would take place later in his workshop or laboratory.

But to return to the matter of motivation. To make a hard-headed professional rob an ancient grave you must supply a special reason. This can probably be done in a way to make it contribute excellently to the plot. You might have this burying-ground the bygone necropolis of a highly mysterious local cult which had flourished a century before, & about whose nature there was a good deal of awed debate. Let it have an evil reputation throughout the countryside—but let it be rumoured that every member of the cult had a large & oddly hieroglyphed tablet of *solid gold* placed in his coffin. Here is your motive. The hardened professional will dare to seek what the rustics have dared not seek. You might allude darkly to mysterious disappearances of human beings & other animals in the vicinity. (For the Nether Things no longer have buried bodies to feed on in that neighbourhood, & cannibalism becomes monotonous!) Your description of the scene is powerful & excellent—one shudders at the dark forest & that which it may conceal.

A second point of criticism is purely mechanical. How did the tunnels manage to get dug—what became of the displaced earth? Very small animals probably burrow without displacing earth, their slight bulk requiring no more of a tunnel than can be made by squirming ahead & packing the soil tighter on all sides. But I don't think human beings could do this. Therefore you must somehow handle the problem of displaced earth. I forget how I handled a similar problem in "The Lurking Fear"—but I think I had the burrows near the surface, with *mounds* indicating displaced earth.

Now for point three—about psychology. You have Matthew[s] doing an incredible thing (going back to the burrows when he has a chance to escape through an old well) *before* you pronounce him mad. Do you think that all his reactions & performances sound natural? Have you tried to estimate *realistically* the response of an actual man of the given type to events such as these?

Another thing—the "mile-wide" cavern is introduced too abruptly & *casually*. This makes almost a sub-climax, & ought to be treated with considerable impressiveness.

At the last, some might consider the detailed explanation from Matthews' dying lips a trifle over-obvious. Also, some might object to the absence of any survivor. If Matthews was killed alone, how has the story reached the reader? This point, however, comes close to pedantry—& is equally violated in Poe's "Masque of the Red Death" & other classics.

In general, don't take my remarks as disparagements of what is really a very promising piece of work. You have the right mood & keynote, & the story certainly produces an ineffably potent & macabre impression. Keep it up! I don't know of anyone else who has done better work at 16!

You are right, I believe, in thinking "Lucian Grey" superior to "The Grave." It reminds me amazingly of one of the juvenile tales I destroyed— "The Picture", written in 1907. That is, the theme reminds me. The tale itself is much better than mine. I had a man in a Paris garret paint a mysterious canvas embodying the quintessential essence of all horror. He is found clawed & mangled one morning before his easel. The picture is destroyed, as in a titanic struggle—but in one corner of the frame a bit of canvas remains . . . . & on it the coroner finds to his horror the painted counterpart of the sort of claw which evidently killed the artist. The idea was good, but the style was so poor that I don't regret having destroyed it a year after its composition.

"Lucian Grey" embodies a fascinating & powerful conception—that of bondage to the Outside Unknown. The mystery of the two lost years offers vast possibilities, & the connexion with dreams is highly effective. Your distinctions in horror shew much thoughtfulness & close analysis.

My principal point of criticism is that more stress & detail ought to occur in connexion with the 2 lost years. This is a major event, & calls for special emphasis. The beginning & ending of the lapse ought to be described, & some hint ought to be given concerning the natural search for information regarding the blank period. What did friends know? How was the absence regarded? What evidence supplied by clothing, personal belongings, &c. at time of emergence from the unknown?

But, trifles aside, the story certainly is a fine performance. Your descriptions of bizarre conditions have a distinctiveness, detail, fresh originality, & convincingness which remove them vastly from the ordinary run of weird images. This is a tale to shudder over & admire. Why not let Derleth, Smith, or others of the group see it & give you the benefit of their advice? The more opinions the better. I certainly enjoyed the story vastly.

Hope your rustic period will prove pleasant. The charm of this ancient house continues to captivate me. Today my aunt is moving in.

All good wishes—
Yr most ob^t h^ble Serv^t
H P L

[A.Ms. Enclosure]

*Weird &c. Items*
Library of H. P. Lovecraft

---

*Poe*—complete tales & poems

---

| | |
|---|---|
| *Dunsany* | Gods of Pegana |
| | Time & the Gods |
| | Dreamer's Tales |
| | Sword of Welleran |
| | Book of Wonder |
| | Last Book of Wonder |
| | Tales of Three Hemispheres |
| | Fifty-one Tales |
| | Chronicles of Rodriguez |
| | King of Elfland's Daughter |
| | Five Plays |
| | Plays of Gods & Men |
| | Plays of Near & Far |
| *Flaubert* | Salammbo |
| | Tempt. St Anth. |

Disraeli—Alroy

*Huysmans*—A *Rebours*

*Perutz*        *Master* of the Day of Judgment

Not in Our Stars—Michael Maurice

---

Owen—The Wind That Tramps the World

---

| | |
|---|---|
| *Machen* | (in addition to non-weird items) |
| | House of Souls |
| | Hill of Dreams |
| | Three Impostors |
| | Shining Pyramid |
| | The Terror (in Century Mag. Oct. 1917) |
| White, E. L. | Song of the Sirens |
| Smith, C A | Star Treader |
| | Odes & Sonnets |
| | Ebony & Crystal |
| | Sandalwood |

| Kipling— | Phantom Rickshaw |
| | Mark of Beast & others |

| M R James | Ghost Stories of an Antiquary |
| | More Ghost Stories |
| | Thin Ghost & Others |
| | Warning to the Curious |

Wright, S. Fowler,  The World Below

*Onions*—Ghosts in *Daylight*

Baudelaire—Poems & Prose Poems

| *Blackwood* | John Silence |
| | ~~Incredible Adventures~~ |
| | Jimbo |

Sitwell, Osbert—Man Who Lost Himself

| *De la Mare* | The Riddle &c |
| | The Connoisseur &c |

Maturin—Melmoth the Wanderer

| *Andreyev* | Red Laugh |
| | Seven Hanged |

| *Bierce* | In the Midst of Life |
| | Can Such things Be? |
| | Monk & Hangman's Daughter (trans. collab.) |

| *Forbes* | Mirror for Witches |

| *Wakefield* | They Return at Evening |
| | Others Who Returned |

| *Level* | Tales of Mystery & Horror |
| | Those Who Return |

| *Chambers* | The King in Yellow |
| | In Search of the Unknown |

| *Doyle* | Tales of Twilight & the Unseen |
| | Tales of Long Ago |

| *Cline* | The Dark Chamber |

| *Beraud* | Lazarus |

| | |
|---|---|
| *Le Fanu* | House by the Churchyard |
| *Marsh* | The Beetle |
| *Busson* | Man who was Born Again |
| *Arlen* | Ghost Stories |
| *Bulwer*-Lytton | House & the Brain<br>Zanoni<br>Strange Story |
| Eddison, E R | The Worm Ouroboros |
| *King* | Spreading Dawn |
| *Pain* | Exchange of Souls |
| *Buchan* | Runagates' Club |
| Beckford | Vathek<br>Episodes of Vathek |
| *Quiller*-Couch | Wandering Heath<br>Noughts & Crosses<br>Old Fires & Profitable Ghosts |
| *Stevenson* | Jekyll & Hyde & others |
| *Haggard* | She |
| *Toksvig* | Last Devil |
| *Bligh-Bond* | Avernus |
| *Jackson* | Gold Point & others |
| *Fouque* | Undine<br>Sintram |
| *James, H.* | Two Magics |
| *d'Aurevilly* | Story Without a Name |
| *Gautier* | Morte Amoreuse<br>Avatar<br>One of Cleopatra's Nights |
| *Merimee* | Venus of Ille |

| | |
|---|---|
| *Benson*, E. F. | Visible & Invisible<br>Man Who Went too Far (in Blue Booklet) |

*Hawthorne*—7 Gables

| | |
|---|---|
| *Hearn* | Kwaidan |
| *Shiel* | Prince Zaleski &c.<br>Purple Cloud |
| *De Mille* | MS. Found in a Copper Cylinder |
| *Russell, Clark* | Flying Dutchman<br>Frozen Pirate |
| *Marryat* | Phantom Ship |
| *Walpole* | Castle of Otranto |
| *Radcliffe* | Mysteries of Udolpho |
| *Reeve* | Old English Baron |
| *Shelley* | Frankenstein |
| *MacDonald* | Lilith |
| *Wilde* | Dorian Gray<br>Fairy Tales |
| *Cowan* | Revi-Lona |
| *Savile* | Beyond the Great South Wall |

*Austin*—On the Borderland

| | |
|---|---|
| *London, Jack* | The Star Rover |
| *Hugo* | Hans of Iceland |
| *Wyllarde* | Stories of Strange Happenings |
| *McKenna*— | The Oldest God |
| *Astor* | Journey to Other Worlds |
| *Pattee*— | House of the Black Ring |
| *Webster*— | Oracle of Baal |

| Birch— | The Moon Terror |
|---|---|
| *Wells* | The First Men in the Moon<br>(others in file of Amazing Stories)<br>War of Worlds<br>Dr. Moreau |
| *Verne* | 20,000 Leagues Under the Sea<br>From the Earth to the Moon |
| Merritt | The Moon Pool (in Magazine) |

*Magazine Files*

| | |
|---|---|
| *Weird Tales* | complete to date |
| *Strange Tales* | " " |
| *Amazing Stories* | First year & a half—1926–7 |

*Anthologies*

McSpadden, J. Walker—Famous Psychic St.
Lynch, Bohun—Best Ghost St.
The Great Weird Stories—ed. by (5) Arthur Neale
9Tales from the German (Hoffmann, Hauff, &c)
Terrible Tales (Italian)
Lock & Key Library 12 vols.
Masterpieces of Mystery 3 vols
3Best 'Psychic' Stories—2 French—Scarborough

| | |
|---|---|
| Selwyn & Blount<br>"Not at Night"<br>Series | Not at Night<br>Gruesome Cargoes<br>You'll Need a Night Light<br>By Daylight Only<br>Switch on the Light<br>Grim Death |

Not at Night—1 Asbury (pirated Am. edition)

7Pub. by Philip Allan
        —Creeps
        —Shudders
8Tales of Mystery (ext. Radcliffe, Lewis, Maturin)—7 Saintsbury
Beware After Dark—4 Harré
Creeps by Night—3 Hammett
Omnibus of Crime (part 2)—8 Sayers
Devil Stories—6 Rudwin

(Occult)

| | |
|---|---|
| 8 | Haunted Homes & Family Legends—Ingram |
| 6 | Haunted Houses—Flammarion |
| 12 | Encyclopaedia of Occultism—Spence |
| 9 | Theory of Pneumatology—Jung-Stilling |
| 10 | Miracles at Knock—MacPhilpin |
| 7 | Magician among the Spirits—Houdini |
| 11 | Demonology & Witchcraft—Scott |
| 2 | Curious Myths of Middle Ages—Baring-Gould |
| 5 | Myths & Myth Makers—Fiske |
| 4 | Age of Fable—Bulfinch |
| 1 | Arabian Nights |
| 3 | Hand of Glory, &c—Blakeborough |

Tale of Terror—Birkhead

| | |
|---|---|
| Poems by Clark Ashton Smith | Star-Treader |
| | Odes & Sonnets |
| | Ebony & Crystal |
| | Sandalwood |

My *Amazing Stories* file contains many Verne, Wells, &c. items as well as later semi-classics like "Station X"[9]

*Notes*

1. HPL jotted these notes, which he called "Books to mention in new edition of weird article," in his commonplace book.

2. I.e., *The Death-Mask and Other Ghosts*.

3. *Tales of Magic and Mystery* 1, No. 4 (March 1928). HPL elsewhere says he sold the story for $17.00 and $18.00.

4. "The Beast in the Cave" (1905) and "The Alchemist" (1908; his "credential"). HPL's mother preserved his very early juvenile stories; e.g., "The Little Glass Bottle" (c. 1897).

5. "In the Grave," *Recluse*, 76–[77]; later rpt. as "The Corpse Speaks."

6. Derleth's "Five Alone" was on the Roll of Honor in O'Brien's *The Best Short Stories 1933* (1933), but "Old Ladies" had been given a two-star rating in 1932.

7. *Marvel Tales* accepted "The Madness of Lucian Grey," but never published it. It was announced as "a weird-fantasy story of an artist who was forced to paint a picture . . . and the frightful thing that came from it." The story seems reminiscent of HPL's "Pickman's Model," the first story by HPL that RB read.

8. HPL read the novel in 1926.

9. By G. MacLeod Winsor.

[6]    [ALS]

66 College St.,
Providence, R.I.,
June 9, 1933

Dear Bho-Blôk:—

Well—yesterday was a day after my own heart—90° in the shade. Haven't felt so well since I was in New Orleans a year ago. I may not have mentioned that I have a sort of tropical physique—have never been too hot (don't know what the term means!) in my life, never feel really good under 80°, can't control my muscles well enough to write legibly under about 75°, & can't do anything but hibernate in winter. I crumple all up, physically & mentally, in the cold, & have actually lost consciousness at +14°. I have to stay indoors any winter day when the outside thermometer reads less than +20°. The only 2 months that I have ever felt really vigorous—uninterruptedly, that is—were those I spent in Florida—May & June 1931. I ought to live in the subtropics, but am so attached to the scenery & traditions of my native region that I can't break away. As a result, I feel really up to par only about 10 days each year. Some day, when added age weakens my resistance, I shall probably have to go south—say to Charleston—which has a fairly warm climate, yet is rich enough in colonial antiquities to keep me from experiencing the extremes of homesickness. But I'm not complaining today! This is my kind of weather, & I'm making the most of it. Have taken several 12-mile walks in the rural regions north of Providence, & spent yesterday writing on the high wooded bluffs of the river Seekonk, about a mile from here—a metropolitan park reservation which has not changed since my infancy.

Meanwhile the new household at #66 gets more & more settled. My aunt moved in June 1st, & her living-room is now in order. It looks even better than my study—& reminds me of our old home, since we are getting old family things out of storage now that we have a place to put them. Over the staircase we are hanging a large oil painting (by an elder aunt who died a year ago—I wish she could have lived to see it re-honoured)[1] which has had to remain out of view since 1904 for lack of adequate display space. We are also planting flowers in the front yard & trying to train ivy (a slip from the Washington estate at Mt. Vernon) up the facade. Incidentally—a recent brochure of the state Educational Commission has a frontispiece showing the ancient hill & college neighbourhood, in which *this house* is plainly visible near the left-hand margin. I am sending a copy (to be returned at your leisure)—which really gives an excellent idea of the neighbourhood in general. You can see the broad sweep of College St. as it climbs the great hill north of the newly-completed (but traditionally colonial) court house, as well as the Brown clock tower, the marble John Hay Library, & the 1770 College Edifice now called University Hall. A magnifying glass will bring out #66 very clearly. Notice the small rear wing—which is really the quaintest part of the house. This is a western view—& the 3d. second-story window from the left (in the main part of the building) is the one at which I am now seated. Notice how the house stands back from the others in College St. I have mentioned that it lies at the rear of a quaint grassy court.

Speaking of pictures—while "intuition" is undoubtedly 100% bunk, it certainly is a coincidence that you had imagined my ugly mug to be much as it is. Actually, it is even uglier than the picture shews—for I *will* not submit to a profile view. In the matter of young Long, your "intuition" missed by exactly one generation—his father, Frank Belknap Long, Sr., *is a dentist,* & a darned good one! That picture, though, doesn't really do justice to Sonny Belknap. In the first place, a profile is, as in my case, though for different architectural reasons, the severest kind of view for him. He ought to have known enough to face the camera. In the second place, he had been caught in a thunderstorm that day, & his clothing—usually ultra-neat—was soaked & wrinkled into a tramplike chaos. Among the enclosures in the present epistle (to be returned) is a face view of Belknap which gives a rather better idea of him. He'd be all right if he'd erase that ambiguous lip-fuzz of his & get a regular guy's haircut—but at present he thinks the black mop & misplaced eyebrow are marks of a "sensitive artist."[2] Boys will be boys—even when they get to be 31 as Sonny now is!

I am extremely glad to see the view of yourself, & am rapaciously annexing it to my permanent collection in the absence of any specific instructions to the contrary. (If, however, it is an only print, I'll reluctantly disgorge.) Later on, if you wish, I'll reciprocate with a snap of Grandpa which you can retain. I don't think your proboscis is even in the running with mine so far as sheer ugliness is concerned. Mine all runs to tapir-like length, whereas yours seems thoroughly well-proportioned. Indeed, without wishing to apply soft soap, I can't help remarking that your visage is a very pleasant & prepossessing one—to an extent that my own dour map never even began to approach. Snaps of me at your age would be excellent material for the comic papers—& without the aid of any Napoleonic hat or rubber cigar! Incidentally, though, I used to be a great hand at rigging up—having a whole makeup kit of bushy beards, fierce moustaches, slouch hats, daggers, pistols, & other appurtenances of the desperate characters toward which my youthful fancy inclined me. Glad that glasses don't bother you—I used to have to wear them all the time, & they kept my nose (which, by the way, is not only oversized but slightly askew since a bicycle accident in 1913) & ears in a state of perpetual irritation. Now I wear them only for steady middle-distance vision—as at the theatre, or at illustrated lectures. I don't see over-sharply at a distance without them, but their absence no longer gives me the headache & dizziness it once did. My rheumy old lamps are a dark brown, though my hide is of an almost chalklike lightness except when laboriously tanned by Florida suns or their equivalent. Like you, I get no exercise save walking, but I'm not as reckless with the food-trough as I used to be. About 12 years ago I began taking on weight—largely through a prolongation of the conscientious stuffing habits enjoined upon me by those who wished to counteract my naturally sluggish appetite. The result was damned uncomfortable—& when I got too much like a brother of the hippopotamus I started a reducing. That was in January, 1925—& in 5 months I had sloughed off *50 lbs.* Merely cut down on the nutrition—the suet melted easily, since it had no business to be there in the first place. Since then I haven't let myself be wheedled into eating more than I want—& consequently have had no tendency to get fat again . . . . . besides which, my digestion is infinitely better than it was before. I get down to 140 or so in summer, when I'm active & out of doors, & go up to 150 or a bit over when I'm hibernating in winter. Right now I'm 144. (Some day, when in a comedy mood, I'll send you a snap or two of Grandpa taken in the 1922–24 period. Can you imagine my trunk hitched to a fat man's face? Incidentally, it was during my fat period that I had my only personal meeting with our friend Moe . . . . what a mental picture he must carry!)

Before quitting the subject of pictures, it occurs to me that you would probably be interested in snaps of other persons whom you know through W.T. & otherwise—hence the enclosed envelope of rogues'-gallery stuff, to be returned at your leisure. You may here get an informal idea of Klarkash-Ton, Belknap, Derleth, Wandrei, Dwyer (a weird artist & writer who is delightfully gifted & appreciative, but who hasn't yet made the grade professionally. N.B.—He's reducing now!), the late Henry S. Whitehead (a delightful chap—my Florida host in '31), Talman, & Two-Gun Bob, the Terror of the Plains. Derleth, as you see, has just a touch of artistic affectation about him—which I'd whale or spoof out of him if he were my son! My only view of Farnsworth Wright is a queer, modernistically treated thing too large for lending. He is about 45, good-featured, trim-figured, & clean-shaven—verging on baldness, & with an immobile expression & awkward motions resulting from a very rare kind of palsy called "Parkinson's Disease" which formed an aftermath to his shell-shock & other war injuries. I've never seen him in person, but Wandrei, Derleth, & Talman have. By the way—Wandrei, Derleth & Talman are all lean six-footers, while my friend Galpin (in Appleton, Wis., whom I may have mentioned to you) is 6 feet 2. Evidently you young fellows go in for height in a big way. Oh, yes—& Dwyer is 6 feet 3 or 4, to which his always ample & sometimes excessive weight adds an atmosphere of giganticism!

Glad to hear that the prospects for the minstrel show are better. About the new W.T.—I haven't had time to read all of it, but what I have read speaks well for the general quality. Klarkash-Ton's "Genius Loci" is great stuff—& the Humphreys reprint is one of my old favourites. I once picked a half-dozen tales as the *most truly & disturbingly horrible* that have ever appeared in the magazine, & I think the list ran something like this:

Beyond the Door—J. Paul Suter
The Floor Above—M. Humphreys      I have a complete file
The Night Wire—H. F. Arnold       of W.T. to date.
The Canal—Everil Worrell
Bells of Oceana—Arthur J. Burks
In Amundsen's Tent—John Martin Leahy.[3]

I also like Paul Ernst's stuff very much. He will certainly be worth watching. Carl Jacobi—a young Minneapolis friend of Wandrei's—is another promising figure. Single-Plot Hamilton is one of the best sedatives I know (The Interstellar Patrol—the menace to the universe—the central machine of destruction—the capture of Hul Jok or Korus Kan[4] &c—the eleventh-hour crippling of the machine—deliverance & thanksgiving . . . . . always the same except when the stock mad scientist takes the place of the Enemy from Outside)—but he *could* write powerful stuff if he only would. In my opinion his best thing is "The Monster God of Mamurth," which was reprinted in the anthology which contained my "Cthulhu".[5] Like Quinn—only more so—he has succumbed to the lure of easy money, & grinds out what he knows the eburneocraniate[6] public & its editorial purveyors are calling & paying for. I regret to say that recent financial stress seems to be leading the very gifted E. Hoffmann Price into that class also.

Klarkash-Ton's "Malygris"[7] is splendid—& it is just like the capricious Brother Farnsworth to turn down a thing like that! The thing is pure poetry in places—indeed, the Dunsanian style suits C A S more than it does me. You'll certainly enjoy the brochure of tales—"The Double Shadow" is especially fine—as is "A Night in Malneant." Speaking of Klarkash-Ton, it occurs to me that you've never seen any of his hellish drawings & paintings—which leads me to enclose an envelope full for your inspection & return. Included is a brief review of an exhibition of his work at Berkeley, Cal. Could Lucian Grey himself outdo the most monstrous of these blasphemous entities? And yet these small grotesques are only the merest suggestions of his really serious pictorial efforts—which are invariably on a large scale, & of which I do not possess any. I have seen some fine specimens in Samuel Loveman's collection, & Klarkash-Ton himself once lent me a splendid assortment, carefully crated.

Glad the book-list proved interesting, & feel free to borrow when you wish. I also found "The Coronation of Mr Thomas Shap"[8] fascinating. About my "Festival"—the waxen masks concealed the indescribable visages of gigantic, bloated slugs or grave-worms which had fed monstrously upon the accursed corpses of long generations of blasphemous necromancers. As for your list of my junk—your choices do not wholly coincide with mine, although they are by no means antipodal. I think "The Colour Out of Space" is my best effort, with "Erich Zann" as a not very close second. I'm surprised that I haven't sent "Erich" before. Here he is—for return at your convenience. I don't share the fondness of yours for "The Outsider". The style is mawkish & overdone, & the climax is too mechanical to be good literature. I also dislike "The Hound"—& don't care for the *present form* of "The Lurking Fear."[9] I like "Mts. of Madness" & "Innsmouth" better than you do—also "Jermyn", "Ulthar", & "Dagon". Indeed, "Dagon" (except for the amateurish *style*) is one of my favourites. "The Shunned House" (get Derleth to send you the set of proofs he has if you want to see it before publication) strikes me, in these latter days, as not so hot. I don't think either of the untyped novelettes would pass muster without revision—in fact, I'm rather glad that I never typed them as they now stand.

About your own work—*don't discourage* that 'introverted self-projection' or 'auto-hypnosis'! It is a quality like that, I think, which gives to all genuine art the vitality & convincingness distinguishing it from mere clever workmanship. The trouble with most cheap weird fiction is that it *doesn't have enough* of this introverted self-projection! The thing to do is not to eliminate it, but to let it operate *in conjunction with* an objective critical sense. Do your dreaming unhampered, & then rigorously apply the test of objective consistency to what you have dreamed—making changes when necessary. That is a sounder policy than either uncriticised dreaming, or objective workmanship without dreaming. I never try to write a story without entering deeply into its atmosphere & feeling keenly the touch of strangeness I am seeking to reproduce—but afterward I endeavour to make the incidents square with reality except for the one supernatural condition postulated.

I like your "Laughter of a Ghoul." The atmosphere is perhaps a little thick with colour; but the idea & climax are excellent, & the tone of menace very finely maintained. Of course the central theme has been used before—you doubtless recall Klarkash-Ton's "Nameless Offspring" in the June 1932 *Strange Tales*—but that does not invalidate it for further treatment. You choose an utterly different climax from C A S's, & phrase it very effectively. This is promising stuff—keep it up! I'll also be glad to see "Sons of the Serpent" & "Nocturne Macabre." And your humorous sketches would greatly interest me, too, even though I could scarcely hope to parallel them myself. Go ahead with your myth-cycle—since I swiped the idea from Dunsany, you can't be any more of a pirate than I am! Your "Glass Eye" is good—as are the verses "Nightmare" & "Weird-Wood." You have a good ear for metre, & the climactic couplet of the second piece is especially effective. Try some of this verse on Wright some time—if accepted, it would bring 25¢ per line!

And so it goes. Hope "Erich Zann" won't disappoint you after my statement that I place it second among my products. It has, by the way, been reprinted four times since its original appearance in W.T.[10]

Best wishes—

Yrs. for the Dark Lore & Elder Sign

　　　　—E'ch-Pi-El

*Notes*

1. The painting was by Lillian D. Clark (1856–1932). See HPL to August Derleth, 5 June 1933: "Over the staircase we are hanging an immense canvas (Rocks at Narragansett Pier) by my late elder aunt (I could curse the damn cosmos that she hasn't survived to see this layout), for which no space has previously been available since the original home disintegration of 1904" (*Essential Solitude* 580).

2. HPL parodies Long's mien in "The Thing on the Doorstep" (21–24 August 1933), the main character of which is loosely based on Long, HPL, and other of HPL's associates.

3. J. Paul Suter, "Beyond the Door" (April 1923; rpt. September 1930); M. L. Humphreys, "The Floor Above" (May 1923; rpt. June 1933); H. F. Arnold, "The Night Wire" (September 1926; rpt. January 1933); Everil Worrell, "The Canal" (December 1927; rpt. April 1935); Arthur J. Burks, "The Bells of Oceana" (December 1927; rpt. April 1934); and John Martin Leahy, "In Amundsen's Tent" (January 1928; rpt. August 1935). It seems that HPL was instrumental in the reprinting of these stories.

4. Nictzin Dyalhis, "The Oath of Hul Jok" (*WT*, September 1928). Korus Kan, a metal-bodied Antarean, is a character in Edmond Hamilton, "Outside the Universe" (*WT*, July–October 1929).

5. *WT*, August 1926; rpt. September 1935. In T. Everett Harré, *Beware After Dark!* (1929).

6. HPL has evidently coined a Latin-Greek hybrid, "ivory-headed" (from the Latin *eburneus*, made of ivory; and the Greek *kranion*, skull).

7. CAS, "The Death of Malygris" (*WT*, April 1934).

8. By Lord Dunsany, in *The Book of Wonder*.

9. HPL always professed he would rewrite the story, but never did.

10. *WT*, May 1925; Dashiell Hammett, ed. *Creeps by Night: Chill and Thrills* (New York: John Day, Co., 1931); rpt. as *Modern Tales of Horror* (London: Gollancz, 1932); and *The Evening Standard* (London), 24 October 1932. Thus, the story was reprinted only three times since its first appearance in *WT*. It was first published in the *National Amateur* (March 1922).

[7]    [ALS]

66 College St.,
Providence, R.I.
June 21, 1933

Dear Bho-Blôk:—

I read all the MSS. with great interest. "Nocturne Macabre" is splendid, though of course the details of phraseology might profit by a bit of polishing. The idea is just what I have recommended for years—having a story told from an unconventional & non-human angle. I had a letter in the Eyrie in 1923 in which I called for stories from the ghoul's or werewolf's point of view, but nobody seemed to get the point.[1] H. Warner Munn *thought* he was following out my idea when he wrote his "Werewolf of Ponkert"[2] (told by a man who has involuntarily become a werewolf, & who regrets his nocturnal deeds), but in reality he wholly missed it. His sympathies were still with mankind—whereas I called for sympathies wholly dissociated from mankind & perhaps violently hostile to it. Your "Nocturne" is the first thing I've seen that fills the bill. It is certainly highly promising—keep it up! "The Soul" has good touches—especially the climactic finale—but is perhaps a bit conventional as weird tales go. "Dr. Lichorn" has merit—especially in its *idea*—though it would take long practice to hit the real Dunsanian keynote which best sets off this kind of conception. "The Feast" forms a very clever union of the macabre & the comic. "The Sorcerer's Tale" is very good indeed—marvellous for a boy of fifteen, as you were in 1932.[3] The style & atmosphere are ineffably Poesque, & the whole thing leaves vivid pictures in one's imagination. It is certainly worth polishing for future use. Probably it would be helped by the presence of more distinct *events*, especially toward the last. More concrete experiences on the novice's part—ending in some marvel or transition even more spectacular than that delineated—would help. And of course a subtle toning-down of the style (economy of adjectives & superlatives, & so on) would form a strengthening element. I return these items as per request. Hope "Sons of the Serpent" turns out well. I find that all stories seem more or less to run away with one—at least they tend to do that with me. Nowadays I can't seem to produce anything less than a novelette.

Thanks for the sketches—which shew a clever hand & a highly Klarkash-Tonic imagination. They're a darned sight better than anything I could ever do in that direction. "Nyarlathotep" just fits my conception, while "The Ghoul" lends a new terror to your "Nocturne." Are these to be returned? If so, they are safe. I appreciated your profile—which, if it scares the infants of today, indicates the growth of a more timid generation than those of my youth! The early snap you mentioned wasn't enclosed, after all. Here, by the way, is a clock-stopping & loathsomely realistic close-up of Grandpa Cthulhu which you can keep if your aesthetic eye can tolerate such horrors in your files.

Glad you've heard from the noble Auguste-Guillaume, Comte d'Erlette. Don't mind if he tears your work to pieces—he may be excessively severe, but even when he overshoots the mark there is often value in the general tenor of his strictures. I'll trust to you not to get scared off as a very promising 19-year-older in Pittsburgh[4] was not long ago . . . . . This youth was so downcast by one of M. le Comte's frank analyses that he won't submit anything else to the Sauk City tribunal! Derleth is a fine chap, but just a trifle cocky & egotistical. The nonsense & egotism will soon wear off, leaving sheer genius. I really think he has the greatest future of any of the gang—& as he himself says, it won't be in the weird, but in general literature. He is primarily a regional novelist with a poetic slant—deeply rooted in rural Wisconsin. Klarkash-Ton—who is 40 years old—won't be as glibly caustic as young Derleth. He, also, will have a better capacity to appraise the purely weird element in your work. I trust, by the way, that you now have his brochure. My copies came 2 or 3 days ago.

I think you are wise not to accept the presidencies offered you; for the more energies you save from mainly social activities, the more you'll have to devote to mainly literary activities. I'll be interested to see some of your humour—as well as such parts of "Sons of the Serpent" as you may send.

Glad you liked "Erich Zann". I'll still stick up for it as my second-best. Advance sheets of my "Witch House" came the other day, & I groaned over the misprints. Here are two gems—"magical LOVE" for "magical LORE"; "HUMAN element" for "KNOWN [chemical] element."[5] Such is life.

I thought Klarkash-Ton's drawings would give you *un nouveau frisson*. But you ought to see his large ones! He illustrated my "Lurking Fear" when it first appeared as a 4-part serial in a wretched rag called *Home Brew*—sometime I'll dig up that set & let you see it. And so the authentic phizzes of the gang proved a surprise to you. Odd, after your excellent guess as to what I looked like! Talman is indeed a poet—having issued a little brochure of verse called "Cloisonné" in his college days[6]—although his recent business career has pretty well ironed the poetic element out of him. He is now assistant editor of the four trade papers of the Texas Co.—the Texaco oil firm—with offices on the 18th floor of the Chrysler Bldg. in Manhattan. Latterly he has been developing into quite an antiquarian—perhaps as a sequel to his always keen interest in genealogy & family legend. He refuses to live in town, but commutes from his Spring Valley birthplace. Yes—Dwyer sometimes blossoms forth in the Eyrie, & is indeed the author of those genuinely weird lines—"Ol' Black Sarah."[7] He has one of the most delicately sensitive imaginations I have ever encountered, & in the course of time will probably pick up enough technique to secure a regular entree into W.T.

I certainly would have revelled in your 96° weather (94° was the best we had in the warm spell of June 8–12), & it would not even have conduced to indolence on my part. Instead, very hot weather increases my activity both physical & mental. Only at about 90° do I really feel any excess of energy— the sort which makes one want to start something active. The cooler it is, the more sluggish do I tend to be. I get positively drowsy under 75°. I certainly need a tropical environment—the cold week following the warm spell has reduced me to a shivering shadow . . . . I often have to sit in the kitchen & light the gas range . . . . but I'm getting my old oil heater fixed up.

Things hereabouts have just been thrown into chaos by a most unexpected disaster. On June 14, while answering the doorbell during my absence, my aunt slipped on the stairs & broke an ankle. Doctor . . . . ambulance . . . . Rhode-Island Hospital . . . X-ray . . . ether . . . . setting in plaster cast . . . . room in Ward K . . . . prospect of 6 weeks in bed & several more on crutches

. . . . . & a financial drain of utterly paralysing magnitude. A truly beautiful thing to happen when one is half-settled in a new home! Well—there's no danger, although restriction to one recumbent posture is rather hard on the back—& on the nerves. My aunt reads, writes notes, & eats with a fair degree of normality. She will stay another week at the hospital, & then decide whether to keep on there or come home with a nurse. Up to now I've been in a mess of arrangements shuttling back & forth betwixt home & hospital; but now a new temporary routine is fairly well worked out. However—in any event the summer is pretty effectively spoiled for the household!

To that list of my weird books add one more item—"Lukundoo & Other Stories", by Edward Lucas White—published in 1927 & very hard to get now. It was a gift from a correspondent in Buffalo.[8] I've read about half of it, & one story—"The Snout"—is a marvellous apex of nightmare! As in the case of his other works, White claims that he actually dreamed these narratives in substantially their present form.

Well—now to work. Thine in the Black Brotherhood
—E'ch-Pi-El

## Notes

1. HPL to Edwin Baird [c. early November 1923]: "Popular authors do not and apparently cannot appreciate the fact that true art is obtainable only by rejecting normality and conventionality in toto, and approaching a theme purged utterly of any usual or preconceived point of view. Wild and 'different' as they may consider their quasi-weird products, it remains a fact that the bizarrerie is on the surface alone; and that basically they reiterate the same old conventional values and motives and perspectives. Good and evil, teleological illusion, sugary sentiment, anthropocentric psychology—the usual superficial stock in trade, and all shot through with the eternal and inescapable commonplace. Take a werewolf story, for instance—who ever wrote a story from the point of view of the wolf, and sympathising strongly with the devil to whom he has sold himself? Who ever wrote a story from the point of view that man is a blemish on the cosmos, who ought to be eradicated?" *WT*, March 1924; rpt. in *Uncollected Letters*, ed. S. T. Joshi (West Warwick, RI: Necronomicon Press, 1986), 8.

2. H. Warner Munn, "The Werewolf of Ponkert" (*WT*, July 1925).

3. None of the works cited here survive.

4. J. Vernon Shea (1912–1981).

5. Cf. *SL* 4.213–14. Neither error was corrected.

6. *Cloisonnè and Other Verses* was printed at Brown University c. 1925.

7. *WT*, October 1928.

8. A gift from William Lumley.

[8]     [ALS]

Crypts of Elder Evil—
Hour of the Scratching on the
Lower Gate
[c. late June 1933]

Dear Bho-Blôk:—

Glad to see the season's produce! I like the new "Lucian Grey" immensely, & think all the changes are in the right direction. The principal remaining defects are mere matters of careless wording, plus one structural weakness connected with the introduction of the climactic final scene. In the latter instance you are too hasty & sketchy about the narrator's forced entrance to the house of horror—the effect being to disturb the tempo of the tale in some subtle way. As for general tendencies—one thing you need to be on guard against is an inclination toward *tautological expression*, both overt & in less literal substance. In "Lucian Grey" you have such repetitious phrases as *past & antecedents, based & founded, blurred & indistinct*, &c—all of which call for elimination. As I read over the copy I added corrections here & there, & it occurs to me that you might wish to incorporate these in the text before submitting the MS. to another critic. Accordingly I am returning the tale instead of sending it on to Klarkash-Ton. I hate to impose a task of re-copying—but you can probably fix up individual sheets without renewing the entire MS. Hope you can decipher my amorphous hieroglyphics—I don't envy you the job! As I think I said before, the central idea of this tale is not altogether new; hence it might meet with obstacles in professional marketing among jaded editors. However, it would do no harm to try it on W.T. I hear that another weird magazine is about to be founded—paying ½¢ per word & using "modern" spectral yarns which are "not too gruesome"—but I don't yet know its name. I'll let you know if I find out first. "The Blasphemy Beneath" is very vivid & colourful, & forms an admirable atmospheric study. I marvel that I never guessed Leng's direful secret before! Of course, some editors would object that, despite the powerful climax, it has no *plot*—but that objection doesn't count with me. My own chief criticism would be, as usual, that the style is a trifle florid & flamboyant—the visible shuddery decoration being laid on rather thickly. *Supreme* horror lies in the black *suggestion* of unnamable blasphemies—& the plainer the language the more ghastly the sense of hideous contrast. However, this is no fatal defect. Another thing I'd mention would be the many instances of *tautology*. I've tried to remove such repetitions as *repellent aspect & repulsive being, putrescent . . . corruption, sombre black, loathsome & disgusting, wholly & utterly, thaumaturgies & sorceries, huge & endless*, &c. In the course of time you'll probably start an anti-tautology campaign & eliminate this repetitious tendency. Oh—one thing more. I see you have Grey read the *Necronomicon* through in a single night—which is incompatible with its supposed *length* as established in tales already in print. You will perhaps recall my citing a very high page number is [*sic*] in "The Dunwich Horror."[1] Accordingly I am calling Grey's copy "fragmentary". Also—you give Howard's von Junzt the praenomen of *Conrad,* whereas at least one printed allusion (which I put in a story I ghost-wrote for a revision-client!) establishes it as *Friedrich.* Howard himself, amusingly enough, did not give von Junzt a first name so far as I know. (Am I mistaken?)[2] Before I forget it, let me enclose (please return) a skeletonic history of the imaginary *Necronomicon* which I prepared for myself in order to avoid self-contradictions in future tales. Since I prepared this, Klarkash-Ton has balled up the works by referring to a surviving *Arabic* copy—but I can fit this into the account by having its survival very obscure & unknown to scholars. Anyhow, C A S had it burn up at the end of his story! ("The Return of the Sorcerer", in *Strange Tales).*[3] Incidentally, the name & meaning of *Al Azif,* as given, are real Arabic—as cribbed from Henley's learned notes to "Vathek."[4] The enclosed copy is one that good old Whitehead typed for me some time before his death.

I trust your "Sons of the Serpent" will develop smoothly when you take it up again, & that your comic material will lend itself readily to dramatic incorporation. You certainly do produce at a great rate—though you have formidable speed & quantity rivals in E. Hoffmann Price, Comte d'Erlette, & Klarkash-Ton. Glad you've had some helpful & interesting epistles from A W & C A S, & that they've shewn you their likenesses . . . . . also that C A S has started you with a collection of his monstrous sketches. d'Erlette can undoubtedly advise you usefully regarding "Nocturne Macabre." As for other promising correspondents interested in the weird—it's hard to predict just who would & who wouldn't prove interesting & responsive, but here's a random list of suggestions jotted down hastily from memory.[5]

*Barlow, R. H., Box 88, De Land, Florida.* Young fellow—great collector of old pulp magazines & enthusiast for weird & scientifiction tales. Has recently attempted weird sketches of his own. Bright but not advanced in achievements. Likeable—& a pleasant correspondent.

*Black, B. C., Box 1061, Prescott, Arizona.* Youngish—& a sort of rolling stone.[6] Has tried writing, but of late inclines more to criticism. Has some rather amusing theories in favour of Philistinic taste, & defends them with a rather naive cocksureness. On the whole interesting—& greatly interested in the weird. Hails from Chautauqua, N.Y., but is now dead broke & on the road. Is quite a semi-professional photographer. Pretty good correspondent.

*Brobst, Harry, 305 Blackstone Blvd, Providence, R.I.* Age 24—alert, bright, adventurous chap. Student nurse in a hospital for the insane. Ex-reporter. Hails from Allentown, Pa. Does not write himself, but is an ardent W.T. fan—his chief idol being Klarkash-Ton. Interested in science. An authority on Pennsylvania folklore. Very pleasant. Had 1 year at Muhlenberg College.

*Dwyer, Bernard Austin, Box 43, West Shokan, N.Y.* Age 34, but looks younger . . . . & feels & acts so. Finely sensitive taste in weird matters, & a slowly increasing power of expression. Pretty good critic in an informal way. Delightful good fellow & interesting correspondent—I'm enraged that fate won't let me visit him this year. Lives in the wild & picturesque Catskills in the farm-house where he was born—& poignantly appreciates the wild, mystical beauty of his native scenery—which he compares to the "wild domed hills & hanging woods" of Arthur Machen's beloved "Caermaen" [Caerleon-on-Usk]. A husky giant, & vastly interested in athletics—swimming, muscular development. Trying valiantly to build up his muscle & work off his fat. A veritable master at the dining-table—I never knew another human being who could hold so much food! Is a pictorial artist of considerable natural skill.

*Lumley, William, 742 William St., Buffalo, N.Y.* An eccentric old man of very unusual qualities. Uneducated, but widely travelled. Probably exaggerates his contact with the Orient & its secrets, but has certainly seen a lot of the world & its queer side. Actually believes in occultism, & claims to have studied ancient & forbidden books like the Necronomicon—also to have seen ghosts. Talks sometimes of being persecuted by enemies—& my madhouse-nurse friend Brobst thinks he may be ever so lightly touched in the belfry. Shews a surprisingly fine taste in weird literature, & has read extensively—both standard works & magazines. A W.T. fan of the first magnitude. Probably has a strong latent literary gift—thwarted by ignorance. Some of his weird verses are really good—even if misspelt & mis-capitalised. An appealingly friendly & generous old boy—he has given me two books in gratitude for slight critical advice. A distinctly interesting character.

*Shea, J. Vernon, Jr., 5705 Jackson St., Pittsburgh, Pa.* Age 20. This is the kid whom Derleth's criticism scared off. Very interesting & promising. Omnivorous reader, & an ardent W.T. fan. Slowly developing as a writer—but in realism (like Derleth) rather than in the weird. Had 1 year at U. of Pittsburgh. Is an enthusiastic devotee of the drama, & has acted in amateur productions. Cinema addict, & voluminous amateur film critic. Very bright & likeable.

*Strauch, Carl F., 812 Washington St., Allentown, Pa.* Age 24. Poet with one published book to his credit. Bosom home-town friend of Harry Brobst (vide supra). Graduate of Muhlenberg College & has acted as assistant librarian there. Authority on Pennsylvania folklore with weird *Hexerei* beliefs. Working on a realistic novel. Delightful & affable—he visited Providence last summer & will probably come again this September. Enthusiast in Germanic literature. Rather anti-scientific by temperament—affording material for heated & interesting arguments with Brobst.

*Wandrei, Donald, 84 Horatio St., Apt. 4B, New York, N.Y.* Age 25. Born & reared in St. Paul, Minn., graduate & former instructor of English, U. of Minn. Disciple & worshipper of Klarkash-Ton—whose cosmic, anti-terrestrial temperament he tends to share. Author of 2 books of bizarre poems & many tales. 2 unpublished novels.[7] Is slowly turning toward realism in literature. Seeking his fortune in the great city, & now almost dead broke. Home address—I fancy he'll be back there soon—1152 Portland Ave., St. Paul, Minn. Very interesting, but may be hard to get started as a correspondent.

Long is a fine chap, but a rottener & rottener correspondent as the years go by. Price would be a good & helpful correspondent if settled down as he was in New Orleans last year, but is now a rather spasmodically articulate rolling stone. Robert E. Howard (Lock Box 313, Cross Plains, Texas) is fascinating when started on the subject of sanguinary Texas folklore. Yes—the world still has quite a bunch of fairly interesting people left in it!

Thanks for the sinister glimpse of Bho-Blôk, the Daemon Lama of Night & Abhorred Leng. Rrrrgh . . . . but all the hidden, festering evil of pathless Thibet leers from those balefully arching brows! I return the likeness herewith, as per request. Thanks, too, for your exceedingly clever drawing of the *other* priest of Leng—who looks very like *me,* if I am any judge. I am adding that to my collection. Drawing your story themes is really an excellent idea, which makes for clear-cut, concrete visualisation. I have done it once or twice—notably when designing nameless monsters like Cthulhu or the denizens of the Mountains of Madness—& I always prepare maps & diagrams where complicated action occurs. Thus I made a complete chart of Innsmouth before finishing the "Shadow". Some day I may try to draw a map of Arkham.[8]

I'm glad you have "The Double Shadow". I knew you'd appreciate it. Whatever Wright rejects usually excels what he accepts! Under separate cover I am sending you—as a loan—the back numbers of W T which you mention. *I* am the writer described by Long in the Space-Eaters—in 1925 I dwelt in a room in Brooklyn Heights much as described.[9] The description of me is good except that my eyes are dark brown. Long is a lax observer, & probably thought light eyes would have to go with such a chalky complexion. I've heard of "The Werewolf of Paris"—founded, I believe, on the actual case of the ghoulish Sergeant Bertrand.[10]

My aunt progresses as expected, though her restriction to one posture is giving her a lame back. In about a week she will probably return home with a nurse. I visit the hospital each day, & am kept so busy that all travel plans are off. I've enjoyed the warmer weather, though our temperatures haven't equalled yours. Have taken some long walks south of the city—one to the quaint & ancient fishing village of Pawtuxet. And of course I do most of my writing outdoors in parks.

Yrs in the Dark Brotherhood—

E'ch-Pi-El.

*Notes*

1. In "The Dunwich Horror," HPL mentions there are at least 751 pp. in the *Necronomicon.*
2. In "The Horror in the Museum" and "Out of the Aeons" (ghostwritten for Hazel Heald), as well as HPL's own "The Thing on the Doorstep," "The Dreams in the Witch House," "The Shadow out of Time," and "The Haunter of the Dark," HPL refers to the author merely as von Junzt.

3. HPL, "History of the *Necronomicon*" (1927). CAS, "The Return of the Sorcerer" (*Strange Tales*, September 1931). HPL's A.Ms. read "Arabic text now lost" (*LAL* 105).

4. A novel by William Beckford. In "History of the *Necronomicon*" HPL defines *Azif* as "the word used by the Arabs to designate that nocturnal sound (made by insects) supposed to be the howling of daemons."

5. RB ultimately came in touch with Barlow, Dwyer, and Shea. His correspondence with Barlow was brief and intermittent; he was in contact with Dwyer until about 1938; and he remained in close touch with Shea until the latter's death in 1981.

6. In early 1936, Black, then in Upland, IN, was planning a little magazine to be called *Nuggets*. HPL was to contribute a brief essay, but the magazine never materialized.

7. Wandrei's two novels, since published, are *The Web of Easter Island* and *Invisible Sun*.

8. See assorted notes, map, and drawings for "The Shadow over Innsmouth" (*CE* 5.249–53), and "Map of the Principal Parts of Arkham, Massachusetts" (A.Ms., JHL), copied by an unknown hand in the *Acolyte* 1, No. 1 (Fall 1942): 26 (as "Map of Arkham"). *Marginalia* (Sauk City, WI: Arkham House, 1944) contains another map preceding p. 279. HPL sent yet another map of Arkham to RB in April 1936 (see RB 59). HPL's notes for *At the Mountains of Madness* and "The Shadow out of Time" have also been published.

9. Frank Belknap Long, Jr., "The Space-Eaters" (*WT*, July 1928). HPL refers to his residence at 169 Clinton Street, which he himself describes in his story "Cool Air."

10. A novel by Guy Endore.


[9]     [ALS]

> Tomb 66—Necropolis of
> Thun. Hour of the Rattling of
> the Nether Grating.
> [early to mid-July 1933]

Dear Bho-Blôk:—

Hope the magazines reached you in good condition. Some 1923 duplicates that I lately sent out disintegrated in the mails like the corpse of M. Valdemar—hence I am rather apprehensive about all ancient wood-pulp shipments.

My aunt returned home in the ambulance July 5, & has since been resting in her own room with a nurse—a much more comfortable arrangement than the hospital. However, it keeps me very much tied down, since I have to be on duty every afternoon while the nurse goes out. My programme is all disorganised, & heaven only knows when I'll have things in order again.

A pleasant interlude—just prior to my aunt's return—was the long-heralded visit of E. Hoffmann Price, who blew in amidst the rattling of a 1928 Ford Juggernaut. During his four-day sojourn festivities were plentiful.[1] Cook stopped in on his way to the convention, & young Brobst was over twice—on one occasion staying all night for a session of triangular literary & philosophical discussion punctuated by a trip to an ancient churchyard (completely hidden from all highways by bank walls & centuried houses) on the hill at about 3 a.m. What we saw, whispered, & intoned in that nighted & legend-haunted necropolis is not for the timid pen to record . . . . . . .[2]

On July 2 Price brought his Juggernaut into the service of antiquarian exploration by taking me to a Rhode-Island region which—despite my lifelong residence less than 30 miles away from it, & my ⅓ ancestral connexion with its ancient families—I had never (through lack of public transportation facilities) seen before with the physical eye. This was the historic "South County" or "Narragansett Country" west of the bay, where before the Revolution there existed a system of large plantations & black slaves comparable to that of the South. The scenery of this territory is ineffably fine, as I had long realised from reading, though none of the choicest areas can be glimpsed from the main trunk highways. On this occasion we began with the marvellously unspoiled colonial seaport of Wickford, & worked southward through the magical land of yesterday. We saw the rambling old snuff-mill where Gilbert Stuart was born in 1755, & the vast Rowland Robinson mansion (1705) amidst its gigantic, centuried willows. The lone, deserted Ferry Church on a windswept headland claimed our notice, nor did we neglect the abandoned "glebe" or rectory of the Rev. James MacSparran (1727), now spectrally overgrown with a lush profusion of vines & briers. We climbed a hill to the well-known "Hannah Robinson's Rock" (around which revolves a pathetic story)[3] & enjoyed what is probably the finest landscape vista in Rhode Island, if not in all New England—winding blue river far below, rich green meadows & woodlands, white headland, church in the distance, & the remote gleam of the half-glimpsed sea. Great stuff! But the climax was the wholly unspoiled colonial village of Kingston—ancient county-seat of King's [now Washington] County, & virtually unchanged since men in knee-breeches & periwigs congregated there for the quarterly assizes. The well-kept, centuried houses, the enormous shade-trees, the venerable court building, & the quaint 1746 inn all remain as of yore to fascinate the beholder. And to think I had never seen this gem of antiquity before! On our way back Price got a typical R.I. shore dinner at the ancient fishing village of Pawtuxet (6 m. S. of Prov.)— whilst I (whose loathing for all sea-food I may have mentioned) got something fit to eat at a lunchroom when we hit town.

Glad my critical observations have proved of some use. By the way—the name of your besetting fault (repetition of words having the same meaning when one would be sufficient) is TAUTOLOGY (not TANTOLOGY). I don't wonder that my infamous script left you in doubt if you didn't know the term. In my day this word was in common use in high-school books on rhetoric— how times change! As for story-construction—a mad narrator scarcely excuses certain extravagances in fictional construction. The primary object of the story is to produce a certain convincing effect on the reader; & if the events & motivation be too weak, the thing falls flat. If the tale calls for a madman too addled to produce a coherent narrative, then the author must refrain from entrusting him with the entire task of narration. But anyhow, the sort of confused perspective, feverish tone, & hallucinative exaggeration a lunatic would ordinarily indulge in would not be likely to resemble the kind of defects against which critics complain. In preparing an horrific description we must make sure that it will *really* horrify instead of merely exciting laughter or evoking a bored sense of gratuitous, unconvincing, & irresponsibly grotesque mendacity. This is best achieved by not laying the colours on too thickly—by darkly & subtly *suggesting* the nameless horrors involved, instead of cataloguing them & rubbing them in. I can speak of this with melancholy eloquence, since overcolouring & extravagance form my own persistently besetting sin. As for the "Necronomicon"— this month's triple use of such allusions is bringing me in an unusual number of inquiries concerning the real nature & obtainability of Alhazred's, Eibon's, & von Junzt's works.[4] In each case I am frankly confessing the fakery involved.

Thanks for the hellish drawings—which really shew a marked aptitude for weird portraiture. That Yuggoth-denizen looks his part every inch, while the Garros admirably illustrates his especial type. The Pan-worshipper gives clear evidence of having glimpsed the Dark God himself.

Glad you like the "Witch-House". As to the question of who will get the vote—it would be amusing if I defeated myself through a victory of "The Horror in the Museum", which I ghost-wrote for a revision-client. But of course the "fan vote" is really no index at all to the merit of a story, since most of the readers are obviously persons without taste or education. When one reflects on the tremendous popularity of Single-Plot Hamilton, Nictzin Dyalhis, & the routine stuff of Quinn, it becomes obvious how little the opinion of the Eyrie commentators really means.

Young Shea, I am certain, will be glad to hear from you. He is a bright, interesting youth, & seems to me exceedingly promising—though not in the field of the weird tale. Old Bill Lumley is an interesting cuss, too—albeit in a different way. He ought to be good story-material himself for anyone with the right kind of skill.

I was much interested in the glimpse of your activities & home life, & regret the financial stringency which necessitates so much tension & curtailment. Let us hope that improving conditions in the economic world will soon produce a more felicitous adjustment. My own financial state is appalling & without promise—so that I hardly know what will become of the College St. household in a year or two unless something turns up. As for details—my aunt has a radio, but I am not very enthusiastic about what comes over it. Indeed, I begrudge every minute not spent in reading, writing, or scenic antiquarian exploration. I'm not much of a cinema devotee, either—scarcely seeing more than half a dozen films in the course of a year. I used to be quite a theatregoer 20 to 35 years ago, but seem to have lost my taste for the drama—a damned fortunate thing for my pocketbook! Architecture & narrative prose seem to be the two aesthetic media

to which I am most sensitive—although I have a decent appreciation of poetry
& have dabbled in random versification myself.

About English courses—it must be that the Milwaukee high schools differ, for I'll swear that my friend Moe at West Division teaches nothing about
which one could justly complain. He seems to keep his pupils keenly interested (I've been in touch with many of them—my friend Galpin was once such),
& generally succeeds in imparting to the brighter ones a very sound & envia-
ble faculty of understanding & appreciating poetry.

As for story plots—that idea of finding a *Thing* in the hold of a long-
sunken treasure-ship is excellent, notwithstanding the existing plenitude of
weird undersea tales. So is the idea of a revival of man's atrophied gills—
indeed, the two ideas might well be combined in the same story. Races of undersea things have often been described, but there would be real originality in
a tale of a *human* civilisation beneath the waves—perhaps populating the
sunken ruins of fabulous Atlantis, Lemuria, or Mu—or hellish R'lyeh. One
could assume a highly scientific prehistoric civilisation (long dead & forgotten) which mastered the art of gill-revival & established vast sea-bottom colonies—colonies surviving long after the decay of the upper-world branch of
the race. I have always been especially fascinated by submarine themes—
using them, as you will recall, in "Dagon", "The Temple", "Cthulhu", & innumerable verses. It's a good idea to send your tales around to various members of the gang, for each critic may have a useful suggestion to give. Some of
the recommendations may be foolish, & many will contradict one another;
yet you can always cull out a useful residue & correlate some of the scattered
precepts into a reasonably unified basis for future development. I think I
agree with you regarding the depth & sensitiveness of *fear as occasioned by
strangeness*. Fear seems always able to gain an ascendancy over any other emotion, & a vast number of our most vital institutions are directly rooted in it. It
has always interested & fascinated me more than anything else—except perhaps the essential element of *strangeness itself,* which most forms of it embody.

Glad to see the samples of humour—whose effect on an audience, if well
delivered, I can readily imagine. They all seem sprightly & adequate—
wisecracking patter rather than deep cosmic irony, of course, but exactly what
is desired for popular presentation. I don't wonder at the success of a minstrel act made up of such material.

I envy you Milwaukeeans your long spell of high temperatures—which
Moe has also mentioned. We have occasional warm spells—it was 94° yesterday—but colder weather comes in between. Early this week I nearly froze—
but have had my oil heater repaired, hence am able to cope with the frost
daemon a trifle better than before. I had gas heat at my former abode, but
here there is no surviving gas connexion except the kitchen range. Today has
been warm, but it is now getting cooler. I am out on Prospect Terrace—a
small park I may have mentioned to you, which is perched near the crest of

Providence's ancient hill (a bit N. of College St.) & commands an impressive panorama of the lower town & of the bordering sunset hills beyond. In summer I do most of my reading & writing in the open—sometimes here, sometimes on a favourite wooded river-bluff (a metropolitan park, immune from urban encroachment & unchanged since my infancy) a mile east of here, & sometimes in the genuinely open woods & fields of the countryside north of the town. This Prospect Terrace is set amidst the colonial dwellings of the hill, & has a peculiar fascination all its own. It has always affected my imagination most profoundly, so that the deepest-seated & most recurrent of all my dream-pictures is that of being on some balustraded parapet high above a strange & marvellous city, looking down on fantastic roofs & spires amidst the spectral & alluring glamour of a flaming, apocalyptic sunset. Sunset-gazing from the Terrace is a favourite local pastime, so that toward evening I do not have the solitude which I enjoy earlier in the day. I generally remain, though—for sunset & the coming of dusk are always worth watching from this unusual vantage point. The great State House dome & St. Patrick's tower stand out marvellously against the fire-streaked west, while the town below is doubly magical as its evening lights begin to twinkle out one by one amidst the deepening violet shadows. ¶ And so it goes. Best wishes—E'ch-Pi-El

### Notes

1. See E. Hoffmann Price, "The Man Who Was Lovecraft," in *Lovecraft Remembered,* ed. Peter Cannon (Sauk City, WI: Arkham House, 1998), 292–94.

2. St. John's Churchyard, one of HPL's favorite places to take visitors from out of town. See also RB 48.

3. Hannah Robinson (1746–1773) liked to gaze out at Narragansett Bay from a large boulder at Tower Hill Road in South Kingston, RI. She had eloped with her teacher, Peter Simon, whom her father had forbidden her to see, and they reconciled over the matter only after Hannah had become deathly ill.

4. HPL, "The Dreams in the Witch House"; Hazel Heald, "The Horror in the Museum" (ghostwritten by HPL); and CAS, "Ubbo-Sathla" (*WT,* July 1933), all mention HPL's *Necronomicon* and the *Book of Eibon* (invented by CAS). HPL's and CAS's stories also mention the *Unaussprechlichen Kulten* of von Junzt (invented by Robert E. Howard).

[10]　[ALS]

> Castle of Udolpho—Hour of
> the Stirring in the Tunnels
> Beneath the Foundations
> [postmarked 22 July 1933]

Dear Bho-Blôk:—

Congratulations on those two drawings! You certainly are crowding Klarkash-Ton for the wreath of upas—& you really come close to tying Bernard Dwyer so far as fantastic conceptions go. The Yuggoth-entity is a genuine knockout, & that hellish sea of faces is really remarkable—you blend the masses & colours with tremendous skill. I'd like to have several rolls of that for wall-paper—fitting up one of the attic rooms of my new Georgian abode as a shrine of horror (with other appropriate hangings & grisly objets d'art) wherein to receive certain select visitors of macabre tastes.

Under separate cover you will receive the June 1930 W.T.[1] The others duly came back, though visibly & mournfully displaying the stress of their return trip. However—I dare say they'll last as long as the rest of the file, the older items of which are almost falling to powder. Glad you found the back numbers of interest. Long's slaughter of me is not the only time one of the gang has bumped another off. In my "Statement of Randolph Carter" the man who goes down into the tomb & does not come up is meant to be my friend Samuel Loveman. I dreamed that story almost exactly as it stands, with Loveman & myself as the characters. That was in 1919. The dream gave me such a punch that I jumped up at once, lit the gas, & made a set of synoptic notes before the first keen edge of the impression wore off. Then later I wrote the story.

I'll be glad to look over "Sons of the Serpent"—& trust that you may encounter no obstacles in its completion. There's nothing like steady practice as a polisher of style & developer of fictional power. Glad you liked "The Shunned House", & hope the public will do the same when Coates issues it as a book. Comte d'Erlette's sketch is rather clever—he has quite a gift at satire, though he doesn't often weave that element into his serious work. As for the new W.T.—I wouldn't be surprised if the Eyrie-herd gave Quinn's rubber-stamp the popularity vote, it being their habit to hand him the laurel whenever he appears.

As for young Jehvish-Êi, the Black Mass Acolyte of Pittsburgh—you'll probably hear from him sooner or later. He is a very spasmodic correspondent, & hasn't written me for considerably over a month. You & he ought to have a good deal to discuss because of your common interest in drama.

Wakefield's stuff is generally very good, & I'm glad you've had an opportunity to read it. Of the tales in the first book my favourites are "He Cometh & He Passeth By" (the villain in which is a sort of caricature of the well-known living mystic & alleged Satanist Aleister Crowley), "The Red Lodge", "The 17th Hole at Duncaster['], & "And He Shall Sing". In the second book I like best "The Cairn", "Look Up There", & "Blind Man's Buff".[2]

Your new plot ideas sound very ingenious—Quinn could certainly keep M. de Grandin & Friend Trowbridge busy over the mystery of the missing bodies! That undertaker could organise a whole army of ghastly zombies—composed of the bodies of Harrisonville's most solid citizens—& their strange antics & depredations could be such as to drive worthy Sergeant Costello to his wits' end. At last the so invincible Jules de Grandin is called in, & voila! A few sprigs of garlic blessed by a convenient priest checks the invasion, while the zombies turn on their evil animator & rend him to pieces! The false devil idea has great possibilities, also. Didn't Price use something vaguely approaching it (at least in spirit) in his "Stranger from Kurdistan"?[3] By the way—I'm enclosing a lately-acquired snap of Price to supplement the rogues' gallery which I sent some time ago. Quite dashing & devilish, as you see!

That N.A.P.A. convention which I couldn't attend saddled me with the chairmanship of the critical bureau—just as I was trying to get rid of responsibilities! Incidentally, one of my recent recruits—R. H. Barlow of Florida—won the story laureateship.[4] You would enjoy that association, I think, if you were to join. You'll recall that I sent you blanks.

So your father has been to the much-advertised Century of Progress.[5] The wretchedly futuristic architecture of those damned exhibition buildings would be enough to keep me away even if I had the cash to get there! I dissent absolutely from the position of those who welcome the new machine-culture involving a complete break with the past. To me there is nothing really civilised in large-scale organisation & spectacular material development—while the modern worship of mere speed & quantity strikes me as being downright decadent. I would prefer a simple, frugal, plain-living society of highly-developed taste & dominantly intellectual & aesthetic activities—a society conscious of its past, & deriving from unbroken traditions a mellow richness not otherwise attainable.

My aunt is now sitting up each afternoon, & in a little over a week ought to have the plaster cast off. Then, however, will come a considerable period on crutches. I've had an invitation to an ancient farmhouse in New Hampshire, but fear I shall have to decline it because of the need of being on hand here.

I have two distinguished guests today—each a fair-sized handful. Little tiger kittens—eyes open, but still shaky in navigation & not playful yet. They belong in the boarding-house whose rear abuts on our back garden, & I fancy I shall borrow one or both of them quite frequently during the various stages of their sportive youth. Probably I mentioned that I am almost fanatically fond of cats. ¶ Well—thanks again for those truly fascinating drawings—& also for the stamps. ¶ Blessings of Sathanas & his Archfiends upon thee!

Thine in the Kshan Ritual—E'ch-Pi-El.

[P.S. on envelope:]

*Late news*

Frank Belknap Long & parents just passed through Providence en route for Cape Cod—also a friend of Klarkash-Ton's, bound for Gloucester.[6] ¶ Owing to the nurse's willingness to stay in next Monday & Tuesday, I shall be able to visit the Longs at Onset, Mass. Belknap was vastly impressed with your weird drawings, & wants me to bring them along to Onset for his further examination.

*Notes*

1. The issue contained HPL's "The Rats in the Walls" (orig. March 1924).
2. H. Russell Wakefield, *They Return at Evening* and *Others Who Returned.* The stories are all addressed in the revised "Supernatural Horror in Literature."
3. "The Stranger from Kurdistan" (*WT,* July 1925; rpt. December 1929).
4. For "Eyes of the God (Maybe the Natives Were Right)," *Sea Gull* 1, No. 7 (May 1933): 5–6; rpt. in Barlow's *Eyes of the God.*
5. The Century of Progress Exposition opened at the World's Fair in Chicago on 27 May 1933.
6. Helen V. Sully.

[11]    [ALS]

Vale of Pnath—
Hour of the Grunting within
the Curiously Asymmetrical
Burrows
[late July 1933]

Dear Bho-Blôk:—

Commiserations & condolences on the d'Erlette critical cyclone! First he puts young J. Vernon to Shea-me, & now he Blochs the aspirations of genius in his own state! What a boy! And now a new victim is lined up, all ready for the axe—the Carl F. Strauch of Allentown, Pa. whom I wrote you about some time ago. However—you ought to see what Little Augie said about the joint effort of Price & myself, which Dwyer forwarded to him the other day. I haven't told Price about that blasting . . . . . I can take it, but I'd hate to see a good fellow like Sultan Malik in a suicide's grave, with moustache, cane, & cravat invaded by the ineluctable worm! However—after one's initial ache has subsided, one can get considerable meat out of M. le Comte's ruthless slashings. Allowing for the exaggerations of youth & arrogance, he really does tend to put his finger on certain weak spots—& several of our gang (especially Wandrei) have really profited by his acidulous advice. Don't get disheartened or throw your critic-riddled tales [a]way. Instead, keep them & analyse them, & use them as the starting points for fresh attempts. Your stuff is very good for a beginner's—& you surely realise that it takes *years* (literally & seriously) for any ordinarily gifted writer to achieve a real mastery of fiction. Hell! You ought to see the crap that young d'Erlette himself was turning out around 1926 & 1927! It took him years to handle language with real accuracy, fluency, & restraint. As for my own early stuff—gawd help us! Of all the junk I scribbled between the ages of 7 & 18, only 2 specimens were worth saving from my great holocaust of 1908. Long was at least 5 years in making the grade professionally—& so on, & so on. Well—I don't believe I need to worry about you, since I see by the note on your envelope that you are at work on a new tale. Let's see it when it's done.

Glad young Jevish-Êi is proving such a good correspondent—I had a whale of a letter from him myself the other day. He is really admirably brilliant, & I think he is headed for something substantial in literature . . . . realism rather than weirdness.

I don't think the N.A.P.A. will disappoint you. If you join, you'll be my second successive *R. B.* recruit—my last having been young R. H. Barlow of Florida, who celebrated his entrance by winning the story laureateship. I have just been appointed chairman of the Critical Bureau—as if I weren't sufficiently oppressed by responsibilities!

My two tiger cubs are now abridged to one—the weaker brother having come to another & better land where fields of catnip stretch away to oceans of salmon-peopled milk. But the remaining cub is surely some boy! Bless me, but how a week & a half has developed the little rascal! He's now strong & agile, & incredibly bright & playful. I borrow him often—so that he is coming to know these colonial corridors exceeding well. As for the canidae—I'm largely indifferent to them, though I have no active dislike. I despise their satellitism & slobbery habits as opposed to the bland independence & instinctive neatness & delicacy of the felidae. A comely black cat with large yellow eyes is to me about the apex of organic grace. Every motion & shade of posture is a poem in line & motion. But I like all the felidae.

Your sketches are certainly great stuff—indeed, that sea of sinister faces has elicited enthusiastic comment from everyone to whom I've shewn it. Casual though they are, your drawings are replete with genuine talent— promising well if you ever care to develop that side of your personality. I shall welcome the further specimens you promise.

About Chaugnar—though Long is quite a cinemaddict, I don't think that Signor Durante's[1] beak is the actual source. Neither—strange as it seems—is my own stupendous proboscis. The real source is a jade-green statue of a Hindoo elephant-god[2] given Belknap by his aunt, who picked it up in the Louvre in Paris—not a theft, but a purchase at the counter where reproductions of noted originals are sold. That statuette—about a foot tall—impressed Sonny profoundly—& the story is the result. By the way, the Roman dream episode in that tale is an interpolated bit of my own—the dream being an *actual* one I had in '27.[3]

Yes—I noticed the debonair tone of your epistle, & am glad that your Casanovian successes have so direct & lasting an effect on your aesthetic processes. But then, I judge from your glowing description that this was no ordinary bit of sheiking. Gilded finger-nails . . . . bless my soul, but what heights of iridescent Antiochan decadence!

I think I mentioned the recent social events on my programme—the visit of Klarkash-Ton's friend, & my trip to Cape Cod to see Belknap & his parents. We had rotten weather, but literary & philosophical discussion atoned for all. And what a kitten they had at the place where we stopped! A ride through the attractive countryside (vide enc.) to Hyannis was our chief material diversion. Just now I'm welcoming to this fair municipality the good old friend I've so frequently mentioned—James F. Morton. That means as festive a half-week as my tied-up status at present will allow. My aunt, by the way, now has half her cast removed; & is learning to walk on crutches. But improvement is damn slow. ¶ Enclosed is a circular of a *new magazine* <to?> *which* Klarkash-Ton & I are contributing. No pay—but it gets us extra lending copies of stuff no paying magazine will take.[4]

> The Peace of Eblis upon thee—
> E'ch-Pi-El

## Notes

1. Jimmy Durante (1893–1980), American singer, comedian, and actor, known for his prominent nose.
2. Ganesha, one of the two sons of Shiva and Parvati.
3. HPL refers to Long's "The Horror from the Hills" (*WT,* January and February/March 1931), which contains HPL's description to Long of his famous Roman dream. Similar accounts were published from letters to Bernard Austin Dwyer (in *Dreams and Fancies*) and Donald Wandrei (in *CF* 3).
4. *The Fantasy Fan.*

[12]  [ALS]

> Sealed Tower of N'kung—
> Hour of the Signal from the Dark
> Nebula
> [c. 22 August 1933]

Dear Bho-Blôk:—

Commiserations on your father's affliction! I can very acutely & vividly sympathise, since I have a relative-patient also. Let us hope that the arm will mend steadily from now onward. My aunt's cast came off a week ago, but the doctor insists on having her rest in bed for a spell before trying her new crutches. I am still closely tied down, & will be even more so when the nurse goes—since I shall then be the sole link with the doorbell & the outside world in general.

Your long picaresque novel of the yacht & its heterogeneous crew sounds highly ingenious—I have often had a roughly similar idea; that is, of some sort of voyage to a long succession of totally distinct horrors & mysteries, ending up outside the known cosmos or in some alien dimension. The plan has vast possibilities; though one must take care to avoid an unconvincing degree of extravagance, & to make each separate background accurate & realistic.

The later & non-human parts sound especially promising. Glad Comte d'Erlette approves of the design. It will certainly be magnificent practice, whether or not the first result is a finished piece of work. Good luck with it!

Yes—I shall have to write a Bubastian story some day—though I am always slow in getting around to any given plan. As a matter of fact I have fully half a dozen plots in mind that deal with the felidae.[1] One of the little kittens next door (which I think I mentioned to you) has been given away, & the other probably will be soon—but meanwhile the remaining one (which was the brighter one anyhow) is a marvellous little companion.

You astonish me when you say you dream but twice a year. I can never drop off for a second—not even in my easy-chair or over my desk—without having dreams of the most vivid sort; not always bizarre or fantastic, but always clear-cut & lifelike. I seldom dream of *recent* every-day things, but tend to hark back 30 years or more to my boyhood—which was by all odds the happiest period of my existence. In nine dreams out of ten I am a kid in short trousers at my birthplace, with my mother, grandfather, & other departed kinsfolk & friends alive. Usually the general setting is quite consistent— horses & carriages, little street-cars with open platforms, &c.— though occasionally modern elements are illogically interpolated into the 1903 atmosphere. At other times modern events are adapted or reconciled to the 1903 period in a way that would be extremely clever if it were conscious work. But besides these comparatively mundane dreams I occasionally have boldly fantastic ones which make good weird-fictional material. Only last night I was with a party of silent, apprehensive men armed with some peculiar occult device like an *ankh* or *crux ansata*—climbing up ladders & picking a precarious way over the huddled, sagging roofs of a rotting & incredibly ancient town, in search of a vague being of infinite & immortal evil which had been afflicting the inhabitants. Once—in the light of a leprous, waning moon—we saw *It* .... a black, large-eared, crouching thing about the size of a large dog, & roughly resembling one of the Notre-Dame gargoyles. In the end It escaped us in a peculiar fashion. Our leader, it seemed, was a very distinguished looking young man on horseback, who did not climb up to the roofs as we did at his orders. All at once, as we chased the Thing from roof to roof & made It cringe at the sight of our shining metal ankhs, It spread rudimentary bat-wings & launched Itself at our leader as he bestrode his pawing horse far below us. Looking down, we saw the Blasphemy merge Itself plastically & hideously with the handsome form of the mounted captain, till in an instant there was but one being where two had been .... a shocking hybrid Thing clad in the silken robe of our captain, yet having in lieu of a face only the black, large-eared snout of the evil entity. It looked up & leered—squealing things we could not understand—& then galloped off on the horse that had been our leader's. We were in confusion—clambering bewilderedly down to the snowless but slightly frozen ground—when I awaked. That's all there was to it—not enough for a story, but typical of the sort of dream I have every week or so—or perhaps twice a week.[2] This kind of dreaming is not as rare as one might think—I suppose you know that Edward Lucas White derives virtually all his strange & highly original stories from actual dreams he has experienced.[3] Did I tell you of the dreams I had at the age of six, when I used to encounter a flock of bat-winged entities to which I gave the name of "night-gaunts"? I may add that all I know of dreams seems to contradict flatly the "symbolism" theories of Freud.[4] It may be that others, with less sheer phantasy filling their minds, have dreams of the Freudian sort; but it is very certain that I don't.

Congratulations on turning your Casanovianism to such practical use! Wish I were young enough to cajole adoring nymphs into doing my typing—I think I mentioned how I loathe the very sight of a machine. I trust you pick your harem for accuracy as well as looks, so that you don't have to waste time on corrections.

*The Fantasy Fan* has just changed its policy, so that after the 3d number or so it will be devoted mainly to weirdness rather than scientifiction. This comes from Editor Hornig's unexpected stroke of good luck in being hired as managing editor of *Wonder Stories*. Naturally he doesn't want to duplicate his activities & be his own rival. If the thing doesn't fail, it ought to carry a good bit of old stuff by Klarkash-Ton & myself. The editor is now looking for articles on weird fiction & reviews of weird books.

By the way—I've just had a letter from the Knopf firm asking to see some of my stuff with a view to possible book publication. *Possible* is good! I've shot along some junk,[5] but after my experience with Putnam & the Vanguard I realise very keenly how little such a request means. These birds are merely scouting around to make sure they don't miss anything. My tripe will come back presently with a polite note of regret.

Haven't had a second to read the new W.T., but hope to get around to it in a week or so. Glad Suter is still up to form—he's an old favourite of mine, though he hasn't been contributing much of late. The commonplace tone of W T is purely a matter of Wright's choice—he could get plenty of really unusual stuff if he would only accept & encourage it. He thinks, however, that the rubber-stamp crap is what his readers want (& perhaps it is, gawd 'elp 'em!); hence moulds his policy accordingly.[6]

I shall be eager to see your new drawings. Klarkash-Ton has sent me quite a few new ones, though too large to enclose in a common envelope. I'll do them up & let you get a look at them in the course of time. By the way— C A S has lately killed two rattlesnakes, one of which had crept almost upon him as he sat writing in the open air just outside his house. He, like me, prefers the canopy of heaven for aestival composition. The thermometer has been up around 108° at Auburn—a thing which excites my keenest envy. 97° is the best we have had. I think I'd enjoy your Milwaukee summers, though the winters are another story. You have greater extremes than we do. The approach of autumn is now mournfully signalised by chilly evenings which drive me indoors from Prospect Terrace & the wooded river-bank. Despite the few warm spells, it seems almost as though we had had no summer.

Had a good visit from my friend James F. Morton—curator of the Paterson Museum. We took many rural hikes; seeing on one occasion a fine old well-sweep in active use, & spending some time in a drowsy village[7] where the spirit of 1820 still predominates. We also visited ancient Warren, down the east shore of the bay, patronising an ice-cream joint where 28 varieties are sold, & thence walking onward to ancient Bristol . . . . . from which we returned to Prov. by train. Another time we went down the west shore to old Pawtuxet—where, as in Price's case, I watched Morton eat a hearty shore dinner. On the final day we took a sail to centuried Newport—exploring the time-hoary town & sitting on the rugged sea-cliffs where 200 years ago Dean Berkeley sat & worked on the MS of his famous "Alciphron; or, The Minute Philosopher." Morton is now climbing mountains in Vt. & N.H.

Has Comte d'Erlette told you about the two new weird magazines which are about to appear? In case he hasn't, here are the publishers as mentioned by him. Names not yet known.

*Rogers Terrill, Popular Publications, 205 E. 42nd St., N.Y. City.*
(reliable. 1¢ per word promptly on publication)

*Jay Publishing Co., 125 W. 45th St., N.Y. City.*
(not so good. ½¢ per word, tardily, after publication.[)]

I shall be on the lookout to see what sort of magazines these newcomers are.

That Price collaboration has now gone to Wright. If—as is likely—he turns it down, I'll let you see the MS. The latter's carbon is now in the possession of Two-Gun Bob Howard.

Sorry you're feeling depressed—but it's no wonder in view of the illness in your household. Things like that are damnably nerve-racking for all hands—I'm all worn out myself with the close confinement, absence of trips, &c. caused by my aunt's break. I've just been invited to New Hampshire, but doubt if I can accept.

Well—I'll have to knock off & get at a depressing verse-revision job which has just blown unexpectedly in. The sordidly commercial has to come first these days—when it comes at all!

With all best wishes, & hopes for your father's quick & complete recovery, I remain
　　　Yrs in the Black Rite of Yaddith
　　　　　—Ec'h-Pi-El

P.S. Just had word of the revival of *Astounding Stories* as a mainly *weird* magazine, to be issued by the standard old pulp publishers Street & Smith, 79–87

Seventh Ave., N.Y. City. Pays 1¢ a word on acceptance, buying shorts up to 7500 words, novelettes to 15,000—no serials. Aims at high quality, & has bought a yarn from Wandrei. Editor, Orlin Tremaine; Asso. Ed. Desmond Hall. ¶ Wright has just rejected the Silver Key sequel written by Price & myself. ¶ Am experimenting with a new story—don't know how it will turn out.

## Notes

1. HPL's commonplace book contains four such plots.

2. J. Vernon Shea incorporated this dream into his tale "The Snouted Thing," in *In Search of Lovecraft* (West Warwick, RI: Necronomicon Press, 1991), 25–28.

3. White speaks of his dream-inspired tales in the preface to *The Song of the Sirens and Other Stories* and the afterword to *Lukundoo and Other Stories*; rpt. in *The Stuff of Dreams: The Weird Fiction of Edward Lucas White*, ed. S. T. Joshi (Welches, OR: Arcane Wisdom, 2013).

4. Cf. "Beyond the Wall of Sleep" (1919): "The greater number of our nocturnal visions are perhaps no more than faint and fantastic reflections of our waking experiences—Freud to the contrary with his puerile symbolism."

5. HPL sent two submittals to Allan G. Ullmann of Knopf on 3 and 16 August 1933.

6. For example, see Farnsworth Wright to HPL, 17 August 1933 (ms., JHL):

> I have carefully read THROUGH THE GATES OF THE SILVER KEY and am almost overwhelmed by the colossal scope of the story. It is cyclopean in its daring and titanic in its execution. . . .
>
> But I am afraid to offer it to our readers. Many there would be . . . who would go into raptures of esthetic delight while reading the story; just as certainly there would be a great many—probably a clear majority—of our readers who would be unable to wade through it. These would find the descriptions and discussions of polydimensional space poison to their enjoyment of the tale. The story is so much more than a piece of fiction, and so far transcends not only the experiences of the readers, but even their wildest dreams, that they would have no point of contact with the ideas and thoughts presented in this opus. [. . .]
>
> It may seem strange that I reject a story which arouses my admiration as much as THROUGH THE GATES OF THE SILVER KEY; but with business as poor as it is now, I feel that we cannot risk discouraging so many readers from buying the magazine, merely by printing a story that is so utterly alien to even their wildest dreams and reveries that they are incapable of comprehending it— let alone appreciating it.
>
> I assure you that never have I turned down a story with more regret than in this case.

7. I.e., Greenville, RI.

[13]    [ANS][1]

[Postmarked Quebec, Canada,
3 September 1933]

Behold where Grandpa is! Having a great time, & dread the end of this 4-day

sojourn. Positively, there is no other place quite as fascinating as La Vielle Québec! Stopped in Boston to look up a 1637 house in the suburbs, & hope to see "Arkham" & "Kingsport" on the return trip. Home Thursday. Am now sitting on the ramparts looking over a scene nowhere to be duplicated in North America. Regards—
    E'ch-Pi-El

*Notes*

1. *Front:* Chateau Frontenac, Quebec, Canada.

[14]  [ALS]

Onyx Cliffs of N'yan above
the viscous sea of half-conscious
Protoplasm. Hour of the bubbling
from below.
[15 September 1933]

Dear Bho-Blôk:—
    No doubt you received my postcard from ancient Quebec. I had a great time there—4 days, & every one predominantly hot & sunny.[1] The old town was as picturesque & fascinating as ever, & I sought out all the familiar sights as well as unearthing some new ones. No other place has quite the concentrated magic of old Quebec. On the return trip I included Salem (Arkham) & Marblehead (Kingsport), whose varied antiquities I never tire of viewing. In Salem I saw something new—a perfect reproduction of the town during its first few years of settlement, reconstructed with extreme accuracy, house for house, in a spacious park. Every type of early building was shown—from the primitive bark & sapling huts modelled after the abodes of the Indians to a well-built board edifice approximating the houses of Europe in pattern & construction. None of the original houses of this period (1626–30) survive—the oldest structures in Salem being gabled dwellings of the 1650 period. On my outbound trip I visited the Deane Winthrope house (1637) in a suburb of Boston—this being one of the oldest buildings in the country. It proved very quaint—with a secret room in the colossal brick chimney.
    Glad your father is better, & hope Chicago's Century of Misdirected Effort won't bore your sister too much. School's opening will no doubt mean a good deal of fun as well as a good deal of application for you—trust the new stunts, lyrics, gags, & costume will be well received. You surely are versatile enough! The V.F.W. convention seems to have formed quite a carnival for your town—& doubtless promoted a vast consumption of that town's most celebrated product. Glad you have found the excitement enjoyable.
    I have read "Lilies" with great interest, & really think it is an excellent specimen of its kind. Derleth is especially fond of this milder type of ghost

story. Of course, the pattern is quite extensively used—but it will always bear repetition in slightly different form. You have a commendably lifelike atmosphere in this specimen. Too bad Wright turned it down—though rejection seems to be his favourite pastime. By the way—the next time you chisel a typing job out of an admiring nymph, tell her to *double-space* it. Editors usually demand double-spacing on all MSS. submitted. I hope to see the new items when they are done—especially the one based on my recent dream.

Meanwhile thanks enormously for the drawings. Both are genuinely good, & I only wish I could turn out something a quarter as clever. Klarkash-Ton thinks you have a very genuine talent—he was enormously impressed with a crayon drawing—"Dine & Dance"—which you sent him. He calls it "powerful", & adds that "the diabolism in it is really startling". Keep it up! I shall be delighted to see the additional drawings you speak of sending—I'm starting a Bho-Blôk portfolio to match my Klarkash-Ton collection. Before long I'll send you the new lot of C A S material—also the tale by Price & me which Wright rejected.

I read the new W T on the train coming from Quebec. It is better than the August issue, though in no way notable. Single-Plot Hamilton has a trace of novelty in his latest offering. I noticed with interest your note in the Eyrie—thanks for the flattery![2]

No news from Knopf—but I really don't expect any favourable action. Glad you've seen the "Lukundoo" book. "The Snout" is one of those tales I wish I could have written.

My aunt is much better now—is getting all over the house on crutches, & will soon graduate to a cane. Of course she can't negotiate stairs yet—but we are thinking of installing an electrical device for opening the front door from the second floor. The nurse ought to be able to be dispensed with in another fortnight.

Recently I've been doing a lot of re-reading of weird classics to see if I can improve my fictional style—I am very weak on plot & incidents. As part of the exercise I am constructing skeletonic analyses of the gist of dozens of standard items—& then comparing them with a view to estimating the relative dramatic value of various elements & types of action.[3]

Enclosed is a circular of a new sightseeing service in Providence. As you may observe, the old burg has quite a few points of interest—& even after Quebec I'm not sorry to be here!

Best wishes—

Yrs for the Sign of Yoth—

E'ch-Pi-El

[On envelope:] P.S. Magazine & new horrors just recd. Transit sure is hard on those old W T's! Saboth & the unclean Rider freeze my blood. Nggrrh . . .! You certainly have a genius for this kind of thing. Just as C A S has a typical kind of rugose, proboscidian head which figures extensively in his work, so are you developing a typical quasi-crustacean visage which blends well with the conceptions illustrated. Good work—keep it up! ¶ Postcard from Price. He has just hit St. Augustine, lucky devil!

*Notes*

1. HPL's trip lasted from 1 to 6 September 1933.
2. RB, in *WT*, September 1933: "Your new issue is superb—the best in some time. Lovecraft scores heavily. Yessir, Grandpa Cthulhu's new story takes the cake—real writing, real background, real horror." Rpt. in Joshi, *A Weird Writer in Our Midst* 76. The story is "The Dreams in the Witch House."
3. This reading resulted in "Weird Story Plots," "A List of Certain Basic Underlying Horrors Effectively Used in Weird Fiction," "List of Primary Ideas Motivating Possible Weird Tales," and "Suggestions for Writing Story" (later "Notes on Writing Weird Fiction"); all in *CE* 5.

[15]    [ALS]

66 College St.,
Providence, R.I.,
Sept[r] 25, 1933

Dear Bho-Blôk:—
          Your card apprised me of the metropolitan trip, & I can well imagine that you must have had quite a time. While the nightmare architecture of the fair would undoubtedly have caused me to see red, there must be scores of sights & exhibits so interesting as to form ample compensation. That old boy of the carboniferous age certainly looks promising—I've seen a *skeleton* of one in N.Y., but a full-size model of the living article is of course something else again. Likewise, I can picture the bizarre effect of the circus when all lit up at night. A city of Yaddith or K'nyan . . . . . or perhaps Klarkash-Ton's trans-dimensional City of the Singing Flame. Glad you also had a look-in on Satrap Pharnabazus of 840 Nuth-Mishav with his evil archives & sinister entourage.[1] There surely must have been ample food for conversation, & I'm glad you had an opportunity of augmenting your file. Hope you had some of your drawings to shew the boys. Anyway, it's a good thing to know them, for they'll now give your MSS. a somewhat more personal consideration when you send any in. It must have pleased them to greet so loyal & gifted a supporter of their enterprise. Naturally I am vastly surprised at learning that Knopf is enough interested in my MSS. to consult Wright about a possible book—although that is doubtless a mere routine process without much conclusiveness one way or the other.[2] At any rate, it gives one an excuse for a temporary feeling of encouragement prior to the inevitable deflating blow. Incidentally—I fear I'd hardly like to trust the choice of tales in a volume to

W.T. readers. Some of their preferences are rather comic, & would possibly include much tripe so bad that I didn't even send it to Knopf.[3]

Thanks for the reimbursement, though there was no need whatever of bothering about it. Here, at last, is the rejected offering of Sultan Malik & myself—together with such Clericashtoniana as I think will be new to you. Don't lose any of this latter stuff under penalty of being boiled in oil, sliced into strips, or treated in some of the subtler ways known to the Black Brotherhood! When you're through with all this, you might send it on to young Jehvish-Êi, the Smoke-Daemon of the Pit, who lately expressed a wish for a glimpse. Tell him to return it finally to Grandpa or incur the direst results. As for this experimental new thing—"The Thing on the Doorstep"—I haven't typed it yet, & doubt if anyone could decipher it in its existing cacographical form. Moreover, I have grave doubts as to whether it is any good. As I think I mentioned, I am profoundly dissatisfied with my fiction, & am now following a sedulous course of re-reading the weird classics to see if I can pick up hints regarding the best ways of handling the basic situations of strangeness & horror. I analyse & make notes on each standard tale as I read it, & endeavour to see what it is that my material lacks. In certain cases I tend to form evaluations of things I have read before—which reminds me that I have just finished enlarging & revising my history of weird fiction for publication in *The Fantasy Fan*. By the way—Klarkash-Ton tells me that there is a *new* nonpaying weird (& scientifiction) magazine about to be launched—*Unusual Stories*, edited by one William Crawford of Everett, Pa.

I've read through your new story[4] with great interest, & must congratulate you on the dark suspense, lurking terror, & febrile pall of cosmic evil hanging over it. The way you lead up to the climax is delightfully effective—having the evil abbot congratulate his guest sardonically on not having encountered the "other" monastery—& the climax itself is powerful . . . . . though I suppose you know there is a sort of taboo against cannibalistic stories among the cheap magazines. Regarding the story as a whole—you realise of course that the evil-monastery theme is a fairly often used one, though always excellent when deftly & originally handled. As for any points to criticise—it is always well to go over the text & see if there are places where one could eliminate awkward or naive phraseology. You are wise in deciding to recast the opening paragraph, & in the next one you might describe the building in less loosely generalised terms—being concrete about its aspect. Was it Romanesque? Gothic? Or a composite of Romanesque foundations & later Gothic work? (Romanesque—with rounded arches would be most ancient.)[5] In describing the black servitors you might see if a less naive-sounding phrase than "intrigued my romantic senses greatly" could be secured. Incidentally— the use of *intrigued* as a synonym for *fascinated* or *captivated* is a neologism which I really think ought to be discouraged. A little later on there is a slightly naive sound in the paragraph where the narrator wonders why the abbey had been built in this wood. Lonely rural monasteries are not very uncommon. If any cause for wonder exist, let it be at certain ruins amidst the trees near the monastery, as if a village had once existed there & had been abandoned at some very remote date—vast trees having grown up inside ruinous foundation-walls. The incident of the strange chanting is *very good.* You get in a fine bit of genuine cosmic horror here. About the decorations—do you suppose you have laid on the richness & ostentation a bit thickly? That is, would not less emphasis on mere *luxury*, & a few vague hints of something bafflingly & subtly *outré* be more to the point? I don't know . . . it's a minor phase anyway. Also—is not the *gluttony* laid on rather heavily? Perhaps not, though. But when you come to the *roast* you must use care. Remember that the guest can see the process of carving—so that it isn't likely any *very well-defined* human member could be served him without his knowing it at the outset. Better let the roast be a flank or thigh which cannot well be identified—at least, let the *first* platter full be such. Of course, all this time the wine is rendering the guest less & less critical . . . . but let him have a certain curiosity regarding some of the bone fragments on the plates. Then have a second platter brought in—smoking hot & smothered in spices. The light tid-bits, as it were. By this time the ribaldry is started, & the guest isn't in a very critical shape. The company is getting sated now, & doesn't pick its bones very clean. And now begin to use your *very choicest subtlety*—for the abbot's sardonic congratulations & tale of the "other" monastery must be managed with the utmost care. Try to have the narration *more gradual,* more a matter of *suggestion*—with less bold & literal *explanation.* It would be just as well to devote a little more space to this sinister narration—making it *very indirect,* oblique, & full of *hints* rather than *statements.* The climax is excellent—it was a good idea to postpone the final revelation till after the narrator's emergence from the abbey, & also to suggest the dream possibility. All told, this is a distinctly strong & promising piece of work, & is well worth a bit of working over. Have you any ideas for *titles*? "The Feast in the Abbey"? "The Remnant"? "Rimmon Abbey"? "The Abbey of Shadow"? "Shadow Priory"? I return the MS. herewith. What kind of a criticism did young Comte d'Erlette give it? Don't get discouraged by these suggestions for change. That's the only way one can ever whip one's style into shape. I'm just as ruthless toward myself—& have torn the first version of my own new tale to pieces fully as severely as I'm tearing this of yours!

Thanks immensely for "Dine & Dance" . . . . ngrrrhh . . . . I can see the aura of diabolism which Klarkash-Ton pointed out! Too bad I can't get a look at some of your larger drawings. You certainly have a tremendous amount of talent in the pictorial field—something I've envied all my life. Not long ago someone quite skilled in art saw your sketches & remarked their immensely promising quality, & Shea lately praised some specimens you sent him.

Congratulations—or commiserations—on your school editorship. You make me think of myself, who have let the chairmanship of the N.A.P.A.'s critical bureau be wished on me this year. Right now I have a stack of amateur journals a mile high to go through & comment on in the next *National Amateur.*[6] But your dramatic & debating activities—together with councilling & Harlequinading work—lie totally outside my experience. In the drama your nearest rival is Comte d'Erlette, who says that he is writing & producing a play for presentation by some parish society to which he belongs.

Price (or did I mention this before?) has changed his mind about going to Florida & has returned instead to New Orleans, where he may again be addressed at 1416 Josephine St. Before leaving the north he had several get-togethers with my friends Long & Morton in N.Y. & Paterson, all three seeming to take to one another with exceptional cordiality.

Whether my own season of activity is ended I'm not quite sure. My aunt is getting on very well, so that I'm not tied down as badly as I expected to be. Did I mention that we have a new electrical device so that she can open the front door from upstairs when I'm not available for bell-answering? If my friend Loveman comes on a visit from N Y next month I may accompany him to Boston for a round of the museums. A week's visit with Long in the canyons of upper Manhattan is likewise not outside the range of possibilities. But both prospects are very problematical—& the chill of autumn is at hand. Just at present the weather is somewhat mild, so that I'm still outdoors a good deal of the time. Have had five good ten-mile hikes lately in the picturesque countryside north of the city.

Well—don't let the Silver Key thing bore you quite to death. If it does, the Klarkash-Ton horrors will revivify you into a sort of malign, soulless life. Best wishes—

> Your ancient Grandsire
>
> E'ch-Pi-El

## Notes

1. A photo of RB with Farnsworth Wright and others in the office of *WT* at 840 N. Michigan Ave. in Chicago appears in *SL* 4 (facing p. 294), but it was probably taken at a slightly later date.

2. Knopf asked Farnsworth Wright if *WT* could dispose of 1000 copies of a volume of HPL's tales. Wright's negative reply was instrumental in Knopf's rejection of the book.

3. In his letter to Allen G. Ullmann of Knopf dated 16 Aug. 1933 (ms., JHL), HPL remarked of "The Outsider" that it was "A great favourite with readers, but rather bombastic in style & mechanical in climax." The letter is full of self-disparaging remarks of this sort.

4. "The Feast in the Abbey," RB's first story to be published in *WT*, although not the first accepted (see RB 29).

5. Cf. HPL's "The Rats in the Walls" (1923).

6. "Bureau of Critics Comment on Verse, Typography, Prose."


[16]    [ALS]

Daemon-Haunted Forest of Gnoph—
Hour that the Boughs move against the Wind
[late October 1933]

Dear Bho-Blôk:—

Betwixt your indispositions (for which, commiserations) & your entertaining activities you must surely have been a busy man during recent weeks! Your stunts have no lack of variety & (if the press photographs be any index of the whole) piquancy, & I fancy good old Lincoln High will miss them sorely when you soar beyond its academic reach. In accordance with instructions I am placing the cuttings in a neat & suitably labelled circulation-envelope & sending on to Bnadvāī-Aā, the genial Behemoth of the wild domed hills, with directions for subsequent & successive forwarding to young Jehvish-Êi, Klarkash-Ton, & Comte d'Erlette. I am sure that all recipients will appreciate the distinction implied in the recognition of your performance by local illustrated journalism. My aunt found the pictures especially vivid, since it is only four months since she was hammered around by the grave & white-clad staff of a busy temple of Æsculapius! Sorry your rubber cigar has been pirated—but imitation is the fate of all great comedians! What artist is ever without his echoes?

Yes—from what I have universally heard, the nocturnal lighting was the real high spot of Chicago's circus de luxe; & there is certainly something imagination-stirring in the thought of such a spectacle springing to life through a beam from *Outside*. In spite of the gas-tank & oil-derrick architecture, I suppose the show had plenty to recommend it—& had I been in Chicago during its existence I would probably not have carried my anti-modernistic attitude to the point of a boycott. Hope your mother will enjoy the thing—although the Dells probably form a much more potent recuperative influence. Thanks for the cards. From all accounts, the Dells must be a tremendously fascinating spot. The United Amateur Press Assn. held its 1918 Convention there, & my youthful correspondent Alfred Galpin (then your age—now a sedate French instructor at Lawrence in his native Appleton, & an aspiring musical composer on the side) sent me quite an assortment of snap shots, including one of himself balanced on a chimney-like monolithic formation which rises dizzily from the depths some distance from the precipitous cliff. His leaps across the bottomless gulf to & from this precarious eyrie nearly shattered the nerves of the spectators! That Indian village must be very quaint—on the order of the Seminole village near Miami, Fla., which I saw (& smelled!) in 1931. This latter was almost too realistic in an olfactory way—but perhaps the noble Sacs & Foxes have higher standards than their southeastern brethren.

Thanks abundantly for the art enclosures. Bless my soul, but you certainly have caught the authentic expression of Grandpa's diabolic & sombrely-brooding countenance! I don't think it looks too old—I have aged like hell in the last 5 years. The fact that you can turn from purely fantastic conceptions & capture an actual resemblance without effort seems to me a most significant indication of pictorial talent. I doubt if many could do the same without a pretty strenuous course of lessons—& even with lessons most would find it damned hard. Your artistic gifts are most emphatically worth developing, & I trust you will spare no pains in following them up. The recent Nameless Entity is a worthy brother to other Spawn of the Pit proceeding from your pen—& I await with keen anticipation the large-sized Blasphemies which you mention as headed my way. Glad you enjoyed the Klarkash-Ton material, which is certainly marvellous stuff. I wish you could see some of C A S's large & elaborate paintings—an assortment of which went the rounds of the gang in a suitable wooden crating device seven years ago. Probably you've heard that Wright intends to let him illustrate his own coming story, "The Weaver in the Vault" . . . . . it's about time, after hearing of his artistic prowess for ten years! But don't let Klarkash-Ton's proficiency overawe you. Remember that he was drawing sinister entities before you were born! If you keep on at your present rate your work will need no apologies when *you* are forty! Bernard Dwyer is another amateur artist of tremendous cleverness, although he has not been practicing much lately. He can draw human figures better than C A S, although he has not the latter's wealth of bizarre vision & unholy imagination.

Glad you're having good debate experience. It's a great wit-trainer, although one must be careful to distinguish between the mere cleverness of one who can argue convincingly, & the actual insight of one who can penetrate accurately & analytically to the truth, irrespective of audience-appeal. I am always a trifle distrustful of the legal & oratorical type of mind, whose prime skill is in bringing others to a given point of view. This type has a fatal tendency to become devoted to a given cause or object rather than to the absolute, impartial, & non-human *truth*—so that when some unexpected shift of evidence alters the validity of a case, the oratorical defender sometimes sticks to the old position blindly, merely because he has come to think of it as "his", instead of following the evidence in the interest of truth & therefore defending the new position as firmly as he formerly defended the old. I also prefer *written* argument to *oral* argument; since the former is always more rationally & maturely conceived, & is far more dependent on the *real strength* of its case, than is the latter. Oral argument always admits of specious vocal overtones & elocutionary flourishes which influence opponents & hearers irrespective of the genuine merits of the speaker's position. A clever natural debater, in oral combat, takes a thousand advantages & effects a thousand forms of insidious verbal browbeating which bring him success even when his case is an absurdly poor one. It is only on "the morning after" that the supposedly beaten opponent sometimes realises that his own position was right all along, & that the nominal victor's "success" was nothing more than a glib & overawing defence of a fallacy. To me a "victory" of that sort wouldn't be a victory at all—since what I am always seeking in an argument is not *to be adjudged right,* but to ascertain (no matter what I may have been thinking) *what is actually so.* Accordingly I always tell the gang that I don't want anybody to accept a verdict of defeat from me if the contest is oral. I never claim to have licked an opponent until I have done it on paper, with no rhetorical tricks, but only a plain marshalling of well-attested data—& with plenty of time for mature analysis, second thought, & unlimited rebuttals on the other guy's part. But anyhow, oral debate is darned good exercise. It gives one speed, agility, & resourcefulness, & helps one in the more serious business of mature written argument. Trust you'll achieve the desired vocal facility. My own voice is rotten—a hellish squawk that tends to mount in the heat of conflict—though I always keep right on arguing in defiance of the aural sensibilities of my victims. I am nearly always in an argument, because my refusal to accept ready-made attitudes causes me to differ on one point or another with virtually everyone else. People usually accept opinions in groups—largely as a matter of fashion—so that he who believes one certain thing generally believes a fixed set of other things . . . . . not because they are *really* connected, but because through unanalytical inertia they *customarily* go together. Thus a conservative in aesthetic standards is (without reason) expected to be a conservative in theology, while a radical in economics is (equally without reason) expected to be equally radical in every phase of sociology & politics. All this conventional expectation seems very unjustified, unrealistic, & asinine to me. I try to derive my basic standards from nature & common-sense, & to refer each problem of life independently to these standards—heeding custom only to the extent of recognising the general importance of cultural continuity & of adherence to certain familiar harmonic patterns in the interest of those illusions (of direction, meaning, & purpose in existence) & apparent points of reference which give to the burdensome process of life its saving sense of zest. This seems to me the only way to get at real facts & solid values—but it certainly does keep one busy arguing!

Glad "The Festival" stood up well on re-reading—though after a decade it seems rather fumbling & overcoloured to me. I criticise in it the same adjectival unrestraint & lavishness which I have criticised in certain things of yours—this florid tendency being a fault which we hold in common. Of the other W T items I like Klarkash-Ton's tale, & think Long's good though not his best (horror too diffused & spread out). There is, I think, unusual promise in the crude "House of the Worm" by an unknown writer—Mearle Prout. This thing is full of rough spots, but it has an undeniably potent atmosphere.[1] Two-Gun Bob, the Terror of the Plains, has a few good touches in his "Pool of the Black One", though other parts cater obviously to herd taste. (Incidentally, Two-Gun has just sent me the most impressive set of snake rattles I ever saw—12 in a row; the equipment of some lethal ophidian patriarch!)

Have you seen the new *Fantasy Fan?* I can send you a copy if you haven't. This enterprise would undoubtedly welcome contributions from you. The other new non-paying magazine—*Unusual Stories,* Everett, Pa—has taken two of my things[2] & several of Klarkash-Ton's. They also would be glad of something from you. Comte d'Erlette is contributing to both. Let me see the dream tale when it's ready. Perhaps it can find a haven in one of these periodicals. *Astounding* doesn't seem as promising as was expected—though the associate editor Desmond Hall has met some of our gang (Long, Wandrei, Talman) & produced an excellent impression. Glad you can stomach the Silver Key sequel—which nobody else seems to like. I really wasn't at my best in that, for Price's mathematical conceptions don't fit my own mood & manner. Anyhow, all my attempts rather disgust me of late—hence the pause for experimentation which I have mentioned.

Glad your expanding correspondence is proving congenial. You'll like Dwyer, I think—a dreamy, amiable giant with a splendidly sensitive imagination & a poignant appreciation of beauty. Shea is a tremendously bright kid— I trust he has kept you posted as to his new temporary address in Cincinnati.

As for my opinion of Herr Hitler—which you evidently derive through young Shea—it is really a complex thing, reckoning basic attitudes & trends rather than single outward manifestations & immediate effects; & is by no means favourable except in contrast with such hasty & all-inclusive condemnations as liberals like Shea & Long echo from the popular press.[3] The whole problem of Nazism & of the deep historical & sociological forces behind it is one so ramified that nothing less than a tome could deal with it properly. Certainly, its overt manifestations have been ignorant, extravagant, ruthless, ill-proportioned, barbaric, & potentially dangerous—but when a force is so mighty & spontaneous we are really obliged to probe beneath the surface if we want the facts. The important thing to remember is that this movement is not a development of normal times. It is merely a type of organised desperation called forth by abnormal conditions, with no claim to being more than a lesser evil. Just as the abnormal oppression of Russian Czardom called forth the desperate & incalculably ruinous force of bolshevism, so has the abnormal burdening of Germany with the twin loads of the Versailles treaty & the adjacent communist peril called forth the desperate & possibly dangerous force of Nazism. Like bolshevism, it is essentially honest in basic intent despite its handicaps of false science, ruthless methods, & ignorant leadership— & it is this undeniable sincerity & single-mindedness which inspires whatever liking one may have for it. Hitler is ill-informed, badly balanced, & neurotic— but he is one of those crude forces which sometimes make history in a blind, fumbling, hit-or-miss way. If one respects him, it is because he is free from ulterior motives, as Lenin, Trotsky, & Stalin likewise were & are in their very different enterprise. That is, his one real zeal is for the welfare of his group rather than of himself. What he wants, to the exclusion of all else, is the escape of his nation from certain perils which he deeply & honestly believes to be real. And a single wish like that, plus the fanaticism which stops at absolutely nothing in the course of fulfilling it, is what makes the messianic type of leader whom people follow—& who, therefore, is significant whether right or wrong. The contrast betwixt this type & the mere calculative opportunist is obvious. Whether any one specimen is a genius or a madman depends wholly upon circumstances—principally upon how nearly right & practical his wishes are . . . . not merely his external wishes, but the basic urges behind the external. In estimating Hitler the best thing to do is not to place too much stress on the crude early acts which all recognise as foolish, ignorant, or barbaric, but to study the deeper relationship betwixt his fundamental attitudes & the profound, permanent psychology & aspirations of his people. It is not a question of whether we like what he does at any given time, but rather of how well or ill he represents the natural & inevitable mood & drift of his national-cultural group. When we stop to analyse, we cannot help noting the vast number of thoughtful & cultivated Germans who accept him as a lesser evil despite their full realisation of his narrowness, crudeness, & atavistic ignorance. They see in him the only valid working focus for the scattered emotions & loyalties of a war-disorganised people, & prefer him to that greater evil of communism which probably forms Nazism's only alternative in Germany.

Now, as to the crucial point—the validity of the Nazi attitudes—one must carefully distinguish betwixt the twisted & extravagant surface manifestations & the broader, deeper feelings & convictions beneath. We know that the surface phenomena are crude & deplorable—& yet it may be that they are erratic & overgrown symptoms of certain positions essentially helpful in the defence of western civilisation; positions involving a resurgence of group-stamina & a healthy reaction against the passiveness & hesitant policy which means decadence & disintegration. If these really are the underlying positions, then it is better to confine one's attacks to the individual extravagances of their crude representatives—refraining from any blanket attack which might rob civilisation of a much-needed defensive influence.

If I read Nazism aright, it has—underneath all the hokum & fallacy & surface cluttering—three main objects: (a) the freeing of Germany from hopeless & unjust disadvantages imposed at Versailles, (b) the rescue of the national aesthetic-intellectual tradition from unmistakably decadent influences, & (c) the defeat of any tendency toward the concentration of disproportionate cultural or sociological influence (through monopoly of such key professions & positions as publishing, the theatre, teaching, criticism, finance, the law, the judiciary, &c) in the hands of any minority group having standards, traditions, & instinctive reactions widely different from those of the larger group as a whole.

Now all three of these objects seem to me both right & important at this stage of civilisation. Whether the Nazis' clumsy & fallacious attempts to further them do more harm than their neglect would do, is hard to say—but we at least ought not to attack the principles themselves in attacking their wrong interpretation & enforcement.

Regarding the Versailles treaty—I am no pro-German, & was all for the defeat of Germany when she challenged Anglo-Saxon dominance, but I do think the peace of 1919 was an absurdly disastrous example of rubbing in a victory. It would have been better to whip Germany more decisively in the field & burden her less afterward—for any incubus like the existing one formed a certain barrier to international recovery. A powerful & vital nation cannot be set upon indefinitely. If Germany can't get better terms, she can never prosper—hence it is only sound patriotism for a German to insist on the revision of Versailles results. Of course Hitler is doing this crudely & tactlessly—but his bark may be worse than his bite. We cannot yet tell how much real war–peril lies in the current Nazi position. It is always to be remembered, though, that such positions are liable to gradual mellowing & modification.

Regarding artistic-intellectual censorship—of course all this exiling & book-burning is childish & barbaric. That goes without saying. And yet it is true that western cultural standards are in the midst of a very ominous decay which ought to be checked if feasible. Jaded & disorganised aesthetes & philosophers are preaching & exemplifying a disintegrative inertia, bewildered aimlessness, & freakish annihilation of all standards & loyalties which makes directly for cultural & national weakness. There can be no question of this—the only problem is how best to check it. What one admires in the Nazis is merely the fact that they dare to tackle the matter at all. All their methods, of course, are dead wrong. They repudiate intellectualism & lapse back into a sort of romantic emotionalism instead of thinking things through & combating decadence with solid reason. But the fact that they enter a protest against current softness, freakishness, & drifting is a point to their credit. They may learn better methods in time.

Regarding the defeat of disproportionate cultural & standard-building influence by sharply-differentiated minority-groups—here again we have a sound principle misinterpreted & made a basis for ignorant, cruel, & fatuous action. There is of course no possible defence of the policy of wholesale confiscation, de-industrialisation, & (in effect) expulsion pursued toward groups of citizens on grounds of ancestral origin. Not only is it barbaric in the hardship it inflicts, but it involves a faulty application of ethnology & anthropology. However—this does not obscure the fact that there is always a peril of the concentration of disproportionate power & articulateness in the hands of non-representative & alien-minded minorities—whether or not of alien birth or blood. Cases are very numerous where small groups of especially active & powerful thinkers have tacitly & gradually secured a "corner" on expression

& value-defining in nations widely different from themselves in natural instincts, outlook, & aspirations. The result has always been unfortunate—either vaguely or quite tangibly—so that no disinterested person could do other than wish for some equitable & workable rectification. Granting freely & sadly that the Nazi policy does more harm than good in its approach to this problem, it remains a fact that nations ought to be able to require some *cultural* (not ancestral or biological) test—that is, a general test of cultural affiliations, as determined by certain significant likes & dislikes, instinctive responses to situations & experiences, natural ethical biasses, typical emotional life, &c. &c.—from persons eligible to key positions in literary, artistic, educational, financial, journalistic, military, legal, administrative, & judicial life. This would work very little hardship to anyone, yet would free the nation from certain tendencies to a very decided strain & potential weakness. Those whom it would debar from certain pivotal positions would be only those who (irrespective of blood) insist on adhering to an alien set of values & loyalties in the midst of the existing order. Even these it would not debar from any save a few crucial activities. No one, I think, can justly maintain that an alien culture ought to be coddled by a nation at the expense of its own. If a group cannot provide a separate nation, through its own strength, for its own culture, it must recognise the inevitable & prepare to accept the cultures of the nations which do survive as nations. Of course the whole problem is infinitely complex, & full of exceptions & variations; but the larger issue is simply that any given nation has a right to defend its own long-seated majority culture against any influence which may seem to be misrepresenting it or bending it in unrepresentative directions. Hitler of course has absurdly overestimated the alien influence of those whom he dispossesses, has adopted an erroneous & actually comic standard of discrimination, & has carried the *extent* of dispossession to extremes unwarranted even where some degree of restriction might be advantageous. So far as the problem of the racial content of a population is concerned, one may only lay down the general principle that *wholesale replacements* by differently constituted stocks are usually to be avoided. Aside from the actually primitive negro & australoid, there is hardly such a thing as superiority or inferiority of stock; although some human branches specialise in the development of certain capacities while others specialise in others. Of the higher races, individuals can very successfully become incorporated in alien majorities; although inconvenience develops where two or more *large groups* seek to inhabit the same territory in close contact. In these latter cases some special modus vivendi has to be worked out. Generally, it is wise for a nation not to encourage a wholesale influx of newcomers whose instincts, appearance, & inherited ideas differ too widely from those of the original stock. Strained feeling & peculiar problems are bound to develop. But of course the observance of such a principle is a long way from the grotesque extremes of Nazism. In the matter of the inferior races, however—

negro & australoid—I think an absolute colour-line is justified. These stocks definitely depart from the norm of homo sapiens in the direction of lower animal forms, & there is no more reason for considering them our equals than there is for considering certain other primitive stem-offshoots (like the extinct Neanderthals) our equals. Any substantial infusion of African, Australian Blackfellow, Melanesian, or black southern Hindoo blood into another stock means the definite lowering of the latter's biological status; hence it ought to be avoided at any cost. Incidentally—I agree with you that the various non-Caucasian races will have to be reckoned with in the course of time. That is why I have great sympathy for any philosophy which tends to arrest softening & decadence in the white powers of the west. Japan is a formidable rival. It has a very superior race-stock, & its psychology contains that almost fanatical stamina & dogged unbrokenness which the west—unless revivified by some new movement—is in danger of losing. Later on, I think a period of Japanese world-empire is virtually inevitable—so that the very best we can do is to stave it off. Hitherto, history has been a succession of white world-empires, but there is no longer any fresh & unexhausted reservoir of white barbarians to take things over when the reigning groups become effete. It looks as if the yellow man's turn were coming, in the end, by default.

Well—this is a helluva lot of space to devote to one topic, but I wanted to make clear the facts regarding my position, lest Shea's quotation represent me as a blind, unanalytical pro-Nazi. Actually, the Nazis would probably kick me out of Germany in five minutes after learning of my attitude toward cultural freedom, religion, & the grotesqueness of their own methods. What I respect in them is simply their blind sincerity. As I have said, Hitler seems to me to express in a groping, awkward way the deepest psychology of Germanic culture—& it is always futile & unwise to expect a national psychology to flow in other than its natural direction. The republic of Weimar was unnatural & forced, & all it brought was general deterioration of morale which might easily have exploded into bolshevism. Now it seems as if the Germans had regained some psychological stability & coherent purpose—hence one would rather see the existing regime mellowed by time & better judgment, than forcibly turned out to make way for one knows not what perilous alternative. The Germans are curious people—one of the oddest culture-groups in Europe. For sheer intellectual force & thoroughness of scholarship they have not a living rival—only the Greeks of classical times being comparable to them. And yet their psychology & civilisation has a certain immaturity & heaviness that stand out quite bewilderingly in contrast. They have not the mellowness of an *old* culture in the sense that France & Italy have—not even the instinctive balance of middle-age possessed by our own Anglo-Saxondom. There is an ineradicable naiveté, romanticism, & insensitiveness somewhere in their cultural fabric— giving them a singular air of adolescence. This may be a healthy sign—implying a youthful stamina & undissipated energy which the rest of the west has lost—but it is occasionally quite perplexing. I think it must be due to the fact that Germany (except the Rhineland fringe) never came under the intellectual discipline of the Roman empire. It does not inherit quite all of the western classical stream which the Latins possess directly, & which we possess through the Norman Conquest. Lacking that heritage, it retains more of the spirit of the old Teutonic tribes—the hordes of Ariovistus & Arminius, & the people whom Tacitus describes[4]—than we commonly realise. In view of this, it is not remarkable that extravagant abuses & misinterpretations of sound principles should arise in times of stress. When settledness is achieved, the thorough Germanic mind will find ways to iron the crudities out.

Incidentally, I may say that I believe some form of fascism to be the only sort of civilised government possible under the industrial economy of the machine age. Laissez-faire industry & commerce are as dead as Carthage & Babylon, since under mechanised conditions all the conceivable needs of the world can be supplied through the labour of only part of the population—& a constantly decreasing part. In order to restore the virtual assurance of every normal adult that he can secure food, clothing & shelter through the exercise of his services—an assurance without which stable society is impossible—the thin spreading of work through governmental oversight over the hours, wages, & conditions of labour is absolutely necessary. I said so ages before the N.R.A. was ever thought of, & I take some satisfaction in seeing such principles actually put in operation. But in order to make the economic system work permanently, distribute resources less unevenly, & satisfy all the varied elements in the community, the extent of governmental oversight will have to be greatly increased. How far & away complete government ownership of large basic industries it will be necessary to go, no one can yet say. It is silly to be bound to specific objectives when free experimentation is the only way to work out a feasible way of life. The important thing—wherever we are headed for—is to avoid such a disastrous break in the cultural tradition as Russia has suffered. We must not allow the romantic & unnecessary ideal of mathematically-perfect justice & equality to lead us into a blind sacrifice of all the intellectual, aesthetic, & personal liberties of the individual (only our *economic* life requires oversight), or to extirpate all those familiar attitudes & inherited folkways which form our normal background & provide the reference-points which give us our illusions of direction, significance, & purpose in a meaningless cosmos. Therefore fascism is the one sound course to follow—each separate nation adopting some form in consonance with its own traditions, & applying it with a minimum of interference with personal life. I think the U.S. has begun excellently—the path being prepared for that gradual evolution which constitutes the best form of transition. In the end, the cumbrous machinery of democracy ought to be eliminated—affairs being administered by commissioners appointed by a dictator seated through an intelligent & educationally select electorate. No one ought to have the vote unless he can understand what he is using it for. Ballots ought to be given only to persons who pass both an impartial intelligence test & a test of economic, social, political, & general cultural knowledge; it being understood that opportunities for education must always be kept equal. While no system can be more than a fumbling—at a vast distance—toward perfection, I feel confident that a government of this kind comes about as close to workable equity & cultural preservation as any government can well come. But of course it will take decades for any nation of the existing sort, steeped in meaningless catchwords & obsolete rule-of-thumb methods, to evolve into anything as calculatedly rational as this.

Coming back to the objective world of 1933—my aunt is vastly better; getting all around on a cane, taking daily walks in the nearby college grounds, & making even longer pilgrimages with my assistance. Last week we even got down the steep hill to the art museum, where an inner court has just been finely developed as a formal garden—with pool, walks, verdure, & a captivating statue of Pan in a niche. Naturally I am freer than before—so much so that I'm thinking of visiting Long in N Y next month. I've been making the most of the autumn scenery through rural walks, though I fear the season for this procedure is virtually over. Yes—I know how splendid your Wisconsin scenery is—Comte d'Erlette having sent me a vast assortment of pictures of it. This autumn I've tapped considerable wild terrain by taking a bus out some main road & then striking out afoot across country till I reach another bus-traversed road along which I can return. In this way I've explored many regions which I never saw before—some of them delectably unspoiled, with narrow rutted roads winding betwixt brier-twined stone walls, ancient gambrel-roofed farmhouses with their barns, byres, & gnarled orchards, primitive well-sweeps & moss-coated water mills, belts of shadowy woodland, distant village spires, & glimpses of curving river-valley . . . all those traditional marks of long, continuous habitation which New England took over bodily from Old England & embellished with distinctive touches of her own. Last week I came on a very ancient farmhouse erected in 1654.[5] It has a great pilastered stone chimney, & is still in excellent condition despite its age. Other recent glimpses of the countryside have come from participation in some of the rides given the family convalescent by motor-owning friends.

Not long ago I took a picture of my colonial abode. Here it is. You might shoot it back some time unless you have a permanent use for it. Saw a demonstration of *television* last Saturday. Vague & flickering, like the early cinema films of 1898 or thereabouts. ¶ And so it goes. Great sunset tonight—I surely appreciate this west-window eyrie! ¶ Regards, & hope to see the dream story in course of time. ¶ Yrs for the Black Seal—E'ch-Pi-El

P.S. In the accompanying picture, the window over the door is of my bedroom. The two at its left are my study's south windows. Study also has two west windows—at the northernmost of which I am now seated.

[P.P.S.] My aunt in the colonial doorway.

*Notes*

1. See Will Murray, "Mearle Prout and 'The House of the Worm,'" *Crypt of Cthulhu* No. 18 (Yuletide 1983): 29–30, 39. Prout's story appears to borrow phrases from several HPL stories.
2. "The Doom That Came to Sarnath" and "Celephaïs." Both were published instead in Crawford's companion publication *Marvel Tales*.
3. Cf. HPL to J. Vernon Shea, 29 May 1933 (*SL* 4.193–95), 14 August 1933 (*SL* 4.235), and 25 September 1933 (*SL* 4.247–48).
4. In the *Germania* (c. 98 C.E.).
5. The house of Thomas Clemence, an ancestor of HPL, outside Manton, RI.

[17]   [ALS]

—Wood of the Black Fungi
—Hour of the Monstrous Multiplication
[November 1933]

Dear Bho-Blôk:—

Your recent bulletin proved, as usual, highly interesting— & I was quite captivated by the monstrous forms of Black Yaddith & Shub-Niggurath.[1] My collection is growing into a marvellous album of nightmare! I envy you your ability—& I fancy that your earlier training in conventional design has a good deal to do with the vividness & disturbing substantiality of your Nameless Things. Dwyer appreciates your drawings immensely, being an aspirant in the same line himself. Has he shewed you any of his things? For sheer grotesque imagination you're in the lead.

I have read "The Merman" with the keenest interest & pleasure, & am returning it with a few annotations & emendations. It is really a fine story— full of atmosphere & tension—& its only dominant fault is that of diffuse language & overcolouring . . . . the pitfall of my own younger days. I trust you'll send this along to The Fantasy Fan or to *Unusual Stories* (a circular of which I enclose in case Crawford hasn't sent you one), & feel sure it will be appreciated there. My changes—the congested script of which I hope you can read—are of two sorts; simplifications of diffuse language in the interest of more direct & powerful expression, & attempts to make the *emotional modulations* more vivid, lifelike, & convincing at certain points where the narrative takes definite turns. You did not seem to mark with sufficient rhetorical emphasis such crucial developments as the finding of the Thing, the discovery of its semi-human nature, & the first sight of its awful kin around the ship. In the matter of language, you must practice simplicity & directness—which I wish I had done when I was young enough to be malleable! Some of your sentences—like mine—have the complex heaviness of the later 18th century.

They remind one of good Dr. Johnson . . . . . do you recall the anecdote of how he expanded his critical comment on Buckingham's "Rehearsal"?[2] He had carelessly remarked, in a racy idiomatic way, "It has not wit enough to keep it sweet"—whereupon, hearing that he had not sufficiently lived up to the classic dignity of a great lexicographer, he caught himself & amended the observation . . . . . sonorously rumbling out, "It has not sufficient vitality to preserve it from putrefaction!"[3] The permanent judgment of posterity does not endorse the Great Bear's weighty afterthought, but recommends rather that the conciseness of the first version be followed. For prose style, the writers of the *earlier* 18th century—Addison, Steele, Swift—cannot be rivalled; the lapse into rococo floridity after 1750 being a decadence of the most unmistakable sort. And I *would* have to pick up that damn'd florid style—probably through a too-early digestion of Gibbon & other exemplars of the 1780's! I hope you will not find my changes in "The Merman" too extensive—only on p. 2 have I indulged in anything like really ruthless substitution. It's a good story, & I wish it a ready acceptance & a cordial reception by its readers.

Concerning activities—hell! I wasn't ironic in referring to your crowded programme. I was expressing a genuine admiration for a schedule obviously much fuller & more varied than any I ever followed in youth. I didn't go in for extra-curricular pursuits at all in high-school—being somewhat of the hermit type, though not an extreme specimen. I put most of my superfluous energies into writing worthless junk—& edited a hectographed astronomical paper (from the age of 8 to that of 20 or 21 I had more scientific than literary interests—geography, astronomy, chemistry, physics, &c) whose appalling childishness quite overcomes me as I look over the file today. I was much less mature at 16 than you are. Just to give you a laugh at the old man I'll enclose (please return) a couple of issues of my pompous *R.I. Journal of Astronomy*—in newspaper form for Sept. 10, 1905, & as a magazine for May '06. Pretty kiddish stuff, even for 15. I'll bet you wouldn't have let such material see the light a year ago! In August 1906 I broke into print—contributing monthly astronomical articles to the newly founded Prov. Tribune, & also dumping reams of callow scientific prose on a rural weekly—The Pawtuxet Valley Gleaner—published in that part of the countryside whence my maternal family came.[4] I never contributed to any school paper—in fact, come to think of it, Hope High didn't have one in my day (1904–08). One thing I used to do was to give illustrated scientific lectures. I had a very good projection lantern—not a kid's magic lantern, but the real thing, taking standard $3\frac{1}{4} \times 4\frac{1}{4}$ photographic slides—& a splendid assortment of slides, mostly astronomical, which I had made for me by an assistant at the Ladd Observatory of Brown Univ.[5] This outfit redeemed my performances from the level to which my puerile text would otherwise have depressed them. Congratulations on your *Quill* editorship—let me see a copy if you have a lendable extra. You'll probably beat the *Comet*—published at my friend Moe's West Division H.S. The dream serial quite captures my imagination, & I think its black Entity is limned with appropriate vividness.[6] You ought to have drawn an illustration of it! The stunts must surely keep you on the alert—but I dare say the enjoyment compensates for the labour. Glad the teacher's convention gave you something of a vacation, & I hope the weather was such as to permit of hiking. I can sympathise with you anent the cold—today is beastly, though the admirable steam heat piped into this joint makes it summer throughout every hour of the 24. I've just found out that although the steam comes in from the library next door, it doesn't originate there. Instead, it is all generated in huge boilers in the college's engineering building—away off on the middle campus over the crest of the hill. The whole college area is heated from the same system—all the university buildings, as well as the nearby private houses on college property. Quite a plan—& perhaps prophetic of a day when houses will all have municipal heat piped in & metered like gas or electricity.

I'd certainly like to see the Wisconsin Dells some day, for I am very sensitive to the charm of landscape. My autumnal walks continued right up to the sinister All-Hallows season—the last three having occurred on consecutive days, Oct. 31, Nov. 1., & Nov. 2. On these occasions I discovered a district of much rural charm which I had never seen before—though it is located on the city's very rim. At one point along a winding hillside road I caught a vista of breath-taking beauty which included a twilight-clad descent of stone-walled pastures, a sunset-litten river fringed with woods, dim violet hills against an orange-gold west, a steepled village in a northward valley, & over the rocky eastward ridge a great round Hunter's Moon preparing to flood the scene with spectral light. Now, however, comes the long hibernation—which on account of my present ancient setting I don't mind so much as I might. My desk is at a west window, & being on a hilltop I get a magnificently glamorous view—ancient roofs & boughs in the foreground, a Georgian belfry & twin church towers in the middle distance, & in the background a strip of far purple horizon with a steeple on a distant hill silhouetted mystically against the sunset.

Glad you've received *The Fantasy Fan.* They'll be glad of any good stories, or of any articles pertaining to weird fiction. *Unusual* will have a much better appearance, though—so you might prefer it as a medium for your choicest works. I hope it lasts long enough to give us ten-year subscribers our story's worth! At present it is having quite a struggle—subscriptions coming in slowly, & news-stand vending being not yet practicable. I think you'll find the N.A.P.A. very interesting when you join—I wish I'd known of it in the youthful days when I was publishing the *R.I. Journal!* There has been some difficulty this autumn, owing to a hitch in the financing of the coöperative mailing bureau, but this problem now shews some signs of straightening out. Had a letter from W T recently, asking to see again the collaborated piece by Price & me rejected last August. Hope it means a reversal of the turndown—Wright is a most bewilderingly capricious cuss!

As for the world situation & my comments thereon—I doubt whether the magazines would care for any such essentially laymanlike comment as I could make.[7] Millions of laymen air their views—around village store cracker-barrels & otherwise—but only the views of special students are worth printing. So far as the situation itself goes—it is certainly a dangerous fallacy to assume that any factor save physical force will ever be the ultimate arbiter of human issues. One may reasonably expect the field of arbitration & compromise to be *extended*—so that many issues formerly precipitating wars will be adjusted without them—but this process can go only just so far. Whenever a group wants a certain thing badly enough, cannot get it through negotiation, & thinks it has any chance of getting it by force, it will most assuredly set out to get it by force. Talk of the abolition of war is simply bunk. War is not a formal institution, but a natural condition resulting from ineradicable human instincts. The formal duel has been abolished—but under other forms men still kill each other when angered enough. War may be outlawed—but groups of men will still offer battle to other groups under suitable provocations, whether the process is *called* war or not. Notions that the primary instincts can be wholly regulated by reason or by the more evolved emotions are based on very misleading misconceptions of human psychology. Idealists wholly lose sight of the natural relative strength of human impulses. Reason & taste can indeed accomplish marvels in removing life from the brutish, unconscious state; but they do this only by influencing a sensitive minority. The masses are always essentially untouched, even though they may seem superficially to follow the lead of the sensitive minority. Whenever aroused by basic emotions of sufficient stress, the herd throws off the cloak of evolved feeling & pitches in for a struggle of the old physical sort. This is something we have to recognise, whether we like it or not— hence the need of being always prepared to defend our especial group & way of life against others. Supine pacifism is a crime & a folly which serves absolutely no worthy end; for since it concerns only one's own fabric—not the other fellow's—it has no effect at all in abolishing war as a whole. It means merely that one's own cherished kinsfolk & habits will be stamped down & dragged in the dust while other groups will conquer & continue to fight— perhaps enslaving us & making us fight for them as we neglected to fight for ourselves. No self-respecting man cares to see his own world & his own people perish—& to serve no end whatsoever. It may be that war—on account of the new terrors added to it by mechanical invention—will eventually cause the collapse of civilisation; but we cannot help that. All we can do is to see that our own group occupies as free & dignified a place as possible as long as the present civilisation does last. Accordingly one can only discourage the hysterical pacifism of the addled younger generation—especially the followers of certain collegiate fashions in emotion—whose attitude means nothing but the degradation & enslavement of our own group, & the consequent triumph of hardier & more militant groups like Bolshevik Russia, Nazi Germany, or

Japan. The world is certainly no pleasant institution, viewed in the long run. And yet there is no reason to expect it to be other than what it is. Indeed, the extraordinary thing is that *homo sapiens* has become as differentiated from other organic species as he has become. How often such a case of differentiation & complex evolution arises in the cosmos is a matter for speculation—the answer depending somewhat on how rare or otherwise solid planetary bodies are. Probably such developments are to be deplored rather than welcomed, since the resultant emotional adjustment undoubtedly brings greater increases of pain than of pleasure. But once it does occur, the natural thing seems to be to carry it as far as possible . . . or at least to try to. The present is assuredly one of the most ticklish moments of history—with internal economic problems aggravating the nations' external problems in an especially perilous way. Just which of many conceivable turns the situation will take, it is impossible to predict. To pretend to see ahead is mere folly, ignorance, or arrogance.

Here is that snap for permanent preservation*—I got more prints the other day. Before long I must try to get some interior views—of the colonial mantels, &c. Again let me thank you for the drawings, & congratulations on the vividness of "The Merman."

Yrs in the Midnight Ritual of Blackest Yaddith—

E'ch-Pi-El

*Notes*

1. See HPL to R. H. Barlow (25 September 1934): RB "has 'Yaddith' as a *person* instead of a *planet*, &c" (*O Fortunate Floridian* 178).
2. George Villiers, Duke of Buckingham, and others, *The Rehearsal* (1672), a play parodying John Dryden, William D'Avenant, and heroic drama generally.
3. The anecdote is recounted in James Boswell's *Life of Johnson*, under the date June 1784. Johnson said "vitality enough," not "sufficient vitality."
4. HPL contributed twenty astronomical articles to the *Tribune* (morning, evening, and Sunday editions) between 1906 and 1908. He contributed 17 articles to the *Pawtuxet Valley Gleaner* (Phenix, RI) in 1906 and may have contributed more in 1907–08, but no issues of the paper for those years have come to light.
5. Cf. *The R.I. Journal of Astronomy* 1, No. 22 (27 December 1903):

> For the past few nights a course of Lectures has been given by this office on the solar system.
>
> It was illustrated by a dozen lantern slides which were made by Mr. Edwards of the Ladd Observatory.

HPL elsewhere identifies this individual as John Edwards (*SL* 4.398).
6. HPL to CAS, 29 November 1933 (ms., JHL): "Young Bloch is using his story based on my mediaeval roof-monster dream as a serial in his high-school paper. I haven't seen

---

*I am assuming that you returned the print as first sent, although I've taken so many returned prints from letters that I can't be sure. At any rate, keep one print.

it, but will be amused to find out what the kid did with the idea." The story does not survive.

7. "Some Repetitions on the Times" (22 February 1933) and "A Layman Looks at the Government" (22 November 1933), unpublished in HPL's lifetime, date to around this time. Both are in *CE* 5.

[18]   [ALS]

ESTABLISHED 1903       H. P. LOVECRAFT, ED.ᵀᴿ·

THE

RHODE ISLAND JOURNAL OF ASTRONOMY, Lᵀᴰ·

BUSINESS & EDITORIAL OFFICES

66 COLLEGE STREET,

PROVIDENCE, R.I.

. . . . . . . . . . . . . . 193 . . . . .

[c. 6 December 1933]

Dear Bho-Blôk:—

Commiserations on the typing ordeal. I have a rebuilt Remington which I bought in 1906—the very year of that magazine-form issue of the R.I. Journal—but I never use it except under compulsion. The whole process of typing is repugnant to me—gets on my nerves. What a pity the stenographic admirer left you flat! But I hope you'll get "The Merman" typed somehow. Glad my remarks seemed useful, & hope that either Hornig or Crawford will look favourably upon the production.

Dwyer certainly can draw! But, by the same token, the Daemon Lama of Leng is no slouch at the same indoor sport! Thanks vastly for the current consignment. You left out the "Golem" illustration mentioned, but I fancy you may send it later. I wish I could get hold of a copy of the book.¹ I saw a cinema of it in 1923,² but never had access to the Meyrink text—although I mentioned it in my article. The heads are tremendously vivid, as usual. You catch resemblances like a veteran—I can recognise the actor in the cinema version (or rather, *per*version!) of "Frankenstein"³ from the pen & ink sketch. Dumballah is surely enough to set any nigger beating his voodoo drums—which reminds me that a friend of Barlow's in Florida has recently witnessed an actual voodoo rite, being one of very few white person to do so. Sort of amateur Bill Seabrook!⁴

I don't wonder that "The Golden Bough"⁵ holds you. It is one of the greatest anthropological works in existence. "Limehouse Nights"⁶ is first-rate fictional pabulum. I must get hold of that Leroux item. Yes—I've seen a few of Comte d'Erlette's Elsinorian chants, & hope he can get a collection of them into print. He surely is a genuine poet—indeed, his profusion of talents is quite bewildering to an ordinary mortal. Enclosed are the old-timers of mine that you wished to see. "Randolph Carter" represents an actual dream I had in 1919—a dream so vivid that I seized a pen the moment I woke up. In the dream I was Carter & my friend Samuel Loveman (who had introduced me to many weird classics such as Bierce & Lafcadio Hearn, & whom I had not then met in person) was Warren. I cannot begin to describe the stark, utter horror I felt in the dream when that thick, gelatinous voice welled up out of the ancient tomb . . . . "You fool, Loveman is dead!" Nrrghrrr. I haven't that much sensation left in me in these latter days of old age! "Arthur Jermyn" (labelled "The White Ape" by W T) is a sort of favourite story of mine, though it is a bit naive & obvious. Gawd help you if you try to copy all this junk!

As to the inevitability of war—I know all about the attitude of collegiates today—which young Shea displays even more violently than you do—but I don't see that this alters the facts of Nature any. Very conceivably certain specific types of war may be minimised through popular disapproval, but there are always extreme provocations which have to be met unless the race is to become an enslaved & subservient body not worth belonging to. You underestimate the natural fight in a normal man under adequate provocation. The recent California lynching[7]—a sheer outburst of pure elemental feeling with no colour-prejudice involved—is a good index of the unquenchable spirit of the species. Of course, irregular outbursts are to be deplored—but if Japan were to demand the right to dump immigrants on California with war in case of refusal, I'll leave to you the "go-to-hell" answer which would follow, & the quick booting in the buttocks which Japan would get in spite of all the idealists in the metropolitan high-schools! The tough old Yankee isn't yet ready to be kicked around & used for a doormat, whatever his lollypop-sucking great-grandsons may elect to do with themselves. However—it is perfectly sensible that the causes of all proposed wars be carefully looked into, with a view to avoiding clashes brought on by merely economic interests.

Sorry to hear of the censor's ban on your dramatic enterprises. Damn that fresh wench—I hope she gets expelled for some other escapade, just to even things up! But after all, adversity may harbour concealed blessings. With more leisure from merely routine activities, you'll probably have better chances to develop your own particular talents. And then again, there may be some modification of the ban when your talents are sorely needed—so that you can pull a neat little Coriolanus stunt! I shall inspect the *Quill* with much interest. Congratulations on the pictorial publicity for yourself & rubber cigar!

Well—Wright *did* take the Price collaboration, for which I am prayerfully thankful. I sure can use my end of the 140! Klarkash-Ton now tells me that he is commissioned to illustrate *another* tale of his—in addition to the "Weaver."[8] Less cheering news is the deflection of the revived *Astounding* from the weird to the science fiction field. No use talking—the public certainly isn't ready to support more than one weird magazine. By the way—have you the new F F with my "Other Gods"? If not, I can let you have a copy. In the course of time you'll get my latest story to read, although I fear it isn't so hot. Dwyer agrees that the first part is weak—obviously a laborious preparation for the final scene which forms the tale's raison d'etre.

　　And so it goes. Best wishes, & good luck with your new tale.

Yrs most sincerely—<br>E'ch-Pi-El

[P.S.] Had my Thanksgiving dinner in Plymouth, where the first one was eaten. Delightfully warm day—& the old town was fascinating as usual. Saw the sunset from Burial Hill—& then the moon shed silver light on the harbour.

*Notes*

1. By Gustav Meyrink. HPL read the novel, borrowed from R. H. Barlow, in April 1935.
2. *The Golem* (UFA [Germany], 1920, silent), directed by Paul Wegener and Carl Boese; starring Paul Wegener and Albert Steinruck. Actually HPL claimed with greater frequency to have seen the movie in 1921.
3. *Frankenstein* (Universal, 1931), directed by James Whale; starring Colin Clive, Mae Clarke, John Boles, and Boris Karloff.
4. For Seabrook see RB 38, n. 3.
5. The celebrated anthropological treatise by Sir James George Frazer.
6. A series of sketches about the Limehouse district of London (chiefly inhabited by Chinese immigrants) by Thomas Burke.
7. I.e., the lynching in San José of two black men, Thomas H. Thurmond and John Holmes, who had confessed to the kidnapping and slaying of a white child, Brooke Hart. A mob broke into the prison where the men were held and hanged them from a tree. See *New York Times* (27 November 1933): 1.
8. CAS also illustrated "The Charnel God" (*WT,* March 1934).

[19]　[ALS]

[postmarked 25 December 1933]

Dear Bho-Blôk:—

　　　　　　　　Before departing on a week's visit to Frank B. Long (during which I shall also see Talman & Wandrei) I must thank you for the generous array of pictorial horrors just added to the Bloch Wing of my gallery. Truly, they're a splendid lot, & I got a great kick out of all of them. That coloured specimen shudderingly embodies your favourite monster-type, as do certain of the others. As per request, I return herewith the sheet with the Yuggoth-denizen, Keebi, & the multi-ocular Lumberer Out of Nightmare. Wrraaahhrr!! but that latter fellow surely is a holy terror! I don't wonder the swordsman's face blanched! I also assume you want the "Golem" illustration returned. Nggrrrhh, but that's a powerful bit! By no means a pleasant little pal to have come looming out of the night at you!

Enclosed is the F F with my *Other Gods*. I think this will form a very encouraging medium for your own work. I guess I told you of *Unusual*'s need of retrenchment—but after all, it will appear in a shape far outclassing the F F. There will be 64 pages, 9 × 6, of common pulp stock—with cover & illustrations. My opening contribution will be "Celephaïs" instead of "Sarnath".1 There will be biographical sketches & portraits of weird writers each month—mine being slated for the third issue. I had a hell of a time boiling down the sad story of my life to the prescribed 900 words!2 The first issue of *Unusual* is now in the press—indeed, you ought to get it almost as soon as this epistle. I'll be glad to see copies of *The Quill*—especially those with the dream tale.

Glad the school upheaval is working out ultimately for the best. How complex are the events of life, & how unpredictable & paradoxical their consequences! Good thing, though, that you're sticking to *The Quill*.

On Shea's advice I saw "Henry VIII",3 & certainly did not feel disappointed. A powerful piece of pageantry—& a poignant human study, too, after the very real pathos of fat King Hal's life begins to develop about half way through the film. Another & still more moving cinematic experience of mine was "Berkeley Square"—which I went to see *twice*.4 Of course some of the uncanny power which this film had for me was due to my especial psychology—the almost disturbing sense of membership in the 18th century, & of alienage from my own period, which has haunted me ever since I could walk or talk. This cinema was freer from anachronisms than any other 18th century drama I have ever attended. The age of Johnson seemed to be taking actual form before my eyes. Providence has many relatively unchanged backwaters like Berkeley Square—indeed, I now live in one! This house is one of the strongest imaginative influences I have ever been exposed to, & it's getting more & more so as the details of furnishing progress. We are constantly getting additional old family things out of storage—just now the living-room fireplace is taking form with an old set of irons & a pair of bellows. I missed "The Invisible Man",5 but will try to take it in when it returns, as it undoubtedly will. I suppose Long & his parents will drag me to half a dozen cinemas, good, bad, & indifferent, during my visit.

Hope you won't let legal likker launch you on too protracted a spree.6 For my part, I never could see much good in alcoholic drugging—& the spectacle of drunkenness, with all the work of millennia of evolution artificially undone, is anything but aesthetic in my eyes. I've never tasted alcoholic liquor, & never expect to during my few remaining years.

Cold & warm weather have alternated hereabouts, & I hope to gawd the latter will predominate during my N Y visit. That Plymouth trip was certainly great—did I mention that the mercury was up to 68° that afternoon?

With best Yuletide wishes—
Yr obt Grandsire—
Ec'h-Pi-El

[P.S] *EXTRA!* KADATH has just come! God! Rrrgh!!!! Truly a magnificent piece of work—design, atmosphere, colour. Thanks a thousandfold!

[P.P.S. on envelope:] The more I look at KADATH the more he fascinates me. I have him propped up beside the fireplace amongst my Yuletide decorations.

*Notes*

1. *Unusual Stories* never published any material by HPL. "Celephaïs" appeared in *Marvel Tales,* May 1934.
2. "Some Notes on a Nonentity" was first published in *Beyond the Wall of Sleep* (1943).
3. *The Private Life of Henry VIII* (United Artists, 1933), directed by Alexander Korda; starring Charles Laughton, Robert Donat, and Franklin Dyall.
4. *Berkeley Square* (Fox Film Corp., 1933), directed by Frank Lloyd; starring Leslie Howard, Heather Angel, and Valerie Taylor. Based on the play by John L. Balderston. See Darrell Schweitzer, "H. P. Lovecraft's Favorite Movie," *Lovecraft Studies* Nos. 19/20 (Fall 1989): 23–25, 27.
5. *The Invisible Man* (Universal, 1933), directed by James Whale; starring Claude Rains, Gloria Stuart, and William Harrigan. Based on the novel by H. G. Wells.
6. Prohibition was repealed on 5 December 1933.

[20]    [Christmas card]

[Printed:] Warmest Greetings and the Good old Wish
A Happy Christmas and a Bright New Year
[Signed] H P L
—1933

[21]    [ALS]

At the Monolith on the Mound<br>—Hour that the Dogs Howl<br>[February 2, 1934]

Dear Bho-Blôk:—

Commiserations on the fountain pen! This contraption of mine still works like a charm—though Cthulhu knows how long it will last. If my shaky script seems to belie the excellence of my stylus, you may attribute it to my convulsive tremors after glimpsing "Baby's Playmate" & "The Music of Chaos". Ngrrrh! Thanks enormously for these monstrous additions to my gallery—truly, they have a diabolic power which I doubt if the younger Wandrei could have beaten at your age. There is a haunting suggestion of *seething* in that evil blue chaos. I was also glad to see the poems, both of which have a genuine force & vividness. The only changes I'd suggest are one or two in the direction of more regular metre. Both are dominantly iambic pentameter, but certain lines fall below or go beyond that stately measure. In "Spectators" I'd suggest that the last line read

> And laugh, & laugh . . . knowing our destined fate.

In "Dreams" the first defective line is the third—which you could bring up to par by inserting some dissyllable in a suitable place . . . . such as *briefly* before *glimpse*. The next line would be better if it started off with a *The* before *splendours*. Stanza II, l. 2 needs another disyllable. How about *mottled* before *daemons*? The next line is redundant—also, *dance* ought not to be set in rhyme with itself. Try the following substitute

> Or visit twilight caves where centaurs prance.

The next line is shy a dissyllable—try *febrile* before *dance*. The epilogue or l'envoi or whatever you call it is all in octosyllabic metre, but I question the advisability of the radical shift. Here is a suggested substitute—in the final line I've changed *until* to *through*, since it is to be presumed that "eternity" begins as soon as one shuffles off.

> Come, let us dream away our futile lives
> Until the day that kindly death arrives—
> When, fetters burst, we shall be wholly free
> To dream in splendour through eternity.

Again let me congratulate you on the excellence of these verses. Shoot 'em along to the F F, U S, & *Fantasy Magazine!*

Howard Wandrei's story was very distinctive, but showed marks of amateurishness. It is clear that drawing is his primary medium. Except for the Merritt reprint, the best thing in the Jany. W T was Klarkash-Ton's "Weaver in the Vault"—with illustration by himself. Next comes the H. Wandrei item, & third is Two-Gun Bob's "Rogues in the House." The Feb. issue is rather poor. Dyalhis & Pope items utter tripe. Price's tale ruined by Wright's demand for an explanatory verbal diagram. Klarkash-Ton's contribution average. Two-Gun's fair. The Rud item passable. And Hectograph Eddie is experimenting with another plot

*Unusual* is certainly having quite a struggle with the printer, & one may only hope for the best. The "advance issue" looks a bit amateurish—but no more so than F F—but the magazine proper will probably be neater. There may be some irregularity in size, for Crawford has his eye on a new printer who can't furnish as large a page as the present one. Hope most of your avalanche of prose & verse will land at its various destinations.

The supplications of your scholastic authorities must be rather a pleasant balm for your ego—perhaps you will condescend to reassume a few of the honours & dignities without undertaking so many as to wreak your own writing & drawing programme. Sorry the affectionate typist is getting quarrelsome—but she'll be back. By the way—the reason you haven't (or *hadn't*—he may have written by now) heard from Bernard Dwyer is that he had lost your address. I've now supplied the missing data, so communication will doubtless flow once more. He appreciated your Yuletide tribute immensely, & says he wants to send you some of his own pictures in return.

As for our energetic contemporary Der Schön Adolf—as I said before, my attitude concerning him is simply one of negative tolerance—as a lesser evil in the absence of any really first-class man with enough leadership & magnetism to keep the German people out of chaos. What Germany really needs is a Mussolini—but unfortunately they can't be found lying around conveniently when the critical time comes. France also seems to be needing something of the sort just now—though I don't think she's as far gone as Italy was in 1922 or Germany in 1932–3. Whether Herr Adolf will do more permanent harm than good in the long run still remains to be seen. So far the outlook isn't especially promising—he evidently lacks Mussolini's capacity for development & mellowing, & his attempted regulation of Germanic culture seems to grow less instead of more rational. He has borrowed the Soviets' idea of a narrowly artificial culture or "ideology" separate from that of Western Europe—& if this concept (with its foundation in definitely false science & rather infantile emotion) lasts long enough to colour a whole new generation, the ultimate result will be highly unfortunate. I was hoping it would settle down into an intelligent attempt to discourage decadence & encourage the normal German main stream—not an artificial, sentimental, & half-archaeological substitute. As for the church question—actually, if Western Civilisation must have some form of supernatural superstition, I really think the old gods are much more appropriate than the pretence of Christianity which we have been externally flaunting since historic & political accident fastened it on us. Christianity has never really fitted us—our whole record is one of actual conduct belying the protestations we make on Sunday. On the other hand the old gods are *really ours*—they were the imaginative product of the same culture-stream which produced our genuine subconscious instincts & folkways. If we openly worshipped them, our habitually ruthless & predatory conduct would not be hypocritical. I'm sure that Thor & Odin seem much closer & more vital than the anaemic, crucified Saviour. However—as a practical issue, it's simply asinine & sentimental to fancy that we can ever set the Valkyries to riding again. Long centuries have taught the herd to embody their ignorance & superstitions in the Christ-

image, & there'd be no advantage in a shift which for most would be meaningless. The trend of reason & enlightenment is toward no gods at all—& it
doesn't matter much which of the old delusions the unthinking cling to. It is
time to separate the problem of law, order, & harmonious conduct altogether
from religion; recognising it as a social & aesthetic matter. As for the economic phase—Hitler's recent moves do look rather bad. We shall see before
long how they operate in actual practice. What a damned muddled world we
have around us! I never thought I'd live to see such a mess!

> Yrs for a Yuggothian Utopia—Grandpa E'ch-Pi-El

P.S. Don't feel disturbed about "apocalyptic"—I'll lend you use of the copyright!

[22]    [ALS]

> Yuggoth—Hour of the
> Rising of the Infra-Red Moon
> [late March 1934]

Dear Bho-Blôk:—

You have my sympathy anent the cold—both climatic & co-
ryzal. Let us hope the latter is now but a memory. As for the former—after a
record-breaking snowfall Feby. 26, decent days have been increasingly prevalent
hereabouts. Even overcoatless sorties down town are now far from uncommon.
After all, the vernal equinox had to bring something along to prove its approach!

Glad to hear the literary news. So old Pharnabazus means to reprint
"Pickman", eh? Well, it's about time he did choose a reprint that he'll have to
pay for! The darned skinflint has so far been using those things of mine
which I sold him in my naive youth, before I knew enough to reserve all but
the 1st North American rights. "The Thing on the Doorstep" is on the way—
it may reach you before this epistle. As you'll see, the "foundling" isn't exactly
of the sort you'd care to adopt & cherish! Glad you're placing some of your
tales & poems in the small magazines. They're really very valuable encouraging influences—bringing your work before appreciative readers, & drawing
criticisms which cannot fail to be occasionally helpful.

Thanks for the pictorial horrors, all of which are effective in their respective ways. The unfinished face of the Zothiquian wizard is impressive even as
it is. I return with suitable reluctance the nameless chromatic entity marked
for such disposal. Ngrrhhrrr!! I'd scarcely like to have that muzzle thrust in
my face at night!

Interested to hear of your gradual return to extra-curricular scholastic activities—undoubtedly a sensible step, since your position in the matter is such an
upper-hand one. You'll probably get enough valuable experience out of the varied doings to make them worth your time & labour. With halved school hours
the pressure won't be as devastating as it would otherwise be. Congratulations

on your departure from the groves of Dionysus—& also on your very advantageous trade of admiring nymphs. Are both of the new ones good typists?

March W T seems to be a rather average issue—I noted your Eyrie letter with interest & agreement.[1] Klarkash-Ton's tale has some exceedingly powerful moments—& his drawing is curiously impressive despite a certain stiffness in the human figure. The cyclopean columned hall, & the two nameless corpse-bearers, form a rather unforgettable combination. Before I forget it—have you a copy of the February F F with my "Polaris" in it? If not, I can let you have one, for Hornig was extremely generous with duplicates.

Have read quite a few things lately—including the celebrated & interminable "Anthony Adverse",[2] lent me by our friend Bnadvai-Aā. It took me 5 days to get through its 1224 pages. Also read Dunsany's latest—"The Curse of the Wise Woman", whose weirdness is very subtle & elusive. And now I've assimilated—at last—Merritt's "Metal Monster" (lent me by Barlow), nearly 14 years after its publication.[3] When it appeared, I passed it over because several readers (the damned fools!) told me it was no good. Boy, what a novel! I can understand now why Merritt deems it almost his best work. Never before have I encountered so utterly perfect & convincing a description of abysmally alien, non-human scenes & phenomena. The human characters & incidents are, alas, sheer pulp hokum—but one forgets all about that in considering the background against which they move. I surely hope Merritt will complete his revision & issue it in book form before long!

Well—blessings of Yog-Sothoth upon thee!

Thine under the Seal of Nyarlathotep

—E'ch-Pi-El

*Notes*

1. RB in "The Eyrie," *WT* 23, No. 3 (March 1934): 390: "The person who objected to a depiction of material decay as an example of weirdness is utterly wrong in his reasoning. Weirdness is a quality—a quality inspiring definite emotion, and having certain definite forms of reaction-patterns. One of these emotions or reaction-forms is fear, the fundamental emotion. Now nothing occasions more fear than the unknown. Death comes under this heading—it is an embodiment, the essence, the symbol of the unknown—a mysterious, awesome, fearful state to mortals. Therefore death as such is weird, because it inspires fear, and the processes of decay that come with death take on that same weirdness due to associative powers. For this reason a skeleton, a grinning skull, or a rotted cadaver is fearful; and if, as in some stories, such a thing is reanimated with unnatural life, fear is born. If decay is not weird, then some of Poe's, Bierce's, Machen's and Lovecraft's best stories are not weird tales. If death and decay and chaos are not weird, then no unnatural transposition of commonplace phenomena can be considered so, for they are simply distortions of matter-of-fact embodiments. Therefore, I fear I must disagree with your critic."

2. An historical novel by Hervey Allen; cf. *SL* 4.379, 390.

3. HPL refers to the original version of the novel, serialized in *Argosy All-Story Weekly*, 7 Aug.–25 Sept. 1920. (This version was reprinted in book form by Hippocampus Press, 2002.) Merritt later revised it as *The Metal Emperor* (*Science and Invention,* October 1927–August 1928) and again for the book publication of 1941.

[23]  [ALS]

April 9, 1934.

Dear Bho-Blôk:—

Congratulations on your minstrel success! You certainly appear to have constituted about nine-tenths of the performance . . . a 12-man cast in yourself! I can imagine the effect of your costume & rendition—plus, no doubt, the widely imitated rubber cigar! I trust that your dramatic appearance of April 2nd proved equally a triumph.

Glad you liked "The Thing On the Doorstep"—& hope Wright will do the same if I decide to submit it to him. Comte d'Erlette's main criticisms turned out to have a rather amusing basis—namely, that he read the story so superficially as to fancy the shooting in the asylum *preceded* the appearance of the Thing in actual *order of events* as well as order of narration! Since the entire denouement depends on the actual chronological previousness of the doorstep appearance—it being this which impelled the narrator to do the shooting—you can see how careless little Augie's reading must have been! However—it is only natural that so feverishly voluminous a reader should be inclined to skip & skim over any individual work . . . . particularly one of no especial importance. Yes—M. le Comte sent me the writeup he got in your local *Journal.* He is certainly headed for success, & I guess he deserves it. I must try to get hold of his published novel before long.

Enclosed is the F F with "Polaris." You'll also be interested in Klarkash-Ton's excellent article on James.[1] Thanks vastly for the glimpse of that pleasant little vampire head, which I return as per request. You certainly have a vast knack in art, & I trust you'll keep on developing it. Some time soon I'll lend you some photographs of the weird drawings of Wandrei's brother—I think you'll find them intensely interesting.

Rather a backward spring hereabouts—I certainly hope I can get to Florida May 1st. Depends on cash.

Robert E. Howard had a bad motor accident Dec. 29—cut & crushed badly enough to kill an ordinary man. But he's all right now—nothing can permanently down the iron physique of Conan the Reaver!

The other day I read Machen's new book—"The Green Round." A bit tame, yet full of the old magic & sense of unreal worlds close to our own. Better give it a once-over.

All good wishes—& hope the spring rush won't get too oppressive.

Yr obt Grandsire
E'ch-Pi-El

[P.S.] Price's garage venture in Pawhuska didn't pay, so he's taking to the road again. Will visit Two-Gun Bob in Cross Plains & Klarkash-Ton in Auburn. I fancy his next tarrying-place will be his native region of San Francisco.

[P.P.S.] New W.T. distinctly above the average. Burks reprint & Black Thirst splendid, Conan & C A S yarns excellent. Klarkash-Ton's design has power despite a certain stiffness.

*Notes*

1. "The Weird Works of M. R. James," *FF* 1, No. 6 (February 1934): 89–90.

[24]   [ANS][1]

[Postmarked Charleston, SC,
28 April 1934]

Greetings from my favourite town! Had a good week in N Y with Long, the two Wandreis, &c—leaving Sunday midnight. Spent Monday morning in Washington, exploring ancient Georgetown section. Afternoon in Richmond, evening in Raleigh, N.C. Hit Charleston at dawn Tuesday. Stopping at Y M C A & doing old town as usual. Marvellous place—18th century survives in every nook & corner. Full summer here—rich green vegetation, hot days, straw hats, & all! In Wash. & Richmond merely springlike, with delicate young foliage. And in N Y it is still wintry, with bare boughs & chill winds. There's a big kick in passing from winter to summer in a few hours. On to Savannah May 1st—& in De Land May 2 unless plans change. Temporary address % R. H. BARLOW, BOX 88, DE LAND, FLORIDA. Trust all is flourishing up your way, & that school activities aren't pressing you too hard. Regards—
                    E'ch-Pi-El

*Notes*

1. *Front:* Bird's Eye View of Broad Street, from Peoples National Bank Building, Charleston, S.C.

[25]   [ANS][1]

[Postmarked De Land, FL,
1 June 1934]
De Land, Fla.

    Great place down here—& Barlow is a splendidly gifted youth . . . . a writer, painter, sculptor, pianist, printer, landscape gardener, book collector, & dozens of other things. He is handicapped by poor sight. This climate braces me up marvellously. Hopes of Havana very dim, but will get a week in St. Augustine anyhow. Shall return north by easy stages.

Best wishes

—E'ch-Pi-El

*Notes*

1. Picture not identified.

[26]   [ALS]

De Land—

June 8, 1934

Dear Bho-Blôk:—

I presume your welcome epistle crossed my card from De Land, since it contains the assumption that I am home again. Such, as you see, is not the case—for the super-hospitality of the Barlow clan has kept deferring & deferring my departure. Young Robert Hayward Barlow is of about your own age, & shares your artistic leanings despite the handicap of abominable eyesight. Sooner or later you'll probably be in touch with him—& I feel sure the contact will be mutually congenial.

I can imagine how busy you have been with your dramatic, scholastic, & other activities, & am glad that success rewarded your labours with the senior play. Thanks for the programme, & for the loan of the pictures. You certainly make an excellent showing in costume, & I can imagine what a hit the minstrel stunt must have scored. Altogether, your school life has been a remarkably brilliant one, & I imagine you will feel both relief & regret at its termination. Let us hope that you will have equally good breaks in the outside world!

Glad you & your household enjoyed the stories. Celephaïs (written in 1920) was *not* retouched except in such an accidental way as was effected by about a dozen misprints. As for "Winged Death"—it *was* virtually written by me; the author being one of my revision clients. Before long you'll see my "Arthur Jermyn" reprinted in W.T. By the way—the April & May numbers of the magazine were unusually good, though the current June issue is rotten except for "The Colossus of Ylourgne."

Thanks for the pictures—all clever as usual. I also read the verses with the keenest interest, & am returning with a few annotations which I hope will prove helpful. I thought them all very good—both the weird & the cynical ones. It flatters me that Nyarlathotep should evoke such a verse-sequence—together with so excellent a portrait. The latter, I am sure, embodies all the salient features of Azathoth's hellish messenger!

No—W.T. has not seen "The Thing on the Doorstep" yet, although I shall probably submit it after I have secured a few more opinions on it.

Dwyer reports receiving it from you. He had seen it before, but the second glimpse won't hurt him.

Glad you're getting out to the countryside a bit, & hope you'll have an enjoyable trip to Chicago & its wonders. Such relaxation will help to put you in the mood for literary & pictorial craftsmanship. My aunt continues to improve in health, & letters indicate that she is almost as active as she was before her accident—which occurred precisely a year ago.

As I said on my card, this region is pleasant in the extreme, & my stay in it has been delightful. The warmth has quite set me on my feet physically. I had a faint hope that I might get to Havana, but this has now virtually vanished. I shall, though, spend a week in ancient St. Augustine if it breaks me! The return north will be by easy stages—I may visit a chap in Macon, Ga.,[1] & in any case I shall pause in Richmond & Washington. In N Y I shall doubtless linger a bit with Long—& if I have any cash left I shall go up the Hudson & pay Bernard Dwyer a visit.

Meanwhile Price has been travelling. The garage venture at Pawhuska proved a failure, so he hit the trail in his faithful Juggernaut & called on Two-Gun Bob at Cross Plains—then dipping down into Mexico & ultimately proceeding to his maternal home in Oakland, Cal. He has since been to Auburn to call on Klarkash-Ton.

Well—I must bring this to a close, since an array of forwarded mail fairly engulfs me. Later I'll show you some snapshots & other souvenirs of my sojourn—including photographs of some of the weird clay statuary that Barlow makes, & bits of skin from various kinds of local snakes.

With every good wish—

Yrs most cordially & sincerely,
E'ch-Pi-El

*Notes*

1. John Milton Samples, an amateur associate and editor of the *Silver Clarion*.

[27]    [ANS][1]

[Postmarked St. Augustine, FL,
24 June 1934]

Amongst my favourite antiquities! Staying in St. Augustine a week, & absorbing ancient atmosphere to the full. North again by the middle of July.

Regards & best wishes
—E'ch-Pi-El

*Notes*

1. *Front:* Oldest Frame House in U.S.A., Located on St. George Street, St. Augustine, Fla.

[28]   [ALS]

Home Again—

July 14, 1934

Dear Bho-Blôk:—

Got back July 10th, & am still lost amidst the chaos of piled-up work awaiting me. Owe 29 letters, & have a stack of papers to read. You last heard from me, I fancy, in St. Augustine. I had a great week there, & then began my reluctant progress northward—spending 2 days in Charleston, 1 in Richmond, 1 in Fredericksburg, 2 in Washington, & 1 in Philadelphia. In Philadelphia I visited the Poe cottage—inhabited by Poe in the late '30s or early '40s, & recently opened as a museum & shrine. A fascinating place—furnished as in Poe's day, & with a notable collection of reliques. When I hit N.Y. I found Long & his parents about to leave for Ocean Grove, N.J. over the week-end, & at their invitation went along with them. Hadn't cash to stay long in N.Y., so didn't look up many of the gang. It was very pleasant to get home & see all the familiar sights—though the chilly evenings of the north seem rather disconcerting after my long absence from such.

I can imagine how busy you've been, but trust that things are settling down more now. Glad all the details of graduation went off well, & shall be interested to see the school magazines covering your activities. Hope the simultaneous plunge into prose, poetry, & drawing will prove fruitful. I am certainly anxious to see the photograph of your "White Ape" statue—& will send you pictures of Barlow's sculptural achievements (Cthulhu bas-relief & Chaugnar statuette) before long. I fancy you'll find young Ar-E'ch-Bei very interesting when you get in touch with him. His latest hobby is trick photography—he has obtained a $5 \times 7$ camera; & with the aid of judicious double shots, models, retouching, &c. expects to achieve some rather bizarre & terrifying results.

Yes—I'd like to get out west some time & see you & Comte d'Erlette & Klarkash-Ton & all the others with whom I have been in epistolary touch so long. Heretofore I've made few trips except when I could combine antiquarian sightseeing with visiting—hence most of my peregrinations have lain along the long-settled & historic Atlantic coast. I know that Wisconsin must be highly interesting in many ways—& Comte Auguste-Guillaume has sent me material which convinces me that it is not without its scenic & historic sides. Sorry you've been having such bad weather. As I think I said, I encountered a typical tropic rainy season in De Land—with ponds & rivers overflowing, & dampness so great that wet clothing almost never dried. On the other hand, my stay in St. Augustine was marked with unbroken sunshine & warmth. When I first came north it was as warm as in Florida, so that I did not suffer any chill. For the last five days, however, it has been cool—especially at night—& I have wished I were back in the south. After the palms & live-oaks & Spanish moss of Florida, the scenery of the north seemed oddly strange to me at first, but I am now getting reoriented to it. Actually, New England in summer probably has the finest landscape—in a quiet way, & from a really artistic point of view—to be found in the United States. It is not unlike some of the Wisconsin landscapes shown in the pictures Derleth sends.

Glad to see your poetic bit—which I herewith reënclose in case it is your only copy. It looks very good to me, & I fancy the completed poem will be quite an impressive production. It's the right idea to work slowly—& never be afraid to revise & re-revise something already written.

Read the new W.T. last week, & fear it's one of the poorest issues yet. Quite a contrast to the excellent April & May numbers.

I am writing this in the open air—in a rural spot not far from Providence's busy centre, yet with a positively idyllic vista of green fields, blue water, & distant village steeple. After all, there's no landscape to beat this—though the tropical vistas of Florida have an intense charm of another sort. I guess I told you about Silver Springs & the Silver River—that bit of jungle which suggests the Congo or Amazon Valley.

But I must cease & continue my attack upon the mountains of unanswered mail.

Best wishes, & good luck with all your ventures.
Yrs in the tenebrous sodality of Yoth
——E'ch-Pi-El

[29]   [ALS]

Sunset—Bench in Roger
Williams Park—July 21[, 1934]

Dear Bho-Blôk:——
I must hasten to congratulate you upon your initial W.T. acceptance—an event which I trust may form the beginning of a successful career as a contributor![1] I knew you'd be making the grade before long, & am anxious to see the horror that turned the trick. Glad if Little Augie & I helped in any indirect way to guide you toward the triumph. All too many of those whom I've tried to encourage have stuck at a certain point & never developed any further!

Glad you had a pleasant time in the metropolis, & that you honoured the W.T. office with your presence. It is encouraging to hear that W.T. sales are picking up. Sprenger's kindly opinion of my stuff is very heartening, & I wish he were in the editorial chair![2]

As for delinquent correspondents—Klarkash-Ton always has pauses now & then, & Dwyer is shouldering quite an arduous programme because of his father's absence on a long visit. You'll hear from both in time. I shall be vastly interested when the art photographs arrive . . . . & Barlow would delight in them. Have I your permission to sub-lend them to him? Before long—unless Barlow has—I'll send you a picture of that Cthulhu bas-relief.

I'm asking Little Augie to send you his copy of "Innsmouth", since mine is out on a long lending circuit, & I don't know who has it at the moment. Hope a second perusal won't disillusion you about it!

I have just heard of a new macabre magazine about to appear on July 25—*Terror Tales,* issued by the publishers of *Dime Mystery.* Probably it will be fearful junk, but one always looks around for possible markets.

Again congratulating you on your auspicious debut—

Yrs for the Black Disc of Kno

—E'ch-Pi-El

*Notes*

1. "The Secret in the Tomb" (*WT,* May 1935).
2. William R. Sprenger, secretary-treasurer of *WT* (see photograph facing *SL* 5.294).

[30]    [ALS]

Necropolis of Khar-Zog; Hour
of the Piping from Below.
[c. late July 1934]

Dear Bho-Blôk:—

Thanks immensely for the existing parts of "The Secret in the Tomb". It really has great stuff in it, & I congratulate Satrap Pharnabazus on the acumen which caused him to accept it. The idea is magnificent, & you develop it in such a way as to bring out the tension & lurking horror with admirable vividness. If I were criticising it from a rigidly artistic angle, I suppose I'd have to recommend that the adjectives & macabre colouring be laid on just a trifle less thickly—but as you know, I like such things personally, & always have to fight a tendency to use them myself. By the way—regarding the quotation from the Necronomicon—in the original version the second line begins with *And* instead of *For*—though it really doesn't make any difference.[1] And look out about the spelling of NECRONOMICON—There's no R in the final syllable. This *does* make a difference, because the word is made up of actual Greek roots, & the -IKON suffix ought to be recognisable. I shall welcome the sight of "Lucian Grey" in its new form—& of other Blochiana as they may appear. Don't try to grind out more than you feel like writing—you'll have ideas enough if you'll only wait for them to dawn of their own accord. One spontaneous story—the sort that demands to be written—is worth a dozen tales deliberately concocted for the sake of writing something. Your allusion makes me very anxious to see Herr Prinn's "Mysteries of the Worm", & I have applied for a copy at the Miskatonic Library in Arkham. If I ever get around to original writing again you may find Ludvig & his hellish volume figuring in some yarn of mine. Nothing like giving these lurking horrors publicity! The librarian at Miskatonic says it will be very difficult to get Mazonides' "Black Spell of Saboth", but that he knows a private individual in Kingsport (about whom he is singularly reticent) from whom a copy of Petrus Averonius' "Compendium Daemonum" (watch your Latin case-endings in coining synthetic nomenclature) may be procured.[2]

I duly received *Fantasy Fan* & *Marvel Tales,* & deem the latter a vast improvement, both mechanically & literarily, over the previous issue. I can't agree that the contents averages poor, since to my mind Long's story alone would make it a notable issue. Wright turned down that yarn, but I insist that it's splendid. Two-Gun Bob also does well, I think, in his "Garden of Fear." Talman unfortunately spoils a good story with cumbrousness, ambiguity, & poor motivation.[3] It occurs to me me [*sic*] that you don't receive the F F regularly. Would you like some of the issues you lack? I have duplicates of lots of them, & would be glad to supply you if you'll send a list of these you already have. Indeed—my bundle of last month's—containing my "From Beyond"— is almost unwieldy!

Haven't written anything lately, & don't know when I ever shall. My programme is all in chaos—& yesterday *another* heavy (but poorly paying) job with a time-limit of Sept. 1st blew in to complicate matters. A whole damn novel to look over, pep up, & supply with a prologue!

I'll be glad to see the sketches & photographs scheduled for future transmission—which reminds me that the nameless head at the beginning of your letter is unusually good. Before long I'll shew you a batch of young Barlow's pictorial horrors. Genius seems to bless the crayons of all Robert B's! Hope little Augie will send "Innsmouth" before long. He has, by the way, just sent me a new (1932) anthology (Strange Assembly—ed. by John Gawsworth) containing two Machen items I never heard of before.[4]

As for weather—it hasn't been above 90° here recently, though reports of considerable heat stream in from the west . . . . &, oddly enough, from inland points in the *north*. Up in Vermont W. Paul Cook claims it has been 114°. No day so far has been too hot for me, & a good many have been too cold. I dread the coming of autumn!

The black kitten across the back garden continues to be a frequent visitor—had him over all yesterday evening. He is certainly an imp from Azathoth's nethermost gulf of tenebrous chaos!

Yrs under the Infra-Red Seal of N'kai—

E'ch-Pi-El

*Notes*

1. Presumably a reference to the "unexplainable couplet" "That is not dead which can eternal lie / And with strange aeons even death may die." The couplet does not appear in the published version of "The Secret in the Tomb"; it may have been an epigraph deleted by Farnsworth Wright.

2. "The Secret in the Tomb" is evidently the first story to mention Ludvig Prinn's *Mysteries of the Worm*. Mazonides' *Black Spell of Saboth* is not mentioned in the published story, but a book titled *Cabala of Saboth* is. Petrus Averonius' *Compendium Daemonum* is not cited.

3. Frank Belknap Long, Jr., "The Dark Beasts"; Robert E. Howard, "The Garden of Fear"; Wilfred Blanch Talman, "A Horror in Profile," all in *Marvel Tales* 1, No. 2 (July–August 1934).

4. Arthur Machen, "The Gift of Tongues" and "The Rose Garden."

[31]   [ALS]

Precipice of Noth—Hour of
the Black Wind from Below.
[11 August 1934]

Dear Bho-Blôk:—

Thanks exceedingly for the noxious "Spawn of the Elder Pits" & the photograph of the tremendously effective Chaney drawing. Such horrors are always welcome, & I await with eagerness the natal tribute to which you allude. I shall also welcome "The Touch of a Corpse"—which I hope may land in one or another of the markets to which it has been sent.[1] Isn't it a bit dangerous, though, to storm two markets at once? If by any chance both accepted, [*sic*] it would be quite an embarrassing matter to back out with the non-preferred one. The editor in question would probably hold more or less of a grudge which might affect his reception of later work from you. It interests me extremely to hear that this tale revolves around that monstrous & forbidden volume to which you timorously & whisperingly referred.

I didn't have quite as many F F's as I thought I had, but here are those I can spare. As you see, brother Charles has taken to coloured covers. Crude as the venture is, it is yet a valuable element in our little circle, & I try to give it (together with its contemporaries *Fantasy Magazine* & *Marvel Tales*) all the encouragement I can. I shall renew my subscription next month.

Haven't seen *Terror Tales* as yet, but am not surprised that you find it poor. I got the new W.T. yesterday, but have not had time even to glance at it. Doubt if it amounts to much except for the Moore & Howard offerings. As for Belknap's M T story—you are right in pointing out the idiot's elaborate soliloquy as the weak spot. This has *two* distinct faults—first, it is an obvious, cumbrous, & undesirable device for conveying certain information to the reader which ought to have been otherwise & imperceptibly conveyed; &

second, it is entirely out of keeping with what an idiot of the given type would have muttered or thought. The passage of almost Dunsanian prose-poetry is especially absurd as coming from an ignorant rural nitwit. All this I have recognised from the first—& mentioned with grandparental severity to Belknap himself—yet in spite of it I consider the story a fine & notable one. It is bigger than its defects—for the restrained suggestion of lurking woodland horrors is ineffably potent. However, it certainly has proved very unpopular. Wright turned it down like a flash, & young Rimel can't find any grain of merit in it. But I still say it's a great yarn—let him dispute who will!

Your lunar hypnosis is surely quite an experience—& one on which a magnificent weird tale could be founded. It makes me think of an alleged prose-poem which I perpetrated a dozen years ago[2] (probably under the influence of Merritt's "Moon-Pool"). I wait to see your sketch of the phenomenon—& later I hope you'll utilise the general idea in a full-fledged weird story.

Don't worry about Klarkash-Ton & Bnadvāī-Aā—you haven't offended them. Instead, each is feverishly busy. Nobody has heard from them—save for hurried postcards—in long weeks. Only the other day Barlow was asking whether Dwyer could be angry over some criticisms of one of his drawings, but I told him his apprehensions were groundless.

Had a most enjoyable visit last Thu–Fri–Sat from James F. Morton, curator of the Paterson Museum—one of the old gang. We covered a good many local points of interest, & went on the final day to ancient Newport—where we saw the U.S. fleet in the harbour, explored the 18th century streets & byways, & walked along the famous oceanside cliffs. We went by boat—the sail down Narragansett Bay being itself no slouch as recreations go.

As usual, I do most of my writing in the open air despite the advent of occasional cool days which drive me in early. This afternoon I've pulled one of my typically damn fool stunts—forgotten my writing pad! Hence this lousy ruled paper, picked up at the only available source of supplies within miles . . . . a rustic roadside stand.

And so it goes. All good wishes, & thanks for the pictures.

Yrs in the ritual of Zaman-ho—

E'ch-Pi-El

[P.S. on envelope:] Back in town—have just bought a Terror Tales. Looks pretty rotten! ¶ Expect to pay a visit near Boston Aug. 23 et seq.—shall see W. Paul Cook & take side trips to "Arkham" & "Kingsport."

*Notes*

1. Neither "Spawn of the Elder Pits" nor "The Touch of a Corpse" survives.
2. "What the Moon Brings" (1922).

[32]    [ANS]¹

[Postmarked Providence, RI,
22 August 1934]

Multitudinous thanks, O Arch-Lama of Leng, for the vast & hellish work of art which arrived to usher me into my 45th year of terrestrial incarnation! Ngrrrhrr . . . y'gah . . . . . I hear it padding softly & purposefully in the night . . . . Really, it's quite a triumph—you certainly know how to sling a mean crayon! My collection of Blociana is getting to be ample & notable. ¶ Also recd. the postal—whose design makes it part of the collection. Shall be glad to see the stories. Glad the F F's duly arrived. A new issue is out, but my extras haven't come yet. ¶ Have just discovered a splendid weird author of the early 1900's—William Hope Hodgson—& have prepared a note on him to insert in my F F serial article.² ¶ Am about to leave for Boston, where I shall visit a friend a few days & incidentally see W. Paul Cook. After that I have a wild hope of getting to Nantucket Island—where I've never been so far, but where the colonial past is said to survive more perfectly than anywhere else in America. I've been meaning to attempt the trip for years. Will let you know if I make it. Trust you duly recd. my epistle of some days ago. Again, thanks & blessings in Yuggoth's name.
E'ch-Pi-El

*Notes*

1. Picture not identified.
2. The insert was to go in Chapter IX, but *FF* ceased publication before that chapter could be published. See HPL's essay "The Weird Work of William Hope Hodgson."

[33]    [ANS]¹

[Postmarked Nantucket, MA,
30 August 1934]

Visited a week-end in Boston, & am now in the quaintest & most old fashioned town in the U.S. A perfect surviving bit of the 18th century—kept as it was through trade decline & island isolation. Here for a week & eating up all the varied antiquities. It is odd that I never visited this marvellous place before—only 90 m. from Providence!²
Regards in the name of Azathoth—
E'ch-Pi-El

*Notes*

1. Picture not identified.
2. Following this trip, HPL described Nantucket in "The Unknown City in the Ocean".

[34]   [ALS]

Valley of Nis—Hour of
the Sounds from Below
[c. mid-September 1934]

Dear Bho-Blôk:—

My Nantucket jaunt certainly was quite an event. Never have I encountered a more complete & unspoiled survival from the past. Toward the last I explored the island on a hired bicycle. It was the first time I had ridden in 20 years—but the process seemed just as facile & familiar as if I had last dismounted only the day before. It brought back so many memories of youth that I almost felt I must hurry home in time for the opening of Hope St. High School!

I hope you'll hear favourably regarding "The Touch of a Corpse" when Wright gets back from Seattle, & that you'll make *Terror Tales* as well. I hear reports of a possible newcomer in the weird field—an avowed rival to W.T.—though details as to name, publisher, & expected date are lacking. There is also a very slim possibility that *Strange Tales* may be revived by Street & Smith with Desmond Hall as editor.

Your programme—with 14 stories on the docket—is surely assuming d'Erlettian proportions, & I trust that all the items may turn out satisfactorily. By the time they are done & supplied with headings, the style & nature of Prinn's "Mysteries of the Worm" ought to be pretty well manifest!

That "birthday card" was surely effective enough, even though you consider it a 'crude & early' specimen. You are surely the arch-interpreter of the ghoulish species—which reminds me that a young chap in N.Y. is making a clay statuette of the Thing in "Pickman's Model".[1] When he finishes & photographs it I'll shew you a print. I thought you'd find Barlow a congenial correspondent. Hope his eyes can be substantially helped by his present Washington sojourn.

I haven't yet read the Sept. W T—nor have I purchased the second T.T., which must have been out a fortnight now. Hope your mother will be able to get you the Not-at-Night with the Rats. Here, by the way, is the new F F—in which you'll find a brief reference to your professional debut.[2]

Glad your latest inamorata is a typist who can help you practically as well as sentimentally. You sure do know how to pick 'em! The throbbing lyric in the d'Erlette vein is very effective, & ought to please the lady vastly. "Dinner at Eight" is likewise powerful in its somewhat different way.

I note with appreciation the hellish entity Kyansita, which heads your epistle. You surely can evolve a company of assorted Shapes that one wouldn't care to meet after dark!

Let us hope that the possible 'startling news' which you mention is good news—& that, in such a case, it may indeed become a reality.

I am now the sole occupant of my ancient quarters—my aunt being in Ogunquit, Maine, for a fortnight. There is a possibility that I may have a visit from one or both of the Wandreis this month. Donald intends to come east & visit a bit, & then both brothers will probably return to St. Paul.

Well—back to work! My programme has been barbarously crowded since my return from Nantucket . . . . & I now face a demand for an elegy, in verse, on a lately deceased member of the National Amateur Press Association.³ I wish the members of that organisation would forget my metrical past!

                   With every good wish—
                         Yrs by the Black Cylinder
                              —E'ch-Pi-El

*Notes*

1. Dean P. Phillips, a friend of Samuel Loveman.
2. F. Lee Baldwin, "Within the Circle," *FF* 2, No. 1 (September 1934): 7: "The youthful Robert Bloch of Milwaukee has sold his first story to Weird Tales. It is titled 'The Secret of [*sic*] the Tomb.'"
3. "Edith Miniter."

[35]  [ALS]

                         Grove of the Pallid Fungi
                         Hour of the Black Moon
                         [early October 1934]

Dear Bho-Blôk:—

I have read "The Touch of a Corpse" with very genuine interest, & believe you have a really fine story despite the possible excess of colouring in places. The central idea is an excellent variant of the Lukundoo theme, & the second horror derived from the first is very effectively prepared for & sprung as a second climax. Also, it was very clever to have the Lukundoo-product *hinted at* in a dream (p. 3) but not directly brought before the reader at any time. I'm sorry Wright turned it down—but can see why he found the style too heavily overloaded with obvious horror-devices . . . . as my style used to be. Let us hope T T will be less exacting—but if it does come back, I'd advise you to tinker with it further. It's a story worth saving—& you'd be surprised as to how much better it will sound when the language is made a bit quieter & more reticent. What the language of a good horror story ought to convey is *hushed tension* or *veiled menace*. Of course the cheap pulp writers don't get this at all—but it can be done. You have the right idea in many ways, but lay on the material just a bit too thickly, as all young writers are prone to do. With experience, I think you'll have a tendency to ease up a bit—yet without losing the dark & brooding quality which all weird prose ought to contain. Later on I hope to see "The Fog"—which I trust M. le Comte d'Erlette has surveyed without total disapproval. Glad the F F proved interesting. I may be partly responsible for that mention of you, in that I told one or another of the Washington boys about your professional debut.

Sorry the startling news couldn't materialise—& hope that both of the theatrical projects, legitimate & vaudevillainous, may turn out well. Good luck, too, with the alumni association. Good idea to keep up reading—"The Old Wives' Tale"[1] is distinctly worth going through. Would you like to be put on the lending list of any weird classics? Some excellent stuff by William Hope Hodgson—& those Williams books which Koenig mentions in his F F article—are going the rounds.[2]

I shall be interested to see the Innsmouth sketches if the vivid likeness of Mr. Vedder is a typical sample! Nggrrrh! That gent has almost reached the stage where retirement from the outside world is necessary!

My programme is all shot to hell—for on top of the previous congestion there is now imposed the further congestion arising from a week-long attack of indigestion which had me inactively abed most of the time. I'm pulling out of that now—but the plethora of piled-up work before me is an appalling thing to see!

Yrs for the inverse Sign of the Shoggoths<br>—E'ch-Pi-El

### Notes

1. A celebrated novel by Arnold Bennett (1908).
2. H. C. Koenig, "The Intellectual Shocker," *FF* 2, No 1 (September 1934): 10, concerning the novels of Charles Williams.

[36]   [ALS]

Necropolis of Nug-Hathoth:<br>Hour that the Uninscribed Stele<br>Grows Phosphorescent————<br>[postmarked 18 October 1934]

Dear Bho-Blôk:—

Congratulations on the Underwood—which is certainly a necessity if you're going to write for publication systematically. Glad to hear that the "Secret" is in type, & hope T T will look kindly upon the "Touch". Good luck with "Feast", "Fog", & "Evil Genius"—though of course rejections preponderate for years in any writer's experience. Glad the Nyarlathotep verses multiply.

Barlow will probably write before long. Dwyer has just enrolled in a C C C camp—though how he managed to do it at 38 I'm damned if I know. So you never saw that mimeographed spoof of last summer? I had a copy but can't find it now—otherwise I'd send it along. It rather amuses me to be charged with the authorship, since the sort of elephantine humour is about the last thing I'd be likely to start![1] Those two Fungi of mine—"Mirage" & "The Elder Pharos"—were set to music 3 or 4 years ago. I've never received a copy of the score, but understand the music is as weird as the text. The composer—Farnese—has a leaning toward the weird, & is now writing an opera based on my synthetic mythology. He wanted me to write the libretto, but I have no experience in dramatic composition, so passed it up.[2]

Indigestion better—though I had a slight relapse yesterday. Commiserations on the cold, & the professional complications it caused. Just now I have a sort of incipient writer's cramp—which hampers my scribbling considerably, though it hasn't driven me to the hated keys of the typewriter quite yet.

Enclosed are the two tales you wish to see. "Erich Zann" isn't bad, but I think the "Horror" one of my poorest. It has touches of absolutely cheap melodrama which I ought to have known better than to write.

So you saw Providence in the news reels, eh? Curious—because the strike disturbances didn't touch this city at all. Of the two riots, one was in Saylesville, 6 miles away, & the other in Woonsocket, 20 miles away. Outside papers probably tended to exaggerate their importance.[3] Both were apparently due to irresponsible hoodlums—entirely outside the ranks of the genuine strikers, & probably stirred up by communistic propaganda. The governor dealt with the situation admirably—refusing to call out troops till it was necessary, but then furnishing enough forces to quiet things up at once. He also closed certain mills—storm-centres of disturbance—till the tension blew over. The whole strike was unfortunate in that it aggravated an industrial confusion already bad enough. It was a pity that the labour unions could not have left the matter for government arbitration—it being amply demonstrated that the present administration is capable of making impartial decisions.

Thanks for the pictorial enclosure—both sides of which possess points of interest. That embattled feline would make an ideal member for the Kappa Alpha Tau fraternity on the shed roof outside my window! The Sleepy Hollow scene is a bit wrong as regards the shape of the church steeple, & the relative positions of church, churchyard, & road. I have been to the place—which still holds much of the past. The old Dutch church dates from 1695.

Yes—I know that the Wisconsin autumn rivals that of New England in beauty. Glad you had a rural glimpse. I've made many trips to the exquisite countryside north of Providence—though it's too cold nowadays to do any reading or writing outdoors.

All right—I won't steer any circulating books your way just yet. I don't blame you for not wanting any extra burdens! But eventually you must know Hodgson. Charles Williams would probably disappoint you, for his stuff is not so much real horror fiction as veiled philosophic allegory. He is artificial & attenuated—& to get a full-sized kick out of him one must take seriously the orthodox view of cosmic organisation. The early Chesterton is perhaps his closest parallel. Possibly M. le Comte d'Erlette would enjoy him. I'm now sending his books on to Klarkash-Ton.

Well—I trust you'll soon get some cardboard & turn out some more nameless Shapes!

Best of luck—

Yrs for the sunken monolith of Gnoph
—E'ch-Pi-El

*Notes*

1. HPL actually did have a hand in "The Battle That Ended the Century," written with R. H. Barlow during his visit to Barlow in the spring of 1934.

2. A reference to Harold Farnese's proposal c. October 1932 to collaborate with HPL on a musical drama in one act set on Yuggoth, to have been called *Fen River.*

3. Workers at textile mills in Woonsocket and Saylesville rioted on 12 September, looting both cities and forcing the Rhode Island National Guard to be called in. One civilian was killed, and dozens were injured. Governor Theodore Francis Green issued a proclamation declaring a state of emergency; as the rioting continued for a second day, he expressed a wish to call in federal troops, something that had not been done in regard to labor unrest since Shays' Rebellion (1786–87). The violence dissipated the next day.

[37]  [ALS]

Burrow of the Dholes
—Hour of the Charnel Feasting.
[late October 1934]

Dear Bho-Blôk:—

Congratulations again! A *second* acceptance certainly forms a great step; for it proves that the first was no mere luck shot, & indicates that more are likely to loom ahead. From now on, I fancy you'll be placing things in W T right along—to say nothing of other magazines of the same nature. Hope *Terror Tales* will prove receptive after all. I don't think everything in it is staff-written, for Carl Jacobi placed a tale there.[1] They have certain standards of their own, though—favouring cheap physical gruesomeness & sadistic cruelty. Yes—let's see one of your recent products. I'll leave the choice to you— send whatever you consider most truly representative. I'd also vastly appreciate a carbon of "Erich Zann" if you're typing a copy for yourself. As you can see from the condition of "Red Hook", stories wear out after many years of lending; & then I simply have to withdraw them from circulation unless I can get fresh copies somehow.

About that libretto—I could never have produced what Farnese wanted. In the first place, I lack all dramatic technique. Secondly, the requirements of music drama are highly artificial & conventional, & involve a claptrap melodrama & sappy romance which I couldn't possibly bring myself to write. Better by far that Farnese produce his own stuff in his own way. He promised to shew me the result, though he has never done so. Perhaps he gave the project up, though he seemed interested enough at the time. Speaking of drama—I'm glad that your "Smiling Through" company has had good bookings.

Glad the F F proved of interest, & that my Yuggothian Fungi struck you favourably. I might grind out more weird verse if I had more time,[2] but latterly I have been utterly swamped by revisory tasks. Haven't written a weird line in metre since 1930. There is no selling these Fungi—only 10 of which W T used.

Dwyer is doing well at the CCC Camp, having been appointed editor of the camp paper. But possibly he's told you about it.

Had an enjoyable week-end Oct. 19–21. On the 20th my host[3] & I explored a section of north central Massachusetts which I had never before visited, & in which I saw some of the finest autumnal foliage & landscape vistas that I have ever beheld. The focus of the trip was West Townsend, where we lunched at a rambling old tavern built in 1774, & patronised the quaintest general store that I've seen in 30 years. Nearby is the Wallis Brook State Forest, where we revelled in wooded hills, rock waterfalls, & leafy gorges of indescribably picturesqueness. On the 21st my host & his wife brought me back to Providence—picking up my aunt at #66 & setting out for the ancient Narragansett country which Price & I explored last year. We visited the venerable seaport of Wickford, & later struck inland to the gorgeously lovely spot where Gilbert Stuart's birthplace—a snuff-mill built in 1750—broods beside the Narrow River. As I probably told you in '33, this centuried structure has been fully restored—wheel & all—to its pristine condition, so that it can grind snuff as well as it did when Stuart's father ran it 180 years ago. The surrounding landscape is doubly beautiful in autumn—& one can fully appreciate it from a heated car!

Yes—the hellish Sabbat draws nigh, & monstrous shadows hover about the lonely hills & the dank wooded ravine here the leprous-white monolith crumbles in millennial decay. I shall watch the glade of the standing stones where the monstrous footprint was seen on the morning after May-Eve. Perhaps I shall survive to tell what I see . . . . but perhaps . . . .

Well, anyhow, let me repeat my congratulations on the placement of the "Feast." May your luck hold—& increase!

Yrs for the Nameless Burnt-Offering<br>—E'ch-Pi-El.

*Notes*

1. Jacobi's only story in *Terror Tales* was "Satan's Roadhouse" (October 1934).

2. "The Book" (I) and "Pursuit" (II) appeared in FF (October 1934). When *Fungi from Yuggoth* was composed (1929–30), HPL professed to expand the poem with more sonnets, leaving XXXIV and XXXV out of his circulating T.Ms. so that if more were in fact added, those two sonnets would close the long poem.

3. HPL's host was Edward H. Cole.

[38]  [ALS]

Chasm of the Watcher
—Hour of the Red Smoke
[early to mid-November 1934]

Dear Bho-Blôk:—

     Well—the three MSS. duly arrived, & I have read them with the keenest pleasure & appreciation. Darned good stuff—all of it! You certainly have the secret of atmosphere & dramatic situation, & your style is improving at a marvellous rate. The tendency toward overcolouring so marked last year is waning rapidly, & your command of effective diction—& of prose rhythm, in the case of the archaic specimens—is becoming more & more dependable. Good work! I wish I could see the output of some of my professional clients improve as fast & as substantially! I have made a few pencil notations, most of which are probably self-explanatory. In other cases, the dictionary will probably indicate the reason for the change—or I'll be glad to explain anything which seems obscure. None of these emendations, of course, is really structural. "The Shambler in the Night"[1] has powerful potentialities, & needs only a little less *indefiniteness* in the theoretical parts—pp 4–5 in particular—to be extremely notable. Keep working on this, & in the end even the capricious Wright will be likely to yield to its malign magic. In places your atmospheric tension & imagery are tremendously powerful—for example: "The frozen moon was his eye, & his limbs were streamers of stars. The snow drifted down like drops of white blood from his body." "The Black Lotus" is another powerful specimen. In places this gets to a really poetic level, & the various turns are excellently managed. The rhythm of the prose is delightful, too. I also like "The Grinning Ghoul" exceedingly. Its dark implications & evil suspense are very potent, while the sense of underground horror is such as I tried to convey in "The Nameless City." The climax has the requisite punch—& justifies the title admirably. I must congratulate you warmly on all three stories—not only because of their great intrinsic merit, but because of the development in your powers of narration which they reveal. You have certainly covered a lot of ground in a year or a year & a half! Keep it up, & you'll undoubtedly become one of the weird magazine standbys—if not a good deal more!

     As for Wright & his capricious rejections—or analogous phenomena elsewhere—don't let any such matters discourage you! Even with long-established writers the percentage of rejections is almost always considerable, while with beginners it is invariably overwhelmingly great. Considering the short time you have been writing, your two existing acceptances form a success of the most decided sort—so that your attitude ought to be one of emphatic optimism & encouragement. I am eager for the publication of "The Feast in the Abbey", so that I may see what changes have been made.

Glad you didn't waste energy copying "Erich Zann". I was astonished to find it reprinted, for Wright had led me to believe that "Arthur Jermyn" would be the next. I haven't had time to read the present issue of W T, but noticed your provocative epistle in the Eyrie.[2] I fear you are just a bit too hard on our distinguished massacre specialist, since some of his stuff has a really distinguished poignancy. Who else can so well convey an idea of unholy antiquity in primal cyclopean ruins? And can anyone deny a certain touch of genuine poetic vision in "The Queen of the Black Coast?" What is more—of all the repeatedly-used stock characters of the W T bunch— Jules de Grandin & so on—it is certain that Conan, hate him as you will, has the most aesthetic justification. He is the least wooden & artificial of all—that is, he reflects more of his creator's actual feelings & psychology than any other. De Grandin is merely a puppet moulded according to cheap popular demand— he represents nothing of Quinn. But in the moods & reactions & habits of Conan we can clearly trace the sincere emotions & aspirations & perspectives of Howard. De Grandin always acts as a synthetic marionette, but Conan often acts as a living & distinctive human being. Of course, the artistry of Howard is only partial. He is not thoroughly trained, & he writes frankly for a popular pulp audience. Much about Conan is indeed mechanical & absurd— but beyond all that there is a certain genuineness & spontaneousness which can't be denied or argued away. However—it is to be remarked that a character of this type is probably out of place in *weird* as distinguished from *adventure* fiction—that is, the *constant exploitation* of such a type is out of place. I can agree with you that the placing of *supreme emphasis* on the head-cracking & gore-spattering activities of a primitive nomad scarcely contributes much to the weird effect of the scenes through which he hews his way. Howard ought to *separate* his two gifts—his command of dark, brooding effects, & his sympathetic understanding of the barbarian mind—into two separate groups of stories; contributing the one to W T & its congeners, & the other to magazines of the *Adventure* class. Of course, he *does* write a great deal of wholly non-weird stuff for things like *Action Stories, Fight Stories,* &c. He has a prize-fighter character called Steve Costigan who seems to be quite a rival of Conan in his virile affections. Actually, as a creator of vigorously self-expressive & more or less sincere & spontaneous fiction of a certain sort, Howard undeniably stands higher than such absolutely [text erased] puppet-showmen & herd-caterers as Edmond Hamilton, Quinn, Kline, & the latter-day Price. Dividing the W T group into sheep & goats, we can't avoid placing R E H in the upper tier along with Smith, Moore, the old-time Price, & the late Whitehead.

I read "The Magic Island"[3] while visiting Whitehead in Florida in 1931. It is certainly a revelation in its way—& we may clearly trace its effect on all fiction concerning Haiti. From the moment of its appearance it has formed an inexhaustible source-book.

So Fritz Leiber is still before the public![4] I had lost all track of him. When I was young he was the most prominent "juvenile" in the company of the late Robert Mantell, & liked his work exceedingly. I recall especially his fine performance of Faulconbridge in "King John"—back in 1911, if I remember correctly. I suppose he is getting along in years now—though not beyond the age at which one may be a standard exponent of the classic drama. He ought to do well as Shylock (as I suppose he is now) in the "Merchant." He used to be Bassanio in Mantell's time. In those days his best chances came in plays where there were two male leads—he was a great Iago in "Othello", & a fine Edgar in "Lear". How the years pass!

As to the Baconian notion—I must say that I don't think there's anything in it. All the claims of the Baconians are based on either superficial concepts of Elizabethan times, or on *supposed* ciphers which have no genuine existence. In cold truth, the internal evidence of the plays clearly indicates the authorship of a careless, half-educated man of the actor Shakespeare's known type. They are lousy with slips & anachronisms which would have been utterly & ridiculously impossible in the work of a scholar like Bacon. Don't get the idea that Elizabethan scholarship was any such lax thing as you'd infer from Shakespeare. Ben Jonson is a better indication of the sort of thing Bacon would have written had he dabbled in drama. Look at "Sejanus" & "Catiline".

By the way—I am not a Shakespearian authority. You probably got the idea from a letter in the Eyrie which contained an erroneous statement to that effect[5] . . . . but I've been busy correcting that report. That letter was written by a boy in the National Amateur Press Assn. who doesn't know me personally, & who evidently got me mixed up with my good friend & fellow-old-time-member Samuel *Loveman,* who is indeed an Elizabethan scholar & author of scenes designed for interpolation into "Macbeth" & "Lear." My own acquaintance with Avon's bard is purely cursory—as a part of a general sketchy familiarity with English literature.

Well—for a wonder, I *have* seen "The Barretts of Wimpole St."[6] Very fine indeed—I surely wish the cinema would turn out more of that quality! Also saw the Barrie play "What Every Woman Knows"[7] in the new cinema version. Good of its kind despite rather naive efforts at modernisation.

Winter draws nigh—though Nov. 5 was warm enough to invite me to a scenic walk. Hallowmass came & went without disaster. ¶ Again, congrats on the new tales. ¶ Yrs for the Sign of Ynagris—

E'ch-Pi-El

*Notes*

1. Probably an early version of "The Shambler from the Stars."
2. RB's letter appeared in *WT* 24, No. 5 (November 1934): 661: "The present issue of WT is rather remarkable in that the short stories by far excel the longer ones—a fact

which each successive issue makes more evident. Conan is rapidly becoming a stereo-typed hero, but I was greatly pleased with Francis Flagg; a real writer, with something to say. I am awfully tired of poor old Conan the Cluck, who for the past fifteen issues has every month slain a new wizard, tackled a new monster, come to a violent and sudden end that was averted (incredibly enough!) in just the nick of time, and won a new girl-friend, each of whose penchant for nudism won for her a place of honor, either on the cover or on the inner illustration. Such has been Conan's history, and from the realms of the Kushites to the lands of Aquilonia, from the shores of the Shemites to the palaces of Dyme-Novell-Bolonia, I cry: 'Enough of this brute and his iron-thewed sword-thrusts—may he be sent to Valhalla to cut out paper dolls.' I would like to see the above tirade in print—I feel sure that many of your readers would support me—at least there is good material there for an argument." In *WT* 23, No. 4 (April 1934): 520, RB had praised Howard though disparaged Conan: "Howard, by the way, is wonderful in this issue; if he sticks to atavism, the ancient Britons and Solomon Kane, and drops Co-nan the Cimmerian Chipmunk, he will maintain his present supremacy in your pages."

3. A book about Haiti by William B. Seabrook.

4. That is, Fritz Leiber, Sr., the Shakespearean actor, father of fantasy writer Fritz Leiber, Jr.

5. Alexander Ostrow in *WT*, October 1933: "Your readers might be interested in knowing that not only is Lovecraft a master of weird fiction, but that he is also an authority on Shakespeare." Rpt. in *A Weird Writer in Our Midst*, 76.

6. *The Barretts of Wimpole Street* (MGM, 1934), directed by Sidney Franklin; starring Norma Shearer, Fredric March, and Charles Laughton.

7. *What Every Woman Knows* (MGM, 1934) directed by Gregory La Cava; starring Hel-en Hayes, Brian Aherne, and Madge Evans. Based on the play by J. M. Barrie and filmed previously in 1921 as a silent.

[39]   [ALS]

At the Pharos in Leng
[22 December 1934]

Dear Bho-Blôk:—

Your account of recent activities is certainly interesting in the extreme—& I congratulate you most sincerely on the many alluring vistas now opening up. Don't mind Satrap Pharnabazus' rejections—it's just an automatic reflex with him! Markets for really popular weird fiction seem to be on the in-crease—the new F F reports a coming magazine to be called *Horror Stories,* run by the *Terror Tales* crowd. And meanwhile (though I haven't seen it) the new Winford *Mystery Novels Magazine* is out. Glad you're keeping up with the humorous work—nothing like flexibility & variety! Hope that radio audition turns out well—let me know whenever you're on the air. With your evident gift for natural, spontaneous satire & ludicrous situations, I don't see why you couldn't put across something as effective as the gags & patter & sly shrewd-ness of Eddie Cantor or Will Rogers or any of the other etheric celebrities!

Your Tuesday evening discussion group sounds admirably interesting & stimulating. In a way—except for the nearly uniform ages, & the possibly greater systematisation of topics—it reminds me of my own old gang in N.Y.[1]—which still ekes out a somewhat shadowy existence though the once-weekly meetings tend to become semiannual or annual. We used to meet around at the different members' houses & argue about everything under the sun—an all-stag group with the utmost heterogeneity of ages. Our youngest—Long at first, & later Talman & Wandrei, successively—tended to be around 22 or so, while our eldest (now dead) was 67 at the last.[2] Good old Jim Morton (curator of the Paterson Municipal Museum)—now 64—was just a decade younger than that during our heyday. Rheinhart Kleiner, Samuel Loveman, & I (now in our forties, then thirtyish) represented the middle generation—& Arthur Leeds was a bit older than we. Thus we typified all shades of chronological influence—from the generation educated in the elegant 80's to the wild young moderns of the terrible twenties. And did we have some swell intellectual free-for-alls on various aesthetic & philosophical subjects? I'll tell the cockeyed world![3] But alas! we were never systematic enough to develop any solid prospects such as those of your club. Your hypnotic experiments certainly sound interesting enough. I suppose there is no reason why clever amateurs or semi-amateurs couldn't produce in certain types of subject that utterly complete concentration of attention which forms the basis of true mesmeric suggestion. Judging from the programme you give, you haven't much spare time on your hands these days! "Is there a Normal Person?" After a long life of observation, I espouse the negative side. Especial congratulations are due you for your chance in "A Midsummer Night's Dream". A highly appropriate classic vehicle for the debut of one of the foremost comedians & character actors of the next generation! Thanks for the book recommendations. I think I've heard of "My First 2000 Years" . . . . by George Sylvester Viereck, isn't it?[4] Shall be glad to see those monstrous new drawings you speak of. You & Barlow surely make a pair . . . did I tell you that his eyes are slightly better & that he is taking an art course at the Corcoran Gallery?

Read the Dec. W T—much better than Nov. As for Conan—while I stand by my general verdict, I must admit that Two-Gun is tending to go stale a bit . . . a conclusion brought home to me by his serial. This damned pulp tradition does "get" 'em all!

Hellish cold spell in Providence—down to 8° or so day after day, & for a week I couldn't venture forth from the house. Prior to that Prov. had an "Art Week" full of lectures. One evening a couple of local artists painted pictures in full view of the audience.[5] One lecture on the cinema would have interested you. Another feature was an exhibition of some of the 700 splendid Japanese prints just acquired by the local museum. ¶ Benedictions—

E'ch-Pi-El

P.S. No—haven't sent in "Doorstep" yet. Am trying to get a new yarn on paper.[6]

[P.P.S.] I may visit Long in N.Y. over or after Christmas.

[P.P.P.S. on envelope:] Nggrrrrh! God!! *It* has come!!! I reel in horror at the monstrous, half-decayed Thing that stares & stares & stares . . . out of the obscene vortex of the dead & the un-dead . . . . Thanks a thousand times—it's really a great piece of work, & will go into the choicest part of my gallery along with last year's scarlet horror. You do manage to get some great effects on a large scale—I'll wager you'd make a prize-winning mural painter! ¶ Season's best wishes!

*Notes*

1. The Kalem Club, most of whose members' last names started with the letters K, L, or M.
2. Everett McNeil.
3. A phrase going back to wartime slang of 1917–18. *The Cockeyed World* (1929), sequel to *What Price Glory?*, was a popular war movie.
4. George Sylvester Viereck and Paul Eldridge, *My First Two Thousand Years: The Autobiography of the Wandering Jew*. First volume of a trilogy also comprising *Salome, the Wandering Jewess*, and *The Invincible Adam*.
5. Hezekiah Anthony Dyer (1872–1943) and John Robinson Frazier (1889–1966).
6. This was "The Shadow out of Time," begun in late 1934 and completed on 22 February 1935.

[40]   [ALS]

Crypt of Zoth
—Hour of the Shadow
[late January 1935]

Dear Bho-Blôk:—

Glad to hear the news! I guess I mentioned the salient facts concerning Yuletide hereabouts—especially the presence of a *tree* for the first time since my boyhood. All my old ornaments were long ago dispersed; but I went on quite a buying spree at good old Frank Winfield Woolworth's, & in the end had a very gaily tinselled layout, glittering with an ample constellation of coloured lights. We liked it so well that it didn't come down till Jany. 10th. But meanwhile I was largely absent—paying Frank B. Long a visit in N.Y. The weather was rather favourable—only 2 days giving me any real trouble. Young Barlow was up from Washington, which gave the sessions something of the aspect of a convention. I saw all the old gang—Morton, Loveman, Leeds, Kirk, Talman, the two Wandreis, &c. &c., as well as Koenig & various other newer acquaintances. At one meeting—at Long's place—we had an attendance of 15. Barlow & I did the museums, bookshops, &c—quite a treat for him, since he had never been in N.Y. before since infancy. Koenig showed us over the Electrical Testing Laboratories where he works—a highly remarkable place, in which all sorts of household electrical devices are tested for their susceptibility to wear & tear. In the realm of book bargains, I found a fine copy of Lewis's "Monk" for a dollar—but Barlow beat me by finding an early edition of George W. M. Reynolds' "Wagner the Wehrwolf" for 15¢! The Wandreis reached N.Y. about the same time I did—Donald landing after a boat trip from California, & Howard coming directly from St. Paul. They have taken an apartment together in Greenwich Village. Barlow's eyes are much better, though his general health is poor. He returned to Washington the day I returned to Providence, & does not expect to be back in Florida till June.

Glad to learn of the stimulating activities of your group, & hope you win your debate with the county committee. The odds would seem to be about even—with the choice of subject & conditions on the other side, but perfect intellectual freedom on your side. Glad you won the previous contest.

It pleases me greatly to see your work getting into print. I enjoyed re-reading "The Laughter of a Ghoul" in the F F, & "The Feast in the Abbey" in W T. The latter seems to have undergone changes since last I beheld it in MS. As it stands, it certainly packs a first-rate punch. Glad "The Black Lotus" will appear in *Marvel*. My own new horror has been stalled by the pressure of other activities. For the past month I have been veritably swamped—& I can't compose anything original unless I have unlimited leisure.

Interested to learn that I figured in a dream of yours . . . . as a sinister ogre, no doubt. About that time—Jany. 3 at midnight (1 a.m. Jan 4. E.S.T.)—Long, Barlow, a chap named Phillips, & I were in the Automat at Broadway & 103ᵈ St., N.Y.C. No doubt some malign overtone of our hellish discourse rode the aether through all the long leagues to Milwaukee!

I read Pitkin's "History of Human Stupidity" a year or so ago. Damned clever—& sensible in spots—though rather marred by a few amusing prejudices & a considerable bias toward the crude commercial ideal. Speaking of stupidity—it certainly is odd that so many failed to get the point of the "Feast." I wouldn't consider the tale as obscure in any way. It seems to have lost most of the extravagance & excessive colouring which I remarked in the MS., & the ending is surely a knockout—whether or not it may be held to involve too strong a dose of coincidence.

Your word-association tests seem based on a generally sound principle, though results are not always conclusive. More people than is commonly realised have no *first* association of any kind—several parallel images occurring to them simultaneously when a word is presented. They are then obliged to hesitate & choose some single word arbitrarily from the group in their consciousness.

Hope to see the new Vampire book sooner or later. Just now I have several borrowed books to read—including the famous "Malleus Maleficarum"[1] & Hugh Walpole's "Portrait of a Man With Red Hair."

Yrs for the Grey Ritual of Khif

—E'ch-Pi-El

P.S. While at Loveman's I saw his collection of about 400 Clark Ashton Smith drawings—some of them unbelievably fine. Barlow, Long, & Wandrei saw these for the first time.

[P.P.S.] Derleth has just told me of a new weird magazine—SENSATIONS—issued by Pierre Publications, 8th Floor, 120 W. 42 St., N.Y. City.

[P.P.P.S. on envelope:] Just bought 2 dark walnut sets of drawers to file papers in—my loose cuttings & documents were getting unmanageable! ¶ And now comes a record-breaking snow to paralyse traffic!

*Notes*

1. Jacobus Sprenger and Henricus Institor [Heinrich Kramer], *Malleus Maleficarum [Hammer of Witches]*, published in Germany c. 1486 as a guide to inquisitors in detecting, examining, and punishing witches. HPL probably refers to the 1928 translation by Montague Summers.

[41]   [ALS]

Northern Slope of Ngranek—
Hour of the Stirring in the Caves.
[c. early February 1935]

Dear Bho-Blôk:—

Well—it was quite a trip! 15 days in all—& what a chaos of piled-up work I came home to! I found my host absorbed in his new hobby of tropical fish, but he still had time to take part in some damned interesting discussions. Also saw the rest of the gang—Loveman, Leeds, Wandrei, Talman, Morton, &c. Met Wandrei's younger brother for the first time, & was almost knocked cold by the progress he has made in his weird art. You & Klarkash-Ton had better look to your laurels, for this kid can draw nameless blasphemies & monstrous Sabbats with a genius & maturity born of the Pit itself! There's no question but that he has gone further with his drawing than any of the rest of us have with our writing. He'll be widely recognised before long—mark an old man's words! Saw the old year out at Loveman's, & was presented with some new objects for my museum—a fine Egyptian *ushabti* of bitumen-covered wood nearly a foot long, a curious little Mayan image of stone, & a carved wooden monkey from the East Indian isle of Bali. Incidentally, I took in most of the museums—seeing the impressive new Assyrian, Etruscan, & Greek stuff at the Metropolitan. Also picked up 2 or 3 book bargains—notably the late Arthur Weigall's "Wanderings in Roman Britain." Saw a good many new people connected with weird writing—including Desmond Hall, editor of *Astounding Stories,* two of the boys behind *Fantasy* (erstwhile *Science Fiction Digest*), the anthologist T. Everett Harré, & . . . . last & preëminent . . . . . the one & only *A. Merritt,* author of "The Moon Pool" & other unique & notable items. Merritt is asso. ed. of Hearst's American Weekly, but is chiefly interested in his own fiction. He proved highly genial, intelligent, & erudite, & outlined the plot of his next story—which will deal with the fabulous city of Ys, supposed to have sunk off the coast of Brittany. The cold spell was a nuisance during the first week, but the protection of the all-extensive subway system—which takes one within 2 or 3 blocks of almost anywhere without exposure to the outer air—enabled me to get by without hibernating. After that the mildness of the days was ideal. The worst N.Y. temperature was -9°, as compared with -11° in Providence & -17° (outdoing even your town) in Boston. However—the lowest temperature amidst which I attempted any doorway-to-subway-to-doorway dodging was +3°. Two blocks of that had my aged heart pumping like a steam-engine!

Yes—I am happy to state that your cheerful little Yuletide greeting came through without a crack or bend! As I said in my previous postscript, it certainly is a tremendously effective piece of work. I displayed it beside my mantel in conjunction with other Christmas decorations, & have now found a safe place for it behind a neighbouring letter-cabinet. Let me once more thank you for this powerful & well-wrought specimen—as well as congratulating you on the genius which produced it. I'll have to frame & hang it some time.

Glad *Unusual* has taken more of your material, & hope it will not succumb to the difficulties now besetting it. I am told that the first issue has been postponed till March. Trust the plan for paying authors will go through—I certainly could use a few more remunerative markets! Good luck with the new tales—which reminds me that *Fantasy* (87-36, 162nd St., Jamaica, N.Y.) is now looking for weird contributions. No pay, but plenty of encouragement. Glad your accommodating & affectionate typist is back. There's one advantage attractive youth has over sour old age!

Your new poems strike me as splendid—quite the best material, indeed, that you have yet produced. Your typical high colouring shews to much greater advantage in verse than in prose. There is real power in these things— apt imagery & a strong dramatic sense—& I think Satrap Pharnabazus was an utter ass to reject them. Send 'em along again some time—for he is apt to reconsider his narrow-margin turndowns. As for changes—you'll note two in "Delirium" & two in "Finis". They are very slight—one in the interest of good rhyme, & the others with a view to removing certain suggestions of flat diction. You certainly seem to have a particular talent for verse of this sort—

keep it up! I'd like to see the two pieces which Comte d'Erlette prefers to the present specimens.

Glad you had a festive Yule & New Year's—though I tend to echo Graf August-Wilhelm's caution against excessive potations. That kind of thing grows on one—till finally one gets to be a perpetually pickled creature like poor Harré, who is now so irresponsible that his publishers have to exert a sort of semi-personal guardianship over him. Still—I guess you generally know when to call a halt.

As for Bnādvai-Aā & Jehvish-Eî—they are probably healthy enough, but merely exercising their accustomed negligence as correspondents. Shea in particular is given to protracted silences—except for a Christmas card, I haven't heard from the young scamp since mid-autumn. (Well, what the Hell! A letter from him has just come!)

Glad that ideas for stories & drawings have been flowing freely. I agree about Winter's nerve-wearing effect—indeed, I generally feel like a limp rag by the time the wretched season is over. Haven't written anything new of late—& shall do some damned thorough stock-taking before making further attempts. Opinions vary on my last story—though returns from readers are still incomplete.

Well—about the best thing I did on my trip was to get this fountain pen whipped into passable shape. I think I've mentioned the perpetual trouble I have with pens—getting them to flow freely enough. This time I went again & again to the Waterman offices for feed readjustments—& behold! At last I have a pen which will glide along finely with almost no pressure. Hope it'll keep up this way.

With best wishes, & hoping that your verse will soon find an entry to W.T., I remain

Yr most ob[t] Grandsire—

E'ch-Pi-El

[42] [ALS]

Kadath in the Cold Waste
—Hour of the Night-Gaunts[1]
[late February?–early March 1935]

Dear Bho-Blôk:—

Congratulations on the new acceptance! You'll have to specialise in "The . . . . of the . . . . . . ." titles if they form such consistent passports to good luck! Glad the appearance of the "Feast" evoked such a cordial response in all quarters—surely a debut of this kind deserves festive recognition! From now on I fancy you'll find W.T. quite a steady market—& believe "The Grinning Ghoul" will probably land when you submit it. My own attempt—"The Shadow Out of Time"—has been held up for lack of leisure to devote to it. I simply cannot produce anything original when my programme is crowded. However—in odd moments I've carried the thing ahead several pages. It is on p. 54 now, & will undoubtedly be a young novel approaching "Innsmouth" in length. I doubt whether it will have any chance with Wright, & am not sure I'll even send it in. There is another story idea in my head which may prove less unsalable—& later on I shall try to develop this . . . getting the necessary leisure through a ruthless subordination of revisory & epistolary activities.[2]

Glad to hear of the prosperity of your group, but sorry you haven't had more time for drawing. Thanks, by the way, for the monstrous head on the envelope of your letter. I've cut it out—giving it a suitable margin—& filed it among other sinister Blociana.

Enclosed is the January F F—which, in view of my fair supply of duplicates, you can keep if it's of any permanent use to you. The weird rhymers surely have a place in the sun this month![3] I shall look for your verses in a subsequent issue.

Hope "The Man on all Fours" won't disappoint you. Let me know at what point you guessed the solution. I did on p. 32—largely through a weary familiarity with the tricks of 'mystery' novelists. Before long I hope to see Comte d'Erlette's next deteckatiff shocker—which he seems to regard as somewhat better than its predecessor.[4]

I trust I can get to see "Clive of India"—since the 18th century is, as you know, my favourite period & (as it were) psychological home. Dickens is not a favourite of mine, but I shall probably pick up "David Copperfield" on one of its return runs. I'll also look for "Iron Duke" & "Last Gentleman". I saw "Chu Chin Chow" as a musical stage spectacle about 1920, & fancy its cinematic reincarnation must be reasonably entertaining. I have seen no cinemas of late, except those to which I was taken during my visit to Long. Of these, "Don Quixote" was the only specimen worth remembering—& that was certainly remarkable . . . one of the most thoroughly artistic screen spectacles I have ever witnessed.[5]

Read the Feby W T lately—a thoroughly mediocre issue. Best thing is the Whitehead reprint. But bless my soul—Edmond Hamilton has got another plot! . . . albeit a venerable one.

And now let me congratulate you most sincerely on the excellence of "Satan's Servants"—which I read with keen pleasure & unflagging interest.[6] Wright was an ass to reject it—for, as I have often pointed out, *plot* in the artificial sense has no place in a weird tale—which should be simply the reflection of a mood. I greatly appreciate the compliment of the intended dedication to me, & would have deemed it an honour to be mentioned in such a way.

Regarding the future treatment of the story—it certainly deserves touching up & further submission for publication. I have taken the liberty to add some marginal notes & made some changes which seemed necessary from an historical & geographical standpoint. Most of these explain themselves.

Roodford had to be outside the boundaries of the Massachusetts Bay Colony, since the strict oversight prevailing within that rigid theocratic unit would never have suffered such a place to exist. Also—the location had to be shifted to some point on the coast where the settlement was not thick. Early New England was colonised with a rush, so that by 1690 the whole coastal region was dotted with thriving towns & almost continuous farmsteads. Two generations of settled life had removed every trace of the wilderness aspect, & (after King Philip's War in 1675–6) Indians were rarely seen. The only place on the coast where a village could exist relatively unknown, would be Maine—whose connexion with Mass. did not begin until 1663, & which was not an actual part of that province till July 1690. I have decided to locate Roodford between York & Wells if that is agreeable to you. Enclosed is a map of N.E. (which you can keep) shewing the new position. That any *wilderness* journey would have to start from Portsmouth & not Boston or Salem, will be obvious from an inspection of this chart. The narrative itself is splendidly vivid—my only criticism having to do with Gideon's *excessively quick* discovery of the nature & horrors of Roodford. It would be much more powerful to have this revelation come with hideous *gradualness,* after days of hellish *suspicion*—as in Blackwood's "Ancient Sorceries". That is what I tried to do (though with a reduced time-scale) in "Innsmouth". In going over the style, it would be well to be on guard against the tendency toward adjectival heaviness which besets both you & me. (In my present attempt I am pausing now & then to cut out bits of involuntary overcolouring which insist on creeping in—references to "monstrous & maddening arcana of daemoniac palaeogean horror" &c. &c.) Occasionally I have changed a word—either because of repetition or because of some doubtfulness in usage. If any such case seems unjustified, I'll be glad to explain it—or the dictionary will shed light on most. Be very careful when representing *archaic language*—for the usual tendency is to overshoot the mark & make the diction *too* ancient. Study the spelling in actual specimens of 17th century printing. I've made a few changes in your principal sample—on page 1. Regarding Governor Phips—he was no witch-finder prior to 1692, but a voyager & soldier of fortune whose career makes interesting reading. Look up the long section devoted to him in Mather's "Magnalia" (probably available at the public library), or read the interesting popular account in Hawthorne's "Grandfather's Chair". At the end of the story I've brought up the point of whether you ought to have the action of this story take place before or after the 1692–3 Salem affair. Certainly, it ought to be *afterward* if you wish to convey the idea that this Roodford business ended witchcraft in New England. By the way—the leading wizard in the Salem trouble, Rev. George Burroughs, came from Wells, Maine, near the relocated site of Roodford. You could make something of that, perhaps, if you wished. Another thing—if you want Roodford farther removed from the outposts of civilisation—so that very little will be known about it—you could have it up some navigable river farther north in Maine.

That would provide for a longer journey through the primal wilderness, & the dark charm of greater isolation. But it's quite all right as now relocated.

Now as to the idea of collaboration—this tale really tempts me more than any other I've seen lately, but I honestly don't believe I could undertake any collaborative job at all at this time. Collaboration is for me the most difficult & exhausting of all work. It entails twice the labour of original writing, & tends to cut off original material which I would otherwise be producing. I have dozens of plots of my own which need developing—& which I could develop much better & more easily than I could develop any externally suggested plot. For example—writing "The Dreams in the Witch House" was a pleasure, which didn't exhaust me at all. I knew what I wanted to do, & didn't have to heed what anybody else wanted. But the collaborated "Gates of the Silver Key" was an irksome & fatiguing task, because I was constantly held to a preconceived scheme of Price's—until I finally broke loose altogether. Under any circumstances collaboration is a harder task than original writing, & the only possible justification is that of wishing some idea to be properly developed which otherwise wouldn't be. Now in the case of "Satan's Servants", I feel certain that you can develop the tale yourself just as well as I could— hence don't feel guilty in suggesting that you try it. During recent months I have had to place a complete veto—in sheer self-defence—on all collaborative projects. I have refused point-blank to do any more such jobs for Mrs. Heald & old de Castro & others—& recently declined to collaborate with Price on a sequel to the "Gates of the Silver Key". I simply can't tackle so much when my time & nervous energy are so limited—& when so many stories of my own are veritably howling to be written.

But as I said before—in this case I feel sure I'm not doing the story any harm by staying out of it. It's great stuff, & you can polish it up just as well as anybody else could. The descriptions of the Sabbat are splendid, & the climax is magnificent. The primary need is to make the traveller's introduction to the horrors subtler & more gradual. One excellent story to follow as a guide is John Buchan's novel "Witch Wood"—which you ought to be able to get at a library. I can lend you Blackwood's "John Silence" (with "Ancient Sorceries") if you like, but unfortunately I don't own "Witch Wood." If you want to introduce more events in the story, you could have Godfrey *suspected* by the evil folk before he unmasks. That episode of the stag could form a basis for such a development—Hell-Friar could come upon Gideon praying in the woods, or something like that. Or some lesser denizen (so as to save H. F. for the climax) could spy on Gideon, & be detected in so doing. Gid could shoot him (at a distance—across a river or something like that) & *fail to find any body* when he reaches the spot. There are all sorts of twists one could work in if necessary. But none of them is really needed. Just make the unveiling of the hellish conditions more *gradual,* & you're all set! I surely hope the tale will achieve eventual placement—illustrations from your pen would make a mighty asset. Incidentally—I feel rather akin to Gideon, since I have an actual line of *Godfrey* ancestry. On Oct. 29, 1732, my ancestor Newman Perkins (b. 1711) was married to Mehitabel, daughter of John Godfrey of S. Kingston, R.I. We may well assume John to be Gid's brother or nephew or cousin!

Weather hereabouts has been atrocious. After all, I fear the present winter is about as bad as its evil predecessor. I've been out of the house only at rare intervals since the middle of January. Again I ask why the hell people ever settled latitudes as far north as this!

Well—again congrats & good wishes

Yrs for the Black Goat—Lhuv-Kerapht

[P.S.] Did I mention that Price has bought a house on a wooded hilltop near the foot of San Francisco Bay? New address Route 2, Box 100-U-5, Redwood City, Calif. And he has acquired a huge black tomcat.

*Notes*

1. Night-gaunts are mentioned in *The Dream-Quest of Unknown Kadath* and *Fungi from Yuggoth*.

2. It is unknown whether HPL even attempted this second story.

3. The issue, designated "the Special Weird Poetry Number," contained the following verses: R. O. P., "Dream"; HPL, *Fungi from Yuggoth:* "The Key" and "Homecoming"; Duane W. Rimel, "Late Revenge"; Natalie H. Wooley, "The Alien"; Robert E. Howard, "Voices of the Night: Babel"; Robert Nelson, "Fragment"; William Lumley (rev. HPL), "The Elder Thing"; Lionel Dilbeck, "The Ghoul's Parade"; and Richard F. Searight, "The Dead World."

4. See RB 54.

5. *Clive of India* (20th Century Pictures/United Artists, 1935), directed by Richard Boleslawski; starring Ronald Coleman, Loretta Young, and Colin Clive. *David Copperfield* (MGM, 1935), directed by George Cukor; starring Frank Lawton, W. C. Fields, and Basil Rathbone. *The Iron Duke* (Gainsborough Pictures, 1934), directed by Victor Saville; starring George Arliss, Ellaline Terris, and Gladys Cooper. *The Last Gentleman* (20th Century Pictures/United Artists, 1934), directed by Sidney Lanfield; starring George Arliss, Edna May Oliver, and Janet Beecher. *Chu Chin Chow* (Gainsborough Pictures, 1934), directed by Walter Forde; starring George Robey, Fritz Kortner, and Anna May Wong. *Don Quixote* (Nelson Film/Vandor Film, 1933), directed by G. W. Pabst; starring Feodor Chaliapin Sr., George Robey, and Oscar Asche.

6. The story appeared *Something about Cats and Other Pieces* (1949) with HPL's notes and suggestions.

[43]   [ALS]

Brink of the Bottomless Gulf
—Hour that the stars appear *below*.
[mid-March 1935]

Dear Bho-Blôk:—

Thanks exceedingly for the glimpse of the two new tales. Both are delightfully effective—especially the "Inn."[1] That piece has a tremendous amount of subtle, insidious atmosphere—& its punch is no less genuine because of the predictability of the climax. Wright's letter of rejection arouses my amusement as well as my disgust. Poor Farny! That censorship of '24 absolutely broke his nerve, so that he has ever since been timid about publishing anything with a corpse over 10 hours old! As you may know, he once rejected my "In the Vault" as "too horrible"—although he did take it later on. It may interest you to know that I revised the now-notorious "Loved Dead" myself—practically re-writing the latter half.[2] Eddy is a Providence man, & I was in fairly close touch with him in '23. I did not, though, devise the necrophilic portion which so ruffled the tranquillity of parents & pedagogues on the banks of the Wabash. The objection to *transpire* is typically Wrightian. Farny does love his precision! But it amuses me to note that his eagle eye missed a *really serious* boner in the *very next line*. In that sentence at the top of p. 3, all the verbs are participial adjuncts of the original *must have*. That is, it is as though the text ran "must have spoken . . . [must have] engaged my room, & [must have] . . . ." Well—as you see, this calls for *gone* instead of *went* in line 2. You wouldn't want to say "must have went"!! I can see how you might make the slip in hasty composition, but it makes me laugh to think that His Pedantic Majesty missed it after delivering a long paragraph's lecture on the minor slip just preceding! Actually, it's just as well to change both words. Correctness never hurt anybody yet! But aside from these minutiae—it's a darned good story, & I feel sure it will land somewhere sooner or later. Wright is hardly a criterion—he's like a dog who cringes & whines at a shadow because some previous shock has broken him. By all means try the tale on the *Terror–Horror* outfit. I don't yet know just what their especial wishes are. They may have some special formula demands—but extreme gruesomeness certainly goes over big with them. Hope "The Grinning Ghoul" lands with Wright after the prescribed alterations. "The Suicide in the Study" is excellent, even though the central idea has been used two or three times before. If any criticism is needed, it would have to do with the same old quality of *possible overcolouring* which we have so often discussed before. But I can't afford to expatiate on this theme, since it is almost impossible for me to write a story of my own without a similar plethora of violent & pyrotechnical adjectives! My new yarn is probably as thickly bestrown with such as any opus of yours. Incidentally, I note with appreciative interest the reference to the mad priest of Bast. If I were you I'd try this around, too—though I fancy the "Inn" will land first. Good luck with the several revisory tasks—including the really impressive "Satan's Servants".

I've finished "The Shadow out of Time", but am so badly dissatisfied with it that I can't bear to type it. It came to some 65 pages before I could finish it. I still like the idea, but vaguely feel that I've developed it rottenly—even though this is the second distinct version. I'm letting Comte d'Erlette see what he can make of the MS—which may not be much, since it is a monstrously, cacodaemoniacally infandous pencil scrawl.

By the way—instigated by M. le Comte, the latter's publishers (Loring & Mussey) have lately written me, asking to see some of my junk with a view to possible book publication. Since this is the *fifth* time (W T 1927, Putnam 1931, Vanguard 1932, Knopf 1933) I have received such a request during the last decade, with no tangible results so far, I am naturally not as naively worked up about the matter as I might otherwise be. Nevertheless I've sent along a parcel of stuff—just for the sake of leaving no stone unturned. I'd hate to think later on that I *might* have had a book published *if* I had responded to the request. I'm expecting my MSS. back any day now.

Regarding W T's slow payment—I received the final half of what was due on the Silver Key thing last month. That makes 7 months' wait in all—the first half coming about 2 months before the other. Wright means to pay sometime all right—but I suppose cash is pretty hard for him to get hold of. Haven't had a chance to read the March issue—but the Feb. was surely the acme of mediocrity. Delighted to note in the March Eyrie that your "Feast" is in the running for first place among the readers. You certainly are making encouraging strides! I fancy a letter from you explaining the impartiality of your criticism of Two-Gun Bob will adequately answer all criticisms such as Mashburn's.[3]

The small magazines have fallen on hard times. Poor Crawford smashed his fingers in his press & was laid up for a time, & now his partner Eshbach has resigned. As a result, heaven only knows when we shall see the next M T. As for the F F—alas & alas! The Feby. issue will be the last, since Hornig could no longer stand the continuous losses involved. This is a genuine tragedy for the weird public, since nothing can replace the vanished journal as a forum for the exchange of information, ideas, & opinions. The roughly similar F M will take over a few features—but this can form only an imperfect substitute, since science fiction always comes first with the magazine in question. Glad the Jan. issue proved of interest. I shudder in anticipation of the monstrous "Fungi" illustrations you so generously promise . . . . especially after viewing & admiring the hellish Mayan gentleman on the outside of your recent envelope!

Hope you can get the use of that machine in time to help your current work. Good luck with the "Sabbat"[4]—& I trust the erudite author of *Cultes des Goules* may duly appreciate the honour of the dedication. You surely have an ambitious programme, & I hope you can follow it out with a maximum of success.

Yes—I did see the "Cleopatra" cinema,[5] & agree that it was a marvellously fine spectacle. The Roman architectural backgrounds gave me a mighty kick—for as I may have mentioned, I have a devotion to classical Rome which amounts virtually to a sense of personal identification. Contrary to your expectation, the Egyptian settings caused me many a groan despite my admiration of their intrinsic beauty & impressiveness. How come? Why, simply because they didn't belong in the *Greek* city of Alexandria! As a moment's reflection will remind you, the Ptolemaic rulers of Egypt were Macedonian Greeks & nothing else but. Alexandria was built on previously unoccupied land in B.C. 332, at Alexander's orders—& was laid out in the most sumptuous Greek fashion by the celebrated architect Dinocrates, who also repaired the damaged temple of Diana at Ephesus. The court & army of the Ptolemies were Greek from start to finish—in language, costume, manners, & habits of thought; very few ideas being picked up from their native Egyptian subjects. The folkways of the Egyptians were always respected, but were never copied. The Egyptians lived their own lives up the Nile, just as they had done in the days of their independence or under the Persian satraps—but Alexandria stayed purely Greek. Indeed, it soon became the virtual centre & intellectual capital of the Greek world. There were, of course, many Egyptians in Alexandria—but they formed a subordinate element in a "native quarter" like the Chinese in Victoria, Hong-Kong, or the Hindoos in Calcutta. To represent Cleopatra as an *Egyptian* queen in costume & setting is just as absurd as to represent a British viceroy of India in a rajah's turban & living in a Hindoo palace. Alexandria & its ruling class were just as Greek as Athens or Corinth or Syracuse. Hundreds of coins show the real appearance of Cleopatra—a Greek matron in coiffure & dress. If she ever put on Egyptian finery it was probably only once or twice a year to impress & flatter her subjects up the river.

Current news—a new coal-black kitten at the boarding-house across the garden. Hope he lives longer than his late lamented brother of last year. I expect to borrow him frequently during the weeks to come. ¶ Heard a good poetry reading last month[6] by Archibald MacLeish, author of "Conquistador." ¶ Excellent lecture on contemporary Russian soviet art. Despite their cockeyed notion of the propagandistic mission of art, the bolshies aren't doing as badly as I had expected. Some of their painters, forgetting sterile politics, retain a lot of the old Russian-Byzantine tradition. And amusingly enough, they aren't nearly as aesthetically radical as the decadent cubists, "abstraction"-hounds, & surrealists of the western world! ¶ Still another lecture on the restored mosaics at St. Sophia in Constantinople by Thos. Whittemore—the guy who scraped the covering off 'em. These date only from the 9th & 10th centuries, though the edifice is of course of the 6th—just 1400 years old, having been built betwixt 532 & 538. A great piece of work for a decadent age . . . Flavius

Anicius Justinianus—what a man! And the old shack certainly has lasted splendidly despite a lot of rough wear!

*[conclusion missing]*

*Notes*

1. It is not clear what story of RB's is referred to, but evidently it does not survive.

2. C. M. Eddy, Jr., "The Loved Dead" (*WT*, May–June–July 1924). The issue of *WT* was banned in the state of Indiana.

3. Kirk Mashburn, "The Eyrie," *WT* 25, No. 3 (March 1935): 396: "A word about Robert Bloch's attacks on Howard's Conan stories: A reader who buys the magazine for entertainment and has no personal stake at issue, has every right to offer whatever adverse criticism he thinks is justified by what he considers the failure of any writer to come up to expectations. But for one writer, while seeking to establish his own footing, to attack another to the editor—that smacks to me of questionable ethics. Polecat ethics is what I mean; but I hope you print the above paragraph in the Eyrie—there are other offenders besides Brother Bloch—and I know you won't, if I use the words I want to. Please take note that I comment upon Mr. Bloch's ethics, and not upon his story in the January issue."

4. Possibly "Wine of the Sabbat."

5. *Cleopatra* (Paramount, 1934), directed and produced by Cecil B. DeMille; starring Claudette Colbert, Warren William, and Henry Wilcoxon.

6. On 3 February.

[44]   [ALS]

Grove of the Gnophs
—Hour of the Windless Rustling
[late March, early April 1935]

Dear Bho-Blôk:—

"The Fountain of Youth" is delightfully effective, & I surely hope it will find professional lodgment. The theme of an overdose of rejuvenation has been used before (cf. "The Elixir of Hate", by George Allan England), but I can't recall any other case where the action is so *sudden*. As for objections—possibly the *swampy* nature of the Everglades has not been sufficiently emphasised. The area is one of shallow water choked with saw-grass, dry land being present only as islands. You could lay this tale on an island (unknown to modern white men) of greater size than ordinary. Don't fail to emphasise the tropical aspect of the scene—the creepers & lush vegetation, the alligators, &c. &c. Also—I doubt if any *paths* mapped in the 16th century could exist today. Better have the map refer to channels among the islands. Another thing—despite modern folklore, the original legend of a fountain of youth referred to something whose magic came from *bathing*, not *drinking*. But these are all small points. It's a fine tale, & I wish it the best of luck among the savages of the editorial jungle!

So the Suicide *did* land! Congratulations! Hope the Inn, Fount, & Ghoul may encounter equal luck. Have you yet tried anything on the new & queerly named magazine called *Doctor Death?*[1] Koenig says it is rather like *Terror* & *Horror*. No—I'm not responsible for the card from *Real America*. I've only remotely heard of the publication before.[2] Hope the vampire yarn turns out well. Comte d'Erlette has my "Shadow"—but I doubt whether either he or you can make out the pencil hieroglyphics. You may think the script of my *letters* is bad enough—but until you know my rough draughts of story MSS., you ain't seen nothin' yet!

Sympathy anent the typing! I abhor the damn machines, & will not use 'em except under compulsion. Hope your Eyrie letter will be used—it'll be only fair of Wright to print it. I trust you'll have a good anniversary session in Chicago— & that Satrap Pharnabazus will look favourably on the Ghoul illustration. Your mention of the Fungi drawings excites my expectant interest! As for synthetic jawbreakers—your new crop certainly has vivid colour! When these get to be hackneyed, you can start on a new crop—like *ptomatophage* or *oneiropomp*.

*Marvel* is certainly pretty poor this time—the best item being the brief tale by John Benyon [*sic*] Harris.[3] My "Sarnath" is a relique of 1919—my period of intensive Dunsanian imitation. But the format is the least amateurish yet. F F's death is a thing to mourn. Naught can take its place!

Your recent reading sounds commendably solid—would that I had the time & energy to keep abreast. The new study group (which I take to be separate institution from the discussion group previously mentioned) sounds tremendously ambitious with its programme extending years ahead. I wish indeed that I might be able to sample its deliberations!

Local weather uneven—one day up to 71° . . . . & that *would* have to be a day when fate prevented my getting out to the countryside! I guess I told you of my 12-mile walk March 6, when the mercury climbed to 65°.

Young Shea seems to be taking life's buffetings valiantly. His family has been hard hit by the depression, & he is now an underpaid serf in a factory owned by an uncle. He is still active literarily, though as yet nothing of his has professionally landed. Everything with him now is realism—he seems to have thrown the weird wholly overboard.

Just got an invitation to contribute to one of the "little magazines" of which Comte d'Erlette is so fond—*The Galleon*, edited by the former associate editor of *Marvel Tales*—L. A. Eshbach, 1337 Good St., Reading, Pa. I doubt if I have anything they'd want,[4] but you might try your luck if you have any choice non-weird pieces floating around. Must be under 3000 wds.

A youthful science fiction fan has just moved from N.Y. to Providence—one Kenneth Sterling—& hopes to found a chapter of the Science

Fiction League here. Bright kid—means to be a biologist. But not interested in the purely weird.

Yrs under the Seal of Poseidonis
——E'ch-Pi-El

*Notes*

1. *Doctor Death* was a pulp magazine containing stories featuring the superhero of the title. It was published by Dell, edited by Carson Mowre, and ran for 3 issues (February, March, and April 1935)
2. *Real America* (1933–36) was a magazine of social and political commentary edited by Edwin Baird.
3. "The Cathedral Crypt," *Marvel Tales* 1, No. 4 (March–April 1935). John Beynon Harris wrote more commonly under the pseudonym John Wyndham.
4. The *Galleon* published "The Quest of Iranon" and "Background." It had accepted but did not publish "Harbour Whistles" and rejected a story, perhaps "The Nameless City."

[45]   [ALS] [corner torn]

Desert beyond Leng—
Hour of the Shapes in the Sand
[c. mid-April 1935]

Dear Bho-Blôk:—

Congratulations on the latest acceptance![1] You certainly are delivering the goods, & will be right in the Klarkash-Ton class for regular contributions before you know it! Glad to know that the monstrous Luveh-Keraph, the sinister Comte d'Erlette, & the darkly brooding Ludvig Prinn are to be confirmed in their immortality. The new stories sound extremely promising, & I trust you have made the aged satanist of Providence an adequately terrifying figure. Hope to see 'em all in time.

Meanwhile let me congratulate you all over again on the vivid writeup in the *Milwaukee Journal!*[2] Hope my friend Moe will notice it. It certainly presents you very strikingly & interestingly, & I don't wonder at the messages & invitations it has brought you. One may pardon its possible slips in view of its manifold merits—& I'm sure Comte d'Erlette & I have no reason to complain because we aren't mentioned. Who is the article supposed to be about, anyhow? I'm long past the age when publicity appears attractive. As a commercialist I suppose Brother Farnsworth will lament the absence of free advertising for his choice commodity! By the way—I think M. Auguste-Guillaume got a writeup in the M.J. a couple of years ago. It was in some metropolitan paper—he sent me a copy, but it was lost by a subsequent borrower.

How you manage to do so many things is beyond me! Glad the debate was successful, & hope the ambitious revue will prove likewise. You & the rubber cigar ought to get the audience roaring loud enough to drown out all eleven pieces of the orchestra! And yet you still have time for your philosophical circles . . . ah, me, the energy of youth!

Your reading sounds well chosen. Glad your advice is beginning to interest the bookshops! As for Merritt's address—it is *Daily Mirror Bldg., 235 East 45th St., N.Y. City.* His office is on the 14th floor—in the quarters of the American Weekly [    ] Hearst Sunday Supplement. The telephone is [VAnderbi]lt 3-4770. Merritt is a pleasant chap—[    ] contemplated deal develop well.

I'm afraid that new thing of mine doesn't amount to much—& there is also a chance that neither you nor Graf August-Wilhelm can decipher the unspeakable cacography with its myriad changes & interpolations.

As for climate—don't envy New England! The promise of last month has not been lived up to very well, & a period of chill & rain has supervened. I surely wish I were in Charleston! No events of great importance to chronicle. A few good lectures—especially a series of three on the late Dr. Benjamin Franklin by Prof. Verner W. Crane of the U. of Mich.—formerly of Brown.[3] Doubt if I can get south this year. Expect to visit Edward H. Cole in the Boston zone May 3–4–5. Later Cook & I may take a motor trip through Vermont.

April W T so-so. "Out of the Æons" is virtually a story of mine—100% ghost-writing. The Bernal idea is clever—I once had a similar idea, but never developed it. H. Wandrei's "O Mecca" has a really weird atmosphere & convincing local colour. Klarkash-Ton is always good. "Shadows of Blood" is full of historical errors—to begin with, the Romans never heard of the Huns till more than 300 years after Caligula's reign.

And now let me thank you most abundantly for the four monstrous nightmares in colour which duly followed your epistle. Ngghahhrrr—Wgggnna . . . !!! Truly, these are great stuff, & I feel flattered by the kinship of some of them to my own private stable of Hellish Things! Now that I know What dictated the Necronomicon, I can better understand why that abhorred & dreaded volume holds certain nighted revelations otherwise inexplicable! Noting the relative size of the Explorer & That Which he has discovered, I am inclined to fear that the venturesome discover[er] will not return to tell what he found at the end of his rocket voyage to Yuggoth. Knaros[?] & The Lurking Fear certainly are creatures one would prefer to behold at a distance, & in the full glare of mid-day! Again let me thank you most appreciatively—my gallery of Blociana is getting to be a striking & notable collection!

Read Merritt's "Creep, Shadow"[4] the other day, but was not greatly impressed. Routine pulp stuff, for the most part—though there are some good hints [    ] *outsideness*, & a vivid series of climactic table[aux.]

Yrs for the Black Seal of Irem—
Luveh-K[eraph]

*Notes*

1. It is not clear what story is referred to.

2. "Milwaukee Youth Writes Horror Tales, Sells 'Em," *Milwaukee Journal* (6 April 1935): The Green Sheet, pp. 1, 3. See Appendix.

3. Crane (1889–1974) was author of *Benjamin Franklin, Englishman and American* (1936).

4. A[braham] Merritt (1884–1943), *Creep, Shadow!*, serialized in *Argosy* from 8 September to 20 October 1934. The novel was a sequel to *Burn, Witch, Burn!*, serialized in *Argosy* from 22 October to 26 November 1932.

[46]   [ALS]

Hellish Sabbat-Night
[30 April 1935]

Hail, O Ludvig Prinn!

Well, here you are! A darned good story, & I'm glad Brother Farnsworth has taken it. His insistence on written permission for any sanguinary annihilation is distinctly amusing. Evidently his native caution has grown in the last decade, since in 1925 he let young Long describe me & leave me as a charred, inert cinder on the floor of my [then Brooklyn] hermitage without so much as a word of consent from Grandpa![1] Well—enclosed is the ponderous document of official sanction—with the signatures of several noted witnesses to make it doubly binding. If Wright wants anything more, I'll have it sworn before a notary public. I've read the yarn with the keenest interest, & am making a few pencil changes (very slight ones) for the sake of greater smoothness & correctness. Most of these, I fancy, will prove largely self-explanatory. If Prinn's immortal work is in Latin, you ought to give the title in that language—hence my change in two places to DE VERMIS MYSTERIIS [Concerning / of the worm / the mysteries]. Also, since knowledge of elementary Latin is so universal, I've modified the statement concerning your limitations in that tongue. Still more—I've supplied just a tantalising fragment of that hellish invocation:

"TIBI, MAGNUM INNOMINANDUM, SIGNA STELLARUM NIGRARUM ET BUFONIFORMIS SADOQUAE SIGILLUM . . . ."[2]
[To the / Great Not-to-be-Named / the signs / of the stars / black / and / of the toad-shaped / Tsathoggua / the seal . . .]

That ought to lend a bit of additional colour. As you see, I've made no major changes—it's a good piece of work, & I surely hope the readers will receive it favourably. Glad to know that "The Secret of the Tomb" is in the coming issue. And I surely appreciate the "Shambler's" dedication.

Your ventriloquial job surely sounds interesting, & I hope it may be the means of introducing you to people who can be professionally & dramatically helpful. Glad to hear of new pictorial monsters in process of incubation—I showed the last batch to a young science-fiction fan named Kenneth Sterling, who has recently moved to Providence, & he was quite impressed by them.

Hope the new short story will develop smoothly. That "Cain to Capone" volume[3] must be quite a fountain of exciting ideas!

As for wars & rumours of wars—it would take a better analyst or a bigger bluffer than I to formulate any predictions. In some ways 1914 seems strangely repeated—but it must not be forgotten that all the nations have the memory of 1914 before them as a warning. It is hard to get beneath the surface & single out really significant elements. Too much stress ought not to be placed on German re-arming, since it was absurd to suppose that any major nation would permanently submit to the grotesque restrictions imposed at Versailles. The rearmament of the Central Powers need not mean any intention to resume aggressive conduct—rather is it a gesture of resumed *equality*, & of the repudiation of post-war handicaps. Naturally the other powers must now be well armed in order to preserve a balance—but what else could be expected? The only way to cut down wars is to cultivate—by slow degrees, of course—a greater economic self-sufficiency among nations. What breeds conflict more than anything else is the desire to promote trades in foreign fields. For example—a war of America & Japan would probably spring largely from the desire of American capitalists to pile up excess profits through extensive trade in China & Manchuria. Of course other factors are present in the present European situation—the nervousness of France, the vindictive sentiments of Germany, & the German desire to regain lost territory & prestige. We can only wait & see what happens. Some nations, I suppose, would welcome a war to eliminate some of the unemployed & distract attention from domestic economic problems—though I fancy they might get more than they bargained for. It must not be forgotten that Russia's bolshevik explosion occurred during a period of war. In America it's hard telling what turn domestic problems will take. I doubt if any system of universal private profit can ever be relied upon to keep the whole of the population busy & fed, hence believe that measures considerably to the left of the present New Deal will ultimately have to be enacted. One may only hope that such can arrive without any violent upheaval—or any lapse into a silly Marxist orthodoxy whose fallacious dogmatisms are even worse than those of Hooverism, Nazism, & other defective systems of the present & recent past. This is certainly a hell of a period to be living in!

I don't wonder that you long for the country—I can't bear urban surroundings myself, & love ancient Providence only because of its curiously village-like aspect. #66 rests amidst venerable gardens, & all around on the hill are rambling green lanes which one would not think of associating with a city. Even so, I prefer to hit the trail for the genuine countryside whenever the weather is favourable.

Spring is here at last—trees & shrubs feathering out with delicate verdure, & forsythias a blaze of yellow. My outing season has begun anew—this time, I hope, quasi-permanently. Young Bob Moe (son of the Milwaukee pedagogue with whom you talked over the telephone) blew in last Saturday morning from Bridgeport, & we put in a strenuous 2 days in his Ford. Saturday we visited old Newport—seeing 2 ancient windmills; a flock of sheep with small lambkins; the home of Bishop Berkeley (1729); the Hanging Rocks where that good cleric wrote his famous Alciphron; or, the Minute Philosopher; the lofty cliffs; a strange rock cleft called "Purgatory", where the sea pounds in; the house where Genl. Prescott was captured by a small party of rebels in 1778; & the venerable town itself—with 1726 church, 1739 colony-house, 1749 library, 1760 market house, & private buildings as old as 1675. Glorious hot day—82° in Providence, though not quite so good in Newport. Took some pictures which I'll show you later if they turn out well.

Sunday we went to ancient New Bedford, the quondam whaling centre which superseded Nantucket in that industry after 1850. Thence—after exploring the N.B. waterfront—to the Round Hills estate of Col. E. H. R. Green (son of the famous old miser Hetty Green) in S. Dartmouth, where the old whaling barque Charles W. Morgan (built 1841) is preserved at wharf—solidly embedded in concrete as a perennial exhibit. We went all over the vessel—which is tremendously fascinating. On the estate is also an ancient windmill which Col. Green moved from R.I. We then explored a region—where southern Massachusetts adjoins southeastern Rhode-Island—which I had never seen before in my life. Splendid unspoiled countryside with rambling stone walls & idyllic, white-steepled villages of the old New England type. Of these latter the best ones—Adamsville & Little Compton Commons—are in Rhode Island. This region was once the seat of the Sakonnet Indians, & originally belonged to the Plymouth Colony. It was first settled around 1673. During King Philip's War the colonists persuaded the local squaw-sachem Awashonks not to join the hostile redskin coalition. At Little Compton Commons there is buried Elizabeth Alden Pabodie—daughter of John Alden & Priscilla Mullins & the first white woman to be born in New England. Her home is still standing—as is that of Capt. Robert Gray, the explorer who discovered the Columbia River on the Pacific Coast. This latter is in Tiverton—through which we passed on our return northward, & in which we obtained some magnificent scenic panoramas. Then Fall River (a dingy manufacturing city) & ancient Warren—at which latter place we stopped off & ate a dinner consisting entirely of ice cream—a pint & a half (comprising 6 flavours) apiece. Finally back to 66—after which I regretfully guided the guest out of town & took a 4-mile walk before returning home. Quite a session!

Well—day after tomorrow another session starts, for I shall be visiting my friend Cole in the Boston zone. Hope to see Salem (Arkham), Marblehead (Kingsport) & various other points of antiquarian interest. Hope the weather will be favourable—though it would be too much to expect conditions as ideal as those attending the earlier outing.

Can't get this in the mail tonight, but trust it will reach you in ample time for the schedule you wish to follow. Hope the few emendations may prove helpful. I shall be on the lookout tomorrow for the new W T with the tomb story. By the way—if anybody criticises the Latin of that interpolated incantation, you can tell him that *bufoniformis* (= toad-shaped) is an artificial coinage of the sort common in the Low Latin of mediaeval & renaissance writers. From *bufo, bufonis,* a toad. *Sadoqua* is the Gallo-Roman form of Tsathoggua (Med. Fr. Sadogui) found in Valerius Trevirus & the early Latin Liber Ivonis.

Good luck——Luveh-Keraph

[Enclosure]

Providence, R.I.,
April 30, 1935

To Whom it May Concern:

This is to certify that Robert Bloch, Esq., of Milwaukee, Wisconsin, U.S.A.—reincarnation of Mijnheer Ludvig Prinn, author of DE VERMIS MYSTERIIS—is fully authorised to portray, murder, annihilate, disintegrate, transfigure, metamorphose, or otherwise manhandle the undersigned in the tale entitled THE SHAMBLER FROM THE STARS.

[signed] H. P. Lovecraft

*Notes*

1. In "The Space-Eaters" (*WT,* July 1928).
2. In "The Shambler from the Stars."
3. A book on racketeering by John McConaughy.

[47]   [ALS]

Necropolis of Khaphnes
—Hour of the Gong from Below
[early June 1935]

My dear Prinn:—

Congratulations on the definite acceptance of "The Shambler"! The dedication will surely give me a momentary illusion of importance! Glad my comments proved of some assistance. I shall welcome the advent of the "Suicide" in the next W T. Yes—you have certainly made progress since the "Secret", although that is none the less clever & powerful for a piece of early work. This rapid development is highly encouraging—& gives you an obvious lead over all the other young experimenters who have been writing for the M T & the late F F. Your place in the W T table of contents along with Klarkash-Ton, Two-Gun Bob, Comte d'Erlette, & Grandpa Nyarlatho-tep surely establishes you as 'one of the family'—if that's any distinction.

Commiserations on the cold! I've had monstrous & devastating visita-tions of the sort in my day. Let us hope that, before the advent of autumn, there will be enough at least half-warmish weather to bake such maladies out of you. Of all long-drawn, discouraging winters this has been the damnedest!

So you have at last read the once-famous "Jurgen". I did once—but failed to be greatly impressed by it. The constant irony was clever—but somehow seemed too obvious & protracted. Cabell strikes me as a sort of a pale-pink Anatole France—with a lot less to say than his prototype had. He is, however, an idol of Barlow's. I mean to read the two Claudius books[1]—right in my line—& shall welcome the cinema on the same theme. Incidental-ly, I'll keep "The Werewolf of London" in mind.[2]

The Fictioneers[3] must be a highly interesting group—& the Farley meet-ing seems to have formed a decidedly red letter occasion. I would have en-joyed the caricature of Satrap Pharnabazus—though I will admit that the latter isn't as consistently fatuous & conventional in his editorial policy as most of the stuffed shirts at the helms of the various pulp rags. The guest of honour, with his wide experience in adventurous quarters, was doubtless a particular hit with those who follow the "action" ideal. Glad your other groups are flourishing. Young Peirce seems to be a very interesting character, & I surely wouldn't mind hearing from him some day. Yes—you spoke of the ventriloquist act. Hope the others go over as well—they surely sound promis-ing . . . full of dramatic possibilities. Don't hurry about the drawings—with your rushed programme, I don't see how you ever get time to do them! Thanks for the lines "Necrophile"—which are really extremely good. I can't understand Wright's dislike of them—unless the title shocked the good soul—since he habitually prints doggerel so unutterably infantile that I won-der how even his half-baked clientele can stand for it. Thanks also for the vampiric title—I've seen titles like that in the bibliographies appended to Montague Summers' two vampire treatises.[4] The subject certainly was a wide-ly discussed one until about a century & a half ago.

Things seem to be going against my MSS. at Loring & Mussey's, & I ex-pect the MSS. back pretty soon. Comte d'Erlette, by the way, doesn't seem to get time to read my undecipherable rough draught of "The Shadow Out of Time", so I'm asking him to pass it on to you. Don't bother with it if you're too rushed, or if the handwriting seems wholly beyond perusal. No hurry—but shoot it back to me eventually. Which reminds me to thank you for shooting the Innsmouth MS. along to Hill-Billy Crawford. I doubt if C. will ever get around to issuing the booklet he has in mind, but there's no harm in giving him every possible chance.

No outings since the frost-bitten 'Kingsport' jaunt described in my last—but there has appeared a vague possibility of my getting south after all. That's about the only way, I guess, that I can ever find my warm weather in 1935! Barlow has invited me to De Land next month—after he returns from Washington—& I'm hoping events will so shape themselves as to permit of my acceptance. Had a 1-day visit May 25 from young Hornig, editor of *Wonder S.* & lately publisher of the F F. He is a very pleasant & intelligent youth—reminding one slightly of Donald Wandrei. He seemed to appreciate very keenly the archaic charm of venerable Providence—which is in some respects not unlike his own town of Elizabeth, N.J. I shewed him most of your drawings, & he appeared to be much impressed by them. Weather was unusually warm & sunny.

Yrs by the Spotted Tentacles of Yith—

Luveh-Keraph

*Notes*

1. Robert Graves, *I, Claudius* (1934) and *Claudius the God* (1935). HPL never read the books, but he cites them in "[Suggestions for a Reading Guide]" (1936; *CE* 2.186).
2. *Werewolf of London* (Universal, 1935), directed by Stuart Walker; starring Henry Hull, Warner Oland, and Valerie Hobson.
3. I.e., The Milwaukee Fictioneers, a group of writers that included RB, Stanley G. Weinbaum, Roger Sherman Hoar ("Ralph Milne Farley"), Raymond A. Palmer, Arthur Tofte, and others. RB's account of joining the Fictioneers and meeting Weinbaum is given in "Stanley G. Weinbaum: A Personal Recollection," in *The Best of Stanley G. Weinbaum* (New York: Ballantine, 1974). The Fictioneers published *Dawn of Flame—The Weinbaum Memorial Volume* (1936), a collection of Weinbaum's stories.
4. HPL refers to Summers's *The Vampire: His Kith and Kin* (1928) and *The Vampire in Europe* (1929).

[48]   [ALS]

Abyss of Noth—
Hour of the Vapour . . .
[mid to late June 1935]

Dear Ludvig:—

Congratulations on the recent acceptance of "Druidic Doom"! You certainly are getting to be a W T fixture . . . taking Grandpa's place, as it were! Was extremely glad to see the "Suicide" in print, & am on the lookout (or will be in September) for the flatteringly dedicated "Shambler".

Glad you had a congenial session in the Land of Pharnabazus—& hope your sketch did not shock that tender soul too violently. You must be careful to devise something very wholesome & cheerful for "The Druidic Doom." Wright's kindly opinion of my stuff rather amuses me in view of his repeated rejections. His attitude toward my most ambitious performance—"At the Mountains of Madness"—is more than half responsible for my slowing up as a writer. However, I'd like to see the cuss—who is probably a much nicer chap than his capricious decisions would indicate. Interested to hear of your meeting with one of the enterprising Binders. As for the errors in his Roman tale—the one mentioned in the Eyrie is really mild as compared with the act of mentioning *Huns* over 3 centuries before there was any such tribe . . . or any such tribe known to the Romans.[1] Sorry you couldn't get over to the Binder mansion . . . . but hope you can make the Chicago meet of July 14th. So Comte d'Erlette's book is landing big . . . . darned glad to hear it! Trust you'll be able to get Satrap Pharnabazus up to Milwaukee before long. Your club surely seems to be a bustling organisation—& the responsibility of being sole weird representative in it must be a heavy one. However, I fancy you are adequate to this not wholly unpleasing burthen!

Regarding the L & M pipe-dream—I no longer expect any results. It is merely a guess of when, & in what condition, my MSS. will come back. Crawford is talking of printing "Innsmouth" & the "Mts" in some form or other— & I shall let him do what he can, although I don't fancy that will be much. Incidentally—some young fellows in San Francisco—Fred Anger & Louis Smith—intend to issue my "Fungi From Yuggoth" as a whole, in the form of a mimeographed booklet. This is part of an informal & economical publishing enterprise, another item of which will be a *complete index of W T* from its foundation to the present. I shall certainly get this last-named item, since at present the finding of any story in a back number is a veritable needle-in-haystack proposition.[2]

Well—as you see, my Florida trip indeed materialised. Barlow returned home from Washington June 3, & I started out on the 5th. I shot straight south with no intermediate stops save ancient Fredericksburg, Va. & my ever-beloved *Charleston*. As you may see by the enclosed cards, both of these places include excellent feeding-grounds for our esurient subterranean friends! After a winter & spring of wretched lassitude, I began to feel a certain strength & comfort the moment I struck the hot Carolina lowlands—& by the time I reached Charleston I was feeling really well for the first time in 1935. I've kept feeling just as well ever since. This is the climate for me, summer or winter . . . & I suppose I'm really an ass to remain chained to the north because of early associations. And yet I would miss New England's scenery & general atmosphere. But the scenery down here is picturesque in another way, as you may gather from one of the enclosed cards. Don't know how long I shall stay . . . there are things I'd like to do in the north next month, but my genial hosts are urging me to prolong my sojourn at least 2 months or so. Such flattering cordiality is hard to beat.

Am falling quite into the pattern of a year ago—for things around these parts are essentially the same. Household a bit larger—Bob's father (Lt. Col. E. D. Barlow, U.S.A. Retired) & elder brother (Lt. Wayne Barlow U.S.A.) being home this time. Most of the old cats are still here—plus 2 magnificent Persians which Bob brought from Washington. Same sort of diversions—rows on the lake, discussion, reading, & experiments in typesetting. Bob means to do some publishing before long. He is building a cabin across the lake, in which he intends to do most of his future printing. I help in various constructive & destructive (clearing away of underbrush & scrub palmettos) operations. Incidentally—you will note in connexion with this epistle some linoleum block work of Ar-Ech-Bei's. The large monster of the letterhead is our old friend Cthulhu, in one of his less usual & more active poses. The little experiments on the envelope have as yet received no name. All were originally designed for the late & sincerely lamented F F.

Speaking of the F F—did I tell you that young Hornig paid me an all-day visit May 25? He came on a night 'bus & left on another, nor was he in the least burthened with excess luggage. A very nice & intelligent chap—he makes me think of Donald Wandrei a bit. His judgment is essentially mature, despite the fact that he is only 18. Later his taste will be still better. He seemed to appreciate the quaintness & beauty of ancient Providence, & I surely hope he will come again. The hidden churchyard of St. John's especially captivated him. On this occasion there was also present the young science-fiction enthusiast Kenneth Sterling . . . . who is about to leave for New York next month. Quite a convention, all told!

Recent issues of W T rather poor, save for a few items of solid merit. It certainly is a weaker magazine than it has been at various periods in the past. However, it is still worth reading—& the only active magazine devoted to the weird in the U S A.

Well—I must cease at last. I don't get much time to write down here, since pleasant activities are always going on. Here's wishing you continued luck in all your ventures. My host sends his best regards, & expresses the hope that he may meet you sometime.

All good wishes—

Yrs most cordially & sincerely—

Luveh-Keraph

*Notes*

1. HPL refers to a letter by Robert B. Baldwin in *WT* 25, No. 6 (June 1935): 779: "I am writing in to question the description of Emperor Caligula's death in Eando Binder's *Shadows of Blood*. According to this highly entertaining narrative, Caligula was as-

sassinated in one of his villas; in a torture chamber, to be exact. But doesn't history teach us that the conspirators, chief among whom were Cassius Chaerea, Bubo, Asprenas, Vinicius, Cornelius Sabinus ('The Tiger'), murdered their mad monarch outside, at midday? Shouldn't we be just a little more accurate about historic detail?"

2. Anger and Smith published neither book, but Barlow commenced typesetting of *Fungi from Yuggoth* and had sent proofs of some pages to HPL.

[49]  [ALS]

> Tropic Tarn of Thok—
> Hour of the Trumpeting Below
> [c. mid-July 1935]

My dear Ludvig:—

Congratulations on the additional sale to the Preadamite Sultan of N. Michigan Ave.! Hope there won't be any weakening change of title. I'll be anxious to see the new story in course of time.

Additional congratulations on the collaboration in commercial ventures—though I hope this pulp-hacking arrangement won't interfere with your production of seriously intended weird tales.[1] Price has suffered as a weird writer because of his commercial work. Derleth actually gets away with both serious & commercial writing—though few people indeed are Derleths!

Glad the Fictioneers continue on their triumphant course—the recent rural meeting must have been a festive event indeed! I'm greatly interested to hear of your meeting with Stanley G. Weinbaum,[2] whose interplanetary tales were first pointed out to me this year. He is probably the only one of the pulp other-planeteers to escape the worst clichés of his province. In his lightly-sketched, half-satirical accounts of non-terrestrial exploration he manages admirably to avoid the usual Martian princesses, evil prime-ministers, & other stock Edmond Hamiltonisms. His "Martian Odyssey"[3] is probably his best thing. In that he displays an inexhaustibly fertile imagination, & keeps wholly clear of the accustomed pitfalls. Congratulations on your collaborative victory with him in the horseshoe tournament—over such learned & capable opponents!

Your Sunday visitors must surely have been entertaining. Darrow,[4] I believe, is just a "fan"—but Binder has surely done some memorable work . . . . even if he did lately refer to the Huns 300 years before such a tribe existed! Interested to hear of the photographs—& hope to see prints of them if they turn out well.

Dr. Stugatche the Goon[5] is a new figure to me, & I am interested to hear of his connexion with the hellish Nyarlathotep. I'll be glad to look over the story containing this sinister figure—though I feel sure you've done right by old Nyarthy. I learn with interest of the Seven Scrolls of Elipidus, the Keeper of the Worm, & the Crawler in the Crypt. The body of monstrous lore & Pantheon of Blasphemous Entities is surely growing!

Sorry you've had such rotten weather—but the north is no place to live, any hour. Only the strongest atmospheric & architectural attachment holds me to New England. Climatic conditions here are ideal for my health, & I dread the thought of going back north—even in summer. My hosts are urging me to stay along indefinitely, & I find myself very easy to persuade in that direction. Bob's cabin across the lake is now finished, & his printing press & other effects have been transferred thither. We row across each day—the trip making good exercise. Not long ago I cut a path through the palmetto undergrowth from the landing to the road on the other side. Our local gang has been depleted by the loss of Bob's brother Wayne, whose furlough expired & who has had to leave for his second-lieutenanting at Ft. Sam Houston. On June 17 (perhaps I mentioned this before) we explored a marvellous tropical river—with leaning palms, sunken logs, twisted cypress roots at the water's edge—&c. &c. &c.—much like the river at Silver Springs which I described to you last year. This ought to make good descriptive material for some tale some time . . . jungle stuff, to use as a background for pre-human ruins, & all that.

Heard recently from C A S—whose parents are better, though still distinctly feeble. He has lately taken up a new hobby—sculptural carving in talc, rhyolite, *dinosaur bone* [of which there is a deposit near Auburn], & other local materials. Some grotesque heads which he has sent to R H B & me are tremendously impressive. Note that his form of sculpture differs basically from R H B's. Barlow *models* in plastic clay, while Klarkash-Ton *carves* from friable solids. The technique is vastly different even though the products are superficially similar. Speaking of art—your envelope design is quite a triumph . . . certainly an improvement over that linoleum stuff of R H B's!

All good wishes—Yrs by the Nine-Legged Goat of Walpurgis—

Luveh-Keraph

## Notes

1. Perhaps a reference to the collaboration of RB and Henry Kuttner in the writing of pulp fiction.

2. Weinbaum (1902–14 Dec. 1935) died of throat cancer at the age of thirty-five. His writing career lasted a scant 18 months, but he is considered one of the greatest of science fiction writers for his realistic portrayal of alien creatures. See also RB 57.

3. "A Martian Odyssey" (*Wonder Stories*, July 1934).

4. Jack Darrow, a science fiction fan. HPL acknowledges him by the term "bursting darohs" in "In the Walls of Eryx" (1936), written with Kenneth Sterling.

5. RB writes of this character: "The name comes from a group of imaginary characters who—believe it or not—were invented to serve as players on teams in a card-game called 'Baseball'—the invention of my friends Herb Williams and Harold Gauer. The game is too complicated to describe here, but involved scoring the games & the performances of the individual 'players.' I later used the name for a central charac-

ter in my story, 'The Faceless God.'" In *The Opener of the Way* and the Chaosium edition of *The Mysteries of the Worm,* the character's name is Dr. Carnoti.

[50]  [ALS]

% Barlow, Box 88,
De Land, Florida.
August 7, 1935.

Noble & Diabolic Dr. Prinn:—

Congratulations once more! It's getting to be a habit! You surely are a W T fixture these days . . . . "the boy who made good"! I shall await "The Faceless God" & other items with keen expectancy, & trust that their reception by the public may prove favourable. Shall be interested to see how good ol' Nyarlathotep fares in your hands!

And so you're getting to be such a notable literary authority that neophytes & aspirants drag you out of bed seeking sage advice! Bless my soul! But such are the responsibilities of fame & competence! Trust you've duly set honest Mr. Leiharder[?] on the right path, & that the Fictioneers will attend to any points you may have overlooked. Which reminds me that Sultan Malik Taus of Redwood City has been entertaining your friend Ralph Milne Farley—showing him around San Francisco & initiating him into the mysteries of the Chinese Theatre. Ask Farley about it when he gets back.

Your recent reading seems to be all in the right direction. Cabell is a great stylist, even though some of his things tend to seem a bit artificial, forced, & repetitious. Huysmans is the supreme classic of decadence . . . somebody has called "Against the Grain" "the bible of the 90's". I've also read his "La Bas".

Glad your farce has been accepted, & hope the other things turn out well. I'll look up that cinema if I encounter it anywhere. Hope your woodland vacation will prove a thorough success—I'll be glad to hear about it later.

I continue to have a good time down here. My super-hospitable hosts are now urging me to remain *all winter*—not going home till next May—but I don't believe I could arrange to do this, much as I dread the physical ordeal of a northern winter. I can't perform serious work without my library & files—hence imagine I'll be at 66 before the month is out. Shall pause at St. Augustine & Charleston if not stone broke. The other day we visited Rock Springs, about 20 m. S.W. of here—where amidst a picturesque wooded valley a crystal stream issues forth from twin black tunnels in the side of a lofty tree-crowned cliff of hard-packed clay. About 60 ft inside the larger of these tunnels there is a vast hidden chamber of eternal night—once used by the Indians as a refuge—beyond which another aperture leads back to unplumbed & inconceivable abysses of inner earth. A great place—hope to see it again.

You'll be sorry to hear of the death on July 22 of young Robert Nelson—author of sundry verses in W T & of "Lost Excerpts" in the F F—after an illness of 17 days.[1] Too bad!

Yrs for the Litany of the Worm—

Luveh-Keraph

*Notes*

1. Robert Nelson, poet and correspondent of HPL, committed suicide on 22 July 1935.

[51]  [ALS]

Ancient St. Augustine

—August 25, 1935.

My dear Ludvig:—

Pardon the paper—all out of the real stuff, & shops closed on Sunday. As you may see, I'm on my way at last. Accompanied the Barlows to Daytona & helped them settle in the flat they are to occupy for a fortnight—then took the coach for ancient St. Augustine. It surely is good to see centuried gables, facades, balconies, & garden walls—& hear the sound of tinkling fountains at twilight, & of cathedral chimes cast in 1682—after 2 months & 9 days amidst rural modernity! Am revelling in the atmosphere of a 370-year-old city—a city founded before Shakespeare could walk or talk, & still containing houses which had 50 years behind them when the Pilgrims landed on Plymouth Rock. Staying a week at my usual cheap but cleanly hotel, & cutting food bill down to a minimum. Spend most of my time absorbing ancient vistas & writing atop the venerable fortress. Moving north tonight—at midnight. Savannah tomorrow morning—then my beloved Charleston—where I hope to hang on at the Y for 4 days. Then Richmond & Washington, Philadelphia & N.Y. Am not sure whether I can stop off in N Y & see the gang. Home in early or middle September. What a trip!

Glad you've also been enjoying the scenic aspects of nature. Your trip sounds idyllic indeed, & I shall welcome the sight of the photographs you mention. Incidentally—many thanks for the clever Yaddith-head!

Glad Hill-Billy is going to print "The Black Lotus". You are surely getting to be almost as widely represented as Comte d'Erlette! Also like him I note that you have a numerical goal for the year. Well—here's hoping you keep up to it! You surely are getting to be astute about placements! Glad the Fictioneers are still going strong. Yes—Petaja is a bright young correspondent of mine. His fiction & poetry are very promising, & if he continues to develop at the same rate he'll amount to something!

Had a pleasant surprise Friday—a call from Barlow, who came up from Daytona for a day's visit to bid the old man a second adieu. I shewed him some local sights he hadn't seen before. He sent you his regards.

Well—now to get packed. Hope you enjoyed the circus. Tomorrow at this hour I'll be in Charleston!

Yrs by the Pentacle of Noth—

Luveh-Keraph

[52]   [ALS]

Home Again

—Sept. 19, 1935

O Mighty Ludvig, Brooder on the Outer Void:—

Hope the Charleston P.O. comes across in the end—damned small of them to hold a card just for a bit of over-writing![1] Well—the trip ended as pleasantly as it began, though from Richmond onward I was bothered by occasional cold days. Hard to get used to the north again! Covered the various Poe sites in Richmond, paused a day in Washington to re-explore ancient Georgetown, & digested some assorted antiquities in Philadelphia. Then N.Y. City—where for nearly a fortnight I was a guest of Donald Wandrei (Howard being away), taking my meals up at Long's. I saw virtually all the gang—Long, Wandrei, Morton, Leeds, Talman, Koenig, Hornig, young Sterling, & the son of Otis Adelbert Kline. Finally home—to confront the most devastating array of piled-up work which the human imagination can conceive! Yuggoth, what a mountain of papers, letters, packages, magazines, & what the hell not! To say nothing of a troublesome verse-revision job! It will be weeks before my programme can be brought around to normal.

Yes—I've seen both W.T. & F.M., & congratulate you upon the excellent work which you have in both. I had read the "Shambler" before, & surely appreciate its dedication. The spoof also is extremely clever—I can recognise myself except for the *pipe* . . . which is scarcely typical of a non-smoker![2]

"Crime & Punishment" certainly is quite a book. The Russians had a curious realism which enabled them to handle psychological problems much better than their 19th century contemporaries. They seemed to escape a certain 'illusionedness' or pervasive sentimentality typical of Western Civilisation—although on the other hand their hysterical neuroticism & alien habits of thought make much of their work seem overwrought & even unintelligible to us. One wonders whether the civilisation which produced Dostoievsky & Turgeniev can ever be reconstructed under the capricious & cramping rule of the bolsheviks.

Your labours surely are Herculean! I see that, like Derleth, you are determined to get your material at first-hand . . . a very sound policy. Hope you won't let the requirements & methods of pulp fiction influence your taste & literary style. Your success in placing material has so far been phenomenal, & I trust it may continue unabated. Prospects certainly seem to be in your favour!

Sorry to hear that Weinbaum has been under the weather, & hope he may soon be fully on his feet again. Pleased to know that he likes some of my stuff. His own work is delightful—forming, as I believe I said once before, about the only pulp interplanetary stuff which isn't hackneyed, puerile, & absurd. I was interested to see his autobiography in a recent issue of F.M.[3]

You'll see "The Shadow Out of Time" in due season. I left my copy in N.Y. for the gang to read, but will soon start it on a circulation route with your name included. Haven't quite decided about submitting "The Thing on the Doorstep." As for the "Fungi"—here's the complete lot,[4] which you can copy & retain at leisure. No hurry so long as the MS. gets back safely in the end.

No—I haven't come across "Mad Love" as yet. Saw two cinemas in N.Y. with Long—"She" & "The Wandering Jew"—both with points in their favour.[5] "She" is scarcely recognisable as the Haggard novel, but contains some impressive scenic effects.

Tomorrow—just as if I hadn't had enough travelling for one year—I shall leave for Boston to pay my friend Cole a week-end visit, during the course of which we shall invade the "Dunwich" [Wilbraham, Mass.] countryside on an errand quite appealing to your ghoulish taste—to scatter the ashes of a deceased old lady on her native soil in accordance with her lifelong wish.[6] I'll let you know of any supernatural phenomena which may accompany this rite.

Cold as hell these days—but I manage to keep alive with the aid of an oil-heater, meanwhile praying for the turning-on of the steam heat. And just to add to my woes, the goddam bathroom ceiling fell down yesterday—occasioning an invasion of plasterers & an exasperating restriction of aqueous facilities. Well—thank Yuggoth I wasn't under the ceiling when it fell! I *did* have such an accident back in 1921 . . . . nearly split my thick skull open![7] ¶ All good wishes—

Yrs for the Black Chant—

Luveh-Keraph

*Notes*

1. This presumably alludes to a postcard so covered with writing that it was held by the post office for insufficient postage.

2. "The Ultimate Ultimatum," *FM* 5, No. 3 (August 1935): 193–94, 212. The sketch purports to report a "big convention" at which "Howard Cthulhu Lovecraft . . . sat in the corner, puffing furiously at a skull-shaped pipe." RB himself smoked a pipe.

3. "An Autobiographical Sketch of Stanley G. Weinbaum," *FM* 5, No. 1 (June 1935): 157f.

4. *Fungi from Yuggoth* comprised thirty-five stanzas (later thirty-six; but HPL's T.Ms. long omitted the final two, in expectation that he would include more sonnets), of which only ten had been published previously in *WT*.

5. *Mad Love* (MGM, 1935), directed by Karl Freund; starring Peter Lorre, Frances Drake, and Colin Clive. Based on the novel *The Hands of Orlac* by Maurice Renard. *She* (RKO Radio Pictures, 1935), directed by Irving Pichel and Lansing C. Holden; starring Helen Gahagan, Randolph Scott, and Helen Mack. Based on the novel by H.

Rider Haggard. *The Wandering Jew* (Julius Hagen Productions, 1933; released in the US in 1935), directed by Maurice Elvey; starring Conrad Veidt, Marie Ney, and Basil Gill.
6. HPL and Edward H. Cole went to Wilbraham, MA, for the purpose of scattering the ashes of Jennie E. T. Dowe (1840–1919), mother of Edith Miniter (1867–1934). HPL had written memorial poems to both women. Edith Miniter and her remote cousin Evanore Olds Beebe (1858–1935) showed HPL the Wilbraham area in 1928.
7. Cf. *SL* 1.151.

[53]   [ALS]

Crest of the Horrible Kaf
—Hour of the Strange Eclipse
[early October 1935]

Dear Ludvig:—

Glad to see yours of Sept. 29 with clever pictorial enclosures. It Which Dwells in Darkness is certainly a good reason for keeping a light going! Glad you're enjoying the autumn scenery. The leaves have only just begun to turn here, though they are farther advanced in inland New England. I'm enjoying the view from my west windows to the full—especially at this moment, when a red sun is sinking behind the antique towers of the hillside.

Busy? You said a mouthful, son! Fancy doing a couple of revision jobs & catching up with a hopelessly lapsed correspondence at the same time that one is trying to read 3½ months of old papers & magazines! Well—last night I completed the back number reading, so one item is off the books! But I have a pile of borrowed books—including the Wells-Huxley "Science of Life"[1]—to dispose of. Heaven only knows when my programme will ever get back to normal!

Glad you've had a chance to get some material to Wright without postage. Long, the Wandreis, & other Manhattan residents save a lot that way, since a large number of the pulps are located in their town. Well—here's hoping your recent shipment won't come back!

Yes—Donald Wollheim is very much all right . . . a real acquisition to the weird & science-fiction group. He is a leading spirit in the "Terrestrial Fantascience Guild" (a rival to the Science Fiction League), & a relentless foe & exposer of the financial policy of Gernsback's publications. He also turns out some fiction that could be a lot worse. Recently he became editor of the Guild's formerly insignificant (& mimeographed) publication *The Phantagraph*, & he is trying to build it up into a sort of successor of the lamented *F F.* This present issue is printed (or misprinted) by Hill-Billy Crawford, & there are some excellent items among the contents—notably an expose of the puerility of pulp science-fiction by one C. W. Lonsdell.[2] I hope very much that Wollheim will get enough support to keep the magazine alive—& trust you'll let him have any spare material which may be lying around.

And so you've heard from little Effjay![3] Interesting to know that you may revise one of his fictional attempts. Is it very bad? Hope the result of your collaboration with Peirce will be successful, & that you'll do ample justice to the plots assigned by The Fictioneers.

Glad you found the rest of the Fungi interesting. They represent an attempt to catch bits of mood & atmosphere—much as my stories do on a larger scale. Sometimes I fancy that poetry rather than fiction is the natural medium for the serious presentation of fantasy—since everything depends on the element of indefinite suggestion. What would be absurd & unconvincing in prose fictional dress might be extremely effective in mystical verse of the right sort. And yet there are fields in which it would be very difficult to replace fiction as a medium.

Well—my Massachusetts visiting was very pleasant, & the ashes were duly restored to their native soil. On Sept. 20 my host & I visited rocky Nahant & ancient Marblehead, undertaking the long Wilbraham pilgrimage on the 21st. The ride into the brooding "Dunwich" hill country was very pleasant, & keenly enjoyed the exquisite vistas which I had not seen since 1928. The region was wholly unchanged in aspect—& I could hardly realise that both of the genial old people who guided me through it & saturated me with its folklore seven years ago were now dead. We went first to Wilbraham village—site of the famous academy—& sought out the Tupper lot in the secluded Dell cemetery. There—on the graves of her father & ancestors, & of her daughter—we scattered the greater part of old Mrs. Dowe's ashes. The cemetery is a spectral place—on hilly ground above a wooded ravine through which a brook runs. There are legends of gruesome encroachments on graves by that sometimes swollen brook . . . . & the great elms & cypresses certainly hint of strange, dank nourishment! From there we climbed over Wilbraham Mountain to the remote region where I visited in '28 . . . . the peaceful farming country locally termed "back o' the maountain". The old Maplehurst farmhouse—a relique of the 1800 period—is deserted now, but is still kept in neat condition by the owners. It looks just the same as when I stopped there, save that the lesser gardens are beginning to be overgrown with briers. Here—near a stone wall where the half-wild remnants of the ancient rose-garden climb—we scattered the rest of the ashes according to the deceased's lifelong wish. Thus the ceremony was over—& the mortal remains which had been born in Wilbraham in 1843 were one with the earth of Wilbraham again. I agree with you in preferring cremation to any other mortuary procedure, & hope that process will be followed in my case. There are, however, no facilities for it in Providence. Our route on this occasion—which you can follow by means of that New England map I sent—was through Framingham, Oxford, Stourbridge, Brimfield, & Palmer. We grazed Worcester on the south, but did not enter it. In Brimfield we saw the classic white church built in 1839 by the father (a contractor) of her whose ashes we bore. I have a letter written by this builder to his wife in which he describes the whole task with much detail. The foliage in "Dunwich" was distinctly autumnal.

Well—on Sept. 22 we reversed our direction & spent the day exploring genial Cape Cod. Here one encounters a wholly different kind of scenery— the flattish seaboard landscape of southeastern New England, with winding creeks, occasional salt marshes & sand-dunes, wind-blown willows, & attractive little coves & seaports. I was fortunate in having this ample & varied dose of New England scenery to acclimatise me after my long absence among palms & live-oaks. We had a picnic lunch just beyond Hyannis, & lounged on the sands of Chatham with only the blue, heaving sea betwixt us & Spain. Cape Cod contains some exquisite villages with great elms, ancient houses, & white steeples. Of these I think *Sandwich* is the most attractive—though much may be said for Yarmouth.

Sept. 23 we were in Lynn & Swampscott—largely in business of my host's—& that evening I returned to Providence. While on the Cape I saw for the first time the new streamlined Diesel train "Comet" which operates out of Providence to Boston & other excursion points, & whose runs average a straight mile a minute. It is possible that I shall have two more scenic trips before the winter sets in—one with my aunt to New Haven in a friend's car, & the other (which is a good deal less probable) with my last month's host over the Mohawk Trail & up into Vermont when the autumn foliage is at its gorgeous best. But even if these don't pan out, I shall feel satisfied at the amount of scenery absorbed this year! The New Haven trip would lead through many quaint Connecticut towns which I know only slightly.

Hope your long tale will land with *Astounding*.[4] I imagine Schwartz ought to make a pretty good agent, since he has been in close touch with all the editors so long. I'm letting him try to market my "Mts. of Madness", though I really have no hope of the manuscript's placement.

Glad you had a chance to talk with Comte d'Erlette over the wire, & hope you'll be able to arrange a face-to-face meeting sooner or later. Howard Wandrei (who was married a fortnight ago) has recently been his guest. Which reminds me that Donald W. has taken a new flat since his brother's wedding—smaller quarters at 88 Horatio St., near where he was a year ago.

You'll be sorry to hear that the mother of Clark Ashton Smith died on Sept. 9. The event was not unexpected, yet it formed a severe blow for all that. It will be a bad thing for Klarkash-Ton's father—who is in feeble health & of advanced years. What plans C A S will make when left alone I don't know.

Haven't yet seen October W T, but hope it's better than other recent issues. You & C A S—& the reprint—are all that redeem the September number.

Well—good luck with all your enterprises.

Yrs by the Column of Cold Fire—

Luveh-Keraph

*Notes*

1. See *SL* 5.256.
2. C. W. Lonsdell, "Is Science Fiction in a Rut? [Part 1]," *Phantagraph* 4, No. 1 (July–August [1935]): [7]–8; [Part 2] 4, No. 3 ([June?] 1936): 13–14. See HPL [to DAW], *Phantagraph* 4, No. 2 (November–December 1935): 1: "Just received *The Phantagraph*, and must congratulate you on an excellent start. That article by C. W. Lonsdell is just what has been needed for years. I've pointed out time and again that the junk in the science pulps is simply a mess of absurd and extravagant hack formulae without substance and convincingness—just puerile words. I hope to see further instalments of this article." The concluding half was listed on the contents of the November–December issue, but the back cover stated that the piece was postponed to the following issue. A similar piece, consisting of an extract from a letter by HPL to Duane W. Rimel, was published anonymously under the title "What's the Trouble with Weird Fiction?" in *Phantagraph* 5, No. 5 (February 1937): 4, 8.
3. HPL and Kenneth Sterling lampooned Ackerman in the story "In the Walls of Eryx" with reference to "efjeh-weeds" and "wriggling" and "slimy ackmans."
4. RB published no fiction in *Astounding Stories*.

[54]  [ALS]

Caves of Mt. Ngranek—
Hour of the Night-Gaunts' Flight[1]
[2 November 1935]

Dear Ludvig:—

Sorry W.T. is such slow pay—but that is what one is led to expect from the reports of Price, Long, Wandrei, & others. The poor old rag has evidently fallen on hard times—indeed, one would sympathise with Wright instead of censuring him if it were not that he is said to draw a full & prompt personal salary from the venture instead of taking his share of the loss with the others. But don't let that deter you from writing! The fact is, it is *better* for a creative artist not to have a cheap professional market, since the latter always causes him to twist & debase his style in compliance with low-grade editorial demands. See what has happened to Long, Wandrei, Price, & so many others! Good writing can have no motivation save the author's desire for expression & harmonic utterance—& the wise beginner who wishes to tread in the footsteps of Poe, Machen, & Blackwood will pay no attention to the styles & wishes of the pulp fraternity. If they'll take what he writes in his own way, well & good. If not, let them go to hell! It is elsewhere—preferably outside the field of writing, or at least outside that branch of writing which forms his serious aesthetic outlet—that the creative author must look for his livelihood. A. Merritt forfeited his best potentialities by allowing himself to be absorbed into the cheap-fiction world & saturated with its hollow & insincere artificialities.

Well—anyhow, creativeness goes in cycles. Don't be discouraged if plots have difficulty in taking form just at present, for pretty soon you'll have an intensive spurt & turn out half a dozen yarns in quick succession. That's the way with most writers, including Klarkash-Ton. They lie fallow for a while—then produce a lot—& then lie fallow again. Glad your stuff has gone to the *Phantagraph* & to the trade journal—but don't let markets, or publication-media of any sort—influence your rate of production.

Glad you're having a good autumn—which seems to be the case everywhere. The outing & tournament must have been enjoyable. New England has had an exceptionally warm season, so that my hibernation-period has been happily postponed. I told you about my excursions of Sept. 20–23, but forget whether I mentioned the outing of Oct. 8 to New Haven. That was a delightful excursion—gorgeous autumnal Connecticut scenery, & 7½ hours to explore a quaint & beautiful old town. I absorbed New Haven's ancient buildings, churches, museums, & gardens, & took especial delight in the *new* Yale quadrangles—each a perfect reproduction of old-time Gothic or Georgian architecture. These quadrangles—isolated from the external modern scene—form glamourous little worlds of the past whose fascination is hard to describe. To wander through them is like walking bodily into a dream. But even this trip did not quite end the season. On Oct. 16 at 6 a.m. my friend Samuel Loveman blew in on the N.Y. boat, & after a brief session at #66 we proceeded to Boston to absorb bookstalls, museums, & general antiquities. Stayed 2 days—concentrating on the Museum of Fine Arts & the colonial sections on Beacon Hill & in the North End (cf. Pickman's Model). Back to Providence at noon of the 18th, & then a round of the local bookstalls—unearthing some I had not seen before. In the evening I reluctantly saw the guest off on the N.Y. boat. Cole still has an idea of trying that trip over the Mohawk Trail & into Vermont, but as the season advances, my enthusiasm for joining him very perceptibly wanes. Still—who can tell? A winter overcoat & well-heated Chevrolet make quite an argument! Meanwhile the warmth of the season has enabled me to take many afternoon walks in the countryside near Providence—a distinctly uncommon thing for late October!

Regarding the Abyssinian situation—that's so damn complex that one has to hesitate before giving a quick verdict. So far as abstract ethics goes, of course, Italy is dead wrong—but we have to remember that if we ourselves had always practiced abstract ethics, the entire North American continent would have remained an undeveloped hunting-ground for the red man, with ourselves increasingly cramped for room—& in need of raw materials—in Europe. The whole history of human progress is one of theft & conquest—the dominance of the strong & developed over the weak & undeveloped. But for this ruthless sweep of power, it is extremely unlikely that any high or stable civilisation could exist. Amusingly enough, our own offences are probably the most flagrant known to history—at least, since the wholesale devastations of the ancient world. For our repeated treaty-violations, slaughter, & land-thefts in connexion with the Indians—from King Philip's War to the days of Oklahoma—there is absolutely no moral or legal excuse . . . nor any parallel in the white man's settlement of Australia, New Zealand, South Africa, India, or elsewhere. And the virtual theft of the whole Southwest from Mexico (whose Spanish conquistadores had pulled the same trick in their day!) is only a milder form of the same principle. Yet who would consider it best for America to remain a savage wilderness? Obviously, we cannot adopt a purely moral (= aesthetic) basis for world politics. Now that we've got all we want—or can conveniently handle—we've acquired the habit of giving moral lectures to other nations who, not having been in a position to grab when we grabbed, are doing now what we did once. Hence the virtuous indignation over Japan in Manchuria or Italy in Abyssinia. But is this quite consistent? The Æthiopians, for all their thin pretence to an ancient civilisation, are basically nothing but a pack of barbaric blacks—wild tribes, held in subjection by a dominant group & having no civilised entity whatsoever. In the culture-scale they probably rate lower than the Iroquois or Pueblo Indians, while racially their nigger strain (amounting to full-blood in many of their tribes) gives them permanent inferiority. They are of no use to themselves or anybody else—yet meanwhile they hold a region whose resources could be of infinite value to European civilisation. Why should they be protected from the inevitable course of things any more than the Aztecs or Mayas or Maoris or Incas were protected? Italian suzerainty would cause them no hardship—as they are, the majority are vassals of the Amhares, & nobody purposes their massacre or enslavement. Under Italy—with the region intelligently utilised—they would certainly be no worse off than they are. Why should Italy be denied that expansion which England, France, & the United States have already had—& to whose gains they still smugly cling? Therefore I cannot see the wisdom of curbing Italy *so long as her object remains solely the absorption of Abyssinia.* But there another story begins. Is this the beginning of a bid for world power at the expense of other European nations? If so, it should be checked at the proper stage. Yet what *is* the proper stage? Is it wise to use the puppet-league (which has blandly ignored Japan & Manchuria) to force a drastic issue *now?* Would it not be better to follow the lines of nature more closely, let Italy do what we've all done, & simply *allow for her greater strength* in the armament & diplomacy of the future? *This purely in the interest of peace.* Abrupt military pressure *now* means an *immediate European war,* whereas a go-slow policy might easily avert any conflict whatever over this issue. Let Britannia show that she will not stand for any encroachment on the Empire, & Italy will probably (with African resources at her disposal) be willing to accept a status of *prima inter pares.* But of course a British gesture through the league is necessary to serve the requisite notification. I guess Sam Hoare & Tony Eden know what they're about! The idea of Æthiopian absorption as the cause of a rising of the dark races seems very fantastic to me. Black, brown, & yellow men are not united & have no effective organisation—except certain of the yellows, who are playing the imperial game for themselves alone.

No striking developments in the weird field. Have you seen Barlow's amateur paper, *The Dragon-Fly?* Just read Comte d'Erlette's new "Sign of Fear"— good indeed! Price is off for Mexico, calling on Two-Gun en route. ¶ Yrs by the Seal of Nug—

—E'ch-Pi-El

[P.S.] Schwartz tells me he has sold my "Mts. of Madness" to *Astounding*. I never expected that would land, but let him have it merely because he seemed anxious to try.

[P.P.S.] Tragic news—Belknap's aunt was instantly killed in a motor accident near Miami Oct. 20.[2] ¶ Barlow has just sent F B the surprise book of the latter's verse which we printed last summer.[3]

[P.P.P.S. on envelope:] Holy Yuggoth! Just got last-minute word that Wandrei surreptitiously submitted my "Shadow Out of Time" to *Astounding*—& they've accepted that, too![4] So you'll read it in print instead of in MS.

*Notes*

1. Mt. Ngranek is mentioned in "The Other Gods" and *The Dream-Quest of Unknown Kadath*.

2. Cassie Doty (Mrs. William B.) Symmes, whose travel book, *Old World Footprints* (Athol, MA: W. Paul Cook [Recluse Press], 1928), contains a preface HPL ghostwrote for Long.

3. *The Goblin Tower* was a small collection of poetry by Frank Belknap Long, published by R. H. Barlow. HPL helped set the type when he visited Barlow in the summer of 1935. See *SL* 5.182, [216], 218, 222.

4. *Astounding* paid HPL a total of $630 for the two stories, $350 (less $35 commission to Julius Schwartz) for *At the Mountains of Madness* and $280 for "The Shadow out of Time."

[55]   [ALS]

Black Cone of Nith—
Hour of the Turning
[mid-November 1935]

Dear Ludvig:—

Thanks for the congrats! The dual luck shot certainly did get the old man all pepped up—for look what came out of the aged bean last week! I was partly set going by the comment of that chap in the Eyrie who suggested that I dedicate a story to you.[1] Well—here goes! In killing you off,

I've been relatively mild. Whereas you had Grandpa all mashed up into a nice viscous red jelly, I've left you as a rigid corpse clutching at a broken pencil & gazing with glassy, sightless eyeballs out a west window—an expression of cosmic, unutterable fear on your twisted features. And as an abode, I've lent you good old 66—as you may deduce from the description. I'm not sure what I'll do with this effort—perhaps I'll try it on Wright, but more probably I'll send it around a circulation list. Such a list will be likely to occur in my next epistle. Possibly the thing isn't much good—I never can judge anything of my own while it's still new.

Glad to hear W T is coming across with at least a bit of cash. April authors are beginning to get theirs—Searight paid for his poem, & Howard Wandrei given half of his O'Mecca money. But before long F W will be in the Gernsback class!

And so you're tackling revision jobs! Accept my profoundest sympathy! Hope you're getting your pay in advance. I've given up doing revision on a speculative basis—with pay only if accepted. If I take a chance with editors, it's got to be with my own stuff, for which I'll get full pay in case of acceptance. One spends just about as much energy revising another guy's story—& getting only half the price—as writing a story of one's own & getting all the cash. The only exception is when the other fellow has some special sure-fire idea which might sell an otherwise salable tale . . . . . but that happens damn seldom!

Sorry your winter has so suddenly & emphatically set in. The autumn has lasted late, & no very violent cold as yet. Out on the Pacific Coast there was a bad cold wave some time ago—green leaves being frozen on the trees before they had a chance to turn.

Glad you continue to find interest in Cabell. Did I mention that the *other* Robert B—youthful sage of De Land—is also a Poictesme-hound? Some of James Branch's stuff is certainly powerful in its way, & apparently destined to survive—& indeed all of it is couched in one of the finest & maturest styles yet found in American prose.

Anent the general warfare question, only time can tell. The really safest policy is to let the powerful & aggressive nations get gradually gorged in a peaceful way, until they no longer feel any acute need of expansion. Of the major powers, England, the U.S. & France are relatively non-aggressive because they have reached the saturation-point. Italy, given a good slice of Africa, might join the same category. Other problems, however, exist in central Europe, where specific conflicting ambitions (Polish Corridor &c) exist. To prevent all wars is of course impossible, but considerable might be done to *localise* them. Embargoes on military supplies in neutral powers have a healthy tendency.

Speaking of Abyssinia—the other day I re-read Father Lobo's old volume, whose English translation in 1735 was Dr. Johnson's first professional literary venture.[2] Lobo was a Portugese Jesuit who tried to convert the Abyssinians to Catholicism in the years following 1624. He describes the country

& people in some detail—& we can see that they were exactly what they are today. The same barbaric raw meat eaters—the same quarrels over the throne—the same treacherous local princes & insubordinate Ras's—the same turbulent Gallas—nothing has changed in 300 years!

Good luck with your radio audition! If you land a berth, I'll tune my aunt's set in on your comedy hour each day—or week. I'll bet you could give some of the widely advertised mirth-merchants a run for their money!

*Later*

Finished typing the story—& am about all in! Here it is—rotten or not. Have decided to circulate it—list enclosed. Am starting out another copy—on another circuit—with Klarkash-Ton. ¶ Just to add to my worries, I find that my typing disturbs the old hen in the flat downstairs. She may, with my compliments, go to hell!

¶ Yrs. by the Sign of the Shining Trapezohedron—
Luveh-Keraph

P.S. Just recd. 2 of Klarkash-Ton's carved images, "The Outsider" & "Hyperborean Snake-Eater". Magnificent—they look like things dug up from primal ruins!

[P.P.S. on envelope:] Hail, Ludvig! Looking over the original MS. of the "Haunter" for a second time, I find a mistake on *page 17, 10th line from bottom.* For "flaping" read *flapping.* Will you please change this on the MS. before you pass it along to M. le Comte? Hope you'll correct any other obvious error you find. After all, such things will escape the most careful reader's eye.

Hastily—
E'ch-Pi-El

*Notes*

1. In "The Eyrie," *WT* 26, No. 5 (November 1935): 652, B. M. Reynolds wrote: "Robert Bloch deserves plenty of praise for *The Shambler from the Stars.* Now why doesn't Mr. Lovecraft return the compliment, and dedicate a story to the author?" "The Haunter of the Dark" is in fact "Dedicated to Robert Bloch."

2. Jerónimo Lobo (1595–1678), Jesuit missionary, wrote an account of his travels to India, Ethiopia, and elsewhere in Portuguese. It was not published in his lifetime. A French translation appeared as *Voyage historique d'Abissine* (1728); this was translated by Samuel Johnson as *A Voyage to Abyssinia* (1735).

[56]   [ALS]

The Windowless Steeple
—Dec. 4, 1935.

Dear Ludvig:—

Glad you found redeeming features in the tale—which I couldn't appraise very clearly myself. Hope other readers will be equally lenient toward it. If you ever want to write a sequel to it, I'll lend you one of the carbons again. Quite a number of the allusions could be used as a starting-point for fresh horrors!

I doubt if Wright would care for "The Thing on the Doorstep." He doesn't *really* like my work—as shewn by his unwillingness to handle long pieces of mine—& the conclusion of the "Thing" would probably strike him as too gruesome.[1] Still, I may try it on him some day—in conjunction with other things. By the way—give "The Fictioneers" my good wishes & thank them for their felicitations anent the *Astounding* placements. You are certainly lucky to have this congenial circle so close at hand.

Your psychological researches are surely interesting—though I trust you realise the unsettled & problematical nature of everything connected with psycho-analysis. That "delusion of birth" complex is one I never had. If I *am* an adopted foundling, I cannot say that my parents (or foster-parents!) picked a brat with a remarkable resemblance to themselves & to earlier figures in their ancestral lines!

Comte d'Erlette told me of the important mission he had delegated to you—too bad it has been balked! I wonder if all newspapers guard their files similarly nowadays? It didn't use to be so—when I was young the Prov. Public Library had files of all the local papers in its stack—even the ancient *Providence Gazette & Country-Journal,* going back to 1763. I read the *Gazette* file completely through . . . down to 1820 or so. Nowadays these files are no longer accessible. Papers prior to 1880 will keep pretty well on account of the better stock, but as soon as the reign of wood pulp begins, maintenance becomes a problem. I have an *Evening Bulletin* of 1876—in as good condition as the day it was printed. By the way—M. le Comte's plan of assimilating the details of the past is certainly ambitious. I've tried to do the same for various periods. It is the best course he could follow if he wants to write a series of really convincing historical novels—with the spirit & substance of old Wisconsin in them. Beyond question, Little Augie is laying the foundations for some very ambitious & serious achievement.[2]

Hope to see the Goon Dictionary in course of time—& am sure it will form an important addition to classical lexicography.

I'll get a look at "Crime & Punishment"[3] if it comes this way. Years ago I wrestled with the novel, & wouldn't mind seeing what the cinema has made of Raskolnikov & his quaint contemporaries! Some good lectures hereabouts lately—heard Prof. Savery of U. of Wash. give a very enlightening address on contemporary American philosophy the other night.[4] On another occasion I renewed my long-flagging acquaintance with the drama through an invitation to see the Le Gallienne repertory company. Couple of mildly clever comedies—in a surprisingly traditional vein—by the brothers Quintero. Smooth performance, but undistinguished material. The *next* night they had "Rosmersholm"[5]—which I would have much rather seen!

Had a 5″ snow Nov. 23, but effects are all gone now. Haven't yet seen Dec. W T, but F M came the other day—with the composite stories. Nothing to brag about—& misprinted to an annoying extent. It amused me to see how quickly Two-Gun converted the scholarly & inoffensive George Campbell into a raging Conan or King Kull![6] By the way—a note in F M apprises me that the "Stern" whose story I admired is really that prolific hack Paul *Ernst.*[7] Only goes to show that many of the routine pulpists *could* do good work if they had the chance. I've seen good things of Ernst's before.

Yrs for the Black Pilgrimage—
Luveh-Keraph

*Notes*

1. Farnsworth Wright always professed greatly admiration for HPL's work and in fact did publish "The Thing on the Doorstep" (*WT,* January 1937).
2. See HPL to L. M. White, Jr. (20 December 1935): "He [August Derleth] will embark on a series of historical novels dealing with his native Wisconsin background. In preparation for this series he is conducting a course of antiquarian research which puts me to shame. He is going exhaustively over all the old records, newspapers, & diaries he can find in local files, libraries, & attics, & is hiring people to copy headlines & topics from the Milwaukee papers of 50 or 75 years ago. He means to know those times as intimately as if he had lived in them—& the result will be apparent when he comes to write the novels." "Letters to Lee McBride White, Jr.," *Lovecraft Annual* No. 1 (2007): 47.
3. *Crime and Punishment* (Columbia Pictures, 1935), directed by Josef von Sternberg; starring Peter Lorre, Edward Arnold, and Marian Marsh.
4. William Briggs Savery (1875–1945), professor of philosophy at the University of Washington (1902–45) and a follower of George Santayana, William James, and John Dewey.
5. HPL saw *A Sunny Morning* (one-act play) and *The Women Have Their Way* (two-act play) by Serafin and Joaquin Alvarez Quintero, starring Eva Le Gallienne. *Rosmersholm* (1885–86; first American production 1904) is a play by Henrik Ibsen (1828–1906).
6. HPL refers to Robert E. Howard's part of the round-robin story "The Challenge from Beyond," *FM* 5, No. 4 (September 1935). His section, the third and longest of five, was quite atmospheric, and was followed abruptly by Howard's action-filled segment.
7. Julius Schwartz, "The Science Fiction Eye," *FM* 5, No. 4 (September 1935): 232.

[57]   [ALS]

Catacomb of Thul
—Dec. 28, 1935.

Honour'd Ludvig:—

      Abundant congratulations on your radio & theatrical triumphs! You are certainly beginning to make a splash in the world of entertainment—with national figures buying your scripts, & agents seeking you out to revivify the jaded diners of nocturnal Milwaukee! Hope the good fortune continues, & that I shall before long be able to pick up your performances regularly on my aunt's radio! Meanwhile I await with interest your lexicographical achievement.

      I was surely sorry to learn of Weinbaum's death—only a few brief months after I was first introduced to his refreshingly original work. I had become an especial fan of his—rejoicing that someone had at last broken through the old interplanetary clichés—& now there will be no more stores of "Tweel"[1] & kindred marvels! Young Sterling—who first brought Weinbaum's tales to my attention, & who is back in Providence over the holidays—was as grieved as I to learn the melancholy news. The fatal illness seems to have been very unusual, since cancer is certainly rare at thirty-three.

      Thanks for the interesting cuttings. I see that the press was not oblivious of your recent dramatic success! I saw that Beacon Hill cult item in the local paper—& in somewhat ampler form. Whether the "cult" amounts to anything more than the orgies of decadent pseudo-aesthetes one can't say—but anyhow, the idea is fascinating. To think I may have been within a stone's throw of a bunch of Cthulhu-worshippers without knowing it! The green cutting told me something I didn't know before—namely, that the Paul Revere house is not the only 17th century house with an overhang left in Boston. I never heard of the Willis house, but must try to find out something about it. I had always thought that the Vernon (1698) & Clough (1695) houses in the North End (the Pickman's Model district) were the only specimens of that sort left besides the Revere edifice. These were demolished in 1933. The Revere house—now restored to its original condition & used as a museum— was built in 1676 on the site of Increase Mather's parsonage . . . after the latter had burned down in one of Boston's historic fires. It will be noticed that the article lists only dwelling-houses. There are, in addition, several pre-Revolutionary public buildings including the Old State House (1713—now a museum), the old North Church (1723—still a church) the Old South Church (1727—a museum) Faneuil Hall (1746), King's Chapel (1749—still a church), &c. Cambridge—outside the Boston city limits—has many structures antedating the Revolution, including some of the Harvard buildings. A census would probably reveal that Philadelphia & Charleston contain the most pre-1775 buildings of any American towns, though Newport & Salem still have many. Providence easily has hundreds of buildings older than 1775.

Tomorrow I expect to depart on a week's visit to Belknap—also seeing Morton, Wandrei, & all the rest of the metropolitan group. Hope the weather will be less bitter than it is right now!

Had a good Christmas—with tree & usual accessories. Among my gifts was an Egyptian scarabaeus, though I can't swear as to its genuineness.

Hoping that 1936 may prove a year of increasing opportunities & good fortunes for you,

I remain

> Yrs by the Eye of Ghatanothoa
> —Luveh-Keraph

*Notes*

1. The alien creature in "A Martian Odyssey" (*Wonder Stories,* July 1934) and "Valley of Dreams" (*Wonder Stories,* November 1934).

[58]   [ALS]

March 14[, 1936]

Plenipotent Arch-Goon:—
I must return your esoteric lexicon—for the loan of which many thanks—before my already hopeless programme gets altogether shot to hell. 1936 is my year of misfortune. Down with grippe in January, so that work piled up on me beyond the possibility of performance, & now my aunt is down with a far worse attack—& with complications & hospital possibilities extending indefinitely ahead. [1] For a month I have had to be primarily a combined nurse, secretary, butler, market-man, & errand-boy—& my own activities have simply slid to oblivion.

Hence this is no reply to yours of 29th ult. I'm glad to hear of the completion of your novel, & hope it may meet with professional placement & success. [2] Glad you have assistance in getting it in shape. This kind of thing may be your natural metier—the grown-up literary equivalent of the cocked hat & rubber cigar! I don't envy you the typing, though!

Yes—I have heard from Kuttner—& day before yesterday snatched the time to drop him a line with a few geographical, architectural, & necropolitan remarks about *Salem,* which he seems to favour as a locale. I congratulate you upon discovering him, for he really seems to be a very unusual find—his prose & verse alike having remarkable force & fluency. His fiction does, as you suggest, display a little imitativeness—& a certain lack of adequate motivation & gradual development—but it has excellent atmospheric qualities & a promising sense of climax. I have an idea that Kuttner will be a rapid learner—whose work will acquire polish & maturity through a series of quick leaps. Glad he seems to be securing a foothold in W T & elsewhere.

I was greatly pleased with the M. of M. illustrations—which far excel the work in W T. The artist must really have read some of the text, since he has perfectly visualised the archaean entities with nothing but a written description to go by. "The Shadow Out of Time", I am told, will appear in the June issue.[3]

Hope the Weinbaum memorial volume will be a success—& that it will contain a good amount of his best work.[4] I shall get a copy. Weinbaum was virtually the only person who gave a touch of freshness & vitality to the interplanetary theme—& it is surely a manifold pity that he couldn't have lived longer.

Rhode Island certainly had a fierce winter—but not nearly as bad as that of the Middle West. Our lowest temperature was 4 above zero, & even that was seldom approached. The worst thing was the failure of the mercury ever to get very far above $+20°$. That caused a piling-up of the cold, & froze many bays & streams which do not often lose their liquid consistency. The cold broke around mid-February, & there has been some really warm weather since. Last Tuesday it was 64°, & the next day 62°. Spring—technically, at least—in 6 days . . . . & you can wager I'm damned thankful! I had a good Christmas—tree & all—& visited Belknap around New Year's. In N.Y. I met a number of weirdists I hadn't seen before—Arthur J. Burks, Donald Wollheim, Otto Binder, &c—& saw good old Seabury Quinn for the first time since 1931. And of course I was in touch with all the regular gang. Saw a copy of Loveman's new book—a circular of which I'll enclose.[5] One of the high spots was the new Hayden Planetarium of the Am. Museum—the most impressive educational device I have ever encountered.

The Goon Dictionary is surely a triumph of its kind—apt, subtle, & iconoclastic metaphor spontaneously coined out of the doings & folklore of the moment. One or two of the expressions seem to have been duplicated in the outside world, but the majority possess the true stamp of Goonic individuality. Utterly Goonique, as it were. The daily conversation of your group must surely be spicy if it includes any large percentage of this special vocabulary!

Under separate cover I am sending a recent product of the National Amateur Press Association which may be of some interest because of its review of Belknap's "Goblin Tower".[6] I think the editor is just a bit severe on the poems. Their defects are genuine enough, but anyone not especially callous toward the weird would recognise the power of their general atmosphere more than he does.

Recent W T's pretty poor—about 1 or 2 good stories apiece in recent issues. Hope to see more of your work there before long.

With best wishes for your novel, & for all your other ventures—

Yrs by the Sign of Gnar—

Abdul Alhazred

*Notes*

1. Annie E. P. Gamwell (1866–1941) actually had breast cancer.

2. Possibly the novel *In the Land of the Sky-Blue Ointments* (unpublished), on which RB collaborated with fellow Milwaukean Harold Gauer (1914–2009).

3. Howard V. Brown illustrated both *At the Mountains of Madness* and "The Shadow out of Time."

4. This was *Dawn of Flame: The Stanley G. Weinbaum Memorial Volume* (1936).

5. *The Hermaphrodite and Other Poems.*

6. [Ernest A. Edkins], "*The Goblin Tower*," *Causerie* (February 1936): 2–4.


[59]    [ALS]

Yuggoth—
Hour of the Buzzing
[April 1936]

Dear Ludvig:—

I would have sooner acknowledged yours of March 18 with its interesting enclosure had I been less harassed by the overwhelming pressure of events. My aunt became worse, & went to the hospital March 17th. She is now finely convalescing—transferred from the hospital to a nursing home & due back here in a week or so—but my added responsibilities are no less devastating. My own activities are utterly sunk—letters unanswered, duties transferred, revision jobs returned unperformed, unread borrowed books piling ceiling-high—in fact, absolute, unmanageable chaos—

"With ruin upon ruin, rout on rout,
Confusion worse confounded."[1]

I read the Kuttner–Wright missives with interest & amusement, & am returning them herewith. Many thanks for sending them. Too bad we had such a devastating effect on Kuttner—but it is evident that mere mortals & novices can't take it where the hellish Entities of the outer void are concerned! The next time we visit Beverly Hills we'll have to feign completely human shapes—except when disposing of guards & other obstacles. Yes—Kuttner is a very bright chap, & I hope to reply to his letter of mid-March very shortly. I intend to lend him some pictures of Salem, in order to correct a somewhat erroneous impression on his part. No—I don't know Bernard de Beauchasne of Chicopee Falls, but I trust he may succeed in his literary ambitions.

Your winter was evidently worse than ours—bad though the latter was. March was warm & springlike here—bring out the birds on the trees prematurely—but April is cold & bleak so far. I hope you'll be able to leave off your overcoat by July 4th—or at least, that there won't be many feet of snow on the ground by then!

Congratulations on the acceptance of "The Creeper in the Crypt". You certainly are getting there! Hope all the other new pieces land successfully. I was glad to see "The Druidic Doom"—a very effective & convincing tale—in the current W T, & shall be looking for "The Faceless God" next month.

Hope Comte d'Erlette will appreciate the "Goon Dictionary". Your Goonic organisation is surely an enterprising branch—& I have no doubt but that *Brutal* will be one impressive magazine. If the Milwaukee April is as bad as ours, I fancy you've postponed your spring festival—but this is no time for the devotees of winter underwear to be shedding the old red flannels! Glad you had an enjoyable Fictioneer meeting. *Which* Binder was present? I haven't yet figured out just how the boys collaborate. They had a splendid yarn in the March W T.

By the way—W T isn't quite as bad as usual of late. Even Hamilton had quite a creditable tale in the March number—which with the Binder & Smith items made the issue distinctly above the average. This month you & Jacobi & M. le Comte carry off the honours.

Hope your Arkham tale develops well. In order not to get mixed up on the geography, you might keep the enclosed crude map in mind. I follow this plan in all Arkham stories to avoid contradictions. Hope you can decipher the thing—a magnifying glass might help.

Sympathy anent the typing—& I hope success on the novel's part will repay you for it.

Crawford is slowly going ahead with the "Innsmouth" booklet, & has secured 4 fine illustrations from *Utpatel.* I've read proofs of 2 sections.

Young Sterling—the science fiction fan—has been desperately ill with an abscess of the lower colon. Operation at hospital—blood transfusion— intravenous nourishment—&c. His life was almost despaired of, but now he's pulling around all right—though he still has to dictate his letters.

Loan exhibit of Klarkash-Ton's grotesque sculpture is going the rounds of the gang. Loveman has it now, I come next, & then Barlow.

With apologies for the inadequate scrawl which my present chaos forces me to substitute for a real letter—

   Yrs by the Sunken Monolith—

     Cthulhu

[Enclosure: HPL's map of Arkham.]

*Notes*

1. John Milton, *Paradise Lost* 2.995–96.

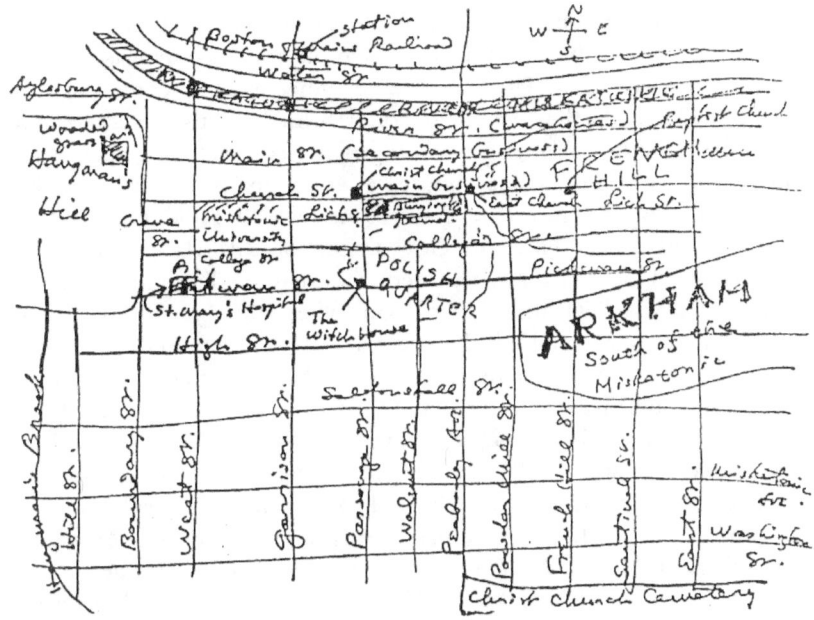

[60]   [ALS]

Extinct Crater of Gno—
Rising of the Eyeless Eaters
[mid-May 1936]

Dear Ludvig:—

Programme still unmanageable, but aunt better. She moved to convalescent home Apr. 7, & returned to 66 on the 21st. Now steadily gaining—takes walks sunny afternoons, & had a pleasant motor ride in the country a fortnight ago. But considerable coöperation still required. I myself am just about exhausted, but warm weather will help to set me on my feet. Spring is really here at last, & the landscape is a thing of beauty. I've taken my work outdoors on several occasions, but have had no time for long-distance rural walks. Barlow has invited me down to De Land again, but there's very little hope of my being able to make the trip.

Some interesting lectures lately—at the college a block over the hill or at the School of Design a block down the hill. Subjects pleasantly varied—Plato's Republic, modern painting, Chinese contributions to western culture, Gilbert Stuart, R.I. silversmiths, archaic Greek art influences, early classical sculpture, philosophy & poetry, Mayan ruins, & the Michelson–Morley experiment. No excuse for being ignorant in this neighbourhood!

On May 4 the R.I. Tercentenary observances began with a parade in colonial costume which started at the college gate—a stone's throw from #66. Later there was a mock-session of the rebel legislature of May 4, 1776—held in costume in the selfsame room of the ancient colony-house (1761) where the original session was held. In this, each old-time deputy was impersonated by a lineal descendant. The acting & costumes were so convincing that one might easily fancy the bygone period returned—with the intervening 160 years merely a bad dream. I was one of the relatively few spectators lucky enough to get into the colony-house & witness the proceedings. In the afternoon—at a ceremony at the State House which I did not attend—Gov. Curley of Mass. presented to Gov. Green of R.I. a copy of the recently adopted resolution of the Mass. Genl. Court rescinding the banishment imposed on Roger Williams in Oct. 1635. After 300½ years, Mr. Williams no doubt highly appreciated this delicate mark of consideration!

Glad to hear of your new work—which surely covers a lot of ground! Wright's cannibalistic objections are nonsense—he ought to see the yarn by Dunsany in the February *Story*—"Two Bottles of Relish"![1] Poor Farny has been timid ever since 1925, when he had a run-in with the Indiana bourgeoisie over a yarn by C. M. Eddy Jr. of Prov., which I revised! Your "Druidic Doom" is a splendid yarn, & has been praised by all my correspondents. Haven't read the May W T as yet, but I agree that Finlay's heading to your tale[2] is a triumph. Mar. & Apr. W T far above average—Jacobi's yarn being a worthy companion for yours. Yes—Wandrei's "Red Brain" is surely great stuff. Wish he could find & publish the rest of the cosmic series to which it belongs! Glad you found the Arkham map useful.

Congratulations on the birthday![3] Hope you'll enjoy the Fiction Guild banquet next month, & that your services at the alumni event will be appreciated. Sympathy on the spring cleaning! I simply *won't* allow my study to be invaded—but I suppose it takes old age to be able to win such immunity!

Glad Kuttner is doing so well. Congratulations to Peirce on his debut![4] Hope you make the *Argosy*, which pays excellently, & to which Wandrei seems to have a settled entreè.[5] I doubt if they'd want anything of mine.

All good wishes, & hopes for a fruitful year

Yrs. by the Weedy Monolith,

Grandpa Cthulhu

*Notes*

1. The actual title is "The Two Bottles of Relish," first published in *Time and Tide* for 12 and 19 November 1932. It is a sardonic detective tale involving cannibalism and is one of the most frequently anthologized tales in modern literature.

2. "The Faceless God" (*WT*, May 1936). See HPL's poem "To Mr. Finlay, upon His Drawing for Mr. Bloch's Tale, 'The Faceless God'" (written November 1936).

3. RB turned nineteen on 5 April.

4. Earl Peirce's first appearance in *WT* was "The House of Duryea" (October 1936).

5. RB published no stories in *Argosy*.

[61]   [ALS]

> Bottomless Well of Yeguggon
> —Hour that the Snout appears.
> [late June 1936]

Dear Ludvig:—

Glad you liked the "Shadow"—which wasn't as badly messed up as the "Mts. of Madness". The hideous treatment of the latter's text utterly sickens me. Damn Tremaine & his methods! I lately corrected 3 printed copies of each tale—in connexion with a titanic tidying-up of my files, made necessary by their completely chaotic state. Congestion her[e]abouts very little abated. I'll never get caught up with things. My eyesight is nothing extra of late—hope you'll be more careful with your own.

Congratulations on acceptance of "The Opener of the Way"—& on the completion of the novel. Hope Schwartz can place the latter as quickly as he did the "Mts. of Madness"! I liked "The Faceless God" as well as "The Druidic Doom"—& felt the potent menace of its atmosphere. Was glad, too, to see "The Grinning Ghoul" in print. You surely are one of the W T fixtures now! Meanwhile I rejoice that your comedy work is receiving favour in such prominent quarters. Long live the tradition of the cocked hat & rubber cigar!

*The Planeteer* [1]—of which I have not yet seen a copy—seems to be a struggling contemporary of *Fantasy Magazine* & *The Phantagraph*. The editors are eager for good material, & I think they are worthy of encouragement. While *The Phantagraph* probably deserves preference, *The Planeteer* might well form a repository for some of your surplus items. Most of the group, indeed, write enough to keep all the fan magazines supplied. By the way—I learn that Hornig has just secured a newspaper job in San Francisco through the influence of good old Merritt. I surely wish him luck. On his way through Indianapolis he stopped to see Miss Moore, who liked him very much.

A good idea—to petition the Mass. General Court to un-hang the Salem witches! Young Kuttner—who specialises in Salem, & to whom I've just lent a Salem guidebook & set of pictures—would be a good one to transmit the appeal to Gov. Curley. I'll let you—as an experienced comic specialist—attend to the matter of making a strip of "funnies" from De Vermis Mysteriis.

Among the recent items in my attempted conquest of chaos was a reading-up of contemporary W T issues. Two-Gun's serial was (your anti-Conan attitude notwithstanding) really splendid despite the "monotonous man-slaughter" & confusing nomenclature. Yuggoth, how that bird can surround ancient megalithic cities with an aura of aeon-old fear & necromancy! His "Black Canaan" is likewise magnificent in a more realistic way—reflecting a genuine regional background & giving a clutchingly powerful picture of the horror that stalks through the moss-hung, shadow-cursed, serpent-ridden swamps of the far south. I have already said how keenly I delighted in your own tales. Comte d'Erlette's "Telephone in the Library" (which I had seen before) has a potency all its own, & Hamilton has surely escaped his formula a bit in "Child of the Winds". Burks spoils his "Room of Shadows" with a certain hack treatment. M. J. Bardine's "Harbour of Ghosts" has promise—& atmosphere. So has Harold G. Shane's "Lethe".

Haven't seen "Things to Come"[2] yet, but am still hopeful. All who have seen it seem to give enthusiastic reports.

¶ Since I began this bulletin I've had a most depressing & staggering message—a postcard with the report that good old Two-Gun has committed suicide![3] It seems incredible—I had a long normal letter from him dated May 13. He was worried about his mother's health, but otherwise seemed quite all right. If the news is indeed true, it forms weird fiction's worst blow since the passing of Whitehead in 1932. No other writer of the group had quite the zest & spontaneity of good old R.E.H.

¶ Other sad additions to the '36 necrology list—Montague Rhodes James, at age of 73; George Allan England, at age of 59.[4]

*Last moment*

Just had word from Two-Gun's father. Sad report all too true. R E H shot himself when he learned that his mother's illness was fatal. Double funeral. The shock to poor old Dr. Howard must be unbearable—wife & splendid only child gone at one blow. R E H's melancholy streak must have run deeper than we thought—for most can take the loss of the elder generation more philosophically. It certainly is cruelly tragic all around. ¶ Best wishes—

Yrs by the Shadow—
Ech-Pi-El

*Notes*

1. A fan publication edited by James Blish and William Miller, Jr. The issue with HPL's material never appeared.
2. *Things to Come* (London Film Productions, 1936); directed by William Cameron Menzies; starring Raymond Massey, Edward Chapman, and Ralph Richardson. Based on H. G. Wells's novel *The Shape of Things to Come* (1933). Wells wrote the screenplay.
3. C. L. Moore had notified HPL that Howard had committed suicide on 11 June 1936.
4. James died on 12 June, England on 26 June.

[62]   [ALS]

Leprous St., Arkham, Mass.
August 12, 1936.

Dear Ludvig:—

The warm spell braced me up considerably, though Rhode Island's summer has on the whole been a cold one. From all I hear, the west has enjoyed a bit more heat than the East. Sorry your eyes & finances have been troubling. I'll pass the word along to Comte d'Erlette when next I write him.

Sorry "Grip of Death"[1] didn't land, & hope to see it in MS. ere long. I'll be looking for "The Opener of the Way" with its Finlay illustration. It's too bad Wright's financial policy is so shaky, but he's promising better things just now. If I were you I'd still give him a chance. Sorry Kuttner is trying to lure you down to the lower depths—though some might be able to cater to the *Terror* group without losing the power to write real stories. Kuttner is an extremely brilliant chap, & it won't be long before he secures a real foothold.

Glad you're helping along the aspiring "fan" editors. The *Planeteer* boys asked me for a translation of the *Necronomicon,* but I couldn't furnish anything at the moment. I was vastly edified by the spoof prepared for Conover[2] (a very earnest & ambitious youth, apparently), & most certainly will authorise its publication. You surely do keep the gags coming thick & fast—I don't wonder that your vaudeville & radio sketches are well received! I return the carbon in case you wish it for your immediate files. The first issue of the *Correspondent,* I believe, will appear in September.

Two-Gun's tragic exit surely is a blow. We shall be seeing many a reminiscence & obituary during the months to come,[3] & many a poem dedicated to the fallen warrior. Barlow has written a fine elegiac sonnet which Wright has accepted for W T . . . alas that Ar-E'ch-Bei's professional debut should have to possess so tragic a background![4] I presume you've heard most details of the melancholy business—including the fact that Dr. Howard has given his son's library to the latter's Alma Mater (Howard Payne College in Brownwood) as the nucleus of a Robert E. Howard Memorial Collection. Of all the persistent pulpists Two-Gun had by far the most vitality. Things like his recent "Black Canaan" shew what was in him, & what he might have developed into. No one can fill his place.

As for the rise of the youngsters—the new generation surely has begun to land in the press with encouraging frequency. Barlow hasn't aimed at the professional magazines very much, since he refuses to adopt popular tricks & formulae. But he'll probably get into W T on his own terms sooner or later—not, perhaps, with any great frequency, but occasionally. Glad the youngsters like Grandpa's work, although I fear some of them tend to overrate it. As an antidote, I am told that the juvenile fan-letterists of *Astounding* are blasting me off the map![5]

Had a call from young Sterling (now in Lynn, Mass., & about to enter Harvard in Sept.) June 30, & hope to see him again before long. Took a Newport trip July 11—an excellent sail. July 18–19 I had an enjoyable visit from your fellow-Milwaukeean Maurice W. Moe, who has been visiting in the East. He came with his son Robert (the youth—now of Bridgeport, Conn.—who was here with his car in the spring of '35), & we covered quite a bit of scenic & historic ground in the all-too-brief span of 2 days. Weather favoured us—for it was warm & sunny throughout, whereas the next day was rainy & cold—forcing me to crouch shivering & heavily blanketed over an oil heater. Later still came another social event—nothing less than the arrival of young Barlow in Providence for a stay of indefinite length. Some property adjustments about the De Land place are occurring, & R H B thought this would be a good time to pay me a visit & make his headquarters in the ancient Arkham region for a while. I surely am glad to see him—& I forgive him even the fierce-looking set of moustachios & side-whiskers he has grown! He has taken a room at the boarding-house across the garden from 66, & will certainly be a most congenial neighbour while he stays. He is full of literary plans—including the establishment of a high-grade mimeographed magazine of distinctive material.[6]

Almost simultaneously with Ar-E'ch-Bei came the loan-exhibit of Klar-kash-Ton's grotesque miniature sculpture, forwarded from N.Y. All the items are truly impressive, & some of them are magnificently suggestive of the products of some sinister pre-human archaeology.

Had an interesting view of Peltier's comet on July 22 at the Ladd Observatory of Brown University—through a 12″ telescope. The object shewed a small disc with a hazy, fan-like tail. I could have seen it through my own small (3″) glass were the northern sky less obstructed in the neighbourhood of #66.

Schwartz has a wild idea about getting some of my stuff reprinted in England (I'm sure it'll come to nothing), & in connexion with this matter I sent my two unsubmitted stories ("Haunter" & "Thing on the Doorstep") to W T in order to exhaust all cisatlantic possibilities first. I expected instant rejections—but to my surprise Wright took both items. When they will appear, I can't say. Haven't yet read the August W T, but doubt whether it amounts to much. ¶ All good wishes—

Yrs by the Black Flame—

E'ch-Pi-El

[P.S.] Old Adolphe de Castro—one-time friend of Bierce & creator of endless fictional junk & learned charlatanry—blew into town Aug. 6. I shewed him around a bit, & he, Barlow, & I wrote rhymed acrostics on Poe while seated on a tomb in the hidden hillside churchyard where the bard of Nis & Aidenn used to roam when visiting Prov.[7]

[Enclosure]

[P.P.S.] Added thought. Would you want to do any fictional collaboration with old de Castro? I notice that you are doing work of that sort, even with minor fauna like Forrest J. Ackerman. Old 'Dolph has written endless reams of stories, none of which is in modern salable form, but any of which might have ideas. He can't revise them himself, & can't pay any reviser who demands cash in advance. But he would like to coöperate with somebody willing to fix up his yarns on a speculative basis—such as half the proceeds in case of sale. You could refuse to tackle stuff which you thought would be unsalable—or which would take as much work from you as a story of your own. De Castro's name might be an asset with some magazines, since he really was a colleague of Ambrose Bierce's in the old days, & was the principal translator of the rather famous "Monk & the Hangman's Daughter". Long wrote the preface to his life of Bierce published in 1929.[8]

In case you're interested, his address is

Dr. Adolphe de Castro,
    461 Ft. Washington Ave.,
    New York, N.Y.

Price had hoped to collaborate with the old boy, but found his own work too pressing. I did his "Last Test" & "Elec. Executioner" in W.T.

*Notes*

1. A collaboration with Henry Kuttner published in *Strange Stories* (December 1939).
2. "A Visit with H. P. Lovecraft." See Appendix.
3. HPL himself wrote "In Memoriam: Robert Ervin Howard" for *FM*. A shortened version, "Robert Ervin Howard: 1930–1936," appeared unsigned in the *Phantagraph*.
4. "R. E. H."
5. Contemporary letters both praising and disparaging HPL's two stories in *Astounding* are now included in Joshi, *A Weird Writer in Our Midst* 110–18.
6. Barlow published only two numbers of *Leaves* (Summer 1937 and 1938), containing HPL's "Cats and Dogs," CAS's "The Third Episode of Vathek," and others.
7. The three acrostic poems, and others by M. W. Moe and Henry Kuttner, were published in David E. Schultz, "In a Sequester'd Churchyard," *Crypt of Cthulhu* No. 57 (St. John's Eve 1988): 26–29. See also NHW 15, n. 4.
8. *Portrait of Ambrose Bierce* (New York: Century Co., 1929). The preface is signed "Belknap Long."

[63]   [ALS]

Citadel of Leng
—Aug. 31, 1936.

Dear Ludvig:—

    Glad you had an enjoyable trip & a congenial session with li'l' Farny. Interested, too, to learn that you've seen galley-proofs of the "Haunter". Hope the old mag will hang together somehow despite its financial difficulties—Price is so disgusted with the present slow payment of authors that he says he'll never contribute again. Congratulations on the new acceptance—& on the originals of your Finlay illustrations. I can imagine the fascinating aspect of these originals, & don't wonder that Wright wanted the "Faceless God" one. If it isn't indeed the finest illustration ever used in W T, it surely comes close to being such. Interested to hear about Finlay & his growing recognition. He surely is going ahead splendidly for one of his age, & may leave all his rivals in the shade before long. Glad he's likely to get some covers to do, & hope that either the "Thing" or the "Haunter" will have the benefit of his embellishment[1]—although I still think that some imaginative quality in Rankin is hard to beat.

Glad to hear of your newly acquired Mephisto. I also acquired a cast recently—that well-known Greek bas-relief of Orpheus, Eurydice, & Mercury—when the old lady downstairs moved away & disposed of a lot of material. In the same windfall came a vast number of books—some of which were new to me, & some of which were good-conditioned duplicates of books of mine which were wearing out.[2]

Hope you can find a lodgment for various products in *Thrilling Mystery*.[3] I met Weisinger[4] briefly last January, at a dinner of the Am. Fiction Guild. Whether you would like New York is an open question. I detest it—but individuals differ. As for the British reprint business—I have no confidence in it, though Schwartz says he worked it for Edmond Hamilton.

Yes—I read "Fantazius Mallare",[5] but thought it rather dull & artificial . . . a conscious & laboured effort to be cleverly obscure. Hecht's real contribution to literature is "Erik Dorn"—the first full-length study of the disintegrated "modern" type to achieve publication in America. It appeared around 1920, & has since been republished in the Modern Library. I wish Hecht had stuck to that kind of material.

Don't bother with old De Castro unless you have the time, & think you could make real use of his ideas. By the way—it turned out that old 'Dolph used to know Henry Kuttner's parents very well, & Kuttner is now in touch with him.

Barlow is still here, but aiming to head westward before long. Aug. 15 we had an enjoyable trip to Newport—repeating my solitary jaunt of the previous month—& on the 20th (my 46th birthday) we explored ancient Salem & Marblehead ("Arkham" & "Kingsport") in company with young Sterling & another friend. Sterling is well recovered from his operation, & has passed his Harvard entrance examinations with highest honours. He has been spending the summer on the shore at Lynn (a city which is close to both Salem & Marblehead), & is as brown as an Indian at present. On this occasion we took in all the antiquarian sights of the Arkham–Kingsport zone—exploring several museum-houses including the prototype of Hawthorne's "House of the Seven Gables", the (18th cent.) Ropes house, the so-called "Witch House"—the erstwhile home of Judge Jonathan Corwin, where several witch-suspects were examined in 1692—the ancient Hathaway house (a typical 17th century edifice, restored), & some others. Some day you surely must get around this way & absorb a few of New England's brooding antiquities—I'm sure you could do it without meeting the fate of your counterpart in the "Haunter". Last Thursday & Friday Barlow visited cousins in ancient New Bedford & saw such things as the whaling museum (with its marvellous half-size reproduction of the barque *Logada* housed in a huge hall), & the actual old whaler *Charles W. Morgan* in its concrete bed on the estate of the late Col. E. H. R. Green. Ar-Ech-Bei starts westward Sept. 1, with probable stops in New York, Washington, & Indianapolis. He will be situated with maternal relations in Kansas City—his future address being % Langworthy, 810 W. 57th St. Terrace, Kansas City, Mo. His visit here has been extremely pleasant—but now I must buckle down to work—with only one more visitor (James F. Morton) scheduled for the season. Hell, but I hate to see the autumn come! ¶ Yrs by the Pillar of Pnath—Ech-Pi-El

*Notes*

1. Finlay illustrated both "The Haunter of the Dark" (*WT*, December 1936) and "The Thing on the Doorstep" (*WT*, January 1937).
2. HPL to R. H. Barlow (23 July 1936): "My library has just been increased by a lot of volumes dumped on me by the old lady downstairs, who is packing to leave for a memorable jaunt (3 years in Germany, after which she'll settle in Newport for life's evening). 10-volume Chambers' Encyclopaedia (falling to pieces), & a stupendous Biblical Commentary (the old dame's father was a clergyman) in 5 huge folio volumes printed in Brattleboro, Vt. in 1835. If you want any fine points of Scripture settled in future, just ask Grandpa! Other items are excellent—& one (a fine Liddell & Scott Greek Lexicon to replace my old disintegrating copy) is a veritable godsend." (*O Fortunate Floridian* 356).
3. RB published only one tale, "Death Is a Vampire" (September 1944), in *Thrilling Mystery*.
4. Mort Weisinger (1915–1978), editor of *Thrilling Wonder Stories*.
5. By Ben Hecht. The book was banned for obscenity upon first publication.

[64]    [ALS]

The Ancient Hill
—Oct. 15, 1936.

Dear Ludvig:—

Yuggoth! So *Thrilling Mysteries* can actually conceive of such a thing as *too much formula of plot*? I'll take your word for it! Here's hoping your nauseous yarn (in its present form or otherwise) finds a readier haven elsewhere. Good luck, too, with "Brood of Bubastis". Glad you have so many yarns awaiting publication in W T, & hope you won't have any trouble collecting the cash for them.

Haven't had time to read the Oct. W T—pushed to the wall with a revision job,[1] & energy all drained away by the cold weather. Now that one comes to think of it, the absence of old-time names on the contents page is a bit remarkable.

Barlow left Sept. 1, & spent considerable time in N.Y.—seeing Long, Sterling, Koenig, & others. Later he got stalled in Chillicothe, Ohio—having lost a ten-spot & being obliged to telegraph his mother for funds. Then a pause in Indianapolis to see Miss Moore. His present permanent address is % *H. M. LANGWORTHY, 810 WEST 57th ST. TERRACE, KANSAS CITY, MO.* Meanwhile I had an interesting visit from James F. Morton Sept. 11–12–13.

He came from Boston, where he had just won the crossword puzzle championship (for which he'll get a silver loving-cup) at the convention of the Puzzlers' League. We had an interesting series of discussions—interspersed with ice-cream-eating contests & sightseeing—& the brief three days passed all too quickly. No—Hamilton has *not* been here. He had, it seems, *thought* of getting around this way, & had asked Conover for my address; but after all he didn't turn up. I'd have enjoyed meeting him—for despite all the hack tripe of recent years, I can never forget "The Monster God of Mamurth."

Glad to hear of your recent sessions with fellow-writers. Milwaukee seems to be evolving into quite a centre of the craft. I've heard of Gallun[2]— & believe I read something of his once which was rather good.[3] I think I met Hubbard[4] in N.Y. last July, but can't be sure of all the various personalities at that Fiction Guild dinner. And so Kline Sr. & another Binder are moving Manhattanward? Belknap will be pleased. I met Kline's son & Otto Binder, & liked both.

Thanks for the glimpse of your two latest portraits—which certainly embody very vividly the distinctive Prinnian type of genius. You ought to have them in the fan magazines—or in one of the professional sheets (like the old Wonder) which use authors' pictures!

Damn Doubleday-Doran! Well—there are lots of other publishers, any of whom may have better sense. It would have been rather odd, anyhow, if a first novel had landed at the very first try! Hope you can collaborate successfully with Kuttner on "The Black Kiss." Glad you still have time for reading—which I don't seem to have despite the piles of borrowed books hereabouts. Hope you can manage to strike a good translation of *La Bas*[5] in course of time.

Congratulations on the sketch by Mooney—& I hope he'll do justice to Kuttner's "Salem Horror."[6] I shall be watching W T for the latter. Which reminds me that I've lately been hearing from young Finlay, who obtained my address from you. A really vivid & remarkable character—& one, I believe, destined for brilliant progress. I've seen some of his poetry—which is the real stuff despite occasional metrical imperfections. He may be one of those rare & lucky characters who can excel in both literary & pictorial art. I'm certainly glad to know that he is doing the heading for "The Haunter of the Dark".

Have recently been hearing from an interesting character in San Francisco— one Stuart Boland, who claims to be a librarian of some sort, & speaks of travels all over the world during which he has seen strange & forbidden books like *De Vermis Mysteriis*. He has most generously sent me a book on Maya-Aztec civilisation, & a lot of photographs of prehistoric ruins which he took in Mexico.[7]

Autumn advances, but I still get out for occasional rural walks. The other night I attended a meeting of a local society of amateur astronomers, & was astonished at the seriousness & scope of their work in fields like meteor or variable star observation.

Lately recd. the mammoth anniversary F M, & noted your column with interest.[8] Did I mention that Conover is going to continue the reprinting of my *Supernatural Horror in Literature?*[9]

Yrs by the Aura of Nyarlathotep—Abdul Alhazred

P.S. Have just read "The Opener of the Way." Damn good! You generally manage to achieve the *mood* & *atmosphere* which the bulk of the pulpists altogether lack.

## Notes

1. Anne Tillery Renshaw's *Well Bred Speech* (1937).
2. Raymond Z. Gallun (1911–1994), science fiction writer.
3. HPL had read Gallun's "Buried Moon" (*Astounding*, February 1936), but had said of it: "'Buried Moon' had an idea in it, though the best opportunities for developing it were wasted" (HPL to Richard Ely Morse, 9 February 1936 [ms., Harvard]).
4. L. Ron Hubbard (1911–1986), science fiction writer and founder of Scientology.
5. By J.-K. Huysmans.
6. Jim Mooney in fact illustrated Kuttner's "The Salem Horror." He went on to have a distinguished career with DC Comics.
7. See Boland's "Interlude with Lovecraft," *Acolyte* 3, No. 3 (Summer 1945): 15–18; rpt. in Joshi, *Caverns Measureless to Man* 37–39.
8. "Funtasy," *FM* No. 38 (September 1936): 18.
9. WC never did reprint the essay (begun in *FF*), nor did he publish HPL's condensation of the first eight chapters. The latter was finally published as *Supernatural Horror in Literature as Revised in 1936* (Arlington, VA: Carrollton-Clark, 1974); in *LAL* 147–53.

[65]   [ALS]

The Ancient Hill
—Dec. 3, 1936

Dear Ludvig:—
Commiserations on the dental siege! If signs hold good, I'll have to have one myself next year, since by a curious fatality such ordeals have always overtaken me in the "2" & "7" years. My last 5 visits to the D.D.S. occurred in 1912, 1917, 1922, 1927, & 1932. That makes '37 rather ominous! But my tusk-tinkerer is a kindly & conservative soul, since he has left me with all my original set of second teeth still in my head! How much he's left in my purse is, alas, another matter.

I guess I mentioned in my last letter how much I liked "The Dark Daemon". Let me add that I got a comparable kick out of "Mother of Serpents"—whose Haitian atmosphere is convincing, & whose climax is magnificently clever, powerful, & unexpected. I also vastly admired Kuttner's "It Walks by Night".[1] It certainly is a fact that a new generation of writers in the approximately 20-year-old class seems to be replacing the approximately 30-year-old set as W T's best consistent producers. You & Kuttner, as I recently pointed out to another correspondent, are almost alone in your ability to catch the atmosphere of genuine horror & weave it into style as well as subject-matter. You can make the feeling of tension & gathering menace manifest from the start, whereas most of the pulp "weirdists" lose all effect through the use of a brisk, casual, cheerfully commonplace medium tempered only by a few laboriously-introduced adjectives. My first crop of "adopted grandchildren"—Belknap, Wandrei, Talman, &c.—are nowadays either going over to hack science & detective fiction or largely (as in Talman's case) quitting the writing field. Assuredly, it is a newer & younger bunch who are now carrying on the tradition of Poe & the Gothic masters. Paradoxically, it is the youngest authors who are upholding the oldest & soundest main stream in macabre writing! By the way—I haven't yet had time to read the Dec. W T through, but am sure that the tales by you & Kuttner are alone enough to make it one of the superior issues. Finlay's illustration for my "Haunter" is intrinsically excellent, but seems somehow to belie the events of the text as given. Which reminds me that I hope to see "The Shadow in the Steeple"[2] when you get it written. Doc Dexter & the box in the bay would make a fine start—& I'll check up all your local Providence references if you wish. But who can be killed off this time? Since you killed me off in the "Shambler" & I you in the "Haunter", the supply of immediately linked victims would seem to be running low! By the way—I'm sorry your typewriter is on the bum, & hope it may be repaired in time to prepare your next batch of MSS. for professional circulation. Good luck with the ideas now under development!

Congratulations on the acquisition of "La Bas" in so appropriate an edition! I probably told you that I once owned this book, but that it was lost amidst the calamities of a friend to whom I had lent it in 1925.[3] Your Goon library is surely becoming quite an institution—I envy you the Claudius books, which I mean to read some time.

I heard of *The Witches' Tales* through several correspondents, but failed to find a copy on any news stand. Now I see that I didn't miss much! I doubt whether it would make much of a market for our gang.[4] By the way—Crawford is finishing up the "Innsmouth" book at last. 32 bad misprints—which will be corrected in a (probably misprinted!) list of errata.[5]

That sketch of the Haitian idol is highly impressive. Its synthesis of traits from diverse cultural sources ought to be good for much speculation! As for voodoo—I'll do the suggested comparing when the new F M blows in.

I'll surely be looking forward to your accomplishment of that Eastern trip—from which I guarantee you a safe return unless you *choose* to remain in certain cryptic & unsuspected burrows beneath some of our elder necropolises.

Recent local events commonplace. I kept up my outdoor trips later in the season than I had thought I could, & discovered a singular number of attractive & impressive woodland regions, each absolutely new to me, within a surprisingly short distance of here.

Not long ago Kuttner showed me a new story—"Hydra"—in which all three of us figure . . . & are disposed of! By this time getting killed off is becoming a positive habit with us! We shall perhaps each die a fresh death at the hands of each member of the gang. Perhaps if good old Two-Gun hadn't begun so tragically & literally with himself, he'd have killed us all off en masse—perhaps having the entire group go down in a red welter of mutual slashing & decapitation! Shea has also slain me in a recent tale.[6]

"Innsmouth" is out—a slovenly-looking job with 34 misprints & a slipshod binding. Just got *Fanciful Tales*—with 59 misprints in my "Nameless City."

Yrs. by the Ebon Casket—

Abdul Alhazred

[P.S.] Just read your voodoo story.[7] Damn good!

[P.] P.S. You mention *enclosures* in your letter—but there were none. Will be glad to see the Finlaiana when you send it along—& will return it directly to Monstro Ligriv.

*Notes*

1. Both stories in *WT,* December 1936.

2. Presumably "The Shadow from the Steeple," a sequel to HPL's "The Haunter of the Dark." It was not published in *WT* until September 1950.

3. HPL probably refers to the translation of *Là-Bas* by Keene Wallis (as *Down There*).

4. *The Witch's Tales* (Carwood Publishing Co., November and December 1936) was a short-lived pulp magazine inspired by a radio program of the same name. Many of the stories were reprints.

5. As predicted, the errata list contained still more errors.

6. See RB 66.

7. Apparently another reference to "Mother of Serpents."

[66]   [ALS]

Citadel of Leng
—Jany. 7, 1937.

Dear Ludvig:—

Congratulations on your dental & typewriterial rehabilitation! Glad to hear of all the new stories, whose titles sound extremely alluring. You seem to practice a judicious rotation of subject-matter—ghouls, Egypt, Druids, &c. About your flying daemon story—are you sure the title is etymologically sound? *Draconibus* is the dative or ablative plural of the Latin *draco,* & thus means "to or for—or with or by—dragons." If it's Greek you're after, the word for dragon (or its daemonic equivalent) is δρακων (drakōn)—or in compounds δρακοντ- or δρακοντο-. The word for a winged creature is πτερον (pteron)—hence a winged dragon would be δρακοντοπτερον (drakontopteron).

In Greek the word *demon* (δαίμον) does not commonly possess an evil sense, but signifies a god—or fate—or a soul or guiding spirit. The sinister meaning is the least common of all. The best all-around Greek word for a "demon" in *our* sense—a hellish, hideous, nameless Thing—Μορμώ (Mormō) . . . usually considered female. The stem is μορμω hence a winged devil would be μορμόπτερον (Mormopteron). You can take these suggestions for whatever they are worth— or look up parallels in some Greek dictionary at the library. If you like, I'll discuss possible titles further—either Greek or Latin, as you prefer.

Sorry W T continues to be so financially backward, & hope Anger's article will forcibly remind Wright of his shortcomings.[1] I'm enclosing the *Phantagraph* containing this article, which ought to prove decidedly interesting to you. Please be sure to return it to me (though there's no hurry), since I am keeping a complete file of the magazinelet. By the way—on Jany. 4 I received half of my pay for "The Haunter of the Dark".

Haven't yet had time to read Jany. W T, but am tremendously pleased with Finlay's illustration for my story. This has the true touch of genuine imaginative genius which places the artist definitely above all competitors. Even Rankin can't strike the Finlay average . . . . or at least, he hasn't yet. I read Rimel's story[2] in MS. a year or so ago, & thought it particularly good. I'm glad to see him breaking into W T, & hope he'll land stories with increasing frequency. He is among the select few who understand what genuine weirdness is, & his craftsmanship improves slowly & surely. Khut-Nhah's "Hydra" did lay things on a bit thick—& just to prove your prophecy of a flood of auctoricidal fiction right, I may mention that young Shea has again left Grandpa for dead on the floor of 66 College—this time as a cleanly-picked skeleton, in a tale called "The Necronomicon." I'm glad, by the way that Shea is again in touch with you, & that his critical asperity is mellowing a bit. If you think he held a light opinion of your early work, you ought to see how completely he annihilated the "Mts. of Madness" & "Shadow Out of Time"! Thanks, incidentally, for your own encouraging opinion of my efforts as expressed in connexion with "The Thing on the Doorstep". I hope to see your "Steeple" tale when you get it done.

Your Goon Library surely is growing most promisingly. I hope to get around to "Smirt" some time, although in general I'm not much of a Cabell fan. The Claudius books I shall *certainly* read. I don't seem to recall hearing of "Finnley Wren"[3] before, but shall certainly keep it in mind.

Congratulations on the new phonograph & records! Music is my aesthetic blind spot—but nevertheless I appreciate the choice collection of weird effects you are accumulating. Some of these I know. Others I hope to hear at some later period. I shall file your list of titles for future reference. I suppose Comte d'Erlette could pick flaws in your taste from an academic standpoint, but if I were you I wouldn't let that worry me. Did I ever mention that a musician in Los Angeles—one Harold Farnese—once set two of my "Fungi from Yuggoth" to weird music? ("Mirage" & "The Elder Pharos") I never had a chance to hear the result.

And so there's going to be some much-needed consolidation in fan-magazine circles, eh? I assume that Conover will merge F M with the S F C if he acquires it. The same thing ought to happen to other ventures—although it would be hard to achieve when every ambitious youth wants to be a full-fledged editor! There really ought to be only *four* "fan" magazines—one of weird news, criticism, articles, &c., one of similar material related to science-fiction, one of original weird stories, & a fourth of science-fiction specimens. Have you seen *Fanciful Tales*? My "Nameless City" has 59 misprints!

Commiserations on the sub-zero weather! Providence has not suffered so acutely—indeed, we had a warm, rainy spell in mid-December. Whether prophecies of a hard winter will be justified during the latter half of that season one can't say—but I hope not. In the South, the winter has been disagreeably cold—chill reaching even down to Miami.

I trust your Yuletide was suitably festive. Ours here was commendably cheerful—including a turkey dinner at the boarding-house across the garden, with a congenial cat meandering among the tables & finally jumping up on the window-seat for a nap. We had a tree in front of the hearth in my aunt's living-room—its verdant boughs thickly festooned with a tinsel imitation of Florida's best Spanish moss, & its outlines emphasised by a not ungraceful lighting system. Around its base were ranged the Saturnalian gifts—which included (on my side) a hassock tall enough to let me reach the top shelves of my bookcases, & (on my aunt's side) a cabinet of drawers for odds & ends, not unlike my own filing cabinets, but of more ladylike arrangement & aspect. Of outside gifts the most distinctive was perhaps that which came quite unexpectedly from our young friend Conover—for lo! When I had removed numberless layers of corrugated paper & excelsior, what should I find before me but the yellowed & crumbling fragments of *a long-interred human skull!* Verily, a fitting gift from a youthful ghoul to one of the hoary elders of the necropolitan clan! This sightlessly staring monument of mortality came from an Indian mound not far from the sender's house—a place distinguished by many striking archaeological exploits on the part of Maryland's "Dr. Stugatche" & his young friends. Its condition is such as to make its reassembling a somewhat ticklish task—so that I may reserve it for the ministrations of some expert mender like Bobby Barlow upon the occasion of a future visit. Viewing this shattered yield of the ossuary, the reflective fancy strives to evoke the image of him to whom it once belonged. Was it some feathered chieftain who in his day oft ululated in triumph as he counted the tufted scalps sliced from coppery or colonist foes? Or some crafty shaman who with mask & drum called forth from the Great Abyss those shadowy Things which were better left uncalled? This we may never know—unless perchance some incantations droned out of the pages of old Ludvig Prinn's *De Vermis*

*Mysteriis* will have power to draw strange emanations from the lifeless & centuried clay, & raise up amidst the cobwebs of my ancient study a shimmering mist not without power to speak. In such a case, the revelation might be such that no man hearing it would any longer live save as one of those hapless entities 'who laugh, but smile no more'![4]

Benedictions—Yours by the Ghooric Key
—Abdul Alhazred

*Notes*

1. "Fantastic Bread & Butter; or, the Mystery of the Missing Authors"; see Appendix.
2. "The Disinterment" (revised by HPL).
3. By Philip Wylie.
4. Poe, "The Haunted Palace" (l. 48).

[67]    [ALS]

The Ancient Hill—
[January 25, 1937]

Dear Ludvig:—

Commiserations on the varied ills! I, too, have been feeling like hell—with my old winter malady of swelled feet (thank Yuggoth it isn't swelled head!) plus a kind of mixed indigestion & general weakness. Here's to an early summer!

Congratulations on the eventual sale of "The Black Kiss"—or something purporting to be such. Hope the novel revision will result in something, & that the other ventures will all adequately mature, each in its particular way.

Thanks for the interesting Finlay pictures—which will go back to their creator in due season. Held up to the light under proper magnification, they make quite a showing—though colour photography is obviously no finished art. I wish I could see the oil originals of those landscapes.

The combined F M–S F C surely ought to be quite a paper, & I await its first issue with much interest. The recent separate issues of its components were both highly creditable. Glad you've seen the new *Phantagraph*. Actually, Wright does not even attempt to answer some of Anger's more telling points—especially about financial policy—but a visible improvement in the W T paying schedule forms a still better answer.

Don't let the would-be collaborators interfere with your original work—but now & then you may find that some of them have ideas which your technical skill & knowledge of the pulp field could advantageously develop. If you want bold & nutty scientific concepts to work on, get in touch with the kid who is about to edit *Supramundane Stories*—Nils H. Frome, Box 3, Fraser Mills, B.C., Canada.[1] Some of his vague & unformulated concepts would do credit to an Einstein or a de Sitter on the one hand, or to an asylum case on the other hand! I've been obliged to decline the honour of collaborating with this fertile young genius—but if you feel like dressing up some highly intricate concepts for *Astounding, Wonder,* or *Amazing,* he's your man!

As to your cheerful little prophecy of a European war by next July, with the U.S. soon in it—all I can say is that it seems to me about a 50–50 matter. It depends on how much the interested nations think they can get away with—& that in turn depends on the impression they get of the way the most powerful less-interested nations will be likely to side. The segregation of the war in Spain, even though millions of Italians and Germans fight on one side & millions of French & Russians fight on the other, is not a complete impossibility. Of course, if a conflict did become general, then the U.S. would be in it sooner or later. But it takes a bolder guy than I to make any prophecies of a definite sort. The stronger the U.S. & Great Britain arm, the better for world peace—whether it be a matter of preserving it or restoring it. Hope for the best, & look to the battleships, aircraft, tanks, & heavy artillery.

Glad you've had some good lecture opportunities—I've heard quite a few spiels this winter, on subjects as varied as Peruvian antiquities, Italian Romanesque architecture, & the relation of biology to philosophy. Congratulations, too, on the growing library.

It certainly pleased me to hear that you & good old Mocrates had got together at last, & I trust that my fellow-greybeard didn't malign me too violently. As for my fondness for ice cream—bless my soul, but I thought you knew all about that! Didn't you see Baldwin's writeup of me in the April '35 *Fantasy Magazine?* I've never been in a real championship contest with other noted ice-creamists like Bernard Dwyer, old Jim Morton or yourself, & have seldom eaten more than two quarts at a time. But some day—when you get east—we'll have to arrange for a series of Battles of the Century. When you pass through N.Y. you can take on Morton, & I'll sign to fight the winner. Then (assuming I win) either to lick Dwyer or go down gamely. Dwyer could lick me on a general dinner proposition—but I'm an ice-cream specialist!

Your Bubastis story is excellent, despite the dubious light in which it presents my beloved felidae.

Yrs by the Vengeance of Bast—
    Luveh-Keraph

P.S. One A. L. Widner, Jr., 114 Co. C.C.C., Waterbury, Vermont asks me to ask you whether you would deign to drop him a line of encouragement. He seems to have aspirations in the direction of fantastic art & literature.

*Notes*

1. Some of HPL's letters to Frome can be found in *Uncollected Letters* 38–42.

*Natalie Hartley Wooley*

# Letters to Natalie H. Wooley

[1]     [AHT]

66 College St.,
Providence, R. I.
July 7, 1933

Dear Mrs. Wooley:—

In reply to your inquiry of the 2nd., which *Weird Tales* has just forwarded, I must hasten to admit that the obscure & sinister volumes so often mentioned by various contributors are entirely fictitious. This included the "Necronomicon" (an idea of mine), the Pnakotic Manuscripts (also mine), the Book of Eibon (a fancy of Clark Ashton Smith's), & the *Unaussprechlichen Kulten* or "Black Book" of von Junzt (an invention of Robert E. Howard's.) Also—the mystical daemons so often referred to in sundry tales—Tsathoggua, Yog-Sothoth, Nyarlathotep, Shub-Niggurath, &c.—are purely figments of the modern imagination, though modelled more or less in imitation of the darker figures of folklore. This creation of artificial gods & lands & fabulous books is by no means new—as attested by Poe's "dark tarn of Auber", lava-swept "Mt. Yaanek", &c, Machen's "Aklo letters", "Voorish domes", &c., Bierce's "Hastur", "Lake of Hali", &c., Chambers' "King in Yellow", & Dunsany's colourful Pantheon of Pegāna. I suppose it is rather confusing to keep this artificial mythology separate from genuine folklore, & fancy it would not be a bad idea if the editor of W.T. were to publish an explanatory note in the magazine. The fact that different writers borrow one another's artificial figures as embellishments doubtless adds to the illusion which makes this material sound like actual legendry.

In view of your interest in weird material I am enclosing a circular of a brochure by Clark Ashton Smith[1] which I think you would find highly edifying. These fantastic tales are especially fine—and better, on the whole, than any which have appeared in magazine form. The poetry volume mentioned—"Ebony & Crystal"—would also be likely to interest you, since most of the contents is in the same weird vein as Smith's prose—especially the long blank-verse piece called "The Hashish-Eater; or, the Apocalypse of Evil."

With every good wish, & hoping that disillusion about the Necronomicon et al. may not decrease your pleasure in the contents of W.T., I am

> Yrs most cordially & sincerely,
> H P Lovecraft

*Notes*

1. *The Double Shadow and Other Fantasies.*

[2]     [AHT]

July 18, 1933

Dear Mrs. Wooley:—

In reply to yours of the 13th I am very glad to say that I *can* recommend an almost endless variety of books which would assist you in developing a weird-fictional style & mood. These are not so much volumes on magic & folklore as actual specimens of spectral fiction itself—for after all, there is no teacher like *example,* & the best course possible for a literary beginner is to read as many really good specimens as he can of the sort of work he wishes to produce. "Dracula" isn't bad—but it is very mediocre as compared with the real classics of supernatural literature. And of course you realise that the contents of *Weird Tales* is largely unutterable, low-grade junk not even touching the fringe of genuine artistic expression.

Now rather than prepare a fresh long catalogue of helpful weird books, I am lending you under separate cover a copy of a long-defunct privately-printed magazine containing a fairly ample survey of the subject[1]—not only a list of titles, but enough historical & descriptive matter to give you some idea of weird fiction in general, & aid you in choosing what you would like to read first. I prepared this article 7 years ago, hence it does not include certain recent items which distinctly deserve mention; but on the whole I think it ought to be helpful in starting a course of fantastic reading. I will add here the titles of the recent or recently noted books which I would include in any second edition of the text:

### *Novels*

~~H. B. Drake—The Shadowy Thing (1928)~~          —after all, I doubt whether this
John Buchan—Witch Wood (1927)                    book quite "makes the grade".
Leonard Cline—The Dark Chamber (1927)
Herbert Gorman—The Place Called Dagon (1927)

### *Short Story Collections*

(only notable items listed)
"Spook Stories," by E. F. Benson—"The Face"
"They Return at Evening" (1928), by H. R. Wakefield—"He Cometh and He
                                                      Passeth By"
                              "The Red Lodge"
                              "The Seventeenth Hole at Duncaster"
                              "And He Shall Sing"

"Others Who Returned" (1929), by H. R. Wakefield—"The Cairn"
"Look Up There"
"Blind Man's Buff"
"The Runagate's Club" (1928), by John Buchan—"The Green Wildebeest"
"The Wind in the Portico"
"Skule Skerry"
"Ghosts, Grim & Gentle" (1926), by Joseph Lewis French—
H. G. Wells—        "The Ghost of Fear"
Ralph Adams Cram—  "The Dead Valley
Guy de Maupassant—  "On the River"
"The Ghost Book" (1927), by Cynthia Asquith
Algernon Blackwood—  "Chemical"
Hugh Walpole—        "Mrs. Lunt"
L. P. Hartley—       "A Visitor from Down Under"
Walter de la Mare—    "A Recluse"

Going back to the printed article—in case it is hard to find a place to start amidst so many titles, let me recommend a few authors & books as especially notable & valuable in the weird-fictional field. These titans are as follows—the best weird work being here mentioned:

Poe—virtually all his short stories—especially "Fall of the House of Usher", "Ligeia", "Metzengerstein", "Ms. found in a Bottle", "Case of M. Valdemar", "Arthur Gordon Pym", & poems "Ulalume", "City in the Sea", "The Sleeper", &c.
Algernon Blackwood—"John Silence—Physician Extraordinary"
"Incredible Adventures"
Any collection containing "The Willows" (long short story)
Arthur Machen————"The House of Souls" (collection—don't miss "The White People" and "The Great God Pan")
"The Three Impostors"
"The Hill of Dreams"
"The Terror"
"The Shining Pyramid"
Lord Dunsany—        "The Gods of Pegana"
"Time & the Gods"
"The Sword of Welleran"
"A Dreamer's Tales"
"The Book of Wonder"
"Five Plays"
"Plays of Gods and Men"

Montague Rhodes James—"Ghost Stories of an Antiquary"
                        "More Ghost Stories"
                        "A Thin Ghost and Others"
Walter de la Mare—      "The Connoisseur & Other Stories" (read
                            "Mr. Kempe" & "All Hallows")
                        "The Riddle, &c." (read "Seaton's Aunt")
Ambrose Bierce—         "In the Midst of Life"
                        "Can Such Things Be?"
Robert W. Chambers—     "The King in Yellow"
M. P. Shiel—            "The Pale Ape & Other Stories" (read "The
                            House of Sounds")
                        "The Purple Cloud"

A fair number of these volumes ought to be available in the libraries of the two Kansas Cities. Later I can send you a list of the weird items in my own collection—any of which I would be glad to lend by mail, as I often do to fellow-strugglers in the weird-fictional field.

Now as for actual magical folklore—the real magical works of the Middle Ages, whose titles sound so impressive when quoted, are for the most part insufferably dull & puerile. One or two of the names I have dragged up are real—such as Remigius' "Daemonolotreia" & Glanvil's "Saducismus Triumphatus"[2]—but they are enough to put any ordinary reader (including myself) to sleep. If you want any of the actual magical formulae used by mediaeval would-be sorcerers, the best things to consult are the numerous works of *Arthur Edward Waite,* or translations of the works of that 19th century Frenchman who called himself *"Eliphas Levi".* Other good items are the books on vampirism & witchcraft by the eccentric living author, *Rev. Montague Summers,* the volume "Demonology & Witchcraft" by *Sir Walter Scott,* and the important anthropological study "The Witch-Cult in Western Europe" by *Margaret Alice Murray.* Another cycle of impressive-sounding folklore or pseudo-folklore is that sponsored by the modern *theosophists.* Some of this is undoubtedly genuine Hindoo myth, but I suspect that the cult of theosophists has mixed with it a great deal of synthetic fakery of 19th century origin. The best books of this sort of thing to read are the following:

    Besant, Annie—The Pedigree of Man
    Blavatsky, Helena—The Secret Doctrine
    Leadbeater—The Inner Life
    Scott-Elliot, W.—Atlantis & the Lost Lemuria
    Sinnett, A. P.—Esoteric Buddhism

More of this stuff can be found in the catalogues of the Occult Society, 604 Locust St., Philadelphia, Pa. Those theosophical mystifications involved vast gulfs of time & cycles of change—pre-human aeons & life coming from other planets—not found in other folklore.

Yrs most cordially & sincerely,

H. P. Lovecraft

*Notes*

1. HPL's "Supernatural Horror in Literature."

2. *Remigius* is the Latinized form of the name Nicholas Remi (1530–1612). *Daemonolatreia* was published in Latin in 1595; there have been two translations, one in German in 1693 and one in English in 1930 (by Montague Summers; as *Daemonolatry*). It is a sort of guidebook to witch-hunting for witchcraft judges. HPL mentioned it in "The Festival" (*CF* 1.410) and "The Dunwich Horror" (*CF* 2.452). *Saducismus Triumphatus* of Joseph Glanvill (1636–1680) condemned skepticism about the existence and supernatural power of witchcraft and included seventeenth-century folklore about witches. It, too, is mentioned in "The Festival" (*CF* 1.410).

[3]     [AHT]

Aug. 6, 1933

Dear Mrs. Wooley:—

[. . .]

However—don't bother with weird fiction at all unless you feel a genuine inclination toward it. It is the most difficult of all material to market professionally, & the circle of those who truly enjoy & appreciate it is always discouragingly small. The only reason I write it is that I virtually can't help it— weirdness & phantasy having fascinated me more than anything else (except perhaps antiquarianism in general, as expressed in architecture & other glamourous [*sic*] survivals of the past) ever since I could walk or talk. It is virtually the only field in which I have anything to say fictionally—hence my restriction to it is scarcely a matter of choice. The demand for weird fiction is always faint & narrow, & on the higher literary levels is so interwoven with special conventions & restrictions that the spontaneous & unconventional writer has scarcely any chance. Again & again I have had some publisher ask to see my stuff with a view to book publication—& then fling it back with a polite note of regret. Just now I've had a request from the Knopf firm, & have sent in seven of my best tales—but I know very well that they will come straggling homeward in the end.

[. . .]

Yrs most cordially & sincerely,

H P Lovecraft

[4]    [AHT]

Aug. 30, 1933

Dear Mrs. Wooley:—

[. . .]

As for the rejection of mss.—experience will demonstrate to you the melancholy truth that certain ones will always come back repeatedly, no matter how proficient a workman you become. The average 'pulp magazine' contributor—like Quinn or Derleth or Long or Howard—gets back about half his mss. several times, & perhaps fails permanently to place ¼ to ⅓ of them. All of the exquisite phantasies in that brochure of Smith's have been rejected 4 or 5 times—by *W.T.*, *Strange Tales, Astounding Stories, Amazing Stories, Wonder Stories, Magic Carpet*, &c. What is wanted professionally is not sheer excellence, but conformity to a certain artificial convention. When a writer lays aside the artistic motive & studies the market cold-bloodedly (as E. Hoffmann Price has begun to do)—analysing editorial whims & deliberately catering to them—his percentage of acceptances rises perceptibly. Not everyone, though, can do this. I can't—& as a result a vast amount of my stuff remains universally rejected. As for editors' reading methods—they usually skim along in haste, but claim to keep on until they find something which makes them certain they can't use the ms. in question. In the larger magazine offices all the preliminary reading is done by "readers" below the status of editor. They are told to reject whatever is flagrantly & obviously unsuitable, but to pass all other material on to an editor for a second & more expert reading. In book-publishing houses it takes the unanimous verdict of a jury of half a dozen or more readers & editors to get a ms. accepted. I ought to know—for I have twice had a collection of tales turned down . . . . once by Putnam's & again by the Vanguard, though in each case I submitted it only at the publisher's request. Just now I have had a letter from the Knopf firm asking to see some things with a view to *possible* book publication—but after my former experiences I realise how little such a request means. These fellows merely look the field over once in a while to be sure they aren't missing anything. I've sent along some tales—merely in the perfunctory spirit of leaving no stone unturned—but they'll come back in time with a note of polite regret. One must become virtually discouragement-proof if one is to persist in professional auctorial endeavour. It is impossible ever to avoid a certain proportion of rebuffs unless one belongs to that rare & happy minority who catch the popular fancy—partly by accident & partly through certain inborn or acquired gifts.

Yrs most cordially & sincerely,

H P Lovecraft

[5]     [AHT]

Oct. 24, 1933

Dear Mrs. Wooley:—

[. . .]

I myself have made the most of the autumn scenery, taking long rural walks nearly every afternoon. I generally ride out some main highway on a 'bus, & then strike across country on foot till I reach another bus-traversed highway along which I can return. In this way I have come upon some very primitive & unspoiled regions; with narrow rutted roads winding betwixt briar-twined stone walks, ancient gambrel-roofed farmhouses (some 200 or 250 years old) with their barns, byres, & gnarled orchards, picturesque well-sweeps & moss-coated water mills, belts of shadowy woodland, distant village spires & glimpses of curving river-valley . . . . all those traditional marks of long, continuous habitation which the older parts of the new world took over bodily from the European world. The other day I came upon a very old house built by a lineal ancestor of my own—Thomas Clemence—in 1654. It has a great pilastered stone chimney & is still in excellent condition despite its age. The autumn here has been exceedingly mild as a whole. The foliage turned late, though with a less vivid splendour than in some years. The gorgeousness is now at its height—some trees are losing leaves, while a few are still green, but betwixt these extremes a kaleidoscope of colour reigns. In town, the crimson of the ivy on ancient buildings & high garden walls is ineffably lovely. I once rode near Chelmsford—a beautiful region, although the city of Lowell is a depressingly ugly industrial centre populated largely by low-grade factory workers—Slav & Latin immigrants.

The fascination of *words in themselves* is certainly very deep & potent for those who are truly sensitive to musical sound & subtle imaginative associations. I feel this fascination profoundly, & try to guard against succumbing to it so excessively that meaning will be sacrificed for mere verbal colour. One can run to disastrous excesses in this direction—Arthur Symons & the later Swinburne being typical victims of the tendency. Still, on the whole I think it is better to err on that side than on the opposite side of barren, unimaginative literalism. My own style is in a state of flux. The earlier things I wrote (like the reprinted "Festival") were undeniably overcoloured, whilst my later stuff ("Witch House" &c.) tends to be diffuse. Just now I am pausing & taking stock, with a view to further experimentation.[1] Absence of much conversation is probably a permanent feature of my style, because the tales I write concern *phenomena* much more than they concern people. The real centre of significance in a weird tale is *not a person but a state of things*—hence it is inadvisable to put too much emphasis on a manner of narration which throws human characters preëminently in the foreground. So much for *conscious* reasons. Actually, much of my preference for non-dialogue text is probably due to the essential old-fashionedness of my literary technique. I am a natural-born archaist in all things,

& the imprint of the 18th century & the Poe period is so strong upon me that I can never escape a certain inclination toward the methods of those times.

   I remain

     Yrs most cordially & sincerely,

         H. P. Lovecraft

*Notes*

1. See RB 14, n. 3.

[6]  [AHT]

                     Nov. 27, 1933

Dear Mrs. Wooley:—

     [. . .]

  As to a good age to be born into—I have my doubts about the future, since in my opinion the existing civilisation has passed its peak & is sliding into a slow downward course like that of Rome in the late Antonine period. My view is pretty well upheld by Spengler in his monumental "Decline of the West". War & graft will never cease, since they are merely the working-out of permanent & ineradicable human instincts. Of course, ingenuity & common-sense may find ways to reduce the number of major armed clashes, & to check up more closely on political thieving—but the old instincts are still at work, & will use just as much cleverness on their side as can ever be used against them. Every individual & group is & always will be out for everything it can possibly get in any possible way. It is all very well to "outlaw" war—but it will inevitably crop out sooner or later, whether we call it "war" or not. Whenever a group wants a certain thing badly enough, & cannot get it through peaceful channels, it will snatch at it by force the first moment it feels able to defeat whatever combination of forces can be brought against it. And too—whenever any loophole for civic theft exists, there will always be plenty of officials to take advantage of it. "Progress" is an illusion. The most civilised period of the world's history was probably the age of Pericles in Athens—around B.C. 450. However—mechanical science, as distinguished from real depth of thought, will certainly advance considerably before the next dark age & fresh start. "Space ships" of the traditional scientifictional sort are perhaps a little beyond probability (the obstacles to their operation being really much greater than popular science indicates), but I certainly think that some sort of rocket voyage to the *moon* (whose extreme nearness puts it in a separate category) will be attempted—first with an untenanted projectile, & later perhaps with a human cargo. Whether any living being could survive such a voyage & return is another matter. Probably all current—& future—ideas of other celestial bodies are wholly wrong . . . . especially the popular ideas of cheap science fiction. In the first place, the number of bodies inhabited by highly evolved organic beings at any one period of the cosmos is probably very small. It takes what amounts to a rare *accident* to produce a solar system, & still *another* rare accident, to produce the stream of biological modifications culminating (so far) on this planet as mankind. It is unlikely that any other planet of this system could have complexly evolved denizens—& other similar systems (if there are any) we can never know. Moreover—the results of complex evolution on other spheres would undoubtedly differ far more from anything we recognise as life than to any of the "Hul Jok" or "Korus Kan" of the indefatigable & repetitious Mr. Edmond Hamilton.[1] There is also the possibility that life is merely a temporary attribute of this one region & period—the complex structure of matter in other sections of space & time being totally alien to the anabolistic-katabolistic cell-pattern which we locally observe & embody. The more we learn of the cosmos, the more bewildering does it appear. Betwixt Einstein & de Sitter (a lecture by whom I've attended)[2] we now have to envisage a cosmos constantly expanding with no future limit in sight—a case of utter waste & dispersal. At this rate it could not have existed more than 5 billion years in the past—& it's anybody's guess what started it & what existed before it. Probably there is some cyclic expansion & contraction, dispersal & re-combination, in the eternal vortex of force-units.

[. . .]

Yrs most sincerely,

H. P. Lovecraft

*Notes*

1. See RB 6, n.4.
2. The physicist Willem de Sitter (1872–1934) lectured in Providence on 9 November. HPL mentioned him by name in "The Whisperer in Darkness."

[7]    [AHT]

Visiting Frank B. Long, Jr., 230 W. 97ᵗʰ St., New York, N.Y.

Jany. 3, 1934

Dear Mrs. Wooley:—

[. . .]

As for the later stages of poetic progress—one must never be in a hurry. Growth is a slow affair; & the more unconscious & spontaneous it is, the further it is likely to go. Let the images & moods *behind* the poems always be your primary consideration. Form is important enough, but the actual imaginative material takes precedence over it. Use the moods most natural to yourself—you have already made a fine start with that delicate, wistful cosmic weirdness which seems to be a characteristic note of your expression.

[. . .]

Yrs most cordially & sincerely,
H P Lovecraft.

[8]    [AHT]

Feb. 19, 1934

Dear Mrs. Wooley:—

[. . .]

Regarding Oswald Spengler's "Decline of the West"—I can assure you that it is not only a real book, but one of the most famous, monumental, & perhaps epoch-making works of the 20th century! Of all contemporary philosophic historians none is more profound than Spengler; & he explains the present chaos of Aryan civilisation in terms of a theory which—if not precisely correct—at least correctly appraises many tendencies. I enclose an old review of the book, which gives a better idea of it than I could. Please return this sometime, though there is no hurry about it. I've read the work, & was profoundly impressed—though I think Spengler pushes the parallel betwixt a culture & a biological organism rather far. The "Decline" was written before the World War. Spengler has a new book out now—"The Hour of Decision"—in which he attacks democracy & calls for a strong Caesarism with aristocratically concentrated wealth & power. He is right in many of his contentions, but I doubt if his solution is correct unless it guarantees a large amount of security to the herd. The Nazis were very fond of Spengler at first, but are now shying off from him because he does not endorse some of the shakily pseudo-scientific concepts on which their regime is based. You'll find parts of the "Decline" pretty dry & involved reading, but it's certainly worth tackling.

[. . .]

Yrs most cordially,
H P Lovecraft

[9]    [AHT]

66 College St.,
Providence, R.I.
Nov. 22, 1934

Dear Mrs. Wooley: —

Glad you found recent F Fs interesting. That story of mine was an old specimen—written in 1919.[1] I liked Smith's "Primal City" exceedingly—both on my recent re-reading & when I saw the manuscript a year ago. I confess that I find something rather fascinating in worms & decay once in a while—in fiction only! Actually, CAS's work is somewhat uneven. Some of the tales fall into routine patterns—but every now & then he soars far out of the rut & achieves something truly impressive. He is certainly, in the long run, the greatest writer connected with W T. I didn't know he had a poem in *Asia*.[2] Undoubtedly it is one which I've read in ms. at one time or another. Frank Owen has considerable skill in delicate fantasy, though there is a certain hollowness or mawkishness about some of his Orientales.[3] He was the especial bane of the late Henry S. Whitehead—but I never shared HSW's harsh opinion. Seabury Quinn, so far as his novel run of fiction is concerned, is not really in the weird class. His tales are obvious mechanical concoctions whose artificiality & superficiality appear in every paragraph—& which have not a single touch of truly weird atmosphere. He knows this as well as anybody else, but writing is simply a money-making business to him. Mrs. La Spina is distinctly mediocre—full of clichés & cheap romantic devices. Two or three of her older stories weren't bad, but her latest attempt was pitifully weak. The real find of the past year is Miss Moore, whose work has a genuine touch of the cosmic strangeness & brooding atmosphere which go to make authentic weirdness. Whether she will keep to her present level or fall into the romantic artificialities of cheap popular fiction still remains to be seen. The insidious cheapness of the pulp magazine tradition always 'gets' a new author if he is not alertly on guard—as witness the cases of Quinn, Price, Hamilton, Williamson, Merritt, & dozens of others who started out as sincere writers & ended up as popular herd-caterers. Right now Long is in the throes of a similar melancholy devolution. No—I did not know that Ella Wheeler Wilcox ever wrote any verse which might be called weird.[4] Hope I can come across some of those illustrated poems. I can well imagine what W. T. Benda would do with a spectral or macabre theme.[5]

I have not read "The Fruit of the Family Tree", though I meant to do so when I saw it reviewed. Wiggam, like Prof. J. B. S. Haldane, believes that much will be done in future toward the artificial development of homo sapiens; but I doubt very much whether such development can ever reach more than a tiny fraction of the extremes they postulate. In the first place, the *complexity* of the laws governing organic growth is enormous—so enormous that the number of unknown factors must always remain hopelessly great. We can discover & apply a few biological principles—but the limit of effectiveness is soon reached. For example—despite all the advances in endocrinology & all the experiments in glandular rejuvenation, there is no such thing as a permanent or well-balanced staving-off of senescence & dissolution. And in the second place, the fact that human beings live by emotion & caprice rather than by reason will probably prevent the widespread application of any unified plan of eugenics. Resistance to organised effort will be tremendous—& can be overcome only in a few instances . . . . mainly in strongly centralised fascist nations. In the United States, for example, the silly & criminal sentimentality arrayed against any rational racial discrimination is of appalling magnitude. What is more—there really is no *one* idea of racial excellence. Even if the *principle* of eugenic control were accepted by a nation, there would remain a constant struggle among various factions advocating different *goals* of development. One group would advocate the cultivation of this or that group of emotions, or the establishment of this or that blood mixture, while another would campaign ceaselessly for a directly opposite result. Thus the Nazis in Germany want to get rid of every trace of Jewish blood, while other groups believe that the highest intellectual qualities in all races come through prehistoric & forgotten infusions of Semitic blood! Amidst such a confusion of objects, what single policy could ever gain an effective ascendancy? However—this is not to say that eugenics will remain utterly neglected. There are, of course, certain lines of action where virtual unanimity exists; & along those lines considerable progress may be expected. It is, for example, agreed that hereditary physical disease & mental inferiority ought not to be transmitted—hence within the next half-century the sterilisation of certain biologically defective types will probably become universal throughout the western world, thus cutting down the prevalence of idiocy, epilepsy, haemophilia, & kindred inherited plagues. The Nazis have already put such a policy into effect. There may, too, be *local* efforts (like the present anti-Semitism of the Nazis) to direct the ethnic strain . . . in cases where a certain approximation of unanimousness exists within single nations. The rise of the inferior stocks at the expense of the superior is becoming so obvious & alarming, that some countries may be veritably scared out of their mawkish equalitarian idealism. Some way of checking the increase of alien elements within nations ought to be devised, & the multiplication of the sound stock ought to be encouraged through a planned economy making it practicable for persons with civilised living standards to rear larger families. As it is, the only persons who can rear large families are either a negligible sprinkling of millionaires, or—at the other end of the scale—low grade proletarians (in America, mainly negroes & foreigners) who do not care what squalor they live in. Under unsupervised capitalism, it is absolutely impossible for the average citizen of good stock to rear more than one or two children with the social & educational advantages which he himself enjoyed, & which are necessary for the maintenance of the great tradition of civilisation. The result in four or five generations is obvious—a complete engulfing of the high-grade stock by the fertile & squalid masses. Regarding the negro—I don't know what the outcome will be. But I greatly doubt whether any general assimilation will occur in the United States. Fortunately the American people seem to have no wavering in their determination to keep African blood out of their veins, so that *nothing* could precipitate such a mongrelisation as occurred in Egypt, & in later years in Brazil & the Caribbean nations. It is no novelty for Aryans to dwell as a minority amidst a larger black population—such has been the case in Alabama & Mississippi for decades, & the upper part of South Africa is having a similar experience. But the effect of this condition is generally to heighten rather than relax the colour-line. The white minority adopt desperate & ingenious means to preserve their Caucasian integrity—resorting to extralegal measures such as lynching & intimidation when the legal machinery does not sufficiently protect them. Of course it is unfortunate that such a state of sullen tension has to exist—but anything is better than the mongrelisation which would mean the hopeless deterioration of a great nation. Naturally, the negro resents his relegation to inferiority—but I doubt if he can do anything dangerous about it. Much as he may increase in the United States, his numbers will never be enough to give him a military advantage over the united white population. And his intelligence could never be equal to a contest with the strategic skill & experience of a massed Caucasian nation. Tragic overturns like that of Haiti could occur only in isolated & ill-protected colonies. All that could make a negro uprising succeed, would be the ardent coöperation of a large faction of the white population itself—& in America there is no white element aside from the numerically insignificant fringe of Marxian communists which advocates complete racial equality. The second generation of European immigrants seems to share the anti-negro attitude, while substantial sections of the Indian population—such as the Osage nation—are beginning to put up the bars against the black blood which has measurably tainted the so-called "civilised" tribes of Oklahoma—Creeks, Choctaws, Chickasaws, &c.—& the pitiful aboriginal remnants (like the Seminoles of Florida, or our handful of Niantics & Narragansetts in southern Rhode Island) of the Atlantic coast. The Osages inflict the most drastic penalties on all members of the tribe forming alliances with Africans. Even if some desperate social crisis were to sweep America into communism, I doubt if the racial-equality plank of the Marxist programme would survive. Blood is thicker than doctrine—the reason the Russians can accept an equality programme with equanimity is that they are already largely mongrelised with Mongol blood, & also that they are not faced with the practical problem of dealing with vast hordes of beings as widely & utterly aberrant as the negro. Of the complete biological inferiority of the negro there can be no question—he has anatomical features consistently varying from those of other stocks, & always in the direction of the lower primates. Moreover, he has never developed a civilisation of his own, despite his ample contact with the very earliest white civilisations. Compare the way the Gauls took on the highest refinements of Roman culture the moment they were absorbed into the empire, with the way the negroes remained utterly unaffected by the Egyptian culture which impinged on them continuously for thousands of years. Equally inferior—& perhaps even more so—is the Australian black stock, which differs widely from the real negro. This race has other stigmata of primitiveness—such as great Neanderthaloid eyebrow-ridges. And it is likewise incapable of absorbing civilisation. In dealing with these two black races, there is only one sound attitude for any other race (be it white, Indian, Malay, Polynesian, or Mongolian) to take—& that is to prevent admixture as completely & determinedly as it can be prevented, through the establishment of a colour-line & the rigid forcing of all mixed offspring below that line. I am in accord with the most vehement & vociferous Alabaman or Mississippian on that point, & it will be found that most Northerners react similarly when it comes to a practical showdown, no matter how much abstract equalitarian nonsense they may spout as a result of the abolitionist tradition inherited from the 1850's. If a Russian-inspired communist dictatorship ever tried to force negro equality on the U.S., there is scant question but that the descendants of Wendell Phillips, Charles Sumner, & William Lloyd Garrison would stand side by side with those of Jefferson Davis & John C. Calhoun in fighting its ultimate implications to the death. *Other* racial questions are wholly different in nature—involving wide variations unconnected with superiority or inferiority. Only an ignorant dolt would attempt to call a Chinese gentleman—heir to one of the greatest artistic & philosophic traditions in the world—an "inferior" of any sort . . . . & yet there are potent reasons, based on wide physical, mental, & cultural differences, why great numbers of the Chinese ought not to mix into the Caucasian fabric, or vice versa. It is not that one race is any *better* than any other, but that their whole respective heritages are so antipodal as to make harmonious adjustment impossible. Members of one race can fit into another only through the *complete eradication* of their own background-influences—& even then the adjustment will always remain uneasy & imperfect if the newcomer's physical aspect forms a constant reminder of his outside origin. Therefore it is wise to discourage all mixtures of sharply differentiated races—though the colour-line does not need to be drawn as strictly as in the case of the negro, since we know that a dash or two of Mongolian or Indian or Hindoo or some such blood will not actually injure a white stock biologically. John Randolph of Roanoke was none the worse off for having the blood of Pocahontas in his veins, nor does any Finn or Hungarian feel like a mongrel because his stock has a remote & now almost forgotten Mongoloid strain. With the high-grade alien races we can adopt a policy of flexible common-sense—discouraging mixture whenever we can, but not clamping down the bars so ruthlessly against every individual of slightly mixed ancestry. As a matter of fact, most of the psychological race-differences which strike us so prominently are *cultural* rather than *biological.* If one could take a Japanese infant, alter his features to the Anglo-Saxon type through plastic surgery, & place him with an American family in Boston for rearing—without telling him that he is not an American—the chances are that in 20 years the result would be a typical American youth with very few instincts to distinguish him from his pure Nordic college-mates. The same is true of other superior alien races including the Jew—although the Nazis persist in acting on a false biological conception. If they were wise in their campaign to get rid of Jewish cultural influences (& a great deal can be said for such a campaign, when the dominance of the Aryan tradition is threatened as in Germany & New York City), they would not emphasise the separatism of the Jew but would strive to make him give up his separate culture & lose himself in the German people. It wouldn't hurt Germany—or alter its essential physical type—to take in all the Jews it now has. (However, that wouldn't work in Poland or New York City, where the Jews are of an inferior strain, & so numerous that they would essentially modify the physical type.) As for Japan—that is still a third kind of problem . . . . not that of inferiority, & not merely that of difference, but that of *difference plus tremendous military power & ambition.* None of the other alien race-stocks involve this factor of aggressive physical might. The Chinese are hopelessly divided, & the other dark races have no coherent national fabric behind them, but the Japanese form one of the greatest & most influential nations in the modern world. Indeed, Japan would probably form a major international problem *even if no racial angle existed.* As a *nation*—aside from all ethnic aspects—Japan represents a first-rate power hitherto balked in its quest for a field of expansion. To sustain its own economic life, it has got to overflow & dominate lands with necessary raw materials, & has got to participate in foreign commerce as freely as the other great powers. Coming late on the international scene, it finds colonial domains & trade routes all preëmpted—so what is it to do? Here is a case of logical ambition opposed by the equally logical ambitions of the western powers. Not a *race* question at all. And I fear the solution will have to be a military one sooner or later . . . . unless the western nations will give Japan an absolutely free hand in the Far East. This they are reluctant to do for two reasons: concern for their own Far Eastern interests, & fear of the upbuilding of Japan as the supreme nation of the world. Of these two reasons I deem the first invalid (for commercial tentacles are not worth defending at too high a cost) but believe the second is sound. Therefore I would advocate acting on the second reason alone—giving Japan all she wants on the Asiatic mainland, but blocking all attempts on her part to secure the highway of the Pacific. That would postpone the final showdown for generations—perhaps for centuries—for if Japan had China to exploit, she would not be thinking about Australia & New Zealand & California for a long while. But the integrity of Australia and New Zealand and California as parts of the Anglo-Saxon world must always be maintained—as long as Western civilisation has the strength to maintain it. In the end—as we grow weak & decadent & self-indulgent—Japan will probably dominate the world; but I'm hoping that that period will be thousands of years in the future. She will probably fight Russia again in the next few years—but if the western world is wise, it won't get drawn into that mess.

   With all good wishes—
    Yrs most sincerely,
      H P Lovecraft

*Notes*

1. "Beyond the Wall of Sleep."
2. CAS had three poems in *Asia:* "Flamingoes" (November 1919), "Palms" (April 1920), and "Beyond the Great Wall" (May 1924).

3. Frank Owen (pseud. of Roswell Williams, 1893–1968) contributed many tales of Oriental fantasy to *WT* and other pulps. HPL owned his *The Wind That Tramps the World: Splashes of Chinese Color,* containing stories originally published in *WT.*

4. Ella Wheeler Wilcox (1850–1919), prolific and widely published poet, generally disdained for the saccharine quality of her verse.

5. Władysław Teodor Benda (1873–1948), Polish-American painter, illustrator, and designer.


[10]    [AHT]

66 College St.,

Providence, R.I.

Jany. 26, 1935

Dear Mrs. Wooley: —

As to writing—there is never any need of hurrying about it. Practice & experiment are as useful as complete story-writing—all these processes aid in the development which one seeks. I'm held up in much the same way that you describe—I have a tale ¾ done but I can't get the unbroken leisure needed to finish it.[1] Congratulations on the sales—but I don't believe you need regret not having framed your first cheque. Such a thing never occurred to me when my first literary remuneration came—in August, 1906,[2] nearly 30 years ago. The fact is, I have never been interested in the commercial side of writing—& am even hostile to it. It is the ruination of sincere artistic expression, & has cut off the literary development of more than one writer of splendid endowments. A. Merritt—Seabury Quinn—Edmond Hamilton—and now, before my very eyes, Long, Wandrei, & Price are gradually losing their literary quality as they buckle to the demands of commercial editors. Somehow or other, writing ought to be kept free from business & the profit motive. I absolutely refuse to make compromises—editors can either take what I want to write, exactly as I write it, or go to the devil. Naturally, I can't make original writing pay—but if I can't keep afloat through other ways I'll cheerfully starve. So, in general, the matter of literary remuneration is not one about which I am apt to wax enthusiastic.

I thought you could scarcely fail to see the power & cosmic strangeness in Smith's "Dark Eidolon". To my mind, that is one of the finest things appearing in W.T. recently. It certainly dominates the January number. Bloch is a kid of 17—who has, indeed, been a fairly persistent FF and Eyrie correspondent during the past year. I've given him occasional hints in the direction of fiction-writing, & in recent months he has developed surprisingly. He is still, of course, frankly a beginner—with a youthful tendency to overcolouring & florid rhetoric—but his progress will be worth watching. He is also a pictorial artist of no mean ability—prone to delineate monstrous entities of the sort envisaged by Smith. Another kid worth keeping one's eye on is little Bobby Barlow. He hasn't made W.T. yet, but his last two stories—still unpublished—show a startling improvement over any of the trifles he has had in the FF & amateur press. He likewise is an artist of sorts. Still another "comer"—albeit a little behind Barlow & Bloch—is young Rimel of your native state. He gets steadily better & better. Robert Nelson—a young FF contributor—has more obstacles to overcome; as has Emil Petaja of Milltown, Montana—a violinist whose verse is increasingly good & whose prose has distinct possibilities.

Yes, indeed—voodoo, black magic, the history of the witch-cult, & everything of that sort is surely of the keenest interest to me. I continually borrow the standard classics on the subject from the ample library of the generous H. C. Koenig. If you are interested in Haitian & African necromancy you ought by all means to read the work of W. B. Seabrook—especially "The Magic Island", which is now available in dollar reprint form. These Sinclair articles of which you speak sound very alluring—though I have never seen them or heard of them before. I certainly would be interested in anything of the kind—though you must not go to any trouble in securing vanished instalments. African witch-doctors (& their West Indian descendants), following tribal customs of incalculable antiquity & working on the minds of ignorant devotees trained from infancy to believe in the wildest forms of magic, do indeed create effects of the greatest marvellousness. They are masterly unconscious psychologists & hypnotists; & when we understand how profoundly the human mind can be influenced by suggestion, we need not wonder at the baffling & startling results they are able to secure. Of course, tales of their deeds become heightened through repetition & through sensational newspaper exploitation. Strange as are the things they *do* accomplish, they never accomplish even half of what they are popularly credited with! By the way—if you ever find any books hard to get in K. C., both Koenig & I would be glad to lend you anything we have. So many promising & deeply interested weird fans live in places where bizarre books are unobtainable—places like Milltown, Mont., Asotin, Wash., Auburn, Cal., West Shokan, N.Y., &c. &c.—that we feel we ought to give them the benefit of whatever volumes of the sort we may chance to possess. Hence a rather active programme of borrowing is carried out among "the gang". And it is not only the small-towners who need to borrow—for even the largest city libraries are sometimes devoid of the most important weird items. Thus Koenig & I lend to each other as much as to any third & fourth & further parties . . . right now I have his copy of the famous old "Malleus Maleficarum".[3]

> I remain
>> Yrs most sincerely,
>>> H P Lovecraft

## Notes

1. "The Shadow out of Time."

2. "The Heavens for August: Celestial Phenomena to Happen Next Month" had appeared in the *Pawtuxet Valley Gleaner* in late July 1906. In *CE* 3.

3. See RB 40, n. 1.

[11]   [AHT]

March 28, 1935

Dear Mrs. Wooley:—

Your expressed difficulty in making a story *as long as* 2000 words—something which young Barlow also experiences—excites my deepest envy & impels reflections on the diversity of mankind. I simply can't write a *short* story these days. Words & images well up & demand to be set down; & if I try to boil the text down to smaller compass, the effect is that of a mere *synopsis,* not an actual story. With me, it takes a building-up process to establish the atmosphere of illusion necessary if the story is to seem realistic & convincing. In short, my methods are wholly of about a century ago. I think & feel, fictionally, in the manner of the 1830's—& if I try to get a story across in any other way, the result is a total failure. I tried to make my newest tale brief—but in spite of me it spun itself out to 65 pages . . . . a novelette. I don't like to use conversation, either. It seems to detract, except under certain limited conditions, from the atmospheric tension of a weird tale. For atmosphere-weaving, there is nothing quite equal to plain narrative prose. However—a few weird *dramas* such as Dunsany's "Gods of the Mountain" & "Night at an Inn" have demonstrated how a natural expert can weave horror, dread, & mounting tension with skilfully managed dialogue. I look upon such productions with admiring envy—for I would flounder helplessly in such a medium.

Your recent reading all sounds solid & excellent. Galsworthy, of course, is one of the real titans—perhaps, with Proust, the sole representative of the first rank of novelists in this generation. There is no question but that British writers are far ahead of American in maturity & excellence. This is only natural in view of America's later start. By the same token, Australia is behind the U.S. In recent years America has made great gains on the psychological side of literature, but has retrogressed badly in the matter of style. The language of some of the younger writers is little more than a harsh patois—a slovenly *sermo plebeius.*[1]

I remain Yrs most sincerely
H P Lovecraft

*Notes*

1. I.e., vulgar Latin spoken by the common people.

[12]  [AHT]

% R. H. Barlow, Box 88, De Land, Florida

June 28, 1935

Dear Mrs. Wooley:—

Yes—Robert E. Howard is a notable author—more powerful & spontaneous than even he himself realises. He tends to get away from weirdness toward sheer sanguinary adventure, but there is still no one equal to him in describing haunted cyclopean ruins in an African or Hyperborean jungle. He has written reams of powerful poetry, also—most of which is still unpublished.[1] Just now R E H is travelling amongst the antiquities of New Mexico & sending me a great deal of valuable pictorial matter. As to Miss Moore—her more recent work certainly lacks something of the spontaneity of the earlier pieces—showing an attempt to repeat earlier successes by presenting the same basic elements in a slightly new dress. That is the fault of all prolific writers for the cheap magazines—& Miss Moore unfortunately wants to be a frequent contributor for the sake of financial returns, even at the expense of quality. It would be a pity if one with such unique natural gifts of imagination were spoiled at the very beginning of her writing career—& yet that is exactly what will happen if Miss M. listens to such advisers as E. Hoffmann Price (who is trying to recruit her for the Am. Fiction Guild) & that little flea Forrest J. Ackerman, instead of Barlow & others who are anxious to preserve her undeniable genius in untainted form. I have recently heard directly from Miss M. for the first time, & can attest that her spontaneous gifts of imaginative perception & fantastic vision are tremendous. I doubt, though, whether her general level of achievement will ever equal Clark Ashton Smith's. Mrs. Heald is a revision client of mine, & all her W.T. material is virtually written by me (like Adolphe de Castro's tales, Mrs. Reed's "Curse of Yig", &c.). I am now, however, cutting out as much of this "ghostwriting" as possible—since it involves too much exhausting labour in proportion to the returns. It is amusing that Wright accepts many of my "ghostwritten" tales while rejecting my signed work. Little Bobby Bloch is quite a boy—& as he gets older his work may be expected to improve substantially. Just now he has the juvenile fault of overcolouring & verbal ponderousness. It is curious how he has managed to outdistance Barlow, Rimel, & Petaja in *professional* placements. Barlow, however, is really ahead in imaginative originality.

Yrs most sincerely,

H P Lovecraft

*Notes*

1. Now published as *The Collected Poetry of Robert E. Howard.*

[13]    [AHT]

In N.Y. visiting Long
Dec. 30, 1935

Dear Mrs. Wooley:—
[. . .]
Speaking of Egyptian things—I see no reason why some legend couldn't be developed around the lotos-flower. I don't know of any existing myth of the sort, but fancy that the flower was directly incorporated into architecture & decoration because of its intrinsic beauty. One must not confuse the *lotos-flower* or water-lily of the Nile with the *lotos-tree* or jujube (really more a shrub than a tree) which bears a small fruit & flourishes in Syria & Libya. This lotos-tree (which is often confused in popular folklore with the Nilotic lily) does indeed support a considerable amount of folklore. All are familiar with the myth that the eating of its fruit causes persons to forget their homes & settle down in luxurious indolence—a legend first encountered in the Odyssey, where we see Ulysses in the land of the Lotos-Eaters. Other legends—in Ovid's Metamorphoses—tell of the transformation of mortals into lotos-trees. Letis, the daughter of Neptune, was so transformed as she fled from an evil pursuer. Long afterward Dryope, a young matron of Œchelia, encountered this tree while walking in the woods with her infant son; & having plucked a flower to amuse the child, was herself changed into a lotos by the gods—who thus punished her unintentional mutilation of the metamorphosed Letis. There was also an Egyptian legend which spoke of a supreme deity as seated on a lotos above the mud of the Nile—& from some references it would appear that the lotos *tree*, not the *flower*, is here meant. The Neo-Platonic writer & reputed magician Iamblichus, who died A.D. 330 (a Syrian), elaborates on this point—saying that the roundness of the leaves & fruit of the tree represent the motion of the intellect, that its towering above the mud represents the ascendancy of mind over matter, &c. &c. Still later, Mohammed said that a lotos-tree stands in the seventh heaven at the right of Allah's throne. Interpreters of Hindoo myth often apply the term lotos to the *nelumbo* tree of India. In developing a new bit of legend, it would be well to use the *flower*—the water lily of the Nile—rather than the tree—both because it has been less overworked, & because it is the source of the Egyptian decorative motif. Before formulating any story it would be well to read up about the plant—in encyclopaedias or other works of reference.
    Glad the Clark Ashton Smith material proved of interest. Of the various volumes, "Ebony & Crystal" is still obtainable from C A S at $1.00, while "The Star Treader" can usually be procured by an enterprising rare book dealer at a somewhat higher figure. Samuel Loveman (12 Middagh St., Brooklyn, N.Y.) could probably get you a "S-T"—or Smith himself might know where to find one. Besides these books, Klarkash-Ton has considerable unpublished material on hand—some of which Barlow intends to publish as a

thin volume entitled "Incantations".[1] Of the merit of C A S's poetry there can be no question. I believe I am right in deeming it the earliest of his media of artistic expression, & he has never quite deserted the Muse even in these days of intensive fiction & (beginning last summer) sculpture. Regarding the amatory verse—which, though good, does not quite equal his fantastic verse in power & sheer originality—I greatly doubt whether any of it was written to an actual damsel cherished above others. While I have never questioned C A S minutely concerning biographical details, I am inclined to think that his admirations have been varied & not too serious—in most cases of course idealised for literary purposes. He may have had real persons in mind when writing some of the odes—but whether any two of the latter were addressed to the same person is another matter. It is thus, I think, with most sentimental lyrists. Some of their products are more or less directed toward genuine objects, while others—& perhaps the best—are directed toward imaginary objects synthesised out of memories & idealisations of all the many real ones. Hence the Pyrrha, Lalagé, Lydia, Phillis, Neaera, Leuconoë, Galatea, Lydé, Chloë, &c. &c. of Horace. Just now, miniature *sculpture*—in the softer stones of his region—forms CAS's principal medium of expression. He lately sent me a hauntingly grotesque head called "The Outsider" (based on my story), & sent Barlow a curious conception entitled "The Hyperborean Snake-Eater".

Naturally, I was vastly encouraged by the two *Astounding* acceptances.[2] I don't see the magazine regularly, but glance over odd issues when any of the gang are represented. Most of the stuff is hopelessly artificial, unconvincing, conventional, & hackneyed; although occasional things by Weinbaum & one or two others are worth reading. The recent cheques were indeed life-savers—so much so that I fear they can't be translated into travel, or anything less prosaic than food & rent! Possibly I mentioned writing a new story— "The Haunter of the Dark"—last month. It has not yet been professionally submitted, but a carbon is going the rounds & ought to reach you soon— from little Kenneth Sterling. No hurry about reading it—& when you're through with it you might send it on to *Richard E. Morse, 40 Princeton Ave., Princeton, N.J.* Hope it won't prove unendurably boresome. It is dedicated to young Bloch, as suggested by someone in the "Eyrie",[3] & leaves that rash youth as a rigid corpse staring out a window with glassy, sightless eyes—upon his face an expression of the most paralysing, unutterable fear! The house & westward view described are genuine . . . good old 66 & what I am now looking at out the west window above my desk. The distant church, however, is a less ancient & less sinister object in real life than in the story. It actually dates from the 1870's, & has no spectral associations—being St. John's Catholic (Irish, though the district has since become Italian) church. Federal Hill (the Italian quarter) as seen 2 miles away from my window is really quite a mysterious & picturesque sight—with the dark bulk & spire of St. John's rising against the remote horizon above the huddled roofs.

Yrs most sincerely—

H P Lovecraft

*Notes*

1. Never published as a book, but represented in Smith's *Selected Poems* (1971).
2. See RB 54, n. 4.
3. See RB 55, n. 1.

[14]   [AHT]

66 College St.,
Providence, R.I.
May 2, 1936

Dear Mrs. Wooley:—

[. . .]

As for religious belief in general—I see no reason for entertaining any. All notions of cosmic consciousness & purpose, & of the importance of man in the limitless pattern of the universe, are plainly myths born of the imperfect information of man's early days. Today we know more about the background of the phenomena around us; & our present knowledge includes nothing which could reasonably lead us to assume the existence of a vast manlike intelligence (the idea is childish, since today we know that the very essence of thought, consciousness, & purpose is the organic brain of highly-developed mammals—a thing utterly inconsistent with vague, unparticled force) in space as a whole. Read the late Ernst Haeckel's "Riddle of the Universe"—translations of which any good library ought to have. Religious superstition is fastened on the race only because of the blind, thoughtless handing down of obsolete myths concocted in ages of total ignorance. Today we not only know the natural forces behind all phenomena once thought supernatural, but realise also the psychological & anthropological forces which caused early man to invent the various myths of gods, cosmic purpose, &c. Modern psychologists know that *any* sort of belief, true or false, can be fastened on the inexperienced emotions of a small child through inculcation—hence realise that religions keep alive only through seizing on each new generation before it can reason for itself, & deliberately hypnotising or crippling its infant judgment in favour of the dominant faith. The very fact that religions are not content to stand on their own feet, but insist on crippling or warping the flexible minds of children in their favour, forms a sufficient proof that there is no truth in them. If there were any truth in religion, it would be even more acceptable to a mature mind than to an infant mind—yet no mature mind ever accepts religion unless it has been crippled in infancy. I believe there should be a law prohibiting religious instruction of any sort for persons under 21. The young mind should be taught only *one* thing—the honest & open search for *truth* irrespective of consequences. Nobody's belief in a given thing means anything unless it is entered into with an open & freely reasoning mind. But religion shrinks from the test of *truth*. It is unwilling to present its case without loaded dice—hence continues to insist that infant minds be crippled in its favour. The fact is, of course, that no active & uncrippled mind could possibly accept any sort of religion in the light of to-day's scientific knowledge. The whole basis of religion is a symbolic emotion-alism which modern knowledge has rendered meaningless & even unhealthy. Today we know that the cosmos is simply a flux of purposeless rearrange-ment amidst which man is a wholly negligible incident or accident. There is no reason why it should be otherwise, or why we should wish it otherwise. All the florid romancing about man's "dignity", "immortality", &c. &c. is simply egotistical delusion plus primitive ignorance. So, too, are the infantile concepts of "sin" or *cosmic* "right" & "wrong". Actually, organic life on our planet is simply a momentary spark of no importance or meaning whatever. Man matters to nobody except himself. Nor are his "noble" imaginative con-cepts any proof of the objective reality of the things they visualise. Psycholo-gists understand how these concepts are built up out of fragments of experience, instinct, & misapprehension. Man is essentially a machine of a very complex sort, as La Mettrie recognised nearly 2 centuries ago. He arises through certain typical chemical & physical reactions, & his members gradual-ly break down into their constituent parts & vanish from existence. The idea of personal "immortality" is merely the dream of a child or of a savage.

However, there is nothing anti-ethical or anti-social in such a realistic view of things. Although meaning nothing *in the cosmos as a whole,* mankind obviously means a good deal *to itself.* Therefore it must be regulated by cus-toms which shall ensure, *for its own benefit,* the full development of its various accidental potentialities. It has a fortuitous jumble of reactions, some of which it instinctively seeks to heighten & prolong, & some of which it in-stinctively seeks to avoid or shorten or lessen. Also, we see that certain cours-es of action tend to increase its radius of comprehension & degree of specialised organisation (things usually promoting the wished-for reactions, & in general removing the species from a clod-like, unorganised state), while other courses of action tend to exert an opposite effect. Now since man means nothing in the cosmos, it is plain that his only logical goal (a goal whose sole reference is to *himself*) is simply the achievement of a reasonable equilibrium which shall enhance his likelihood of experiencing the sort of re-actions he wishes, & which shall help along his natural impulse to increase his differentiation from unorganised force & matter. This goal can be reached only through teaching individual men how best to keep out of each other's way, & how best to reconcile the various conflicting instincts which a hap-hazard cosmic drift has placed within the breast of the same person. Here, then, is a practical & imperative system of ethics, resting on the firmest possible foundation & being essentially that taught by Epicurus & Lucretius. It has no need of supernaturalism, & indeed has nothing to do with it. However, an ethical system is always hard to enforce, so that moralists are constantly looking for powerful agents of compulsion. Some favour armed force (& armies & policemen will always be needed), while others look to pride or fear or reason or aesthetic taste. Primitive man used force as a matter of course, but he also realised the powerful compelling nature of superstition. If he could hook up ethical precept with the myth (in which he then believed) of cosmic purpose & will, he would have the most potent of influences working with him to make people accept his preferred code of conduct. It was easy for him to persuade himself & others that the gods liked the various instincts & types of conduct & rational compromises (kindness, honesty, non-encroachment, coöperation, &c.) which make for general harmony among men, & that they disliked the various lawless instincts & types of conduct (egotism, treachery, cruelty, encroachment, lack of social coöperation, &c.) which act in an opposite direction. Hence arose the illusory concepts of "right", "wrong", & "sin" as cosmic matters—& the general popular tendency to identify religion & ethics. Really, of course, there is no essential connexion between religion & ethics. Ethics can stand on its own feet without religion, & the time has come in which it must do so to an increasing degree. Its enforcing agencies—aside from physical power—should be reason & taste & pride; as indeed they are now among the enlightened. It is interesting to observe that many of the world's religions tacitly recognise the lack of connexion between faith & ethics by loftily ignoring the latter. Hellenic religion tended to leave ethics more or less to the philosophers, while even Protestant Christianity had its Antinomian sect (in Massachusetts Bay Colony in 1638 et seq) which proclaimed that "salvation" was a matter of sheer faith irrespective of conduct. Religion has served its purpose, & is meaningless in the light of today's understanding of the universe. We now perceive *that there is no "why" of things*—that, indeed, the whole concept of a "why" is based upon an obsolete perspective. Things simply are—forming momentary phases of ceaseless rearrangement of forces which always have existed & always will exist. Why should they be otherwise? The existing patterns are merely basic conditions of entity—which have nothing to do with the transient ideas & wishes of the negligible organisms of our planet. We now understand the origins of those ideas & wishes, & realise that they are simply automatic nervous phenomena having nothing to do with reality. If it amuses any childish mind to juggle words & apply the name "god" or "the gods" to the automatic principle of regularity in the cosmos, no one need object. Words are pretty things to play with. But we must remember that this pattern principle has not the slightest resemblance to the various deities of traditional religions. It is not a "mind". It has no consciousness or purpose. It doesn't know we exist or care what we do.

It has nothing to do with the aesthetic or utilitarian human concepts of "right" & "justice". It is simply a *condition*—like the existence of an atmosphere around the earth. Epicurus vaguely realised all this when he said that although the gods may exist, they never concern themselves with the affairs of mankind.

Today time spent in considering religion is simply wasted. What is needed is *scientific social vision* & *coöperation,* with the rational happiness & balanced development of men, individually & collectively, as its sole object. That is, we need to cultivate a practical morality based on common sense, good taste, & modern sociology . . . doing which, we may well leave supernatural belief & the grovelling worship of unconscious force-patterns to the ignorant & the hyper-emotional. Read H. L. Mencken's "Treatise on the Gods"—& also Nietzsche's "Genealogy of Morals". The various brochures of Joseph McCabe, published by the Haldeman-Julius Co. at Girard in your own state, are also enlightening. A good article on the vanishing of religious belief among modern thinkers will be found in *Harper's Magazine* for August, 1934—"Religious Beliefs of American Scientists", by James H. Leuba, Prof. of Psychology at Bryn Mawr.

However—despite my disagreement with its philosophical assumptions, I appreciate none the less the grace & excellence of your essay "Intimations—The Hand in the Dark", which I return herewith plus a few very trifling changes of text. This sketch is extremely well-phrased & imaginatively developed, & certainly ought to quiet any apprehensions of yours regarding the quality of your writing. I hope it may eventually appear in print—either in the N.A.P.A. or elsewhere. My objections are solely against the logic of certain assumptions—for example, I see no reason why the ability of the human imagination to conceive certain aesthetically impressive & emotionally gratifying passages of literature (an ability fully explained by materialistic psychologists) should be regarded as "proof" that man has a 'divine spark' or that he cannot (as he certainly will) become 'drifting dust on a burned-out planet.' What this imaginative ability proves is merely that man is a very complexly organised form of matter—that he stands very high in the scale of development as measured by degree of removal from primitive unorganised substance. This, no one wishes to deny. Man is indeed by far the most advanced product of the cosmic flux of which we have any direct knowledge—*but what has this high status to do with the quality of permanence* (i.e., the mythical condition of "immortality") *or with the kind of relationship which the species has with the basic force-patterns of cosmic entity?* It is absurd to think that any being very highly developed must be essentially different *in principle* from beings of much lower development . . . . or, conversely, that it is a slur upon the greatness of a high species to declare that it is not the especial & eternal pet of a conscious & personified cosmos. Joseph McCabe has aptly & truly said that there is no difference *in kind* (despite the enormous difference *in degree*) between the howl of a dog & a symphony of Beethoven. Still—all this doesn't make your concept any the less poetical, or your essay any the less graceful. Congratulations on a good piece of work!

Regarding the "Knickerbocker" History of New-York—this is the famous (originally anonymous) work of Washington Irving which gave rise to the popular use of the word "Knickerbocker" as a term for the New-Amsterdam Dutch & their present descendants. Nieuw Nederland is the *Dutch* form of the name New-Netherland. Irving's form (Nieuw Nederland*es*) is not correct, but was perhaps suggested by the debased Dutch of the province. This book[1] was originally written in 1809, & is primarily a comic or satirical performance . . . . a parody on history, although it includes many actual facts & dates among its broad caricatures & grotesque invented anecdotes. The book is something of a classic, & did much to advance the fame of Irving. It deserves a reading by everyone—side by side with some actual history which will furnish the facts travestied by the author. The Dutch have never liked this volume, alleging that it ridicules them unjustly. Certainly, Irving takes pains to present those aspects of Dutch life & personality which seem most grotesque in Anglo-Saxon eyes. As to the age of the *edition* of the book you have—it is not very great. This is a relatively modern reprint, as shown by the format & typography—which follow the pattern of Burt's Home Library, a series designed in the 1890's. On a guess, I would say that this edition is about 30 to 40 years old—a product of the early 1900's. I shall return it very shortly—& I trust that its 20th-century date may not lessen its importance in your eyes. After all, the *text* is just the same as that of the original edition published 127 years ago! It is interesting to note how whimsical comedy sometimes anticipated sound reality. In this book Irving begins with a mock-pompous account of the origin of the world & of mankind—as a prelude to the history of New York. In his day such a connected view of history was a good joke—yet today our scientific knowledge teaches us that all historic events are closely knit, & that no phase of life can be adequately considered except in relation to the general world background. Hence Wells's "Outline of History" begins with just such a cosmic perspective—the joke of yesterday having become the serious historic philosophy of the present!

> Yrs most sincerely—
> H P Lovecraft

*Notes*

1. *A History of New-York,* as by "Diedrich Knickerbocker."

[15]  [AHT]

Nov. 21, 1936

Dear Mrs. Wooley:—

[. . .]

In this criticism I am perfectly candid about the bard's status as a beginner, & fully outline the need of elementary technical training, wider reading in really good poetry, & efforts to produce something more than utterly trite & wornout sentiments couched in flat prosaic language. Naturally, I make the usual effort not to be discouraging, & do not emphasise the quality of *hope-lessness*. I simply state conditions as they are, & dwell on the need of improvement—giving the same lot of recommendations that I usually give to a beginner: to read the sort of poetry contained in the Golden Treasury, the Oxford Book of English Verse, or modern anthologies like Untermeyer's,[1] & to study technical treatises like Brander Mathews' "A Study of Versification", Teter's "An Introduction to Some Elements of Poetry" (46 p. brochure obtainable for a quarter from Moe), & Anne Hamilton's "How to Revise Your Own Poems" (a new booklet of 80 pp. obtainable from the author at 6413 W. 6th St., Los Angeles, Cal. I don't know the price, but it's excellent despite one or two mistakes.) I wasn't sure at first whether you wished the criticism & mss. sent to you for forwarding, or sent directly to the bard—but a re-reading of your letter seems to indicate the latter. Accordingly I'm sending the material off by this post, & if it earns me a hostile comeback I can do no more than reiterate the truth of my estimates & politely indicate to the sweet singer of Springfield where she can go if she doesn't like 'em!

Glad to know that you've been in touch with Kansas City's brilliant new citizen,[2] & hope you'll be able to meet the little imp in person before long. He is certainly one of the brightest & most promising kids I have ever seen—gifted alike in literature, art, & various forms of craftsmanship—& despite his present scattering of energies in different fields I think he will go far in the end. His studies at the Art Institute will undoubtedly be very good for him, & help him to establish a sort of aesthetic orientation. Hope he'll meet your uncle amidst the academic maze—though the size of the institution doubtless minimises the chances of accidental contact. Barlow has been growing fast in a literary as well as artistic way—as you doubtless deduced from his "Dim-Remembered Story" in *The Californian*. A still later tale of his—"The Night Ocean", also scheduled for *The Californian*—shows an even greater advance, being really one of the finest atmospheric studies ever written by a member of the group.

On July 28 I was quite bowled over by a surprise visitor—none other than our young friend Barlow (plus a fierce set of black moustachios & side-whiskers—which you'll doubtless see soon) come to investigate ancient Providence amidst his transition from Florida to your part of the world. He took a room at the boarding-house across the back garden, & proved an incessant & congenial caller at #66—likewise lapping up all the local libraries, bookstalls, & museums. He made himself very useful mending books & other objects, & I was able to help him a bit with his new fiction. We had an interesting time Aug. 6–10, when old Adolphe de Castro (once a collaborator of Ambrose Bierce—now 77—for whom Long & I have done much revision) was here also (stopping at a local hotel); & on one occasion the three of us sat on a tomb in the hidden hillside churchyard north of #66, writing rhymed acrostics on the name of *Edgar Allan Poe*, who 90 years before used to wander through that selfsame necropolis while on visits to Providence. The church-yard session, incidentally, gave rise to an amusing series of echoes. Though it would never have occurred to Barlow & me to submit our results for publication, our shrewd old colleague *did*—& secured a W.T. acceptance from Wright! After that Bob & I did send ours in—but they were turned down because of old Dolph's priority. Now that the ball has been started rolling, we've let the new *Science-Fantasy Correspondent* have our specimens. Meanwhile correspondents began to emulate. Young Kuttner has devised a splendidly poetic acrostic, & Moe (who saw the churchyard in July) prepared a very clever academic version—& has incorporated all the acrostics into a hecto-graphed booklet for use in his classes. Nor is that all. Derleth is editing a Wis-consin poetry anthology for a N.Y. publisher,[3] & having seen Moe's specimen, decided to include it in the volume. All this from Barlow's idle no-tion of writing acrostics while seated on an ancient tomb on a summer's af-ternoon![4] On Aug. 20th—my 46th birthday—Bob & I set out to explore Salem & Marblehead, pausing in Lynn to pick up little Sterling, who was recovering from his operation of last spring & preparing to enter Harvard in September. The day was ideal, & the kids formed a better idea of early New England ar-chitecture than they had ever had before. On Sept. 6 Barlow left Providence, thereafter spending some time in N.Y. confabulating with Long, Koenig, Loveman, Howard Wandrei (Donald is back in St. Paul), &c. He then headed west in earnest, pausing in Indianapolis for a very congenial call on Miss Moore. After a brief period in Leavenworth he settled down in Kansas City—& is henceforward likely to be a fellow-townsman of yours for a considerable time.

  I remain

     Yrs most sincerely—
      H P Lovecraft

*Notes*

1. Francis T. Palgrave, ed., *The Golden Treasury;* Sir Arthur Quiller-Couch, ed. *The Oxford Book of English Verse, 1250–1900;* Louis Untermeyer, ed., *Modern American Poetry: A Critical Anthology.*

2. I.e., R. H. Barlow, who had just moved there.

3. *Poetry out of Wisconsin.*

4. Adolphe de Castro, "Edgar Allan Poe" (*WT,* May 1937); R. H. Barlow, "St. John's Churchyard," and HPL, "In a Sequester'd Providence Churchyard Where Once Poe Walk'd" (*Science-Fantasy Correspondent,* March–April 1937). HPL's poem was reprinted in *WT* (May 1938) as "Where Poe Once Walked: An Acrostic Sonnet." Maurice W. Moe published his own, HPL's, Barlow's, and de Castro's in *Four Acrostic Sonnets on Poe* (1936).

# Letters to Robert and Mrs. Elmer Nelson

[1]     [ALS]

66 College St.
Providence, R.I.
Octr. 19, 1934

Dear Mr. Nelson:—

I note yours of the 8th with much interest, though I can't second your endorsement of the Wright letter in the Eyrie.[1] Certainly, only a very few of the WT stories have even a rudimentary claim to mature literary standing. The conceptions are trite, the characters artificial & wooden, & the development slovenly & mechanical. This weird stuff follows a set of lifeless & meaningless formulae just as closely as does any other pulp junk. However—Smith, Howard, Whitehead, Moore & (less often) others occasionally get beyond this welter of mediocrity—& produce things worth remembering. In the October issue "The Black God's Kiss", "The Seven Geases", & (very possibly) "Old Sledge" are worth saving from the waste-basket. (Also, probably, "The People of the Black Circle"—though I'm waiting for its completion before reading.)

In time I think you'll realise, that you've been overvaluing this sort of material—& undervaluing the soberer, more realistic material in the more solid publications. After all, phantasy is only a very narrow & minor field of expression. The highest literary art is the expression of emotion through the ordinary events of daily life. And when phantasy does become art, it is as though flamboyant extravagance but through the careful presentation of such moods as people actually feel when confronted by those illusions of unreality with which nature abounds. "The Willows", "The White People", & a few other tales really catch these moods & thus achieve a serious status. Some of the few better tales in W.T. *approach* such a capture, though I can hardly agree that they quite accomplish it. Some touch of crudity, obvious mechanism, or concession to cheap popular standards generally spoils the completeness of the effect. Smith comes the closest to success of anyone.

As for the hypothetical high-grade weird magazine I suggested—*of course* the WT group, including myself, couldn't get in at the present stage of development. They ought not to—for their technique is full of crude spots, & their conceptions blurred with cheap fictional standards. But the magazine would set a new goal & example; & in the end would probably help the best writers of the group recognize their own crudities & immaturities (as I'm trying to do), be that they might ultimately gain a foothold in the pages. An influence like that is needed—for one of the reasons our best WT fantaisistes don't develop their talent is that they know there is a market for mature work. However, it will probably never come—for such a venture can never be self-supporting. There is not enough of a public for it.

I certainly hope you'll succeed in your ambition to produce literature—& am sorry your environment is not sympathetic. If in any way possible, I'd advise that you look about for some means of subsistence other than writing—for when anyone depends on his pen for daily bread, the usual result is deterioration. He has to write tripe to please low-grade editors—& as time passes, the pattern gets so fixed that he can't produce anything else. Indeed, most lose even the *desire* to produce anything else . . . . Thus Quinn, Hamilton, Price, Williamson, & so on—all brilliant chaps who *could* create splendidly if freed from external suggestions & obligations. This stifling of artistic sincerity & frustration of real literary creation is really a major tragedy—a fatal flaw in the system of commercial barbarism around us some are ironic enough to call "civilisation." Only occasionally do we come across a personality so intense that it *can't* be wholly crushed by commercialism.

All good wishes—

Yours most sincerely,

H. P. Lovecraft

## Notes

1. See *WT* 24, No. 4 (October 1934): 527–28: "Wilfred D. Wright, of Toronto, writes: 'As a consistent reader of your monthly story-books for twelve years, I wish to express a few brief comments and opinions. A.—Your periodical has no real competitor as far as material goes, and its writers surpass all other types of contemporary magazine writers in literary skill. B.—The taste of genuine weird tale readers should be wide. Hence different types of weird stories, by different writers, have their own appeal; viz., Mr. Quinn, by comparison, is not truly weird, yet the tremendous personality of Jules de Grandin is so human and likable that one misses an old companion when he is not among the pages of WT. I suggest that Mr. Quinn's stories be titled as An Adventure of de Grandin as related to, and set down, by Seabury Quinn. C.— Those covers . . . my remark is: Who cares? Tear them all off if you do not like them; Weird Tales is my magazine, covers or no covers, printed or painted. Other than appreciation of Brundage's or any other illustrator's art, I got over being influenced by pictures when I finished reading *Mother Goose*. . . . I shall continue to read WT as I have in the past, because of the gripping, eldritch tales of elder times by Lovecraft and Smith; for the imaginative thrills of the future adventures of Hamilton and Moore; for the lovable personality of de Grandin by Quinn; for the thrilling old barbarian Conan of Howard; for Mr. Eadie, Mr. Long, Mr. Cave, Mr. Wandrei, Mrs. La Spina, and all those old and new writers of the genuine weird story as found only in your magazine, WEIRD TALES.'"

[2]   [ALS]

66 College St.
Providence, R.I.
October 27, 1934

Dear Mr. Nelson:—

Bless my soul, but you needn't feel sorry about having ventured opinions regarding weird fiction! What can anybody give but an honest opinion? As time goes on, most of us change the bulk of our opinions about various things—but we needn't feel ashamed of the old ones merely because new facts have caused us to form news ones. Nor could it be sensible to expect anybody to refrain from forming opinions till he had become deeply erudite in a given field. We can't keep holding opinions at all stages of the game—justifiably or not—& the most one can ask is that we keep our views open & tentative . . . subject to change as we acquire new data for judgment. Some of the views I held 10, 20, & 30 years ago make me laugh today—& yet I don't worry about having held them once. By the same token, I shall probably laugh 10 or 20 years hence at some of the views I hold now! All we can do is to keep as open-minded & rational as possible & striving at times to exercise a sense of proportion. We shan't hit it right every time, but our errors can always be rectified when more light is shed. More, it would be folly to expect.

So far as the field of weird literature is concerned, the only sensible thing to do is read everything in sight & draw whatever tentative conclusions seem to be warranted at the moment. The only obligations are those of sincerity & open-mindedness. Don't take any opinions from others. If others challenge views you hold, simply let the challenge serve as an incitement to fresh research & appraisal on your own part. Then, if you find the other fellow correct, well & good. You can change your view as needed. But if you don't find the opposing view justified, you don't have to change. But be your own arbiter in the long run.

My own views are simply the conclusions drawn from a survey of different kinds of writing. I may be wrong in many ways, but for the moment I feel strongly the sharp line of demarcations between writings which form disinterested self-expression (Blackwood, de la Mare, James, Dunsany, Poe, Bierce, Machen, &c) & those which (like most magazine fiction) are artificially designed to suit certain demands of the superficial & conventional reader. I wouldn't wish to impose my views forcibly on anyone else. Rather would I suggest that others look over the ground themselves, & see if they don't naturally draw similar conclusions of their own accord. That is the real crux of all my arguments. Even if carelessness makes me sound arbitrary & dogmatic at times.

I'm glad you like "Beyond the Wall of Sleep"—though this is an old story written in 1919 & scarcely representative of my present style. I fear you are far too charitable about the value of my stuff, for the more I study my past performances the less I am satisfied with them. Just now I can't feel satisfied with more than two of my attempts—"The Colour Out of Space" & "The Music of Erich Zann." Whether I'll ever produce anything of real value still remains to be seen. I'm taking a rest now—as I did between 1908 & 1917.

I trust your own work will keep on developing despite obstacles, & hope you will try pieces on the various magazines. The FF, *Fantasy Magazine,* & *Marvel Tales* furnish excellent & encouraging havens for matter which the remunerative magazines won't accept.

All good wishes—& don't worry about the opinions you express at any stage of your progress. Just be sincere & open-minded!

Yrs. most cordially—H. P. Lovecraft

[3]   [ALS]

66 College St.,
Providence, R.I.
Jany. 16, 1935

My dear Nelson:—

Glad to hear that you had a pleasant Christmas, & the coming year may prove a fruitful & congenial one for you. I shall be looking for more of the "Lost Excerpts"—as well as other material from your pen. Don't be discouraged merely because you don't produce Poe-like masterpieces at the outset. No one ever wrote a great story or poem without years of experience & apprenticeship. You have done very well indeed—keep it up! Regarding copyrights—I never bothered with such things. The chances of pirating are really very remote & when a piece is professionally published, the magazine holds the copyrights—with reservations indicated by the author on the upper right-hand corner of his ms. In sending a ms. for publication it as well to append the phrase "First North American Serial Rights Only." This means that you are selling *only the first printing.* If an anthology copies the piece, or if the magazine decides to reprint it, more pay is due you—though re-sale prices seldom equal those for a first printing. Re-sales sometimes count up quite impressively—my "Erich Zann", for instance, has been used six times in America and England.[1]

Regarding philosophic matters—I doubt profoundly anything involving extremes, or suspicious conformity to human wishes. All religious or other systems assigning mankind an important place in the universe are obviously primitive myths—no matter how widely & persistently perpetuated. So far as any real evidence goes, the cosmos is simply a perpetual field of interacting streams of force, amidst which the galactic universe, the solar system, this tiny Earth, the principle of animal life, & the human species are nothing more than momentary accidents. The cosmos at large knows nothing & cares nothing about the trivial incidents of human existence. "Beauty" & "goodness" are mere local human concepts which have nothing to do with the universe.

The only real, permanent & universal things are the laws of mechanics, chemistry, & physics which we learn slowly & gradually through the impersonal observation of external nature. The conditions resulting from these laws can never be changed. What we *can* do toward diminishing our painfully chaotic adjustments to nature, is to study these laws assiduously, & then see how closely we can steer our own courses in conformity with them. To do this, we must pay especial attention to those phases of natural law which govern the actions of our bodies & thought-processes—biology, psychology, anthropology, &c.—so that we may ascertain what may & what may not be expected. Perfect adaptation to nature can never be looked for; since our various instincts were all accidentally evolved, & include many permanently conflicting tendencies. But reason & experience can probably—through long courses of trial & error—cut down many of the conflicts now existing. The subordination of religious delusions will form one great step in advance. As to war—it can never vanish as a whole, since it is merely the expression of a natural human instinct. Any individual or group will always try to get whatever it wants in any way it can—& when peaceful means fail, it will fight if it believes it has any chance of winning. We can scarcely imagine any alignment of human forces which will make it impossible for some group to challenge all opposition at one time or another. Wars there will always be—as long as animal life exists—but on the other hand, it is quite conceivable that reason will succeed in cutting down the *number* of them very considerably. Many of the present specific causes of war can undoubtedly be removed in time. Alas, I think that individual economic distress will vastly diminish under the social & political conditions of the future. Life is a matter of mixed chance & mechanics, & there is as little reason to be a pessimist as to be an optimist. Scientific detachment is the only sound attitude. ¶ All good wishes—Yrs, sincerely—HPL

P.S. Had a pleasant time in N.Y. around New Year's. Saw Long, the Wandrei boys, Talman, Koenig, Leeds, &c., &c.—& also young Barlow, who was up from the South. Quite a convention, all in all!

*Notes*

1. It is uncertain what the sixth sale is to which HPL refers. See HPL to CAS, c. 31 May 1933: ". . . my "Erich Zann' has had another sale—its *fifth!* . . . This sale is to the publishing firm of Denis Archer, London, for a new cheap anthology of weird material. . . . The other four sales were (1) to W. T., (2) to Creeps by Night, (3) to the British ed. of Creeps, & (4) to the London Evening Standard. 3 British to 2 American, including (5) the sale to Archer." Though paid for, the story was not published by Archer.

[4]    [ALS]

Thursday
[17 January 1935]

Dear Nelson:—

Yrs of the 15th impels me to add a postscript to my note of yesterday. Bless my soul, but I didn't see anything "over haughty" or otherwise amiss in your former letter! Don't worry so much about the impression you create—what the hell does it matter, anyhow? The world isn't important enough to make it worth anybody's while to bother about such trifles. Simply jog along, observe the ordinary rules of civility as you understand the, & let the other fellow go sit on a tack if he doesn't like the way you speak or write! As to being "insignificant"—hell! so are we all, except perhaps some 5 or 6 percent of the human race . . . . the really capable & creative men who sustain the burden of our civilization. So far as the weird-fiction group is concerned, we're all insignificant together, & no individual need worry a moment about his own especial insignificance! When we reflect on the actual stature & nature of the cosmos—just a perpetual welter of electrons & streams of force aimlessly changing positions according to blind, fixed laws—we see how useless it is to attach any real importance to human events. What the hell! Everything is automatic, predetermined, & actually uncontrollable by ourselves anyhow. The whole mess means nothing—a gigantic piece of naïvete which an external eye would perceive as a titanic jest or a bitter mockery. "Life", said old Horace Walpole a century & a half ago, "is a tragedy to those who *feel*, but a comedy those who think."[1] Cultivate analytical thought rather than emotion & join the laughers! Remember that it was old Democritus, the acute analyst & atomic materialist, whom antiquity called "The Laughing Philosopher". When we first begin to realize the triviality of existence & insignificance of mankind our traditional pride & may get a jolt; but on second thought we ask ourselves, 'why the devil should we mean anything in the damn'd old universe? What good would it do if we *did* mean anything?' As soon as this sensible attitude sets in, we begin to acquire something of the placidity & contentment of controlled mice who scamper happily about a granary without resenting in the least their negligible status therein. There is less to worry about once we realize the truth. Why in thunder need we bother about anything except keeping fed & clothed & housed, & observing the common rules of rhythm of our environment which make for beauty & social adjustment? If others don't like it when we do our best, what the hell of that? Why need we concern ourselves with what others think of us? Human feelings & relationships have no meaning—they are mere biochemical phenomena like the growth of weeds or the motions of fishes—so why waste time & emotional energy in bothering about them? Once we perceive the triviality & meaninglessness of the whole business, an immediate burden is lifted from our nerves. I thumb my nose at the whole cursed cosmos & let it stew in its own damn grease!

However, I know what a nervous tension is, & can sympathise most acutely with your present state. That's why I urge you to apply realistic philosophy & reason yourself out of it as far as possible. While we can't always conquer a *predisposition* toward neuroticism, we can generally apply sound horse sense & remove many of the irritants which cause that predisposition to become painfully manifest. I know whereof I speak—since my whole youth was punctuated by nervous breakdowns which prevented my attending college & wrecked my career generally. I'm an old fossil of 44 years—but a damned sight better off nervously through sheer conservation, appraisal & reflection. The lesson brought by the years is *to take things lightly.* Nothing in the universe matters much—& the existence of organic life on this planet is only a momentary accident which will soon vanish, leaving things just the same as if it had never been. Amid such an ironic comedy of blind cosmic drift, who are we to worry about trifles?

Glad you like "Erich Zann"—which has had 6 printings in various magazines and anthologies. I like it second best among my stuff—"Colour Out of Space" being first. Sorry the disillusion about the "Necronomicon" was a jolt—almost all fantastic authors (Poe, Bierce, Machen, Hodgson, Shiel, &c) have invented such fictitious background items. ¶ Well—cheer up & don't worry about things!

Yrs most cordially——HPL

*Notes*

1. "This world is a comedy to those that think, a tragedy to those that feel." Horace Walpole (1717–1797), letter to the Countess of Upper Ossory (16 August 1776).

---

[5]    [TLS]

66 College St., Providence, R.I.,
September 19, 1935.

Dear Mrs. Nelson:—

I was indeed pained and shocked to hear last July of your son's sudden and untimely death—the news coming from my friend R. H. Barlow, whom I was then visiting, and whom you had notified. Every now and then I have been on the point of dropping you a line of sympathy for what must be a devastating blow indeed.

I had heard from Robert as late as July 3d, when he mentioned that he might some time travel through the east and stop in Providence to see me,. In replying I told him how glad I would be to welcome him in this ancient town—but the next I heard was the sad news which Barlow transmitted to me.

I had been hearing from Robert at irregular intervals for a period which must add up to three years or more. Meanwhile I had noticed with appreciation the clever and increasingly competent verses and prose-poems which he had in media like WEIRD TALES and THE FANTASY FAN. I presume you have a file of this material. His promise in the field of literature seemed to me very considerable; for despite the marks of youthful contraction—indefiniteness or overcolouring now and then—his work had a distinct imaginative richness and atmospheric power which was rapidly improving through criticism and self-discipline. I expected to see him develop like other youths whose careers I have watched—August W. Derleth, Donald Wandrei, Frank B. Long, etc.—who are now well-established figures in the world of weird writing. Barlow shows me the unpublished "Lost Excerpts" which you sent him, and which will sooner or later be published in some appropriate medium. These all have touches of the brilliancy and power which were becoming characteristic of their author. Needless to say, you will receive copies of whatever magazine publishes them. Barlow, by the way, was prompt in informing the "fan" magazines of the unfortunate occurrence, so that at least one has printed a brief notice.

My correspondence with Robert was not of a business nature, but had more to do with points of criticism connected with weird literature. We discussed standards, methods, and individual stories and poems off and on; and I believe I once or twice offered suggestions in connexion with lines of his. I remember the pains I took to make clear the gulf between cheap magazines stories (the WEIRD TALES sort in general) and genuine weird literature like the books of Arthur Machen, Algernon Blackwood, and M. R. James. He appreciated this difference more, I think, than the average follower of the popular magazine press. In all his letters he showed an admirable courtesy and considerateness. Himself obviously very sensitive, he went to almost elaborate lengths to avoid giving offence whenever his opinion differed from that of his correspondent. He was liked by all the persons to whom he wrote—and by the one member of the group (Charles D. Hornig, editor of WONDER STORIES and THE FANTASY FAN) who had the pleasure of meeting him in person. Hornig was particularly saddened by the news of his premature departure.

So once more let me express my profound sympathy—at the same time emphasizing the fact that Robert did not lack for appreciation and esteem despite the tragic brevity of his life and writing career. Only the other day I had a letter from young Petaja—out in Montana—reiterating his sorrow at the loss.

With every good wish, and the hope that time and philosophy will help to lessen the acute pain which you and Mr. Nelson must now feel, I am

Yours most sincerely,

H. P. Lovecraft

# Letters to William F. Anger

[1]     [ALS]

66 College St.,
Providence, R.I.,
Aug. 14, 1934.

Dear Mr. Anger:—

Glad to learn from your recent note that you have found some of my stories interesting. Your favourite "Dunwich" was rather well liked—it got an O'Brien 3-starring in 1929—though I really think "The Colour out of Space" (*Amazing Stories,* Sept. 1927) was better.[1] None of my stuff really satisfies me, & the rejection of some of my best work has been rather a discouraging influence in latter years. I agree with you as to the failure of the recent collaboration[2]—any restraint on my own imagination means a total flop for me. I hate collaborative writing, but Price was so eager for a sequel to my "Silver Key" (W T Jan. '29) embodying certain mathematical concepts of his that I couldn't civilly refuse!

Regarding the dreaded *Necronomicon* of the mad Arab Abdul Alhazred—I must confess that both the evil volume & the accursed author are fictitious creations of my own—as are the malign entities Azathoth, Yog-Sothoth, Nyarlathotep, Shub-Niggurath, &c. Tsathoggua & the *Book of Eibon* are inventions of Clark Ashton Smith; while Friedrich von Juntz & his monstrous *Unaussprechlichen Kulten* originated in the fertile brain of Robert E. Howard. For the fun of building up a convincing cycle of synthetic folklore, all of our gang frequently allude to the pet daemons of the others—thus Smith uses my Yog-Sothoth, while I use his Tsathoggua. Also, I sometimes insert a devil or two of my own in the tales I revise or ghost-write for professional clients. Thus our black pantheon acquires an extensive publicity & pseudo-authoritativeness it would not otherwise get. We never, however, try to put it across as an actual hoax; but always carefully explain to enquirers that it is 100% fiction. In order to avoid ambiguity in my references to the *Necronomicon* I have drawn up a brief synopsis of its "history"—the supposed dates of its original writing (under the Arabic title *Al Azif*), of its translation into Greek as το Νεκρονομικον by the Byzantine monk Theodorus Philetas, &c. &c.[3] All this gives it a sort of air of verisimilitude.

I'm interested to hear that you have written weird fiction yourself, & hope you won't let yourself get easily discouraged. Professional magazines, of course, are very hard to make; but have you heard of the three little semi-amateur magazines which exist for the encouragement of the weird & science fiction enthusiast? They are:

*The Fantasy Fan*, 137 W. Grand St., Elizabeth, N.J.

*Marvel Tales*, 122 Water St., Everett, Pa.

*Fantasy Magazine*, 255 E. 188th St., New York, N.Y.

All of these are very hospitably disposed toward the beginner—accepting MSS. (of course, without pay) which the professional magazines often decline. They contain many things by writers well known in the professional press as well as by novices—for even the most experienced veterans have repeated rejections. If you like, I'll send you samples of *Marvel Tales* & the *Fantasy Fan*—of which I have a number of duplicates.

Speaking of weird authors—I suppose you know that Price & Smith are fellow-Californians of yours. Both would undoubtedly be glad to see you if you ever chanced to drop around in their direction. Price's address is 5314 E. 12th St., Oakland, & Smith's Box 385, Auburn.

With every good wish—& hoping that your knowledge of the fictional nature of the *Necronomicon* won't wholly destroy your interest in it,

I am

Yrs most cordially & sincerely,

H. P. Lovecraft

*Notes*

1. See RB 2, n. 2.
2. "Through the Gates of the Silver Key."
3. "History of the 'Necronomicon'" (1928).

[2]     [ANS][1]

[Postmarked Nantucket, MA,
31 August 1934]

Dear F A:—

Yrs of the 22nd has just been forwarded to me—I am spending a week in the quaintest & oldest-fashioned place in America. Antiquarianism is my supreme hobby, & visiting old & historic towns my greatest pastime. Oddly, I had never been to Nantucket before—though it is only 90 m. from my own doorstep.[2] It is a perfectly preserved Yankee seaport of a century ago—not a thing changed! ¶ Glad you're in touch with both Price & Smith. Price certainly is tremendously genial & helpful. Hope your "Sentient Clay" will be accepted. I'll probably submit that "Doorstep" thing soon.[3] Haven't written anything lately—pausing for a fresh start, & swamped with nerve-wracking revision jobs. I'll send you a few issues of *The Fantasy Fan* when I get home—you'd enjoy it.

All good wishes—
                    H P L

*Notes*

1. *Front:* Harbor view, Nantucket, Massachusetts.
2. HPL soon after wrote about Nantucket in "The Unknown City in the Ocean."
3. I.e., "The Thing on the Doorstep," which HPL must have sent to Anger before the first extant letter to him (hence the remark "Glad to learn from your recent note that you have found some of my stories interesting" in WFA 1). HPL did not submit "Doorstep" to *WT* until July 1936.

[3]   [ALS]

66 College St.,
Providence, R.I.,
Dec. 29, 1934.

My dear Anger:—
                    Glad to hear from you again! Sultan Malik has mentioned you from time to time, & I congratulate you on your ride in Mighty Juggernaut.[1] I had the honour of riding in that imposing relique last year, when the Peacock Sultan was in Providence—though since that time I believe the venerable chariot has undergone much expert tinkering.

I hope exceedingly that you can get to see Clark Ashton Smith; & that when you do, you'll give him a writeup like the one you gave Sultan Malik. Yes—Wandrei was there lately, & the two seem to have had a highly enjoyable session. I read your Price interview in the F F with much pleasure, & congratulate you on having made it so piquant & interesting. Knowing just what details to select for such a presentation is an art in itself. F. Lee Baldwin is now trying his hand at a similar account of myself—data being gleaned through correspondence. It will be illustrated with a linoleum block cut made by young Rimel from a photograph which Barlow took last June.

I don't believe Wright is worrying very severely about my work. He rejected two of my last things—"At the Mountains of Madness" & "The Shadow Over Innsmouth"—on the ground that they were too long,[2] & might be uninteresting to his precious readers. This & similar incidents have discouraged me so much that I'm not writing any more for the present—except in an experimental way.

Don't get up too lofty expectations about "Sarnath". It's one of my oldest & most-rejected specimens—written in 1919 or 1920, when I was so much under the influence of Dunsany that most of my work tended to be imitative. *Marvel Tales* may develop into quite a thing—though Crawford's taste is lamentably crude & undeveloped in spots. In the recent issue the story by Keller—"The Golden Bough"[3]—was the only really good thing. Did you receive Crawford's booklet with the "White Sibyl" & "Men of Avalon"?[4] The former tale is splendid, though the latter inclines toward mawkishness & artificiality.

The December W T is much superior to the November issue—Smith's "Xeethra" plainly taking first place. I hear of new weird magazines on the market—*Mystery Novels* & *Horror Stories*—but am assured that they are very crude & valueless.

I trust you had a pleasant Yuletide. My own was exceptionally delightful—with a *tree,* which I haven't had before since childhood.

Hoping you may enjoy a happy & fruitful New Year—I remain
Yrs most sincerely,
H. P. Lovecraft

P.S. Am going to N Y tomorrow to see Long. Barlow & Wandrei are also in the metropolis, so it'll be quite a gathering.

*Notes*

1. I.e., E. Hoffmann Price and his automobile, a 1928 Ford Model A.

2. Cf. *SL* 3.395 regarding the rejection of *At the Mountains of Madness.* As for "The Shadow over Innsmouth," HPL wrote to Farnsworth Wright on 18 February 1932: ". . . my new 'Shadow over Innsmouth' is three typed pages longer than 'Whisperer in Darkness', & conventional magazine standards would undoubtedly rate it 'intolerably slow', 'not conveniently divisible', or something of that sort. For the present I don't think I'll submit any new material anywhere" (*SL* 4.17). Unknown to HPL, August Derleth later submitted the story to *WT,* but Wright predictably rejected the story because it was too long to publish in one installment and could not published in two parts without disrupting the mood (Farnsworth Wright to August Derleth, 17 January 1933; ms., Wisconsin Historical Society). Wright rejected the story again in 1939 for the same reason.

3. David H. Keller, "The Golden Bough," *Marvel Tales* (Winter 1934) .

4. CAS and David H. Keller, *The White Sibyl* [by Smith] *and Men of Avalon* [by Keller] (Everett, PA: Fantasy Publications, 1934; *LL* 815).

[4]     [ALS]

66 College St.,
Providence, R.I.,
Jany. 28, 1935.

Dear Anger:—

Glad you've had another glimpse of the Peacock Sultan—who has been outlining his real estate venture in a series of bulletins. Hope he gets settled before long as a complete rural 'squire—it will help his output, without doubt. His rate of production—which has transcended all manual recording & reached the dictaphone stage—certainly gets me dizzy!

That Crawford booklet is worth getting for the sake of "The White Sibyl"—though Keller's "Men of Avalon" isn't so hot. Smith is certainly the greatest of them all—as his magnificent "Dark Eidolon" in the current W T well attests. I certainly hope you can get to Averoigne[1] to see him, & that you can contribute a bit to his recognition. Wish Sultan Malik could get around oftener to break the monotony of his days—he works too hard, & doesn't get enough relaxation.

As for Wright's acceptances & rejections—I've long ago given up trying to find any central thread of reason in them. They are clearly governed by caprice, pure & simple. One of his favourite tricks is to reject a tale & then recall it for acceptance. As to the work of C. L. Moore—I don't agree with your low estimate. These tales have a peculiar quality of cosmic weirdness, hard to define but easy to recognise, which marks them out as really unique. "Black God's Shadow" isn't up to the standard—but you can get the full effect of the distinctive quality of "Shambleau" & "Black Thirst".[2] In these tales there is an indefinable atmosphere of vague *outsideness* & *cosmic dread* which marks weird work of the best sort. How notably they contrast with the average pulp product—whose bizarre subject-matter is wholly neutralised by the brisk, almost *cheerful* manner of narration! Whether the Moore tales will keep their pristine quality or deteriorate as their author picks up the methods, formulae, & style of cheap magazine fiction, still remains to be seen. A. Merritt fell for the pulp formula, hence never realised his best potentialities. Miss Moore may do the same. But at present she certainly belongs in the upper tier of W T contributors along with Smith, Howard, &c.

What you say of Julius Long[3] is interesting. It would seem a fact that most of the pulp hack writers are confirmed hard drinkers—just why, I'm sure I don't know. The anthologist T. Everett Harré lives virtually every moment in an alcoholic stupor. I've never been able to understand the psychology of drink—just why people consider it desirable to spend most of their time in the clutch of a poison which sends them back several million years along the evolutionary scale! I'm 44, & have never touched alcoholic liquor. Somehow or other, my imagination seems to function in its humble way without external aid!

Speaking of assorted Longs—I visited my friend Frank Belknap Long in N Y over New Year's, & met all the local group—Morton, Loveman, Kirk, Kleiner, Leeds, Koenig, Talman, &c. &c. The event became something of a convention through the simultaneous presence in Manhattan of young Barlow & both Wandreis—Donald having just arrived from California, where he visited C A S, & Howard coming directly from St. Paul. The brothers have taken a very attractive flat at 155 W. 10th St. in Greenwich Village. This was Barlow's first visit to the metropolis since infancy, hence Belknap & I were kept quite busy introducing him to the museums, galleries, & bookshops. We had a meeting of the clan at Belknap's Jan. 2 with 15 present. Later we assembled at Loveman's, & he exhibited some 300 or 400 splendid drawings by Clark Ashton Smith—the most notable array of such material outside Auburn. I hadn't seen this collection in years, & it was absolutely new to Long, Barlow, & the Wandreis. On another occasion Koenig (now in Florida) showed Long, Barlow, & me through the Electrical Testing Laboratories,[4] with which he is connected. A rather fascinating place, full of bizarre-looking devices for testing the safety & durability of every sort of electrical household appliance. The weather was fairly decent—only 2 days being so cold as to give me serious trouble. Home Jan. 8, & struggling ever since with accumulated work. Now & then the cold keeps me imprisoned within doors—yet I fancy the winter isn't as bad on the whole as the preceding one. Just now we're digging out after a record-breaking snow storm.

All good wishes—& regards to the Sultan when you see him.
Blessings & the Peace—
Abdul Alhazred

*Notes*

1. I.e., Auburn, California. CAS set several of his stories in the fictitious medieval land of Averoigne.
2. C. L. Moore, "The Black God's Shadow" (*WT,* December 1934); "Shambleau" (*WT,* November 1933); "Black Thirst" (*WT,* April 1934).
3. Julius Long (1907–1955), American writer of detective and fantasy fiction.
4. The Electrical Testing Laboratories were located at 2 East End Avenue at 79th Street in New York.

[5]    [ALS]

66 College St.,
Providence, R.I.,
Feby. 16, 1935.

Dear An-Gha, Hierophant of Lemuria:—

I envy you your prospective visits. Accounts of the lord Malik's palace of necromancy atop the horrible Kaf sound highly alluring—& I am interested, too, in the voracious white daemon of feline exterior which has been acquired as a guardian of the outer gate. The Peacock Sultan certainly does break all records in taking editorial citadels—& I trust his present streak may continue unbroken.

I wish, too, that I could be in on the expedition to Placer County, where the thousand-mile shaft to evil Tsathoggua's nighted abode hits the surface of the planet. Needless to say, the High-Priest Klarkash-Ton will be glad to see you all. It will be a good thing for him—breaking the monotony of a very prosaic & uneventful existence. When you get there you'll see an even larger collection of pictorial horrors than I saw last month—for C A S has kept the best of his products himself. Ngrrhh! but I'd like to get a glimpse of some of those that Wandrei (who was there in November) told about! You'll find Auburn an interesting place, full of the history & early traditions of your state. It was one of the first gold camps, being known as Woods' Dry Diggings until renamed by some Goldsmith-lover in 1849.[1] Some of the pioneer buildings are still standing in older sections. During the 13 years of our epistolary acquaintance, Klarkash-Ton has sent me numberless postcards illustrating the region.

I am very glad that Bernal is receiving such recognition, & am sure he will respond nobly to the encouragement. I recall his "Man Who Played with Time" three years ago—though not till recently did I realise that a fifteen-year-old was responsible for it. It is truly a remarkable thing for a boy of that age to write. I shall be interested to see what Bernal's later work is like.[2]

Regarding the Moore stories—one has to separate the undeniably hackneyed & mechanical romance from the often remarkable background against which it is arrayed. "The Black God's Kiss"[3] had a vastly clever setting—the pre-human tunnel beneath the castle, the upsetting of gravitational & dimensional balance, the strange, ultra-dimensional world of unknown laws & shapes & phenomena, &c. &c. If that could be taken out of the sentimental plot & made the scene of events of really cosmically bizarre motivation, it would be tremendously powerful. The distinctive thing about Miss Moore is her ability to devise conditions & sights & phenomena of *utter strangeness & originality*, & to describe them in a language conveying something of their outré, phantasmagoric, & dread-filled quality. That in itself is an accomplishment possessed by very few of the contributors to the cheap pulp magazines. For the most part, allegedly "weird" writers phrase their stories in such a brisk, cheerful, matter-of-fact, colloquial, dialogue-ridden sort of style that all genuine sense of shadow & menace is lost. So far, Miss M. has escaped this pitfall; though continued writing for miserable rags like the current pulps will probably spoil her as it has spoiled Quinn, Hamilton, & all the rest. The editors will encourage her worst tendencies—the sticky romance & cheap "action"—& discourage everything of real merit (the macabre language, the original descriptive touches, the indefinite atmosphere, the brooding tension, &c.) which her present work possesses. Nothing will ever teach the asses who peddle cheap magazines that a weird story *should not & cannot* be an "action" or "character" story. The only justification for a weird tale is that it be an authentic & convincing *picture of a certain human mood*; & this means that *vague impressions* & *atmosphere* must predominate. Events must not be crowded, & human characters must not assume too great importance. The real protagonists of fantasy fiction are *not people but phenomena*. The logical climax is not a revelation of what somebody *does*, but a *glimpse of the existence of some condition contrary to nature as commonly accepted.*

Just got around to reading the Feby. W.T., & find it rather mediocre. Edmond Hamilton has left his single plot for another—but unfortunately a decidedly venerable one! I wish a really good weird magazine could be established & supported—something able & willing to use material of the Machen-Blackwood–James calibre.

All good wishes—

Yrs for the Black Apocalypse—
E'ch-Pi-El

*Notes*

1. HPL alludes to the poem "The Deserted Village" by Oliver Goldsmith (c. 1730–1774), which opens "Sweet Auburn! loveliest village of the plain . . ."
2. A[rthur] W[illiam] Bernal (1913–1991), "The Man Who Played with Time" (*WT,* March 1932). Bernal published four more stories in *WT:* "Vampires of the Moon" (May, June, and July 1934); "The Man Who Was Two Men" (April 1935); "Satan in Exile" (June, July, August, and September 1935); and "So Very Strange!" (April 1937).
3. *WT,* October 1934.

[6]     [ALS]

66 College St.,
Providence, R.I.,
March 27, 1935.

Dear An-Ghah:—

Yours of March 7 duly received, & I note all the various observations with interest. Regarding "Julhi"[1]—I wouldn't tend to give it an extreme classification in either direction. It certainly displays very well the author's peculiar power to evoke images & conceptions of utter strangeness, & to suggest monstrous gateways from the tri-dimensional world to other spheres of entity, yet somehow doesn't have quite the concentrated explanation, & the central idea is largely a repetition of "Shambleau" & "Black Thirst". There is too much literal & concentrated power of the Shambleau theme. I would tend to rate it above "Black God's Shadow", but below "Black God's Kiss". It is hard to measure a story absolutely—there are so many points to consider. The real test is simply that of ability to awake & sustain a certain mood in the discriminating reader. "Julhi" falls short of certain other Moore yarns because there is something just the least *expected* about the various twists & touches—& of course a sort of conventional romanticism hovers over the whole thing. However—the story of course rises miles above the lifeless, mechanical tripe forming the bulk of W T's contents. As for the illustration—it is of course nothing notable, though it would have to go a long way to take the cellar championship from some of the other "art" work in the magazine. The best thing Wright could do is to cut out all illustrations—unless he can provide material equal to Rankin's better products. The new illustrator[2]—whose name I didn't know till you mentioned it—is a good realistic draughtsman in the usual tradition, but lacks the subtle quality of fantastic imagination which one could wish in work of this kind. He beats Hammond, though. Of all the illustrators who have worked for W T I think Rankin is the best, with Brosnatch as a fair second. Olinick is far & away the worst—with Doak not far behind him.[3] Occasional good work has appeared from the less frequent artists—Joseph Doolin & J. Allen St. John. I wish Wright would accept work from Howard Wandrei, who draws magnificently in the Sime–Harry Clarke tradition, but so far he has rejected all offerings from that quarter—thereby proving that he is more favourably disposed toward the usual than toward the truly excellent. By the way—Klarkash-Ton has the purest essence of the weird in his drawings, though his difficulty with human figures & with the pattern element hamper him somewhat in the realm of illustrating. Have you ever seen his crayon & water-colour sketches in blasphemous entities & hellish trans-galactic vegetation?

Regarding "The Feast in the Abbey"[4]—I really don't know how much of its fan vote was deliberately whipped up. Of course it was absurd to compare anything in the issue with "The Dark Eidolon"—& yet not only the Bloch item but two more . . . a wretched Quinn thing & the rather uneven "Charon"[5] . . . were cited as first-place rivals. After all, the vote of the readers means almost nothing—including as it does vast hordes of the ignorant, the tasteless, & the superficial.

As for the intrinsic merit of the "Feast"—I think you're a bit too severe on it. Of course Bloch is a 17-year-old beginner still frankly in the imitative, traditional, & experimental stage—but I don't think he's done badly for his years. I saw the first draught of the "Feast" about a year ago, & can assure you that the improvement in the present version is striking. Give the boy time . . . & not in San Quentin, either! His worst fault is exactly like my own—a tendency toward *overcolouring*—laying the adjectives on too thick in scenes of horror & mystery. Undoubtedly he'll outgrow a good deal of that—I was vastly worse at his age. The very traditional beginning of the "Feast" can hardly be condemned without qualification. Of course these storm openings are undeniably usual—but they are somehow so perfectly suited to their purpose that one hesitates to rule them out with a blanket edict. In various parts of this tale there is a certain sinister authenticity of mood—a touch of half-convincing dread—which marks it off from hopeless routine items. Despite the mechanical climax one feels that the author knows both the principles of dramatic suspense & situation, & the basic essence of the cosmic horror mood. There is promise present. He doesn't use his materials to full advantage yet, but he has them in a way that a lot of other minor contributors haven't. The story ought to be judged merely for what it is—a beginner's product. It was really unfortunate that it won prominent mention & thus seemed to come into competition with mature work.

Well—the worst rigours of winter seem to be over. Derleth has just sent me his new novel, "Three Who Died", but I've had no time to read it as yet.

One of the youthful science-fiction fans of N.Y. has just moved to Providence—Kenneth Sterling, an astonishingly bright & precocious lad.

All good wishes—& trust you'll get to see C A S soon.

Yrs for the Black Seal—

E'ch-Pi-El

P.S. Sorry to note the discontinuance of the *Fantasy Fan*. Nothing can quite take its place, though *Fantasy Magazine* will probably handle certain of the features.

*Notes*

1. C. L. Moore, "Julhi" (*WT*, March 1935).
2. John R. "Jack" Binder.
3. I.e., H. R. Hammond, Hugh Rankin, Andrew Brosnatch, and G. O. Olinick. "Doak" was a pseudonym (and middle name) of Hugh Rankin.
4. RB, "The Feast in the Abbey" (*WT*, January 1935). The story won the readers' vote as the best in the issue.
5. Seabury Quinn, "Hands of the Dead"; Laurence J. Cahill, "Charon."

[7]     [ALS]

66 College St.,
Providence, R.I.,
April 24, 1935

Dear An-Ghah:—

Regarding W T illustrations—I hope I didn't do Binder's work an injustice. He is really an excellent artist. I merely tried to point out that for weird work certain special imaginative qualities & a certain adroitly nebulous technique are desirable—& that of the W T regulars, Rankin has these attributes most strongly developed. The O'Mecca picture is surely excellent—though I wish you could have seen the one which Howard Wandrei himself drew for the story.[1] Wright turned it down—for some capricious reason past fathoming. I suppose you know that Howard W. is a weird artist of the very first quality—wholly above the pulp illustrator's level. Fiction is a relatively minor interest with him—though he is now doing a vast lot of cheap hack work for Street & Smith & others. Olinick—who flourished in 1926–7—is undoubtedly the worst "artist" W T ever had. *Doak* was next worst. I wish they wouldn't attempt to have any pictures—in most cases the drawings misrepresent the text & cramp the reader's imagination.

Don't take my "Sarnath" too seriously—it's an old piece, surviving from my period of Dunsany discipleship. The current M T represents a vast improvement in format, though the contributions are only mediocre. Hope Crawford can keep it up—he is having a hard struggle. I'm advising him not to divide his energies—to abandon the crazy idea of starting *another* magazine

(*Unusual*) before he had this one established![2] It would also be well for him to go easy on the booklets—though a few of those wouldn't be as bad as another attempted magazine. The demise of the F F was certainly a tragedy—but if Hornig couldn't float it, I don't know who could!

I liked "The Man Who Was Two Men"—exceedingly clever idea. Indeed, the idea so resembles (& goes beyond) one of my own that I've removed the latter from my plot-book. I didn't read "Vampires of the Moon"[3]—pulp serials are a little too much for my patience unless I know in advance that they are unusual. "O'Mecca" was really fine—genuine weird atmosphere & ample regional colour. Since Wandrei comes from Minnesota, I fancy he draws his characters correctly. "Shadows of Blood" was rather painful because of the glaring historical inaccuracy. The Romans never heard of the Huns till around 375 A.D.—more than three centuries after the time of Caligula. Klarkash-Ton's story is excellent—I read it in MS. a year ago. By the way, C A S is having a hard time these days—with both parents ill & requiring his care, & his own health nothing extra. Yet he has finished several new tales—all of which, fortunately, Wright has taken. Hope you can get to see him during the summer.

I saw that Wollheim article dealing with Hugo the Rat[4]—through the kindness of a bright young member of the Science Fiction League, Kenneth Sterling, who has recently moved to Providence. It was nothing new to me—for more than one friend of mine has been robbed by that thieving son-of-a-beachcomber. He printed a story by Frank B. Long in the Spring 1930 *Wonder Stories Quarterly*,[5] & neither paid the author nor gave any attention to letters about the matter. I advised Long to take drastic steps, but he thought the sum wasn't large enough to bother about. Others I know—including C A S—have recovered cash from the Rat only through legal action. There's no real answer that Gernsback can make to the Wollheim exposé—all he can do is to keep quiet. But his shifty tactics will overreach themselves & wreck him in the end. Meanwhile he relies on suckers, pays two or three contributors whom he can't afford to lose, & counts on the MSS. of writers who don't care whether they're paid or not. I wouldn't mind a non-paying magazine if the editor would honestly call it such—like the F F, F M, & M T. It is his masquerading as a remunerative publisher which makes Hugo such a damn'd thief! Fortunately he is an exception. Street & Smith, the *Terror Tales* & *Dime Mystery* firm, & Wright are all honourable in their dealings. Wright is sometimes slow, but he always pays in full in the end. By the way—speaking of the S. F. League & its members—have you seen their mimeographed parody on the science fiction magazines—*Flabbergasting Stories*?[6] It is really extremely clever & witty—Sterling showed me a copy. If I recall correctly, Wollheim is the editor.

With all good wishes—

Yrs for the Avatar of Tsathoggua—

E'ch-Pi-El

*Notes*

1. Howard Wandrei, "The Hand of the O'Mecca" (*WT*, April 1935).

2. Crawford published an "advance issue" of *Unusual Stories* in March 1934, then two issues in May–June 1935 and Winter 1935.

3. The story was by A. W. Bernal. Cf. RB 45: "The Bernal idea is clever—I once had a similar idea, but never developed it." Presumably HPL refers to his commonplace book. At this time, HPL had in his possession only the typed version of the notebook as prepared by R. H. Barlow in May 1934. The T.Ms. shows only one crossed-out entry—the entry that suggested "The Shadow out of Time." The "Cassius" entry ("Man has miniature shapeless Siamese twin—exhib. in circus—twin surgically detached—disappears—does hideous things with malign life of his own.") may be the entry to which HPL refers. It was not "removed" from his notebook but flagged for Barlow with the title of Henry S. Whitehead's story. Many entries in the commonplace book deal with loss of identity in various ways, and "The Man Who Was Two Men" certainly deals with that theme. The other stories mentioned in this paragraph are in *WT* (April 1935).

4. I.e., Hugo Gernsback. DAW's exposé of Gernsback's failure to pay authors for work published in *Wonder Stories* (including himself, for the story "The Man from Ariel" in the July 1934 issue) appeared in the April 1935 *Bulletin* of the Terrestrial Fantascience Guild, a science fiction fan club. In "In the Walls of Eryx," HPL and Sterling poked fun at Gernsback by reference to "ugrats" (*CF* 4.601) and to the Science Fiction League (Sci-Fic League) as mud-dwelling "sificlighs" wriggling in a corpse (*CF* 4.615, 616).

5. "The Thought Materializer" (*Wonder Stories*, Spring 1930).

6. A parody of Gernsback's *Wonder Stories*. See *SL* 5.152.

[8]　[ANS][1]

[Postmarked Providence, RI,
28 April 1935]

Glad the Price trip was so enjoyable—Sultan Malik said you had been around, & that he was glad to see you. Nimrod,[2] from all accounts, must be a great fellow. Glad you & he get along well. You ought to take the friendship of so valiant a warrior as a great compliment! Old Jug, too, is a distinguished veteran—who seems to thrive on sundry repairs & replacements. ¶ Congratulations on the "Thirsty Blades"[3] illustration! Barlow, who collects such things, will be envious when he hears of it. ¶ Glad you like "Out of the Eons"—which is practically ghost-written by myself. I've done oceans of this work for various writers. ¶ I read "Ishtar" & "Satan"[4] at Barlow's last year, but did not like either very much. They are both full of the hackneyed perspective of popular pulp fiction. Don't know where the Ishtar story could be picked up reasonably—but any bookseller in a large city could find you a copy in the end. You could also get a new edition from the publishers. ¶ Am having a guest[5] over the week end, & going on historic & antiquarian tours (Newport, New Bedford, &c.) in his car.

All good wishes—

    Yrs sincerely

        Ech-Pi-El

*Notes*

1. *Front:* The [Augustus Stout] Van Wickle Gates, Brown University.

2. E. Hoffmann Price's cat.

3. Otis Adelbert Kline and E. Hoffmann Price, "Thirsty Blades" (*WT,* February 1930); illustrated by Hugh Rankin.

4. A. Merritt, *The Ship of Ishtar* and *Seven Footprints to Satan.*

5. Robert Ellis Moe.

[9]    [ALS]

                          66 College St.,

                              Providence, R.I.,

                                  May 19, 1935.

Dear An-Ghah:—

    Glad to hear that the fantastic fans of Oakland & Berkeley are numerous enough to hold meetings. There aren't many places where such a first-hand exchange of ideas can be effected—New York perhaps being the principal one. Possibly the Science Fiction League will help to unite the various devotees of space ships & death rays . . . but the ghoulist & vampirist are still left out in the cold.

    So you saw Baldwin's sketch of me. It was indeed very cleverly done—combining a questionnaire with the remembered trifles of some 3 years' correspondence—& I'll tell Baldwin of your high opinion when next I write him. He seems to have a natural aptitude for this kind of thing, & is now at work on Robert E. Howard.[1] Rimel's linoleum cut was also very skilful—I never knew anyone to get such elaborate results from linoleum before. The picture, however, tends to look more youthful than I do—since linoleum is not very well adapted to catch the nuances of greying hair & the insidious facial hardening of the forties. It was made from an excellent photograph which Barlow took last June.

    Yes—I have a complete W T file of a sort, though some of the issues are almost falling to pieces from age & decay. Pulp paper was not made to last—& I fear I haven't taken very good care of my specimens. Barlow has an almost complete file . . . duplicate files, in fact, with the issues of the best one wrapped individually in cellophane. He takes the most elaborate care of them. Derleth's file is also not far from complete. I'll surely let you know if I come across any duplicate early issues. Some of the dealers who advertise in the fan

236 @ Letters to William F. Anger

magazines could probably help—some report good results from Carl Swanson of Coleharbor, N.D., though they say he is sharp & given to high prices. Yes—Burks used to have some great Haitian stuff in W.T. He was much better in the early days, before he went in for formula stuff & quantity production.

Yes—others have thought it odd that one born in the midst of a famous sea-food region should have such a detestation of marine products . . . but actuality has nothing to do with neat consistency. Rhode Island clams & clambakes are celebrated the world over—& when our friend the Peacock Sultan was here in old Juggernaut in 1933 I introduced him to a typical clam dinner in a quaint fishing village near Providence down the west shore of the bay. Narragansett Bay is likewise famed for oysters. It would be odd if your supply came from here!

Read the May W T recently, & found it sadly dull. I fear the average is considerably below what it used to be—with Whitehead dead, other standbys gone over to conventional hack work, & Wright more capricious than ever about his acceptances.

May get down to De Land again to visit Barlow after the latter returns home in June. Trip is still doubtful, however. The spring has turned out a wretchedly late one, so that my scenic & antiquarian outings have been very few so far.

All good wishes—

Yrs most cordially

E'ch-Pi-El

[Enclosure][2]

[PROSPERITY CLUB
"In God We Trust"]          more or less

[name and address obliterated]

| [Mr. W. W. Whitehead | 1943 Broadway #201 | Denver, Colorado |
| Mrs. Shirley Whitehead | 1943 Broadway #201 | Denver, Colorado |
| Mrs. Geo. J. Scott | 1660 Logan St. #7 | Denver, Colorado |
| Mrs. Mildred Miller | 3402 Josephine St. | Denver, Colorado |
| Miss Margaret Sylvester | 4515 East 25th Ave. | Denver, Colorado] |
| H. P. Lovecraft | 66 College St. | Providence, R.I. |

[FAITH—HOPE—CHARITY]     & naiveté

[This chain was started in the hope of bringing prosperity to you.

Within three days, please make five copies of this letter—leaving off the *top* name and address, and mailing to five of your friends to whom you wish prosperity to come.

When omitting the top name, send that person ten cents (10¢) wrapped in paper as a charity donation. In turn, as your name leaves the top, you will receive 15,625 letters with donations amounting to $1562.50.

Now is this worth a dime to you?

Have the faith your friend has and this chain will not be broken.]

Here's something amusing, the prototype of which came the other day. I suppose you've read of such devices recently. When this arrived I resisted my ordinary impulse to chuck it into the waste-basket & decided to pass it along just for the fun of it . . . as a sort of test of human psychology, and expression of contempt for the conventional economics of the dying social order. So I sent a dime to the first person whose name appeared & struck off the rest with 4 carbons to unload on various correspondents with a sense of *humour.* Don't bother with it if you're busy. I, of course, am not bothering with the 3-day limit. It will be amusing to see how far one or two chance transmissions of such a thing can go—though I doubt if anybody will be overwhelmed with any welcome avalanche of dimes!

*Notes*

1. Baldwin does not appear to have published any sketch about Robert E. Howard, although Duane R. Rimel prepared a linoleum cut for it.
2. Text not within square brackets are HPL's comments. Other recipients of this chain letter were R. H. Barlow, W. Paul Cook, Woodburn Harris, and Frank Belknap Long, Jr.; see HPL to Barlow, [11? May 1935] (*O Fortunate Floridian* 266–67).

[10]   [ALS]

66 College St.,
Providence, R.I.,
June 1, 1935.

Dear An-Ghah:—
Yrs. just recd. Yes—Sultan Malik told me of the replacement of old Jug by Terraplane, & I was sorry to learn of the passing of the veteran which had once wheezed up to my door . . . & in which the Peacock Sultan & I had explored some of the picturesque spots of southern Rhode Island. But it had to be—for in the venerable frame of old Jug were lodged the seeds of a fatal malady. The new chariot, I understand, is much less thirsty than its predecessor. Hope the proposed trip to see Klarkash-Ton turns out well. I haven't heard from the Temple of Tsathoggua in a month—but presume C A S would have notified me of any unfavourable development regarding his parents' health.

I'll keep a record of the W T's you seek, & hope that Barlow or somebody may be able to supply at least a few of them. Eventually I trust your file may become complete—or at least nearly so. Absolutely complete files are quite rare. I have one, but it is falling to pieces from old age. Barlow—who has a nearly complete file—keeps his copies sealed in cellophane & has duplicates for reference.

Glad you have such a group of weird devotees in your region. Aside from this group—& the small bunch in N Y—such nuclei are virtually non-existent . . . in marked contrast with the numerous local clans of science-fiction fans. I'm sure your Dutch-treat plan of banquet-financing will contribute greatly to the economic stability of the band.

*Tales of Magic & Mystery* must be rather hard to get at this late date! It wasn't much of a magazine, & they paid only $17.00 for "Cool Air".[1] Hope you can find a copy. The thing ran for only 4 or 5 issues—& I haven't them all. My copy of "Cool Air" is rather seedy. Glad you liked "Arthur Jermyn". It really doesn't amount to a great deal, but I somehow have a sort of sneaking fondness for it.

Glad you had a chance to see "Tobacco Road".[2] Long & others in N Y took it in, but I missed it. From all accounts it's a pretty grim & powerful bit of realism.

I am greatly interested in Lewis Smith's[3] new propositions, & hope to purchase a copy of the W T index—a convenience I greatly need. I've about worn my file out pouring over it for stories which I can't place within 5 years' range. Barlow & others will prove almost certain customers.

Now as to mimeographing my "Fungi"—I'm sure I'd be glad to have it done. Barlow has had an idea of printing them, but I doubt if he'll ever get around to it—he has so many other irons in the fire. I doubt if there'd be much profit—but I wouldn't be rapacious about percentages if there were. First you'd want to defray your own expenses—paper, postage, use of mimeograph, &c. I am enclosing all 35 of the Fungi as written in 1929–30. Probably you haven't seen all of them. I think a booklet ought to contain the whole thing if it is to be issued at all. If you decide to use the stuff, please be tremendously careful about mistakes. I don't know whether the mimeograph process allows of anything like proofreading, but if it does I hope you'll let me read the proofs. Please return the original MS. in the end. Accuracy is really essential, for the slightest error—even of punctuation—sometimes plays the very devil with a piece of verse.

Had an interesting visit from young Hornig, lately editor of the *Fantasy Fan,* a week ago. He is a very nice chap—reminding me slightly of Donald Wandrei. He seemed to appreciate the quaintness & beauty of Old Providence very keenly. Young Sterling (who returns to N Y later this month) was also on hand, making quite a convention of the event.

It is likely that I shall be heading south in a few days to visit Barlow—though all first-class mail addressed here will be forwarded. When I get down there, my address will be % R. H. Barlow, Box 88, De Land, Florida. Hope to take old Charleston & St. Augustine en route, though limited cash will force me to cut intermediate stops down to a minimum. Barlow himself will return home from Washington next Monday.

All good wishes—

Yrs most cordially & sincerely,

E'ch-Pi-El

[P.S.] Give my regards to Sultan Malik & Klarkash-Ton when you see them!

*Notes*

1. See RB 5, n. 3.
2. Jack Kirkland's dramatic adaptation of Erskine Caldwell's novel *Tobacco Road* premiered on Broadway on 4 December 1933; first book publication New York: Viking Press, 1934.
3. I.e., Louis C. Smith, WFA's associate; so spelled in WFA's letters to HPL.

[11]   [ALS][1]

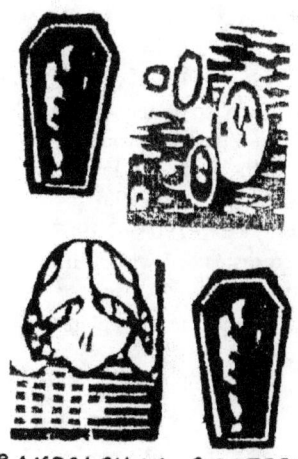

RANDOLPH W. CARTER

% R. H. Barlow,
Box 88,
De Land, Fla.,
June 20, 1935.

Dear An-Ghah:—

Glad to hear that everything arrived in good shape, & trust that your venture may progress successfully. Let me thank you most sincerely for your offer of W.T. Index #1—an item which will be vastly appreciated, constantly used, & sedulously treasured. This index is one of the most-needed things I can think of, & ought to sell widely among the devotees of our hobby. By the way—Barlow wants to order a copy of the catalogue at current prices—so put him down as an original subscriber.

I appreciate all your mimeograph difficulties, though I never used this instrument myself. When I was 12 & 13 & 14 I issued a sheet (The R.I. Journal of Astronomy) on a common hectograph—[printing the text like this,[2] and using a multiplicity of inept and obviously juvenile illustrations—] but that was a considerably simpler device than the *Multi-stamp* you mention. Well—good luck!

I thought some of the Yuggothian Fungi would be new to you. Don't hurry on this proposition—but try to have the text accurate when you get around to it. I'm interested at hearing about the cover design[3]—& hope to have a glimpse of the text before the possibility of correction is revoked.

Glad "Tobacco Road" is doing so well in your part of the country. Down here in Florida one sees many groups of natives who correspond more or less to the decaying type depicted by Caldwell. There are retrogressive groups in the north, also—as you'll recall if your read my "Dunwich Horror" in W T a few years ago.

Well—as you see, my trip *did* materialise. I left Providence June 5, & shot straight south—pausing only in ancient Fredericksburg, Va. (boyhood home of Genl. Washington) & in my favourite old city of Charleston, S.C. As you know, I am supremely fond of early-American architecture & the atmosphere of old towns. Down here everything is as delightful as it was last year. The subtropics always benefit my health—indeed, I am now feeling really well for the first time in 1935!

With every good wish, & hoping that success may crown the mimeograph venture, I remain Yrs for the Elder Sign—
    E'ch-Pi-El

*Notes*

1. Written on stationery designed by R. H. Barlow. See HPL to A. W. Derleth, 16 June 1935: "Observe my classy new-last-week-in-spring stationery—cuts of which were designed by my artistic & enterprising host. I am especially proud of the Coffin of Lissa motif in the N.W. & S.E. corners. Other parts typify the Fungi from Yuggoth, permeated by subtle colours out of space." (*Essential Solitude* 698).
2. HPL published the *Rhode Island Journal of Astronomy* from 1904 to 1907 (plus two issues in 1909). Here HPL printed the bracketed text instead of writing it in script to illustrate how he prepared his publications for printing.
3. Louis Smith suggested that a cover be designed around the bookplate Wilfred B. Talman designed for HPL.

[12]    [ALS]

% Barlow, Box 88,
De Land, Florida,
July 22, 1935.

Dear An-Ghah:—
            Glad to hear from you—& shall await with interest the report of your trip with Sultan Malik to the Temple of Tsathoggua. I know you'll find Klarkash-Ton vastly interesting, & hope you'll acquire enough biographical material for an ample article in F M.[1]

No hurry about the Yuggoth stuff—but if Smith changes his mind about bothering with it, Barlow will be glad to take the job off his hands. In fact, Barlow is rather hoping it will come his way. His idea is to add the sonnet "Recapture" (of the same nature as the Fungi—in W T for some late month in 1929 or some early month in 1930) to the rest of the text, making 36 Fungi in all.[2] Hope the W T index progresses well—I'm certainly anxious for a copy! Sorry you've had so much trouble getting old W T issues, but the 1923 ones surely seem to have become rarities.

So you don't care for San Francisco? Some day I hope to get out to your region & see for myself. It seems to me that almost any *hilly* city would have to be picturesque—especially if old & historic. S.F. has a glamourous tradition & the right sort of geography—though of course commonplace architecture can detract from this. Providence is a hill town 300 years old, & with surviving houses as old as 1742. (Farm houses within limits as old as 1735 or earlier.) I live on the crest of a virtual precipice—adjacent to the Brown University campus—in a house 130 years old.[3]

Have read only part of the July W T & find it distinctly mediocre. But then, it never is much good. Received Hill-Billy Crawford's *Marvel Tales* the other day, & must admire the persistence with which the poor chap puts out his semi-illiterate venture. He surely has stamina, however crude his taste may be!

I'll be on the lookout for "The Werewolf of London",[4] despite my rather discouraging past experiences with alleged "horror" cinemas. Thanks for the tip!

    All good wishes—

    Yrs most sincerely—

        E'ch-Pi-El

*Notes*

1. Anger does not seem to have published an article on CAS in *Fantasy Magazine*.

2. Before "Recapture" (written November 1929) was incorporated into *Fungi from Yuggoth* as no. XXXIV, "Evening Star" and "Continuity" had been tentatively designated XXXIV and XXXV in HPL's A.Ms. HPL had not included the two poems in the T.Ms. in the event that he might write more sonnets, as he professed to do (he never did), thus leaving these two poems the penultimate and ultimate in the series, no matter the final number of poems. They became XXXV and XXXVI. After Smith and Anger abandoned the plan to publish the poem, R. H. Barlow set type for and printed eleven sonnets in mid-1936. He also designed a title page for the book with artwork by CAS. Barlow, too, was unable to complete the book and shipped the printed sheets to the Futile Press for completion, but the book never was published.

3. The Samuel Mumford House, built c. 1825.

4. See RB 47, n. 2.

[13]   [ALS]

(next address me at)

66 College St.,

Providence, R.I.,

August 14, 1935

Dear An-Ghah:—

Yes, I heard from Sultan Malik of the blasted voyage to Klarkash-Ton's. C A S surely is in a tight place with two infirm parents on his hands. His responsibilities are enough to break any ordinary person down—& yet he continues his work in literature & the arts. You surely must meet him sooner or later.

I envy you the trip to Mt. Hamilton (named, no doubt, from good old Single-Plot the Cosmic Wizard!) in such appropriate company. I've never looked through any telescope longer than a 12″ (of the Ladd Obs. of Brown U.)—& that in the mediocre air of Providence. With a 36″ atop a clear-skied California mountain, you surely came pretty close to the stamping ground of the Interplanetary Patrol! Interested to hear that Hectograph Ed outlined his formula for pulp concoction.

Thanks for the prospectus of the W T contents pamphlet. Smith sent Barlow a sample page of the enterprise. It surely is a useful thing—though it is not quite what I expected. I thought it would enable one to place a story at once—by listing all the titles alphabetically in one solid column covering the entire file—thus:

Space-Eaters, The, by F. B. Long                              Vol.... p.......

(September 1928)

Well—the existing thing forms an extremely valuable aid as far as it goes, & I hope the sale will be wide. I certainly want a copy. Tell Smith to send it to my home address. I believe he is passing the Yuggothian fungi on to Barlow.

Your trip to Martinez must have been interesting. The Peacock Sultan has told me something of yon dauntless Juggernaut—worthy successor to his own late veteran of the road. I can keep track of your trips rather well now, by virtue of the excellent California maps which Sultan Malik has been sending me. These new bridges over S.F. Bay must indeed be impressive sights.*

I've never read "Dr. Krasinski's Secret", but vastly admire other things of Shiel's. "The Purple Cloud" is a marvellous specimen of the last man theme, while "The House of Sounds" (in the volume called "The Pale Ape & Other Stories")[1] is one of the most powerful weird things ever written. But Shiel is very uneven. Some of his stuff—especially that written before 1900—is discouragingly affected & extravagant.

Glad you like "In Amundsen's Tent"—to my mind one of the best things ever published in W T. Leahy's stuff is usually rather mediocre—but

---

*That cemetery sounds like an exceedingly quaint place.

for once he certainly rang the bell! I haven't read the Ernst serial—which looks distinctly unpromising. Indeed, I no longer waste time sampling pulp serials unless some qualified judge assures me they are worth tackling. Yes—I liked Klarkash-Ton's tale exceedingly.[2] He never disappoints!

Glad you were interested in the N.E. travel notes, & hope you can visit my part of the country some day. I'll send you cards of other ancient places when I acquire some.

On Aug. 18 I shall begin my northward journey—pausing as long as possible at St. Augustine & Charleston. Don't know whether I'll have cash enough to stop in N.Y. I've certainly had a great time down here, & hope I can make the trip again next year. I dread returning to the cold nights & occasional cold days of the north.

Hope you can get the early W T's from Hamilton. Curious that he does not value them! You'd have strong competition if many know of the opportunity!

Charles D. Hornig has been in California, but didn't have time to meet many of the weird group. He was rather pained at hearing of the death of Robert Nelson—whom he had met personally.

All good wishes—
  Yrs for the Elder Sign—
    E'ch-Pi-El

*Notes*

1. See *SL* 1.255 re *The Pale Ape*.
2. John Martin Leahy, "In Amundsen's Tent" (*WT*, August 1935; orig. January 1928) and CAS, "The Treader of the Dust." HPL presumably refers to Paul Ernst's story "Doctor Satan" in the August 1935 issue (it was not a serial). Ernst's most recent serial was "Rulers of the Future" (*WT*, January, February, and March 1935).

[14] [ANS][1]

[Postmarked Providence, RI,
1 October 1935]

Yrs recd. in the midst of the chaos caused by my homecoming amidst piled-up work. The accumulations were prodigious, & I shan't be straightened out again for weeks. Back from the south Sept. 19. I stopped in N.Y. 2 wks. as guest of Donald Wandrei—seeing all the gang. Later took a brief Massachusetts trip—to the "Dunwich" country & Cape Cod. Now I'm wrestling with the work which I've neglected so long. ¶ You'll be sorry to hear of the death of Klarkash-Ton's mother Sept. 9. ¶ Glad you're helping Price toward popularity—he surely is a versatile quality producer! ¶ I've just recd. the *Phantagraph*, & hope it can be kept up & form a successor to the F F. Sent in 2 of the old Fungi recently.[2] ¶ W T surely is getting impossible. I read only 1 or 2 items in each issue. As for M T—the increased size is encouraging, but I can't see that the literary standard amounts to much. There is no good weird magazine to-day. ¶ Hope Lewis Smith's index will develop & appear in a reasonable time.[3] All good wishes—

E'ch-Pi-El

*Notes*

1. *Front:* Benedict Temple of Music, Roger Williams Park, Providence, R.I.
2. "The Dweller" and "Night-Gaunts."
3. Louis C. Smith to HPL, 7 July 1935 (ms., JHL): "I have managed . . . to get five more pages done on it, which brings the total up to twenty-nine, or only five more to do. After that the book will be ready to mail,—before July 15, anyway—as there will be only the gathering of the sheets, and stapling."

[15]    [TLS]

66 College St., Providence, R.I.,
Jany. 16, 1936.

Dear An-Ghah:—

Glad to receive yours of the 1st.—which came as I was spending a week in N.Y. with Long and incidentally seeing a good many of the weird and science fiction group. Met Arthur J. Burks, Otto (of "Eando") Binder, and Maurice M. Kaplan (Jacques Bartel)[1] for the first time, and saw Seabury Quinn for the first time since 1931. Also, of course, was in touch with the regular gang—the Wandrei boys, and old friends of general literary rather than weird-and-science affiliations. Oh, yes—and I also saw young Wollheim, of The Phantagraph, in person for the first time. Some of these meetings took place at a dinner of the Am. Fiction Guild—an organisation of which I am not a member, but to which Sultan Malik belongs. Visited the new Hayden Planetarium of the Am. Museum for the first time—a very impressive device.

Sorry Smith did not complete his venture—but after all, a mere set of tables of contents was only the beginning of what ought to be done. The thing which would be really valuable would be a genuine *index,* listing all stories alphabetically and indicating the number and page in which they appear. That, of course, would be a large undertaking—and it is open to question whether anything as cheap as W.T. fiction would be worth it.

By the way—did Smith send the MS. of my "Fungi" on to Barlow? It has not been returned to me, and I need it very badly—in fact, I have no MS. of these verses now. Barlow is about to print them, and I need something to read proof by—for I hate to decide all the fine points of phraseology and punctuation over again. I must ask Barlow when I write him.[2]

I was very glad of the stroke of luck whereby two of my novelettes landed with Astounding. Such a thing might never happen again, but the incident is pleasant in any case. The placing of the "Mountains"—rejected by Wright in 1931—was particularly gratifying. Hope the story won't disappoint you.

Glad you had such a good time with the Peacock Sultan—he mentioned his outing with you, and sent me a Chinese paper in commemoration of the occasion. I must brush up on my Cantonese! With the new canine addition, the household atop Mt. Kaf must be developing into a menagerie! Glad you have the original illustrations to such important stories.

Enclosed is a circular advertising a new book by a friend of mine—Samuel Loveman, who stands on what might be called the rim of the weird group.[3] It is he who first put me in touch with Clark Ashton Smith back in 1922. This isn't actually weird verse, but touches the borderline of strangeness in places. I read the proofs of this volume three times last September, so it ought to be reasonably accurate!

All good wishes—
Yrs most sincerely,

E'ch Pi-El

*Notes*

1. Maurice M. Kaplan, who wrote under the pseudonyms Jacques Bartel, Philip J. Bartel, and others, published stories in *Wonder Stories, Amazing Stories,* and *Future Fiction.*
2. In early February, HPL wrote to Barlow: "Damn Louis Smith for not returning my Fungi! And I wish I knew where the *old* MS. is. I patched it up & lent it to somebody—but I can't remember whom. That is the only one with annotations as to where the various items have appeared" (*O Fortunate Floridian* 319). Barlow was typesetting the book in June and HPL was reading proofs; since a T.Ms. of *Fungi from Yuggoth* resides at JHL, we can assume it was eventually returned.
3. *The Hermaphrodite and Other Poems.*

[16]  [ANS][1]

[Postmarked Providence, RI,
17 February 1936]

Greetings! I think—in fact, I'm quite sure—that the Fungi MS. which I sent Smith was a carbon copy, so rest easy on that score. However—Barlow (under date of Feby. 3) says he has not received *any* Fungi MS. from Smith, so there is a hitch somewhere. Hope I'll get the copy back somehow, since I'm now without any MS. of the verses. ¶ Read the last two W Ts lately. Moore stories are the best items, but "Norn" is quite notable. ¶ Crawford is thinking of publishing "Shadow over Innsmouth" as a book or booklet, & hopes to get illustrations from Utpatel. ¶ A new (non-remunerative) magazine which might form a good haven for rejected MSS. is *Nuggets*, about to be issued by one B. C. Black, Box 53, Upland, Indiana.[2]

Best wishes—

   H P L

*Notes*

1. *Front:* New Providence County Court House, Providence, R.I.

2. The magazine does not seem to have been published.

[17]   [ANS][1]

[Postmarked Providence, RI,

2 September 1936]

Greetings! Glad your group liked "Mts. of Madness"—which was so hopelessly mangled toward the end that I consider the story virtually unpublished. ¶ "Cats of Ulthar" was just a private edition of 40 copies which served as Barlow's '35 Christmas card. Don't believe any extras are available. No volume of my verse will appear for a long while, since Barlow is moving to Kansas—doesn't know when he can get at his printing & binding apparatus again. Glad you've seen the Goblin Tower.[2] ¶ Barlow visited here from Jul. 28 to Sept. 1, & became quite acclimated to ancient New England. I showed him around Providence, & we also explored Salem & Marblehead (Arkham & Kingsport) in company with young Sterling. He likewise saw New Bedford. In doing some local genealogical research Barlow found he is my 6th cousin, by virtue of common descent from one John Rathbone, born in 1658.[3] ¶ Early in August old Adolphe de Castro (one-time friend of Bierce) was here—& on one occasion he, Barlow, & I sat on a tomb in a hidden hillside churchyard & wrote rhymed acrostics on the name Edgar Allan Poe[4]—who 90 years ago used to wander in that selfsame necropolis when on route to Providence. ¶ Sultan Malik told me of your recent visit, & of your appreciation of K'hi-K'hi Conquering Lion of Judah. Hope your joint article will develop well & see print.

Best wishes—

   E'ch-Pi-El

*Notes*

1. *Front:* Campus, Brown University, Providence, R.I.

2. See RB 54, n. 3.

3. See *SL* 5.301, and also p. 343.

4. See RB 62, n. 7.

# Letters to Kenneth Sterling

[1]    [AHT]

Haunted Jungle of Kled-Yaddith
—Hour of the Carrion Wind from the
Cyclopean, Ivy-Gown Ruins:
[July 1935]

O Mighty Booleywag:[1]

    I am tardy in acknowledging your appreciated missive, but can probably be pardoned because of the crowded programme amidst which I find myself. The trip from ancient Charleston was pleasant & uneventful. I slept soundly in Jacksonville on the night of the 8–9th, & in the morning took the De Land coach—which whirled me through the truly subtropical scenery marking my journey's end . . . . a type of scenery not to be found as far north as Charleston, despite the presence of small palmettos & more or less Spanish moss there. I could not find the particular post cards you wish, but have stumbled on some new & very attractive specimens—three of which I am enclosing. My eyes, however, are still peeled . . . & I'll probably have some of the desiderate views before I've finished making the rounds of local stationery emporia. Hope these gaudy lures will succeed in dragging you down—I'm sure you & Florida would find each other congenial! You'd realise, if you saw this place, that my trip was a matter of attraction at the southern end rather than of flight at the northern end. Indeed—my aunt & everyone up north can prove that my drowsy drooping is a settled geographico-physical phenomenon just as marked (if not more so) before you were born as since that felicitous event! Well—down here I'm feeling great . . . & shall probably continue to do so until the chill of the north shrivels me up once more. Not merely in general pep & alertness, but in specific things like digestion & nasal phenomena, I am utterly transformed by the healing & vivifying magic of the subtropics.

    Well—Barlow met me at the De Land coach station, & I found things about as they were last year—except that the household is a bit ampler. Col. Barlow is now at home, & Bob's elder brother is here on a furlough from San Antonio—where he is stationed as a 2nd Lieutenant of the army. Feline population interesting—most of my 1934 friends on hand, plus two lordly Persians (yellow) brought down from Washington by my young host. Our programme is about the same as '34—book discussion, boating on the lake, monkeying with type & press, &c. &c. &c. Bob is such an active young devil that I hardly have any time to write letters . . . . & if I wait till he retires, I'm too damned sleepy to write coherently! Maybe I'll use these conditions as an excuse for dropping some of my correspondence!

As for courses in penmanship—gawd knows I need a dozen of 'em, but I doubt they'd do me any good. I had all that in school, & it simply went out the other ear. The point is that I couldn't get all my MSS. & letters written if I had to pay attention to any set of rules or stop to form my individual letters. With me, perforce, the *word* or even *phrase* or *sentence* is the primary unit which makes its bid for recognition—not the *letter*. That's what my uncle used to say about his writing . . . . although you insist it wasn't as bad as mine. However, if you know of any magical book on the subject, send it along & I'll give it the once-over. No harm in trying anything! Actually, though, some of the type-writer-spoiled decadents of this indolent generation ought to learn *how to read handwriting* . . . . . that is, how to read all the various specimens that come along in a day's work . . . the good & the bad alike. People *used* to be able to do it—you know the anecdotes of Balzac's & Darwin's proofs, & all that. They took a broad view & considered each word in relation to the *context*—acquiring such an instinctive & automatic command of *general* appearances that they didn't often go wrong. For example—when anybody sees a symbol like *lhr* between such words as move & chair he knows damn well the thing means *the*. One doesn't have to stop & ponder whether the *t, h,* & *e* are per-fectly defined as separate units. What of it? It's perfectly clear according to the rules of common sense that any symbol of the given *approximate* shape in the given location *must,* barring a miracle, be *the* & nothing else. It's a matter of sharp observation & quick common sense—& in the old days people were expected to use both of these qualities. Only in the last 2 decades, since the complete ascendancy of the typewriter, have people 'laid down on the job' & refused to employ ordinary vigilance in recognising assorted forms of script. I know my own script is lousy, but the greater number of my correspondents seem to have no trouble with it—not even Barlow, a member of your own generation. Oddly enough, the one who complains *next* most loudly of my cacographic hieroglyphs is a member of my generation . . . Edward H. Cole.

Glad you have the "Nemesis" copies—thanks endlessly for the self-sacrificing care given the magazine, & for the carbons you intend to bestow upon the Old Gentleman. As for those carbons—I don't care how they're folded, but they might as well be dumped at 66 as sent down here. I have no immediate correspondential use for them—& Barlow has the magazine any-how. But again, thanks, & all that!

No hurry about the books—I shan't know the difference whenever they reach 66. By the way—Barlow no longer takes the science-fiction magazines, so that I won't be able to follow reading suggestions as closely as I otherwise might.

Glad you've given the elderly critic of West End Ave.[2] a good dressing-down, & hope he'll take the lesson to heart. He's a nice chap—bright & intelligent—but a little to erratic & impulsive in his judgments, & a little too proud of his birthdays.

Thanks for the bouquets regarding "Nemesis"—but I'm afraid it won't make the school readers for many a year. I'm glad you like those lines

"Where the black planets roll without aim—
Where they roll in their horror unheeded, without knowledge or lustre or name."

—because they are favourites of my own, born of a very potent visual & imaginative concept, which nobody has ever singled out for praise before. It certainly gives me satisfaction to know that I've really put across something with that image. The primary concept is one of vast nighted worlds holding unimaginable concepts known to no other parts of space, & so hideous that any one of them would explode with horror if made conscious of the other's hellish arcana. As for the identity of the "sin" from which all this daemoniac pursuit stems—I must admit that I haven't the least idea what it could be! Probably some affront against the governing powers of the cosmos—some insult to Azathoth or Nyarlathotep or some of those boys—since it is that sort of a "sin" which the weavers of mythology seemed generally to classify as least pardonable. The affront must be *conscious*, so that I fancy the mere *losers* of CAS drawings are not condemned in this fashion. What would happen to a *deliberate destroyer* of Clericashtoniana is another matter—& one perhaps too monstrous to record! [. . .]

Yrs for the Grey Litany of Yoth—E'ch-Pi-El

*Notes*

1. L. Frank Baum's *The Road to Oz* (1909) has a character known as the "Head Booleywag" (p. 222).
2. I.e., Frank Belknap Long, Jr.

[2]    [AHT]

% Barlow, Box 88,
De Land, Florida
August 3, 1935.

Obeisances & Genuflections, O Grand Exalted Booleywag!
Iä! Shub-Niggurath! The Goat with
a Thousand Young! Cthulhu
ftaghn . . . Yog-Sothoth!
IAOPUMUMFSTFPUSA
        [. . .]
        [. . .] Congratulations on your capture of second prize in the W.S. cover contest! Who got first—or don't you know yet? If that rat Gernsback overturns Hornig's decision & deposes you from your well-earned eminence I shall advocate his immediate eradication . . . or conversely, if he boosts you to *first* prize I shall recommend the forgiving of all his multiform sins! Regarding

that point about the "northern" hemisphere—if the asteroid has an axial inclination like the earth's, it naturally follows that one of its poles will be directed to the same part of the sky toward which the earth's north pole is directed. Hemispheres will roughly correspond—so that the asteroidans will have a word to express *"the hemisphere turned toward that part of the sky containing Ursa Minor, Ursa Major, Draco, Cassiopeia, &c."* The *word* will not be the English word "northern"—but it will *mean* the same thing . . . & the corresponding hemisphere of the earth will naturally be called by that word. In asteroid-language the term may be *lgtyggh urghphnn* . . . but the only way you can make the reader understand it is to use English & say "northern hemisphere". Surely Wollheim realises that we habitually use terms like this in connexion with other planets. We constantly speak of the *north* polar cap of Mars, & the *northern* hemisphere of Jupiter. Roughly speaking, we carry a mental picture of the solar system with the ecliptic in the middle, & with the side toward the Bears & Dragon arbitrarily known as "north", & the opposite side known as "south". Inhabitants of any solar planet would do something like this—having a certain sense of "up" & "down" in surrounding space . . . depending on the hemisphere they inhabit. There would be some generic way of differentiating the hemispheres of any planet whose axis approaches a perpendicular to the orbit—the side toward the Bear & Dragon having one name, & the side toward the Octant & Southern Cross having another name. And the counterparts of those names in our language are certainly "north" & "south". Of course this confuses the average plane of all planetary orbits with the *equator* of the sky (the latter a prolongation of the *earth's* equator in space), but the difference is not great enough to matter. That is, the difference in orbital inclination of all the major planets is not extreme, & the variation of the earth's axis from a perpendicular to the average orbital plane is not radical enough to annul the general idea of direction involved. To sum up—it is both legitimate & natural . . . if not well-nigh inevitable . . . for the inhabitants of one solar planet to use terms roughly corresponding to N. & S. in connexion with the entire solar system. The terms N. & S. would likewise have a *certain* meaning to persons outside the solar system yet near enough our part of space to have most of the constellations as we see them. To one from the ultimate outside reaches of space-time the terms would be meaningless. One might make quite a study of directional notions in ultimate space. I'll say more on this subject after reading the story. Well—I hope the story appears with a minimum of misprints, & with at least a half-decent illustration. I'll be looking for it. With *two* acceptances, you are surely on the high road to authorship![1] Good luck with Dr. Zorn & the Martian war! [. . .]

    Yrs for staples, omnipresent & eternal—
      The Whipplegob.

*Notes*

1. KJS's first story sale was "The Brain-Eaters of Pluto."

[3]     [AHT]

Burrow of the Whipplegob
—Oct$^r$ 6, 1935

Invincible Booleywag:—

[. . .]

[. . .] Glad you've read "Pegāna". Of course it has not the keen interest of "A Dreamer's Tales", since it is essentially a pseudo-mythology instead of a set of stories. It lays the foundations for the volumes which are to come. Here we learn of the gods & of their prophets, & of the wise words spoken by such great prophets as Imbaun. In the next volume, "Time & the Gods", the theme is expanded, & we hear certain tales of gods & men in the morning of the world. Then comes the age of heroes & of marvellous strange lands, & we have "The Sword of Welleran" & "A Dreamer's Tales". But as the world grows old, the spirit of childlike faith & eager wonder & adventurous expectancy fades out of it—& we behold the growth of flippant scepticism & irony & hints of *conscious* myth-weaving & rational explanations. In such a mood was "The Book of Wonder" conceived. Nor do we ever again see the old, naive Dunsany in quite his pristine mood, though there are occasional brief backward flashes. Of his recent work I like best "The Curse of the Wise Woman—which is an almost realistic sketch of a 19$^{th}$ century boyhood in Ireland. Yes—you might some day write a tale about the Iaop pantheon of dark daemon-gods—Booleywag, Cocolorum, Whipplegob, & Bazoolah. You could tell how the Bazoolah finally dispersed into a diffusive vapour of words—having been found to consist of nothing else. [. . .]

Yrs by the Black Stone ——— E'ch-Pi-El
Cesarically Apotheosised Whipplegob


[4]     [AHT]

The Ancient Citadel—
Oct. 23, 1935

Invincible Booleywag:—

[. . .] Regarding the crucifix—I remarked at the time how utterly hackneyed such a device is, but of course I realised (as you will upon reflection, remembering the typical forms of comparative mythology) that the cross-symbol is by no means confined to any one religion. It is, indeed, one of the earliest magical signs known to anthropologists, being generally associated with life & fertility, & probably having a remotely phallic origin. Surely you recall the "ankh" or Egyptian crux ansata is ♀—which incidentally (with a slight lowering of the horizontal line) has become the astronomical symbol of the planet Venus (♀). The Swastika or hooked cross 卐 goes back to prehistoric times in India & elsewhere, while various cruciform types figured so largely in Aztec-Mayan religious iconography that the Conquistadores thought the natives were half-turned to some variant of Christianity! Belknap knew all this when he wrote the story[1]—though I dare say the hackneyed literary custom influenced him more than the anthropological background. Some sort of symbol (or spoken ritual) seems desirable to use in most cases of conjuration, since that has been the virtually universal custom among superstitious mankind since the beginning of the species. Something in the basic mental & imaginative makeup of the human animal seems to call for tangible symbolism—or audible incantation—in approaching or invoking the imagined powers of the cosmos—hence the menhirs & cromlechs, idols & obelisks, crosses & pentacles, horseshoes & rabbits' feet, amulets & onangas, saints' bones & holy water, prayers, hymns, & rituals, &c. &c. &c., which figure throughout the field of mythology. But when I write a story I try (save in pseudo-folklore bits like "Psychopompos") to be reasonably original & unhackneyed in choosing a symbol for such purposes. [. . .]

When last I wrote you, I believe I mentioned that my aunt & I were about to get a ride to New Haven. Well—the trip came off brilliantly on Oct. 8. I had 7½ hrs. for exploration while my aunt visited a friend. The day was ideally sunny (though I could have wished it warmer), & the ride through rural Connecticut scenery (100 m = 2½ hrs) delightful. New Haven is not as rich as Providence in colonial antiquities, but it has a peculiar charm of its own. Streets are broad & well-kept, & in the residential sections (some of which involve hills & fine views) there are endless stately mansions a century old, with generous grounds & gardens, & an almost continuous overarching canopy of great elms. I visited ancient Connecticut Hall (1752—oldest Yale college building, where Nathan Hale of the class of 1773 roomed), old Central Church (1812—with an interesting crypt containing the grave of Benedict Arnold's first wife), the Pierpont house (1767—now Yale Faculty Club), the historical, art, & natural history museums, the Farnam & Marsh botanic gardens, & various other points of interest—crowding as much as possible into the limited time at my disposal.

Most impressive of all the sights, perhaps, were the great *new* quadrangles of Yale University—each an absolutely faithful reproduction of old-time architecture & atmosphere, & forming a self-contained little world in itself. The Gothic courtyards transport one in fancy to mediaeval Oxford or Cambridge—spires, oriels, pointed arches, mullioned windows, arcades with groined roofs, climbing ivy, sundials, lawns, gardens, vine-clad walls & flagstoned walks—everything to give the young occupants that massed impression of their cultural heritage which they might obtain in Old England itself. To stroll through these quadrangles in the golden afternoon sunlight; at dusk, when the candles within the diamond-paned casements flicker up one by one; or in the beams of a mellow Hunter's Moon; is to walk bodily into an enchanted region of dream. It is the past & the ancient motherland brought magically to the present time & place. The choicest of the quadrangles is Calhoun College—named from the great Carolinian (whose grave in St. Philip's Churchyard, Charleston, I visited less than 2 months ago), who was a graduate of Yale. Nor are the Georgian quadrangles less glamourous—each being a magical summoning-up of the world of

2 centuries ago. Many distinct styles of Georgian architecture are represented, & the buildings & landscaping alike reflect the finest taste which European civilisation has yet evolved or is likely to evolve. Lucky is the boy whose formative years are spent amid such scenes! I wandered for hours through this limitless labyrinth of unexpected elder microcosms, & mourned the lack of further time. Certainly, I must visit New Haven again, since many of its treasures would require weeks for proper inspection & appreciation.

You would have enjoyed especially the natural history museum (belonging to the college), with its special biological exhibits illustrative of evolution, & its absolutely unique geological & palaeontological section. In this latter there are illuminated models shewing the world in previous geologic ages—mesozoic landscapes with tyrannosaurs & stegosaurs fighting, & brontosaurs wading in rivers; Cretaceous scenes with giant cycads, & carboniferous swamp panoramas with tree-ferns & other primitive vegetation. All are tremendously realistic—though necessarily on a somewhat small scale (making a brontosaurus about a foot & a half long). There is also a good collection of prehistoric bones (great stuff for a ghoul after old Centre Church's crypt & the Grove St. cemetery are exhausted!)—though it doesn't equal the American Museum's hall of skeletons.

But even this New Haven jaunt didn't quite end my 1935 travels. Last Wednesday at 6 a.m. my friend Samuel Loveman blew into town, & after a session at #66 we both started out for Boston to absorb books, museums, & antiquities. Stayed 3 days—stopping at Technology Chambers in Irvington St. Took in quite a few things (including the cinema "Last Days of Pompeii"[2]— quite a spectacle, though infantile as a story), but had no time to look up Cole or anybody else in the group. Back to Prov. Friday afternoon, & browsing in local bookstalls. Then I regretfully saw the guest off on the Colonial Line boat. Incidentally—don't ever try to use this line. It has gone to the devil lately, & Loveman found the rabble of drunken fellow-passengers almost unendurable! [. . .]

Yours by the Sign of Nug—
Ech-Pi-El

*Notes*

1. Apparently "The Space-Eaters" (*WT*, July 1928).
2. *The Last Days of Pompeii* (RKO Radio Pictures, 1935), directed by Ernest B. Schoedsack and Merian C. Cooper (uncredited); starring Preston Foster, Alan Hale, and Basil Rathbone.

[5]    [AHT]

Caverns of Kai
—Nov. 20, 1935

Mighty Booleywag:—

[. . .] As for the higher grade of magazines—I don't think I'm wrong in my belief that none of them have any use for weird fiction. The spirit of the age is directly opposed to fantasy of any type, & it will be years before the fashion changes. Fantasy is the expression of subjective instead of objective life— moods instead of events—& the sort which I write represents moods coloured by tradition. This is wholly against modern taste. Today the demand is for reali- ty—if not objective reality, then the sort of mood-analysis which excludes tradi- tion & deals more with raw emotion [&] psychological complexities than with sheer constructive imagination. There's hardly any denying this—a glance at the current standard magazines shews the state of thing. Of fantasies in the tradi- tional vein, virtually nothing is used except the exaggeratedly light, humorous trifles of the later Dunsany, & the allegedly "smart", pseudo-allegorical, symbol- ic junk of triflers like Cabell. It seems to be a fact—& others agree with me in so regarding it—that the opening for serious weird material is *book publication; &* my stuff simply isn't good enough to make the grade in that direction. [. . .]

[. . .] About rockets—certainly I realise that the major experiments in- volve really serious research. They can probably get higher up in the strato- sphere than anything else ever can, & it is surely fitting that all their possibilities be investigated. But I trust that repeated accidents will cause ex- perimenters to take additional precautions—excluding spectators when any- thing problematical or of unusual magnitude is attempted. The *newness* of all this business is quite bewildering to an old man—when I was young the rocket principle was never heard of in connexion with locomotion, so that in writing my ponderous essay "Can the Moon Be Reached by Man?" in 1906 I enumerated only three possible motive powers—shooting from a cannon, screen to cut off gravity (if such be ever discovered), & some future manipu- lation of electrical repulsion. How times do change!

Thank god my elucidation of relative Harvard–Yale merits arrived in time to prevent your signing up with that gilded temple of showy illiteracy in New Haven! As for the Peabody Museum—its strongest point is the scope & ar- rangement of the exhibits. I know the American has a good lot of anthropologi- cal stuff—Polynesian, African, Esquimau, Peruvian, Mexican—scattered around here & there; but it's harder to get a connected panorama than in the Peabody. And more—the best Am. Indian stuff is in a separate museum at 156th St. However, as a museum of natural history in general, I guess the American does lead all competitors. I recall those glass models of marine organisms. Hope the management suitably corrects that case of mis-labelling (or mis-labelling of a case) which your eagle eye so unerringly spotted! I must see that planetarium the next time I traverse Manhattan's teeming ways—& I'd like to see the Philadel-

phia one also. Glad you've witnessed the spectacle at last. Seems to me Wollheim isn't the only hyper-critical bird if you object to not seeing (in an arrangement supposed to represent the heavens as seen without optical aid) Uranus,
Neptune, & Pluto! But wait—possibly I'm getting the various types of exhibition mixed. If there is a performance which displays the solar system as a pure
diagram—& *does* shew the satellites of Mars, &c.—then it is odd that no attempt
is made to shew the three outermost orbs. I doubt if any useful end would be
served by showing any object as improbable as Dr. Lescarbault's "Vulcan"[1]—
although they might have included a couple of possible trans-Plutonians whose
presence is suggested by the location of certain cometary aphelia. Uranus is just
on the limit of naked-eye visibility—on the 6th stellar magnitude. But when you
stop to think of the number of such faint points of light peppered around the
nocturnal heavens, you can realise why it is considered, for all practical purposes, as invisible. [. . .]

    Yrs. for the Apocalypse of Yuun
        —Ech-Pi-El

*Notes*

1. Edmond Modeste Lescarbault (1814–1894), French doctor and amateur astronomer best remembered for his claimed 1859 observation of the planet Vulcan.

[6]    [AHT]

                                    Peak of Mt. Ngranek
                                        —Dec. 14, 1935

Illustrious Kheh-Es:—

    [. . .] Well, well, so Sonny Belknap thinks Grandpa is interested only by
the very great or the very dumb, eh? I'd never noticed that before, although
upon reflection I can perhaps see what the young scamp means. For all my
fellow-numbskulls in the depths I have of course a sort of fraternal feeling—
loyalty—or "class consciousness" as the Marxists would say. When I see another goof whose density is a trifle greater than mine (I have met 3 or 4 such
in the course of a long life), or who is dense in different spots, I take a sort of
fraternal delight in giving him a boost so that he can shew the critics something for once in his life. The reward is gratified class pride. Thus it makes me
chuckle to think that I've put over a story by old Bill Lumley. Let us dubs pull
together, & the smart guys can't always keep us down! "They laughed when I
sat down to the typewriter" . . . & all that! Well, at the other end of the scale I
simply admire intrinsic quality when I see it. All that makes the bipedal pri-
mate homo sapiens at all notable among the other apes is his reason, & I like
to see a guy who can really use that quality—as so few ever do. Thus I find a
sequence of truly rational & discerning accomplishments—& its performer—
of very genuine interest, albeit a different kind of interest from that fraternal

tie which binds me to the Lumleys and Bivonae.[1] One has to admire the Newtons & Einsteins & Bertrand Russells & Kenneth Sterlings at a respectful distance! Now as contrasted with the kindred boneheads & the distant luminaries, how little of interest there is in just the average egg! With a peck measure of beans at hand, who can be especially interested in any one of the beans, even though it be a very fair & typical specimen? So with the average citizen. He is a very worthy product of a mould, but haven't we seen thousands of such products before? We know his folkways & psychology in advance—his tastes, shibboleths, habit-patterns, &c.—& there is no especial fun in seeing these repeated over & over again. We go to the zoo to see yaks & zebras because we don't encounter them often—who could expect us to be equally interested in cows & horses? Or rather, who could expect an old geezer like grandpa to be so interested? I understand that to the younger urban generation of bottled milk & motor users, cows & horses are indeed in the pink rhinoceros & duck-billed platypus class!

Well, boiling the matter down, I guess the real secret of interest with me is *unusualness*. I like a guy to be original—to be himself, & not merely the 987654321st impression of his civilisation's rubber stamp. Belknap isn't quite right in thinking that the person of average *capacity* doesn't interest me. What bores me is the person of average *tastes & attitudes & performances*. I don't care what any bird's I.Q. is, so long as he is as original, independent, & sincere in his attitude & work as his own particular cerebrum will let him be. Of course, as I've said, I feel a bond of fellowship with the Bivonae & the Olsons, & a respectful admiration for the Aristotles, the Descartes, the Sterlings, & the Belknaps; but aside from these little partialities I'm scarcely less interested in the chap of average endowment *who is equally original & distinctive* in thought & expression.* Let me see if I can cite a case. Well—take Bob Howard. There's a bird whose *basic mentality* seems to me to be just about the good respectable citizen's bank cashier, medium shopkeeper, ordinary lawyer, stockbroker, high school teacher, prosperous farmer, pulp fictionist, skilled mechanic, successful salesman, responsible government clerk, routine army or navy officer up to a colonel, &c. average—bright & keen, accurate & retentive, but not profound or analytical—yet who is at the same time one of the most eminently interesting beings I know. Two-Gun is interesting because he has refused to let his thoughts & feelings be standardised. He remains himself. He couldn't—today—solve a quadratic equation, & probably thinks that Santayana is a brand of coffee—but he has a set of emotions which he has moulded & directed in uniquely harmonious patterns, & from which proceed his marvellous outbursts of historic retrospection & geographical description (in letters), & his vivid, energised & spontaneous pictures of a prehistoric world of battle in fiction . . . . pictures which insist on remaining distinctive & self-

---

*It is possible, though, that complete originality is commoner in dubs & geniuses.

expressive despite all outward concessions to the stultifying pulp ideal. It is, therefore, piquant & enjoyable to exchange ideas with Two-Gun or to read his stories. He is of about the same intelligence as Seabury Quinn—but Yuggoth, what a difference! And yet, of course, when I say *distinctiveness*, I mean *genuine & harmonious* distinctiveness. I have no use for the shallow, self-conscious freak who grows long hair, or wears windsor ties, or cultivates boorish or affected manners. That isn't originality, but merely standardised mediocrity's effort to ape originality. I like a person to be quiet & unobtrusive, but really *individual* in his tastes & perceptions & intellectual or artistic expression. Nor do I like freaks whose differences from the average—even if genuine—are merely the result of callousness, stupidity, or disease . . . . the anti-social criminal or bum or ruthless leader, or the sadist or sissy or general sloppy mess. That isn't harmonious imaginative independence, but merely bad construction or malfunctioning. Perhaps I could define my favourite type by saying that it is a person of basically normal natural personality, with a strong sense of fitness, harmony, & social obligation, who is sincere in his thoughts & imagination & who refuses to let these qualities be modelled, dulled, or standardised by herd psychology or other irrelevant outside influences. He may be a damn fool, or an average guy, or a genius—but if he has this balance of qualities shewing in his correspondence or conversation or accomplishments I generally find him more or less interesting. I haven't yet attempted to determine the West End philosopher's place on the Bivona-to-Bergson mental scale, but fancy he is comfortably removed from the cellar rungs despite the occasionally visible follies of youth & hasty judgment. Which reminds me that I surely hope his *Phantagraph* will succeed.[2]

Turning to stratosphere balloons & their use as rocket-launchers—I imagine that during the infancy of the device each launching would pretty well wreck the bearer of the recoil, but that later on some floating device of less destructibility might be invented. Not that it wouldn't need a great deal of overhauling & strengthening after each use. I honestly don't know how well a *parachute* can ever be used a second time or more. In *any* case I fancy it would require expert renovation & reinforcement, but the exact amount would seem to me to differ according to the kind of flight & landing it had undergone. Often, of course, it would be so banged & dragged that there could be no question of second use. Glad you heard a good rocket lecture. I don't doubt but that this form of propulsion is getting to be more & more a thing of exact & dependable study. Yes—I saw an item about the Lindbergh–Guggenheim backing of the Goddard experiments. I always realised that Goddard was a serious investigator.[3] Glad the latest victim you observed is now on his feet again.

About Belknap's assertion that I might attempt hackwork with a "plot genie"—I'd call it *ancient memory* rather than pure imagination. In view of the hack work which I have done in the course of revision, some of which has proved salable, I often used to ask myself whether I could not with equal effectiveness devise low grade formula hashes on my own hook, & reap all instead of part of the returns. Of course I lack all skill in the synthetic, jack-in-the-box *plots* demanded, so that some mechanical boost, like the "plot genie" or its equivalent would be an understood necessity. Well, in pursuance with this theory I bought one or two of the cheaper devices on whose principle the "genie" is based;[4] but soon saw that any practical use of them would be impossible for me or anyone remotely like me. The wholly meaningless mechanical points called "characters", the unmotivated word-messes called "action"—& everything of the sort—were so utterly vacuous, repellent, & abhorrent to me that I saw I could do nothing in such a field. Even the conventional jargon demanded in place of civilised English (it makes me crawl & shiver to see Belknap & Wandrei using it so callously nowadays!) nauseated me so violently that I realised my inability to have anything to do with it. When I *revised* the kindergarten pap & idiot-asylum slop of *other* poor fishes, I was at least *not creating* any fresh slobberings. I was, in a microscopic way, putting just the faintest bit of order, coherence, direction, & comprehensible language into something whose Neanderthaloid ineptitude was *already* mapped out. My work, ignominious as it was, was at least in the right *direction*—making that which was *utterly* amorphous & drooling just the minutest trifle less close to the protozoan stage. While I left substantially untouched the repulsive mob-catering points which made the wretched thing salable, I was spared the supreme degradation of having to think up such simian devices myself. I *could* revise crap—but the attempt to *construct* such stuff was beyond me. Well— this truth sank in gradually, & didn't impress me fully until a couple of winters ago. Up to that time I used to harbour vague, always-postponed plans for getting a plot-machine & trying my luck—& I see that Belknap remembers them. I think the last time I ever discussed that theme with him was August, 1933, when I visited the family at Onset, near Cape Cod, where they were briefly aestivating.[5] But it's an obsolete issue now. As I told Price in a letter only the other day, I couldn't possibly write a detective story of the common type—or any other, for that matter. I have, to begin with, not the faintest interest or natural aptitude in the given field. Secondly, I know very little about the requisite details of the forms of contemporary life involved—the world of modern inventions, business procedures, & so on. Thirdly, the prescribed attitude, character-&-action formulae, methods, & language concerned are so overwhelmingly repulsive to me that the emotional handicap would leave me helpless. [. . .]

[. . .] That lecture by Durant must have been very interesting. I've read— in fact, I own—his "Story of Philosophy"; & he seems to me to be a very wide scholar & gifted expositor, although he has a slight tendency to truckle to hard aspirations & favour illogical popular attitudes of optimism & baseless belief instead of coming right out with the stark & cheerless known facts about the universe & man's negligible & transient place therein. He may, though, have changed somewhat in the decade or so since his book was written. What he says concerning multiplication of inferior stock at the expense of superior is a tragic truth—& something which can never be corrected until religion (with its crazy opposition to birth-control, sterilisation, & all other sensible eugenic measures) is curbed, & democratic irresponsibility replaced by some more select & unified form of government. I doubt, though, whether even the most tremendous increase in the general mental level could do more than palliate the dilemma of unemployment in an industrially mechanised world; since the *primary* cause of the trouble is not that the majority aren't equal to the tasks which need doing, but that there can never again—with modern machinery—be tasks enough *of any kind* to go around. Only a relatively few persons—& this includes both the intelligent planners & the inferior operatives—will ever be needed in order to perform adequately all the tasks which will normally need performing in the future world . . . . even if the general standard of living is immensely raised. The point is that, once a certain type of article has been designed & produced, it is possible to keep right on *duplicating* that article (as in meeting a higher standard, with more people buying or needing any given article) with only a *few* more employes than those needed to produce a small supply. Increasing demands for *goods* will *not* call for any *even comparably corresponding* increase in *employment.* It may as well be understood that unemployment on a colossal scale will persist just as long as industry remains in private hands & without a strict governmental regulation of the hours, distribution, conditions, & remuneration of labour. Nor would any increase in mass intelligence help more than a trifle. While of course the shrinking of employment throws the dull & inept out of their jobs *first,* so that we commonly associate inferiority with unemployment, the brilliant & competent feel the pinch soon enough. Those who retain jobs in hard times present a higher *average* than those without them, since the latter group *includes* the less-efficient & chronically unemployable element. But when we analyse the jobless & lower-averaged group we find that it is not homogeneous—being composed of two distinct elements: first, the inferior who were the first to go; & second, the superior who were forced out later, when jobs grew too few to accomodate all the superior people. Since firing in the upper levels is not always a precisely quality-graded process, it is safe to say that a good part of the *later* victims of unemployment are not a whit inferior in quality to the people who remain in jobs. Today the jobless professor, engineer, doctor, executive, &c. is a familiar sight. There are simply not enough jobs to go around, & the number of the jobless would be scarcely less even if *all* the unemployed, instead of only *part,* were of reasonably superior intelligence. Perhaps a wider superiority of intelligence would enable many persons to *change* jobs—thus producing a flow of labour from crowded to uncrowded fields—but in times of depression this would be no more than a drop in the bucket, since *all* fields are more or less overcrowded under such conditions. The fact is that laissez-faire capitalism is just about done for. It cannot survive, for its constant drift is toward a greater & greater impoverishment of the majority. Not all the diffused intelligence in the world could check the steady concentration of wealth among the handful of proprietors who control the tools & materials of industry, & the relentless crowding out of more & more persons for whom no place among the proprietors & exploiters is left. Only a few people are able to buy of the producers, & the troughs of the "natural" business cycle get deeper at each successive depression. The only way the capitalists can keep afloat themselves is by virtually forcing the people who still have money under the tightening system to buy all sorts of tawdry luxuries which they don't need, & by making goods so inferior that they need frequent (& really unnecessary, if the things were well-made) replacement. The result can be seen around us any day—the appalling *waste* of materials while millions suffer for lack of anything, & the intolerable tawdriness & vulgarity of the *psychological atmosphere* caused by the continual pressure on people to buy things which they don't need, & the consequent ill-bred exaltation of material possessions, acquisitive ability, & extravagance. The fact is, that plutocracy is as destructive culturally as it is physically. And in the end, of course, it destroys itself. Marx saw this nearly a century ago, & there is no questioning the epoch-making nature of his discovery even if we reject the particular deductions from it—& proposed applications of it—which he & some of his followers have made. The *main features* of this mounting disharmony or accumulating social stress could not be altered by any rise in the level of public intelligence. What intelligence *would* do, however, is to make possible a rational modification & ultimate replacement of the system without any such hellish mess as the Russians have experienced. Higher intelligence would recognise the asininity of the *profit* principle as distinguished from the *reward-for-service* principle, & would get rid of any system which makes the maintenance of essential productive services conditional upon the heavy piling-up of a surplus profit not needed for the securing of new materials or the remuneration of labourers & executives. It would not duplicate the bolshevik absurdity of exalting manual labour over directive & administrative work, or of dragging culture down to the level of the factory-hand. With the basic industries publicly owned, it would continue to remunerate high-grade service amply & low-grade service less amply. Traditional institutions would continue unhampered. But it *would* get rid of the eternal quest for *extra profit*—a quest which breeds the paradox—or crime—of *waste*. Under a non-profit economy the feverish *encouragement* of material extravagance & needless buying would cease. The idea would not be to make as many things as possible, & then cram them down people's throats whether they want them or not, but to make *what the people want* in just the quantities wanted. Fewer things would be made, sold, & used—life would be freed of many needless & ostentatious luxuries & gadgets, & everything (being made honestly & without the profit motive) would last longer. Thus *waste* (about which Stuart Chase has said so much)[6] would be cut down to a minimum. The atmosphere would be freed from the stultifying element of acquisitive commercialism—from the waste of human skill & effort on mere needless personal surplus-accumulation, & from the false ideals whereby street-gamin *sharpness & * money-seeking business enterprise are today praised as ends in themselves. At the same time the *amount of production & activity* would scarcely be decreased, since the wider spread of resources through publicly regulated employment conditions (including old-age pensions & unemployment insurance) would cause nearly everyone to share more widely in the surviving staple products of industry. People wouldn't buy so many gewgaws & trick machines, & they wouldn't buy razor-blades & electric-light bulbs & motor cars so often—because the old ones would last longer. But *more* people would be buying motor cars & good clothing & solid furniture & ample food than were ever able to buy them before. Each person would work less time than a full-time employe of today, but more people would be working. Humbler employes would receive more pay than they do now, middling employes about the same as at present, key executives slightly less than now, & large "owners" nothing at all because there would be no individual large owners. Nothing really radical—merely putting all large industry on the *present* basis of city water & postal service & fire, police, & military protection in the U.S., of the railways in Mexico, of the telephone system in New Zealand, & so on. There would be no reason to disturb small trading & retail shopkeeping at all. In a word, there could be an intelligent *socialism,* based on the known *facts* of Marxian economics, without any of the idiotic & murderous tyrannies & restrictions & cultural convulsions of bolshevism or "orthodox Marxism" as preached by the Stalins & Briffaults & Belknaps of today. There is no question at all of the ability of such a system to function if a majority of the people were of even fair intelligence. It might even function with our existing bunch of nitwits *if it could once be put into operation.* But there is the rub. How to sit on the greedy at both ends of the economic scale—the capitalists & the beggars—& how to set in motion the necessary administrative steps—there, gentlemen, is a full-time problem for better brains than ours! No wonder that so many impatient minds have flopped over to the general communistic position which despairs of any change save through revolutionary violence. Under a rational socialism a dominantly low-grade population could get along better than under capitalism—assuming, of course, that the government *was* rational . . . . that the vote & office-holding privilege were restricted to persons able to pass stiff educational & psychological tests, that executive processes were unified & simplified, & so on. In the course of time—after long campaigning against silly folklore prejudices—steps toward the improvement of the biological level might be taken through rational eugenics. And even from the first *one* improving factor would be operative—i.e., the virtual certainty of most high-grade people to have more children under an economic system granting them greater security. There is no question but that the leading cause of small families among superior people is the impossibility—under present conditions—of educating & rearing children in a manner suitable to their heritage. No man of average income gets enough money to send 5 or 6 children through a university—& if he did get them through he couldn't be sure of their all finding suitable places in life. Give this man a substantially increased security—perhaps no greater direct salary, but special subsidies for each child, free university education, & (most of all) guaranteed positions for the whole of the new generation—& the size of his household will almost certainly increase. Special subsidies for children would of course be strictly limited to parents of good biological stock. But in the end, of course, the improvement ought to come from *both* directions—increase in the sound stock, & limitation of the unsound stock through birth control & sterilisation. As for the supposed conflict of socialism with human nature—I don't take much stock in that. The whole trouble is in *getting the thing started*. Once the initial objections are overcome, & *money out of proportion to services* made impossible (through the playing of one private selfishness against another) to get, the same old instincts can operate much as usual—only details & proportions being changed. Although the principle that *more* work (chronologically measured) will always bring more money cannot always operate—since a small amount of work will always have to be artificially apportioned—the principle that *better* work will bring more money will indeed still be operative. Higher-grade jobs will bring higher-grade pay—& wage differences based on differences of efficiency in performing the same job would be equally certain. The one supreme problem is *how to get away from the present set-up & start moving toward a peaceful & enlightened socialism*. I'm damned if I know how to do it, since the people wouldn't vote for a decent plan if such a thing were worked out & presented to them next November. They grumble & shake their grimy fists at anybody in power—yet won't take a chance on anything that looks different from what they have. They are radical only when aroused by blind fear or fury. Paradoxically, they'd probably *vote down* an intelligent social programme (& Norman Thomas has something not widely remote from that) on the 3d of November 1936—yet, if by any fluke of hypnotic propaganda a Hoover-like administration were to slip in & commence starving & rebuffing the masses, these same dumb sheep would probably later stampede under the spur of radical oratory & start a revolution ending in something a damn sight *more* unfamiliar than what they were afraid to try at the polls! Can you beat it? That's mankind! Well—I see just *two ways* out of the present impasse aside from a general social revolution. One is a comparatively bloodless fascist or socialist coup beginning with a march on Washington & the various financial centres. This would be less like the Russian or French revolution than like a South American turnover. Not many would fight—because only the numerically small plutocrat group would bother to resist the installing of a new group of officials with a relatively mild

& non-upheaving programme. The other—& I believe preferable—way is gradual change in a fully legal fashion—a steady leftward veering of the properly elected government. Since the people—except in emotional moments—are afraid of sharp change, the only course is to *try the very mild remedies first*—changing to bolder measures when it is seen that the possibilities of the milder ones are exhausted. First the cautious steps of the New Deal—governmental supervision of private industry & commerce. Then—when the recalcitrance of business or the inability of restricted private enterprise to carry on becomes apparent—a gradual taking over, one by one, of the larger industries and services by the government. No theatricals—no cultural upheavals—no repudiation of tradition—no people turned out of their houses—no jazzed-up education or wild-eyed "ideologies—no stirring-up of discord in other countries—none of the bull-in-a-china-shop stuff to which Belknap so eagerly looks forward. Simply a logical extension of the gradual evolutionary process which has been at work ever since man stopped depending on hunting & fishing & began to keep flocks & herds. Can it be done? Ask me another! But for the present I am for the methods of men like Roosevelt or La Follette or Thomas rather than for the imported methods of Messrs. Lenin, Trotzky, Stalin, & their colleagues, successors, & sympathisers.

As for the element of *ethics or morality*—that is actually less pressing than the element of economics. Indeed, to some extent morality depends on economics. Remove the savage financial stresses & maddening insecurity of contemporary life, & diminish the importance of monetary possessions, & it is almost certain that property crimes could be cut from ⅓ to ½. Likewise a vast number of crimes of violence, in which various economic conditions indirectly figure. As a broader psychological proposition, a great deal of anti-social feeling comes from a clinical & despairing realisation that existing society itself is merely a grab game based on primitive greed & strength. A Morgan cornering resources for his own benefit & forcing men out of jobs is merely an Al Capone or Dutch Schultz with the accepted rules on his side & with a little thicker veneer of suavity & sanctimonious self-justification. Under such a system is it any wonder that respect for the prevailing rules—& the supernatural mumbo-jumbo advanced to bolster them up—is rapidly waning to a minimum? Respect for the folkways & regulations of the community will inevitably increase to a vast extent as soon as the community can give evidence of being organised & maintained with the general welfare as its primary goal. Only when a man feels that the social fabric is beneficial & honest in its relation to him, is there any logical reason why he should feel any obligations toward that fabric. Dishonesty & crime will of course persist; but with certain goals universally established & popularly supported, the harm done by these things will probably be less than that today done by "moral & legal" plutocracy at its best. Naturally, the police & army are still going to be on the job; & the gentle grafter will find that *his* kind of Utopia has not been attained. As to the less ponderable factors—the psychological mood of harmony which underlies the subtler niceties & deeper motivations of ethics—it may reasonably be expected that these will be favoured by a state of society in which education & aesthetics will inevitably play an increased part. Better social education, a heightened artistic sense, a well-organised legal & police system, & *most of all* a governmental & economic organisation which the average citizen can respect, & *for which he can see a hopeful future involving himself & his descendants* (i.e. a society which he feels to have a significant & favourable direction & purpose), will form better moral influences than all the gods & devils & fairy-tale rewards & punishments that the combined ignorance, fear, imagination, & charlatanry of mankind have ever invented. Man must have a norm which he can *really consider worth following*—& in this age of scientific information the only effective norm is necessarily a practical, favourable, & attainable way of life.

Regarding *religion*—I do not think there is the slightest reason for regarding it as a major ethical agent. It is today almost negligible in that capacity, & never was more than an enforcing & popularising device tacked on to pre-existing social & ethical concepts. Ethics has its origin in social necessity & expediency (see Nietzsche's "Genealogy of Morals" or any work on primitive man), & later acquires niceties & overtones from aesthetics—when the elements of grace, harmoniousness, &c. in personal adjustment begin to figure though the growth of imagination. As can be seen from any analytical study of western civilisation, the deepest concepts of conduct come from a sort of enlightened selfishness. We know that the individual has to be regulated if he is to reap the benefits gained through social organisation. If each does not at least outwardly conform to such regulation, he has no chance of inducing others to conform. Therefore it is good sense to give up certain individual liberties which one might or might not be able to seize if physical strength & cunning were the only arbiters. By such a relinquishment, we gain certain advantages & guarantees which far outweigh anything we would be likely to lose. It pays to subscribe to a code, & to make that code hard to evade. And it pays to live up to it; since if we are caught beating it, it becomes logical for others to try to beat it, & we end up by having none at all. So much for the purely practical. Later the aesthetic principle develops, & we avoid certain moods & arrangements which have come to have an harmonic or symbolic value for us. There is also another aesthetic or semi-aesthetic factor—that of *pride*. Types of action approved by the group come to be associated instinctively with *personal superiority*, while disapproved types are identified with *inferiority*. Thus a man can make himself superior by conforming to the pattern which the group praises, while those unwilling to conform are regarded as inferior. Egotism works on the side of morals. In certain special fields additional pride & ego factors operate—especially in the field involving *honesty & veracity*. It is plain that these qualities are worshipped by the group because they tend to enhance the working value of *all* the group's agreements & regu-

lations. Without them, the struggle to evade regulations previously agreed upon—to dodge what you've persuaded the other fellow to do—would be
ceaseless. Therefore the highest honours are paid to the man who can prove
himself most strongly truthful & dependable, & the deepest contempt visited
upon the man who cannot. But there is even more to the matter. Obviously,
group regulations can be broken in two ways—by open & defiant physical
strength, & by sneaking undercover stratagem & treachery. Now those who
break regulations in the *first* way are naturally men of the type otherwise most
attractive to a vigorous social order. They are strong & superior & confident
in the main—only a little twisted from the idolised type of valiant leader &
defender in battle. Their anti-social act, therefore, is regarded as a relatively
*mild* offence—a peccadillo, glossed over by overtones of imagination. On the
other hand those who break regulations in the *second* way are of the type *least
liked* in a healthy community—the weaklings & skulkers & schemers; the men
who cringe & run & obey as opposed to those who defy & fight & command.
They are too weak to *seize* what they want, so they *trick & lie* their way to it.
They deprive others of their share without bravery or boldness, & without
running any risk or paying the price of combat. They wriggle like worms &
beat the game. They choose a typical weakling's way. Catch a *man* in a bad
position, & he'll tell you to go to hell & fight his way out. Catch a *sneak* in the
same position, & he'll smirk & say "I didn't do it" in the hope of dodging responsibility & escaping without taking his medicine. Thus *dishonesty* has come
to signify *weakness & inferiority* to an extent true of no other anti-social mani-
festation. Most men will cling to the concept & appearance of honesty even
when all other restraints are openly thrown overboard. Honesty & bold truth-
fulness—with all those overtones combining to form the aestheticised abstraction *honour*—come to be the inseparable sign of a *strong & courageous man,*
the type most respected & idealised in the western world. It is probable that
in western Europe & America, where the heritage of Teutonic feudalism
dominates life, the old Northern concept of *honour as the badge of a strong man* is
an infinitely more powerful & genuine ethical factor than any of the attenuated & wishy-washy abstractions of our thin Christian veneer. Catch a man
breaking most of the nominally-acknowledged biblical commandments, & he
grins it off as a joke. But call him a *lying sneak* or *cheating dog* & he'll turn red
& sail into you with both fists. *That* is what gets him where he lives & sets
the old adrenals working! Not theistic Christian "virtue", but old-fashioned
Teutonic-warrior *honour,* is the chief force which in our civilisation backs up
the legal, utilitarian, & aesthetic factors in establishing social behaviour. One
may add that the working of the whole range of ethical-superiority feelings is
very subtle. We do not merely try to play to our external audience. According
to well-known psychological laws we dramatise ourselves in our own eyes &
for our own benefit. We get a rare feeling of thorough superiority by con-

forming to the social code even when nobody is watching. It is very pleasant to pat oneself on the back & say into the mirror, "See what a great guy I am!"

So, as I have said, the *religious* factor in ethics is almost never a dominant one. It varies in different civilisations, & is of course a result of the group's attempt to buttress social regulations with an alleged cosmic or magical authority. "Do what I say, or what the group needs, or else the bogey-man will get you!" "Be a good boy & Cthulhu will give you a gum-drop!" It must always be remembered *that most religions are not primarily ethical at all.* Religion in its strictest sense is merely *an emotional attitude toward the supposed causative principles of visible cosmic & terrestrial phenomena.* It may be no more than a fear of the anthropomorphically or daimonomorphically personified unknown—whereby terrible beings are to be placated by prayers & drum-beatings & sacrificial food—or an orgiastic pleasure in the personified bounties of nature, whereby benignant paternal & maternal gods are rewarded or sued for favours with songs & incense & dances & less publicly mentionable exercises. Moreover, some of the religions in which theistic imperatives & duties to the gods are most fanatically stressed are not especially concerned with *conduct among mortals.* The set of stern duties owed to the supernatural shadows often has nothing to do with the social behaviour of the worshippers toward one another. Even in Greece, where the pantheon *did* look rather sternly on such crimes as its own members did not commit, the supreme guardian of ethics was *human philosophy*—as utterly distinct from religion. Theologically, the worst "sins" were those which involved ὕβρις or outrage *toward the gods* rather than anti-social dealings among mortals. *Virtue* was identified not with religious fervour but with *knowledge, beauty, & rational moderation.* And it is from this Greek world, rather than from the Teutonic world of feudalism or the Hebraic world of Christianity, that the working fabric of our civilisation is derived. The strong ethical sense of the early Roman was pretty well Hellenised before the great age of classical antiquity out of which the modern world was born.

Actually, the only primarily ethical religions are the Hebraic group—Judaism & its two children Christianity & Mohammedanism. Buddhism *began* ethically, but was thinned out considerably. Confucianism is *ethics only*—with no active theism. "Respect the gods, but have as little as possible to do with them." Through the sheerest accident, western civilisation had an ethical religion tacked on to it—but the natural temper of the culture was so unsuited to the outward faith that the latter's acceptance was never perfect. At first, when the adoption was new, Christianity filled the imagination of the western world & prompted all manner of grotesque deeds & laws & customs. Stylites on his pillar, the martyrs of the arena, & all that. But even so, the phenomenon was one of painfully adopting an unworkable system to the needs of the group, rather than one of changing the group to fit the new & exotic system. People didn't change much. They began to call the Saturnalia "Christmas" & transfer the rites of Diana & Cybele to this or that "saint", but it was largely a matter of nomenclature. The new ethical emphasis likewise meant only a verbal change. With an Hebraic religion they had to make excuses before indulging in the anti-social conduct which the new faith prohibited—but the matter ended just about there . . . . or at the scarcely more advanced stage of making an emotional fuss & then going ahead & doing what they pleased. Thus the mediaeval nations cheated & murdered & oppressed & whored & robbed just as they classical nations did—the only change being that they had a new set of catchwords, a new theme for art, & new habit of mumbling apologies to crucifixes & statues of the Virgin, or giving money to buy beer for fat monks & their wenches & bastards, before or after slitting throats or despoiling peasants or poisoning relatives. Sometimes, though, they capitalised their new faith as a cloak for sadism or political ambition or commercial rapacity. If a group of simply-living purists like the Albigenses in southern France seemed to imperil baronial or churchly revenue, they could be very conveniently massacred as heretics. And if the rising Moslem tide cut off eastern trade routes, the Pope & Kings could start a set of Holy Crusades to wipe the infidels out.

However, it is undeniable that religion did get associated more or less with every-day ethics, verbally at least. This was especially true, of course, after the rise of Protestantism—which really formed an effort to get back to the long-forgotten ethical essence of Christianity. The Puritan movement in England & New England constituted about the apex of religious ethics in the modern world—something comparable to the attitude of tribal, non-Canaanitist Israel, or to the more ascetic & fanatical Fatimite or Wahab sects of Islam. It would be hard to say just how widely religion affected conduct. The main code of the Puritans was the heritage of Saxon England—the legacy of Odin, Thor & the Aesir—modified by such classical influences & cynically verbal popish Christianity as the Normans brought in. Saxon-Teutonic feelings predominated. But the reversion to Hebraic ethicalism in faith undoubtedly produced a grimmer conscientiousness & rectitude for a few generations, leaving even to this day certain cultural traces manifest in British & New England art & literature & politics. We may give superstition its due—although at the same time we must regret that it usurped a position as titular authority for all conduct. The evil of this usurpation lies in the fact that superstition cannot continue to function in an age of wide knowledge & accurate philosophical & psychological analysis, whereas ethics remains necessary in any age or culture. It was a mistake—though an unconscious one—to give morality the appearance of depending largely on a doomed & obsolescent system of belief. This illusion of dependence leaves ethics in a distinctly weakened position now that the supernatural fancies are crumbling & withering. But that weakening does not, of course, imply *extinction*. As we have seen, ethics does not in the least *need* religious backing. It is only through an unfortunate chain of accidents that religion has come to be regarded as an ethical essential in the western world. Once we begin to teach moral conduct as a realistic sociological necessity & a powerful aesthetic asset—backing up such teaching by at least some attempt at maintaining a decently ethical political & economic fabric—we shall not need to worry about the absence of religion. The decline in Roman ethics after the Punic Wars had little to do with any change of belief. Rather was it an effect of contact with the decadent Hellenistic culture. The old Roman faith was strongly ethical—involving a curious idea of *bargaining* with the gods. But it didn't help Roman morals when Greek social influences crept in. The later decline of the whole Graeco-Roman world was not essentially an ethical decline. Classical ethics probably reached a low point around the 1st century A.D.—the rise coming through the greater ascendancy of rural society, through a happy accident of good government—the Antonine Emperors—, & through the shift of cultural influences to western & northern provinces—Spain & Gaul—less touched with decaying Hellenism. The temper of the people is not to be judged by the imperial court, which seldom drew its reigning luminary from the soundest strata of the social fabric. No major ethical effect can be traced to the adoption of Christianity—which won only by a nose against the Persian systems (Mithraism & Manichaeism ... the latter persisting into the Middle Ages as a pseudo-Christian "heresy") which rivalled it in popularity. The people had become soft & submissive, & wanted a highly emotional religion of the Oriental type to cater to their changed mood. This decadent reaching for mysticism had its forerunners in the mystery cults—Apollonian, Dionysiac, Pythagorean, &c.—which sprang up in the Hellenistic times & contributed many typical features to the Christian ritual. The new religion, by weakening patriotism, exalting spineless meekness, & laying emphasis on a future instead of a present world, undoubtedly helped to wreck the classical civilisation. But it was not the main cause of the decline. The original loss of stamina in the people—softness, indolence, weariness of mind & emotions—played a great part. A curious cultural senescence which sometimes overtakes a social group. And worst of all was the political-economic set-up—a slow, relentless concentration of wealth in a few powerful hands, & a steady impoverishment of the majority which drove even landed gentry to serfdom, suicide, or flight to the barbarians. The vast, unwieldy imperial fabric did not know how to administer & allocate its own prodigious resources. The parallelism between the decay of the Roman world & the present state of our own western world is startlingly great. Many factors—mechanised industry, modern warfare, &c—make a difference, but it is not a favourable difference when all points are considered. Our only advantage is a greater understanding of what is going on—which may or may not do us any good. The softness & the increasing economic stress are both present.

As to whether it would be proper or practicable to attempt to bolster up a dying religious belief now known to be meaningless & without any foundation in reality—my present opinion is strongly negative. It does not pay to try to found any important aspect of society on a demonstrated fallacy. Once we have the facts, belief in an exploded system can never be depended upon to serve as a stable foundation for anything. The truth will creep out here & there—subtly & inadvertently—as the bulk of mankind faces the cosmos in the light of modern knowledge & sees again & again the lack of support of anything in the primitive legendry. To tie as important a thing as ethics to a quaint mythology unsustained by any fact of nature, & losing its hold more & more on the conscious & subconscious mind of the population, would be like placing a priceless treasure in a sinking ship. There is no prospect whatever that the expiring mythology can ever help morals—so the plain duty of the community is to rescue morals as quickly as possible from the superstitious affiliations which are tending to bring them into discredit. More & more people realise consciously or subconsciously that religion is false; hence if ethics is closely linked with religion, ethics likewise will be deemed false. The best thing which can be done for morality is to prove that it is demanded & justified by the plain laws of society & the clearest principles of aesthetics. *Give it a backing which can stand the test of time & rational philosophical analysis.* No need to persecute the dying fragments of religion. Just insist that ethics is a material social-aesthetic necessity, irrespective of any fanciful value it may derive from traditional mythology. Build up the material foundations steadily & thoroughly, as Aristotle & others built them up in Greece. Then, when the flimsy scaffolding of supernaturalism falls, the useful social reality will remain in place with a genuinely solid grounding.

The dying influence of religion is no mere theory, but a constantly observed fact. No one in western civilisation now acts from a religious motive, no matter what his conscious, external, & professed belief may chance to be. Even among the most persistently religious class—the ignorant Catholics— conduct is virtually unswayed by any regard for Christian morals. This is because *subconscious* doubt has already become strong through the constant confrontation of the people with facts contradicting the traditional mythological assumptions. The visible facts of nature, & the instinctive attitudes filtering down from the thinking classes, all pay their part. Now & then religious precept will take *momentary* effect—just enough to hinder & retard various social measures (such as birth control, sterilisation, &c.) needed by the community—but it will never again be a really profound or consistently influential force. Those who heed it one day in a year will disregard it 364 days in a year—& are doing so now. The idea of religion as an ethical agent is not merely theoretically obsolete—the breakdown of religious motivation is today an universal & accomplished fact. Whatever future support of any value we can get for morals will have to come from another source. The bulk of remaining theists no longer believe in immortality with its rewards & punishments—except perhaps the peasant Catholics, & what *they* believe has no effect on their conduct. Casual observers fail to realise the widespread & subtle psychological principle whereby people can *believe & not believe a thing at the same time*—or rather, can "believe" it *so far as they know,* but harbour enough subconscious doubt (based on widespread evidence against the belief, on the sight of thousands of sensible disbelievers, & on the fact that nothing in existence really confirms the belief) to make that belief wholly or partly inoperative as a conduct-moulding factor. The ancient Gauls *really* believed in the immortality-myth, & would contract debts to be paid in the future life. The Egyptians likewise based practical deeds on the expectation of an elaborate series of shadow-world events. The most fanatical Moslem sects took immortality so seriously that they actually regarded death as a relatively minor incident—this myth seeming so real to them that the basic instinct of self-preservation was completely side-tracked. Hence the hordes of devotees of the prophet who poured recklessly over the Near East & North Africa & Spain in the 7th and 8th centuries—facing & overcoming armies with the courage of madmen because they actually didn't care much whether they were in "this life" or the "next". Today nobody believes in the magical legends of folklore as implicitly as that. Sober philosophy frankly recognises the absense of any reason to believe in an order of being outside the physical, & the overwhelming improbability of any such thing as consciousness, personality, or will outside the transient cerebral cells of the complex material organisms. The masses get echoes of this—for you can't suppress vital facts indefinitely—& are waked up just enough to notice that no real evidence for their mythology is visible. Tradition & sheep-like conventionality often make them persist in outward belief, but their *real inward faith* is so shaken that they are no longer profoundly affected by what they think they believe. They go to church—but conduct their business, political, & personal lives as if no church existed. Now & then they let the church persuade them into the assumption of certain positions (often highly anti-social & detrimental to progress)—but their hearts are not in the matter, & their tenure of these positions is artificial, capricious, & variable. And most of the people who maintain these positions in public, violate them in private. As a living & dependable social force, religion is dead. And *permanently* so, since a deep, spontaneous popular faith in a palpable fallacy simply cannot be bolstered up in the absence of real evidence. Many social experimenters like the Nazis & Spanish conservatives & Coughlinites[7] try to use an artificially whipped-up religious belief as part of their programme, but it doesn't get them very far. I used to think that a perpetuation of the popular myth among the lower orders would be socially useful, but I now doubt this extremely. The ethical side of religion is played out—indeed, the only religion which is likely to have any future in the western world—Catholicism—is that which has always been the least effective ethically. Of course, the fact that people formerly linked ethics & religion, & neglected all ethical instruction save through religion, makes it inevitable that the decline of faith shall speed up to some extent the decline in morals. But the way to fight that is not through bolstering up childish & primitive legends. Instead, we should publicise & inculcate the *real bases* of ethics, sociological & aesthetic, & give people *a truly adult & rational reason* for adhering to certain codes of honesty, non-encroachment, harmonious action, &c. For the masses, police pressure & herd example will be enough to produce as great a conformity as the masses have ever possessed. If ever the thinking classes evolve a new ethic *in which they can really believe, & which they can follow hopefully & spontaneously,* the crowd will quickly pick up the emotional contagion & accept the code as fully & effectively as they have accepted any of the codes of the past.

It is easy to see why ethics has declined. The fact is, that it has never rested on solid foundations in the modern western world. Many of the ethical concepts commonly preached—the virtue of acquisitive enterprise, the evil of leisure, the justice of a system which enriches a few & starves many, the desirability of competition rather than coöperation, the legitimacy of sacrificing life (in war & otherwise) to protect the private gain of a few, &c. &c.—are so fundamentally rotten & ridiculously illogical that one wonders they could ever have been accepted & endorsed by an adult group of normal mentality. What, then, preserved them for centuries? In some cases, a local emergency expediency. More often, sheer mental laziness or bewilderment on the part of the majority. Somebody had shouted that these things were so, & the poor simps hadn't the skill or the acuteness or the philosophical-scientific technique to analyse & appraise for themselves. We can hardly realise how *new* the habit of widespread logical analysis of our folkways & concepts—& the demand for practical justification, common sense, & consistency in them—actually is. The most absurd beliefs & ideals & standards used to get by merely because we were too dull to investigate their claim to authority, or to demand that they harmonise with themselves & with nature. Another preserving influence was *religion.* Tack the fetish of mumbo-jumbo on to even the most grotesquely asinine or criminal concept, & the herd will piously swallow it as good ethics as long as they remain in magic-besotted condition. Hence the world of complacent injustice & absurdity into which we were born.

But now a change has come. New & increasingly rigid standards of truth & consistency have arisen with the growth of a scientific habit of mind. The old loosenesses & glossings-over & hushed-up inconsistencies will no longer be accepted. Moral codes have been dragged out of the twilight of mysticism into the light of day & given a close & honest looking-over . . . . & the hollow lousiness of a good part of them has become common knowledge. At the same time the bolstering hypnosis of religion is steadily dissolving & crumbling.

Well—it is only natural that the good should be imperilled along with the bad. The fact that a large part of our moral belief has been revealed as either silly or evil in the light of modern knowledge has caused the whole ethical fabric to fall under suspicion. The prestige & widespread acceptance of morals as a serious cultural & social factor can be restored only by rescuing the idea of them from the wreck of an exploded faith & attitude, & by giving them a genuine & adequate motivation in the social & aesthetic necessities of today & tomorrow. Evolve a way of life which really rests upon rational social & economic adjustment, & which really promises a decent & hopeful future to those who participate in it, & you can secure a genuine popular acceptance of the rules & ideals & attitudes underlying it. No other hope for any real morality exists. People cherish a code, & harbour feelings & aspirations based upon it, only when they are convinced that it represents a line of action or form of organisation *really worth upholding & promoting*. Infantile legendry & plutocratic oligarchy no longer form anything which the bulk of the people inwardly deem worth upholding & preserving.

Of course there is always the question of *how ethics ought to be inculcated*. Sometimes one hopes that the various religious organisations of yesterday & today—to which ethical teaching has been traditionally entrusted—can eventually evolve into permanent schools & rallying centres of morality by gradually casting off their supernatural beliefs & devoting themselves to the sociological & aesthetic elements which really underlie desirable attitudes & behaviour. It would be pleasant to think of our white-steepled New England churches as continuing (or rescuing!) that character-building function which was associated with them in past centuries. But the more one thinks about the matter the less one hopes. These traditional sects are incredibly narrow & irrational, & will probably die off before they shake free of their mythological incubus. Only a few—like the Unitarians—will ever be likely to make the transition. Then, too, it may be that in a modern & scientific age a complexly-linked principle like ethics ought not to be taught as a separate isolated thing. Since it depends dually upon sociology & aesthetics, it ought perhaps to be taught only as a part of sociological & art courses. Possibly it can never seem fully motivated or justifiable except when correlated with its sources & backgrounds. It is the tendency of the scientific & philosophical mind to accept things most readily when their place in the general pattern—their relationship to larger wholes—is most clearly emphasised. On the whole, I'll have to leave the matter to wiser men than I. But I do feel sure that the present slump of shifty amorality & callous opportunism—a typical concomitant or social-political-economic decadence—will be measurably mitigated if ever the world can hit upon a stable & workable plan for the equitable allocation of its resources & the rational & effective administration of its affairs. [. . .]

[. . .] Thanks for the compliment of naming me as an Harvardian reference. It gives a sort of solid-citizenly, authoritative feeling to be invoked in such a capacity! All right, I'll type my reply—lest the praise I wish to give be interpreted as derogation. I can see where my script would be a bit perilous . . . thus . . . "Mr. Sterling is in all ways an _____* thinker, an _____**

scholar, & a_____*** of _____**** character &_____******
personality." [. . .]*

   [. . .]

Yrs. by the Green Shadow
E'ch-Pi-El

*Notes*

1. Bivona is unidentified.
2. HPL alludes to Donald A. Wollheim, who at this time lived at 801 West End Avenue in New York City.
3. Robert H. Goddard (1882–1945) was an American engineer who built the first liquid-fuel rocket in 1926. His work was supported by a grant of $100,000 by financier Daniel Guggenheim and also by aviator Charles Lindbergh.
4. HPL to CAS, [22 October 1933]: "I sent for that "plot Robot", but find it is nothing at all I could use in my own work. All it concerns is the purely conventional hack junk—with hero, heroine, obstacle, crisis, & all that. But it may come in handy in revising commercial trip for dumb clients—certainly, it gives a very forceful idea of the artificial hokum called "plot" & considered an indispensable factor in pulp fiction."
5. HPL to Arthur Leeds, 19 June 1934 (ms., JHL): "I think I will send for that plot stuff—the free information, that is—if you'll let me have the address. I've forgotten the place I sent for the Plot Robot. I also sent somewhere else in California for something called a 'plot graph'—which wasn't so hot, either." The Plot Robot was the invention of Wynclffe Hall. The plot graph has not been identified.
6. Stuart Chase (1888–1985), American economist who wrote *The Tragedy of Waste* (1925) and later served as an advisor to President Franklin D. Roosevelt.
7. I.e., the supporters of Father Charles E. Coughlin (1891–1979), a radio preacher who founded a political organization called the National Union for Social Justice that advocated various economic reforms. He later discredited himself by revealing anti-Semitic tendencies.


[7]    [AHT]

Pinnacle of Fear———
Jany. 15, 1936

Mighty Kheh-Es:—

---

*Note: in the transcript, HPL's two variants are typed one upon the over, as strikeovers.
*ACUTE or OBTUSE?
**EXCELLENT or EXECRABLE?
***YOUTH or YOKEL?
****SOLID or SOILED?
*****PREPOSSESSING or PSYCHOPATHIC?

[. . .] Glad you were able to meet some more of the group, old & new. That evening marked my own first sight of Binder[1]—who is surely a very prepossessing chap. About Kleiner—he is one of the old-time amateur journalistic group about which I have told you. He is some 43 years of age, & a light versifier of genuine distinction, who has had occasional bits in the columns of Christopher Morley, F.P.A.,[2] &c for the last 15 years or more. He is a booklover of quiet tastes, with a considerable leaning toward the 18th century classics of which I am myself so fond. He is also an ardent admirer of Charles Lamb. His occupation—when, in these times, he is able to have any—is accountancy & bookkeeping. If he were pushingly mercenary, he could probably place considerable light verse material professionally; but he is too much for an old-fashioned scholar & dilettante for that. His mastery of technique is extremely thorough, & he has always been a valued critic in the National Amateur Press Association. He was born in New York, & has lived in the Bushwick section of Brooklyn ever since he could talk & walk. His present address is 116 Harman St., where he dwells with his aunt & cousin. He is one of the oldest members of our informal local group—he & Belknap & the late Everett McNeil (writer of boys' books) being among the first to assemble on Friday nights for discussion in the old days—back in 1922. A delightful person in his quiet way. Leeds has had a full & eventful life south of the boundary. During the war he was a volunteer in the Canadian army. He was connected with the cinema industry in its early days—both as actor & as scenario writer—being one of the old Edison Co. which vanished before you were born. He can tell you all about the stars your parents saw in their youth. At another time he held a position with the Home Correspondence School of Springfield—being quite an expert in the technique of the short story & scenario as they were known 20 years ago. He is co-author with Dr. J. Berg Esenwein of a text-book still in print. His own stories once had a moderate sale, & he was one of the leaders of the old Writers' Club which met in lower 5th Ave. Like most of our gang, he has no money-making aptitude, & for the last 15 years or so has always been on the ragged edge of poverty. His wife & children—the latter doubtless grown up by this time—live in Chicago, but he lacks finances to keep the home together. He himself is utterly devoted to New York—being my precise opposite in this respect. He has at various times worked in book shops, been connected with correspondence-course dealers, &c. &c.—& has even been a sideshow barker with a travelling circus. He is now working in the writers' W.P.A. project—digging up historical material for the proposed American guidebook, & doing it damned well. A great old boy is Arturo—there's nobody quite like him. He must be 55 or more now, but he certainly doesn't look it. Of his stories, the best beyond doubt is "The Return of the Un-dead" in W.T. a decade ago.*

---

*He has travelled extensively—even been to Egypt.

[. . .] Well—I have seen "The Informer" at last (for 15¢), & certainly agree that it's a great picture.[3] Indeed, I've seen very few cinemas even approaching it in grim, relentless power. This is real tragedy—the stuff of which the Elizabethans throve! That dank, miasmatic aura of the Dublin slums, & the brooding coils of fear that wind tighter & tighter around the pitiful lump of brainless flesh which is Gypo Nolan, make an effect which no appreciative spectator will ever forget. No—I didn't notice the Sennwald rating—in fact, I don't follow the cinema columns very closely. But I did see "Ah, Wilderness"[4] the other day & revelled in it. Yuggoth, but it made me homesick for 1906! Naturally, it wouldn't have an equal appeal to you or Barlow or others of your generation. [. . .]

See you later—pax vobiscum—    E'ch-Pi-El

*Notes*

1. Otto Binder—the "O" of the writing team "Eando" [E and O] Binder.

2. Franklin Pierce Adams (1881–1960), American columnist and wit, known for his syndicated newspaper column "The Conning Tower."

3. *The Informer* (RKO Radio Pictures, 1935), directed by John Ford; starring Victor McLaglen, Heather Angel, and Preston Foster. Adapted from a story by Liam O'Flaherty and dealing with the Irish Civil War (1918–22).

4. *Ah, Wilderness!* (MGM, 1935), directed by Clarence Brown; starring Wallace Beery, Lionel Barrymore, and Aline MacMahon. Based on the play (1933) by Eugene O'Neill.

[8]    [AHT]

Edge of the Abyss—
Jany. 21, 1936.

Mighty Kheh-es:—

[. . .] No—I have yet to be introduced to Coblentz's[1] fiction. But let us hope I shall have a chance to fill this grave lacuna before many months have gone. I think the cinema of "Ah, Wilderness" differs greatly from the play, although I have not seen the latter. With the greater latitude of the film, the screen version gives all sorts of typical 1906 glimpses, including an old streetcar, a primitive steam automobile, &c. It was photographed in Grafton, Mass.—roughly between here & Worcester—where the passing years have taken little visible toll. You won't think adolescence so uninteresting 30 years from now. It represents the last period at which a person retains that glowing sense of adventurous expectancy which makes youth so golden. Nothing will ever give you half the pleasure in 1966 that some of the commonest things give you now—or gave Richard Miller & your father & myself in 1906. I have yet to see the man of my age who wouldn't give his eye-teeth to be 16 again. And the most ironic thing is that we never realise what we have when we have it. All adolescents want to be old—but the minute they're old they wish they were adolescents! That's the way with life—just a succession of mockeries & ironies! Get two or three old geezers together in informal conversation, & the chances are nine out of ten that they'll be harking back to their early days before the passage of half an hour. I hadn't been in De Land a week last spring before Bobby Barlow's pa & I were howling duets of the songs we used to know in 1895 or 1900 or 1905. That's why it's hard for us dodos to realise how sensitive you young fellows are about your ages. We envy you, damn it all! However, I really *don't* recall telling Schwartz your age. During our one conversation last September he said something about your youth, but I can't remember doing more than point out that one shouldn't judge intellect or attainment in terms of mere years. I am always amused or exasperated by the contempt for earlier youth shown by fellows just a few years older. These older youths, of course, aren't old enough to know the value of what they're about to lose, but on the other hand feel akin to the younger chaps & resent the competition they offer. Their apparent scorn of a fellow 3 to 5 years younger is usually based on jealousy—because the younger chap has advanced to their status or beyond quicker than they have. A counterpart of this situation in later years is when a young man forges ahead & attains honours usually won only by older men—as in the case of 30-year-old Senator Holt, &c.[2] Then you'll usually see the old fossils wagging their beards & whining about the "young incompetent".

So Sonny Belknap claims he isn't guilty of those eclipse & Palestine-in-Egypt boners, eh? The little rascal! He can't put any of that whitewash over on his old Grandpa! Yes, I know he's all full of mystical nonsense despite his orthodox Marxism. In the old days he took all sorts of religious pap seriously, & he was fascinated by the symbolism & ritualism of popery. He studied all the various vagaries of theological imagination with owlish seriousness (as if one were to study the Ptolemaic theory of the universe or the phlogiston theory of combustion seriously today), & once gravely avowed that it was of more importance to know about the Gnostic & Manichaean heresies than about the facts of physics or biology. Some boy—but a great chap for all that! And so he says his Grandpa is also a changeable & illogical cuss? Well—of course my opinions of things have evolved with the years, as indeed they ought to. Why shouldn't one change beliefs as new evidence arises? Every time my field of knowledge widens, there are new facts to be correlated with the old—& this often necessitates a revision of existing concepts. I certainly would hate to have remained static ever since 1919 or 1920, when I first knew Belknap! All that I try to preserve is a fixed regard for truth & harmony. In actual fact, my profounder, more basic conceptions of the cosmos & its values are about the same as they have been since 1898 or so. What changes is my interpretation of external facts as related to these conceptions. It is also to be noted that certain specific details on my interests—love of ancient things, sensitiveness to architecture & scenery, fascination by the strange & weird, addiction to scribbling, respect for the sciences, &c. &c., have remained unaltered since my earliest recollections. I am more like my 1896 self than most persons are like their six-year-old selves. But hell, this isn't an autobiography! Anyhow, you can see that both Belknap & Grandpa are pretty bad eggs—at least, if you are to judge one by the descriptions of the other. Probably our lasting congeniality is just the natural affiliation of worthless & crack-pated dubs. [. . .]

Yours by the Sign of Tsathoggua—E'ch-Pi-El

*Notes*

1. Stanton A. Coblentz (1896–1982), American author and poet, writer of satirical science fiction.
2. Rush D. Holt, Sr. (1905–1955), U.S. senator from West Virginia (1935–41).

[9]    [AHT]

The Ancient Hill—
May 25, 1936

Illustrious Kheh-Es:—

[. . .] That lecture I told you I was going to attend May 4 was extremely interesting. It was by Prof. Dayton C. Miller,[1] the present chief authority of the oft-repeated Michelson-Morley experiment, whose *supposedly* negative results form the basis of the Einstein theory. Miller contends that the results of the famous experiment are *not* negative, but that they merely yield a quantity (always the same, & *too constant* to be dismissed as error as the relativists dismiss it) vastly *less* than that demanded by the traditional pre-Einstein view of the cosmos. Without being dogmatic, he suggests *that the old-time concept may be right;* & that the failure of the experiment to show the *full expected* difference in the velocity of light as produced by the motion of the observer may be caused *by some of the ether* (which he refuses to rule out of court) *itself*—some drift which causes a portion of it to be carried along with the moving earth, thus affecting the apparent velocity of light as related to the earth's motion. Miller produced some impressive data, & showed that many widely-accepted accounts of the Michelson-Morley experiment (including Eddington's) are definitely erroneous. Just how the leading relativists regard Miller I don't know—but he surely sounded like one not easily disposed of. Is our view of the universe due for another jolt? We shall see!

Speaking of astronomy—I've just stumbled on a whale of a *genealogical* discovery: one which gives me a bigger kick than any other I've ever made! Believe it or not, I find *I am the great-great-great-great-great-great-great-great-great-grandson of the astronomer who introduced the Copernican theory into England!* Usually I'm not much of a genealogist—merely taking what's on my charts & letting it go at that. The other day I ran into a caller of my aunt's—an old lady related to us in the Field & Wilcox lines—& she mentioned how proud I ought to be of our common forbear, *the astronomer John Field or Felde.* That quite floored me, since our charts carried the Field line back only to the original Providence settler John Field, who died in 1686, & I knew that bird was no star-gazer! Well, it soon turned out that the ancestry of this settler has been known for ages to genealogists, though I had no inkling of it. The astronomer—an Elizabethan whose 1557 Ephemeris had the 1st English account of the Copernican system, & who has been called "The Proto-Copernican of England"— was the Prov. colonist's *own grandfather*—hence *my* 9-times-great-grandfather. It sure gave me a kick to get a real *man of science* in my pedigree—which as a general thing is lousy with clergymen but short on straight thinkers. Later I looked up the standard Field genealogy[2] at the library & found out all about the line (orig. Counts de la Feld in Alsace. Sir Hubertus de la F. took lands in Lancashire 1069. The Prov. stock comes from branch in W. Riding of Yorkshire)—tracing my Field ancestry back 20 generations to Roger de la Feld of Somerby, born in 1240. But it's the *astronomer* who interests me, & about whom I must learn more. I have a triple shot of Field blood, being descended from 3 of the Prov. settler's grandchildren.

Well—I hope your normal strength is pretty well back by now. Don't study *too* hard!

Yrs by the Green Eidolon—E'ch-Pi-El

*Notes*

1. Dayton C. Miller (1866–1941), American physicist and astronomer and opponent of Einstein's theory of relativity.
2. Frederick Clifton Pierce (1855–1904), *Field Genealogy* (Chicago: W. B. Conkey Co., 1901).

[10]   [AHT]

The Ancient Hill
— June 20, 1936

Mighty Booleywag:—

[. . .] Well—news of the weird world is sad indeed. It seems to be my bad fortune to have to act as your necrological informer again—unless the following depressing & staggering item has otherwise reached you. I got it—without particulars, & as relayed from Texas—on a card from Miss Moore day before yesterday . . . . & the purport is that Robert E. Howard—good old Two-Gun, whose moustachio'd portrait I so recently showed you—is dead by his own hand. It seems incredible—for I had a long, normal letter from him written May 13. He was worried about his mother's health, but otherwise seemed perfectly all right. If this news is indeed true, it forms fantasy fiction's worst blow since the passing of Weinbaum[1]—& strictly *weird* fiction's worst blow since good old Whitehead's death in '32. Nobody else in the gang had quite the driving zest & spontaneity of Brother Conan. 1936 surely is the champion hoodoo year! Old Two-Gun had gifts of an order even higher than the readers of his published work could suspect, & in time would have made his mark in real literature with some folk-epic of his beloved southwest. He was a perennial fount of erudition & eloquence on this theme—& had the creative imagination to make old days live again. It is hard to describe precisely what made his stories stand out so—but the real secret is that *he was in every one of them,* whether they were ostensibly commercial or not. He was greater than any profit-seeking policy he could adopt—for even when he outwardly made concessions to the mammon-guided editors & commercial critics he had an internal force & sincerity which broke through the surface & put the imprint of his personality on everything he wrote. Seldom if ever did he set down a lifeless stock character or situation & leave it as such. Before he got through with it, it always took on some tinge of vitality & reality in spite of editorial orders—always drew something from his own experience & knowledge of life instead of from the herbarium of dessiccated pulpish standbys. He was almost alone in his ability to create real emotions of fear & of dread suspense—as I can appreciate with double force after reading his recent work. For among other items in my attempted conquest of chaos has been a reading-up of contemporary W T issues. His serial, "Hour of the Dragon", is a sustainedly potent performance. How he could surround those primal megalithic cities with an aura of aeon-old fear & necromancy! "Black Canaan" is likewise magnificent in a more realistic way—reflecting a genuine regional background & giving a clutchingly compelling picture of the horror that stalks through the moss-hung, shadow-cursed, serpent-ridden swamps of the farther south. Contrast any of this with the essentially thin & synthetic material forming the bulk of the magazine. This loss will just about finish W T as a magazine worth reading. No author—even in the humblest fields—can excel unless he takes his work very seriously—& Two-Gun did just that, even when he claimed & consciously believed that he didn't. And this is the giant whom Fate had to snatch away whilst hundreds of insincere hacks continue to concoct phony ghosts & vampires & space ships & occult detectives! I can't understand the tragedy—for although R E H had a moody side expressed in his resentment against civilisation (the basis of our perennial & voluminous epistolary controversy), I always thought that this was a more or less *impersonal* sentiment—like Belknap's rage against a capitalistic world. He himself seemed to be pretty well adjusted—in an environment he loved, with plenty of congenial friends to talk & travel with, & with parents whom he obviously idolised. His mother's pleural illness imposed a great strain upon both him & his father, yet I cannot think that this would be sufficient to drive his tough-fibred nervous system to self-destructive extremes. Nor was his financial state desperate so far as I know. I wonder if he was alive when my last letter arrived—some 10 days ago. Probably he never saw its bulky contents . . . 32 pages of argument ending with an enthusiastic tribute to "Black Canaan", which I had just read. Hell! Well, anyhow, I think he realised how keenly his work was appreciated. I hope Wollheim & Share-Cropper Shep had told him about their plan to issue his "Hyborian Age" as a separate booklet. That ought to prove popular among Conan's thousands of admirers. Wright certainly must run some sort of obituary; & since Price is the only one of us who ever met Two-Gun in person, I'm telling him he ought to write the tribute—as I did for Whitehead four years ago. But alas, all the tributes in the world wouldn't bring good old Two-Gun back! [. . .]

[. . .] I see by the old Farmer's Almanack that summer begins tomorrow—but I'd never suspect it from the grey, chilly days now prevailing! The long, cold spring has worn my energies down to the vanishing-point, & I feel as if I were on the brink of some nervous explosion! An aggravating influence is the loss of my two best friends. Three weeks ago both Mr. John Perkins (black, born Feby. 14, 1935. You saw him last year) & the Earl of Minto (black & white—born last October) succumbed to some malady which is afflicting the local felidae—a thing which may be an obscure epidemic propagated by what you biologists call "filterable viruses", yet which may be the malign activities of some contemptible poisoner. The sad end of the brothers seemed connected with some digestive disorder. If this *is* the work of some wretched neo-Borgia, I hope to hell somebody feeds him poison a thousandfold more painful than that with which he has subtly supplied his innocent furry victims! For a time it looked as if there would never be any more kittens at the house across the garden—since a couple of months ago the white-&-black matriarch of the clan was given away to the psychological laboratory of Brown University . . . . where it was assumed she would round out her days in ease & luxury & academic dignity (together with other felidae, canidae, &c.) in tests of instinct, intelligence, perception, &c. for the benefit of successive generations of students. However, after the great dual bereavement the master of the establishment got her back—& now she roves the ancient garden once again, drawing the admiring glances of sundry black & tiger & maltese swains of the neighborhood. I hope she will prove true to the lean, black Mr. Perkins Senior, since I'd like to see another little black handful of fur like the late Johnny around here some time in the autumn! [. . .]

Yrs for recovery, progress, & wire staples—E'ch-Pi-El

*Notes*

1. See RB 49, n. 2.

[11]  [AHT]

The Antient Hill
—Septr. 16, 1936

Invincible Booleywag:—

[. . .] And so you did give the bolshies their nickel after all! Well—there's no harm in being in right when the revolution comes! I read the old Communist Manifesto many years ago; & even though then wholly out of sympathy with it, was impressed by some of the isolated points it brought out. Today I would sympathise on more counts—but even so, would not give it a 100% endorsement. There is no question of the vast intelligence & farsightedness of Marx & Engels, & of the basic importance of the large economic principles which they discovered & formulated. The only mistake is to think that every ramification they developed, & every inference they drew, is infallibly accurate & worthy of slavishly literal following under every conceivable set of circumstances. The major discovery as to general drift is sound—but the derived system of "dialectical materialism" with its fantastic economic interpretations of everything, its linkages of totally dissimilar fields (art, science, &c.) with economics, & its assumptions (disregarding dozens of potent historic & psychological factors) of the utter inevitability of certain courses, is no more to be accepted uncritically than are the kindred philosophic generalisations of the mediaeval schoolmen. Some people seem never able to realise that no great discovery comes forth without attendant clouds of error & half-truth. The biological deductions of Darwin were *essentially* sound—though they included many minor slips & ignored important factors later discovered. The psychological principles of Freud are fundamentally important—but they are overlaid with provoking amounts of bias & absurdity. So with Marx. The essence of his discovery is of deep & permanent value; but in building upon it both he & others were occasionally misled by a variety of inevitable factors—ethical feeling, lack of foreknowledge of mechanical developments, lack of psychological & historical perspective, irrelevant traditions of preëxisting radicalism, &c. &c. The notion of international commerce as a pacificator is patently fallacious—while the dictum that revolution would come first in a highly industrialised country has been directly reversed by the facts. The notion of the community of women is a mere dream of irresponsible extremists—repudiated by Russia, & today probably held by nobody save the Spanish anarchists. Actually, no one theory ought to be followed in planning the future of a state. Each nation & culture-stream has different desires & needs & habitual methods; & we should consult theories only in seeking guidance as to the most practicable means of attaining the individual goals chosen by each . . . . . provided, of course, such goals were not at variance with the obviously universal principle that every citizen of a state has a right to a job affording decent self-support.

As to the question of whether the whole western world is facing the ultimate alternative of communism or "fascism" (as that term is understood at the moment)—I think it is yet early to decide, despite certain indications in that direction. Local habits of thought & action play a great part, & the Northern nations with their long-standing traditions of *gradualism* might well stand apart from the world of totalitarian dictatorships even if France were swept in. A good deal depends on the extent to which normal evolution is opposed by the reactionary classes. If the old plutocrats can keep their senses about them, & realise that they must relinquish their special privileges one by one, there is distinct hope for orderly progress. If they don't, then one must expect that irrational & violent tactics, likely to end in communism, will be used against them. The nations of Scandinavia form a very hopeful sign—for there the plutocrats are gradually backing down under the combined pressure of increased government supervision & the competing system of consumers' coöperatives. England is also well on the way. The United States has the handicap of a lawless pioneer tradition which exalts individual gain to a grotesque extent—but even here the North-European temperament has softened the savagery of reaction. We do not find—except among a few blustering old-timers, the old women of the D.A.R., & certain backward fundamentalists of Ku Klux or Black Legion calibre—much of that organised & unscrupulous reaction among us which has produced the Royalist & Croix de Feu movements in France, & the present revolt in Spain. Even the Republicans have softened their platform to such an extent that Landonism looks like a washed-out 1932 version of the New Deal. Reaction—despite certain temporary spurts—is slowly giving ground among North-Europeans; & I believe that only some unforeseen retardation, or some disastrous involvement in a new world war, will check the gradual movement toward some reasonably rational & more or less socialistic form of political-economic organisation. Just *how* rational & liberal such an organisation will be, we cannot of course guarantee. It may be that attempts to mould opinion will extend too far, & clash to a greater or lesser extent with the ideal of disinterested education—though I rather doubt it. In any case it is inconceivable that the grotesque scholarship-tampering of Soviet Russia or Nazi Germany could result. Intellectual regimentation comes naturally to Central & Eastern Europeans; but among the Northwestern peoples powerful hereditary culture-factors operate against the tendency—despite the partial manifestations appearing as anti-evolution laws, teachers' oaths, plutocratic pressure on college curricula, &c. All of which reminds me that Sinclair Lewis's "It Can't Happen Here" is now running as a syndicated serial in the *Bulletin*—causing me to read it day by day, though I'd never have tackled it as a book amidst my present feverish programme-congestion! Regarding contemporary Europe—the important thing just now is to keep other nations out of the Spanish mess. My sympathies are all with the liberal Madrid government—but I'd rather see it licked than see all Europe (if not all the world) go up in flames. The sacrifice of *one* nation is better than the ruin of *all*. Therefore I heartily endorse the efforts of Premier Blum to keep France neutral despite communist pressure. His is the only sane attitude—& I surely hope he can keep his moderate government in office. Just what a continuance of the strikes will do, I can't quite figure out. It *might* saddle France with an ultra-radical government which would mix into the Spanish crisis at once. Yet it might merely cause a shuffle driving centre elements toward the right & seating a reactionary government which would suppress the strikes, keep out of Spain (or tacitly aid the rebels), & lay the foundations for fresh internal trouble. It sure is a hell of a world—& if even half a century produces much definite improvement I shall (or would if I were alive) feel distinctly surprised. And even if internal things get straightened out a bit, the spectre of a general war (though distinctly lessened by non-capitalistic regimes in all the stronger nations) will always be hanging over mankind. Lucky will be those who—with a minimum of contacts with the bitternesses of class & nation—can spend their lives in the pursuit of universal aspects of truth & beauty. I don't wonder that you long to get back to your microscope—for if protozoa & bacteria haven't the sense of human beings, neither have they the follies & delusions! Here's hoping that no government or social order will ever hold up your disinterested quest for pure fact by demanding that your findings accord with "proletarian 'truth'", "totalitarian 'truth'", or something of the sort! [. . .]

Yrs by the Elder Chaos—E'ch-Pi-El

[12]  [AHT]

The Antient Hill
—Septr. 26, 1936

Trans-Terrestrial Booleywag:—

[. . .] Under separate cover I'm sending some more nefarious bolshevik matter. Do you want me to destroy marks of origin on this stuff, or is the traditional Harvard liberalism broad enough to stand for it without comment? Considering that Harvard bred John Reed,[1] I fancy the peril is not vast.

As to the whole social-organisation question—I think that all set formulae are misleading. Adam Smith & Marx both leave out important local & psychological elements. I don't think the scene of various revolutions can be predicted without reference to local history & tradition, nor do I believe in such things as one definite proletarian revolution. In each nation the oppressed elements will seek amelioration as their special ills & special conditions dictate—& no one revolution can form the key to any other. If future events in Spain ever parallel those of Russia, it will be because of certain basic similarities in their backgrounds—in each case a predominantly mediaeval & authoritarian nation plunged from its agricultural stage into the present with no intermediate experience of industrialism or bourgeois democracy. The curve in the northern nations, with their vastly different history, will be infinitely different.

I am profoundly sceptical of all the dogmata of the Marxists (as also of those of the plutocrats), for they seem to me founded on certain 19th century artificialities of philosophy. There is a tremendous overemphasis on "class"—regarding as fixed & typical something which in Europe is more or less fluid, & only one element among many—& a tremendous underemphasis on loyalty to the national or cultural group. The plain natural fact that *any* Englishman would stand up for England against *any* outside foe of any "class" whatsoever—a fact behind which stand a profound & complex range of biological & psychological causes—is overlooked in the anxiety to stress another kind of division of mankind. It is true that Englishmen suffering oppression hate the more fortunate Englishmen responsible for their state; but this hatred is *less* than is their hatred of any serious disruption of the traditional English fabric (speech, mode of daily life, freedom from control outside England, &c. &c.) around them. They would never join in any concerted action with alien proletariats—whose similar economic plight in no way lessens their basic dissimilarity & incomprehensibility in all the major departments of life. And this goes for the proletariat of all nations having a settled history & well-defined culture-stream. Their own group—their family, as it were—comes first. House cleaning is an internal process to be accomplished in one's own way. "Internationalism" is a delusion & a myth except so far as an intelligent policy of non-aggression, compromise, & conciliation is concerned.

"Class-consciousness" I hold to be a vicious principle—vicious alike in the nobleman & in the stevedore. "Classes" are something to be got rid of or minimised—not to be officially recognised. The only human units which merit recognition are the individual & the state—which latter ought to coincide as much as possible with a general culture-group. It is the business of the individual to see that he obtains a decent adjustment—proportionate to his loyalty & to his willingness & ability to contribute service to the state. If he cannot secure this adjustment without combining with other individuals at a similar disadvantage, well & good. Temporary alliances are often necessary in desperate struggles. But it should be for his rights as an independent, unclassified citizen—not as a member of some artificial "class"—that he fights. And alliances with other oppressed individuals *outside* one's own nation are often dangerous. If in some general clash of 'have-nots' with 'haves' the whole cultural unity of a group were to perish, the physical survivors would not have enough left in existence to make continued life worth enduring. Life is satisfying & tolerable only when lived amidst the traditions & environmental landmarks out of which one normally developed. In correcting economic evils we must not destroy all that makes life worth living.

I think the northern nations will probably evolve in the direction of a more rational order—according to cultural patterns existing since the days of

Caesar & Tacitus & before—except when some sudden disaster sweeps a group off its feet & into some artificially fostered mould. The future of fascist dictatorships seems still problematical. A really good one—which guaranteed comfort to the masses even while reserving power & plenty for a few—might last almost indefinitely, if skillful propaganda kept a favourable emotional atmosphere paramount. I rather doubt the success of red activities in the present fascist states, since so large a majority of the people seem reasonably satisfied. But in Spain (granting rebel victory) I think it will be another story. There the new rulers will follow mediaeval royalist rather than modern fascist patterns, & will fail to provide decent conditions for the masses . . . hence probably a future communist revolution.

Yes—the unjustified dogmatism of laymen in economic & political matters is surely ludicrous. It is only human, though, to be irrational about what touches our daily life. Pure science doesn't, but economics does! And all this is *encouraged* by the absurd catchwords of democracies—where any oaf can cast a ballot.

Yrs. by the Blue Light on Leng —— E'ch-Pi-El

*Notes*

1. John Reed (1887–1920), American journalist and social activist, best known for his treatise on the Bolshevik Revolution, *Ten Days That Shook the World* (1919). He graduated from Harvard in 1910.

[13]  [AHT]

The Antient Hill
—Oct. 18, 1936.

Tovaritch Kheh-Es:—

[. . .] About sleep—7 rather than 8 hours per noctem is my average. Different individuals, I believe, require different amounts—as may even the same individual at different ages. I don't often stage 60-hour wakeful sessions as I did (through necessity) last month,[1] & in recent years I have resorted less & less to my old time-saving device of cutting out a single night's rest occasionally. I'm glad to hear, by the way, that your health is improving, & hope you'll be free of all extraneous tubes by next summer. Your fellow-sufferer Edkins is mending slowly. His wound temporarily closed a fortnight ago, but inflammation developed nearby & it has reopened to some extent. This will not, however, prevent him from getting to Florida around Nov. 1.

Glad that college isn't as unrelievedly Republican as you had feared—but I'll continue to disguise the source of any vile treasonable propaganda which may reach me for forwarding. As to this *class* matter—there is sense in what you say, & my difference from your position may involve more of mere *nomenclature & psychology* than of basic conception. I agree that most of the motive force behind any contemplated change in the economic order will necessarily come from the persons who have benefited least by the existing order; but I do not see why that fact makes it necessary to wage the struggle otherwise than as a *fight to guarantee a place for everybody* in the social fabric. The just demand of the citizen is that society assign him a place in its complex mechanism whereby he will have equal chances for education at the start, & a guarantee of just rewards for such services as he is able to render (or a proper pension if his services cannot be used) later on. Now this does not apply merely to the stevedore & elevator-boy. It applies equally to the artist & professor & administrator. The same social principle which assumes that positions should be artificially allocated to men of the factory-hand level of accomplishment, assumes also that positions should be artificially allocated to men of the trained executive level; each individual to be given a return determined by the kind & quality of the service he renders. The man of executive calibre benefits as much as the man of the factory-hand calibre in point of security, so we cannot truly call the principle a "class" issue. If *anybody* might call it a "class issue" it is the man of executive calibre, who feels that he loses more than he gains—since under the old order he was fairly sure of a job anyhow, & generally received a larger return (in unearned profits) than the just one which the new order would allot him. Well & good. If the enemy want to talk "class" (notice how the plutes complain that Roosevelt, in merely denouncing unjust special privilege & urging justice for *all*, "pits class against class" or "arouses class hatred"!), let them talk & be damned! But the *real aim* of the socialist is essentially a classless one. He is not thinking of benefiting this special group or harming that special group. He is simply thinking of ensuring just placement to *everybody*—& if his conception of just placement doesn't measure up to the wishes of any certain group, then the "class issue" is the "injured" group's—*not the socialist's*. This, I believe, is a far sounder conception than the "class-conscious" one. The war is not of any one "class" against any other "class". It is of *the people*—each human being considered as an equal unit irrespective of the amount of so-called "property" attached to him—against anybody & everybody who would obstruct a programme guaranteeing each member of the people security & opportunities commensurate with his skill. This may, of course, mean—in terms of contemporary society—a struggle in which the low-paid wage-worker & the unemployed predominate on one side whilst the highly-paid businessman & inheritor of wealth predominate on the other side; but I think it is more socially wholesome—more favourable to a rational mood & perspective, & better adapted to the psychology of the future order aimed at—to think of the matter in general human terms than to think of it in terms of the *present* industrial status of the majority of participants on either side.

　　This may sound very sappy & attenuated, but I believe there is much to be said for it. It is better to fight *for a just deal for all the people* in the name of *all the people* (& who cares if some of the people refuse to be represented?) than in the name of any special "working class". In a decent society everyone is a "worker"—but if we use the term too narrowly today, we shall find that it creates mental overtones & images not at all favourable to the best type of development. There will be a tendency to exalt & idealise the contemporary low-grade worker *just as he is,* instead of to insist that his attributes be radically changed through the extension to him of a security & body of cultural privileges he has never possessed before. There will be a tendency to hate & injure the refinements & amenities of high-grade life, & to subordinate the cultural traditions which mean so much to sensitive persons, simply because these things have not hitherto been enjoyed by those classifiable as "workers". Excellence in human personality will be opposed, slighted, or jeered at as something hatefully "aristocratic" or "bourgeois"; whilst many of the crude & repellent folkways & attitudes of the *present* working "class" [folkways & attitudes which would not exist if justice prevailed] will be exalted as great national values. Now all this is very bad, & makes for increased bitterness. There ought not to be any rallying around the standards & ideals of the contemporary workman, together with a massed hatred of the standards & ideals of the contemporary aristocrat. Standards & ideals should not be associated with one "class" any more than with any other "class". Keeping well-groomed & talking grammatically & enjoying Horace & possessing sensitive honour—in brief, being a gentleman—ought not to be associated with the inheritor of a fortune any more than with an intelligent mechanic or miner. *We must learn to divorce the idea of human status & attributes from the relatively trivial concepts of remunerative occupation & financial position.* There will always be *natural* aristocrats & men of taste, & there will always be crude clods; but in a rational society it may be that the aristocrats will include people whose *purely economic* activities are relatively insignificant—miners, mill-hands, 'bus-drivers, &c— whilst the crude clods will include highly-paid industrial administrators. The big idea is *to substitute the idea of personal excellence for that of economic position*—& in order to do that, we must not encourage any hatred or repudiation of those high qualities which are at present (through long injustice) associated with the "ruling class". Heaven knows, there is too much "class consciousness" in our *present* order! Listen to any average discussion of a stranger, & see how infallibly his economic status is brought up & dwelt upon! Read any news item about an accident, an arrest a marriage, or a death, & see how infallibly a mention of *economic occupation* is tagged on to each person named . . . John Smith, grocer, age 50 . . . William Jones, insurance agent. . . . George Brown, labourer . . . &c. &c. &c. . . . . . As if the principal thing about John Smith were the fact that he is a grocer . . . . as if he had no rounded individuality or complex personality of his own; no likes & dislikes; no taste in art or literature; no philosophic position or social belief . . . . . They never say "John Smith, admirer of Greek sculpture" or "John Smith, phenomenalist", or "John Smith, student of astronomy" . . . . it is, instead, always "John Smith, grocer"! This, mind you, is the vice of the *old* order—thousands of years old. I don't accuse the Marxians of inventing it. I merely think the rational socialist out to *repudiate* it instead of *clinging to it & intensifying it!*

I'm not against any rational appeal to individuals who fare ill under the present system to join forces—on the avowed basis of their common disadvantage—as a common bloc in a war (preferably parliamentary, otherwise if absolutely necessary) against the system. Really, I am quite with you in principle. My objection is to *the psychological & cultural effect of calling this struggle a war of "workmen" against another specific group of individuals.* Actually, the reluctance of many persons to line up with socialism against capitalism is because of this persistent identification of socialism with nigger roustabouts & surly coal-miners & illiterate bricklayers as opposed to people who shave daily, read *Harpers,* & live in tastefully furnished (even if cheap) homes. If the Marxians would lay less stress on the literal hammer & sickle & lay more stress on the *general circumstance of prevailing inequality & injustice,* they would win over more of the ill-paid professors & bankrupt small grocers & corporation-fleeced inventors & booted-around bookkeepers of whose continued capitalistic sympathies they so justly complain. *The big mistake of the Marxians is that they blind themselves to all non-economic factors.* They expect a man to act primarily according to his *economic* status, whereas in reality his primary reaction is determined wholly by his *culture* status. We act first & instinctively with *the sort of people whose tastes & background are like our own.* Only with difficulty & in mature years are we generally able to think & act independently of our hereditary culture-milieu—& all too few of us can ever achieve that independence. Most of the dispossessed non-workmen are products of the general culture-milieu which also produced the "ruling class", hence they can never be expected to act as enemies of that "class" *as a class*—especially if those who invite them to do so are conspicuously & avowedly the representatives of another & frankly inferior culture-milieu. If socialism wishes to create a really effective "popular front" against the system of special privilege, it must cease to represent any particular proletarian type. It must stand forth simply as the dispenser of real justice & best hope of the *economically* disadvantaged, & must abandon all traces of hostility toward the *culture* of the lucky propertied elements on whom, in practice, it will be waging war. This for two reasons: because that culture is one also shared by many of those it wishes to win over, & because that culture must eventually, in all essentials, form the general culture of all the people. Probably socialism *will* more or less broaden in the right direction. Even now the conscious "have-nots" are acquiring an increasingly impressive stream of recruits from the ranks of the traditionally cultured; & although many of these recruits profess to be converted to the one-sided ideology of proletarianism, the net influence of the influx is all in favour of reconciling the socialistic movement with the hereditary culture of the race. More &

more a socialist may be well-born person who thinks & feels as a gentleman, & whose warfare is that of a just & responsible gentleman upon a *system* (not a group of men) which viciously denies part of the community the basic rights which taste & logic demand for all. Look at such popular leaders as F D R, Bertrand Russell, Karl Marx himself, Oliver Baldwin, Norman Thomas, Leon Blum, Rexford G. Tugwell, & scores of others—all products of the general culture of the "ruling class", & none in all probability desirous of enthroning any new culture opposed to its non-economic phases. (Briffault & some of the extreme left theorists are another story). Persons of this general type are more numerous in the ranks of the socialists each year, & the result will probably be a good one. If there ever has to be something corresponding to a "class war", it will probably be waged on purely economic lines, & not fall into the incidental tragic pattern of a war of plebeian coarseness & ignorance against patrician taste, intellect, & refinement.

Yes—after all, I pretty much agree with you. There must be a widespread education of all types of people as to the need of new distribution-patterns, & somehow the *blind fear of the word "socialism"* must be broken down, so that progressive parties will not have to conceal, euphemise, & compromise in order to secure any effective popular support. It is pathetic to note how at present the New Deal's campaigning has to soft-pedal social evolution & stress conservatism in order to rebut the dead-slogan persuasiveness of the reactionaries & stand a chance for success! Certainly, the forward fight will be hard & long—& we can afford to be patient with a little slowness if that will save us from what Russia has been through & what Spain will be going through for the next few years. A Popular Front is certainly a great desideratum—but in order to gain the cautious & traditional, it will have to crack down on the wildest extreme-lefters . . . the people who preach like Belknap & Briffault. [. . .]

Well—don't let the Czarist secret police get after you! All good wishes—Yrs. for the Cause—Ech-Pi-El

*Notes*

1. HPL worked 60 hours without a break to finish his work on Renshaw's *Well Bred Speech* (see RB 64).

[14]   [AHT]

The Ancient Hill
—Dec. 9, 1936.

Increasingly Erudite Kheh-Es:—
    [. . .]
    [. . .] Yes—I heard something about an election. Who was it that got licked? Lemke, Langhorne, Lampson, Long (no—he's *physically* dead), Landsdowne, or

something like that.[1] Anyhow, I ain't got no kick comin'. While of course the general result was apparent long in advance, the extent of the triumph surely was a gratifying surprise! I did—for the second time in my life—what I did on the night of Nov. 7–8, 1916, when the fortunes of Hughes & Wilson hung in the balance ["He kep' us outa war"] . . . . went to a late cinema show [Loew's State . . . . in '16 it was the Emery in Mathewson St.—now the Carleton, where your revered sire & I saw those Spanish comedies last year][2] where returns were announced. The national results were plainly indicated from an early hour, but the State & city figures took longer to settle . . . . Mayor Dunne having quite a close squeak.[3] By the time the show closed—2:45 a.m.—there was no danger of any contrary report next day as there was 20 years ago. On that occasion, as you may have read, the nation went to bed believing Hughes elected, but had that belief shattered the next day. All in all, the recent election was a memorable victory. The feeble arguments, obvious hokum, absurd accusations, & occasionally underhanded tactics of the Republicans acted against them, while some obscure instinct of common sense seemed to keep the extreme radicals from wasting their votes on obviously hopeless tickets. It amuses me to see the woebegone state of the staid reactionary reliques with whom I am surrounded—the old-school group away from whose past-drugged ideology it is impossible to pull my aunt. Around election-time I came damn near having a family feud on my hands! Poor old ostriches! Trembling for the republic's safety, they actually thought their beloved Langford or Langtry (or whatever his name was) had a chance! However, the alert university element was not so blind. Indeed, somebody quoted one of the professors as saying just before the election that his idea of a bum sport was a man who would actually *take* one of the pro-Landis (or whatever his name was) bets offered by the white-moustached constitution-savers of the Hope Club easy chairs. Well—even the most stubborn must some day learn that the tide of social evolution can't be checked for ever. King Canute & the waves! I think I told you on a postcard of my sight of Pres. Roosevelt on the morning of Oct. 20. In spite of the crowd, I obtained some excellent & fairly close glimpses.

Well—now we shall see what the ensuing years bring forth. If all the evidences of modern economics are correct, capitalism is doomed to automatic defeat because of the paradoxes inherent in it. To maintain profit, artificial scarcity is necessary; & as costs drop & produce a free circulation of goods, a certain lowering of profits counteractible only by dangerously low wages (which modern workmen will not endure) or labour-saving methods & machinery (which produces unemployment & unrest) tends to set in. Cyclic depressions are inevitable under capitalism unless goods can be kept scarce, at the same time that avenues for keeping producing machinery busy can be kept open—which means that more & more wealth must be concentrated in the producers who already have it, & that they must find markets for an increasing stream of products outside their own economic world—i.e., in foreign or colonial trade (which must often be secured & maintained by warfare) where the produced goods will not pile up & lower prices. In other words, the capitalistic principle is unstable—incapable of *ever* attaining any workable equilibrium. All that keeps it alive is a *constant expansion*—hitherto possible because of increasing needs & the opening up of new territory, but manifestly incapable of indefinite prolongation. The universal *plenty* talked of by Hoover & other sincere dupes of the system is a definite impossibility under capitalism. It would kill profit & wreck the system. Any attempt to see that the bulk of the population has what it needs tends to reduce profit so greatly that producers may find it impossible to keep on producing as capitalists. Then comes the test—will the government try to enforce hardship & artificially save capitalism for a few more years, or will it courageously meet the issue & provide for the gradual & peaceful absorption of increasingly profitless industries for nonprofit operation under social control? Straws in the wind like the Mussel Shoals power venture tend to arouse hope despite the lip service still paid to capitalism by the New Deal. It would be distinctly possible for a rational government to socialise large industry little by little without any real disturbance or upheaval of the national culture—provided desperate & effective opposition is not encountered. Can we count on the New Deal's aims & guidance—& upon the absence of savage obstructionism, armed or otherwise, among the defeated reactionaries? How will the weathervane point in 1940? I'm by no means a pessimist where the orderly northwestern nations are concerned. They have a natural knack for muddling along through orderly trial & error & getting what they need without shedding rivers of blood & tearing down all their art & folklore & way of life & traditional heritage. I think they can do it if they are let alone & not dragged into the vortex of any general war. If the latter—gawd help the whole damn planet! But my main point is that a workable socialism ought certainly to be attainable without the accompanying savagery, grotesqueries, & extravagant charlatanry of orthodox bolshevism. And that's what we have a chance of getting if the ill-advantaged will be patient, & the over-advantaged not too stubbornly recalcitrant. To hell with "class consciousness"! Instead of "liquidating" the "bourgeois exploiters" simply absorb their industries so that they cannot exist as such. When they are put on a salaried basis for such service as they render, & when the educational opportunities they once monopolised are guaranteed to every person of requisite capacity without regard for origin or economic status, the resultant population will tend so naturally to homogeneity of culture-status & of social adjustment that any separate ex-bourgeois class will crumble away for sheer lack of *raison d'etre* & distinguishing marks—& without the need of any massacres or "purges" or official disadvantages. Of course, groups of the cultivated & tasteful, & groups of the crude & ignorant, will always exist within society. But can the flexible & natural groupings be even for a moment compared to the rigid, irrational, birth & wealth & occupation-determined castes now artificially existing & flaunting (the low as well as the high!) their existence & solidarity? The real ridiculousness of the class idea is not the presence in the community of different elements with different habits & interests. There will always be different elements like this. The absurdity lies in the *emphasis* now placed on the class idea; the arbitrary, capricious, & irrational criteria of grouping; & the childish pride taken in membership in this or that class even when the proud member has none of the individual tastes or abilities which would rationally determine his status as high or warranting self-satisfaction. Groups of persons with similar interests & points of view are inevitable—but the habit of attaching grave importance to such grouping, of assuming group-superiority, of making the group difficult of access, of shewing hostility to non-members, & of advocating non-intercourse with non-members even when the latter may in certain fields be more congenial than fellow-members is simply damned nonsense. The moment a "class" seeks to overstress its existence, or begins to clamour for legal recognition, it becomes absurd & potentially anti-social. Gawd knows that the natural smallness & puerility of mankind create more than enough "class-consciousness" for one planet without the adoption of a deliberate gospel of caste at either end of the social scale.

Well—I'm glad you believe in a reasonable amount of kindness for the poor old bourgeoisie. They'll appreciate that comfortable place under the table, although I fear their traditional acquisitive instinct will make them quarrel for the scraps you throw them—with the rugged individualists getting the bulk of these, & the rest starving! As to the general appreciation of intellectual & aesthetic opportunities—I fear that all the present "classes" leave a good deal to be desired. The cheap interests of millions in every group—involving, often, a tremendous waste of human potentialities—argue not only an inherent inferiority in many, but some grave basic defect in education all along the line. However, all this should be approached in a spirit of gradual evolutionary reform—not in the sadistically upheaving spirit of Briffault or Sonny Belknap or other would-be over-night world-reorganisers.

Tugwell's exit from politics—not permanent, I hope—surely does have something anticlimactic about it, as you & the cutting suggest. But my acute sweet tooth forbids me to consider the molasses industry as ignominious![4] On the contrary, I could enjoy a good sticky flood of the amber delicacy on a slice of bread any day! Glad you had a glimpse of—& an earful from Prof. Frankfurter, who is one of the most rational & moderate social thinkers of the age. Let me know what Nearing—yesteryear's academic storm-centre—is like.[5] I haven't kept track of him in recent years. Has he gone completely communist? Incidentally—not a bit of seditious propaganda has showed up for you at 66 since my last communication. Do you suppose the Comrades have expelled you from the Worker's Council for lax attendance or non-payment of dues or something of the sort? [. . .]

[. . .] As for current events—I believe my last bulletin was the card I dropped you on Oct. 20 just after my glimpse of F D R, & during a delectably warm spell which helped me prolong my season of outdoor explorations. As I think I said in a preceding epistle, the unique feature of these autumnal rambles was that I succeeded in discovering several splendid rural regions within a three-mile radius of here *which I had never seen before* in the course of a long life I mentioned the woods over the crest of Neutaconkanut Hill (on the western rim of the town, at the end of the Plainfield St. car line), & spoke of their shadowy & almost spectral charm. Well—I utilised the warm 20th & 21st of October in exploring a hitherto untapped region down the east shore of the bay, where the Barrington Parkway winds along the lofty bluff above the water. I found a highly fascinating forest called the Squantum Woods— where there are great oaks & birches, steep slopes & rock ledges, & breath- taking westward vistas beyond the trees. On both occasions there was a fine sunset—then glimpses of the crescent moon, Venus, & Jupiter . . . & the lights of far-off Providence from high places along the parkway. On my ex- pedition of the 20th I ran across *two tiny kittens* in the heart of the woods (they doubtlessly belonged to a nearby hospital), & they trotted companionably af- ter me during the entire hour & a half I was there! Oct. 28 I reverted to the Neutaconkanut region—extending my voyage of discovery to the country west of the hill, & to the western slopes of the eminence itself. At times I was in places fully half a mile from any spot I had ever trod before. This terrain is full of magnificent views of rolling meadows, ancient stone walls, hoary groves, & distant cottage roofs to the west & south. I crossed the hill (it is really a small plateau or tableland) eastward to the parts I knew before, occa- sionally skirting the wooded edge where dark valleys slope down to the plain below, & huge balanced boulders on rocky heights impart a spectral, druidic effect as they stand out against the twilight. Finally I came to more familiar ground—where the grassy ridge of an old buried aqueduct gives the illusion of one of those vestigial Roman roads which traverse the woods & fields of old England—& stood once more on the cityward slope which I have always known (& which, indeed, is visible from the window at which I am writing). Country like this—high & rocky, in utter contrast to the low-lying, windmill- studded sea-plains of the Newport & Little Compton region—well illustrates the extreme geographic diversity possible within Rhode Island's minute area. Our autumn, though, was notably lacking in visual splendour. Not as prema- turely cold as I had feared, but with the dullest October foliage within my memory. Half the trees were swept bare by heavy rains as soon as they began to turn, whilst the other half remained green for an anomalous length of time—the leaves then falling almost as soon as they did turn. *Red* hues were especially rare. The result was a tremendous loss of glamour—although we heard of gorgeous woodlands at points not many miles distant, while the Vermont & New-Hampshire leafage is said to have been of unparallelled magnificence. Comte d'Erlette also told of riotous autumn colours in Wisconsin. We had snow as early as Nov. 24, which was uncomfortably early for these Plantations. Hope the winter won't be a bitter one—but hibernation is my lot in any case, & I thank Yuggoth for the generous steam heat supplied by our academic landlords. Lectures come now & then to the college, but cold weather (under +20, my deadline of physical safety) prevented my getting to the two I wished most to hear. The other night my aunt & I attended a fine address at the School of Design on the colonial restorations at Williamsburg (which I saw only in an incipient stage in '29 & '31)—delivered by the son of the landscape gardener responsible for the restoration of the elaborate formal gardens. This titanic archaeological project—the greatest single task of the kind attempted outside Pompeii & Herculaneum—is a work of the Rockefeller millions, & one of the few remaining justifications of a dying capitalism! An intelligent & tradition-revering socialistic government, however, could have done the same thing—indeed, on a smaller scale the U.S. government *is* doing such things, as in the restoration of the Morristown & Valley Forge camp areas, & similar projects. I believe even the goddam bolsheviks, having had their fill of landmark-burning during the wilder days of the their regime, are about to restore the magnificent Byzantine church of St. Basil in Moscow. [. . .]

[. . .]

Yrs by the Headless Eikon—E'ch-Pi-El

*Notes*

1. The reference is both to Alf Landon, the orthodox Republican candidate for president, and to William Lemke, a third-party candidate supported by the radical political activists Charles E. Coughlin and Francis E. Townsend.
2. See RB 56, n. 5.
3. James E. Dunne, mayor of Providence (1927–39).
4. Rexford G. Tugwell (1891–1979) served in various capacities in FDR's administration during his first term (1933–37) but resigned at the end of 1936 and became vice president of the American Molasses Co. He subsequently served as governor of Puerto Rico (1941–46), then taught at various universities.
5. Felix Frankfurter (1882–1965) was a professor at Harvard Law School before being appointed to the Supreme Court by FDR, where he served from 1939 until his death. Scott Nearing (1883–1983), American radical economist, educator, and political activist, was indicted in 1918 under the Espionage Act for opposing US entry into World War I but was found not guilty in 1919. By the 1930s Nearing, who had progressed from socialism to communism, was living in rural Vermont.

[15]   [AHT]

The Ancient Hill—
Jany. 10, 1937.

Noble Kheh-Es:—

[. . .] Getting around to destructive propaganda & ideologies—I note the advt. of the new book by Belknap's favourite. Briff can think all right, but I still regard him as just a bit too eager to start tearing-down activities. As for the *Times* & España—one can hardly blame anybody for shuddering a bit at some of the elements which are getting control of things at Valencia & Barcelona . . . but even so, I guess sympathy will continue to go to the harassed government rather than to the rebels. The outcome will be bad enough in any case; but since so much bloodshed has *already* occurred, one cannot but hope that the victor will be the side toward which the nation would ultimately drift anyhow. A soviet Spain would probably be no worse for the outside world than a savagely reactionary one—& might be a good deal better. One would wish, though, that the original liberal regime of Azaña could have run its course & prepared the way for a liberal & democratic transformation to ultimate socialism. I realise, of course, that it is the reactionaries & not the socialists who started the present cataclysm—& have that much less sympathy for them. Altogether, I side wholly with the loyalists, & hope they have a chance of winning. Last summer I thought they were licked, but they surely have shewn staying-power! The biggest problem of all is how to keep the rest of the world out of the mess. Hell only knows what each new day's headlines will announce! The Nearing lecture must have been of keen interest, & I fancy I'd have received it much more favourably than I would have a year or two ago. There is no doubt but that Russia's economic system is less wholly insane—& less of a potential dynamite charge—than is laissez-fair capitalism; that the nation is rapidly improving & becoming rational; & that the desperate resistance of the old regime occasioned & perhaps justified much of the violence of the original revolt. I have reached the point of admitting that perhaps the Russian revolution is as beneficent a thing as could have happened (in view of local conditions making orderly evolution impossible) *in Russia*. That, however, does not convince me that a parallel phenomenon would necessarily be the best thing for *other* countries. Whatever good Russia has achieved, has been achieved at a tragically high cost whose horror & injuriousness cannot justly be minimised. The bloodshed & human suffering have been appalling, while the damage to independent thought & creativeness will take generations to repair. It would certainly pay any other nation to be tremendously patient, & to experiment long & earnestly with mild evolutionary processes, if thereby the transition to final socialism could be effected without any of this hideous destruction & tragic intellectual aesthetic sacrifice. There is no reason to think that the necessary concessions cannot be extorted gradually, step by step, from the reactionaries of the more liberal & parliamentary nations even if those reactionaries put up all the resistance in their power. Certainly the process will have to slow—but we may well excuse slowness if we can thereby escape wholesale slaughter & dictatorial tyranny, & the even temporary enthronement of an insane philosophical & artistic tradition which contradicts nature, common sense, & beauty at every turn. After all, *we do not need absolute justice & rationality in society all at once.* The one immediate & important step is to see that everybody has a decent quota of food, shelter, warmth, clothing, & endurable surroundings. This need not mean that we all get what we deserve, but simply that we get a tolerable modus vivendi which we can afford to bear for an indefinite time while we work slowly & steadily toward the more complete, more logical, & more equitable final adjustment. If anybody thinks the western nations are not getting the rudiments of such a first step into effect, let him compare the America of 1937 with the America of 1932, or the England of the whole current generation with the England of 1900. Ten years more—even five year more—will have a story to tell. Of course the reactionaries will fight this progress with all their might. But who on earth thinks they could ever muster together the elements needed to launch a successful coup d'etat of the sort now labelled "fascist"? Sir Oswald Mosley may organise a few parades & riots in London—but where is his movement as a whole? Coughlins & Huey Long successors may combine with Hooverites over here—but how did last Nov. 3 show them up? Nobody says these birds may not cause a bit of trouble now & then—but who fancies they could either set up a Nazi regime in London & Washington, or precipitate a civil war of the sort now raging in Spain? When the plutes thunder about how they're going to abolish the New Deal & block social evolution, one feels like giving them the colloquially classic reply, "Oh yeah, you an' who else?" They'll doubtless keep on fuming, & will make all sorts of alliances—as with the Catholic church—to combat progressive ideas. But just watch the election returns in 1940 & 1944 & 1948 & 1952 & so on. And can you picture (to use the German parallel) any Coughlin growing a trick moustache & working up a Nazi ecstasy, or (to use the Spanish parallel) any Col. Teddy Jr. importing a lot of Filipinos & Moros, rousing up an army of Ku Kluxers & Black Legionites, & laying siege to his Cousin Frank in Washington?[1] They just naturally don't do things that way in Anglo-Saxon countries. Where the bolshies go wrong in prophecy is in ignoring *the overwhelming differences in the various national culture-streams.* Their pathetic & illusory assumption of a non-existent international similarity blinds them to the salient truth that no two nationalities ever react alike to the same situations. Thousands of years of habituation to certain types of feeling, thought, & action—types transmitted from generation to generation by all the overwhelmingly powerful forces of tradition . . . . cradle songs; childhood tales; boyish games; family records & folklore; ballads & schoolbooks; existing laws & social institutions; moral & religious attitudes; national myths, songs, & legends; every form of literature & art; &c. &c. &c. . . . . have given to each separate nationality or culture-group a psychology & set of quasi-instincts so intensely peculiar to itself that comparison with the psychology & instincts of any other nationality or culture-group is futile & foolish. The Russian revolution could have occurred only among Slavs of Byzantine culture-heritage—& the present Spanish nightmare is purely Iberian (the old Visigoth-Moor complex) in its psychology & methods. To imagine similar phenomena among northwestern Nordics is simply humourous. Italian fascism has deep roots in a never-quite-dead Roman psychology. German Nazism is the surface outcropping of a mystical tribalism always latent in such Teutons as were not reached directly or indirectly by classical culture. Orthodox bolsheviks, trying to deny nationalism out of existence by merely shutting their eyes, miss all this—& accordingly go wrong on their theories & predictions. The basic economic assumptions of socialism are probably correct. Marx was about 75 or 80% right, & we know that an inevitable drift from capitalism to collectivism is under way. But he who lets no dogma enslave his mind & emotions knows that the change will be accomplished in a different way by every different nationality or culture group. And the northwestern way is not the Russian or Spanish or German or Italian or Turkish or Hindoo or Chinese or Japanese way. *Single incidents & episodes* may be duplicated in diverse culture-groups. Thus riots & uprising might be precipitated anywhere. But it would take more than a Cromwellian or Washingtonian revolt—or a possible march of some "hunger army" on London or Washington—to make a Russian or Spanish shambles. What distinguishes national methods is not so much the things they start, as *the way those things are carried on*. A parliamentary evolution might well be accompanied by certain sporadic hostilities—but who could imagine such hostilities as attaining the ruthlessness or cultural destructiveness typical of the upheavals in eastern & southern Europe? History shows that they are rare among us, & that even a Sherman's march to the sea never equals the savage fury of a Mola's or Franco's devastations.[2] Probably we can go through our changes without open warfare—but even if warfare appears, it will be something less than a holocaust of social & cultural disintegration.

France, culturally, occupies such a dual position that any of several courses might be open to it. Although stemming institutionally from Teutonic kingdoms, & inheriting much of the parliamentary tradition, it likewise retains so much of the aboriginal Celtic capriciousness & excitability—never extinct in the Gallo-Roman—that curious departures from the northwestern norm sometimes occur. Thus the excesses of 1793. However, recent European developments seem to have emphasised the logical & evolutionary side of the French; so that one may hope they will follow the orderly northwestern route. The course you outline as a roseate but unlikely possibility may yet be the chosen one—nor does it need to have such specific administration & time limits as you assign. I hope France will have the sense to keep the present Popular front government in power as long as possible. Blum has given the nation a damned good start in the right direction.

I'll say more of dictatorships, & the tendency of the bulk of the continent to split into communist & fascist camps, after I've read Dutt.[3] It seems to me, though, that commentators tend to overlook the differences between different kinds of communism & fascism as they might be practiced in different nations. Much of a nation's desirability from the standpoint of the outside world depends on the extent to which it will mind its own business & refrain from international interference. Judged by this standard, some fascist states might be vastly better neighbours than some communist states.

The outcome of a world war would depend much on some still unsettled factors of alignment. That certain nations—echoing the spirits of the Holy Alliance over a century ago—would like to see Russia crushed is obvious. But how many would actually line up for battle? Russia looks as if it could beat off some very formidable combinations, & I don't believe England & America—or France—could conceivably be lined up against it. If Russia won, or could hold out long enough to discourage & demoralise its attackers, revolutions of various sorts might be staged within the latter. Nearing seems to be talking sense in this matter.

Baldwin's speech also sounds interesting & far from wild. I suppose, by the way, that you know his wife is a cousin of Belknap's—that is, a first cousin of Sonny's mother.[4]

There is much in what you say of Russia's present & future—as to its having already been through its major transformation to a state of relatively stable equilibrium. It surely would seem to have great advantages over the other continental nations—assuming that they will never accept a path of peaceful evolution. Yet but for war, many nations *could* exist almost indefinitely under a fascist regime—were that regime mild, rational, & generous. Such a regime could be conceived, even if not now very well exemplified. But more of this after reading Dutt. I can less readily comprehend the success of an *anarchical* regime—though I presume the only surviving brand of anarchy, the Spanish sort mixed up with syndicalism (which I take to be a sort of trade-union-ocracy), is really not anarchical at all, but essentially dictatorial. However—I don't think this principle has a chance beside one or another of the forms of socialism. This bird Kelly must have been rather an interesting character. Our friend Morton used to be an anarchist back in 1900 or so.

Well—the first thing to do is to keep up the stiffest defences of our own civilisation, so that we may be free to accomplish our own social evolution in our own hereditary way without encroachment or interference from any outside source, & to maintain the fruits of 1500 years of Anglo-Saxon cultural habits & experience. Meddle with none—& let none meddle with us. And when we have finally muddled through I fancy we shall have a far richer & finer fabric than can be possessed by any nation making a sharp break with its normal stream of inherited folkways & intellectual & aesthetic habits.

[. . .]

Yours for the millennium—E'ch-Pi-El

*Notes*

1. HPL refers to Theodore Roosevelt, Jr. (1887–1944), son of the president. He served as governor of Puerto Rico (1929–32) and governor-general of the Philippines (1932–33). He resigned upon the election of Franklin D. Roosevelt, to whom he was distantly related. "Moros" are ethnically indigenous Muslims in the Philippines.
2. Don Emilio Mola y Vidal (1887–1937), a Nationalist leader in the Spanish Civil War who ordered systematic executions in captured cities as a means of inciting fear in the populace.
3. HPL apparently refers to *Fascism and Social Revolution* (1934), by the British journalist and communist R. Palme Dutt (1896–1974).
4. Stanley Baldwin (1867–1947), prime minister of England (1923–24, 1924–29, 1935–37). His wife was Lucy Ridsdale (1869–1945).

[16]  [AHT]

The Ancient Hill—
Jany. 27, 1937.

Multipotent Booleywag:—
And so the West End Sage is a political reactionary? Well—he may take a violent leap to the other extreme some day, like another wise youth who used to live only a few doors above him on the other side of the street! Yes—I'm with you on the loyalist side of the Spanish revolution, for no matter what kind of government it may favour in the end, it certainly represents a less backward & dangerous influence than any regime the rebels would be likely to establish. The idea of a united front among progress-seeking elements is a good one, & can be achieved in many nations if all leftist parties will be rational & realistic. The number of goals & ideals held in common by socialists, communists, syndicalists, & liberals of various other kinds is really enormous, & any of these groups ought to prefer the triumph of one of its fellows to the triumph of blind reaction. What each must do in order to secure the support of the rest is to abandon any individual features which may be specifically abhorrent to one or more of the others. The sacrifice of a few small points would surely be justified by the ultimate victory, not otherwise securable, of a regime whose basic principles are of the general sort desired. The loyalists are certainly holding out magnificently—& it will be curious to see how long the conflict can be kept isolated in Spain despite the increasing influx of foreign military elements on both sides. Despite the loss of face involved, I don't think either Germany or Italy—or both in concert—would really wish to launch a world war by refusing to accept the consequences of a clear-cut loyalist victory. Regarding the current Russian trials—I can't even make a plausible guess as to what really lies behind the scenes. The whole business looks grotesquely stage-managed & unreal—yet the executions appear to be grimly

real enough! The fantastic nature of the various confessions, & the peculiar—
even insistent—readiness of all the defendants to incriminate themselves in
the most spectacular & theatrical possible way, seem to savour more of fiction than of real life. If it weren't for the apparent reality of the death penalties, I'd say the entire thing was a piece of gigantically-scaled propaganda,
with each actor rehearsed in a role calculated to impress the naive & uneducated. Yet that explanation would obviously be a misleading oversimplifica-
tion. Something is really going on, without doubt—& the nearest thing to a
guess I can give is that the defendants are making their set speeches under
Stalin's orders in accordance with a pressure involving more than their individual lives. That is, they are probably told that they'll be killed anyhow, but
that if they don't tell the stories prepared for them their families & associates
will suffer persecution & possible death. It's my guess that there is a real undercover rebellion on—launched by the more extreme bolsheviki who resent
Stalin's realistic swing to the right, & who want to restore the old (& suicidally
fallacious) international aspect of Soviet policy. Stalin is probably right in
ruthlessly putting it down, whatever one may think of his method of doing it.
Trotzky's connexion with the business I deem very doubtful—indeed, I believe the government is merely using his name as a focus for popular fear.
Undoubtedly the malcontents represent Trotsky's school of thought as opposed to Stalin's, but that the exile is really behind all the plots looks a bit
fishy to me. Probably he'd like to see Stalin out, but in his exiled & watched
position I doubt whether he would find it physically possible to develop &
coördinate any worldwide scheme of the sort mentioned at the trials. As for
Bukharin—the enclosed item includes all I've seen.[1] I also enclose a
BULLETIN editorial on the trial—none of this material to be returned. By
the way—you ought to be interested in Max Eastman's article on Russia in
the new HARPERS.[2] Eastman—the same old firebrand as when he edited
THE MASSES a quarter of a century ago—is a Trotskyite, & claims that Stalin is actually abandoning socialism! I admire Eastman when he sticks to literary topics & lets politics alone. I return the interesting Browder cutting.[3]
Thanks! Here's hoping you & your pa won't get lined up along with Sonny
Belknap & Little Bobby Barlow & shot at sunrise! Actually, I fancy Browder
must be a very good sort in this way—& surely no more twisted in one direction than the Republicans are in the other direction! Nevertheless I tend to
favour the in-betweens. I realise the backward pull of the reactionaries under
a policy of gradualism, but believe that this drawback is a small one compared
to the more disastrous drawbacks of violent revolution. Read the little sketch
by Elmer Davis entitled "The American Way of Life" in the Lion's Mouth
section of the February HARPERS.[4] We shall batter down private ownership
by degrees, despite all the kickbacks. Efforts to marshal "save-the-constitution"
sentiment will persist—but how far did such get last year? A steady popular
pressure for the government control of industry exists. Crises will develop—

but when private owners refuse to continue under he social-welfare conditions imposed, the people will not stand for retrogression. They will at least
be willing to back up a programme of governmental absorption. No two cases
will necessarily be alike, but the trend will be unmistakable. We shall get to
where Russia is getting—but without the hideous waste & sacrifice which has
occurred in Russia. Life will go on unchanged—we shan't have any wild-eyed
educational upheavals or campaigns against hereditary folkways or seizures of
private homes or inculcation of crazy scientific fallacies such as one sees in
Nazi Germany & Soviet Russia. The general structure of society & national
continuity will persist despite the elimination of unearned profits & the guarantee of work or security to all. Revolution in this country would really postpone rather than accelerate a better social order, for the bulk of the people
oppose it so bitterly that it would make them rally under any old-time American banner, no matter how reactionary. The sure way to get reactionary fascism in America is to start a Marxist revolt under international auspices.

Well—here's hoping I see you soon. Viva Caballero![5]

Yr obt Grandsire—HPL

[P.S.] About the motor strike—I think, in view of the autocratic power of a
corporation employing 200,000 men that the cause of the employes is to be
preferred. The sit-down principle is really illegal, but in social crises one can't
stand on the finer points of law. The company ought to waive technicalities &
agree to governmental arbitration.[6]

## Notes

1. Nikolai Bukharin (1888–1938), a central figure in the Bolshevik Revolution of
1917, was arrested on 27 February 1937, tried and convicted the next year, and executed on 15 March 1938.

2. Max Eastman, "The End of Socialism in Russia," *Harper's Magazine* 174 (February
1937): 302–14. Eastman (1883–1969) was an American writer and political activist
who in 1913 became editor of the socialist paper *The Masses*. It was shut down in 1918
as a result of the Espionage Act.

3. Earl Browder (1891–1973), leader of the Communist Party USA (1934–45). He ran
on the party's ticket, nominally opposed to FDR, in the election of 1936.

4. Pp. 329–32.

5. A reference to Francisco Largo Caballero (1869–1946), a leader of the Spanish Socialist Workers' Party and prime minister (1936–37) of the Second Spanish Republic
during the Spanish Civil War.

6. A sit-down strike in Flint, Michigan, organized by the United Automobile Workers
against General Motors began on 30 December 1936. On 11 February 1937 General
Motors agreed to recognize the union as the exclusive bargaining representative for
the auto workers.

*Donald A. Wollheim*

# Letters to Donald A. Wollheim

[1]     [*Cosmic Tales*]

[May 1935]

Regarding my non-belief in the supernatural—I think on the whole that a majority of those I know share it—including weird writers. Last Autumn I made a sort of tabulation of the beliefs of all the close correspondents about whose opinions I had any real information. Listing them in age groups, I find the result a significant commentary on the progress of disillusionment in America. These correspondents are scattered all over the country from Florida to Washington, Massachusetts to Texas, Pennsylvania to California. [I omit age groups ever 35 since only a small minority of fans are over that age. DAW] Out of a total of 23 persons between 17 and 35—

Orthodox Christian—1; Liberal Christian—1; Other definite supernatural beliefs—0; vague & Liberal—no recognized religion—1; Open minded & undecided agnostic—8; complete agnostic or atheist—12.

Summarized we get three positive believers in some form of the supernatural against 20 doubters and absolute disbelievers.

[2]     [ALS]

% R. H. Barlow,
Box 88, De Land, Florida
July 9, 1935

Dear Wollheim: —

Glad indeed to hear from you—even though my crowded visiting programme may prevent me from doing full justice, in this reply, to your highly interesting letter. Pleased to know that the two stories proved of interest. I wouldn't call either my best effort—or even nearly such—though "Pickman's Model" might be worse. You are right, I think, in pointing out that *ghouls* have not been used as extensively as other fabulous terror-shapes in current weird fiction. One of the new writers for WT, however,—young Robert Bloch—is rapidly atoning for this deficiency by specialising in ghouls . . . as you will see when more of his tales are published. The human "ghoul" or body-snatcher makes a good central figure for certain sorts of gruesome tales, but the best variety is the genuine corpse-eating burrower as featured in the Arabian Nights. Of the human churchyard-haunters one of the most repulsive & abnormal specimens (in actual life) was the Frenchman Bertrand, whose exploits were performed a century ago in Paris. I believe this creature

303

was recently fictionalised in a novel by Guy Endore (which I haven't read) called—heaven knows why—"The *Werewolf* (!) of Paris".[1]

*The Galleon* is published by L. A. Eshbach, whose address is (so far as memory dictates) 1337 Good St., Reading, Pa. "Iranon" has not yet appeared, but is announced in print for the next issue. Don't get your expectations up—for it's a poor & mawkish thing; a left-over from my most imitative Dunsanian period.

Regarding the supernatural—I certainly think that no reason exists for believing in it. The whole concept—including the really uncalled-for act of seeking a *why* in a cosmos of infinite extent & duration & perceptual rearrangement— seems to me very obviously a product of primitive imagination . . . . a natural & inevitable thing in the race's infancy, but redundant & untenable in the light of our own present knowledge (fragmentary though the latter still is) of space, matter, & energy. The whole series of attitudes favourable to supernatural belief— of which "why-asking" is a typical & prominent example—has obviously been fastened upon us merely through traditional folklore—blindly repeated under emotional conditions & fastened on each new generation before it is old enough to resist irrational suggestion or exercise independent intellectual judgment. During recent generations new knowledge has come to light which makes theistic concepts doubly absurd, & which has naturally loosened the fanatical force with which the elders used to cripple the judgment & emotions of each new generation. No person born since 1900 has been subjected to the almost hypnotic thought-warping of earlier times—hence all have had a better chance to exercise their natural intelligence in the light of existing knowledge than their forbears had. As a result, there is less belief in baseless myths which would never occur to anybody soberly surveying the existing field of information without externally imposed bias. Religion is something which no sane person could well concoct from any of the realities of nature as now understood. It is purely *vestigial*—a hangover from days of greater ignorance.

However—considering how slow mankind is to adopt any new idea which clashes with a preëxisting emotional bias, it is only probable that certain vestiges of religion will continue to hang on for many centuries. The ignorant herd will accept the grossest superstitions as before—while the educated will cling to increasingly denatured & attenuated forms of theism. Only the consciously analytical will be completely atheistical for a century or more. I doubt, though, if any really civilised people still accept such concepts as the "sacredness" or "inspiration" of certain books (Koran, Bible, Avesta, Rig-Veda, Book of Mormon, &c.—according to accidents of affiliation), or the reality of the various miracle-myths (virgin births, swarms of bees around infants' lips, dead & ill restored to health, &c.) peddled by the several surviving brands of organized magic.

Still—as you point out—religious accidents & illusions have tremendously affected the course of history. The survival of Jewish culture as a compact tradition is one instance, & the birth & spread of Islamic culture is another. Just as, but for religious accident, the Jewish civilisation would have merged into the Hellenistic world; so would the people of Arabia have lived & died without spreading their culture from India to Spain, had it not been for the life & dreams of Mohammed. That which moulds history more than anything else is *fanatical mass emotion well disciplined & directed*—& up to the present time religion has formed the chief excitant of human fanaticism & determination.

But—as you also point out—the day of this kind of thing is declining. The minute distinctions & laboured ritualisation of the various brands of magic no longer have the emotional hold on mankind which they used to have. Moulding influences in future will be those of the larger historic culture-units rather than those of traditions dependent upon special faiths. Because of geographical-cultural intertwining with the several groups of western culture, the present Jewish group will almost undoubtedly become absorbed into these groups & share their traditions. Islam may or may not disappear. Its more westernised fringe, as represented by Turkey, & possibly Egypt & other Levantine districts, will probably enter the western cultural stream. Certain parts, however—Arabia, Mesopotamia, &c—seem likely to remain culturally distinct for a long time. Hindoo culture—highly antipathetic to the west & strongly integrated geographically—seems destined to drag its rather squalid course along for centuries. Chinese culture deserves a continuance of its long life—& I hope it can secure such. It is virtually immiscible with western culture, & will only be harmed by vitiation & amalgamation. Japanese culture will be hybridised with westernism—more & more as Japanese conquest increases the nation's contacts with the west. It is a pity, because Japanese aesthetic traditions are among the finest in existence.

Telepathy is, perhaps, an open question—though so far the anti-evidence has impressed me more than the pro-. This bird Pritchard must be a curious character.[2] Sometimes the line between self-delusion & conscious hoaxing wears very thin—but I still think that conscious fakery exists in many cases ordinarily attributed to delusion. I think that psychology has been rather slow in calling attention to a certain peculiar human impulse which bears every evidence of being a definite one—the feverish desire (irresistible on the part of many) to foist evidence of unreal & impossible phenomena on other people ... to make people believe things which aren't so. There are probably profound & natural reasons behind this desire—reasons based on symbolism, & on a frantic desire to escape from the galling limitations of reality. These same causes promote the survival of religion—& the writing of weird fiction!

Regarding the relative average mentality of ancient & modern races—I still think the ancients had it on today. This is no original opinion of mine—many have held it since the dawn of scientific anthropology & psychology, & it was almost as axiom with Sir Francis Galton, the father of rational eugenics. The point is that the ancients could think more clearly, connectedly, & extensively from a given array of data than the moderns can. The moderns have the benefit of all the principles that the ancients discovered for themselves, & of all the accumulations which have piled up in the intervening ages. Naturally, they have more knowledge & more gadgets to play with—but the history of science & philosophy seems to prove that the ancients were capable of dealing more acutely with any stated set of facts or conditions than moderns would be. Despite the way moderns draw accurate conclusions from intricate data, they cannot begin to equal the ancients in exercising judgment, determining practical values, & constructing systems of rational & self-consistent philosophy. Where is the modern Epicurus, Democritus, Plato, or Aristotle? And where is the modern public capable of appreciating such minds? Where is the modern public which could avidly demand & understand & enjoy the dramas of Æschylus, Sophocles, & Euripides as the Athenians did? Of course all qualitative comparisons are doubtful & difficult, but there are certain probabilities which seem very significant in themselves unless some specific evidence arises to contradict them.

As for machines—I do not see that they form anything of real importance. Certainly, accurate knowledge in certain directions depends upon instruments of precision & complexity which cannot exist without machinery; but such accurate knowledge is not essential to a mellow culture—a mature & aesthetic adjustment to the existing environment—of the highest order. The race which knows the most facts & has the greatest number of electrical toys is not always (one might even say not often) the most truly civilised. Indeed, any nation which attaches importance to mere mechanical conveniences— things having to do only with such meaningless things as *quantity* and *speed*— shews itself by that very attitude as lacking in a mature sense of proportion— & therefore as essentially defective in civilisation. Machines are capable of contributing to a real civilisation, but they do not constitute one. And the moment they transcend their province of supplying real needs—the moment they begin to create *artificial* wants & to cater to them—they become potentially anti-cultural. The trouble with this age is that it is immensely skilled in mechanics without having the least adult notion about what to do with all the trivial tops & concrete playthings created by all that mechanical skill.

The theory you recently heard described—about the unconscious elimination in each age of the human type it most values—certainly seems to be borne out to a startling degree by the record of mankind, although I'd hardly consider it a safe basis to dogmatise on. In the present age the limitation of growth among the literate & cultivated, & the concomitant unlimited multiplication of the inferior, ignorant, & unfit, is certainly something about which we may be alarmed. It is rapidly producing a race of lower & lower level—not really extinguishing civilisation, but retarding it & injuring it seriously. The cause, of course, is dominantly economic. If it requires more money than any high-grade man is likely to possess to rear 5 or 10 children in a manner suitable to a high-grade man's children, who can expect him to have that many? Can anyone be expected to rear a brood of children which he can never educate to his own level? On the other hand the inferior have no level to maintain—they spawn like rabbits & have no motive not to do so. It will take extensive & deep seated social & economic legislation to make it possible for the generality [of] persons of high intelligence & cultivation to rear large families. In former times the cost of education was less, & the difficulty of meeting expenses also less. Opportunities for acquiring & conserving a decent competence were certainly vastly greater in past generations than they are now. Today a good mental endowment & habits of industry & thrift no longer form any guarantee of financial independence. Concentration of wealth in a few places & increasing meagreness elsewhere is now the rule . . . . a real fact, & no mere demogogic claim of the Coughlins & Longs & bolshevik nuts.

Regarding the two New Yorks—the cleavage seems to me very clear. Nor can there be anything but hostility between the two. No culture suffers itself to be displaced without a struggle—nor does any new culture fail to dislike the resistance displayed by its predecessor. It was so when the Achaians displaced the Minoan culture of prehistoric Greece—so also when the Teutonic tribes occupied the ruins of the Roman Empire—so also when the Saracens & Latin-Gothic Spaniards struggled for control of the Iberian peninsula.

Thus in considering the real New-York versus the replacement New-York. I said at the outset that a stranger from Mars might find the intruding city as important & potentially meritorious as the city it has displaced. So it may be when Japan conquers a softened western world & imposes its culture upon the regions now European, American, & Manhattanese in civilisation. The future Japano-European culture may be as important & great as the present European culture from an impartial outsider's standpoint—yet it's a safe bet that Europeans won't welcome its advent. When one is *not* an impartial outsider, the academic aspects of the question do not count heavily. Everyone *fights for his own*, right or wrong—& no group or region gives up its dominance or cultural integrity without a death-struggle. Even when the change is one of insidious penetration instead of conquest the same struggle exists—though generally transferred from the military to the economic or cultural plane. No self-respecting member of any group allows any part of his fabric to be weakened or detached without offering the strongest fight he can put up. That is why the great empires retain so much of their power—those which give up easily are pushed to the wall, while the instinctive & joyous fighters survive.

When subtlety replaces force a complex situation is created, but new ways of meeting it are devised. We cannot *reconquer* New York because it simply *slid away* from us—without the conscious aggression of those responsible for the loss. There is no specific enemy to strike at. Therefore a new sort of tension arises . . . a cultural cleavage involving an insulation of the parent fabric against alien & uncongenial influences proceeding from the seceded or infected part. It is recognised that the changes occurring in the lost territory cannot be legally annulled, so the infected limb is culturally amputated. It is given up as a bad job, & efforts are made to check any spread of the malady to other parts of the body. All this, obviously, tends to prolong the natural hostility engendered by the original struggle for cultural control of the lost region. It need not involve any denial of the possible intrinsic merit & importance of the intruding culture, but simply forms a normal defensive attitude on the part of the older culture still dominating in the surrounding region. As time passes, & the defences of the older & larger fabric become complete, the tension will tend to relax. When the intruding culture no longer forms a source of possible vitiation to the main fabric, it can be looked upon like any other foreign civilisation—& appreciated according to its merits. By that time the sense of loss on the part of the parent nation will be less acute, for no living persons will remember the time when the lost section belonged to the main fabric—assuming, of course, that no active irredentist movement is kept alive. Also—as you point out—as the centuries pass the new culture has a chance to acquire genuine mellowness of its own & to win a higher place in the esteem of its neighbours . . . including the fabric from which it has been detached. All of these points were, I thought, specifically conceded in my last epistle. I freely admitted that the nascent replacement-culture of New York might have as much potential intrinsic merit as any other culture, & that the centuries might conceivably refine & develop it into something of unique excellence—as interesting & non-repugnant to us as Chinese or Saracenic culture. Whenever I referred to hostility I referred only to the *present* attitude of a member of the main American civilisation—a specific local phenomenon without any bearing on the cosmic or intrinsic external aspects of the case.

I did not say that the existing New York ought to be exactly like an old & established city. I merely pointed out that the shouldering aside of an old established city by this new growth, & the existence of this growth on soil where an old & established city of our own used to stand, is bound to be resented by us. We don't expect a raw, nascent thing to be like a finished product—but we lament that accident that has precipitated a raw, nascent, & alien thing—without any cultural relationship to our own lives & history & instincts & aspirations—into our physical midst. If the new growth were in Africa or Borneo we would wish it well & admire its progress—but who can love a new baby in the next apartment when its squalling annoys us? Even if that baby is destined to grow up into a new Alexander or Shakespeare, its infantile crudities are no less irritating—especially so if it seems destined to feel feelings, do things, & speak a language alien to one's own feelings & acts & language.

In the case of New York, time will probably heal a good deal of the existing hostility. The region will be recognised as a sub-culture—a geographical island of variant civilisation, not expected to be like our own fabric—& will be amicably regarded on that basis . . . as the Greek cities of southern Italy were regarded by the Roman population of the bulk of the peninsula. What makes New York *seem* offensive at present, is the maintenance of the myth that it is still part of our fabric—a myth which makes us expect it to be like us, & which causes us to judge it by standards not applicable to it. Also, we are irked by the economic & commercial survivals which cause New York influences (influences no longer representing us) to control many of our avenues of cultural expression . . . books, magazines, drama, art criticism, museum treasures, &c. As it is, the expression of our people is modified in its utterance & formulation by commercial & editorial manipulations not in sympathy with us—so that we have the feeling of an unjustified influence exerted in & upon our civilisation by a culturally seceded group no longer part of us. This condition—& the irritation which goes with it—will have to be allayed by the growth of a new commercial & cultural centre for America proper . . . probably Chicago after the construction of the St. Lawrence canal—which peanut politicians can't delay many generations more. As many important financial activities are transferred to Washington with the growth of that socialisation essential to national survival, so will the publishing & educational activities of the larger American people probably shift westward to the centre of the country, & come into the hands of leaders shaped by the historic American tradition of the whole national fabric. The transfer of museum treasures westward to American soil as the balance shifts in that direction is not beyond conjecture—though less important & less critically certain. And all this will help New York just as much as it will help America, since it will tend to normalise an abnormal situation & eliminate a mutually galling strain. It is distinctly undesirable that any vast cultural fabric should entrust its major channels of expression to a section wholly detached & antipodal in feelings & aims. 7,000,000 people cannot continue to misrepresent 120,000,000 people of utterly different temperament, heritage, & purposes. Our avenues of publication, standards of criticism, sources of uttered philosophy, policies of education, & centres of aesthetic absorption must be in the hands of persons & interests sprung from our own soil & inheriting the same emotions & purposes that the overwhelming bulk of our people inherit. As soon as we fully recover these functions, & are once more an integrated cultural fabric with an homogeneous expression of our own, we shall be able to look more complacently upon our exotic neighbours—even those whose territory has been carved from ours—& appraise their life & achievements with an objective, impartial justice now manifestly beyond the range of possibility.

To touch on specific points—I have no intrinsic case to present against New York (as a disinterested Martian) except that its intensive urbanism seems to be a bad sign. Spengler is certainly not wholly off the track in pointing out the relative vulnerability & decadence of urban-commercial-sceptical-cosmopolitan-intellectual civilisations as opposed to rural-military-naive-nationalistic-emotional cultures. If New York conquers more territory from

America & loses some of its intensive urbanism, it may be able to achieve an almost fabulous greatness. Otherwise it may have to pay the price of complacent cockneydom & fall prey to one or another of the various forms of enfeeblement or disintegration. Among fantastic possibilities, its reconquest by America is not wholly to be laughed aside as a remote, perhaps accidental eventuality. The consequences of the destruction of the existing city in the course of warfare—either from an attack from a non-North-American foe or through a social revolution precipitated by the brooding radical element so strong in Manhattan's immigrant underworld—offer a wide field of conjecture. Urbanites have poor powers of stability & recuperation, & in any cataclysm involving readjustment or re-colonisation elements from America proper would have a fresh chance for dominating Manhattan Island & its environs & restoring the civilisation of 1623 et seq. All this, though, is frankly in the science-fiction-futurity class!

Only one more point. Your historical parallel of Boston in 1630–35 & New York in 1930–35 fails to work, for the very important reason that Boston was *not* an exotic growth of a pattern alien & unfamiliar to the people of New England. That is, it fails to work so far as *I*—an English colonial of this region—am concerned. It is valid enough from the standpoint of the *Indian* who previously inhabited the territory . . . indeed, *his* position with respect to Boston in 1635 was much as *ours* with respect to neo-Manhattan is in 1935. In the earlier clash of cultures, we occupied the position which you & Long do today . . . . whilst King Philip & Weetamoe & Awashonks & the Wampanaug, Narragansett, Pequot & other native tribes correspond to our modern selves. King Philip in 1675–6 fought us desperately—with every ounce of his strength—& died like a man, cursing the invaders. We today—less menaced as a group (for we grabbed *all* of the natives' lands, while you've grabbed only one of our numberless cities) & with less occasion for a physical clash—fight with the same basic intent, though with the different weapons & objectives dictated by the different detailed conditions. But in 1635 Boston was *not* a new & alien town to *us*. We had simply brought to those virgin shores the old, familiar integrated culture which we had known for some 570 years—ever since the Norman Conquest fixed the pattern of life & feeling in our own Kent & Devonshire & Lincolnshire & Norfolk & Gloucestershire & other source-regions of the determinant bulk of the people. Boston & Providence & Newport were to us merely what Cleveland & Chicago & Denver & Salt Lake City & Seattle were to our descendants—new extensions of our own cultural fabric, where under fresh roofs the same thoughts & feelings & objects & social organisation existed unimpaired & unmenaced. Boston & Providence . . . & Jamestown & Philadelphia & Charleston . . . . were crude & physically new, but they were not garish nor gaudy nor blatant nor mushroom-like nor alien nor incomprehensible nor unsympathetic. They were ours. We made them, & transferred our institutions to them, & they expressed us. Our settled ways of

550–600 years went right on—subject only to the minor modifications of physical environment & slight, previously-agreed-upon, purely voluntary social change. Our languages, furniture, architecture, utensils, customs, trades, ideals, purposes, & everything else went straight on according to the natural lines worked out by 600 years' inheritance & experience. When, in the course of time, local differentiation developed, & other sorts of settlers were added to ourselves, the modifications were so gradual that the original pattern was never destroyed. The evolutionary relationship to the original culture-stream was never sacrificed, so that no deadlock of clashing goals & no hopeless disparity of folkways & expression ever developed save when New York gradually drifted off. Newcomers were engulfed in the settled preëxisting fabric, & familiar standards & objects were transferred over distances of thousands of miles. As a result—& notwithstanding outwardly vast heterogeneities of aim & custom & attitude—the overwhelming bulk of the American people from Maine to California & Florida to Alaska all share a certain roughly identical nucleus of perspective & emotional habits & social axioms & instinctive goals—a nucleus in many phases utterly & antipodally opposed to the congeries of concepts & folkways evolved by the inhabitants of neo-Manhattan. The Indians resented our intruding culture—but in vain, for our superior physical strength engulfed them. Today we resent any threat to our culture— maintained 600 years in the Old World & 300 more in the new, a total of nearly a millennium—from any source whatsoever . . . . . . & would fight as desperately as the Indians if we thought it in danger. However—the balance of forces is a little different this time, since we have *all* the physical & military advantage ourselves, & could crush to fine powder any claimant threatening our dominance. This being so, we can afford to relinquish for the time being the cultural adherence of a small bit of territory whose withdrawal was, after all, an automatic phenomenon involving no defiance of the larger culture & no offence or evil intention on the part of those unconsciously responsible. No equitable course save a recognition of the status quo—plus safeguards against further withdrawals of territory—can be at the present moment conceived. Thus, whilst we hate the new & intruding culture *as a whole*, we cannot hate its individual members, who we know are not responsible for the drift affecting their local fabric. Individuals cannot be hated or punished for an automatic movement which sweeps them along. Thus the situation is not quite like that between a national fabric & its *deliberately seceded* fragments. The hatred is impersonal & institutional only—& will for that reason be modified the sooner when America regains its channels of expression & comes to regard New York as something frankly alien despite its political bonds . . . . a kind of northeastern Puerto Rico or Hawaii or Philippine group. In the remote future we shall regard & visit New York with the same appreciative interest which we now display in regarding & visiting Rio de Janeiro & Cairo & Yokahama.

Turning to M. R. James—while I don't scan the obituary columns with an altogether eagle eye, I can safely say that the good old ex-Provost of Eton was hale & hearty as recently as 2 or 3 years ago. If he has slipped out of the world since then, I'm damned sorry![3] Glad you've read his complete works. Of his various tales I think "Count Magnus", "The T. of Abbot Thomas", & "An Episode in Cath. History" are the best—in the order named. *Weird Tales*—like all the other pulp junk—is hopeless. The June issue was pitiful. Haven't see July, but doubt if it will be much better. The thing never was worth much (despite its mountainous superiority over crap like *Terror* or the old Macfadden–Hersey *Ghost*) & now it is very nearly a total loss. If it attempts to duplicate the field of *all* the pulps—detective, science, &c.—it will end up by suiting nobody at all!

Glad the feud between you & Hornig (of which Sterling spoke some time ago) is healing gradually.[4] To my mind Hornig is a very nice chap—who certainly can't be blamed for the swindling tactics of that old reprobate Gernsback. Having taken a job with the Gernsback outfit (& who could refuse any reasonably legitimate job these days?), he seems to me to be following as correct a course as anybody could. Not that I know all the details of the business—but that such is a reasonable impression. He certainly deserves a lot of credit for handling a responsible position at an age when most wouldn't be equal to it. And he did struggle valiantly with the late FF. I guess I mentioned that I had a very pleasant visit from him on May 25—when he spent the entire day in Providence. Glad also that you've met your neighbour Frank B. Long. Did I mention that he used to live at 823 West End Ave. cor. 100th St—the old Hanover apartment house torn down in 1927? (There is no 823 now—the door of the H's successor is 825) Another neighbour of yours is T. Everett Harré the anthologist ("Beware After Dark") who hangs out at the Hotel Paris—West End & 97th St. I think you'll like Belknap. You'll probably meet Koenig later—at some meeting of congenial spirits at Long's. I believe you've met the brothers Wandrei.

Congratulations on your editorship of *The Phantagraph!* Having seen *Flabbergasting Stories*[5] in Sterling's files, I feel certain that the magazine will not lack sprightliness. Hope the typographical deal with Crawford will prove successful—& wish you could build the periodical up into a real successor to the FF. Good luck, anyhow! About "Fungi from Yuggoth"—I am pained to say that at this date every one of the 35 is either printed or pledged![6] However—if you wouldn't mind using specimens whose only publication was in a local Providence daily nearly 6 years ago, I could let you have 2 or 3 of the very best. Nobody outside Providence has ever seen them in print, & the *Journal* wouldn't do any bothering about the copyright. Whether you'd care to use these is up to you . . . I'd be glad enough to see them in a fan-reading magazine. But by the way—would their prospective appearance in collected form—as a booklet—form a further objection? Two young weird fans of the San Francisco region—Fred Anger & Louis C. Smith—intend to publish such a booklet either in printed or mimeographed form. (Another & very desirable venture of theirs is a *complete index of WT* from the first issue to June '35.[)]

I think I can get something for you from Barlow, & am asking CAS what he can send in the line of poems or pastels. Koenig ought to have bibliographical notes of interest—& I suppose Nelson (whose address is 1030 Elm St., St. Charles, Illinois) could furnish some of his promising (though slightly naïve & overcoloured) verse. Other possible sources of material are:

William Lumley, 742 Williams St., Buffalo, N.Y.

Duane W. Rimel, Box 100. Asotin, Wash.

Robert E. Howard, Lock Box 313, Cross Plains, Texas.

Robert Bloch. 620 East Knapp St., Milwaukee, Wis.

Emil Petaja, Box 85, Milltown, Montana.

These are all old FF contributors. Any use for drawings or linoleum blocks? Barlow & Rimel could fit you out in that line. Also try Bernard Dwyer, C.C.C. Camp 25, Peekskill, N.Y. Here's wishing you success—& I surely hope Hornig won't perceive any fraternal rivalry to lead him into an unfavorable position.

Having a good time down here—summer or winter, this is the climate for me! The Barlows' place is on the edge of an attractive lakelet—across which, in a picturesque oaken grove, Bob has built a neat cabin to house his printing & other activities. Local scenery is very attractive—palms, live-oaks, Spanish moss, &c. Last month we visited a winding tropical river (tall cypress jungle—leaning palms—twisted roots at water's edge—pallid flowers & leprous fungi—black earth—sunken logs—snakes & 'gators—lush vines & creepers) which strongly suggested the Congo or Amazon. Don't know how long I shall be here—though my super-hospitable hosts insist on my staying till August. Stopped at Fredericksburg, Va. (Genl. Washington's hometown) & Charleston, S.C. (marvellous 18th Century survival) on the southbound trip, but hope to take in St. Augustine, Savannah, more of Charleton, Alexandria, & Philadelphia on my return. My health is so much benefited by the warmth of this region that I hate to think of returning north. All good wishes—

Yrs most cordially & sincerely,

H P. Lovecraft

## Notes

1. The protagonist of Endore's novel is one Bertrand Caillet.

2. Kenneth B. Pritchard, a believer in paranormal activity; see, for example, "The Words in the Sky (A True Experience)," *Fantasy Fan* 1, No. 7 (March 1934): 107, and "A Disembodied Shadow (A True Experience)," *Fantasy Fan* 1, No. 12 (August 1934): 190, 192). His "The Electric World" appeared in DAW's *Fanciful Tales*.

3. James did not die until 12 June 1936.

4. See WFA 7, n. 4. Hornig had become involved in the feud between DAW and Hugo Gernsback because Hornig was managing editor of *Wonder Stories*.

5. See WFA 7, n. 6.

6. "Expectancy" (XXVIII) did not appear in a periodical until decades later. HPL later modified his claim a bit; see DAW 6.

[3]     [ALS]

66 College St.,
Providence, R.I.,
Septr. 20, 1935

Dear Wollheim:—

I seem to be a hard person to locate these days! Even now I am on the move again, having picked up your letter just as I was leaving for Boston to visit a friend & accompany him on a trip to the "Dunwich" region of central Massachusetts. This reply is written in the Boston zone, but I'll hold it till I get home in order to enclose those Yuggothian fungi you wish.

All in all, the big trip was decidedly enjoyable. I left De Land August 18th, & had a week in ancient St. Augustine & several days in Charleston. The charm of these places is almost impossible to describe—one must see them & drink them in gradually & detailedly. Had a day each in Richmond, Washington, & Philadelphia, & paused several days in New York as the guest of Donald Wandrei. During my metropolitan sojourn I saw many of the weird fiction group & got a brief glimpse of Sterling—who returned from Brookline just before I left. You can find him at the *Hotel Commander, 240 W. 73d St.*—though by this time you may have located him yourself.

No—I have not seen *The Phantagraph* as yet, hence must postpone replying to all questions pertaining to it. I certainly hope you can make a success of it, for some publication of that sort is badly needed. Yes—I told Barlow about the venture & fancy you can count on his support. Pritchard must be a curious cuss—though many have a superficially general education coupled with amazing lacunae of ignorance & credulity. About Nelson—I had so little correspondence with him that I really feel inadequate as his biographer. The fact is, I scarcely know anything about him. The place to get data on his life is his home—indeed, I think his mother (Mrs. Elmer Nelson, 1030 Elm St., St. Charles, Illinois) would be very glad to furnish information. She has been writing those whose names she has found on her son's correspondence list. As for unpublished work—there may be some at his home, while Barlow has 3 or 4 of the "Lost Excerpts" on hand. I believe Barlow has some destination for these things more or less in mind, but you might write him & see whether his decision is final. I'll be glad to give Nelson a writeup if you'll get the necessary biographical data from his mother. His work was obviously immature—tending toward chaos & extravagance—but it had an atmospheric quality arguing considerable promise.

Hope you can get plenty of cuts of the right sort. In addition to Rimel, I think you'll find Barlow & young Emil Petaja (Box 85, Milltown, Montana) very clever at this kind of illustration. Glad you're using Ferguson[1]—whose work seems to me extremely good.

Regarding the Anger–Smith duo—they have dropped the idea of publishing the "Fungi" . . . which Barlow may print later on. Their "index" is now (I believe) available at 35¢ per copy, but is a bitter disappointment to those who have waited expectantly for it. I haven't seen a full copy, but sample sheets tell the story . . . . & explain the quotation-marks I have used around the noun. For the "index" would seem to be merely a transcript of the various *tables of contents* . . . a mildly useful thing indeed, but of course not a true *index* at all—& lacking the most important functions of the real thing. An actual index is yet to be made—& I hope somebody will do it some day. But both Smith & Anger seem to be very nice chaps. Price knows Anger, & thinks him very pleasant. Glad he has come to your aid in the science fiction war.

Congratulations on the "Creeps" discovery! Those volumes are excellent things to have, though some of them include matter one is likely to have elsewhere. I have two of them—"Creeps" & "Shudders".[2] The discovery of a complete W.T. file in a bookshop is surely an important event, & one which will create excitement when generally known. I suppose the dealer wouldn't consider breaking it up. Barlow would sell his soul for certain 1923 issues . . . . & he wouldn't mind taking bound volumes which might involve duplication. If I had the fifty I'd be tempted myself, for my file is in execrable condition. It will probably fall to pieces sooner or later.

Yes—WT certainly seems to be going to the dogs. I haven't tried to read the "Dr. Satan" junk[3]—the most cursory glance classifies it all too ruthlessly! But I disagree with you about "The Monster God of Mamurth". To me that story has a distinct grip. It is out of the pulp tradition, & somehow achieves a slight aura of convincingness. It is the one good thing Hamilton has ever done. "Vulthoom" has its moments, but falls a bit beneath Klarkash-Ton's best level. I fear the pulp editors have subtly harmed Smith by their constant objections to his originally poetic style & exotic vocabulary. By the way— you'll be sorry to hear that Smith's mother has just died after a long illness. I fear he's in for a double bereavement, for his father is in extremely bad shape.[4] CAS has faithfully cared for them both in their illness—in the face of obstacles which would have disconcerted a less sturdy & determined soul.

Yes—I liked Bloch's "Shambler" . . . & not merely because it was dedicated to me. Bloch is an extremely promising kid, & I only hope the pulp formula won't "get" him as it has Hamilton, Wandrei, Long, & many others. He surely gave the old gentleman quite a vivid end in his story—but I'm used to that. A full decade ago Long left me as a bit of charred cinder on the floor of my chamber in Brooklyn Heights . . . cf. "The Space-Eaters", published in W.T. some time in the middle or later 1920s. Bloch's sketch in *Fantasy* was very amusing—he has a comedy side which contrasts curiously with his weird predilections. One of his favourite pursuits is organising comic shows & appearing in them, clad in a curious costume involving epaulets, cocked hat, & rubber cigar. I imagine he must have been the premier cut-up of Milwaukee's Lincoln High School! Yes—I wish that Rankin might have illustrated the "Shambler". To my mind he is the only illustrator of the bunch who has any real imagination. As for Dwight A. Boyce—I must admit that I never heard of the gentleman before.[5] I can't take the "art" work of the pulps seriously, & seldom notice the various designs & alleged pictures. It had been my impression that most of the tailpieces were left-overs from Andrew Brosnatch, the main illustrator of a decade ago, who did some pretty good work in his day. One or two are by Frank Utpatel, a friend of Derleth's who could become an interesting rival of Rankin's if Wright would give him a real chance.

So W.T. has a special Canadian edition, eh? Your reference was the first I had heard of it. Whether this is an influential factor in the growing financial precariousness, I really can't say—but nearly all close observers seem to think that the poor old mag is getting pretty shaky. The Wandrei boys lay the trouble to Wright's poor story judgment—to his insistence on detective & adventure stuff when his readers would obviously prefer real weirdness. Alas, the miserable rags of the Terror–Horror group have cut into sales. Probably WT got a good deal of its support from ignorant dullards of the crudest type—who now turn avidly to *Terror* & *Horror*, where this kind of pabulum appears in greater quantity & more undisguised form.

About "Supernatural Horror in Literature"—at a guess, I'd say that the FF had published something like one-half. I surely would like to get the rest of it to the weird-fiction circle somehow. It has been vaguely half-promised to a pair of youngsters who have a future magazine in mind (who have asked me to keep the matter confidential in case the project does not materialise),[6] but I fancy I could secure a release if any certainty of more immediate & dependable publication became possible. Let me know when you've mapped out your programme & estimated various possibilites in detail.

I am very anxious to see *The Phantagraph*, & hope a copy will be awaiting me upon my return home. If I find one, I'll continue this epistle & let you know what I think of the contents. I shall try to be impartial & candid . . . & feel sure I won't have to be as tactfully non-committal as I perforce was when Hill-Billy Crawford asked me what I thought of the quality of his latest giant *Marvel Tales!* Meanwhile I'll try to dig up & copy those "Fungi" which appeared in the *Providence Journal*—enclosing them in this envelope.

Hope I haven't overlooked any point. For several weeks I shall be an especially rotten correspondent, since I'm utterly engulfed by the mountains of tasks I found awaiting me upon my return from the south. To begin with, I have 3½ months of old periodicals to read up—& on top of that are endless letters (my mail didn't get forwarded toward the end of my absence) & an especially tough verse-revision job to cope with. A score of malignant fates have converged with the apparent determination to sink me!

Hard work getting used to the chilly northern climate after enjoying the genial mildness of the south—I don't feel half the energy I felt in Charleston or Florida. But today is an exception—gloriously hot, despite the imminence of the autumnal equinox. Our trip to "Dunwich" tomorrow will include some delectable rural scenery of the old New England type—a thing for which I'm avid after my long stay amidst palmettos, live-oaks, & Spanish moss. Our mission, however, is a pensive rather than festive one—for we are about to take the ashes of a deceased old lady to North Wilbraham, Mass., to scatter on her native soil in accordance with her lifelong wish.[7]

And so it goes. Au revoir for the present . . . though I'll add postscripts, no doubt, when I get home & prepare the enclosures.

All good wishes—

> Yrs most cordially,
> H P. Lovecraft

P.S.—Sept. 26.

Home again—& into *another* maelstrom of massed correspondence! But here are a couple of Fungi—perhaps the best of the lot. They appeared in the Prov. Journal in 1929, & have not been elsewhere published.[8] Night-Gaunts are actual dream-creatures of mine. They used to haunt my sleep when I was 6 years old—so badly that I would try to keep awake to avoid seeing them. They persisted in recurrent dreams for years—not wholly disappearing till I was 10 or more. I invented the name "Night Gaunt" myself at the time of maximum persecution.

The "Dunwich" trip was highly enjoyable despite our melancholy mission. Scenery was exquisite—the hills of the Connecticut Valley, & all the vistas of outspread, white-steepled countryside that go with such regions. It was very little changed since my visit of 1928—& I could scarcely believe that both of the persons who guided me & told me the ancient folklore on that pleasant occasion are now dead.[9] We scattered part of the ashes in the Wilbraham cemetery, over the graves of the deceased's ancestors, & the rest among the neglected rose-gardens of an estate (now untenanted) which she had known & loved. The day was appropriately grey, & the foliage had begun very perceptibly to turn.

Sunday my host, his family, & I had a picnic on Cape Cod—enjoying a gentle, marine type of scenery sharply contrasting with the remote ruggedness of the "Dunwich" country. We loafed at length on the sands of Chatham, with nothing but the Atlantic between us & Spain. Foliage—as in Rhode Island—not greatly turned.

Thus I am after all—despite my long absence—getting well saturated with the varied essences of New England scenery this year. There is the bar-est possibility of a later trip—over the Mohawk Trail & across into Vermont—though this is vaguely tentative.

Well—I hope the enclosed pair of Fungi won't disappoint you too badly. Good luck—& let me see a copy of *The Phantagraph* when it's convenient.

Most sincerely yrs—

H P L

*Notes*

1. (H.) Clay Ferguson, Jr. (1914–1995), designed the cover of the single issue of *Fanciful Tales*.
2. Anthologies anonymously edited by Charles Birkin.
3. Paul Ernst (1899–1985) wrote a series of Dr. Satan stories for *WT* in 1935–36.
4. CAS's mother, Fannie (Gaylord) Smith, died 9 September 1935 at the age of 85. His father, Timeus Smith, died 26 December 1937 at the age of 82.
5. Dwight A. Boyce (1910–2003) contributed at least fifteen illustrations to *WT* from 1935 to 1946 and had several letters published in "The Eyrie."
6. It is not clear who HPL is referring to here.
7. See RB 52, n. 6, and RB 53.
8. HPL submitted "Night-Gaunts" and "The Dweller" at this time. DAW reprinted the five sonnets that had appeared in the *Providence Journal,* four in *The Phantagraph* and "Background" (as "A Sonnet") the fifth, as the only content in *The Lovecrafter*.
9. I.e., Edith Miniter and Evanor Beebe.

[4]     [ANS][1]

[Postmarked Providence, RI,
1 October 1935]

Just recd. *The Phantagraph*, & must congratulate you on an excellent start. That article by C. W. Lonsdell is just what has been needed for years. I've pointed out again & again that the crap in the science fiction pulps is simply a mess of absurd & extravagant stock formulae without substance or convincingness— just puerile words. I hope to see further instalments of this article. ¶ Interested in your sketch of the origins of science fiction. ¶ Your statement that I 'was once director of the Providence observatory'[2] flabbergasted me a bit, insomuch as (a) I have never been director of any observatory, or even connected with one, & (b) there is not & never has been any "Providence Observatory". Then, after a moment, it dawned on me that you must have seen one of my kid publications of 30 or more years ago—when I used to call my own small telescope & other astronomical & meteorological apparatus "The Providence Observatory" & 'publish' (by hectograph or on the typewriter) important-looking "bulletins" & "annuals". Thus do the exaggerations of youth bear misleading fruit in old age! ¶ Glad Tremaine is favorable to your society & publication.[3] All good wishes & thanks—HPL

*Notes*

1. *Front:* Benedict Temple of Music, Roger Williams Park, Providence, R. I.
2. So stated in *Phantagraph* 4, No. 2 (November–December 1935): 3.
3. By "society" HPL probably refers to the Terrestrial Fantascience Guild, a group founded by DAW as a rival to the Science Fiction League (see RB 53).

[5]    [ALS]

66 College St.

Providence, R.I.

Octr. 7, 1935.

Dear Wollheim:—

Here is something which Two-Gun Bob says he wants forwarded to you for *The Phantagraph*, & which I profoundly hope you'll be able to use.[1] This is really great stuff—Howard has the most magnificent sense of the drama of "history" of anyone I know. He possesses a panoramic vision which takes in the evolution & interaction of races & nations over vast periods of time, & gives one the same large-scale excitement which (with even vaster scope) is furnished by things like Stapledon's "Last & First Men".[2]

The only flaw in this stuff is REH's incurable tendency to devise names too closely resembling actual names of ancient history—names which, for us, have a very different set of associations. In many cases he does this designedly—on the theory that the familiar names descend from the fabulous realms he describes—but such a design is invalidated by the fact that we clearly know the etymology of many of the historic terms, hence cannot accept the pedigree he suggests. Price & I have both argued with Two-Gun on this point, but we make no headway whatsoever. The only thing to do is to accept the nomenclature as he gives it, wink at the weak spots, & be damned thankful that we can get such vivid artificial legendry. Howard is without question the most vigorous & spontaneous writer now contributing to the pulps—the nearest approach (although he wouldn't admit it himself) to a sincere artist. He puts himself into his work as none of the regulation hacks do.

Thanks for the *Phantagraph* which you sent. Now I have *two* copies instead of *none!* I must subscribe as soon as I'm out of my present financial arrears.

Best wishes—

Yrs most sincerely,

H P L

*Notes*

1. "The Hyborian Age," first published in part in the *Phantagraph* "Supplement" (October–November 1936) and then issued as a booklet (1938).

2. Note that DAW published HPL's "The Shadow out of Time" and Olaf Stapledon's *Odd John* in his *The Portable Novels of Science* (New York: Viking Press, 1945).

[6]    [ALS]

66 College St.,
Providence, R.I.,
Nov. 13, 1935.

My dear Wollheim:—

Very glad to hear that so many of the old group have responded to your invitations, & hope *The Phantagraph* will build up & retain a solid clientele as loyal as the FF's & even more numerous. The purchase of a press is surely an encouraging step—& it will certainly relieve you of the greatest financial burden a magazine has to bear. As you wish, I'll keep the new plans confidential until you are ready to announce them. In the course of time I'll be looking for *Astonishing Stories*—a thing filling just as great a need in its own field as *The Phantagraph* fills in another.[1] I trust you'll maintain a higher standard of neatness than Crawford's—& I hardly need say that you'll undoubtedly have a higher standard of literary taste than *Marvel* has hitherto shewn! Regarding contributions—anything now knocking about these diggings is at your disposal.* Just now there isn't a damned thing in the way of fiction available—though there probably will be plenty of odds & ends if ever I get at that long-deferred writing session. About the Fungi—nearly all *have* been printed in magazines, but if you don't mind things used locally & long ago there are a few more to which you're welcome. In the matter of *book* publication—I would never be able to finance such a job myself, so it's merely up to some publisher (Barlow, yourself, or anybody else) whether he wants to take the risk of breaking even on the venture. Personally, I doubt if such a brochure would pay its own expenses—& I have so warned everyone who has suggested a venture in that direction. Whether Barlow will ever get around to the edition he contemplates, I'm sure I don't know. After a certain length of time all obligation on my part would vanish—leaving the verses free for book publication by anybody else rash enough to take the risk. Barlow's edition of Long's "Goblin Tower"—which I helped print last summer—will soon be available. I think Ar-Ech-Bei will bind up copies as he receives orders. The next venture will be Klarkash-Ton's "Incantations". Bob is undoubtedly a better starter than finisher, but he *does* come through with something once in a while. His little magazine *The Dragon Fly*, published in connexion with the National Amateur Press Association, is a gem of its kind.

———————————

*The article on weird fiction which the FF used as a serial is now definitely free for publication if you have any use for it. And I may be able to get "The Nameless City" again.

Just heard from Eshbach, who says that *The Galleon* has become a strictly local magazine devoted to regional material. He has resigned as editor. I can't say that "Iranon" amounts to much. It is mawkish & imitative—just an experiment of my intensive Dunsanian period.

Glad "The Hyborian Age" will be used in the P. Of all the prolific pulpists, Two-Gun easily leads in vitality & genuineness. His prehistoric world is a consistent reality to him—& some of his poems have amazing power. Lumley, Petaja, CAS, Koenig, Bloch, Rimel &c. will all make good contributors—& sooner or later you'll probably hear from Barlow. I recall that he hasn't a very high opinion of your partner. From certain dealings connected with back numbers of weird magazines he has picked up the idea that Shepherd is rather a sharp, self-interested kind of negotiator—indeed, he said he hoped you'd watch out pretty closely for your own interests if you attempted any joint venture with the enterprising Alabaman. No doubt the feud has its two sides—for we are all prone to hasty & premature judgments.

About that "Iranon" MS.—I am submerged in the deepest shame! With a thousand & one things clamouring for attention, & damn near 75 correspondents on my list, I simply *forgot all about the matter* & gave the item in question to the omnipresent & prehensile Barlow! No excuse—just the failing memory of senility! Well—you'll certainly get the next MS. I produce (not, however, that such a thing has any genuine value) just as soon as the text of it is printed.[2] And I hope it will be of a better story than "Iranon". I surely hope you can pardon the lousy memory which has made me an unwitting promise-breaker!

Anent addresses—Derleth's is just *Sauk City, Wisconsin*. His first *serious* book, "Place of Hawks", was published last summer & has received some fine reviews. Indeed, it has gone so far toward establishing him as a real author that Scribners may take over the publication of his future books. He plans a long series of novels of the soil, based on the slowly unfolding history of his region from the earliest times. Meanwhile his latest detective novel—"The Sign of Fear"—is just out, & it is probably better than any of its three predecessors.[3] Derleth has the most promise of anybody in our group.

Price's address is Route 2, Box 100-U-5, Redwood City, California—but he is now in Mexico City during the course of a long motor trip. Before the trip is over he will call on Two-Gun Bob at Cross Plains.

Klarkash-Ton is slowly emerging from the shock of his bereavement, & gaining perceptibly in health. He has not written anything lately, but is doing wonders in the field of weird carving or miniature sculpture—working in the various sorts of friable stone found in his region. He promises to send me some photographs of his new carven monsters before long. Three of them—"Cthulhu", "The Outsider", & "Dagon"—are named from fictional horrors of mine.

Tragedy has just touched Belknap's family—his aunt, Mrs. Cassie Doty Symmes, having been instantly killed in a motor accident near Miami Oct 20. It was she who financed his first book of poems, "The Man from Genoa", & to whom that volume was dedicated. Grimly enough, Barlow was binding a copy of Belknap's next collection—"The Goblin Tower"—for her when the blow fell. She herself had published a small book—"Old World Footprints"—in 1928.[4]

Yes—our sprightly young friend the Booleywag[5] confessed that it was he who exploited Grandpa's bygone & juvenile "Providence Observatory". He has the jocose constructive imagination of youth! A brief explanation might un-puzzle some readers of *The Phantagraph*—though I was pleased to observe that a good many recipients seem to have overlooked the innocently misleading paragraph!

The sale of both "Mts. of Madness" & "Shadow" certainly took me completely by surprise. Wandrei hadn't told me he was submitting the latter—& I gave the "Mts." to Schwartz only after enthusiastic solicitation & with not the slightest hope of results. I don't see yet how the damn things ever landed, for neither makes the least approach to the pallid formula ordinarily demanded by Tremaine & his ilk. Undoubtedly it's just a sheer coincidence—a pair of random luck-shots that couldn't be duplicated in a decade. But just the same the dual incident is distinctly encouraging—forming a psychological antidote to the effect of many rejections elsewhere. It promotes my resolution to try to snatch the time for some more yarns . . . even though these future yarns may receive a uniform cold shoulder. I've tentatively finished one now.

I'd like to see what the Canadian edition of Farny's Folly looks like! If it succeeds while the U.S. edition languishes, Wright had better move up to Toronto & make it his headquarters. For the cleaner advertising pages, I fancy Canadian government regulations rather than Farnsworthian idealism must be held responsible! The economics of publishing are altogether beyond me—but everyone seems to think that poor old WT is in a bad way.

New England has had a remarkably warm autumn, so that my hibernating season suffered a happy postponement. Made a trip to New Haven Oct. 8 & spent the day in enjoyable antiquarian exploration, & on Oct. 16–18 I visited Boston with my friend Samuel Loveman (poet—a collection of his will shortly be published by the Caxton Printers)—absorbing bookstalls, museums, & Georgian architecture in generous measure. And on many afternoons I have taken my work out to the woods & fields, just as I do in summer!

Just glanced though the Nov. WT—which is somewhat above the average, with 3 stories worth reading. "The Way Home", by Paul Frederick Stern (a new writer to me)[6] takes the lead because of its mood & atmosphere. Price's story is the best thing of his which I've seen in 3 years—while Two-Gun displays his customary vitality.

Clark Ashton Smith lately sent me two of the grotesque carved images (of friable stone) in which he is nowadays specialising, & I found them vastly impressive. His technique clearly catches some of the tricks of primitive sculpture, so that one could easily imagine many of his products to be things excavated from primordial ruins.

Well—here's wishing you luck with all your magazine enterprises. I must send in a *Phantagraph* subscription before long. Rimel & Petaja speak of literary & artistic contributions they are making, & it looks as if you were well on the way toward establishing an important & meritorious journal.

Every good wish—

Yours most cordially,

H P Lovecraft

*Notes*

1. An issue of *Astonishing Stories* appeared in May 1935, edited by Wilson Shepherd. The bimonthly *Astonishing Stories* (1940–43) edited by DAW's fellow Futurian Frederik Pohl may have been the outgrowth of the initial plan. DAW had a story published in the magazine.

2. This proved to be "The Haunter of the Dark." However, the whereabouts of the manuscript now are unknown.

3. I.e., *Murder Stalks the Wakely Family* (1934), *The Man on All Fours* (1934), and *Three Who Died* (1935).

4. HPL ghostwrote the preface to the book for Frank Belknap Long.

5. I.e., Kenneth Sterling.

6. See RB 56, n. 7.

[7]    [TLS]

66 College St., Providence.

Feby. 7, 1936.

Dear Wollheim:—

Yours of the 23d found me in a state of utter disorganisation—with a programme hopelessly crowded with unperformable tasks, and health close to the breaking-point from nerve-strain and grippe. For about a fortnight I could hardly stay up many hours at a time, but I am now rather better—though still so shaky in the muscles that you'd probably find my script unreadable. Hence the typing.

No need to feel contrite about the lack of ceremonious adieux at the Long meeting. Holy Yuggoth! With the vast gangs that sometimes assemble, and the diverse destinations and hours of departure, nobody ever thinks of formal bowings and scrapings! I was very glad to have seen you, and sorry the brevity of my sojourn prevented further colloquies. Next time I hope we shall have ampler opportunities for discussion.

The Phantagraph duly arrived, and I have read it with interest and appreciation. While the typography here and there betrays Shepherd's inexperience with a press, it is really very neat indeed—and I am glad the linoleum cuts came out so well. If I were you I'd insist on proofreading privileges, for

Shepherd is evidently a bit free and easy. I notice that he repeats the error of printing "Memnon" as "Memmon".[1] A different and larger type for headings, a more harmonious sort of ornament, and a little more neatness in matters of spacing and page arrangement would also help. But all this will come gradually to Shepherd as he becomes more familiar with printing and acquires more type and accessories. Ruppert—and even Crawford—now have the fruit of considerable experience. One thing more—it would seem neater if the cover were a double size sheet folded over the back, instead of two small sheets with the back of the magazine gaping open. However, these are all minor mechanical matters. The contents seem well selected, and the cover catches the eye admirably. I am now looking forward to the next issue, with its "Lonsdell" article and the first instalment of Two-Gun Bob's "Hyborian Age".

Anent the "Fungi"—I've really forgotten which ones (aside from "The Dweller") I've sent you—but here are some more which have seen the light only in the Prov. Journal 6 years ago. If they duplicate any previously sent, pardon me. I may later be able to dig up some still older junk from my files of amateur papers—but when I come to re-read it I may decide it is too bad for re-publication. These things would probably average longer than the Fungi—being macabre sketches in the octosyllabic couplet. Meanwhile I've asked both Rimel and Petaja to send you "The Nameless City", which they may have done ere this.

As for the "Haunter"—ask Sterling to lend you the typed copy when it reaches him on its rounds. I typed this particular MS., but many have no serious trouble reading my writing. Barlow, Hornig, and others very seldom get held up. The secret is, perhaps, a dual one. In the first place, people used to reading handwriting accept the *word* rather than the *letter* as a unit. Before the age of the typewriter nobody but schoolchildren ever thought of making each letter separately and carefully. *Words* had a certain characteristic formation in every-day script, and one became familiar with their appearance. This brought in the second principle—alert attention to *context.* The script suggested the word, and context clinched the matter. Of course, inattentive, non-comprehending reading was difficult—but when one knew what to expect in the ordinary course of language, the very structure of the sentence proclaimed at once which of several similar-looking words any given written symbol might be. Printers acquired a kind of instinct for difficult types of handwriting, and could easily decipher things which would utterly baffle their soft, typescript-pampered successors of today. No writer could possibly have prepared long MSS. in the round, copper-plate, separate-lettered hand of the schoolboy. It would have taken aeons to complete any sizeable work, and the slow medium would have held up the very processes of thought. Sometimes in making—or having made—a "fair copy" of a completed work, greater pains would be taken—but this was generally left to copyists whose time was of no particular value. It is very curious to me how the younger generation has lost the old facility to read handwriting. Again and again I am handed MSS. by others which various persons complain they can't read, but it is only once in a long while that I ever get held up by such a thing. Regard for the word unit plus attention to context usually makes all but the most interlined and re-corrected MSS. fairly plain. However, my own much-corrected rough draughts are probably worse than the average—although Barlow can read any of them. Whenever I have a MS. typed, I tell the copyist to leave blank any place where a doubtful word occurs. Of course, I go over all finished MSS. myself, rectifying words, spelling, punctuation, etc.

Glad you enjoyed the "Mts. of Madness." There are some misprints—like "palaeocene" (a meaningless and self-contradictory word) for "palaeogean", etc., but I fancy a general idea of the text can be obtained. I liked the cover and illustrations very much. The artist surely read the text, since the representation of the polar entities is almost precisely like my own visual concept—and like the sketch I made for my own guidance when writing the story. As for the names of the ships—since the expedition was from Miskatonic University and financed by Arkham citizens, I think no more natural appellations could have occurred to the organisers. Precedent can be found in many famous expeditions of actual history. And I don't think realism could frown on the dissection of one of the various species which *may* have formed a background for the legends of the "Elder Ones". I have been very elastic in throwing out some of those mythological hints, and may have contradicted myself in different stories. As for the Thing on the cover—if I remember rightly (it is long since I have read the tale except for a hasty skimming to reconcile some of the facts to Byrd's latest discoveries), it is a shoggoth, or something closely related to that species of abomination. At any rate, it is something so unwholesome that the barrel-like beings are delightful every-day companions in comparison! Yes—the Ellsworth flight makes antarctic tales rather timely just now.[2] No—the area covered by the flight is entirely different from that in which the Mts. of Madness claw hideously at the sky. Ellsworth started in Graham Land—under South America, about 65° S. Lat. and 60° W. Lon.—and flew to Little America— under the Pacific, about 78 S. Lat. and 160 W. Lon. The Mts., on the other hand, are in that totally untouched and almost limitless expanse west of Victoria Land—the vast continental expanse below the Indian Ocean and the coast discovered by Wilkes in 1839 or so. I purposely chose the most inaccessible possible region, so that early discovery would not "date" my story as other antarctic tales are now "dated". The seat of the imaginary peaks is 76 S., 113 E.—not on the way from anywhere in particular to anywhere else, hence very unlikely as a route of aeroplane flights for many years to come. I deliberately pondered to find the remotest and most inaccessible spot on this planet. It is, roughly speaking, inland from Sabrina, Budd, and Knox Lands. I probably put more into this story than into any other I ever wrote—for the mystery and fascination of the Antarctic have haunted me persistently ever since I was ten years old. That is why its rejection and cold reception in 1931 did so much to discourage and slacken all my fiction-writing. It interests me vastly to learn of your own flyer in antarctic fiction—expecially [*sic*] since you say my Yuggothian Fungus inspired it. I'd like to see it some time. I believe I sometimes place Mt. Kadath in the antarctic—in fact, I'm not sure that I don't mention it somewhere in the "Mts". Well—I hope later instalments won't disappoint you. My primary object is to convey something of the feel and aura of the hideous white south and its brooding mystery, but I can't tell yet how clearly I have succeeded—or how far from success I have remained. I'd like to read some really good antarctic tales, but have found most sadly flat and unconvincing. Poe's "Arthur Gordon Pym" still seems to me the best of the lot—the only one which sticks in my memory. I refer to it repeatedly in the "Mts".

About the Feb. Astounding in general—not being a follower of that magazine, I can't very well compare the current issue with others. However, it seems rather less uniformly dull than most of the science pulps. Long's story— if divested of the hack romance—will be found to embody many very clever and vivid concepts, and there are ideas in "Mathematica", "Buried Moons", [*sic*] and "The Shapes".[3] "Mathematica" certainly has a bold and ingenious scope, though it tends just a little bit too close to the abstract and the conventional to be overwhelmingly convincing.

Glad to hear that you've obtained good material for Fanciful Tales, and hope the supply will keep up. As to addresses—some of those you wish I don't know myself, but I append a list of those I do know. Price can put you in touch with Hamilton and Mashburn. I don't know Merritt's residence as distinguished from his office.

About those problems of identification—Leeds was the darkish, fairly thick-set, rather bald middle-aged chap with the moustache (a real one, not a shadow like the Belknap–Howard Wandrei brand). He was the only person at once moustached and bald. He didn't get into much conversation with our group at the end of the room—although later on he, Loveman, Kleiner, and I held a session at the Sherman Cafeteria which lasted until just 3:07 a.m. by the beanery chronometer. He is a dashing and interesting character—ex-soldier, ex-actor, ex-circus barker, ex-text-book author, and what have you. He was once connected with the Home Correspondence School as an authority on the short story and cinema scenario, and fifteen years ago was a big figure in the old Writers' Club which met in lower 5th Ave. He does not have much published work nowadays, but his one W.T. story (published a decade ago) "The Return of the Undead" was memorable. Just now antiquarian research is engrossing him. He must be 55 or more, but certainly doesn't look it. Kleiner was the lean, stooped, clean-shaven fellow with the kindly gnome-like face—of about my own age and degree of greyness . . . . . the chap who horned into our questionnaire discussion and floored even our omniscient young friend Sterling with some literary queries. He is a light versifier of extreme grace and facility, who has had pieces in all the popular "colyums"—Conning Tower, Bowling Green, etc. As a metrical technical and gentle Horatian satirist he has few peers, and this year he is serving nobly as verse critic in the National Amateur Press Association. He has a mellow literary knowledge which includes the classics of the past to a degree not often found in the younger generation . . . . . he and I often lament, as elders will, the decline in civilisation since we were young. He is an accountant by profession—not unlike his literary idol Charles Lamb. It is through general literature and old-time associations that Kleiner belongs to our circle, since he has not the faintest interest in the weird or the "scientifictional".

Well—let me know in advance when you can get to Providence, and I'll see about meeting you and guiding you to my ancient hilltop citadel. I had the pleasure of another series of sessions with Sterling this month, and I trust he has brought you my regards.

With all good wishes, and hoping to see both Fanciful and the next Phantagraph in the course of time, I remain

Yours most cordially and sincerely,

H P Lovecraft

[A.Ms. Enclosure:]

*Addresses*

Don't know Merritt's *home*, but his *office* address is Daily Mirror Bldg.—
25 East 45 St., N.Y.C.
14th floor—Am. Weekly.
Tel. VAnderbilt 3-4770

Richard Ely Morse,
40 Princeton Ave.,
Princeton, N.J..

Miss C.L. Moore,
2547 Brookside Pkwy., S. Dr.,
Indianapolis, Indiana.

Seabury Quinn,
34 Jefferson Ave.,
Brooklyn, N.Y.

Edmond Hamilton
Newcastle, Pa.
ask E. Hoffmann Price, Route 2, Box 100-U-5, Redwood City, California.
ask Price also for addresses of W. Kirk Mashburn—who is somewhere in Texas

Richard F. Searight,
    19946 Derby Ave.,
        Detroit, Michigan.

other addresses unknown & clueless so far as I'm concerned.

*Notes*

1. Referring to CAS's "The Memnons of the Night," *Phantagraph* 4, No. 2 (December 1935).
2. American explorer Lincoln Ellsworth (1880–1951) and British explorer Herbert Hollick-Kenyon (1897–1975) made a trans-Antarctic flight from Dundee Island to the Ross Ice Shelf on 23 November 1935. In the course of the flight, the airplane ran out of fuel, forcing the pair to land at Richard E. Byrd's then-abandoned camp at Little America. The pair were rescued only after two months, on 16 January 1936.
3. *Astounding Stories,* 16, No. 6 (February 1936) contained Frank Belknap Long, "Cones"; John Russell Fearn, "Mathematica"; Raymond Z. Gallun, "Buried Moon"; R. DeWitt Miller, "The Shapes," and the first installment of *At the Mountains of Madness.*

[8]    [ALS]

                66 College St.,
                    Providence, R.I.,
                       April 19, 1936

My dear Wollheim:—

        You will probably excuse this delayed reply to yours of March 12 when you learn the reason therefor. When I last wrote I was just pulling out of a grippe attack & facing a formidably congested programme. Well—scarcely was I on my feet when my aunt came down with an infinitely severer version of the same malady—tying me up at once as a sort of combined nurse, butler, market-man, secretary, & errand-boy. Complications set in, & the patient had to go to the hospital—a step which merely shifted rather than lightened my added responsibilities—but I am glad to say that she is recovering finely; transferring on April 7 to a convalescent home, & being due back here on Tuesday. All my own affairs are in utter chaos. Letters since February unanswered, amateur duties transferred to good old Kleiner, revision jobs returned unperformed, borrowed books piled up unread, & everything generally gone to seed. Nor am I in any shape for coping with the mess—my energies being at a low ebb, my eyesight giving me trouble, & a devil of a cold now having me in its grip. However, I don't forget that the whole siege has been a darned sight worse for my aunt than it has for me! Sorry to hear of your own grippe—all effects of which I trust are long past.

        I was delighted to hear of your advent to amateurdom, & at once sent you a copy of the best current journal—*Causerie,* published by the splendid old-timer Edkins. Glad you've been receiving other items. Yes—Barlow has been a frequent contributor for 3 years—though I regret to say I can't recall where all his many pieces have appeared. Bradley's *Perspective Review* has had several, Segal's *Sea-Gull*[1] at least one or two . . . . but there my memory slips. I've passed most of the smaller papers on to others. I know, though, that he hasn't had anything in non-National papers. He is not a member of the United. He himself could probably give an idea of the various journals through which his numerous sketches have been scattered.

As for the various journalistic & political crudities you have observed—I believe I warned you in advance that the institution of amateurdom is a very free-&-easy & heterogeneous one. It has its high spots & it has its blots—papers as fine as *Causerie* and as trivial as *The Proof Sheet;* scholars as splendid as James F. Morton (whom you met in person at Belknap's) & dumb poetasters as bad as Norman Quillman;[2] organisers & parliamentarians as solid as Edward H. Cole, & politicians as turbulent as Ralph W. Babcock.[3] We have to take it as we find it—occasionally putting in a few licks toward improvement—but most of us agree that it forms a distinctly helpful & encouraging influence. Though always somewhat heterogeneous, it has periods of quite brilliant achievement—& right now we are making particular efforts to raise the qualitative level. The one thing to do about the peanut politics so seriously discussed by Babcock, Trainer, Hanson,[4] et al. is to forget it!

It undoubtedly is un-ethical of Detrick[5] to send strictly U.A.P.A. material to National recruits—& it is certainly injudicious of him to include cheap political sheets exhibiting the very worst side of amateurdom's activities. Many prospectives, as you say, would tend to be alienated by such a flood of irrelevant & puerile matter. If the official situation weren't already in such a state of tension I'd be tempted to recommend a polite rebuke for such slipshod procedure—or if I knew Detrick at all (which I don't. I've never exchanged even a postcard with him), I'd do some tactful suggesting myself. Well—anyhow—he has only 2½ months more in office! The division of amateurdom into rival associations is unfortunate but seemingly incurable. When I joined in 1914 there were *3*—*two United Associations* resulting from a split in 1912. I was first a United man—in the United not now existing. We called the present "United" the "pseudo-United", & they called us the "rebel United". Actually, it would be hard to say which was the more legal. Qualitatively, though, my United was away ahead of its rival—& of the National as it has been since 1900. (1885–95 was the N.A.P.A.'s heyday or Golden Age) Although I was desultorily a National member from 1918 on, & president in 1922–3, my first devotion was to the *old United* until it became abeyant amidst the general amateur depression of 1927. I tried my best to keep it alive, but the prevailing apathy was too powerful. Only in 1930 did I again become at all active in amateurdom. I then chose the National because it had been less an enemy of my United than the pseudo-United (= present so-called "United") had been, & because it was intrinsically the better of the survivors. Since then both surviving associations have had quantitative revivals. It now remains for the National to regain its qualitative status of 40 or 50 years ago. The "United" of today is prospering after a fashion, but is relatively crude, & in the clutch of a Noel[6] dictatorship from which Il Duce, Der Führer, the Ghazi, et al. could learn much! But there's more good than bad in amateurdom, & if you'll exercise a sense of proportion & selection I believe you'll manage to enjoy it. It was a great help to me 20 years ago, & I'd still hate to drop out completely.

I shall be glad to see the next *Phantagraph,* & trust that Shepherd's command of typography will gradually increase. It pleases me immensely to know that Rimel is illustrating "The Nameless City", for I like his cuts very much. When you need more verse I'll dig up some ancient things which I can guarantee no weird fan can ever have seen in print. Many were published (in amateurdom or local papers) before the bulk of the present generation was born!

About handwriting—of course, the "Haunter" & any much-corrected MS. designed for no eye but my own is hardly a representative sample. However, I do not think I was wrong in assuming that the younger generation read varied average samples of script less readily than their pre-machine elders. I have heard other oldsters remark the same thing, & when I classify the source of the curses & complaints I receive the same thing appears. People active a generation before me—the septuagenarians & octogenarians of to-day—scarcely ever express any difficulty with any but the worst extremes of bad script. These are the old boys who *never saw* typewriting in their youth. My own generation—semi-mechanised, with all business but few personal letters typed—produces a few complainers. But then—coming down to the young fellows who grew up since the war—a sudden leap develops. These boys fairly bombard me with plaints & imprecations regarding my "unreadable" script—& when one glances at the virtually universal typing habits of the present, an inference does not seem unreasonable. Others have pointed out a curiously parallel phenomenon—the apparent fact that post-war youths' own handwriting tends to retain juvenile or immature characteristics in adult years because of its relatively slight use. On this point I am not fully prepared to pass—although several cases within my field of vision seem to sustain it to some extent. What I do feel surer of is that more people hesitate over an average bit of script in 1936 than was the case in 1896. I can't see the force of your argument against this contention. You say that the boy in school uses script exclusively—but you forget that the *kind* of script involved is the slow, conventionally formed, exaggeratedly clear script of pedagogy . . . which is just as legible as typing, but which because of its slowness would be useless for wide employment. Of course the pupil often lapses from the model, especially in note-taking, &c.—but in this case the loose, rapid script he reads is mostly *his own,* to which he quickly becomes used. He certainly could not compete with his father, who habitually read the loose, rapid script of scores of *different* personal correspondents; or with his grandfather, who came up against every conceivable variety of scrawl in his business, professional, & civic, as well as personal contacts. You can't imagine how sharp the eyes & correlative senses of the oldsters were—how executives went over long reports in different scrawls; how compositors set type from MSS. that would torment a modern youngster out of a year's growth; how publishers read long novels that would look like Sanscrit or Amharic to their grandsons. Don't fancy that the varying practice of *schools* is of any significance in this matter. What is learned in school is only a drop in the bucket of one's general equipment. *School* instruction certainly was grotesque enough in the past*—but that hadn't the least bearing on the fact that everybody *in actual practice* soon began to read unconsciously *by words* & never thought of reading any lesser unit. Modern formal education has merely begun to recognise & encourage what was always the general practice. About the difficulty of different handwritings—of course one has to go through a quick orientation process on encountering a strange script, but this is infinitely speeded up by a judicious use of common sense as regards *context*. Certain words tend to have certain probable positions in relation to other words; & since *a few* words of virtually *any* script are *always* recognisable, we can easily infer what certain of their less obvious neighbours are. Get the *logic* of a paragraph & a few words form a key to virtually all. Thus suppose you had written a certain sentence of yours in bad longhand:

$$\text{1} \qquad\qquad \text{2} \qquad\qquad\qquad \text{3}$$

    "But a word (squiggle) script *never* (squiggle) the same in more than (squiggle) person's manuscript."

The words enclosed in rings are illegible—but (in view of (a) their *place* & (b) their *approximate* form) could any mistake be made regarding them? What *could* word #1 be *except "in"*? Could it *sensibly* be "on" or "an" or "or"? And could #2 be other than *looks?* How much sense would "lacks" or "locks" or "lunches" make? It was *really* this specific principle of identifying words by their *collective outlines* (aided by logic) which I had in mind when referring to *word-reading*—although this of course *includes* the more general principle.

But remember that I was only laying down broad tendencies. Scores of people in the old days used to get held up by anything short of copperplate Spencerian, while scores of youth today *can* decipher loose script as readily as their elders. Barlow & Hornig, for example, are veritable wizards of this kind of thing—though distinctly of today's generation. Yes—I know that a lot of contemporary writers compose on the machine, but I couldn't help thinking their style is the worse for it. The rigid conditions of typing militate against the utter

---

*I suppose you know how *spelling* was taught in the days before the Civil War. The hopeless youngster had to recite his oral spelling *by syllables,* repeating in a sort of "House that Jack Built" fashion until the last one was reached. Thus: *incomprehensibility* i-n, in; c-o-m, com, *incom;* p-r-e, pre, *incompre;* h-e-n, hen, *incomprehen;* s-i, si, *incomprehensi;* b-i-l, bil, *incomprehensibil;* i, i, *incomprehensibili;* t-y, ty, *incomprehensibility!!!!!*

freedom which the hand writer possesses—especially the freedom to reconsider words & constructions *at once,* when the impulse is fresh; & to transpose, delete, interpolate, & replace *immediately & to an infinite extent.* The obstacles—partly physical but even more psychological—are the imprisonment of the sheet in the machine, the hesitancy involved in suddenly going back to an earlier bit of text or skipping all around, the lack of minuter letters for interpolations (of course, most authors *do* correct their typed MSS. in handwriting), &c. Subtler though nearly as grave is the effect of the noisy *false rhythm* (a measure determined by letters & word-lengths, not by the actual phonetic value of the words, sentences, & paragraphs) of the keys & line-changings on the delicate *true rhythm* of language. Really well-condensed, harmonic prose is a rarity today, as the styles of dozens of contemporaries attest. The music of a pure style is impossible to achieve amidst the boiler-factory clatter of false rhythms inflected by a machine. Let us hope that the new silent typewriters will tend to ameliorate this tendency, & restore to the writer the ability to let his aural imagination work. Meanwhile the best stylists of today—like Dunsany—are those who compose by hand.

Glad the later parts of "Mts. of Madness" proved of interest. I think I meant the obscure *greater* barriers of the *other* mountains to concern emissaries from other parts of space—very terrible emissaries of nameless overlords. Perhaps I'll write a sequel called "The Slopes of Schizophrenia". By the way—Price asked me to ask you *not to quote in print* his expressed opinion of Wright's rejection of the Mts. He wants to keep on the good side of old Pharnabazus! The artist—Howard V. Brown, so Sterling tells me—did extremely well with the story—indeed, I never had a tale better illustrated. Crawford meanwhile is slowly going along with "Innsmouth"—having obtained 4 excellent illustrations from Derleth's friend Utpatel. I've read 2 sections of proofs, but doubt whether the book will be ready for a month or two. The March & April W T weren't as bad as usual—even Hamilton getting away from his formula for once. Binder & Klarkash-Ton appear to advantage, & Kuttner—who lately wrote me—is a promising newcomer. Jacobi, Derleth, & Bloch do well in the current number.

Kleiner's name isn't on the N.A.P.A. list because he isn't in a position to pay dues just now. I wish we could tactfully get him back on the list without fiscal formalities—heaven knows he's giving valuable service enough! Long used to be a member but lost interest. Leeds never was. Klarkash-Ton joined the *old* (not the present) United just before it became abeyant, but has never been a National member. But Morton (whom you met) has been a leading amateur since 1889. No weirdists besides those you've named are amateurs. Derleth, like CAS, joined the *old* United toward the last. Loveman was a prominent amateur from 1902 onward. He is now off the list, but I am trying to get him back. Barlow, Rimel, & Mrs. Wooley are all my recruits to the N.A.P.A. My still newer recruits Shea & Miss Sylvester are weird *fans* but their writing is not in the weird line. I'm now trying to recruit Koenig & Sterling. By the way—our young friend Kheh-Es the Booleywag certainly has been through a frightful siege. His parents were badly worried, & it's a relief to see him definitely getting on his feet again. Hope some miracle can enable him to catch up in his studies, as he's desperately anxious to do. He & my aunt were in their respective hospitals at the same time, & are both recovering at about the same rate.

Hope to see you in Providence before long. Let me know when you're coming, & I'll give any needed directions & be sure to be on hand. There's a good deal in the old burg which ought to interest you! ¶ Regards, & best wishes—
Yrs most sincerely—HPL

P.S. Barlow has sent the whole file of his 1932 correspondence with Shepherd, & from the original documents his position stands vindicated. Shepherd offered to trade him a complete 1923–4–5 WT file for a bound set of *Amazings*. Barlow sent the *Amazings* & received only some junk in return. Then Shepherd bluffed & pretended he'd never offered the WT's. His illiterate letters to Barlow are a revelation. RHB asked me not to pass the file around, but I'm asking his permission to show a concise digest of it to those persons who have heard Shepherd's version.[7] It will be an eye-opener for you! Shepherd pretended to have certain magazines to trade which undoubtedly never existed!

[P.]P.S. A travelling loan exhibit of some of Klarkash-Ton's is now at Loveman's—& will later visit Providence & De Land. Why don't you get in touch with Loveman & arrange to see it? His home address is 17 Middagh St., Brooklyn.

*Notes*

1. Chester P. Bradley and Harold Segal, both youthful amateurs. For Barlow's publications in these and other amateur journals, see the bibliography in *Eyes of the God* (2002).
2. Norman Quillman, a Michigan amateur.
3. Ralph W. Babcock, Jr., president of the NAPA (1934–35).
4. George W. Trainer, Secretary of the NAPA; Edgar Hanson of West Concord, NH, editor of the *Proof Sheet*.
5. Charles L. Detrick, secretary of the NAPA (1934–35).
6. Clyde F. Noel was part of the so-called [J. F. Roy] Erford–Noel UAPA faction headquartered in Seattle, WA. He was president of the faction in 1925. The split between this faction and the Hoffman–Daas faction to which HPL belonged occurred in 1912.
7. This is "Correspondence between R. H. Barlow and Wilson Shepherd of Oakman, Alabama—Sept.–Nov. 1932."

[9]     [ALS]
66 College St.,
Providence, R.I.,
July 6, 1936.
Dear Wollheim:—
I am sorry I could not be prompter in acknowledging yours

of June 27th, but the chaos & congestion around me utterly precludes speed of any sort. However, in one sense you are not the loser; since up to last Friday I could have given no first-hand information regarding the Howard tragedy. I have now had a letter & local papers from R E H's father—& am forced to confirm the very sad rumour of his suicide. By this time you may have had confirmation from other sources—but I will repeat the salient facts in case you have not.

After a year of intense worry over his mother's grave pleural illness, Howard shot himself through the head at 8 a.m. June 11, when told that his mother would never recognise him again & would not live more than 48 hours. He lived for 8 hours without regaining consciousness, dying at 4 p.m. His mother—also without being conscious—died 30 hours later, on the night of the 12th. One can imagine the intolerable sorrow of poor Dr. Howard— with wife & splendid only child gone at a single blow. A double funeral— with identical coffins—was held on Sunday, June 14. REH's books have been given to his alma mater in Brownwood as the nucleus of a Robert E. Howard Memorial Collection.

Even now I can hardly believe the thing. It is like a nightmare from which one ought to be able to wake up. I had a long normal letter from good old Two-Gun as recently as May 13, while Price had a cheerful postcard mailed June 3. I had known of his worry about his mother's health, but never dreamed it would reach this tragic culmination. Evidently his moody & melancholy streak—the trait manifested in his lifelong hatred of civilisation— went far deeper than any of us realised.

The loss to weird fiction is staggering—for REH's vivid & compelling tales were leaving all competition behind. I've told Price—the only one of us ever to meet Two-Gun Bob in person—that he ought to write the main obituary for *Weird Tales*—just as I wrote Henry S. Whitehead's (I was the only one to have seen HSW in person) four years ago. About a *Phantagraph* obituary—I hacked out the enclosed notes yesterday, but if you find them too long you can manipulate them at will provided you don't use my name in connexion with them. You can, if you like, combine them with a news item containing the salient facts of the tragedy. "The Hyborian Age" will have a sad significance in the light of what has happened—& if (as Shepherd suggests) you ultimately issue an edition in booklet form you surely ought to present a copy to the Memorial Collection. Such a booklet ought to be very popular among the thousands of Conan-fans in WT's clientele. I've just written Dr. Howard a letter of sympathy—though I realise the futility of words in the face of the double grief he is enduring.

I am glad to hear of the new plans for *The Phantagraph*, & believe a regular monthly schedule will help vastly in promoting interest & increasing circulation. As for verse items—are the enclosed any good? The "October" thing may not be weird enough, although it has certain suggestions of weirdness.

Would you be willing to copy matter from old amateur papers if I should lend you the latter? There is a good deal in the issues of 15 to 20 years ago that I'd be glad to let you use if you'd save me the ordeal of transcription—an ordeal well-nigh impossible to endure in my present state of exhaustion. The stuff sent to *The Planeteer* consisted of a couple of carbons of some mediocre junk written & published in 1925.[1] I've never seen a copy of the magazine, though the youthful editors inform me that I've been honoured with a free subscription in exchange for my immortal quatrains. About CAS material—he's under a worse strain than I am, but I fancy he'll send you some material as soon as he can. Most certainly, he is not offended in any way! Concerning that article on interplanetary fiction[2]—I'd be glad to let you have it if it weren't already given to Crawford. The fact is, it was written especially for Crawford two years ago. He doesn't seem to use it, & if you can get him to transfer it to you I'd be glad to have it appear in your mimeographed bulletin. Actually, I don't see what use he can make of it, since *Marvel Tales* is an all-fiction publication. You can tell him I recommend his passing it on to you. If you use the text in *The Californian* be on the lookout for misprints. There's one tricky specimen (which I can't recall just now) toward the end. Regarding news items—there's hardly anything of importance to relate apart from the Howard tragedy. Price has just had a pleasant visit from W. K. Mashburn. Howard Wandrei's wife was injured in a motor-bus accident en route back from Minneapolis & is now in the hospital suffering from cerebral & spinal concussion. No—not a single distinctive thing to relate!

I had the pleasure of a call from our young friend Sterling a week ago, & was delighted to see how well he had weathered his truly frightful ordeal. It must have taken tremendous fortitude to get through a horrible experience like that without going all to pieces nervously. His basic architecture has certainly altered in the year-&-a-third since I first saw him, & the designation of "cherub" is surely obsolete! His scholastic prospects still look promising, & I wouldn't be surprised if he made Harvard next autumn despite the obstacles of the past winter. Without question, he is one of the brightest youths I have ever encountered, & I fancy he'll outdistance the bulk of our group before many years have passed.

Glad you had a chance to survey the "low-down" on the great Barlow–Shepherd bout of '32. That illiteracy of Shepherd's was no mere matter of typing—you ought to see the pencil scrawls! But I agree with you that he has changed radically since those days. His recent letters to me show real solicitude for your joint magazine enterprises, & a real determination to achieve typographical improvement; nor do I think he would try to lure any more customers through promise of non-existent "Interplanetary Storys" files for 1915! Accordingly I offer all possible encouragement when I reply—or carefully refrain from evoking the spectres of 1932 except among the two or three persons (you, Sterling & Koenig) who had not heard both sides of the matter. He is really doing splendidly—learning fast, & showing more persistence than most fledgling printers. I surely wish him—& the whole chain of enterprises—the best of luck!

About the new *Wonder*—I haven't seen a copy, but am afraid from what I hear that its quality has not been improved by its divorce from Hugo the Rat.[3] No—I haven't yet tried anything on it, though I had a letter from Margulies last February inviting me to do so. I doubt if the old FF material would be suitable for sending. In the first place, it isn't science fiction; & in the second place, I fancy the previous publication (even in the absence of any copyright) might involve legal barriers.

I was glad to see *Queer* in the recent N.A.P.A. bundle, & am pleased to note your rapid absorption into the fabric of amateur journalism. It somewhat astonishes me to learn that the Noel association has advantages over the National. I'd join it but for the haunting ghost of *my* United, which pined away in '27. The split of 1912 was caused by an election so close that each faction thought itself the winner. It really seems to have been a tie—which only a wizard could untangle. Each group called itself *The* United, & carried on as before. For 15 years there were two *United Amateurs*. Actually the rival groups became very different in nature—the one I joined having a serious literary quality. Haggerty was *not* in my United, but always on the other side. If there was any political "moving spirit" on our side (to correspond to J. F. Roy Erford in the enemy's camp) it was Edward F. Daas of Milwaukee—the chap who first recruited me to amateurdom in 1914. Glad you've joined the N.E. Club—which I haven't done as yet. You'll get more N.A.P.A. papers now that your name is on the list. *Manettism* & *Perspective Review* are no longer issued.[4] There *is* a spring *Californian*, & a summer one too. You'll undoubtedly receive both sooner or later. Have you received the *second Causerie* & *both* issues of *The Dragon Fly?* If not, let me know. I can supply you. I can't agree with you about amateur politics. To me they have always seemed trivial & irrelevant.

Yes—it looks as if I'd be in Providence throughout 1936, & I'd surely enjoy seeing you some week-end when you can get around. Let me know ahead, & I'll be sure to be on hand—& will send directions for reaching 66, or arrange to meet you at whatever terminal you select. Hope you can make it! Barlow may get up this way during the late summer.

Well—do as you like about the obituary. I'll be looking for the July *Phantagraph*. ¶ All good wishes

—HPL.

[Enclosure: "Robert Ervin Howard: 1906–1936" (A.Ms.).]

[On back of envelope:] *Phantagraph* just arrived. Glad to see it. Multum in parvo!

*Notes*

1. See WS 11. Six issues of the magazine appeared, but that of September 1936 (with

HPL's material) was not completed.

2. "Some Notes on Interplanetary Fiction."

3. On 21 February 1936, Gernsback sold *Wonder Stories* to Ned Pines of Beacon Magazines. In August 1936 the magazine changed its name to *Thrilling Wonder Stories*.

4. Published, respectively, by Clarke W. Walton Monroe of North Carolina, and Chester P. Bradley of Michigan.


[10]  [ALS]

July 9 [1936]

Dear Wollheim:—

Just a few notes amidst a chaos of engulfing duties. I've sent the old amateur papers with my verses, together with some newer stuff. Of all this material, only the *old* material (as follows) need be returned:

*Tryout Jul 1919* (with "Oceanus", "Clouds", & "Mother Earth")

*Vagrant Oct 1919* (with "The City" & "Psychopompos")

*Vagrant Dec 1919* (with "The Nightmare Lake")

*Philosopher 1920* (with "The House")

"Ward Phillips", signed to some of this stuff, is an old pseudonym of mine. You won't want anything as long as "Psychopompos" now—but if you ever do, let me know & I'll supply a MS. embodying some revisions. I can't find any more junk just now, but perhaps I'll have dug up some more by the time you get around to these parts.

I've looked over your own verse with much interest, & am herewith returning it with a few emendations. You might try it on Wright again, or use it in one of your various magazine projects. The metre was all right, but some of the wording didn't fall quite within the poetic tradition. It is hard to explain just what needed doing—for the only way to get the real hang of poetry is to saturate oneself with the best specimens. I enclose a little N.A.P.A. booklet of mine which you can keep if you like.[1] Better still would be a perusal of Brander Matthews' "A Study of Versification".

I am also sending #2 of *Dragon-Fly* & *Causerie*—for your permanent retention. You ought to have received them directly, but mistakes will happen. I've also enclosed all the recent *Tryout* duplicates I can find, since you say that good old Smithy (who will be 84 next October) hasn't favoured you yet. A quaint little bundle of errors published by a delectably naive patriarch. Glad you have the new *Californian*—in which I was glad to see your article on Pure Fantasy reprinted. Barlow's contribution is magnificent stuff—& I don't say so merely because it is dedicated to me. Splendid rhythm, poetic imagery, emotional modulations, & atmospheric power. Literature is certainly the kid's forte (you ought to see his elegaic sonnet on good old Two-Gun which arrived yesterday!), & I wish he'd stop scattering his energies in a dozen other hobbies!

Good luck with your press club![2] You surely *are* in amateur journalism! Convention seems to have been a great success. Did I give election returns? Martin Pres., Bradofsky Ed., Boston Convention Seat.[3] No—I haven't yet joined The Fossils, though my old *R.I. Journal of Astronomy,* published over 30 years ago, makes me eligible. I envy you that bound volume of *The Fossil.*

I enjoyed the new *Phantagraph* exceedingly—nor did I mind the small type. Indeed, I wish it were *all* in small type, so that longer material could be used. As I used to tell Hornig, the big thing is the *contents*—to hell with mere *appearance.* For my part, I'd rather see a large mimeographed paper than a small printed one. Do you use verse in *Fanciful Tales?* I'm enclosing a couple of items from young Morse, which he wants placed in the *best* possible magazine.[4] Shoot 'em back to *me* if you can't use them to advantage—I can in that case try them on Crawford or others. Morse asks that the publisher be sure to retain his dedications. Another thing—what is your maximum length (in any of your ventures) for non-fictional prose? Price wants to prepare some personal reminiscences of Two-Gun (something apart from my obituary), & has asked me what "fan" magazine is best able to handle such a thing. I shall ask all the fan editors & see who can offer the largest space.[5] Hell! I'm getting to be a regular literary agent! Have you heard of the new fan sheet—*Science-Fantasy Correspondent,* about to be published by one Willis Conover, Jr., of Cambridge, Md.? Old Bill Lumley is still going strong, & would be glad if you could accomodate any verses of his. I trust you've sent him the issue with his poem. Did I tell you that a story of his—"The Diary of Alonzo Typer"—was accepted by WT? This reminds me that I haven't kept track lately of the acceptances reported by various correspondents. I'll try to jot down & report future items of the sort. One thing, though—Wright has taken a couple of things of mine—"The Haunter of the Dark" & "The Thing on the Doorstep". I expected rejections, but wanted all chances exhausted before letting Schwartz have them for some British reprinting project which he's agitating. And so you've seen Crawford? I wonder if he'll ever get out that long-awaited MT—& if so, whether he'll stop at a single issue. His projects have a way of petering out. If you can get that interplanetary article out of him, you're welcome to it. Hornig? He went west to seek his fortune, & is now in Los Angeles with a clerical job tentatively in sight. If he doesn't land it—or another—he'll be back in ancient Elizabethtown in the course of time. Present address—820½ Carondelet St., Los Angeles, Calif.

How well any of my junk would fit in the new *Wonder* I can't say—but the reprint of the Merritt item seems to clear up one point.[6] If typing weren't such a nightmare I might try some of those old FF items. I must get a copy of the new venture & see what it's like.

Glad the REH obituary & data I sent will be of use. The poems by Two-Gun himself will be sadly appropriate[7]—& I hope "The Hyborian Age" can ultimately come out as a pamphlet. The tragic event surely seems to contradict the usual idea of Two-Gun as a hard-boiled, hairy-chested, eat-'em-alive guy—but who can untangle the complexities of the human mind & emotions? I'd hardly criticise his act as *cowardice,* since it really takes guts to overcome the blind animal clinging to life which most of us possess, & to make an artistic exit when the appropriate time comes. Every person's life is his own, & there's no valid obligation to remain alive when no reason for living exists. I certainly shan't continue to live if circumstances ever deprive me of the surroundings & possessions necessary to my reasonable contentment. What I criticise in Two-Gun is simply his *judgment.* He had youth, health, an admirable & affectionate father, & good literary & financial prospects. With maturer reflection, he would have realised that all of us have to bid farewell to the olden generation sooner or later, no matter how sorrowful the inevitable parting may be—& would have taken his loss more philosophically. And of course it was desperately myopic of him to forget the blow he was inflicting on his father. But he was in no mood to reason. For months he had been losing sleep while acting as nurse to his mother, & at the last he had watched her bedside for three days & nights without closing his eyes. This strain, joined to the already-existing moody streak in his nature—& perhaps to an overdeveloped maternal devotion—was enough to overrule all reflections & inhibitions. He had been worrying for a year, & the final disaster was simply too much. The act was to some extent planned, as remarks to the agent Kline, & some papers at his home, attest. Dr. Howard was going to have him watched incessantly after the death of his mother, but did not suspect he would make the attempt *before* the end. The whole thing is certainly ineffably tragic—& to Price, who twice visited in the happy & harmonious Cross Plains household, it seems well-nigh unbearable. The present bravery of old Dr. Howard excites one's admiration. He is still going to live on in the old home alone & keep up his practice—meanwhile founding the Robert E. Howard Memorial Collection (in which "The Hyborian Age" certainly must go) at his son's alma mater.

Some decent weather at last! 92° here yesterday, & just as comfortable today. I've done more work in the past 48 hours than in the whole fortnight preceding. It takes about 90° to pep Grandpa up to the pitch of real accomplishment!

Best wishes—& try to be careful of the various loan-items, though there isn't the least hurry about their return.

Yours most sincerely,

H P L

## Notes

1. *Further Criticism of Poetry.*

2. HPL may be referring to the American Amateur Press Association (AAPA), which was being formed around this time. DAW's colleague Wilson Shepherd was extensively involved in this organization.

3. Margaret Nickerson Martin, poet and literary critic based in Jackson, MI, was president of NAPA in 1936–37, succeeding Hyman Bradofsky. Her publication was called the *Literary Record*.

4. "Dark Garden," dedicated to CAS, and "Mad Dream," dedicated to HPL.

5. E. Hoffmann Price's memoir "Robert Ervin Howard" appeared in *Diablerie* (May 1944); rpt. in the *Howard Collector* (Summer 1961) and in Price's *Book of the Dead* (Arkham House, 2001).

6. Merritt's "The Drone Man" (*Fantasy Magazine,* September 1934) was reprinted in *Thrilling Wonder Stories* (August 1936).

7. Howard's poems "Always Comes Evening" (August 1936) and "Song at Midnight" (August 1940) appeared in the *Phantagraph*.


[11]    [ANS][1]

[Postmarked Providence, RI,
23 August 1936]

*The Lovecrafter*[2] duly arrived, & I must hasten to express to you & Shepherd my keen & sincere appreciation of your joint thoughtfulness. It's surely a compensation for the advance of old age to become an editor & publisher without one's knowledge! ¶ Barlow—whose presence in Providence I guess I mentioned—is still here. A fortnight ago there was another guest—old Adolphe Danziger de Castro (one-time friend of Ambrose Bierce & later a revision client of mine), to whom I shewed the sights of the town. One afternoon he, Barlow & I sat on a tomb in the hidden hillside churchyard & composed rhymed acrostics on the name of *Edgar Allan Poe,* who 90 years ago roamed that selfsame necropolis when on visits to Providence. ¶ Barlow & I took a Newport sail Aug 15. On my birthday we explored ancient Salem & Marblehead (Arkham & Kingsport), stopping in Lynn to add young Sterling & a friend to our party. The Booleywag is looking very well these days—& is as brown as an Indian. If Barlow pauses in N.Y. on his way to Kansas (whither he is headed) you'll probably see him. ¶ All good wishes—& thanks again for the thoughtful anniversary remembrance.
Yours most sincerely—
H P L


*Notes*

1. *Front:* Witch House, Salem, Mass.

2. Actually a broadside, purporting to be Vol. 47, No. 1, and dated 20 August 1936, HPL's forth-sixth birthday.

[12]   [ALS]

66 College St.,
Providence, R.I.,
August 30, 1936.

Dear Wollheim:—

Glad my former letter safely reached you, & that the Morse sonnets proved acceptable. Hope you'll soon get the printing schedule of *The Phantagraph* settled. No hurry about the borrowed amateur journals so long as they're safe. I can understand what a crowded programme is—being driven virtually to the wall with various tasks at the present moment! Glad the revisory touches in your verses proved acceptable & hope to see the result in print eventually.

Interested to hear of your session with—& lodgment of—young Conover. He seems to be a very earnest & ambitious chap, & I hope his new magazine will succeed. But I do wish some of these various sheets could be *combined*, with everybody working for the success of one or two good publications. Large numbers of publications involve wasteful duplication of material & impairment of individual subscription lists. Somebody recently said there were as many as *15* fantasy fan sheets in existence or planned. That is really a suicidal situation—for such a scattering of subscriptions means extinction for all. It's up to you young editors to get together somehow! Sterling tells of a new magazine of which I haven't otherwise heard—name unknown, but published by one Robert A. Madle, 333 E. Belgrade St., Philadelphia.[1] Ever hear of this bird? Yes—there is certainly a singular & commendable tendency toward cordial fellowship among fantasy devotees—as among amateur journalists. No doubt it exists because such persons realise that their tastes are rather out of the ordinary—that they are unlikely to encounter kindred spirits every day, hence must make the most of those whom they do run across.

No—Hill-Billy Crawford ain't done git nowhars on "Innsmouth" in the last few weeks. I've had proofs of about half the story—& there matters seem to rest. Hill-Billy is a raht-smart starter, but has a way of getting all muddled up in the middle of everything. He has told me about his Lindbergh-case book—some insane crank-theory of the sort which grow up among the naive after every prominent crime. I still await *Marvel Tales,* which will soon be having to change its publication schedule from annual to biennial!

I note your remarks on the disposition of Sultan Malik's reminiscences of Two-Gun Bob. He is himself undecided, & is reluctant to let any one sheet capitalize on sorrow by announcing "exclusive publication" or anything like that. A present plan of his is to make many carbons & release them all simultaneously to the various "fan" magazines like a syndicate feature—letting each one print or not print, according to inclination. In such a case the various editors might well get together & decide just who shall handle the item. Another thing about Two-Gun which ought to be printed is P. Schuyler Miller's bibliography & history of Conan the Cimmerian.[2] This is a list of all the Conan stories arranged in proper chronological sequence, together with a stream of comment outlining the development of the hero from his first appearance at 15 to the height of his kingship of Aquilonia at the age of about 40. Wright lent me a MS. of this, though I doubt whether he intends to publish it in WT. It was prepared before the tragedy, & REH himself had a chance to inspect & approve it. Shepherd—in a letter of Aug. 17—speaks of a plan for publishing a book of REH's tales by subscription—an excellent idea if it could be developed on an adequate scale & with proper mechanical excellence.

As for the present whereabouts of the peripatetic young Booleywag—he is now leaving Lynn for a brief period in N.Y. preparatory to entering Harvard in late September. It is an open question whether he'll require a second operation—this time a very minor one—before being in shape for the winter. The decision of the doctors in this matter will determine the extent of his availability for social & literary contacts during his Manhattan period. In any case he'll be around again by mid-September, but if the final tinkering is decided, he'll be in the hospital for the bulk of his metropolitan stay. Barlow's pause in N.Y. depends to some extent on whether the Supreme Booleywag will be at liberty to serve as guide & philosophic arguer. The place to get fresh tips on Sterling's plans is his temporary N.Y. headquarters (after Sept. 1—or rather, beginning then)—% Mack—Tel. SChuyler 4-5800 (Suite 806). I have a vague idea that this is the Hotel Park Crescent at Riv. Drive & 87th St. Kenneth, a friend of his named Rogers[3] (a law student in Lynn), Barlow, & I had a most enjoyable trip to Salem & Marblehead on my 46th birthday. We went through several ancient houses (of the "Witch House" sort) & sat on a tomb in the Charter St. Burying Ground in Salem—gazing at the giant willows engulfing a gravestone which formed the nucleus of my story "The Unnamable".

Yes—I surely enjoyed *The Lovecrafter,* & must thank you again for the thoughtful tribute. I rather imagined that the edition was a strictly limited one.

Barlow starts westward Sept. 1st—headed for Kansas City, where he will probably reside for an indefinite time. He'll undoubtedly call you up if he stays in town—though his plans in this respect are very unsettled, & dependent to some extent on the liberty of the Booleywag. About Long—he was away at Ocean Grove N.J. at last reports, but may possibly be back by this time. Conover, though he saw nearly everybody else, did not get in touch with him.

Sorry to hear of Shepherd's fresh accident. Hope he can arrange to publish the WT index on which L. C. Smith fell down. Haven't heard from Klarkash-Ton for a long while, but know he is having a hard struggle managing the place & taking care of his increasingly feeble father. Wandrei is home in St. Paul for a while, but I can't think of any news from Price, Derleth, or the others. Edkins is just pulling out of a serious second operation.

I had an interesting visit from good old M. W. Moe & his son Robert July 18–19. We covered most of the local sights & had a good time generally.

I hadn't seen Moe since 1923, & found him much less changed than myself. Barlow blew in July 28, & has been busy seeing sights, buying books, & looking up ancestors at the local libraries. He has found that he is my *6th cousin* by virtue of common descent in 7 generations from one John Rathbone of Block Island, R.I., born in 1658. Thus:

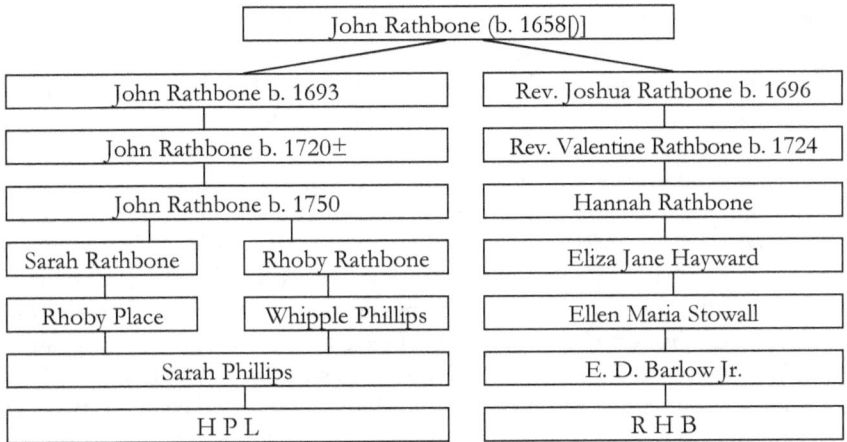

It is curious to note that although Ar-Ec'h-Bei is young enough to be my son, he is descended from our common forbear in precisely the same number of steps. Bob's great-great-grandfather, Dr. Barzillai Hayward, (husband of the Hannah Rathbone mentioned above) attended Brown University—in a building still standing only a stone's throw from #66—with the class of 1807. On his mother's side Barlow is a collateral descendant of Pres. James Monroe of Monroe Doctrine.

Another recent Providence visitor was old Dr. Adolphe Danziger de Castro, one-time associate of Ambrose Bierce & author of a biography (with preface by our friend Belknap) of that gifted figure. Old 'Dolph was a revision client of mine some years ago (you may recall his "Last Test" & "Electric Executioner" in WT), & is always trying to saddle me with unprofitable speculative jobs. He was here for 5 days—returning to NY from Boston, where he had been discharging the melancholy duty of scattering his late wife's ashes over the sea in accordance with her last wish. We shewed him the principal sights, & on one occasion he, Barlow, & I sat on a tomb in the hidden hillside churchyard (of which the Grand Booleywag has doubtless shewn you pictures) & wrote rhymed acrostics (at Barlow's suggestion) on the name of Edgar Allan Poe—who 90 years ago wandered in that selfsame necropolis when on visits to Providence. I expect a visit from Morton in a fortnight or so. He is now in New Hampshire, & will later pause in Boston to attend the Harvard Tercentenary & collect some genealogical data.

Barlow visited cousins in New Bedford Thursday & Friday, & was shewn all the sights of the ancient seaport—the whaling museum (with its impressive half-size model of the barque *Lagoda* in a lofty hall), the actual whaler *Charles W. Morgan* in its concrete bed on the estate of the late Col. Green, &c. &c. He sets out Tuesday morning for points west, & will probably stop in Indianapolis to see Miss Moore. His future address will be ℅ H. M. LANGWORTHY, 860 W. 57th St. Terrace, Kansas City, Mo.

Thanks for the copy of the *Mid At Am*—& here's hoping your local society can get organised before long. [anent your geographical limit—why exclude D.C. . . . is it to keep old Hadley out?][4] Interested to hear of the local United chapter. Yes—the Erford-Noel pseudo-United has always gone in for the long-haired -ism stuff rather crudely & naively. Glad you're roping some fantasy fans into amateurdom. Sorry you've failed to receive *Tryout* & Babcockiana. I'm notifying old Smithy—though Babcock's a hopeless case. Bradofsky's backing down is most unfortunate after his clear-cut vindication at the polls. He is inexcusably "temperamental" & hypersensitive—& ought to control his caprices better. He fancied he was not receiving suitable coöperation—whereas the current obstacles were only an editor's usual tribulations. He has done much for amateurdom—& received a very dirty deal last year—but this year the trouble is of his own brewing. Townsend, I think, will make a good editor.[5]

Best wishes, & hope to see a *Phantagraph* soon.

Yours sincerely,

—H P L

P.S. As for *trying* to increase my list of correspondents—hell! I wish you'd tell me how to trim it down & keep it under control! The reason I always try to encourage young editors is that I think they need such encouragement at the outset. A very little help means a good deal to them at that age, & it doesn't cost very much to give it.

*Notes*

1. This apparently was the *Fantasy Fiction Telegram*.
2. P. Schuyler Miller and John D. Clark, "A Probable Outline of Conan's Career," appended to *The Hyborian Age*.
3. Unidentified. HPL's handwriting is difficult to read here, and the name may not be *Rogers*.
4. HPL apparently refers to a copy of the *Mid Atlantic Amateur* sent to him by DAW. "Hadley" refers to Edwin Hadley Smith of Washington, D.C., a leading figure in the NAPA.
5. Clyde G. Townsend, official editor of the NAPA (1924–26) who took over as president for the 1936–37 term after Hyman Bradofsky resigned.

# Letters to Wilson Shepherd

[1]    [ALS]

66 College St.,
Providence, R.I.,
April 29, 1936.

Dear Mr. Shepherd:—

Yours of the 23ᵈ—& the second *Phantagraph*—have duly arrived, & I am glad to note the improvement in the magazine. An enterprise like this must develop slowly—especially if one is new at the business of editing & printing. One learns by experience as one goes.

I like the *Phantagraph* very much, & believe it is entirely on the right track. So far as the nature of the contents is concerned, I doubt if any preferable policy could be adopted. A magazine like this is no place for long original fiction, but is logically an avenue for discussion & criticism & news connected with fantastic writing. Articles on different phases of the weird, reviews of weird books, news of magazines & authors, brief verses & sketches in the same vein—all of them are what such a magazine ought to have, & what indeed *The Phantagraph* does have. The kind of progress to be striven for is simply one of expansion & improvement in the existing direction. More & better material of the same kind. Specific suggestions which one could give are very few. Possibly a sort of weird *reading guide* would be a good idea—a list of the really best books & stories in the given field. Many of the younger devotees are very slow in learning of the finest work—which is never found in magazines except for occasional reprints. *The Phantagraph* ought to introduce the beginners to authors like Blackwood, Machen, Dunsany, M. R. James, Walter de la Mare, William Hope Hodgson, H. R. Wakefield, Hanns Heins Ewers, &c. &c. If I were editor I would pay less attention to the pulp authors (though never neglecting the high spots of the magazine field) & more to the standard classics. But possibly that is just the course you *are* planning. Altogether, I think *The Phantagraph* has made a very good beginning, & I surely hope it can keep up its development without interruption.

Regarding the *printing*, I can't give any sort of expert opinion, since I know nothing at all about practical typography. I couldn't print any sort of an issue. But judging purely as a layman, I'd say you were learning the art very rapidly. I assume that you were new to printing when you started #1. This naturally shows the unavoidable defects of beginner's work—the frequent misprints, the sometimes awkward spacing, the occasionally crude-looking headings (like that ⌈ ⌉ one), the lack of graceful arrangement & of type of the proper size & style for various other headings, the use of rather primitive ornaments (such as ❧ & 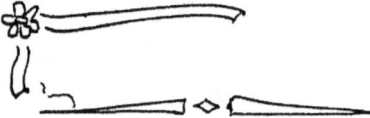), the mixing of black & blue pages, the occasional poor impressions (uneven or faintly inked), &c. &c. Some of these things are undoubtedly due to the lack of ample typographical equipment, & will disappear when you get more fonts of type for headings, better ornaments & borders, & other things of the sort. Indeed, I can see the difference which the new heading type (of the right size, but not quite heavy enough to match the body type), & the increasing number of linoleum cuts by Rimel & Petaja, have made in the second issue. Possibly these young artists could design you some conventional ornaments of the right sort—borders for headings (something on this idea):

or tailpieces of various kinds—roughly like this:

A tailpiece ought to be either a regular panel or something which tapers downward. The bracket work which you use is not quite the thing—& anyhow, ought to be the other side up—like this:

Avoid ornaments which plainly show themselves to be common printing devices—like brackets of this sort.

However—a good many of my remarks may be needless, since the *much* better spacing & ornamentation of the second issue shows that you are learning fast. The heading of Howard's article could scarcely be improved upon, & if you could make the rest of them as tasteful & well-arranged as that you would need no advice!* The contents page, I think, is a little crowded. Have you any *small caps*? If so, I think you ought to use them for authors' names in the "by-lines". The *spacing* of #2 is much better. Indeed, one could sum up by saying that *headings* are probably the weakest point, & that *ornaments* form the next-weakest. And of course you ought to strive constantly for fewer & fewer misprints.

When you can, you ought to get some typographical criticisms & pointers from really qualified critics—which I am not. I see that you carry the N.A.P.A. device on the contents page—which reminds me that you could get

---

*the heading of the Lonsdell article is also very well arranged.

great help from the printing experts in the Association. Send a copy of the latest *Phantagraph* to our official typographical critic (Helm C. Spink, 513 Belgravia Court, Louisville, Kentucky), or to Ralph W. Babcock, Carnegie Institute of Technology, Pittsburgh, Pa., with a request for helpful advice. Either would be glad to give you some pointers. And try to get on the mailing list of the Kelsey Press Co's free paper, *The Printer's Helper.*

But as I have said, you are already headed in the right direction. #2 is a vast improvement over #1, & I am sure the good work will keep up. Let me congratulate you on a very creditable issue! ¶ Later I hope to see *Fanciful Tales*—a venture in which, as in the earlier one, I wish you the best of luck! ¶ With best wishes,

Yrs most sincerely,<br>H P Lovecraft

[2]     [ALS]

66 College St.,<br>Providence, R.I.,<br>May 10, 1936.

Dear Mr. Shepherd:—

I duly received yours of the 1st, & am very much interested in your remarks concerning *The Phantagraph's* policy. I am sure that you have the right idea of the magazine's proper function, & that all contemplated development is in the right direction. I'll be very glad to assist in the listing of good fantastic reading, & will send in some outlines when I get time to compile them. Koenig will also be a willing coöperator in such matters—in fact, he tells me of his intention to furnish an article on William Hope Hodgson—an author whom he virtually rediscovered so far as our circle is concerned.[1]

The best weird books are generally rather hard to obtain—not only in small places but even in large cities with extensive public libraries. The New York Public Library, for example, has no copy of "Melmoth, the Wanderer". Both Koenig & I are willing to lend to responsible persons the few weird books which we own, but these do not include some of the most desirable.

It is an undoubted fact that science-fiction is vastly more popular than weird—especially among the young. This is really quite natural; since weird fiction appeals only to certain types of temperament, whereas science-fiction represents an exaggeration of the inventions & discoveries which everyone knows about & in which most persons (especially the young, who have grown up in the midst of an age of applied science & remember no other period) are keenly interested. It is hard to say that either of these two fields is intrinsically "better" or "worse" than the other. Weird fiction—because of its grounding in certain basic human moods—can be developed on a higher plane than the essentially fact-bound & mechanical science-story, yet very few weird tales in the magazines rise to such a height. The best weird magazine tales are probably a bit better than the best science magazine tales, but do not excel the fine science-fiction work of H. G. Wells, S. Fowler Wright, & W. Olaf Stapledon (author of "The Last & First Men"). Of the poorer grade of stories, I fancy the weird & science specimens are about equally bad—although the science ones may *seem* the more boring because they are more plentiful.

I am sure you have no reason to feel dissatisfied with your printing progress—considering the improvement between #1 & #2—& believe the magazine will look still better when you gradually enlarge your equipment. Your two decorative woodcuts look very promising, & I fancy you can do wonders in this line after you've studied the subject of typographical ornament more thoroughly. Don't rely on my judgment in such matters, for I am no specialist. Those designs which I suggested were merely the crude ideas of a layman. Real experts in printing can tell you just what sort of decorations belong best in spaces of a certain size & shape, & in relation (as regards headings) to certain styles of type. Another good thing to use—when you have the proper facilities—are *ornamental initial letters* at the beginning of articles & stories. There are several distinct kinds of these, & at least two different ways to use them . . . some printers preferring to have them sunk ⊥IKE this, & some preferring to raise them *above* the general level of the type ⌐IKE this.

About type—yes, I think Caslon italics would make the best "by-lines" if you have no small capitals. Some might even prefer them to small caps. But either full capitals or ordinary body type are rather bad to use. There are lots of details of taste connected with the use of type—especially as regards the *mixing of styles* in body & headings & title (or contents) pages—some styles going well together while others tend to clash in appearance. I'm not a very good judge of these matters, but real experts can give very definite & valuable advice. Yes—proofreading is surely an art in itself, & requires both a sharp eye & a ready willingness to use both the dictionary & common sense. Some authors submit erroneous copy, & it often takes cleverness to straighten this out.

Glad to hear of plans for *Fanciful Tales*. You're lucky to get illustrations from Ferguson, who really does the best line drawing of anybody outside the professional ranks. He'll probably land in the professional magazines sooner or later. There surely is room for a high-grade semi-professional weird magazine—& many splendid MSS. can be obtained, both from beginners & from more established writers. Rimel, Howard, C. A. Smith, Barlow, Bloch, R. E. Morse, Kuttner, Derleth, & many others would undoubtedly be glad to coöperate. But the commercial launching of such a magazine will be difficult—as Crawford's experience has proved. By the way—I don't know just when C. can finish that "Innsmouth" book. I haven't read half the proofs yet. I'll be interested to see Wollheim's coming N.A.P.A. magazine.

About the new *Wonder*—I can't tell yet what it will be like, since I see conflicting reports. I've never seen any of the other publications of the

Margulies group, though I hear they're pretty bad. My friend Long writes blood-&-thunder junk for them. Some say that *Wonder* will try to combine two extremes—each issue having *one* or *two* good stories to attract the better readers, but being otherwise given over to the favourite "action" junk of the mob. One can judge better when the first issue appears.

As for ink-colours—I think *black* is best in the long run, & believe the majority would prefer it. But the most important thing is to have the *same* colour throughout each issue.

All good wishes for both magazines. Later I'll send some reading suggestions, which I hope may prove acceptable.

Yrs most sincerely—

H P Lovecraft

*Notes*

1. H. C. Koenig, "On the Trail of the Weird and Phantastic: More Notes on William Hope Hodgson," *Phantagraph* 5, No. 4 (January 1937): 4–6.

[3]     [ALS]

66 College St.,

Providence, R.I.,

May 29, 1936.

Dear Mr. Shepherd:—

Thanks very much for the proofs of Rimel's cuts, both of which are splendid specimens. Rimel is probably the best linoleum artist to be found outside the ranks of the professionals, though Petaja is a close second. Utpatel is ahead of them—a veritable magician—but he is now definitely professional. In line drawings Ferguson is hard to beat, but he says he does not care to handle weird work, being a science-fiction specialist. If you are on the lookout for good amateur artists (line—not linoleum), it would pay you to write *Bernard Dwyer, C.C.C. Camp 25, Peekskill, N.Y.*—who is very clever & versatile, & has a keen fondness for the weird.

It is indeed a fact that the devotees—as well as authors—of fantastic fiction are exceedingly scattered. Someone in the W.T. Eyrie suggested the idea of local clubs such as those of the science fiction fans—but I doubt whether more than two or three such could be organised. For the most part, if weird fictionites wish to exchange opinions & compare notes they must do it by mail. For such a scattered circle, some unifying forum or official organ is a necessity—& *The Phantagraph* has the field clear to become just that. I hope you'll win better support than Hornig did for the late *Fantasy Fan*. He put his best into that, yet never got more than *60* paid subscribers. One advantage you have is that you do your own printing, so can stand a small subscription list better than he could. The continual expense of Conrad Ruppert's press work was what made the FF so impossible to continue. But no magazine of the sort can really meet expenses unless a decent proportion of the fans will *actually subscribe.* Your lower price will be a help—for people will pay a half-dollar more readily than they will pay a dollar. Meanwhile you ought to try to get in touch with as many weird fans as possible. Do you suppose Wright would give you the addresses of his Eyrie contributors? You might also get in touch with this chap Hopkins[1] who wants to organise local clubs. As soon as you get an issue which really satisfies you in appearance, you ought to print a lot of extras to distribute as samples. An actual good-looking issue is the best possible advertisement.

I'll probably have a list of weird books ready for you as soon as you have space for it. Meanwhile I have already prepared a brief article on the tales of William Hope Hodgson[2] at Koenig's request—which he will send you in connexion with a biographical article of his own. He has just dug up a considerable amount of new data concerning Hodgson.

About weird books—a nation-wide mail-service circulating library would be a real asset if anybody had the capital & enterprise to start one. As it is, both Koenig & I try to help out in a small way by lending our own books free to any responsible person who wants to see them. But we couldn't do this on a large scale. Even the few loans we make wear out our books very badly—& if we supplied a very large circle we would soon be without any books to lend! A really practical library for the fan group ought to have fees—out of which postal & replacement costs could be paid. It ought, too, to have a wider range of books than can be found even in the combined libraries of Koenig & myself. Whether such a thing could ever be founded, remains to be seen. You might broach it in *The Phantagraph* some time. It ought not to try to make money, but should strive to support itself—to break even.

About the popularity of science-fiction—you are correct in comparing it to the rage for western stories which began a couple of generations ago & is still going strong. Young readers like stories dealing with anything which represents pioneering & adventure. In the 1890's their idea of adventure was the opening up of new lands in the west—digging gold, fighting Indians, & all that. Today the same sort of glamour hangs around the laboratory of the applied-science specialist, who is always turning out new marvels in one field or another—aëroplanes, radios, & all sorts of things which upset old notions & extend our knowledge of the universe. But of course the cheap science fiction of today gives just as inaccurate a picture of real science, as the cheap western fiction of yesterday gave of real western life. Amusingly enough, most science fiction merely takes over the old formulas of western fiction without changing anything but names. The average interplanetary tale is just a camouflaged "western" with the pioneers & soldiers called "space-explorers", & the Indians called "Martians" or "lunarians" or something like that. The same cheap "action" stuff lies at the bottom of both.

And cheap weird fiction is in no better state. W T is certainly going down—perhaps because of the new magazines you mention. Of these newcomers I have read almost none—only the second issue of *Terror Tales* a year or so ago. That was wholly worthless trash, & I suppose the others are just about like it. Whether a really good weird magazine could succeed—without drawing on the low-grade reading elements to whom Wright is catering more & more—yet remains to be proved. But anyone who tries to issue such has my good wishes!

About printing methods—home-made wood block decorations are certainly a great idea. You can learn from books or typographical critics just what designs to use for certain spaces or specific purposes, & then you can make them in wood. Your newspaper friend can undoubtedly give you dozens of useful hints—& various critics in the N.A.P.A. are expert in some of the fine points. One whom I forgot to mention in my earlier letter—a fellow who is getting a foothold in the professional field—is *Carroll D. Coleman, 110 W. 11th St., Muscatine, Iowa.*[3] Another who might help is the old-timer *Charles A. A. Parker, 114 Riverside Ave., Medford, Mass.*

I certainly wish *Fanciful Tales* all possible success, & congratulate you on the interesting variety of contributions obtained for the opening issue. I've read Rimel's "Forbidden Room" & like it very much. Hope you'll take care with the proofreading—which is certainly tricky work. If you'll send me proofs of "The Nameless City" I'll be glad to read them. Fifty pages will make quite an issue—& I'm sure the decision to use black ink is a wise one.

The commercial problem will be a tough one—but as in the case of *The Phantagraph,* you have the advantage of home printing, so that you can afford to hang on while slowly building up a circulation. 1000 is a pretty high goal to set—but I presume that is ultimate rather than immediate. As with *The Phantagraph,* advertising & popularisation will have to be gradual—& might be promoted through sample copies of some especially good-looking issue. It will be very difficult to get the magazine on the news stands, as Crawford's experience has proved—but perhaps you're not trying for that. Crawford himself, by the way, will probably not form any particular rival, since his *Marvel Tales* will (if he is ever able to issue it regularly) specialise in science fiction while you can make it a point to specialise in the weird. This same distinction will also give clear & separate fields to *The Phantagraph* & to Schwartz's *Fantasy Magazine.* By the way—what is this *Baroque* which I see announced on your stationery? If I were you I wouldn't divide my energies among too many magazines. It's wiser to stick to one or two, making these ample & regular.

Thanks for the blotter—which ought to be good advertising. I hope to see Wollheim's amateur paper soon. He's a very brilliant chap, & ought to stir up the N.A.P.A. considerably.

With best wishes for all the various ventures,

Yrs very sincerely,

H. P. Lovecraft

*Notes*

1. Julius Hopkins, a prolific contributor to the "Eyrie," claimed to belong to a group of weird fiction enthusiasts in the Washington DC area called "The Necronomiconists." In the July 1937 *WT,* he promised the group would be issuing an "official organ, *The Scarab."*
2. "The Weird Work of William Hope Hodgson."
3. Carroll D. Coleman (1904–1989) was proprietor of Prairie Press, and a printer of fine editions of poetry known for their elegant typography and small print runs. He published twelve books by August Derleth between 1939 and 1970.

[4]     [ALS]

66 College St.,
Providence, R.I.,
June 20, 1936

Dear Mr. Shepherd:—

Congratulations on the splendid cover for *Fanciful Tales,* which certainly ought to help greatly in promoting & popularising the venture. As requested, I am not showing the design to anyone. It ought to go finely on the red paper—& will really give the magazine a more mature & professional-looking appearance than any of the rest of the "fan" group can boast. I don't believe you'll have any difficulty in getting adequate art work. You really don't need a great amount, since *good fiction* is what makes a magazine. A relatively simple heading is all that a first-rate story requires. About Utpatel—here is the set of drawings he made for "The Shadow over Innsmouth". Pretty good, I think. He is very versatile, & some of the designs he has made for Derleth's work in *Weird Tales* are totally unlike these. But Rimel & Petaja will do for a while. They are very clever, & are constantly improving. I surely hope that *Fanciful* can become a sort of headquarters for the best & most serious type of weird fiction, & believe it has a very good chance of so doing—if it can keep afloat on very small receipts. Serious fantasy can never be a really paying proposition, & anything steadily featuring it will have to place the profit motive in a secondary position. As to getting publicity & circulation—your *Phantagraph* experience surely would seem to argue against the sample-copy idea, though as a matter of fact that Crawford-printed issue wasn't nearly as neat & prepossessing-looking as some of the issues you can eventually get out yourself. The large-paged, thin format had a kind of clumsy effect, & the typography was essentially commonplace. Moreover, it was mailed in a doubled-up, unprotected fashion which left its appearance anything but neat. A trim-looking issue mailed flat in an envelope has twice the appeal of a carelessly folded sheet, loosely wrapped & likely to reach the reader in a frayed & tattered state. However, even with the handicap of appearance reckoned in, I suppose the very poor response to the first issue makes a good argument against sample copies. It is too bad that you can't get access to the Eyrie list—but I've noticed that smallness in Wright. Incidentally, though, when a letter-writer's address is a rather *small town* (as discovered by looking it up in a population list), it might be worth taking a chance & sending him a circular or sample even in the absence of a street or box or R.F.D. address. But in any case, it will take time, patience, & persistence to build up anything like a satisfactory clientele.

Meanwhile I hope *The Phantagraph* will become the standard forum for devotees of the weird. Certainly, such devotees are mainly scattered about in widely separated places—so that periodicals & correspondence will always have to take the place of face-to-face discussion among them. As to the lack of weird addicts in your part of the world—there is a young chap in Birmingham from whom I hear occasionally (Lee White, Jr., 2834 Bush Blvd.) who used to be interested in the weird, even though he is now going over very largely to general literature of an emphatically modern type. He is the son of a Baptist clergyman, & is now attending Howard College—where he edits the student publication, *The Quill*. You might send him samples of *Phantagraph* & *Fanciful*, for he probably retains some trace of his old interest.

I hope to fix up that book list before very long—& meanwhile you will doubtless see the Hodgson material which Koenig will send. Glad to hear of the new type & accessories. The styles used on the envelope are surely very pleasing.

It seems to me an excellent idea to print "The Hyborian Age" as a separate pamphlet. You might even advertise it in W T, since a good many of the readers must be curious about the background of Howard's numerous tales. However, if the edition is not large, it might not pay to do any wide advertising.

Plans for *Baroque* sound very interesting, & I will be careful not to give any hint of the venture. I believe you'll find weird verse very easy to get—& some specimens are pretty effective. A new writer who might have some for you (as well as prose tales) is Henry Kuttner, 145 South Canon Drive, #3, Beverly Hills, California. (Pardon me if I've given you his name before).

I shall be looking for Wollheim's *Queer*. Amateur journalism is a loosely organised affair, with plenty of crude spots, but on the whole I think it's worth belonging to. It can give a lot of help & encouragement when one gets to know the members & becomes an integral part of the fabric. The rivalry between different associations is unfortunate but unavoidable. There were once *two* "Uniteds"—the result of a split in 1912—& one of them (now in abeyance, & of course deeply hostile to the one now surviving) attained a splendid literary development between 1914 & 1922. That was the first amateur press association I ever joined, & I was sorry to see it go out of existence in 1927. Only since its disappearance have I been principally devoted to the National. Both surviving societies are riddled with cheap politics, but the only thing to do about this is to ignore it except when working for reform now &

then. I'm sure a paper from you would be very welcome if you could find time to issue one.

Thanks very much for the cutting—which might well form the basis of a story some day. Cases like this show that "Nameless Cults" are by no means mere inventions of the fictionist. Indeed, the Black Mass is a repulsive reality in many large cities, while the rural European "witch cult" with its hideous "Sabbat" rites in lonely woods on April 30 & Oct. 31 was also an actual thing up to about 200 years ago. Today Europe is full of groups trying to revive bygone & primitive institutions, & this Hungarian case resembles a sect in Germany which is trying to revive the worship of the old gods Odin & Thor.

You have certainly had bad luck in lending books! Koenig & I have fared rather well—for most of the fan group are pretty conscientious & dependable. Sometimes books are kept a long while, & the wear & tear is considerable; but there has been very little real carelessness, & no vandalism at all. The worst piece of luck I ever had was 7 or 8 years ago, when 3 or 4 of my Machen books were burned in a fire at the home of a borrower—a blaze which also ruined many books of his own.

Yes—I read a collection of Service's verse once, & liked a great deal of it. Taken as a whole, he is not as subtle & original as poets of the first rank; but he has a music & smoothness all his own, & many passages are undeniably power & beautiful. I recall the stanzas you quote—all of them excellent. Some of the images are extremely vivid—& it interests me to note the poet's repeated use of the *gibbous moon*. There has always seemed to me to be a certain weirdness in this lunar phase, & I have used it several times in tales & verses of my own—long before I ever heard of Service. If I write Koenig soon I'll ask about your verses—though you'll no doubt hear from him directly ere long.

With all good wishes, & trusting to see both F T & another *Phantagraph* in due season,

I remain

> Yrs most sincerely,
> H. P. Lovecraft

P.S. Just at this last moment I've had a most depressing & staggering message—a postcard with the report that Robert E. Howard has committed suicide. It seems incredible—I had a long, normal letter from him dated May 13. He was worried about his mother's health, but otherwise seemed quite all right. If the news is indeed true, it forms weird fiction's worst blow since the passing of Whitehead in 1932. No other writer of the group had quite the zest & spontaneity of good old R.E.H.

[5]   [ALS]

66 College St.,
Providence, R.I.,
July 14, 1936.

Dear Mr. Shepherd:—

Thanks exceedingly for the advance sheets of "The Nameless City". Misprints are gratifyingly few—only 8, including two which concern only the punctuation. One thing I might mention—you twice spell *led*—the past tense of *lead*—with an "a" in it, as if it were formed like the past tense of *read*. This is a tricky point worth being on guard about. The appearance & arrangement of the pages are very prepossessing, & seem to indicate steady typographical progress on your part. The announcement page is very neat—though I believe it might have been advisable to capitalise each *important* word in the heading—thus—*A Word from the Editor*. As it is, there is a tendency toward ambiguous reading—as if the heading were *AWARD from the Editor*. This, though is a very trivial point. About the cover—red & green would be excellent, but now that you mention it I can see the advantages of yellow & black. The latter would certainly be the more *distinct*—& I'm not sure but that it would be preferable all around. The design is certainly splendid, & I see no need for varying it from month to month. The fact is, I like a fixed cover-design or arrangement—which is the rule among all the high-grade magazines like *Harpers* & the *Atlantic*. The *contents* forms the big point—& illustrations may well be secondary. Utpatel is good, & so is Finlay. But I think *Rankin* has the most fertile imagination of them all. I never saw a design by Muller[1]—indeed, I've never seen an issue of *Amazing* under its present management. For the present, small neat headings—plus the cover—are all that you need to think about; & the linoleum artists like Rimel & Petaja seem pretty well able to take care of these. You surely seem to be starting out soundly & cautiously, & I don't see why you can't eventually attain the modest success at which you aim. Hope the circulation campaign will pan out well. A close study of the W T Eyrie will certainly bring to light a great many "fan" addresses—& an advertising campaign using a judicious blend of circulars & sample copies ought to produce at least tolerable results.

I won't mention the coming change in *The Phantagraph's* printing until the time is ripe—but I think the idea is on the whole a good one. The besetting trouble of most small publishers is that they tackle too much at one time—just as Crawford has tied himself up with more responsibilities than he can possibly manage. If you print *Fanciful Tales* regularly, & a few other things occasionally, the regular issuance of *The Phantagraph* would certainly be a tough burden, & one likely to cause a general clogging-up of your whole programme. A regular monthly *Phantagraph* of 8 pages seems to me an excellent plan—for regularity & frequency are more important than sheer size. Long waits kill public interest in a periodical sooner than anything else. Glad to hear of your new press, which will certainly form a great step in advance.

With a 7 × 11 chase, you can set up two pages of your present size at a time—& print large pages if necessary.

Hope you'll find young White congenial—although, as I pointed out, he seems to be turning from fantastic literature toward general literature of an ultra-modern type. He is experimenting in poetry in the manner of Dr. Donne.[2] About the amateur press associations—the way to enjoy them is to ignore their politics & just go ahead with one's own literary or publishing programme. What they need are more papers of high quality—& more debates on literary & other vital topics instead of mere schoolboy squabbles about trivial personalities.

Yes—the Black Mass has certainly been practiced continuously in many large cities since the middle ages, being especially prevalent in Paris 40 or 50 years ago. Much information regarding its incredibly repulsive details can be gleaned from the novel "La Bas" [or "Down There"] by Joris-Karl Huysmans. The ritual you quote sounds authentic as far as it goes—though of course it is only a fraction of the whole nauseous procedure.

I surely wish the Howard suicide report* *would* turn out to be a fake like the Tucker hoax, though I fear that is hoping too much. I don't know of any practical joker who would be likely to start such a thing. If true, it is certainly a major blow for weird fiction. I'll let you know anything further that I hear. I've written a sketch about R E H & his work—a sort of obituary—which I shall probably send to *The Phantagraph* if the tragedy turns out to be sadly genuine. Another recent loss to weird fiction—in the wider field—is that of Montague Rhodes James, who died a fortnight ago at Eton at the age of 73. His tales include some of the most powerful in existence. Also—George Allan England lately died at the age of 59.

Wishing you the best of luck with the coming *Fanciful,* I remain

Yrs most cordially,

H. P. Lovecraft

P.S. Just had word from Howard's father. Sad news is all too true. R E H shot himself when he learned that his mother's illness was fatal. Double funeral. The shock to poor old Dr. Howard must be unbearable—wife & splendid only child gone at one blow. R E H's melancholy streak must have gone deeper than we thought—for most can take the inevitable loss of the elder generation more philosophically.

*Notes*

1. Evidently P. Muller, who illustrated for *Amazing Stories* and perhaps other pulps.
2. See HPL's revision of White's "[On John Donne]" in *The Ancient Track* (p. 475).

---

*As coincidence would have it—Sterling tells me that the young science-fiction writer David R. Daniels, who died this spring, also committed suicide.

[6]    [ALS]

66 College St.,
Providence, R.I.
August 11, 1936.

Dear Shepherd:—

The only pages of "The Nameless City" so far sent me are the first three—numbered 5, 6, & 7 in the magazine. I'd surely be glad to see more. Mistakes certainly will creep in—though some could be avoided if you could devise a way to let the various authors read proof. I guess a red cover printed in green or black will be all right—& again congratulate you on the design.

Your remarks on the various illustrators are very interesting, & I am grateful for the glimpse of Muller's work. His method certainly seems highly original—& stands out sharply from anything else commonly met with. The faces are very effective—& if this is a typical sample of his art I can easily see why you give him so high a rating. Again, thanks for the glimpse.

Hope all will prosper in the issuance of *Fanciful Tales*. Your idea of sending notices to people who have praised certain authors in magazine departments is a very clever one, & I am glad it seems to be yielding results.

Yes—I now have the first of the monthly *Phantagraphs,* & am greatly pleased with its neat appearance. The transfer of the printing will surely help clear the deck for *Fanciful Tales*. Hope the larger press is by this time fully installed, & that it is living up to expectations.

Glad to hear you are entering amateurdom. I don't know much about the present "United", but Wollheim seems to like it better than the N.A.P.A. A paper from you (circulated, I hope, in both associations) will be very welcome. As to pre-human civilisations—in all truth, there is scarcely any chance that such could have existed. Everything we find in the earth, & everything we know about life & geology, seems to indicate that man is the first animal of very high evolution to appear on this planet. Nor is it likely that any human civilisation could have existed before 15,000 or 20,000 B.C. Virtually all tales of incredibly ancient lost lands & civilisations bear the plain earmarks of myths.*

About the Huysmans novel "Down There"—I really don't know where it could be obtained, although I believe it is still in print & no longer under the ban of the censors. Any large bookseller could undoubtedly tell you where to get it. Yes—dark rites of one sort or another surely do have a tendency to survive among certain groups—either decadent aesthetes in large cities, or simple & primitive people in remote & secluded regions. Probably the "hexerei" among the rural Pennsylvania Germans is the most consistently developed case of the kind in America.

---

*As for *coming* changes—I don't believe they'll exceed those occurring at certain crucial times in the past—such as the fall of the Roman Empire.

Robert E. Howard's suicide surely is a tragic event—& the loss to weird fiction is irreparable. A Conan book would surely be a most desirable item— as would a brochure of "The Hyborian Age." R E H's father is establishing a Robert E. Howard Memorial Collection in Brownwood, Texas, & wants Price to come to Cross Plains to look over his MSS. & act as literary executor. (E H P isn't sure he can—though he would like to.) You'll learn more of R E H when you read some of the coming obituaries. Somewhat to my surprise, Schwartz says he is going to use a rather longish one of mine in an early issue of *Fantasy Magazine.*

Your verses on "Death" have a very clever idea & development, & the Ferguson illustration surely seems to blend very well—even though the artist hasn't given Death the sable cloak you mention. Just now the lines do seem to have a decided applicability to R E H. I am returning this material as per request—with a few emendations to eliminate certain technical defects. Most of the changes are explained on the margin. If any seem obscure, I'll gladly elucidate further. Thanks very much for the glimpse.

All good wishes—

Yrs most sincerely,

H P Lovecraft

[P.S.] Lately received a loan-exhibit of Clark Ashton Smith's grotesque miniature sculpture. Some of the items are splendid.

[7]    [ALS]

66 College St.,
Providence, R.I.
Sept. 5, 1936.

Dear Shepherd:—

Before acknowledging yours of Aug. 14 I must thank you for your share in the delightful birthday remembrance which reached me on the 20th.[1] That forms the first time I was ever an "editor & publisher" without my knowledge! The choice of material to reprint was surely an apt one, & the whole thing was splendidly appropriate to the occasion. Again let me thank you sincerely. I've dropped Wollheim a postcard of acknowledgment.

Thanks for the additional Nameless City sheets. I haven't had time to look through them yet—but that really doesn't matter, since everything is too late to be changed. It surely will be advantageous when proofs can be sent to the various authors. Glad the advertisements seem to be exerting a steady if not spectacular pull. I wouldn't mind criticisms of *The Phantagraph's* size. Of course, the larger a paper can be, the better—but a little is vastly to be preferred to none at all, & a small & frequent magazine has advantages over a larger but irregularly issued one. Congratulations on the new large press— though I'm sorry it started in by crushing your finger. Hope the injury won't prove lasting—& that the press may redeem itself through subsequent good conduct.

About primal or pre-human civilisations—of course whatever conclusions we draw are no more than extreme probabilities; but the fact remains that any sort of civilised life before the settling-down of existing mankind 15,000 or 20,000 years ago is at least very unlikely & is wholly unsuggested by any evidence. There was probably *time* for such a civilisation between the dawn of true mankind & the opening of history; but a variety of circumstances such as the existing lore of all nations, the absence of elaborate pre-glacial artifacts even in well-preserved deposits, the disturbed state of the earth in early geologic periods, &c. &c. make its existence overwhelmingly improbable. We can be *certain* that many popular myths of early civilisations are false. Thus all tales of "Atlantis" or any lost land in the Antarctic ocean fall to pieces when we see that no land connexion between the separated islands of that ocean could possibly have existed since the dawn of the age of mammals & man. We know this latter fact because such separated islands have no similar plants & animals belonging to any recent geologic period. If they had been connected by land in such a period, they would still have a common flora & fauna belonging to it. However—we needn't let the scientific probabilities bother us when we want to write an imaginative tale of dim aeons. All that the fictionist needs is an air of consistent plausibility.

I looked over your new verses with much interest, & believe the idea in them is very clever. As before, I've done a little straightening out & added some marginal notes. Hope you'll like the new version, & that it will get into type some time. [*Note in margin:* I've supplied a new title, & a sort of climactic ending, for the verse.] Some good books to read on the subject of verse construction are "A Study of Versification" by Brander Matthews (obtainable at most public libraries) & "An Introduction to Some Elements of Poetry", by George E. Teter. This latter is a medium-sized booklet, & can be obtained for 25¢ postpaid from Maurice W. Moe, 1810 W. Wisconsin St., Milwaukee, Wis.

Glad you're in touch with Kuttner, & hope he can furnish *Fanciful* with a number of good items. He seems to be an extremely brilliant young man.

A book of Conan stories would certainly be a very welcome item, & I hope such a thing can be published some day. It ought, I think, to be a pretty large & inclusive thing—& might form quite a problem to a publisher with limited equipment. It seems to me that for an *immediate* volume a collection of Howard's *best* stories—irrespective of their membership in the Conan cycle—would be the wisest venture. R E H's best weird tales, without question, were the short "King Kull'['] series—though perhaps *some* of the Conans & Solomon Kanes, plus the recent "Black Canaan", fall into that category. Certain Howard enthusiasts ought to be consulted about the contents of such a book—*Price* being especially well qualified to pick selections. Financing would be a rather hard problem (I'm utterly broke!), but a large number of small subscriptions secured through advertisements in the fan magazines might help. Your scale of estimated prices is very helpful in forming an idea of the problem—as is the set of paper & cover samples. A 100-page volume ought not to be impracticable in the end—& might conceivably hold all the "King Kull" tales. Art work can sometimes be secured quite reasonably—Utpatel having done four drawings for my "Innsmouth" for only $15.00. A sketch or line drawing of R E H would make a good frontispiece—& as a model I'd suggest one of the 1931 snapshots (I could lend a small print). These are more typical, I think, that the stouter, moustached snaps of R E H's last days. But all these points could be discussed by the editorial board—pictures, title, scope, size, selections, &c. I'd suggest your getting in touch with Price on the subject, & also with R E H's father.*

The *Conan* stories—as a unit—would probably make a huge volume . . . . or two smaller volumes. They are not all of equal merit; though each has something to recommend it, while the best are truly magnificent. An abridged collection, with material carefully selected, would be very welcome if an unabridged volume were found impracticable. But it would want to be a sizeable tome in any case.

By the way—have you seen the article & bibliography about Conan which P. Schuyler Miller has prepared? It is a very clever thing—listing all the Conan tales in chronological order, & adding some running comment on the development of Conan from a raw Cimmerian youth of 15 to the period of his Aquilonian kingship around the age of 40. Wright lent me a copy of the MS., & I hope he will use it. If not, I hope one of the fan magazines will print it.

Had a very interesting letter from Virgil Finlay the illustrator the other day. He seems to be an extremely pleasant as well as brilliant chap.

All good wishes, & thanks again for the thoughtful birthday remembrance.

> Yrs most sincerely,
> H. P. Lovecraft

P.S. Wollheim said something about an additional accident to your hand. Hope it wasn't serious.

*Notes*

1. See DAW 11, n. 2.

---

*Dr. I. M. Howard, Box 313, Cross Plains, Texas.

[8]  [ALS]

66 College St.,
Providence, R.I.,
Octr. 1, 1936.

Dear Shepherd:—

Glad to hear that you are fully recovered from the press accident, & hope no more will occur.

Yes—I surely appreciated the birthday greeting, & would be grateful for a few others to give away. It was indeed a thoughtful idea—& a highly appropriate one. The sonnet "Background" fitted in very nicely—although I wasn't thinking of birthdays when I wrote it. Again, my thanks & appreciation!

About the possible purchase of a linotype—I'm no kind of a business man, hence couldn't advise very intelligently; but from mere hearsay & layman's judgment I'd advise you to go slow & look far ahead. Linotypes are without question very expensive, & require a substantial amount of "overhead" to operate. The very cheapest—at second hand—would probably amount to over a thousand dollars, & the power needed to run it would certainly be heavy. I'd say that it all depends on the *size* of the printing business you expect to run. So far as I can see, a linotype is very profitable to a *large business,* but a heavy drain on the profits of a *small* one. Its great advantage is that it's a labour saver—but in order to make it pay for itself you've got to have a heavy enough business to keep it working a good part of the time. The profits of a small business aren't enough to defray the heavy cost & upkeep. So it seems to me that it all boils down to the question of how big a business you'll find it practicable to undertake next year. I'm no expert, but I'd venture the guess that a "fan" publishing enterprise wouldn't be enough to make a linotype profitable unless you could swing a brisk job printing business on the side. And you're the only one who can judge of that—knowing the conditions around Oakman, & estimating the speed with which you could learn all the details of professional typography. Your business would probably have to be primarily local, although (if able to quote low prices) you might get a certain amount of outside work from amateur journalism & from fantasy "fan" publishers. Your difficulties would be those of any relative novice founding a new business in the face of existing competition (for I presume Oakman is already well covered by printing facilities). It would be a pure gamble—with your chances of success depending on how much free capital you might have to tide you over until you could gather a profitable amount of business. Since the times are bad, & since you would have older & more experienced printers to compete with, I'd say it would be wise to ponder deeply before plunging in. At least, seek the advice of people who know more about the matter than I do. One good chap to advise you is my old friend *W. Paul Cook, 5720 Westmoreland Place, East St. Louis, Illinois,* who has had charge of the presswork of newspapers—also handling job printing—for 30 years. Tell him I referred you to him, & he'll give you sound advice. Regarding the cost & upkeep of a linotype—ask the amateur journalist *Vincent B. Haggerty, 21 Stegman Court, Jersey City, N.J.* Haggerty purchased a linotype several years ago with the idea of handling large amounts of amateur printing, but found it a costly drain & had to get rid of it. If Wollheim is an equal partner in the venture he could call on Haggerty in person & learn all the particulars face to face. So that's all I can say—go slowly & cautiously, & calculate very carefully the amount of business you'll be able to get. You might indeed succeed—but remember that a linotype costs like hell & is fitted only to large-scale enterprises. In any case I wish you luck!

I hope that the Howard book may duly materialise. Price's address is *Route 2, Box 100-U-5,* Redwood City, California. The financing will be difficult, since so many of us are dead broke. Koenig, Derleth, Wandrei, Searight, Miss Moore, & perhaps others might be worth consulting. Advertising in the various magazines contributed to by Howard would be the best method of marketing. The Miller article & Hyborian Age wouldn't go so well in a first or general book as in a separate brochure heralding a later Conan volume. You ought to see the Miller thing—which is very interesting.

As to the question of lost prehistoric civilisations—of course there is no absolute proof that such could not have existed. It is all a question of *probability.* Certainly, the idea is eminently fit for fictional use, & it will continue to form a standby of fantaisistes. Glad you liked "The Shadow Out of Time", which wasn't as badly misprinted as the "Mts of Madness", although Street & Smith's lousy style-sheet (which capitalises words like *Moon* & even *Moonlight,* & does other absurd things) makes it look rather odd.

Glad you found the verse revision acceptable. If you enjoy occasional verse-making, it would pay you to brush up little by little—as chances appear—on the technique & traditions of the art.

Kuttner is a very bright chap—as is Bloch. If the professional magazines all reject "The Torture-Master" you may yet get it for F T.[1] Better ask Bloch about it before some other "fan" editor gets ahead of you. As for sending my stuff to *The Argosy*—I might try it when I have something on hand, but at the moment I'm absolutely cleaned out. Not an available story anywhere, & too much revision work to give me time to write more. However, I doubt the suitability of my stories for *The Argosy.* This magazine seems to demand formula material vastly different from mine. I have only once tried a story on *The Argosy*—that being "The Rats in the Walls." R. H. Davis—then editor—rejected on the ground that it was too horrible to print. *Weird Tales* accepted it, & it was very well received— being copied in an anthology & later reprinted in the magazine.

Haven't had time to read the Oct. W T—utterly swamped with a complicated (& ill-paying!) revision job. Worked 60 hrs. without sleep on it last week.[2] Heard again from the illustrator Finlay—a tremendously brilliant & picturesque chap, only 22. He writes poetry as well as draws, & some of his verses are astonishingly good despite certain technical defects.

Hope F T is progressing well. No particular hurry about its appearance—better well done & a trifle late, than hastily patched up & early. Think over the linotype business carefully, & don't act till you've sought the advice of experts like Cook & Haggerty.

Best wishes for all your enterprises—
Yrs most sincerely,
H. P. Lovecraft

[P.S.] I was glad to see the new *Phantagraph* with its ample material by & about R E H.

*Notes*

1. Apparently a nonextant story by Bloch.
2. See RB 64, n.1.

[9]    [ALS]

66 College St.,
Providence, R.I.,
Nov. 3, 1936.

Dear Shepherd:—
Yours of Oct. 4 duly arrived, & I must thank you for the extra *Lovecrafters* & sample sheets of *Fanciful*. The new type is very pleasing. Of course, one can't crowd so much into a small space with it—but the vastly improved appearance more than makes up for this. "Umbriel", by the way, has a tremendously original idea. I wish Wollheim had developed it at greater length, & explained how an organic being could decompose amidst the airlessness of interplanetary space.

Glad to hear that the issue is progressing well, but sorry to learn of the canine pi-ing incident![1] I have once or twice had occasion to straighten out chaotic heaps of type, & realise how hard it is. Lucky it wasn't the type you are currently using!

I'll be interested to hear what you decide regarding the linotype matter after receiving advice from Cook, Haggerty, & perhaps others. Your plans—which I will of course keep confidential—sound excellent in general; although I fancy the difficulties of deriving profit from small magazines are many & varied. A book venture might succeed—if you got the right titles & were able to sell at a low cost. But general commercial printing would probably be necessary—at least at first—in order to meet the expenses of a linotype. A second-hand outfit at $300.00 sounds like an incredible bargain—but it would be well to get some experienced printer's advice before committing oneself. I'm sure Cook & Haggerty will be very conscientious in their recommendations. By the way—the cost of maintenance which you cite is rather less than I had imagined. In any case, best wishes! Yes—this Cook is the quondam editor of *The Recluse*.

Hope all will develop well regarding a R E H volume. Such a thing ought to be well done if done at all—& I fancy your rapidly increasing skill will enable you to turn out something creditable.

About style-sheets—I never object when a magazine changes my especial form of *spelling* to some other standard & well-recognised system. But I *do* object when some eccentric or silly practice (like capitalising *Moon* & *Moonlight*) is adopted, or when the *punctuation* & *paragraphing* are monkeyed with. As you say, a change in punctuation will sometimes ruin the whole meaning of a passage—& editors often do this because of their lack of understanding of the original meaning.

Hope you get the Bloch thriller. Your reports on *The Argosy* are highly interesting—I must look that old-timer up afresh some day. So far I haven't found *The Witches' Tales* on the stands, but I'm still on the lookout. I'll keep in mind the stories you recommend.

Fan magazines certainly multiply bewilderingly. *Fantasy* seems to be staging a comeback, & will probably dominate the science-fiction side of the field, while *The Phantagraph* & *The Science-Fantasy Correspondent* take care of the weird side. The latter is continuing my "Supernatural Horror in Literature", begun in the late lamented F F. *Fanciful Tales* & *Marvel Tales* will divide the purely fictional field between them. The others—magazines published by Frome, Madle, Blish & Miller, & others will probably amount to relatively little. But just now it does look as if there were a separate magazine for every "fan"!

As for a 60-hour stretch of toil—of course, I could not repeat a thing like that too often. It leaves one rather limp, & a repetition without a long rest would hardly be advisable. Nor would it be wise to prolong even one session much longer. Cutting out two nights of sleep is about my limit—although I have sometimes gone a week or two with only brief sleeping periods—2 to 5 hours—each night.

Haven't had a chance to read the new W T yet, but I see that the illustration to my story belies the text a bit. However, it's an intrinsically good drawing, & does Finlay credit.[2]

Cold weather is shutting down at last—though I took occasional woodland rambles all through October. Work has piled up so badly that it's just as well I can't get off on outings any more! Read final proofs of "Innsmouth" the other day, & fancy Crawford ought to have the book ready before long. It's about time!

All good wishes—

Yrs most sincerely,

H P Lovecraft

*Notes*

1. "Pi-ed type" is loose type that has been spilled or tossed into an unsorted heap.

2. I.e., Virgil Finlay's illustration for "The Haunter of the Dark" (*WT*, December 1936). The illustration appears to depict Robert Blake's discovery of the skeleton of the reporter Edwin M. Lillibridge *outside* (rather than inside) the Starry Wisdom church.

[10]  [ALS]

66 College St.,
Providence, R.I.,
Dec. 15, 1936.

Dear Shepherd:—

Hope matters at the office will soon get adjusted, & that the type-sorting job may not prove too hard. Glad to know that the new type is almost as economical of space as the old. Your news on commercial printing prospects sounds cheerful, & may indeed justify the purchase of a linotype in the end. It is fortunate that you have a friend in the linotype business—who can keep you posted on bargains. He probably wouldn't try to persuade you into any deal you couldn't manage, since such a move would be bad for him as well as for you in the end.

Price spoke about his opinion regarding the Howard book, & I think he is right in the end. As I suggested in the first place, it would be really unwise to launch such a volume (which would naturally be regarded as a sort of memorial to R E H) unless there were an assurance of sufficient cash to make it of ample size, & of accurate & artistic typography, workmanship, & binding. The plan is distinctly worth keeping in mind, but the time is not yet ripe for action on it.

I haven't yet been able to see a copy of *Witches' Tales,* but several correspondents have done so & are unanimous in reporting that it is very bad indeed—worse even than the magazines of the Rogers Terrill group. Of course, it may develop into something better—but its start is surely inauspicious enough!

The trouble with the "fan magazine" situation is that there are too damned *many* of them. I've counted a full dozen, & some one else reports the existence of fully a dozen more than that! They divide the buying public so badly that the circulation of each one suffers. Also, they scatter the contributions which might all go to one magazine, & involve a foolish amount of duplication & waste so far as the printing of news is concerned. I've seen only a small fraction of them, but suppose the others really *do* exist. Your deal with Blish sounds interesting. I never saw his *Planeteer,* though I contributed two pieces of verse to it. I wonder if he ever printed the stuff! He wrote me recently that he had changed the name of the paper to *Curious Stories,* & at his request I sent him some more stuff (a short prose sketch) for that. Does your deal do away with *Curious Stories,* or is that a new thing he is starting after having sold you *The Planeteer?* I give it up! Too complicated for me! Conover & Stickney are doing great work, & Stickney is breaking all records for *typograph-*

*ical accuracy.* How long they can carry on is of course another matter. If only they & you & Wollheim could all get together on a single magazine, the result would be something memorable! Crawford is very careless in his methods, & habitually undertakes more than he can handle. Yes—"Innsmouth" is out at last, but is not a very impressive production. There are 34 bad misprints—corrected by means of a printed list of errata.

Sorry the cold weather reached down as far as your region in November. Up here we had a sizeable snowfall Nov. 24—which is very early for Rhode Island. Hope that isn't typical of what to expect all through the winter!

Well—*Fanciful Tales* came at last, & I was very grateful for the three copies—which I have carefully corrected. The magazine really makes an excellent appearance for a newcomer—the cover being a marked asset, & the printing testifying to your increasing experience. I like the contents immensely—especially R E H's splendid posthumous poem. Derleth's story is good, though Keller's is rather undistinctive. The Sykora & Pritchard items could have been spared. I have said before that I liked Rimel's tale, & the idea in Wollheim's.[1] Hope the misprints in the next issue can be cut down—there are 59 in "The Nameless City" [led—the past & participial form—is repeatedly spelled "lead" &c.] If young Stickney—a 14-year-old—can turn out the accurate text he does, others will surely be able to do so in time! But as I said, this issue makes a fine beginning, & I wish it every sort of luck. ¶ Yrs most sincerely—H P Lovecraft

P.S. "Pickman's Model" is to be reprinted again—this time in a "Not at Night Omnibus" to be published in London next spring. ¶ Only recently saw the Jan. W T. Finlay's illustration for my "Thing on the Doorstep" is splendid.

*Notes*

1. Robert E. Howard, "Solomon Kane's Homecoming"; August W. Derleth, "The Man from Dark Valley"; David H. Keller, "The Typewriter"; William S. Sykora, "The Globe"; Kenneth B. Pritchard, "The Electric World"; Duane W. Rimel, "The Forbidden Room"; and DAW, "Umbriel."

[11]   [ALS]

66 College St.,
Providence, R.I.,
Jany. 21, 1937.

Dear Shepherd:—

Glad to hear that your difficult book job was finished successfully & on time. It undoubtedly formed good practice work, & will help the typographical quality of future jobs in the magazine & book field. Odd that the larger type packs in more closely than the smaller—but I suppose it is expertly designed to do just that, with letters made in such a way that less space is wasted on mere breadth of shank. The increase in available work is surely encouraging, & I hope you will be able to expand your mechanical equipment to keep pace with it.

It certainly would be wiser to wait a while about the R E H book. Better not to begin until there is an assurance of carrying the matter through successfully & producing something of adequate size & appearance. A poor-looking book would hardly form a fitting memorial to as fine an author as R E H. Nothing is more unsatisfactory than a volume which retains the earmarks of amateur workmanship—either in printing or in binding. You'll see what I mean when you inspect a copy of "The Shadow Over Innsmouth". Cautious planning, adequate advance financing, & careful, practiced workmanship are the things to strive for. Delay can do no harm—but an inadequate job could. As for the grade of paper—I doubt whether anything like what is commonly known as "pulp" would be suitable for a book, but there are fairly cheap papers which might do. The kind of paper used for the *Science-Fantasy Correspondent* ought to be all right. Page size ought if possible to approximate the regular professional dimensions—something line [*sic*] 7½ × 5 inches. And the binding ought to be cloth—& well done. The slovenly cloth binding of "The Shadow Over Innsmouth" is a good example of how a book should *not* be bound. Illustrations really aren't much of a necessity—& whether to have R E H's picture as a frontispiece depends on how much the *memorial* element is to be stressed. If such a picture *is* included, it should be made from the fine large photograph which Dr. Howard recently sent to Price & me. Any illustrations for the text ought to be done by Finlay—who can without question furnish the best work of anyone not charging a large sum. Certainly, there'd be no harm in gradually investigating prices & estimating the cost of such a job. Indeed, it is impossible to make plans until the approximate figures are known.

Haven't yet seen a copy of *Witches' Tales*, but unfavourable reports about it predominate. I'll pick up a copy & judge for myself whenever I see one. It will be interesting to see whether it keeps afloat or not. I believe the other low-grade weird magazines—*Terror* & *Horror*—are still going.

And so my random guess of two dozen "fan" magazines was conservative rather than extravagant! Well—there's going to be still another one now, for I've had a request for material from one James [*sic*] J. Weir of South Amboy, N.J., who says he is starting something of the kind. The other day I received a copy of *The Fantasy Fiction Telegram* (hectographed), published in Philadelphia, which I had never seen before. One Nils H. Frome, of Fraser Mills, B.C., seems to be full of ambitious plans for *Supramundane Stories*. This profusion of little sheets all trying to do the same thing certainly does much to create a deadlock, & I hope some of the existing & proposed consolidations will strengthen the papers concerned. Glad you have absorbed the Blish ventures—which reminds me to ask whether you know what has become of the contributions I sent Blish—two pieces of verse, "The Wood", & "Hallowe'en in a Suburb", & a prose fantasy entitled "Ex Oblivione". Have any of these been published? And if not, have you the MSS.? If you have the MSS. you're at liberty to use them as you like—or if you don't want them, just shoot them back, since I am constantly getting requests for stuff. The future of the Conover–Stickney venture will be worth watching. I doubt whether the grandiose advertising plan will pan out, but with good luck, the S F C might break even on its own merits. The careful typography, general neatness, & attemptedly high standard of contents are all favourable signs. Someone (I can't recall who) passed along the rumour that Conover & Stickney mean to take over *Fantasy Magazine* from Schwartz, but I don't see how they could possibly handle that. Any such plan must surely be dependent on some other plan for different printing arrangements. However—any steps toward consolidation are welcome. If all the semi-amateur publishers could pool their cash & energies & concentrate on three or four good magazines—a weird "fan" sheet, a science-fiction "fan" sheet, & either one or two all-contribution magazines (like F T & M T) to carry original stories & poems in the various branches of the fantasy field—the result would certainly be beneficial in every way. Of course, I see the obvious obstacles—scattered personnel, & so on (although some teams such as you & Wollheim, & Conover & Stickney, seem to do well in spite of distance)—but in any case, a narrowing of the wide array of papers will be beneficial. The two really important outfits—if Schwartz gives up—will be yours & the Conover–Stickney one. Crawford's projects will never get anywhere, & the others are too small to be real rivals . . . although they will of course drain off a certain amount of potential circulation.

Sorry the F T subscriptions haven't been coming in faster—but as I remarked long ago, all the semi-amateur magazines seem to encounter the same difficulty. Hornig's *Fantasy Fan* had only 60 paid subscribers. How to build up a really solid clientele is a problem beyond my solution. Very low price is probably the greatest appeal of all—but of course that can't get below costs. All told, F T's first issue is highly creditable—& the weak Sykora & Pritchard items are surely no worse than many a professional magazine has carried. R E H's poem is a genuine high spot—& the Derleth & Rimel tales are excellent. The cover is ideal—& will doubtless be still more impressive when it overlaps less & can include colour. By the way—your recent linoleum cut is really tremendously clever, & ought to make a good illustration for some story. If you can always turn out work of that grade, the problem of illustrations & decorations ought to be quite easy. Better paper & page-evenness will help to give the magazine a good appearance, as will also the new heading-type matching the body-type. And of course every increase in typographical accuracy forms a tremendous asset.

Kuttner is certainly doing finely with professional fiction, & I hope that eastern trip of his will materialise. A convention of fantasy fans would surely form a notable event—& there is of course as good a chance of arranging one is [*sic*] there is of arranging N.A.P.A. & U.A.P.A. conventions. That's an event I would surely try to attend.

That "Satanist temple" in Los Angeles must be quite a place—though of course it merely forms another phase of the persistent charlatanry & cult-ism which seems to find its most congenial habitat on the Pacific Coast. About that "review" of a "new Necronomicon translation"—all I had was a typed copy, & I discover to my dismay that this has perished or vanished. It was merely a clever spoof, although seriously written & actually published in a paper in some village near N.Y. City. I never saw a copy of the printed text. I'm sorry I can't name the author, but I was asked not to tell.[1] The one who sent it to me was not the writer, but he said the latter wished his identity kept a secret. In certain particulars, this "review" contradicts the fake "history" of the imaginary volume which I prepared some years ago. Since you seem to be interested, I'll enclose an outline copy of that "history"—which is of course merely a lot of mock-scholarship cooked up about a book which does not exist.[2] I invented the name "Abdul Alhazred" when a very small boy enthralled by the Arabian Nights—applying it to myself. Years later I had a dream about a strange book called the "Necronomicon", & for various reasons conceived the idea of mentioning it in fiction as a Greek translation of some Arabic original by old Abdul. My first use of the idea was in "The Nameless City"—written in 1921. Please return the "historical" synopsis some time—although there is no hurry. I may mention that I have never tried to put the "Necronomicon" across as a serious hoax. I am always perfectly candid concerning its fictitious nature.

Hope you had an enjoyable Yuletide. We had a decorated tree, & the weather was gratifyingly mild. Of gifts, the most distinctive was perhaps that which came quite unexpectedly from young Conover—for lo! When I had removed numberless layers of corrugated paper & excelsior, what should I find before me but the yellowed & crumbling fragments of a long-interred human skull! It came from an Indian mound not far from Conover's home—& its condition is such as to make its reassembling a somewhat ticklish task. Reflective fancy strives to evoke the image of him to whom it once belonged . . . a sanguinary sachem? A crafty medicine-man? Who knows?

All good wishes—

Yrs most sincerely,

H P Lovecraft

*Notes*

1. DAW was the author of "THE NECRONOMICON as *Translated and Abridged from the original Arabic of Abdul Alhazred*, by W. T. Faraday."

2. "History of the 'Necronomicon.'" Shepherd ultimately published the piece as a pamphlet after HPL's death.

[12]  [ALS]

66 College St.,
Providence, R.I.,
Feby. 17, 1937.

Dear Shepherd:—

Sorry the recent book job included some financial difficulties, & hope you managed to collect at last. The practice, however, was undoubtedly very beneficial—so even if you didn't get your pay the loss would not be *quite* total.

About the R E H book—it is certainly well to go slow. You're welcome to any suggestions I can offer, although my lack of publishing experience would make my advice no better than any average layman's.

Hope I'll have a chance to see your article on the fan magazines—although I've never received a copy of *The Science Fiction Fan*. As to the best policy to pursue toward the innumerable young editors who ask for contributions—it's rather hard to decide offhand. Of course, the more magazines there are, the less any one of them will prosper (aside from the few which don't overlap in province)—but on the other hand, a little encouragement might make a loyal & permanent fantasy devotee out of someone who would otherwise drift away. In actual truth, most of these miniature hectographed things can never survive anyhow, so that it really isn't hurting the more substantial editors to give the kids a pat on the back. One realises how one would have felt oneself in childhood when playing at editorship. I know that I was always overwhelmingly grateful for any recognition accorded my little *R.I. Journal of Astronomy*. Of course, one couldn't send more than a trifle or two to each editor—or keep it up if by chance any of the sheets in question reached a second or third issue. But this question doesn't seem to arise very often. Most of the "magazines" to which I have sent trifles (always old junk dug up out of files of 20 or more years ago) have, so far as I know, never appeared at all! By this time I haven't much left to send, so that the problem will be automatically solved so far as I am concerned. By the way—I hope Wollheim is taking good care of the old amateur papers with my stuff which I lent him for copying. Some of those could never be replaced, & if they were lost, I certainly would feel like raising hell!

There is probably room for 2 to 4 fan magazines. With 2, one would be a news & criticism & general article sheet like *The Phantagraph* or the *Science-Fantasy Correspondent,* while the other would be a fiction & poetry magazine like F T, welcoming the literary attempts of the fans themselves. With 4, this general type of division would also exist, but in each of the two classes there would be separate magazines for weird & science fiction devotees. It seems to me that there ought to be some sort of general convention of the more responsible publishers, involving a voluntary partition or division of activities— that is, one person or group would agree to put all his energy into one sort of magazine, while another specialised in another sort. You & Wollheim, for example, could take the fictional field with *Fanciful Tales,* & Conover & Stickney could agree to eliminate fiction from the S F C. Then, if you dropped *The Phantagraph* or allowed it to be merged into the S F C, you would have the field clearly divided. Or you could keep the *Phantagraph* & restrict it to the weird while Conover restricted the S F C to science. Anything to secure harmony & avoid duplication. It may never come to pass, but something of that sort would surely be helpful. Just how much Crawford will figure in the field, I can't say. He always has ambitious plans, but they generally come to nothing in the end. If he started a fiction magazine & could keep it going, he would need an editor with some ability to judge fiction. Incidentally, I didn't know that Wright gave Ackerman free W T copies. That kid surely knows the art of ballyhoo! A few years ago he was selling snapshots of himself for a nickel, & generously offering to correspond with such persons as would send stamps to cover his replies! Starting a paying magazine is a tough proposition, & a great deal depends on sheer luck. Probably 2 or 3 *regular* issues (not scattered like Crawford's) & a certain amount of advertising would be necessary before one could tell whether or not a magazine would really "take". There would also have to be a good deal of sounding-out as to the sort of policy most in demand—whether material of substantial grade is wanted, or whether the readers want a magazine open to their own contributions amateurish or otherwise. There certainly is a definite place somewhere for a fantasy magazine welcoming reasonably good amateur work—like the early attempts of Bloch, Rimel, Kuttner, Petaja, &c.

If that linoleum cut was a first attempt, I'd say that you must have considerable natural aptitude for the process. Let us hope you will cultivate the gift.

I never saw the magazine *Thrilling Mystery,* but know that Long & Kuttner contributed. The item by Blackwood must be either a reprint or a syndicate feature offered by his American agents.[1] Certainly, it can't represent his best & most serious work—for no magazine of the "Thrilling" grade would want a really good item.

I hope Kuttner can get east for a sort of general convention. He is among the brightest & most promising of the newcomers. I imagine he's right about the Pacific Coast as a sort of nut centre, for nearly all the crack-brained New Thought & Rosicrucian & Theosophical & similar cults seem to have their headquarters there. I suppose one or two of these eccentric groups started the thing, & others followed as the reputation of the west coast as a haven of mysticism grew. The presence in Southern California of a lot of gullible old people—retired business men & their wives from all over the country seeking a sunny climate—helped to provide a large sucker supply for the Yogis & mahatmas. Now I suppose the cinema element—flashy, over-emotional, & usually ignorant show-offs for the most part—still further increases their credulous circle of dupes.

About the *Necronomicon*—Kuttner is trying to have some fun with you. If you want to get even, pretend to believe him & add that you have heard of the book from Birmingham dealers. Quote him some of the names & dates in that fake synopsis, which I'm pretty sure I've never showed him. That fake review was by someone who hadn't seen the synopsis, hence contains statements which clash with it. I wish I could find the typed copy which Conover (*not* the author) sent me. Abdul Alhazred is a name I used as a kid when I used to play Arabian Nights. Years later I thought it would be amusing to use it as the name of the author of a "hellish & forbidden" book. The *Necronomicon* isn't supposed to be at all obscene, but is supposed to tell of all sorts of pre-human horrors on earth & of monstrous forces in the outside universe—something like the book in Henry Hasse's recent W T story.[2] There isn't any such kind of book in real life—the nearest thing to it being the compilations of ancient & mediaeval magical rituals (which in truth sound more childish than terrible) made by scholars like Arthur E. Waite & Alphonse-Louis Constant ("Eliphas Levi"). Also, some early Hindoo chronicles might have something of the same general tendency. Thanks for the copy of the synopsis.

About a circulating fantasy library—one way such a thing could be founded would be to have all participants list whatever books they would be willing to put into it, & appoint a general librarian to take charge of the requests. A catalogue including all volumes would be issues, [*sic*] & a scale of borrowing rates decided upon. Then all borrowers would apply to the central office or librarian, who in turn would pass on the order to whoever happened to own the book asked for. This owner (to save postage) would send the book direct to the borrower, records of dates being carefully kept. Upon finishing the book, the borrower would send the latter back to the owner, but would send the fee to the central librarian. The latter would keep a certain percentage of each fee to defray expenses, transmitting the rest to the owner to defray wear & tear. Of course, a central librarian *might* be dispensed with—all owner-participants combining to issue a joint catalogue, but having individual transactions absolutely separate in each case, with the owner of the books getting full fees. In the catalogue the owner of each book would be listed—fees being made uniform, though perhaps higher for rare & non-replaceable books than for routine items. You might get Koenig's ideas—he & I have done a great deal of free lending in the past, & have our weird books catalogued. Neither he nor I, however, would let our choicest books go out to any & all borrowers—fee or no fee. We want to know that all recipients are careful & responsible. Probably we would each let *certain items* in our private catalogues be listed in a collective library catalogue. Clark Ashton

Smith has a fair collection which might cause him to participate. Of course, I dare say this plan would not entirely cut off free loans to certain deserving persons. Indeed, we are hardly likely to turn misers over night! But it would open up our facilities to comparative strangers—to whom we could not extend free services without sooner or later going broke. A reasonable cash fee would defray our postal expenses (bad enough as it is) & provide for the occasional replacement of worn-out books. If we adopted the central library plan, we could go still further—occasionally collecting funds for the acquisition of certain desired books which no private member happens to own— these books being kept with the central librarian & their fees going wholly to him for library use—after refunds to contributors. I'm no business planner, & couldn't predict how such a thing would work in practice—but the matter is worth discussing at leisure.

Sorry to hear of the many Yuletide accidents & near-accidents, & am glad that yours remained in the latter class. The school reunion must have been quite an event—& the gifts sound all in the right direction. You'll find the filing case a great asset. I began accumulating sets of drawers a couple of years ago, & don't know what I ever did before that.

Winter hereabouts has continued to be mostly very mild, so that I can get out on most days. My health, however, has remained very poor—the lingering touch of intestinal grippe keeping my strength at such a low ebb that I can attend to only the most necessary things.

*Later*

Down at last. Doc has me taking 3 different medicines at once, & am up only a little while at a time. Shall have to curtail all activities drastically during the balance of the winter.

Best wishes—

Yrs most sincerely,

H P L

*Notes*

1. The Algernon Blackwood "The Man-Eater," *Thrilling Mystery* 6, No. 2 (March 1937): 32–40, an original story about a were-tiger; posthumously collected in *The Magic Mirror,* ed. Mike Ashley (Wellingborough, UK: Equation, 1989).
2. "The Guardian of the Book" (*WT,* March 1937).

*Willis Conover, Jr.*

# Letters to Willis Conover, Jr.

[1]     [ALS]

66 College St.,
Providence, R.I.,
July 9, 1936.

Dear Mr. Conover:—

Yrs. of the 7th recd—& I am very glad to hear of the founding of a new "fan" magazine. Since *Fantasy Magazine* leans so heavily on the side of science-fiction, I hope you'll have a corresponding leaning on the weird side—thus making your publication (like *The Phantagraph*) something of a successor to the sincerely lamented *Fantasy Fan*. Your list of contributors is indeed promising. What is your limit of length for prose? E. Hoffmann Price has it in mind to write a set of reminiscences of the late Robert E. Howard (who shot himself June 11 on learning that his mother was about to die. Price is the only one of us who ever met R E H in person.), & wants to put it in the "best" of the fan magazines, whichever that is. I don't know which one to steer him to, but will ask all the editors about their space limitations. *The Phantagraph* has become so diminutive that I fear it will have to be counted out.

Now as to something from me—many thanks for the invitation! I haven't a thing left in prose, since recent conditions have kept me from writing, while the last of my unpublished things has been placed. There is, however, a bit of verse knocking about—& here is a specimen which you may or may not find too bad to use.

I shall be looking for your opening issue, & wish you all success.

With best regards,
Yrs most sincerely,
H P Lovecraft

[Enclosure: A.Ms. of "Homecoming."]

[2]     [ALS]

66 College St.,
Providence, R.I.,
July 21, 1936

Dear Mr. Conover:—

Sorry to hear my previous letter went astray, & hope the post-office will be more careful about this one![1] Glad the verses were found suitable. Surely, a year's subscription to the *Correspondent* forms a very adequate remuneration for an effort of that length. No need to return MS. after publication. Later on I hope I shall have more material suitable for your magazine.

I note your space limits with much interest, & will mention them to Price. However, I rather fear that his R E H reminiscences have been tentatively promised to *Fantasy Magazine.*[2] Schwartz seems eager to honour the memory of our late colleague—& is about to use a very ample obituary which I wrote without any expectation of its unabridged publication. However, we shall see. Sorry E H P didn't answer your letter, but I fancy he has no material on hand. He writes virtually nothing save full-length stories, & most of these secure professional acceptance.

By the way—you might say in a note somewhere that the Robert E. Howard Memorial Collection (at Howard Payne College, Brownwood, Texas) is eager to receive as donations any books, MSS., or other material written by friends of R E H or on subjects (weird fiction, folklore, southwestern history, Celtic history & antiquities, Oriental history, &c) in which he was particularly interested. Material to be sent to his father—Dr. I. M. Howard, Lock Box 313, Cross Plains, Texas. The loss of R E H is certainly a tragedy of the first magnitude!

I shall be on the lookout for the first issue of the *Correspondent,* & hope the venture may meet with success. There is room for a good magazine devoted to the interests of weird fiction—though of course it is hard to establish any new venture on a profitable or even self-sustaining basis.

All good wishes—

Yrs most sincerely,

H. P. Lovecraft

*Notes*

1. HPL's letter had been misdirected to Cambridge, MA (Conover lived in VA).
2. See DAW 10, n. 5.

[3]    [ALS]

66 College St.,
Providence, R.I.,
July 29, 1936

Dear Mr. Conover:—

Very glad to hear that letters of mine have proved helpful in your venture, & sorry that some others have been able to respond only briefly. No objection at all to answering your questions—though I fear you may find the facts regarding "ancient & forbidden books" a bit disillusioning.

As to myself—full name HOWARD PHILLIPS LOVECRAFT—born AUGUST 20, 1890. Have never really started out to write under a pen-name, (i.e., in professional magazines. Years ago I wrote voluminously for the *amateur* press under a dozen or more different aliases) although some of my revisory or "ghost writing" jobs for others virtually amount to stories of mine written under other names. Don't mention this latter point in print, though, for it would be rather bad professional ethics to claim virtual authorship for work done for clients. No stories in magazines other than of the weird or science group—except a fantasy in *The Galleon* a year or so ago.[1] Bits of verse here & there at very infrequent intervals. Am also active in the National *Amateur* Press Association (of which I'll send you details if you like), contributing criticism etc. My library contains a fair amount of standard weird *fiction*—which I have catalogued & am always glad to lend to responsible enthusiasts who can't get the items elsewhere—but is rather weak on actual folklore & occult reference books. I have, however, Lewis Spence's "Encyclopaedia of Occultism". You could find much more occult folklore stuff in the library of H. C. Koenig, 540 E. 80th St., N.Y. City—whose notes you have probably seen in the "fan" press from time to time. He also is glad to lend any items to the right persons. His collection includes a good many reports of mediaeval witchcraft trials.

Now about the "terrible & forbidden books"—I am forced to say that most of them are purely imaginary. There never was any Abdul Alhazred or *Necronomicon,* for I invented the names myself. Robert Bloch devised the idea of Ludvig Prinn & his *De Vermis Mysteriis,* while the *Book of Eibon* is an invention of Clark Ashton Smith's. The late Robert E. Howard is responsible for Friedrich von Junzt & his *Unaussprechlichen Kulten.* So far as Albertus Magnus goes—there was such a person, but he never wrote any such thing as "Egyptian Secrets". The latter must have been merely one of the cheap occult compilations (like the 7th Book of Moses &c.) which borrow impressive-sounding names to delude the public & attract attention. The *real* Albertus Magnus (Albrecht von Bollstädt or de Groot) was an ecclesiastic and philosopher of the 13th century, whose subtle speculations & knowledge of physical science caused ignorant people to regard him as a magician or devil-worshipper, & to associate his name with all sorts of things he never did & all sorts of books he never wrote. He was born in Swabia—at Laningen on the Danube—in 1193, & was educated at Padua in Italy. He joined the Dominican Friars in 1222, & was made Provincial of the order in 1254. He taught at Cologne, & had the famous ecclesiastical philosopher Thomas Aquinas as a pupil. He was made Bishop of Regensburg in 1259, but resigned three years later. Only 4 years ago—in 1932—the Catholic Church made him a saint. His works were first printed in Lyons & Leyden in 1651, by the Dominican friar Pierre Jammy. They amount to 21 large volumes, but some of these are probably spurious. The genuine ones relate wholly to philosophy & physical science, in which he was a follower of Aristotle. He founded a distinct school of Philosophy, called the "Albertists". What gave Albertus his reputation for magic & alchemy was probably—aside from his philosophical speculations—his unusual scientific experiments. The Middle Ages—as the case of Roger Bacon shows—feared & distrusted experimental science, & tended to regard experimenters as wizards or diabolists. Enemies accused him of black magic, & circulated all manner of legends concerning him. In his old age he fell into a sort of dotage, & may have made eccentric utterances & demonstrations which bore out the popular legendry. The most famous story about Albertus is that of his dinner to King William of Holland in 1240, in the garden of his monastery. It was *midwinter*, & the King was astonished at being asked to dine outdoors. But when the party adjourned to the garden, they found it full of flowers & greenery, & gay with singing birds. This naturally sounded like magic to the Middle Ages, but the truth is that the garden was probably a *greenhouse*, roofed over with some transparent substance & powerfully heated. However, the anecdote (if true) shows that Albertus liked to astonish people. The habit of calling Albertus an *alchemist* probably arose from a passage in his *De Rebus Metallicis et Mineralibus*, where he speaks of testing the gold which an alchemist claimed to have made, & of finding it very infusible. This alchemical reputation grew to such an extent that Michael Maier (alchemist & author of *Musaeum Chemicum*) declared that he had actually found the "Philosopher's Stone" & had given the secret to his pupil Thomas Aquinas. All of which shows that Al was quite a boy—though he never wrote some of the miscellaneous fantastic junk attributed to him—either the book you mention, or the better-known *De Secretis Mulierum*.

As for seriously-written books on dark, occult, & supernatural themes—in all truth, they don't amount to much. That is why it's more fun to invent mythical works like the *Necronomicon* & *Book of Eibon*. The magical lore which superstitious people really believed, & which trickled down to the Middle Ages from antiquity, was really nothing more than a lot of childish invocations & formulae for raising daemons &c., plus systems of speculation as dry as the orthodox philosophies. It was merely a lot of ill-assorted odds & ends—memories of Graeco-Roman mystery-cults, Pythagorean speculation (embodying ideas from India), Egyptian, Babylonian, Persian, & Jewish magic, & the Neoplatonism & Manichaeism of the late Roman Empire. The Alexandrian Jews were probably most active in keeping it alive—hence the preponderance of Jewish Kabbalism in the puerile mixture. The Byzantines & Arabs also clung to such stuff—to which was added the scraps of popular European superstition (Latin, Teutonic, Celtic), & the dark lore of the furtive Dianic cults (responsible for witches' Sabbats &c.) which perpetuated the revolting remnants of a lost pre-Aryan nature-worship. All this lore was disconnected & fragmentary, & there was never any especial *book* holding a large amount of it. The so-called "Hermetic Volumes" of "Hermes Trismegistus" are simply a set of metaphysical scraps from 3d century Neoplatonism & Philonic Judaism. It is not until *modern times* that we see any attempt to collect & codify these scraps. What the mediaeval & renaissance philosophers & "magicians" wrote is mostly namby-pamby stuff of their own devising—plus the popular folklore of their day (cf. Paracelsus, &c). The first serious collection of ancient magical scraps was Francis Barrett's "The Magus"—published in 1805 or so & reprinted in 1896. The first *really scholarly* material of the sort was the work of the eccentric Frenchman Alphonse-Louis Constant (middle of 19th century), who wrote under the pseudonym of "Eliphas Levi". More compilation of the same kind has been done by Arthur Edward Waite (still living, I believe)—who has also translated "Eliphas Levi's" books into English. If you want to see what the actual "magical" rites & incantations of antiquity & the Middle Ages were like, get the works of Waite—especially his "Black Magic" & "History of Magic". Sorry I don't own these—if I did I'd be glad to lend them. Other stuff can be found in Waite's translations of "Eliphas Levi". There is a more popular history of sorcery by "Sax Rohmer" (Arthur Sarsfield Ward), whose title I forget.[2] But you will undoubtedly find all this stuff very disappointing. It is flat, childish, pompous, & unconvincing—merely a record of human childishness & gullibility in past ages. Any good fiction-writer can think up "records of primal horror" which surpass in imaginative force any occult production which has sprung from genuine credulousness. The crap of the theosophists—which falls into the class of conscious fakery—is interesting in spots. It combines some genuine Hindoo & other Oriental myths with a subtle charlatanism obviously drawn from 19th century scientific concepts. Scott-Elliot's "Atlantis & the Lost Lemuria" & Sinnett's "Esoteric Buddhism" are rather fascinating. Clark Ashton Smith knows a lot of this stuff, & E. Hoffmann Price read up on it rather extensively some years ago.

Pseudo-scientific or semi-charlatanic stuff forms a class by itself. Among this material (all of which is good fictional source-reading) is the "Atlantis" lore promulgated by Le Plongeon, Donnelly, & Lewis Spence, the "Mu" books of the late Col. Churchward, the miscellaneous effusions of Charles Fort, &c. &c.[3] Some of these authors are plain fakers, while others are self-deluded "nuts". But even this kind of thing can't equal a really well-written story.

Price is a fine chap—a war veteran, West Pointer, & former army officer. As to the origin of our collaborated "Gates"—it is something like this. Price liked my old story "The Silver Key" (WT Jan 1929), & urged me to write a sequel. I didn't feel like it, hence postponed the matter. Then Price wrote a sequel himself & sent it to me to look over. I found it so different in spirit from the original story that I re-wrote it extensively, & added a new part longer than Price's. The result was something perhaps ¾ mine—entirely so in wording— but embodying in the central portions certain mathematical concepts of Price's. The later cosmic section is entirely mine both in idea & words. This story has never satisfied me, since I had to twist so many events to suit Price's ideas. I have struck it off the list of my work. Collaboration is not in my line, & I was once wise enough to refuse a similar venture with the late Henry S. Whitehead.

Well—I trust this disposes of the current queries . . . & am sorry my information on "ancient lore" has to be so disillusioning. By the way—biographical notes about me wouldn't be exactly new in the "fan" field, since an article of the sort by F. Lee Baldwin appeared in *Fantasy Magazine* a year or so ago. If you haven't seen this (& if I can find a duplicate), I'll send it to you some time.

All good wishes, & awaiting the *Correspondent* in course of time—Yrs most sincerely—H P Lovecraft.

*Notes*

1. The *Galleon* had published "The Quest of Iranon."
2. *The Romance of Sorcery.*
3. Augustus Le Plongeon (1826–1908), author of *Vestiges of the Mayas* (1881), *Sacred Mysteries among the Mayas and the Quiches, 11,500 Years Ago* (1886), and other works. He proposed a now discredited theory that the Maya had been in touch with the lost continent of Atlantis and were ancestral to Ancient Egypt. Col. James Churchward (1852–1936) wrote several books on the supposed continent of Mu, which sank in the Pacific—see *The Lost Continent of Mu, the Motherland of Man* (1926), *The Children of Mu* (1931), and *Cosmic Forces of Mu* (1934)—in which he claimed to have discovered an ancient language called Naacal. HPL mentions Churchward and the Naacal language in "Through the Gates of the Silver Key" and "Out of the Aeons."

[4]    [ALS]

66 College St.
Providence, R.I.
August 2, 1936.

Dear Conover:—

I feel guilty in having sent you on so many wild-goose-chases for the *Necronomicon* . . . . but am glad that the quest has served to introduce you to some less mythical volumes of spectral interest. Montague Summers' vampire books are splendid source-material—very scholarly despite their learned author's naive belief in the occult. I'll be interested to hear of your own contribution to horrific bibliography. Perhaps I'll mention it some time in a tale, since members of the WT group frequently use one author's synthetic daemons & forbidden books as background-accessories. About the illegible words in my former letter—here's the correct text. (1.) FRIEDRICH VON JUNZT: UNAUSSPRECHLICHEN KULTEN. This latter is the German for "Nameless Cults". Howard didn't know German, but Derleth supplied the requisite words. (2.) PIERRE JAMMY. (3) MANICHAEISM. This is a religion which arose among the Persians in the 3d Century A.D. as a result of the teaching of Mani or Manichaeus. It added certain Buddhistic and Judaeo-Christian concepts to the orthodox Zoroastrian faith. Mani was finally killed by Zoroastrian priests, but his faith became widely popular in the Roman Empire, rivalling Mithraism & Christianity. Late Manichaeism became merged into Christianity, forming a sort of heretical sect of the latter. Its influence survived into the Middle Ages, & was bitterly opposed by the orthodox Christian church. Sects professing it were savagely massacred by the followers of the Pope—the murders of the Albigenses in Southern France in 1209–1245 being a typical persecution. (4) ROMAN. (5) HERMES TRISMEGISTUS. This was the Greek name of the Egyptian god Thoth. Certain sacred books arising in Egypt at a late (Hellenistic) date were naively ascribed to this deity & called the "Hermetic Books". Fragments of these survived to the Middle Ages—by which time the ignorant populace had begun to regard "Hermes Trismegistus" as a *Chaldaean philosopher* (just as they thought Virgil was a magician) & the founder of alchemy! The association of this name with alchemy—or chemical procedure—survives to this day in the term "hermetically sealed". (6) PARACELSUS. This is the assumed name of the physician and chemist Theophrastus von Hohenheim, a Swiss who lived from 1493 to 1541 & was a professor at the U. of Basel. He was a bit of a charlatan & alchemical dabbler, yet is one of the chief founders of the modern physician's & druggist's arts. (7) A. P. SINNETT, author of "Esoteric Buddhism". (8). LE PLONGEON. Sorry my writing is so bad. I ought to type my letters—but mortally hate the process of typing.

"Egyptian Secrets" must be a quaint old volume—none the less interesting because of the spurious authorship.[1] It is probably a product of the 18th century—& is perhaps akin to Hohman's "Long-Lost Friend", so famous in the annals of Pennsylvania "hexerei".[2] Thanks endlessly for the generous extract, which is infinitely entertaining.

Yes—Bloch is a very good correspondent of mine. I'm sorry he doesn't like Howard's work, but realise his right to an opinion of his own. The Conan tales sometimes failed to be truly weird—becoming mere chronicles of adventure & (as Clark Ashton Smith put it) "monotonous manslaughter"—but some of them were great, while all of them had a rare spontaneous vigour & zest.

"Elemental"? Well—the best definition is "a kind of semi-material embodiment of one of the four supposed principles of nature—earth, water, air, & fire—as recognised in ancient & mediaeval times." Concepts of these things vary greatly—some regarding them as shapeless horrors, while others have conceived of them as legions of delicate & sometimes beautiful beings more or less like mankind—gnomes of the earth, undines of the water, sylphs of the air, & salamanders of the fire. *Paracelsus* had something to say about them, but the best account is to be found in an early 18th century treatise by the French priest Abbé de Villars, entitled "Comte de Gabalis". In fiction, Blackwood's "Nemesis of Fire" used the first concept, while LaMotte Fouqué's "Undine" embodies the second.

R. H. Barlow (whose stuff you've probably seen) is in Providence for an indefinite stay. He makes a very congenial neighbour.

Best wishes—Yrs most sincerely—H P L

[P.S.] I'll send you that issue of *Fantasy* with my biography as soon as I can find my stack of copies, now mislaid.

*Notes*

1. Possibly *Albertus Magnus: Being the Approved, Verified, Sympathetic and Natural Egyptian Secrets; or, The White and Black Art for Man and Beast* (n.p., 19—), a translation of *Bewährte und approbirte sympathetische und natürliche Egyptische Geheimnisse für Menschen und Vieh.* The work is almost certainly not by Albertus Magnus.

2. John George Hohman, *Pow-Wows, or the Long Lost Friend,* published in German in 1820 as *Der Lange Verborgene Freund* (*The Long-Hidden Friend*), and later in two English translations: the first, a crude translation by Hohman himself (*The Long Secreted Friend or a True and Christian Information for Every Body,* 1846), the second a more fluent translation (*The Long Lost Friend: A Collection of Mysterious and Invaluable Arts and Remedies for Man as Well as Animals,* 1856). The name *Pow-Wows* was added in late 19th-century reprints.

[5]     [ALS]

66 College St.,
Providence, R.I.,
August 14, 1936

Dear Conover:—

No excuses needed for leaving off such frills as "Mr." I don't give a hang for ceremonial niceties of any sort. Glad your quest for the *Necronomicon* had its compensating features. Since your enquiry, two more persons have asked about the Mad Arab & his hellish & forbidden tome . . . . so that I fear I've become a wholesale hoaxer despite my innocent intentions. However, I continue to disillusion all enquirers very conscientiously.

Bloch shewed me that account of his imaginary visit,[1] & I certainly agree as to its side-splitting qualities. He is especially clever at that kind of thing, & has sold considerable amounts of comic dialogue to sundry "gagsters" of the radio & vaudeville stage. The description of me is what one might call a slightly idealised one—insomuch as I've been clean-shaven ever since I had anything to shave, while I seldom eat people alive except for Sunday dinner. As a general thing, I prefer human flesh cooked—& I usually avoid *authors* as a diet, since they tend to be lean & tasteless. I never devour guests as long as they are well-behaved—indeed, Barlow is still alive & intact after more than a fortnight in my necropolis!

Comte d'Erlette's *Cultes des Goules?* An invention of Bloch's. The name Comte d'Erlette, however, represents an actual (& harmless) ancestor of August W. Derleth's, who was a royalist emigré from France in 1792 & became naturalised in Germany under the slightly Teutonised name of *Derleth.* His son, emigrating to Wisconsin in 1835, was the founder of the Derleth line in America.

About the Conan tales—I don't know that they contain any more sex than is necessary in a delineation of the life of a lusty bygone age. Good old Two-Gun didn't seem to me to overstress eroticism nearly as much as other cash-seeking pulpists—even if he did now & then feel in duty bound to play up to a Brundage cover-design. Speaking of Conan—he is on a fair way toward becoming a popular folklore hero among the fans. P. Schuyler Miller recently prepared a bibliography & chronology arranging the Conan stories in their proper time-sequence & providing a running comment on the history & development of the doughty Cimmerian from his first exploits at the age of 15 to his last recorded deeds as King of Aquilonia around the age of 40. This extremely clever document (which REH saw & praised shortly before his tragic exit) is now in Wright's hands (he lent it to me), but if he doesn't use it in WT you ought to get hold of it for the SFC. It would be a good rival to "The Hyborian Age", now running in *The Phantagraph*. No—I won't repeat your opinion of the Conan tales, nor give away your Eyrie pseudonym. I'll be looking with interest for "Mr. Ryan's" contribution in the next issue![2]

About reproducing parts of letters—I don't know of anything especially private in mine, except that I wouldn't wish any opinion or implication derogatory to a fellow-writer to appear. But you *can* print if you wish that my 'Mountains of Madness' was atrociously and injuriously mangled toward the end, and that the style-sheet determiner of *Astounding* is an absolute ass for capitalising words like *moon* & *moonlight,* for changing words like *dinosaurs* to *Dinosauria,* and for illiterately altering *subterrene* to *subterrane*—the latter a word having no existence as an adjective![3]

About the relation of the word *hermetic* or *hermetically* to the god *Hermes*—I hope I made it plain that it was a very *indirect* one. The mediaeval alchemists who coined the word thought that *Hermes Trismegistus,* supposed author of the *Hermetic Books,* was a Chaldaean philosopher. Actually, *Hermes Trismegistus* was simply the Greek name of the Egyptian god *Thoth,* to whom the books in question were attributed by the later ancients. (The books themselves were not older then the 3d century A.D.) Now *Thoth* & the real Greek *Hermes* were not exactly the same thing. The Greeks & Romans always tried to identify the gods of foreign races with corresponding deities of their own, but the relationship was often forced & far-fetched. Sometimes, when two races were close enough to have inherited similar streams of Aryan mythology, there was a *genuine* resemblance between the different gods declared to be the same. Thus the Greek *Hermes* was indeed very much like the Latin *Mercury* with whom he was identified. But when it comes to *Thoth* the parallel is a bit stretched. Thoth was a pretty different bird (bum joke. Thoth had an ibis's head!) from Hermes, even though he did preside over speech, art, science, & literature. However—the fact that the Greeks *thought* that Thoth was their Hermes established the *verbal* linkage . . . . & it doesn't matter much, since the books have no more real connexion with the one mythical figure than with the other! Greek god—Egyptian god—Chaldaean philosopher . . . . it's all the same. None of these hypothetical bearers of the name ever existed! The name *Trismegistus* means merely *thrice-greatest.* The books themselves were nothing more than scrambled extracts from the more mystical parts of Neo-Platonic & Alexandrian-Jewish writings of the 3d century A.D. They treat of science, art, religion, medicine, cosmography, &c., & embody more than a hint of Pythagoreanism. They tell of the creation of the world from fluid, the formation of the "soul" from life & light, the indestructibility of all things, the origin of all suffering in motion, the transmigration of the "soul" from body to body, &c. &c. Their connexion with *alchemy* is very thin—but the uncritical mind of the Middle Ages (which made a Chaldaean philosopher of the supposed author . . . & deemed Virgil a magician!) could imagine anything.

Yes—one can certainly dig up a lot of varied information merely by following out all the threads of association connected with this or that word!

No—Providence seems to have no permanent weird-tale enthusiast save myself. Ours is surely a widely-scattered clan! Of all the devotees of the group I've met less than half in person. Robert E. Howard never met any fellow-weirdist except E. Hoffmann Price. Clark Ashton Smith has met only Price and Donald Wandrei. Derleth, too, has met very few. Thanks for the Keller news—possibly I'll send for that volume, though I buy very few items by the pulpists.[4] About *science-fiction* of mine before the "Mts"—there was nothing which could really be called such, although "The Colour out of Space" was printed in *Amazing* (Sept. 1927). That is my only old item in a science-fiction magazine. As for my file of weird magazines—I have WT complete, *Amazing* from the beginning through 1927, *Fantasy Fan* complete, *Strange Tales* complete, *Fantasy Magazine* since Jan. 1934, & all that have appeared of *Marvel Tales* (& *Unusual*) and *The* (printed) *Phantagraph*. By the way—I hope you duly received the FM with my biography in it. Keep it if you like—I found quite a few duplicates. The picture is rather poor—looks younger than I do. Glad to hear of your increased word-limit for SFC contributions. Congratulations on the Finlay sketch & drawing! Yes—organ music with weird fiction is quite an idea. More could be made of music by weird authors. As for more of my stuff in WT—Wright *did* recently accept two stories. He will not, however, take anything of substantial *length* from me. He rejected "Innsmouth", "Mts. of Madness",[5] &c. About the *spelling* I use—I don't give the matter much thought, but adhere to what seems the most universal & conservative. Not that I copy the moment's usage in London, but that I stick to what has been used for the longest time over the bulk of the Anglo-Saxon world. No—I'm not of British *birth,* although my paternal line is closer to Old England than that of the average Yankee. The Lovecrafts are a Devonshire family, the only ones of whom to come to America were my great-grandfather Joseph Lovecraft & his five children. They came in 1827 to New York State—the child who became my grandfather being then 12 years old. Thus on my father's side I am only of the 2nd American-born generation. *My mother's* ancestors, on the contrary, all came to New England between 1630 & 1656. Amusingly enough, I am a

*6th cousin* of young Barlow, both being descended in the 7th generation from one John Rathbone of Block Island, who was born in Roxbury, Mass. in 1658.

Your catalogue of hellish & forbidden books sounds highly impressive, & the very names make me shudder. Of only one have I ever heard before—this being (can I bring myself to write the dreaded words?) Mülder's infamous *Ghorl Nigral.* I even *saw* a copy of this once—though I never opened or glanced within it. It was many years ago in Arkham—at the library of the Miskatonic University. I was in a shadowy corner of the great reading-room, & noticed a huge volume in somebody's hands across the table from me. The reader's head was completely hidden by the massive tome, but on the book itself I could descry the words "Ghorl Nigral" in an archaic Gothic lettering. What I knew of it made me shudder—& I felt vaguely alarmed when others began glancing at the silent reader & quietly edging out of the room one by one. When I saw that I was wholly alone but for the unspeaking page-turner, my feeling of disquiet became almost overpowering—& I too edged toward the door . . . . keeping my eyes resolutely away from the reader for some unknown reason or other. Then I saw that the room was growing very dark, though the afternoon was by no means spent. I stumbled over a chair, & gave vent to a wholly involuntary cry—but heard no answering sound. At this point came a horrible glare of lightning & a deafening stroke of thunder, though those outside the building observed no sign of a storm. Attendants came running in, & someone brought a candle after the lights were found out of commission. The man who had been reading was dead, & his face was not pleasant to contemplate. He had a queerly foreign look, & his hair & beard seemed to adhere in unhealthy patches. The book, from which all eyes were sedulously averted, was tightly clasped in his brown, bony hands—& the attendants seemed slow in trying to dislodge it. When at length they did so, they encountered something very singular. For the hands, instead of releasing the book, came irregularly off at the wrists amid a cloud of red dust—whilst the body, pulled forward by the attempt, collapsed suddenly to a powder, leaving only a heap of greenishly mouldering clothes in the chair. Those clothes were later identified as belonging to a man found buried 30 years before—whose tomb in Christchurch Cemetery was found to be empty. Never since that day has the "Ghorl Nigral" been taken from its locked vault in the library basement.

I gave your regards to Barlow & he sends his to you. We had a third member in our literary group last week—Dr. Adolphe de Castro, one-time friend & colleague of Ambrose Bierce (Long wrote the preface to his Bierce biography), & occasional WT contributor. One afternoon, he, Barlow, & I sat on a tomb in a hidden hillside churchyard just north of #66 & composed rhymed acrostics on the name of *Edgar Allan Poe*—who 90 years ago used to wander through this selfsame churchyard when visiting Providence. Next week Barlow & I hope to get to Salem & Marblehead—pausing in Lynn to pick up young Kenneth Sterling for the expedition. Amidst all these social activities my work is going to the devil—I'll have to buckle down to it in earnest soon!

All good wishes—Yrs most sincerely,

H P Lovecraft

[P.S.] Loan-exhibit of Clark Ashton Smith's grotesque miniature sculpture is here. Some of the figurines are diabolically impressive.

*Notes*

1. "A Visit with H. P. Lovecraft"; see Appendix.

2. See "The Eyrie," *WT* 28, No. 3 (October 1936): 381–82: "Joseph Allan Ryan, of Cambridge, Maryland, writes: 'Do WT readers ever stop to observe how far Weird Tales has traveled since its inception? Let's take an early issue of WT—the October 1925 one, for instance—and compare it with the latest one. First of all we have J. U. Giesy's humorous pseudo-scientific tale, The Wicked Flea—a highly illogical story of a flea that grew to a gigantic size and went chasing big dogs all over the country; it relied on silly names and one solitary pun to give it humor (?). Then there was Seabury Quinn's The Horror on the Links, the first de Grandin story. Although this story showed Quinn's superiority in the field of weird story writing, it was not so interesting as are his present de Grandin tales, for it gave a scientific explanation to each phenomenon, whereas today we find only indications of the occult in Quinn's masterpieces. The Prophet's Grandchildren, by E. Hoffmann Price, was, though interesting, not weird, for it merely retold a legend of the Moslems . . . The Fading Ghost, by Willis Knapp Jones, started as though it was going to be a real WT short-story classic, but it ended up with a surprize ending which explained everything as a mistake which could never be incurred. Tom Freeman's The Death Shower was the only a cleverly constructed detective story, not weird; while A Mind in Shadow, by Tessida Swinges, was a simple child's story, related in baby-talk, which could not have been even remotely connected with Weird Tales—it should have been rejected, instead, by Child Life Magazine. The Weird Story Reprint, Wilhelm Hauff's The Severed Hand, had a touch of weirdness to it, but was ruined by a weak ending; moreover, the title bore little relation to the story. There were other stories by authors who were, no doubt, prominent and popular at the time, but most of whom have dropped into the background. The illustrations, both inside and on the cover, were all done, very crudely, by a sole illustrator, Andrew Brosnatch. Compare his efforts with the present exquisite work of Virgil Finlay and Mrs. Brundage, with the detailed, clear-cut drawings of Harold De Lay, the shadowy, mysterious grease-pencilings of Hugh Rankin. Notice, too, the wide variety of artists—the early WT's had but one. The July, 1936, issue was almost a direct contrast to the early issue of 1925 which I reviewed. Clark Ashton Smith's scintillant gem—Robert E. Howard's tale of the barbarian, Conan—Edmond Hamilton's fascinating weird-scientific tale of the near future—Thorp McClusky's different vampire thriller—August W. Derleth's narrative of spirit return, proof of his never-failing mastery—the handsome Manly Wade Wellman's short tale of stark horror, nearly approaching the point reached by Kuttner's The Graveyard Rats—the beautiful inside illustrations and the excellent cover—the usual array of interesting letters in the Eyrie—all these rounded up an issue which was as nearly perfect as an issue

can be, and which was yet typical of the standard maintained in the last five years. And still some readers yearn for the 'good old days'!"

3. Conover did in fact publish extracts from HPL's letters under "Odds and Ends" in *Science Fantasy Correspondent*.

4. Probably David H. Keller's *The Waters of Lethe* (Great Barrington, MA: Hayward S. Kirby, 1937). A book by Keller did appear in 1936—his novel *The Eternal Conflict* (1949) was published in a French translation as *La Guerre du lierre* (Issy-les-Moulineaux, France: La Fenetre ouverte, 1936)—but it seems unlikely that this is the book referred to.

5. August Derleth had submitted "The Shadow over Innsmouth" surreptitiously to *WT*, since HPL refused to submit more stories following the rejection of *At the Mountains of Madness*.

[6]     [ANS][1]

[Postmarked Providence, RI,
17 August 1936]

Yrs. just recd. Congratulations on the vacation! You surely have met a vast bunch of editors & writers, & ought to have material for many columns of personal notes. I never saw Tremaine—& am interested to learn that he has supplied science fiction plots. "Colossus"[2] was an obvious repetition of an old Ray Cummings idea—that's the only one of the lot I've read. I simply can't stand cheap hack "scientifiction". I never met Cummings, either. Met Binder once & Quinn several times—both are extremely likeable. Long & Wandrei are old friends of mine—hope you met them. ¶ I've read all of Merritt's published stuff, but have seen none of the cinemas. All of the so-called weird cinemas are infantile & unconvincing—at least, all I've ever seen. By this time you have my letter. Glad the *Fantasy* duly arrived. You can keep it if you have any use for it. ¶ Barlow is still here. We went to Newport Saturday, & Thursday we hope to join young Sterling in Lynn & visit "Arkham" & "Kingsport" (Salem & Marblehead). All good wishes—H P L

*Notes*

1. *Front:* Betsy Williams Cottage, Roger Williams Park, Providence, R. I.

2. By Donald Wandrei.

[7]     [ALS]

66 College St.,
Providence, R.I.,
Aug. 29, 1936.

Dear Conover:—

Very glad to learn of your ambitious plans for S F C. You surely have been accumulating a valuable background, & I hope the new venture will profit by your erudition. If you want to read the rest of my

"Supernatural Horror in Literature" I'll be glad to lend you the original version in *The Recluse*—plus the added notes bringing it down to date.

My birthday was the 20th, & I spent it in ancient Salem & Marblehead ("Arkham" & "Kingsport") with Barlow & young Kenneth Sterling. We explored many old gabled houses of the witchcraft period, & sat for a long time in the centuried burying-ground mentioned in my story "The Unnamable"—where the giant willow is slowly engulfing a 250-year-old slab. Many thanks for the good wishes. I seem to be tolerably hale & hearty at 46—with all my teeth, fair sight & hearing, a few spears of hair, & strength enough to totter around a good part of the day. But the years tell on one! You young fellows don't know how lucky you are!

Glad to hear of your interesting visit with Quinn. He has invited me to 34 Jefferson several times, but I've never been able to get around there. Whenever I pass through N.Y. I'm always rushed to the limit, since I know so damned many people there. No—I don't recall Quinn's having mentioned any experience in New Orleans. I haven't seen his library, but believe he said it was covered with framed cover-designs of his W T stories. In view of the average "art" standard of this periodical, I can't say that I envy him his decorative scheme!

I'll be interested to see the second-person Binder story, & hope you can get other distinctive items. Congratulations on the Keller material.

Long ought to be back from his vacation in Ocean Grove by this time. Better try calling him up before you leave the metropolitan zone. His telephone is RIverside 9-3465. His address is 230 W. 97th St.—cor. of Broadway. Take the West Side Interborough Subway to 96th St. Wandrei has gone home—perhaps for good. Not Indianapolis, but *1152 Portland Ave., St. Paul, Minnesota.* Haven't seen Hamilton yet—but hope he'll show up later. It would be pleasant if he arrived before Tuesday, when Barlow sets out for Kansas City. R H B will probably stop briefly in N.Y., & Washington, & Indianapolis—calling on Miss Moore in the latter place.

No—that cut in FM didn't do me injustice. I do *it* injustice—being a haggard old geezer as compared with the relatively spruce individual (who might be a son or nephew of mine) shown therein. Where do I keep Yog-Sothoth at night? Alas—I *can't* keep him anywhere, since his plastic & occasionally gaseous constitution enables him to evade all terrestrial restrictions. I once tried to rent him to a vindictive fellow-scribbler, but he resented it in a curious way. The scribbler is buried in the hidden churchyard here. As for sic'ing him on to Master Ackerman—I tried that, too, back in '33, but he was very balky. Said it was an insult to set an immemorial daemon of outer cosmic space to the task of fly-swatting. Hope you'll safely ship Darrow his baby ghoul. Sorry I can't relay the information, but I'm not in touch with Darrow. About the pronunciation of the Outside word roughly given as *Cthulhu* in our alphabet—authorities seem to differ. Of course it is not a human name at all—having never been designed for enunciation by the vocal apparatus of homo sapiens. The best approximation one can make is to grunt, bark, or cough the imperfectly-formed syllables *Cluh-Luh* with the tip of the tongue firmly affixed to the roof of the mouth. That is, if one is a human being. Directions for other entities are naturally different. By the way—Cthulhu isn't a *she* but a *he*. He'd feel deeply enraged if anyone regarded him as sissified!

Thanks in advance for the snapshot of your gang. Would you care for the loan of some snaps showing all (or rather several) of the fantasy group? They include Long, Derleth, Talman, the late Robert E. Howard, Price, &c.

All good wishes for the S F C—& hoping the residue of your visit will be as delightful as the early part—

Yrs most sincerely—E'ch-Pi-El

[8]     [ALS]

66 College St.,
Providence, R.I.
Sept. 1, 1936

Dear Conover:—

I'll rush this off in order to give you Miss Moore's address—which is 2547 Brookside Parkway, S. Drive, Indianapolis, Indiana. Hope you get a good contribution from her. Enclosed are the pictures I mentioned—not a group, but separate views. Sorry some are so old—but these are doubtless better than none. I include pictures of two deceased persons—three, reckoning the late Robert E. Howard—on the assumption that you've seen their work. Sorry there are no good ones of Long & Derleth (the enclosed of AWD is a hellishly sappy one, dating from his callow days of juvenile affectation), but all the best snaps of these two are lent to Rimel for linoleum reproduction. Rimel isn't so bad as a portrait artist—indeed, I don't see how anybody can catch a resemblance in a medium as rough as linoleum. The trouble is with the medium itself. No hurry about the return of these views—& sorry the assortment isn't wider.

About "Supernatural Horror in Literature"—the complete treatise *is* in existence, & was published entire in 1927. The notes I spoke of are merely inserts to bring the text up to the date when I sent it to the *Fantasy Fan*. Hornig returned the whole thing, of course, when the FF failed. If you'd like to continue reprinting the article, beginning where Hornig left off, I'd be superabundantly glad. I'll mark where to start on the copy. Doubtless I'd better postpone sending this item till you get home. Incidentally—you might glance over the parts you're supposed to have read, since the FF version was full of misleading misprints.

Clark Ashton Smith is badly oppressed by circumstances this year, & has not written to anybody in months. His father is feeble, his cash is low, & the care of his place (including the fetching of water ¼ mile each day, & the care of 40 hens) is tremendously burdensome. It's a wonder he can get anything done—& we must forgive him any lapses in correspondence. As for the question of how I keep up with my own correspondence—I'm damned if I know, & I certainly shall have to cut it down before long if I expect to do anything else! It's a thing that insidiously gets hold of one—one doesn't know where to begin the process of elimination! Enclosed, by the way, is the note for your partner which you requested—although I fear it isn't a very interesting one. I fear that you & he place too high a valuation upon the rambling scrawls of a nonentity! I wonder if Stickney is descended from Jonathan Corwin the witchcraft judge of 1692, whose house in Salem is still called "The Old Witch House"? I showed this place to Barlow & Sterling last month. Also—have you relatives in Southern Ohio? I used to be in touch 15 years ago with a Howard R. Conover of Cozzaddale—later of Cincinnati—in the old United Amateur Press Association.

About "The Skylark of Space"—I've never read it, since a vast majority of the mature critics who have tell me that it has no serious literary merit.[1] From what I hear, it has some clever theories as background, but is essentially a juvenile adventure-action story with the usual artificial stock characters, conventional situations, mechanical thrills, &c. &c.—like the bulk of current pulp science-fiction or like the "Jack Wright" & "Frank Reade" nickel novels of my youth. In view of your favourable opinion, I may have done it an injustice by heeding other opinions—but one can't spare the time to read everything. I've never read the others you mention, either. The fact is, that virtually all magazine science-fiction is synthetic tripe not worth a grown-up's time. It is simply a mess of bright ideas dragged down by infantile handling—hackneyed & lifeless plot-devices & figures—just boys' wild west stuff given an interplanetary setting with handsome young space-pilots instead of cowboys & sheriffs, & "Martians" & "moon-men" instead of Indians & outlaws. And of course the usual superfluous rag-doll labelled "beautiful heroine". The only serious science-fiction is that outside the cheap magazines, & at the moment I can think of only three persons who produce it—H. G. Wells, S. Fowler Wright, & W. Olaf Stapledon.

No—I didn't tell Cthulhu about your mistake. Long experience with daemons & cosmic entities teaches tact! Has Yog-Sothoth a pedigree? No. He always existed. Since he has no parents, I've never met 'em. He isn't housebroken, so I generally try to chain him outside. When he sends forth a pseudo-podic tentacle (which can pass through the most solid walls) & begins to grope around inside the house, I usually call his attention to something going on in another galaxy—just to get his mind off local things. Yog doesn't *always* have long, ropy arms, since he assumes a variety of shapes—solid, liquid, & gaseous—at will. Possibly, though, he's fondest of the form which does have 'em. I've never encouraged him to scratch my back, since those whom Yog-Sothoth touches are never seen again . . . at least, in any recognisable shape. It is not even safe to speak the name of Yog-Sothoth aloud.[2] If we *seem* to have done so, & yet remain alive, it is merely because our merciful ignorance has caused us to mispronounce it. Yog-Sothoth's wife is the hellish cloud-like entity Shub-Niggurath, in whose honour nameless cults hold the rite of the Goat with a Thousand Young. By her he has two monstrous offspring—the evil twins Nug & Yeb. He has also begotten hellish hybrids upon the females of various organic species throughout the universes of space-time (cf. "The Dunwich Horror"). Sorry Mr. Darrow couldn't afford a real baby ghoul, but hope Mr. Ackerman will prove an effective substitute. It would be highly gratifying to discover some real use for Mr. Ackerman.

Concerning Wollheim's exaggeratedly flattering estimate of me—I can only comment with amusement that I didn't know I put up such a good false front! Actually, my ventures into the languages haven't led me far from the dictionaries & grammars (I couldn't even invent a good "original" name for REH's "Nameless Cults"—it was Derleth who thought up *Unaussprechlichen Kulten*), & my scientific information is the merest layman's smattering. As to lack of *push*—in my day a gentleman didn't go in for self-advertising, but left that to the little parvenu egotists. However, I probably am a good deal less practical than the average. Regarding *stories*—the reason my placements are so limited is that my work simply doesn't fit many existing periodicals. No—I'm under no contract, but no magazine save W T exists which prints material of the sort I write. I have no skill at all in insincere artificial writing—the sort which produces conventional pulp tripe & succeeds in the cheap magazines. When it comes to mechanical work of that grade, I have to turn to *revision* instead. And so far as *high-grade* writing is concerned—I simply don't measure up to it. Six or seven times book-publishers have asked to see my stuff with a view to collected printing, but in each case they've turned it down in the end.[3] By the standards of real literature, I simply don't exist—& that is equally true of all the routine hacks who fill the pulp magazines. We are the most negligible of small fry, & anyone who mistakes us for real authors is simply wasting his esteem. Pulp fiction is not the product of art, but of a sort of calculative commercial cleverness about on a par with that of a skilled mechanic or small business man. I'd rather be a *good* plumber or bookkeeper or post-office clerk than a popular scribbler of science-fiction hokum. If you want to see *real artists* in fantasy, look outside the magazine field—at Dunsany, Blackwood, Poe, Machen, de la Mare, Bierce, the late M. R. James, &c. The nearest approach to really serious matter in the pulps may be found in certain stories in *Adventure*, & in the few choicest pieces of such exceptional writers as Clark Ashton Smith, Miss Moore, the late Henry S. Whitehead, & the late Robert E. Howard. Derleth is coming along—but his best work is not fantasy.

About W T covers—they are really too trivial to get angry about. If they weren't totally irrelevant & unrepresentative nudes, they'd probably be something equally awkward & trivial, even though less irrelevant. The "art" of the pulps is even worse than its fiction, if such be possible. Rankin, Utpatel, & Finlay are the only illustrators of W T who are worth anything. I have no objection to the nude in art—in fact, the human figure is as worthy a type of subject-matter as any other object of beauty in the visible world. But I don't see what the hell Mrs. Brundage's undressed ladies have to do with weird fiction! However—I seldom notice what the cover-design of any cheap magazine is. Only once in an age does anything worth a second glance appear. If Wright were to use a really effective weird design the bulk of his half-illiterate readers wouldn't know what it was all about, & would write scornful & ungrammatical letters to the Eyrie. The average W T fan never even heard of the great fantastic & macabre illustrators—John Martin, Sime, Harry Clarke, Arthur Rackham, &c. He may have heard the name Doré—but probably thinks it means a kind of a row boat!

All good wishes—Yrs most sincerely—H P L

P.S. Barlow left for N.Y. this morning. Hope you & he can get in touch before you both leave N.Y. for your respective destinations. Long can put you in touch with him. ¶ Yes—I recall that Binder graveyard story.

*Notes*

1. *The Skylark of Space* by E. E. "Doc" Smith (1890–1965) is one of the earliest novels of interstellar travel and the first example of "space opera."
2. Jews came to believe that YHWH, the divine name of God, was too sacred to be spoken, and ceased uttering the ineffable name aloud.
3. To the list in RB 43, one can add the William Morrow Company, to whom HPL sent stories at the behest of Wilfred B. Talman.

[9]    [ALS]

66 College St.,
Providence, R.I.,
Sept. 23, 1936.

Dear Khono-Vhah:—

The *Recluse* containing Sup. Horror in Lit. has gone forward under separate cover. I've marked where Hornig left off reprinting, & shall certainly be glad to see the rest appear. If any of the interpolated portions are illegible, ask me what the doubtful words are. Meanwhile I'm submitting—through your partner—some of the recent churchyard acrostics I told you about. You can do as you like with these. By the way—copies of the *Recluse* are so scarce that I wish you'd return mine after the serial is finished. I'd rather like to have the article in its compact form.

About length of letters—I believe my longest has been around 70 or 80 pages 8½ × 11. These were parts of historical, philosophical, literary, political, or scientific discussions, hence partook a good deal of the nature of the essay or article. I haven't time for such elephantine missives nowadays. As for the curtailment of my correspondence—as I'm telling Stickney (from whom I received a very pleasant note), this will not mean any abrupt policy of arrogant & neglectful silence. It will mean rather a cutting down of the *length & promptness* of such letters as do not absolutely demand space & speed. I immensely enjoy the new points of view, varied ideas, & diverse reactions afforded by a wide correspondence, & would be infinitely reluctant to have any drastic or large-scale elimination. Long has repudiated all correspondence except important business letters—but *I* certainly wouldn't aim for any such extreme! The one thing I *shall* have to do is to learn how to turn down requests for free revision & extended criticism. I always like to help a fellow-struggler along when I can—but correcting stories & poems is too exhausting & time-consuming a process to undertake lightly. Those who make these requests undoubtedly don't realise what a burden it is—but I shall have to dodge such responsibilities none the less.

This reminds me of your enquiry about my sadly microscopic income—an enquiry which is all right in this case, although some questionees might indeed find it a bit personal. The answer is that my professional attempts apart from fictional junk consist of just that sort of revisory work which my curious correspondents are so anxious to have me perform for them! At the moment I'm trying to whip into shape a textbook on English usage—for the head of a school in Washington.[1] Since revision jobs are always irregular—with long gaps between—and so exhausting that one can't do them justice without a vast amount of time & energy, it follows that they aren't a very profitable source of income. If I didn't piece out by slowly using up the last few dregs of my existing property (& after disasters in 1904, 1911, & the present, those dregs are *damned* few!), I wouldn't be eating very much. But what the hell *is* one to do? I'm naturally uncommercial—I despise trade & haggling & competition & smallness in general—& good positions are few & hard to secure. If I were young again, I would take some clerical training fitting me for lucrative work—but 46 is 46! Certainly, I could not become a cheap fictional prostitute like the pulp boys—the basic idea of concocting synthetic rabble-ticklers is so nauseous to me that I *couldn't possibly* do it even if I were willing to! It's my mistake that I never thought about money when I was young. There was no immediate want then, & I always thought it would be easy to slip into some modestly paying niche when the need might arise. I did not realise the vast gulf between sincere fiction & commercial fiction. Today I would jump at any *regular position* paying $10.00 per week or more—that being the minimum sum enabling me to eat & maintain quarters large enough to house my library, pictures, & basic family heirlooms. Whether I shall ever get such—or whether I can ever manage to make $10.00 per week *regularly* through revision & stories—I'm sure I don't know. If I can't, there's always Robert E. Howard's solution awaiting when the end of my resources is reached. Meanwhile I have developed *economy* to a fine art within the last eleven years—this being the period in which I have most fully realised my increasing peril. I do most of my own laundry, cut my own hair with a patent device that hitches on to a Gillette razor, never spend over $2.00 or $2.50 per week on food, & wear my clothes for ever. Of my 4 suits, 3 date from 1925 & the newest from 1928. My overcoats are of *1915* & 1932—& my raincoat is an old topcoat of *1909*. Amusingly enough, I don't especially mind these economies—for I began them late enough in life to make them seem like a rather humorous & interesting *game*. My great anxiety isn't to have *more,* but to hang on to what little I *have.* If I *did* have more cash I'd probably continue my present economies & spend it on travel. An old man doesn't need to be a gourmet or a dandy. But all the same, I wish I *could* get hold of some regular job (of any damn kind from running an elevator to editing a magazine, or from drug-clerking or night-watchmaning to teaching English or history) paying ten bucks per week or over! (N.B.—needless to say, *none* of these personal details are for publication!)

Returning to long letters—20 to 25 pages closely typed was not unusual for Robert E. Howard. He used to expatiate on Southwestern history, & to present extended arguments in favour of barbarism as opposed to civilisation. Poor old Two-Gun Bob—it's tough to think that I'll never get another fat envelope from Cross Plains! My last letter to him was of 32 pages—this size—but it probably arrived too late to be read.

About Bloch's age—I *did* know once, but can't be certain at the moment. It can't, however, be far from 20. He graduated from high-school in '35, if my memory is correct. In any event he's a tremendously bright youth, & one may be certain that he'll make his way in the world.

I'm interested in the way you prefer human flesh. De gustibus non disputandum est—but I like mine well-done. I'm particularly fond of the canned brand sold by the Black Man of the Arkham witch-cult coven & prepared in the secret cannery at Innsmouth. It is prepared only from plump, healthy bourgeois specimens (usually those sacrificed at the Sabbats & Estbats in the forest behind Arkham), & is seasoned very highly with forbidden spices grown by non-human gardeners in the walled lamasery of Leng. I don't care overmuch for vampire-blood, but share your taste for embalming-fluid. As for authors—of course some are fairly plumpish, but they have an unpleasant flavour for all that. Probably because of the saturation of their tissues with alcohol.

I noticed the "Ryan" criticism, & am not sure how well I agree with it. The old WT issue you chose for comparison was rather below par—& I certainly think most of the new ones are just as bad. The Aug–Sept one, for example, had almost no redeeming feature except the instalment of Two-Gun's serial. In the July issue you are too kind to Hamilton's routine filler & to the utterly lousy hash entitled "Loot of the Vampire". However—the letter is very pleasing & well-written, & certainly puts over the old-timer idea most convincingly. About Miller's address—sorry, but I don't know it. I've never been in touch with PSM—the Conan sketch having been lent me by Wright. Old Farny can undoubtedly put you on the track.

As for the *Ghorl Nigral*—if you really feel you *must* see it, & are not afraid of certain obscure consequences, you *might* make arrangements at the library of Miskatonic University. About the spoof in my earlier letter—I'm afraid that wasn't much of a *story*, & don't believe you'd better use it under my signature. You could quote it as from the letter of some anonymous Arkham-ite—or if you wanted to make a pseudo-story of it you could sign it with some fictitious or fantastic name & pass it off as a parody on my style. Nine readers out of ten would attribute it to Bloch. Indeed—why not sign it with the name of his synthetic magician Ludvig Prinn? That is, if you think it wise to waste space on such crap. After all, there's a good deal of serious material needing to get into print.

Thanks immensely for the transcript of Wollheim's spoof—about which he had never breathed a word. If the *Necronomicon* legend continues to grow, people will end up by believing in it & accusing me of faking when I point out the true origin of the thing! That's what happened to Machen in connexion with the legend of the "Angels of Mons"—a legend originating with his short story "The Bowmen", published soon after the battle. It must get hold of this Faraday translation—even though it is probably a fake. As you will see by the accompanying historical sketch (which please return), there is no Arabic original in existence. Other errors probably originate with the reviewer—for example, Alhazred came *after* Mohammed, & the Greek as well as the Latin text of his hellish work has been published. By the way—pardon the repetition if I've ever lent you this mock-learned outline before. *Azif* is a real word—I cribbed it out of Henley's learned notes to "Vathek". No—I won't give Wollheim away in this matter.

Sorry you missed Long & Barlow, both of whom are very interesting. Barlow nearly missed both Long & Koenig, who were away when he hit N.Y., but they got back before he left. I imagine he must have met Wollheim, since he spent most of his time with Sterling, who is quite a close friend of the young reviewer.

Glad you found the snaps interesting. No hurry about their return so long as they come back safely in the end. I can lend you better ones of Long & Derleth when Rimel returns those lent him—& of myself when I come across the now-misplaced original (taken by Barlow in '34) of the Rimel cut in *Fantasy*.

When did I find that Barlow is my 6th cousin? Well—we determined the exact degree of kinship last month, when tracing his Rathbone line in the standard Rathbone genealogy at the local Hist. Soc., but I had long known that he had some sort of a R.I. Rathbone line. The question was merely how his (not then traced) hitched on to mine. Incidentally, Bob's great-great-grandfather Dr. Barzillai Hayward (who married Hannah Rathbone, whose great-grandfather John R. [b. 1658] is also my lineal ancestor) studied at Brown University (class of 1807), only a stone's throw from this house. The old college edifice (built 1770) which he frequented is still standing in the best of condition.

As for science-fiction, & the dividing-line betwixt literature & tripe—I think the latter can be drawn with rough accuracy, even though all lines are hazy & surrounded by a broad twilight or ambiguous zone. A work is primarily literature when it presents events in a really convincing perspective—with adequate emotional preparation for each development, honest delineation of character (without inappropriate, conventionalised, or misproportioned emotional reactions, &c.), plausible developments & motivations, absence of artificially handled melodrama & synthetic "adventure" clichés, & the sort of artistic craftsmanship which uses language gracefully & fastidiously & weaves an atmosphere of logical unfolding & momentary reality about the recorded scenes & happenings. When a work departs markedly from this standard—following cheap "action" patterns suited to juvenile taste, having absurd & inappropriate emotions figuring in the pattern, harbouring rubber-stamp characters & strained motivations, & written in an ignorant, slapdash newspaper style—it certainly is *not* even approximately literature. I leave it to your common sense, & to your interpretation of the age-statistics of the "fan" element, which sort of material preponderates in the gaudy pulps on the news-stands. If there has been improvement, it is too slight to be perceptible to the adult readers of the latest science-fiction rags. Two or three persons who waded through some of the *Astoundings* containing my recent things said the magazines were hopeless. I didn't even try to read them—although I did begin a story a few months ago (I forget its name) without having the patience & martyrdom to finish it. Not everything, of course, is equally bad—& the best of the Weinbaum stories were really good. Sterling introduced me to these—in fact, he lent me a large envelope full of them. But of course the distance between all this & Wells is unbridgeable. I'm not saying that Wells hasn't modern successors—indeed, I especially mentioned S. Fowler Wright & W. Olaf Stapledon. There may be others—probably are. The only point I'm trying to make is that such reputable material seldom if ever gets into the pulp magazines. And this is not *my* guess. I don't read the damned things, except for my very desultory skimming of WT alone. I merely repeat the consensus of the few mature friends of mine who *do* try to wade through some of them.

Do I ever use 'quotations' (I think you mean *conversation or dialogue*) in my stories? Very rarely to any extent, although snatches of it occur in several. My whole theory of fantasy fiction opposes the use of dialogue on a large scale. In fantasy the *characters* are subordinate—the *massed atmosphere & phenomena* being the important things. Third-person narration—or straight narration, anyhow—is the best way to convey atmosphere. Look over the bulk of Poe's & Dunsany's tales. Human prattle generally tends to weaken the impression. When I *do* use a bit of dialogue I am always careful to make it *realistic* rather than absurdly conventional in the usual pulp fashion.

As to WT covers—the reason I deem them "trivial" is that the whole damn magazine is too *far* from perfection to have any mere added touch of lousiness count for anything. On the average, no single issue ever contains more than two stories worth reading, while *one* is still more typical. In perhaps 3 or 4 issues out of the annual twelve, there is absolutely *nothing* of merit. The "art" headings are jokes except for a few Rankin and (lately) Finlay efforts . . . . & amidst all this crap who gives a hang about the extra drop-in-the-bucket formed by a typical Brundage cover? I expect the worst in any pulp rag, & am grateful when some redeeming feature like a Klarkash-Ton or Moore or Howard story stands out as a rare exception. However—I recognise the *practical & utilitarian* side of the Brundage question, as related to the horror of stern parents or the quizzical glances of fastidious & uninitiated friends. My aunt has seen too many of these messes to notice them, but I did have to chuckle a year or so ago when a prim old lady asked to see a recently published story of mine & was confronted by the usual attireless damsel on the exterior! The good soul was obviously taken aback—though, being prepared for horrors anyhow, she bore up bravely. She's dead now—I hope the Brundage chromo wasn't a contributing cause! Incidentally—the current St. John cover is certainly a damned sight more truly *weird* than anything Ma Brundage's limited range of fancy could evoke. This chap St. John isn't at all bad—though he isn't in it with Rankin & Finlay. I had a very pleasant note from young Finlay the other day—he says he's illustrating my forthcoming "Haunter of the Dark". I'm not sure but what he'll beat them all in time. Utpatel is a fine artist, but his best stuff never appears in WT.

Yes—Yog-Sothoth doubtless has his embarrassing moments . . . like Jove, when Juno got on to some of his terrestrial diversions. As for little Nug & Yeb (only 10 feet in diameter when in their average form)—the *are* a bit destructive sometimes, though it's only a playful, good-natured roughness. I like to have the little fellows about (even though they sometimes do dissolve visitors & passers-by, & cause occasionally troublesome enquiries), for they are basically very friendly & companionable. I imagine they must be somewhat like Howard, the baby ghoul—in temperament, though not in appearance. Too bad Mr. Darrow couldn't accept Howard, since the latter seems (except for his excessive kindness toward my junk) to have rather more literary discrimination than his substitute Little Forrie. I hope you have some picturesquely ancient graveyards on the Eastern Shore, so that Howard may become familiar with the best background & traditions of his species.

No—Hamilton hasn't showed up in these parts, although that doesn't necessarily argue his non-receipt of your letter. Developments in his itinerary may well have shunted him elsewhere. I'd have been very glad to see him—for despite his latter-day hack-scribbling I'll never forget "The Monster God of Mamurth". Price has met him & likes him exceedingly.

Hope all goes well with the *Correspondent.* The field is overcrowded, but there's always a chance for a really good magazine to achieve a permanent place. Too bad all the young publishers can't band together & eliminate the waste of duplication & the handicap of a divided circulation.

Best wishes—Yrs by the Black Monolith
　　　　　—E'ch-Pi-El

P.S. Just received a snapshot from young Kuttner, which I'll add to the travelling rogues' gallery now in your possession. Just put it with the others & return it when you return them.

*Notes*

1. Anne Tillery Renshaw's *Well Bred Speech.*

[10]　[ALS]

66 College St.,
Providence, R.I.
Oct. 24, 1936.

Dear Khono-Vhah:—

　　　　　Glad everything duly arrived. Must have been a helluva job retyping all that Sup. Horr. in Lit. stuff. I had no idea you'd attempt it, but thought you'd set type from the book & notes. About Kipling—certainly it would be just as well to bring the tenses up to date.[1] Indeed, not previously doing it was a mere oversight on my part. You'll note that I *did* revise the M. R. James passages in the same way. In fixing the Kipling paragraph better do it this way: (p. 48 Col. 1 near bottom)

　　　The late Rudyard Kipling often approached it, & despite his omnipresent mannerisms handled it &c. &c &c.

This involves (a) inserting *The late* before *Rudyard,* (b) striking out *has* before *often,* (c) substituting a comma for a semicolon after *approached it,* (d) striking out *has* & a comma before *despite,* (e) changing *the* to *his* after *despite,* & (f) striking out the comma after *mannerisms.* Correction (e) is not part of the tense-changing, but merely a general improvement which occurred to me.

Thanks very much for the life subscription—which I'll duly keep quiet. Wonder who'll last the longer—the SFC or I? Later on I'll undoubtedly have more stuff for you, so that I'll more or less "airn my keep". Yes—I'll be glad to put in a good word for you the next time I write Brother Farny. I think he ought to give you some good publicity—which I believe he did to both FF & FM. If anybody of the WT group cares to finish Sup. H. in Lit he ought to know where to find it!

No need to get permission about Sup H. from Cook—he's glad to have any *Recluse* perpetuated. That goes for Wandrei's poem & all the rest. Incidentally, he might be glad of a complimentary copy of your opening issue if you can spare him one. Address: 5720 Westmoreland Place, East St. Louis, Illinois. The law about reprinting depends on what arrangements the author made with the magazine. If he reserved all but first rights, he & not the publisher has the say. I'm sure, by the way, that Wandrei would be glad to let you use "In the Grave", which is indeed very good.[2] He's home at present, so address him at 1152 Portland Ave., St. Paul, Minn. Yes—use the Necronomicon "history" if you like, though in a spoofing way revealing its really imaginary nature. I don't want to confuse any sincere folklore student by pulling a misleading hoax. Only the other day I had a letter from a San Francisco librarian asking about the Necronomicon.[3] It's really a dirty trick to add to the already great bewileringness of antiquarian scholarship!

About one of REH's argumentative letters—he always used to ask me to keep them confidential, but I don't know that he'd have objected to their posthumous publication. They'd need editing, since they are all replies to specific arguments of mine. My letters to him are in the Memorial Collection at Brownwood. I'll see how some of the epistles look when I am less desperately rushed than at present.

Commiserations on the intermittent light. I've met that trouble in the past—indeed, a case of it last year gave me the main idea for my tale "The Haunter of the Dark".

Your dreams were surely winners! I've always had very vivid & picturesque dreams, although they seldom concern contemporary persons & places. Most of them hark back to my boyhood & boyhood home. Incidentally—cars *used* to go up College St. (cable cars—the hill being too steep for trolleys), but do so no longer—a tunnel through the hill having been cut in 1914.

Price told me of the article he sent you. Glad you found it interesting. We surely had quite a time over that story, & it's hard to tell you just who the author was!

Stickney sent me sample pages of SFC, & I was most favourably impressed. I learn with great interest the history of the magazine & the society behind it. Here's wishing it a long & vigorous life! I'm sure it was quite all right to include "Mr. Ryan" among the promising young authors—for who will identify him as Ye Ed? And some assistant ed. might have written the paragraph anyhow!

As for age—I fancy different people have their best time at different ages. I think I was happiest when around 11 or 12 or 13.

About McClusky—his *new* story is as *good* as that Vampire thing was *rotten*.[4] Evidently he's like Ernst & Hamilton—a gifted writer who *chooses* to be a hack.

I'll look for "Prinn's" Ghorl Nigral yarn. Hope the process of changing from epistolary form won't be too difficult. Good luck with the conversion of your teacher. Yes—one often encounters bright youths in the science fiction field, for despite its literary limitations this kind of stuff attracts active young minds because of its subject-matter. I'll send you those other photographs as soon as I get hold of them again. Sorry the local pickings don't nourish Little Howard adequately, & hope you & he can apply suitable pressure to the necropolitan authorities. Never mind about careless text in your letters—mine are probably even worse. I never read over the scrawls I fling out—if I did I'd be swamped even worse than I am.

About the passable stories in the last few WTs—I'll jot down a few as I see them. I don't think any of them quite make the real literature class—although the Smith & Moore items, & REH's "Black Canaan", come near it. In the following list, the bracketed items *just get by* as promising or half-passable:

*April*

Face in the Wind—Jacobi
Hour of the Dragon—REH
Druidic Doom—Bloch
Rajah's Gift—EHP

*May*

Faceless God—Bloch
Child of Winds—Hamilton
Red Brain—Wandrei

*June*

Black Canaan—REH
Tel. in Lib—Derleth
Grinning Ghoul—Bloch
(Lethe—Shane)
(Harbour of Ghosts—Bardine)
Brain in Jar—Searight-Hammerstrom

*July*

Necromancy in Naat—CAS
Red Nails—REH
Lost Paradise—CLM

*Aug–Sept*

Not a damn thing!

*Oct*

Opener of the Way—Bloch
(Lost Door—Quick)

(Doom of H. of Duryea—Peirce)
Tree of Life—CLM
Secret of Kralitz—Kuttner

*Nov*
Black Hound of Death—REH
Crawling Horror—McClusky
Dark Demon—Bloch
(Brother Lucifer—Whipple)

Yes—"Witch House" was the tale whose cover design so floored the old lady. I've forgotten what the picture was, but none of Ma Brundage's creations appeal especially to Victorian gentlewomen!

Before I forget it—here's Barlow's *latest* address, annulling all others: ℅ H. M. Langworthy, 810 West 57th St. Terrace, Kansas City, Mo.

Thanks exceedingly for the loan of the picture containing your likeness. I'm glad to learn that the SFC has such a prepossessing-looking chief! Later I'll be glad to see the other photographic items which you promise for the rogues' gallery.

By the way—have you heard of a new weird magazine called *The Witches' Tales*? Several correspondents have mentioned it to me, but I haven't been able to find a copy on the local stands. Probably it's merely another rabble-tickler like *Terror & Horror*.

The advance of autumn has largely put an end to my outdoor reading & writing sessions, but I still get out for frequent rural walks. Oct. 20 & 21 were phenomenally warm—& I improved the occasion by taking quite a pedestrian trip down the east shore of the bay, & exploring a delightful wooded tract of whose existence I only recently learned. I've also lately taken to exploring a wooded hill—Neutaconkanut—on the western rim of the town (& visible in the distance from my window) whence a series of marvellous views of the outspread city & adjacent countryside & blue bay can be obtained. I had often ascended it before, but have only recently examined & appreciated the exquisitely mystical sylvan scenery—curious mounds, flower-starred meadows, & hushed hidden valleys—beyond its crest. It shall henceforth be a favourite goal of mine.

The other night I attended a meeting of the local organisation of amateur astronomers—"The Skyscrapers", which functions more or less under the auspices of Brown University—& was astonished at its degree of development. It is now contemplating the purchase of a well-known private observatory with 8″ refractor in the western part of the state. Surprisingly systematic work is done—largely in the variable star & meteor fields. At the recent meeting there was a lecture on early R.I. Astronomy, & the reflecting telescope used here in observing the transit of Venus on June 3, 1769 (& owned by the college since 1780) was exhibited.

All good wishes, & high hopes for the future of the S F C
　　　　　—Yours most sincerely—
　　　　　　　　　　　H P L

*Notes*

1. Rudyard Kipling (b. 1865) died on 18 January 1936.
2. "The Corpse Speaks," *Recluse* No. 1 (1927): 76 (as "In the Grave").
3. Stuart M. Boland. See RB 64, n. 7.
4. "The Crawling Horror" (*WT,* November 1936).


[11]　　[ANS][1]

[Postmarked Providence, RI,
18 November 1936]

Just recd. the Correspondent & must extend congratulations on its excellence. It is the most correctly printed of all the small magazines, & the quality of the paper improves its appearance. ¶ Contents extremely interesting & meritorious. I like the delicate & elusive wistfulness of your "Lost Chord". Williamson's article is very ably written, & your partner's story has an ingenious & original idea. The Keller tale would make a notable psychological document if less clumsily written. He ought to revise & re-cast it. Too bad you didn't cut out the false word "thusly" & correct the bad spelling of impostor.[2] ¶ And before I forget it, let me make an apology concerning my verses "Homecoming". The other day, in going over my files, I found I had used this piece in the old *Fantasy Fan*—though I firmly believed it was unpublished when I let you have it. Rest assured that I'll be doubly & triply careful about any further contributions! ¶ Again, congratulations & best wishes. Yrs sincerely, H P L

*Notes*

1. Drinking Fountain, Roger Williams Park, Providence, R. I.
2. Willis Conover (as Joseph Allan Ryan), "The Lost Chord" (25–26); David H. Keller, "The Perpetural Honeymoon" (4–13); Jack Williamson, "Psychology and Characterization" (18–22); and Robert A. Madle and Corwin F. Stickney, "Brain, the Creator" (14–17).


[12]　　[ALS]

The Hilltop Mausoleum
　　—Dec. 4, 1936

Dear Khono-Vhah:—

　　　　Glad you liked "Pickman's Model". Yes—the College St. house mentioned in the "Haunter" is #66. All the geographical touches are literally accurate except for some details anent the church. Right at this moment I'm looking westward at the dim slope of Federal Hill & more or less shuddering at the darkly-outlined church tower. (Actually, the steeple was struck by lightning & taken down over a year ago).

Finlay's werewolf was surely splendid—indeed, I singled it out to mention to him as especially striking.[1] I never saw the *transition* stage so well depicted before. Yes—Bloch draws as well as writes—at least, he used to. Some of his crayon-coloured horrors would send even Little Howard back to his burrow trembling.

Glad to hear of SFC plans. I'll surely mention my liking for the magazine the next time I write Satrap Pharnabazus. Glad he's already giving you favourable mention. I'm interested to hear of the features scheduled, & really think you'll lead all your legion of rivals in the end. Glad Price is coöperating. He's a great chap indeed—I met him in New Orleans in '32, & again here in '33, as perhaps you know. Glad your prejudice has abated. He writes anything that will sell, & his pot-boilers are not to be regarded as parts of his personality at all. I never saw one of his bawdy tales. His real metier is the adventurous Orientale.

Well—you started something when you spoke of a summary of the earlier parts of "Sup. Hor. in Lit."! Look at the enclosed! I looked at the question all ways, & tried to decide what the best course was. First, how many of your clientele would be likely to have seen the old FF? Hornig had a circulation of only 60, & even allowing for free copies & passing-around, not more than 100 to 150 persons can ever have read it. Now of this 100 or 150—dating between October '33 & February '35—how many are likely to be represented on your list? The regular gang—Long, Wandrei, Price, &c.—don't count anyhow, since they've read the whole thing in *The Recluse.* How many, then, who have read *only* the FF instalments, are likely to be among those to see the resumed article? Enough, let us say, to make it advisable for you not to go back to the beginning & print the whole thing over. But how about the vast majority who know nothing about the article? Here's the rub! For one who has never seen it before, the latter half alone does look damned incomplete. But what good will a merely nominal skeleton synopsis do? What advantage has a brief, uninformative paragraph over nothing at all? A person either *has or hasn't* seen the FF instalments. If he *has,* he doesn't want *any* synopsis. If he *hasn't,* he won't get much good from anything not detailed enough to round out a picture which will match well with that of the coming sections. Well, in the end I prepared this condensation, which runs to about 2500 words. It is short enough not to set the article back more than 2 or 3 instalments, but long enough to work the reader into the spirit of the theme, give him some idea of what it's all about, indicate the most important works to be read in the given section of the field, & prepare him to go on with the new sections without any sense of lapse or interruption. It isn't as good as the equivalent full text would be, but it's the shortest thing (or so it seems to me) that's in any way better than nothing. In any case, I prepared it, and am sending it along for any fate you may select. But if you don't want it, you might send it back for filing—since it might be good to lend some time.[2] I don't know just how long you mean to have your instalments, or just how much you would object to stringing out the serial to the extent of this extra 2500 words. I leave it all to you. If you preferred to have no actual summary but merely a table of important weird books & stories covering the equivalent field we might discuss that. The duality of the situation—the fact that a few of your readers will have read the early parts while most will not have—is indeed perplexing. But to my mind the 2500-word summary is the best compromise. It makes the article reasonably complete for the new reader—who is in the majority—yet does not set the whole thing back for the old reader as badly as would the reprinting of the complete early text. Anyhow, it's up to you. I'm interested to hear of your school address on horror-fiction, & of the service afforded by the article. You are evidently becoming quite a local authority on the bizarre—but don't be too ready to flatter us WT hacks by coupling our names with the classics!

Your recent dream was surely vivid & interesting, & the subsequent verses form a vigorous reflection. That basic idea of a city or region wiped out for its hellish misdeeds is a perennially useful one, & has figured in mythology & literature from the earliest ages down. Dunsany's "Fall of Babbulkund" is a good modern embodiment. Your verses show considerable metrical aptitude, & will doubtless be still better after revision. If you deal much with verse, it would pay you to study some of the many excellent treatises on the subject. You might read Brander Matthews' "A Study of Versification"—obtainable at any library—or send for an excellent recent manual, "How to Revise Your Own Poetry", by Anne Hamilton (obtainable from the author, 6413 W. 6th St., Los Angeles, Cal.—I don't know the price), which many clients of mine have found useful. Another very useful aid is George E. Teter's booklet "An Introduction to Some Elements of Poetry", obtainable for 25¢ postpaid from M. W. Moe, 1870 West Wisconsin Ave., Milwaukee, Wis.

Your potential story plot—about the evil sculptor & his dire end—certainly has possibilities, & I hope you can arrange for its eventual development, collaboratively or otherwise. I myself could hardly undertake it—for I have learned from long experience that collaboration is *infinitely harder* than original writing. Unless I have perfect freedom in ideas & style alike, I am hopelessly handicapped—and I see no use in making things harder for myself when I'm already strained to the breaking-point. In the past I have allowed myself to be persuaded into a few collaborative ventures—to please the other guy—but the results have never been satisfactory. Now I am compelled by sheer necessity to call a halt. I have more ideas of my own than I have time to develop, & what little time & energy I *can* spare must go into these. Collaboration in serious writing does not pay anybody who has an adequate stock of original ideas. The only ones for whom it is at all profitable are the commercial formula-experts who can effortlessly adapt any idea to a saleable hack framework.

With them it is a different kind of game—but I have none of their mechanical skill. Your best bets for collaborative aid are young Bloch & Kuttner, whose pulp work has given them much practice in technical manipulation. Other possibilities are Rimel & Petaja, both still more or less in the amateur stage. Meanwhile don't forget that a single-handed development on your own part wouldn't be a bad idea. The best way to acquire the various twists of technique & solve the various problems of narration is by actual practice.

Congratulations on securing the darkly potent Monstro Ligriv as an illustrator! I'm sorry, though, that the reproduction of his drawings will prove costly. About that autograph idea (which Price had mentioned)—let me thank you for the compliment of regarding my obscure scrawl as possessing value![3] Really, the request gives one a momentary illusion of importance! I don't think you'll get very high prices for my rooster-scratchings—except on a cheque, where they can appear all too seldom—but if you want to try the game, don't let me discourage you! Is the enclosed what you want? If not, let me know & give closer specifications, & I'll prepare another set. And if you ever dispose of this batch I'll prepare you as many more as you like. Bless my soul, but autographs (when not mixed up with the responsibilities of legal documents) are the easiest of all commodities to create!

Yes—I certainly hate to see winter come. We had a snowfall here as early as Nov. 24. As for being outdoors—hell! I'm never under a roof on any good summer afternoon. I always take my work in a black bag & make for some congenial region. Congratulations, by the way, on your recent expedition with its osseous loot. Hope you'll get a complete skull next time! Our similar deposits up here are pretty well worked out.

As for mail—5 to 10 epistles is perhaps the daily average hereabouts. The trouble is that many of them require research, work, or extended argumentative replies. I must take drastic steps toward reducing this flood, & cutting down responsibilities generally.

Glad to hear news of Little Howard, & to learn that he has at last secured some really worthy & congenial associates of his own age. You'll find the best class of ghouls in the more ancient churchyards. The unmasking of the caretaker doubtless involved a good deal of a shock, but I'm glad that a reasonably workable adjustment has been effected. Accept my best wishes for the local Guild chapter's drive against these sullen & intractable older feasters of the commoner cemeteries! ¶ Well—I hope I haven't overlooked too many points. Let me know what you think of the enclosed. ¶ All good wishes—Yrs by the Ghorl Nigral—Abdul Alhazred

P.S. Thanks for the cliché article, which I return.[4] It will surely help to liven up my literary style! I enjoyed it particularly because one of my recent jobs involved the compilation of a list of stock phrases. I wish I'd had this article then!

Just saw new WT. Finlay's illustration for my "Thing on the Doorstep" is really splendid! Glad to note Wright's allusion to SFC in the Eyrie.

My "Pickman's Model" is going to be reprinted again—in England, in a "Not at Night" omnibus.

[*Separate note:*] Here's something Sultan Malik sent for my censorship. I'm not doing much to it—merely bringing it in line with precise facts. He has me an inch too short, & hasn't seen me since my hair has done most of its greying. I looked perceptibly younger in '33.

Best holiday wishes

—E'ch-Pi-El

[*Enclosures:* "H. P. Lovecraft: Viewed by E. Hoffmann Price" and "Supernatural Horror in Literature" (summary of preceding parts published in *The Fantasy Fan*).]

*Notes*

1. HPL refers to Virgil Finlay's illustration for "The Woman at Loon Point" by August Derleth and Mark Schorer (*WT,* December 1936).

2. See RB 64, n. 9.

3. WC had suggested that HPL sign his name several times on a sheet of paper, so that *SFC* could sell the autographs as a way of raising money. See *LAL* 142.

4. WC had sent HPL a clipping of Frank Sullivan's "The Cliché Expert Takes the Stand" (*Reader's Digest* 27 (November 1935): 65–66; condensed from *New Yorker,* 31 August 1935).

[13]   [ANS]

[24 December] 1936

Greetings—& a thousand thanks for the delightful mortuary relique! It arrived, thanks to the careful packing, in what was probably very much its condition when shipped—the upper part in two large & joinable sections, a third large section, & a sizeable array of smaller fragments. I shall have an interesting time trying to piece the latter together—a sort of picture puzzle de luxe—& wish I had the aid of a clever reconstructive expert like Barlow . . . who last summer completely reassembled & restored a cherished Chinese vase which I broke. This will certainly form a most delightful & appropriate embellishment for my ghoulish lair, & I surely appreciate your thoughtfulness in sending it. I presume you were assisted by Howard the Baby Ghoul in excavating it—& must congratulate him on his keen scent for good specimens! ¶ Have just finished decorating a Christmas tree. ¶ Season's best wishes— E'ch-Pi-El.

[14]  [ALS]

Hellish Plateau of Leng
—Jany. 10, 1937.

Dear Khono-Vhah:—

Yours of Dec. 26 arrived while I was still admiring, with all the zest of fresh acquisition, the gruesome loot of Howard the Infant Ghoul. Don't worry about the fractures—I'm sure a little Duco cement will work wonders when the proper skill is applied. Certainly, Chief Thunder-Under-the-Ground isn't going into any ash-can, by a long shot! As for one of the Chief's legs—thanks for the idea of sending it, although the dome itself forms a pretty generous quota. If any other logical claimants exist, you might supply them in preference. Otherwise, I'm sure I'd keenly appreciate such a monument of mortality at some time when its sending might prove convenient. I shall keep a careful watch on the Chief's cranium, & will let you know of any curious agitations occasioned by resentment at the various indignities accorded his disjecta membra. At the moment, he seems singularly—perhaps deceptively—peaceful. Meanwhile let me thank you afresh for what is certainly my most distinctive Yuletide gift of recent years![1]

Glad you like "The Thing on the Doorstep"—although, as a critic, I must protest (logically rather than modestly) against your flatteringly high valuation of it. In actual truth, I think it has a sort of middle rating. It is better than my "Haunter of the Dark", but not so good as my "Colour out of Space". Nor is it even in the running with such standard weird masterpieces as Machen's "The White People", Blackwood's "Willows", Poe's "House of Usher", Shiel's "House of Sounds", & dozens of others I could name. Don't get your standards mixed. Some of my stuff—and that of other W T hacks—may be as good as the *poorer* work of Blackwood & the other big-timers, since all weird writers seem to be singularly uneven. But nobody in the W T group has ever approached the *best* work of the standard fantaisistes. To compare any of my stuff with Machen's "Hill of Dreams" or Blackwood's "Incredible Adventures" or Dunsany's "Bethmoora" or M. R. James's "Count Magnus" or Poe's "Ligeia" would be simply to subvert the soundest principles of criticism. It is safe to say that Blackwood is the greatest living weirdist despite vast unevenness & a poor prose style. Machen, with an incomparably superior style, comes next. Dunsany—with the greatest style of all, could perhaps top them all if he would stick to the relatively serious vein manifest in "A Dreamer's Tales", "Time & the Gods", & "The Sword of Welleran". About the name "Pickman"—no, I don't know any bearer of it, but it is especially common in *Salem*, which as you know is the vague prototype of my "Arkham". In all my tales I try to be very realistic, using surnames typical of the regions involved. Thus in a Charleston tale I would have Izards, Pinckneys, Rhetts, Manigaults, Ravenels, Mozÿcks, &c.—in a St. Augustine tale Seguis,

Pappys, Masterses, Sanchez's, Genovars, etc.—and so on. If you've ever seen my "Shunned House", you will have noticed the local Providence names.

I'm vastly interested to learn of your plans for the SFC—its consolidation with FM, its increasingly large editions, & its publication of the *entire* "Sup. Horror in Lit." Regarding the latter idea—while to the old FF readers it may seem like duplicating a lot of ground, I can easily grasp your point of view. After all, the microscopic FF clientele of from 3½ to 2 years ago doesn't count for much in relation to the public at which the SFC–FM will be aimed—so that this intermediate printing scarcely means more today than the original *Recluse* printing of 1927. I'm sure *I'll* be glad enough to see the first half repeated—since the misprinted FF version was in many places more misleading than illuminating. Whether you'll want to use the condensed synopsis later, will perhaps depend upon circumstances. At any rate, there's perhaps no harm in keeping it on file. If you do use it, though, you'll want to trim it down (or piece it out) to end at the logical place instead of in the middle of a chapter as determined by the FF's chance moment of suspension. Or I might finish the summary as you suggest. About the text of this synopsis—which was carelessly typed & of which there is no carbon—the following renderings of the points you question are correct: (1) *fantaisiste;* (2) *Hanns Heinz Ewers;* (3) *Gustav Meyrink's.* That latter name was given in caps in the margin merely to elucidate a rendering originally somewhat illegible (not misspelled). About the usage to follow—I never insist on any particular spelling except that I detest the cheap extremes of ultra-modern faddism such as *"thru", "medieval", "sulfur", "prolog"* &c. &c. &c. (ugh!) My spelling is simply that of the majority of books in my library—of all dates, & printed on both sides of the Atlantic. It is what I regard as the norm or most widely diffused standard of the Anglo-Saxon world, without modernisms or localisms. About following the style sheet of *The Recluse* in every detail—I fancy it might be better to let me go over each instalment myself before printing . . . unless you can arrange to avoid copying & print directly from the text. While I'm too busy to attempt any wholesale revision of the treatise, there are some extravagances & vagaries of a decade ago that I wouldn't mind correcting if I had the chance (indeed, I *did* tone them down in the synopsis); hence if you could send the text of each instalment in double-spaced typing, I could improve it considerably in spots . . . . making my corrections very neat & legible wherever they might have to occur. There's one point of usage which I'd like to change all through the text—this being the capitalisation of unimportant words (articles, conjunctions, prepositions, &c.) in quoted titles. For example, the style-sheet of the *Recluse* version would say *The House And The Brain,* whereas I now believe that *The House and the Brain* forms a preferable usage. With your careful eye for detail, you might be able to attend to this point yourself—but I'd just as soon undertake the responsibility. Incidentally, I'm not sure that the *Recluse* text is entirely free from misprints & mis-punctuation. Knowing how Ruppert would mangle the thing anyway, I didn't bother about this point during the former reprinting; but in your careful version it would be a shame to perpetuate yesteryear's errors. This is another thing which I could straighten out if I saw the text of each instalment in advance. But follow whatever policy you find most practicable and convenient. In any case we may be assured of a text infinitely better than the mixed-up & boner-strewn FF version! That article really should be thoroughly overhauled—expanded, reproportioned, & rewritten—but I'm never likely to have time for such a process.

Your general programme for SFC–FM is surely ambitious enough, & I hope sincerely that the essential points may duly materialise. The matter of what title to use, & how to number the issues, is something which you & Stickney ought to debate at considerable length, & after getting a symposium of opinions from old-time fans. FM is an old & established sheet as "fan mags" go, & its tradition is of course an asset. On the other hand, the SFC represents something very different & of much higher grade; so that you might not wish a label with different implications. If you *do* let the FM name predominate (or even if you don't), the question of *numeration* also deserves debate. The clean-cut definiteness of *Vol. I No. 1* has certain advantages—yet there are other advantages in figures which imply a solidly established quality. Many magazines, when they absorb others, are careful to choose the *oldest* as a basis for their reckoning, so that they may lay claim to a long continuous ancestry. How really fair this is when great changes of policy are involved, would require quite a delicate bit of judgment. Presumably, the future SFC–FM won't be much like the *Science Fiction Digest* of September 1932—yet you will, by the absorption of FM, acquire the legal & ethical right to trace back to that. With some readers, a 4½-year record would count considerably. Others would prefer a fresh start. How to decide between these alternatives surely is some job. I'd hate to have the responsibility of casting a vote!

The contemplated changes in material seem to me all in the right direction. I didn't even try to read "The Great Illusion", but all of these composite stunt stories (including the one I contributed to) are just so much unalloyed tripe.[2] Any decrease in emphasis on hack formula fiction, together with any corresponding increase in emphasis on really serious work (reviews of reputable weird novels & collections, bibliographies of standard fantastic material, critical or other essays on the genuine fantastic literary artists of the past, resurrection of forgotten or obscure authors & books [W. H. Hodgson—Shiel's "House of Sounds", &c.], accounts of fantastic geniuses in pictorial, sculptural, & musical fields, tracing of bizarre elements in standard general literature, &c. &c. &c.) is greatly to be welcomed; although I suppose you couldn't pass over the magazine crap entirely without losing ¾ of your potential subscribers. Reprints of any of the *good* weird or (if any) science material in magazines would be an excellent idea—& Price's early stuff could scarcely be excelled for the purpose. See if you could get Quinn's "Phantom Farmhouse"—which to my mind is much better than his "House of Horror".[3] Notices of works on dark folklore (like Summers', Miss Murray's, &c.), together with articles on various superstitions, would always be acceptable—as would be a department on such developments in actual human knowledge (astronomy, physics, psychology, geology, geography, exploration, anthropology, archaeology, history, &c.) which carry fantastic implications. That is—discussions of whether meteorites could carry living bacteria, accounts of Prof. Rhine's telepathic experiments at Duke University, reports of theories affecting our concepts of the universe or of conditions on other planets, reports of undersea surveys, hypotheses touching our mental pictures of the earth's geological past, new light on prehistoric (or early historic) civilisations, &c. &c. &c. A whole department of mythology & folklore would be desirable—bringing in, among other things, all the pre-human, root-race, & lost-continent stuff of the theosophists. Price & Klarkash-Ton could give you endless data in that line. Another department might well handle scientific fakery, charlatanism, & delusion—Charles Fort stuff, freak religions like the cult of Koresh,[4] astrology & alchemy (though these belong also in folklore), & all the Atlantis, Lemuria, & Mu theories pedalled by fanatics (sincere or otherwise) like Le Plongeon, Ignatius Donnelly, Lewis Spence, & Col. James Churchward. In the field of scientific prophecy, Wells, J. B. S. Haldane, the Huxleys, & others furnish enough material for discussion. Indeed, there could never be any trouble in finding enough material for a small fantasy magazine without resorting to the exploitation of pulpdom's trash & trivialities. You could well afford to cut cinema material down to a minimum, since virtually all so-called weird films are simply infantile nonsense. The two or three I've yawned through have cured me of all desire to see any more. Of course there has never been any real criticism or adult comment on such things in the "fan mags". In reality, all that the cinema has ever offered in the way of valuable weird effects are certain *scenic & atmospheric settings* (to be regarded only as momentary visual spectacles) occurring either in the course of predominantly non-weird films or as parts of utterly puerile pseudo-weird shockers. The Wells film "Things to Come"[5] may have certain real merits, but I haven't seen it. Indeed, I scarcely see more than half a dozen cinema shows in the course of an average year. Here's hoping Fearn will show some discrimination. Well—in general, I wish your venture the very best of luck all around. Prospects surely are favourable—with your high standards, competent accuracy, & acquisition of the FM tradition all working together. You have every chance to seize & maintain the lead among fantasy fan publications.

As for Little Forrie, the demon fanscicinemattoid & lett-eyrieonant—bless my soul, but I'm sure he must be a bright & delightful kid underneath the surface! He has merely been carrying a bit too much ego & exhibitionism for his years, & is even now apparently mellowing down into something very different from the enfant terrible of three years ago. He will never, in all probability, be a literary enthusiast or connoisseur—but that's not saying he isn't a pleasant chap, & one who will probably succeed in some chosen field like advertising, press-agenting, salesmanship, promotion, & so on. I'm no enemy of his—& indeed would probably chat cordially with him if I met him. The other day someone was suggesting that Little Effjay ought to be sat on again, because of his verbal antics & constant Esperanto-pushing; but I replied that I saw no reason whatever for bothering him. There's no harm in his rattling on concerning his special interests—& so long as he doesn't attack serious writers, it doesn't hurt anybody to let him see his name in print (or hectograph) as often as he likes. Live & let live. My campaign of '33–'34 against him was over a single definite issue—the merit of Klarkash-Ton's work, which he had wantonly & destructively attacked. Now that he isn't doing any harm (on the contrary, he's providing useful service with his magazine-back-number business), I haven't a thing in the world against him. Long may he wave! Incidentally—I surely won't repeat your critical estimate of his film "reviews"!

About the "Rats"—most certainly it's all right for Bordley[6] to sub-lend it to you, since I'm sure you'll exercise due care concerning the preservation of this last remaining copy. No hurry at all—but shoot it back to me when you're through with it. This story was rather well liked in its day, although I can't get highly enthusiastic about it. If you'd like to see more of my old junk, I'll send you a list of all my tales—apart from collaborated or repudiated items—& you can check off those you haven't read. I could then lend you, a few at a time, such of the stories as I possess in transmissible form. I am constantly receiving requests for such loans, & have worn out copy after copy of my tales in so doing. Re-copying is rather more than I can attempt; but I sometimes strike bargains whereby I get fresh copies typed, while I always strive to get extras when my old things are reprinted. Now that I see how heavy & steady the borrowing is, I am trying to get more copies of each story published—& have secured five each of "The Haunter" & the "Thing" from Wright, in exchange for the privilege of reprinting tales to which I hold rights. I had three copies of both of my *Astounding* items, but last month a slovenly borrower so nearly ruined "The Shadow Out of Time" with grease spots & pencil marks that I believe I'll have to get another if they're still on sale. I'm glad I spotted the qualities of this bird before lending any valuable books or recommending that Koenig do so!

Hope your collaboration project will work. You'll find either Herr Ludvig or Khut-N'hah an able & conscientious fellow-worker. Glad Price's article duly reached you—but there's no hurry about publishing such a thing in view of the fact that another writeup of the same old coot occurred in FM less than two years ago. As for a title—"The Sage" sounds a bit flattering, so why not say "The Hermit" or "The Ghoul" or "The Patriarch" or something less unmerited?[7] However—you're free to do your own choosing. Williamson on Hamilton would make quite a popular item, as would the reverse. Sultan Malik could do a splendid one on the late REH if he chose—& I hope he will choose before long. He's the only one of the group who ever met good old Two-Gun in person. Barlow (810 W. 57th St. Terrace, Kansas City, Mo.) could give Miss Moore a writeup. So far as I know, he's the only one of us who has ever seen her. Wandrei could do Derleth, & vice versa. Rimel is now—at long distance—preparing an article on Long for *The Phantagraph*. Altogether, you'll find no shortage in brief personal sketches of the sort you wish.

Glad Prinn has furnished some good material on weird music. His article ought to be excellent, since he is quite a connoisseur on the subject & has recently acquired a large number of macabre phonograph records. Monstro Ligriv's autobiography will form another valuable asset. I was glad to see his finely-rendered cover on the Feb. WT, & hope he will continue to dominate the magazine. The contents of SFC–FM #1 in general would seem to promise excellent balance, & I hope that Herr Dr. Prof. Mülder's startling "Ghorl Nigral" sequel will be ready to start in that issue. I didn't realise that this savant was still living—& hope he will be after the publication of his revelations, despite Yog-Sothoth's well-known vindictive tendencies. I'd be interested to learn his address—not the old Heidelberg one, of course, since it goes without saying that the Nazis must have exiled anybody with his type of scholastic & literary activity! Well—let us hope that he will not share the fate of his too-audacious compatriot Herr Dr. Friedrich-Wilhelm von Junzt nearly a century ago! One pays a penalty for the knowledge which goes into compilations like the "Ghorl Nigral"!

Glad the autographs proved acceptable—though I fear the market for such may not turn out to be quite as favourable as you anticipate. Let me know if you ever need any more—& meanwhile congratulations on the response from other sources. Give my regards to Hamilton, & tell him I hope he can make Providence—& #66 on the Ancient Hill—the next time he passes through New England. I may not be able to give him a skull, but I can show him a pretty ghoulish hidden churchyard with interments dating back to 1723.

I dropped your friend Saari the encouraging message you requested . . . even though your letter contained my first intimation of the gifted young gentleman's existence.[8] Just to make the thing seem more genuine (I must have the makings of a first-rate hypocrite in me!), I used a local picture postcard—which surely must have banished all suspicion of Cantabrigian prompting! Genuinely, though, I'm sure from your description that Saari must be a nice chap, & I sincerely hope he *will* succeed. I must ask Wandrei to look him up.

Congratulations on your 16th natal day! I really thought you were older—though the achievements of youngsters like Stickney, Sterling, et al., ought to have shown me that the present generation is getting off to an early start. It seems to me there weren't so many bright youths in my day. I'd hate to let you see the kiddish hectographed paper I was publishing when I was your age. I had made print just before my 16th birthday—with some astronomical articles—but oddly enough, I kept right on with my painfully juvenile magazine enterprise for at least a year. My fiction of that period was unspeakably naïve & pompous. When I was 18 I dumped most of it—saving, indeed, only two specimens . . . "The Alchemist" & "The Beast in the Cave". The latter dates from my 15th year, & begins like this: "The horrible conclusion which had gradually been obtruding itself upon my confused yet reluctant consciousness had now become an awful certainty. I was lost—hopelessly, irrecoverably lost—in the vast & labyrinthine recesses of the Mammoth Cave."[9]

Hope you'll investigate the subject of verse technique some time—you'd undoubtedly enjoy a mastery of it. I think you could procure that Matthews book at the public library. Another excellent manual is Gummere's "Handbook of Poetics".

You surely are quite a dreamer—and it's curious (to me) how quickly your new experiences & correspondents get translated into visions. Hope I succeeded in saving you & Herr Ludvig on that cliff—it would be a pity for two such promising celebrities to be lost in 'the unreverberate blackness of the abyss'![10] My own dreams usually go back very far in time, & it takes a long while for any new experience or scene or acquaintance to get worked into them. At least ¾ of them are laid at my birthplace, where I haven't lived since 1904, & involve those who were living in those days. But the real scenes frequently merge into unknown & fantastic realms, & include landscapes & architectural vistas which could scarcely be on this planet. At times I also have *historical* dreams—with a setting in various remote periods. Occasionally—but not often—a dream of mine forms a usable fictional plot. Such was the genesis of "The Statement of Randolph Carter". Many of my "Fungi from Yuggoth" are actual dreams versified.

I'm interested to hear that Bordley is an artist, & hope you can use his talent advantageously in FM. I knew he was clever with *makeup,* since he lent me several snapshots of himself in extremely vivid & fantastic disguises. Yes—I'd like to see his idea of "Pickman's Model" some time—& see whether it tallies with mine or with Rankin's or with Barlow's—all different. Haven't seen the new *Life*—indeed, I don't believe I've seen any copy of the magazine for 30 years. I don't follow the periodical press very closely, save for *Harpers* & a few other solid old-timers.

Glad the first half of the winter proved mild along the Eastern Shore. We haven't had the early & severe winter that was predicted—at least, not so far. Hope the coming weeks won't afford a contrast. Klarkash-Ton reports intense cold out in California.

All good wishes, & thanks again for the monument of mortality—Yrs by the Elder Sign—E'ch-Pi-El

*Notes*

1. See RB 66, p. 183.

2. "The Great Illusion," *Fantasy Magazine* 6, No. 4 (September 1936). A composite story by Eando Binder, Jack Williamson, Edmond Hamilton, Raymond Z. Gallun, and John Russell Fearn. HPL participated in a similar round-robin tale, "The Challenge from Beyond."

3. Seabury Quinn, "The Phantom Farmhouse" (*WT,* October 1923; rpt. March 1929); "The House of Horror" (*WT,* July 1926).

4. Cyrus Teed (1839–1908) founded the Entero (Florida) Hollow Earth cult, taking for himself the name Koresh.

5. RB 61, n. 2.

6. [Thomas] Kemp Bordley, a mutual friend about whom little is known.

7. Price's article "H. P. Lovecraft: Viewed by E. Hoffmann Price" was in fact published as "The Sage of College Street," *Amateur Correspondent* 2, No. 1 (May–June 1937): 6–7.

8. WC had asked HPL to send congratulations to Oliver E. Saari for the sale of his first story to *Astounding Stories* ("The Stellar Exodus" in the February 1937 issue).

9. Here WC typed the entire opening of the story with spaces between every letter, to mimic HPL's deliberate printing of the text.

10. The last line of Dunsany's "The Probable Adventure of the Three Literary Men."


[15]   [ANS][1]

[Postmarked Providence, RI,
11 January 1937]

P.S. to my letter—just recd. second S F C, & am delighted with its trim & tasteful aspect. Contents well-balanced, too. There has surely been no falling-down after #1. Keep it up! Finlay's cover decoration is splendid, & reproduced very clearly. ¶ Also received last old-regime issue of F M with announcement of the coming consolidation.

All good wishes

———E'ch-Pi-El


*Notes*

1. *Front:* No picture.


[16]   [ANS][1]

[Postmarked Providence, RI,
12 January 1937]

P.S.'s thick & fast! Just recd. your card—& you'll find some of the points touched on in my letter . . . including that of the capitalisation of titles. As I've said, the *Recluse* text certainly contains many slips—& I think you'd better send me the double-spaced typed copy of each instalment for a final going-over before publication. ¶ About *cabbalism*—the double-b spelling has always been at least *permissible* (see Stormonth &c.), & I prefer it in cases where the actual superstition of the *kabbalah* is involved. If I were using a word of this type in an ordinary metaphorical sense—as when referring to some unknown mysterious design as a *cabalistic* symbol—I'd follow the single-b fashion; but when considering the actual superstition of the kabbalah or cabbala I think the more closely etymological form is preferable. The matter is not important, & if you prefer the more usual single-b form I have no objection to its use. It is undeniably the more traditional—following the French *cabalisme* &c.—through which it entered the English language. However, the edition of the Encyclopaedia Britannica (9th) which I have not only prefers *cabbalism* to *cabalism*, but prefers *Kabbalism* to either. I really think it is desirable to distinguish the special literal use of the word from its common figurative use. But do as you like—Best wishes—H P L

*Notes*

1. *Front:* No picture.

[17]   [ALS]

Pharos of Leng—
—Jany. 31, 1937.

Dear Khono-Vhah:—
            Being half down with some cursed variant of grippe or what-the-devil, I have just about the strength of a wet rag, & shall hardly be able to do justice to your recent epistle. I am, however, making an effort to get the Sup. Horr. in Lit. text back to you in good season. At first I meant to send only the first section, but later thought I'd get it all out of the way. I didn't change as much as I expected—words here & there, a bad punctuation style where dates follow titles of stories, a boner regarding "The Golem", & a bit of over-florid writing in the Poe chapter. To explain that Golem business I must confess that when I wrote the treatise I hadn't read the novel. I had seen the cinema version, & thought it was faithful to the original—but when I came to read the book only a year ago . . . Holy Yuggoth! The film had nothing of the novel save the mere title & the Prague ghetto setting—indeed, in the book the Golem-monster never appeared at all, but merely lurked in the background as a shadowy symbol. That was one on the old man! I ought to have corrected this before sending you the *Recluse*—but jest nachelly overlooked it. Probably the later sections will need more changes, for I think I can recall passages with lots of flourishes which would bear ironing out. We shall see—there surely being no hurry about the matter! By the way—are you or *The Recluse* (my copy is lent to Finlay) to blame for the repeated rendering of *didacticism* as *"didactism"*? Anyhow, I've straightened the matter out. And I'm adhering to a 2-b *cabbalism*, since virtually all uses of the word in the text seem to involve the actual superstition of the *Kabbalah*.
      Thanks tremendously for the snapshots, which I am adding to the travelling gallery with the utmost pleasure. You & Stickney surely make a prepossessing editorial team, & I'm sure the more serious infant ghoul isn't formidable enough to do really permanent petrifying among the case-hardened members of

the weird fan circle. Of course, if the question were one of circulation amongst the general lay public, more caution might be advisable. Speaking of grim visages—here at last is the horrific original of that flattering linoleum cut. Note the proboscidian effect—my only local rival in that field being the elephant at Roger Williams Park. Keep this curio if it's of any use—I ordered 6 prints from Barlow. It is—gawd help me—actually a pretty good likeness—the wear & tear of the intervening 2½ years having done their aging in a subtler way than so sketchy & Rembrandtesque a snap could well record. Incidentally—here once more is that group picture which you sent me & which I returned. This time it came from Finlay—in the battered state which you will observe & lament. The accompanying design is certainly tremendously clever.

And now let me advert to that incredible document on which you wasted so much hard copying labour, & which stares at me with so alien an air across the gulf of 13 long years![1] Hell, no—I had no copy of the thing, & probably forgot it within a year of the time I wrote it. Where on earth did you ever run across that chap Henneberger? Don't let him rope you into any professional proposition, for although he means well his ventures always explode & leave not only himself but his colleagues holding the proverbial bag. If you don't believe me, ask Long!

Well—about that damn letter—I gape with mortification at its egotistical smugness, florid purple passages, ostentatious exhibitionism, ponderous jauntiness, & general callowness. It wouldn't be so bad if I had written it at 13 or 23—but at *33!* What a complacent, self-assured, egocentric jackass I was in those days! All that gabble about the shaping & development of—the world's most perfect cipher! Well—the excuse, if any, is this: that the invalidism & seclusion of my earlier years had left me, at 33, as naive & inexperienced & unused to dealings with the world as most are at 17 or 18. As you see by the letter, I had only just burst out of a shell of retirement, & was finding the external world as novel & fascinating as a kid finds it. I was drunk with a sense of expansion, as it were—fascinated by new scenes (I'd just been to New Hampshire, Salem, Marblehead, New York, & Cleveland for the first time) & allured by the will o' the wisp of literary success (first WT placements the year before—& the future easily imagined)—so that my whole psychology was that of a belated adolescence, with the usual egotism, pompous writing, jauntiness, & show-off tendencies of the callow. It is hard for me to recapture the mood of that far-off age—but very obviously, I thought I was quite a guy. Probably—in fact, certainly—I had a better time then than I have now . . . but only because I didn't realise what a vacuous, snobbish, & complacent ass I was. Well—the one consolation is that I'm not quite as effervescently sappy a dub in '37 as I was in '24. I may be bad enough now—but at least, the years have been able to focus my sense of proportion a bit, so that I would scarcely be capable of *quite* such an orgy of blah as this nauseous spouting which the past has just yielded up. I groan to think of the energy you have wasted in typing this interminable carload of slop! Nevertheless I'm extremely grateful for the copy—which brings back the past very vividly, & helps to reconcile me to the present. I shall keep in on file as a horrible example. There are some evident mistakes in the text—places where the absence of connective words is plainly manifest—but I may have made these myself as I typed the damn thing. The place you have marked as doubtful—where I speak of *scientific leanings* [i.e. *inclinations*]— is correct so far as I can see. "Scientific *learnings?*" would be a meaningless & unidiomatic phrase, whereas *leanings* is perfectly idiomatic. I don't see why this phrase should have appeared doubtful. As for the "long ſ"[2]—it is curious that you should associate this with a *lisp*. No other mode of representing a nonterminal lower-case S existed till about 1800, & I always prefer a book with the long ſ to one without it. I learned the art of versification from such a book (we had dozens of them in a spectrally fascinating 3d story room without windows called the "trunk room", which I used to visit by the hour by candle-light), & can't yet feel perfectly at home with modern short-s volumes. I suppose you youngsters associate the long ſ with the lower-case *f,* forgetting that the cross-bar does not extend to the right of the upright stroke. In handwriting (where, by the way, the long ſ was not as universal as in print save as the first of a double-s), the long ſ was distinguished from the *f* by the fact that the lower loop was toward the left instead of toward the right. By the way—in my old letter did I try to represent the long ſ with a plain lower-case f, or did I take pains to scratch out the cross-bar on the right of the vertical line?[3] Incidentally—remember that the long ſ was *never* used on the *end* of a word. In the body of the text it had certain combinations (do printers call these things *ligatures?*)—fi, ffi, ft, fl, ffl, ff, fh, fk, & very rarely fb. The combination ct (*never* st. This latter, as found in some pseudo-artistic modern fonts, is a sheer affectation without traditional justification) was universal, & lasted about a decade longer than the long ſ. Up to about 1780 all *proper names* were set in italics. Up to about 1750 all nouns were capitalised. Up to about 1700 the capital U was simply an enlarged version of the lower-case one. The *e* was often (*always* in verse) elided with an apostrophe in the past & participle forms of such words as aſk'd, paſs'd, walk'd, obſerv'd, &c., when the final *-ed* was *not* meant to be pronounced as a separate syllable. The older pronunciation of such verbs was aſk'-ed, paſſ'-ed, walk'-ed, ob-ſerv'-ed, & the memory of this condition was so strong that it became necessary to mark the elision when the shorter & newer pronunciation was meant. The shorter pronunciation was originally a free-&-easy, half-colloquial form never used in formal reading or solemn discourse. As such, it was popular as early as the Elizabethan age; & during the 17th century it gained ground & became the dominant form except in sermons & ponderous orations. The older form hung on in theological circles till nearly 1800—many an 18th century divine thundering about the dam'-ned Souls that the Lord *Jehovah* had deliver-ed unto eternal (pronounced *e-tär'-nal* up to around 1750) Wrath. The form Yᵉ for The, seen in many modern imitations of old writing, was *never used in print,* being confin'd wholly to script. *And it was always pronounced as "the"*—the "Y" being merely a convenient imitation in the Roman alphabet of the old *th* symbol Þ (thorn) in the Anglo-Saxon alphabet. Yᵗ was an equally common script abbreviation for *that*. All such affected, pseudo-archaic spellings as *Olde, Shoppe, Fayre*, &c. are fakes if meant to apply to anything much newer than Shakespeare's time. Very few hung on beyond the time of the Commonwealth, & many had begun to wane even before Shakespeare. 18th century spelling did not differ greatly from ours—words like gulph, landſkip, ſhoar, perſwade, antient, wou'd, cou'd, meer, cloaths, publick, smoak, chryſtal, &c. forming the principal departures. The interchange of u & v (and he went vnto Prouidence), & the use of ff in place of capital F (Jnº ffield; Richd ffoster; ffrancis Browne, &c.) did not survive the Restoration except among the half-illiterate town clerks in the colonies. Incidentally, I suppose you know that I & J, as well as U & V each pair forming variants of a single Roman letter) were always listed together in indexes & dictionaries up to about 1830 or 1840—thus:

| | | |
|---|---|---|
| James | Valley | |
| Iäpetus | Vane | Points like this are |
| Icarus | Udolpho | worth remembering if |
| Joſeph | Virgil | one wishes to form |
| Ipſwich | Ulthar | any sort of real picture |
| Jud'a | Volume | of bygone days. |
| | Utrecht | |

Cheap writers—&, alas, a few good ones—make insufferable asses of themselves trying to deal with the past ignorantly. A recent WT story "The Album" is a laughable tissue of anachronisms—especially the attempt to represent late 18th century English. But I digress. As for ever printing that 1924 crap—good gawd, no! I'd hate to have anybody who *can* be kept in ignorance know what a pompous ass I was as recently as 13 years ago! If I were important enough to justify it, I suppose it would be all right to use a few brief selections; but as things are, I feel that even these would be excessive. It doesn't do to give too much publicity to one who isn't prepared to justify it with substantial performances—& I am distinctly slipping out of the field. I haven't the time or energy these days to produce anything new—& if I did, it probably wouldn't be any good. Too much mention in print would be inappropriate under the circumstances. I had a biography in FM in '35, & now both the Bloch spoof & the Price article are appearing in the SFC. That ought to be enough for me—especially unless I get going again aesthetically. Any further personal articles or items would be merely empty build-up—always unjustified & ultimately ironic.

As for taste in authors—yours will develop as fast as you get hold of the right stuff. Someone spoke of a Blackwood tale in *Thrilling Mystery* (I never see these lousy scientifiction rags), but I'm sure it can't be more than an inferior reprint or syndicated pot-boiler.[4] Blackwood must be judged by his best, not his worst, material—the more so because he is admittedly uneven. Read "The Willows", "Incredible Adventures", & "John Silence". As to the magazine stuff—I quite diametrically disagree with you on the merit of Moore work, for the early tales ("Shambleau", "Black Thirst", "Black God's Kiss") have magnificent atmosphere & cosmic unreality, whereas the later tales (I've seen none except in WT) tend to be commercialised hack work. About the illustrations to "Mts. of Madness" & "The Shadow out of Time"—I thought them all clever, although the Shadow ones belied the text in several ways. The artist, however, has none of the imaginative genius of Finlay, Rankin, Utpatel, or Howard Wandrei. About "The Tree"—send it to *John J. Weir, 223 John St., South Amboy, N.J.,* who was asking me for copy a couple of days ago. It ought to do for the mimeographed sheet he is planning.

"Rats" came safely—many thanks. My criticism of the tale is not the same as yours, for I approve of leisurely development. To me the climax now seems crudely & sensationally handled—my typical 1923 stuff. About other tales—here's a list of all my published & unpublished stuff—such as I haven't repudiated. Check off the things you *have* seen (I've checked a few, but will leave others to you, since I'm not sure about many) & return the list, & I'll gradually lend you such items as I have in available form. Your friend Bordley has about a half-dozen of my tales (I can't recall which ones, except that the "Shunned House" is among them), & you might find out what these are—having him pass on to you for perusal & return to me any which you haven't read. The "Colour" surely *will* be the last, since Schwartz has my only copy in connexion with some agent scheme of his. I really must get it back, for I'm certain the idea he has (of placing a collection in England) will come to nothing. Other MSS. of mine are also tied up in the same venture. Your offer to type dying MSS. some day is generous indeed, but I wouldn't impose on you unless I had some service or commodity to offer in exchange (a contrast to the guys who send me their stories for a free criticism or revision which sometimes takes all night!). About the offender who mangled my "Shadow out of Time" MS.—it certainly isn't anyone you'd ever run up against—just a WT reader outside the "fan" circle. In view of the abject apologies & promises of future carefulness which I've received (backed up by the intact return of matter lately sent) it would seem almost unfair & embarrassing to post the quondam culprit on a blacklist—but I certainly *will* issue a warning *if* any second case of trouble develops. Chances are against your ever making such a loan—but a second offence (& more tests are at hand!) would cause me to caution you anyhow. This joint certainly is a circulating library!

Your recent dreams surely seem up to the usual standard—that one about the hidden room & the *not wholly alive* sleeper being a winner! You ought to make a story of that! I feel greatly complimented by my inclusion in the time-juggling dream, & am glad of the data on my 1910 whereabouts. I was very ill (with a bad case of the prosaic malady *measles*) early in 1910, & have only a hazy recollection of things for some time during that year. Now I know where I was! Undoubtedly I had gone down to the Eastern Shore to recuperate—or to draw vampiric nourishment from centuried Indian mounds. With this memory-jogging, I distinctly recall that prepossessing visitor from the future—although I'll admit I didn't believe that time-travelling stuff. I thought you were just spoofing—indeed, I never thought I'd be alive as far into the fabulous future as 1937. Pray accept my belated apologies for that scepticism of 1910! Incidentally—I used to do a little rowing here as well as in Maryland.

Enclosed is a Barlow MS. which I hope you'll like for the SFC.[5] This is an experiment in really artistic fantasy-weaving—just a word-picture with no plot, no climax, & no specific ending. Barlow is coming along rapidly—his "Night Ocean" in *The Californian* being one of the finest weird bits I've ever seen.

Weather hereabouts remains warmish, & I get outdoors once in a while. ¶ Thanks for snaps & letter transcript—& good luck with Sup. Horr. text.

Yrs by the Ghorl Nigral—E'ch-Pi-El

*Notes*

1. WC had acquired, and typed, HPL's letter to Edwin Baird of *WT* of 3 February 1924. In *LAL* 200–11.
2. That is to say, the "long s."
3. [The bar was scratched from each letter.—W. C., Jr.]
4. See WS 12, n. 1.
5. "The Root-Gatherers," *Polaris* 1, No. 2 (March 1940): 7–9.

[AN Enclosure *LAL* 224–25:]

*Tales of H. P. Lovecraft*

(exclusive of juvenile, collaborated, experimental, and disavowed stories, & of essays or prose-poems.)

| | |
|---|---|
| * Professionally published | □ Semi-professionally published |
| † In an anthology | § O'Brien 3-star |
| ¶ Minor year-book mention | # O. Henry 1st place |
| Δ Reprinted in magazine | ■ Brochure or small book |

1917—The Tomb *
1917—Dagon *
1917–18—Psychopompos (rhyme)
1918—Polaris □
1919—Beyond the Wall of Sleep □
1919—The White Ship *
1919—The Doom That Came to Sarnath □
1919—The Statement of Randolph Carter *
1920—The Tree <[1]

1920—The Cats of Ulthar * Δ ■
1920—The Temple *
1920—Arthur Jermyn * Δ
1920—Celephaïs □
1920—From Beyond □
1920—The Picture in the House * ¶
1921—The Nameless City □
1921—The Quest of Iranon □
1921—The Moon-Bog *
1921—The Outsider * Δ
1921—The Music of Erich Zann * † Δ
1921–2—Herbert West—Reanimator *
1922—Hypnos *
1922—The Hound * Δ
1922—The Lurking Fear * Δ
1923—The Rats in the Walls * † Δ <
1923—The Unnamable *
1923—The Festival * Δ
1924—The Shunned House ■
1925—The Horror at Red Hook * †
1925—He *
1925—In the Vault * ¶
1926—Cool Air *
1926—The Call of Cthulhu * †
1926—Pickman's Model * † ¶
1926—The Silver Key * #
1926—The Strange High House in the Mist * #
1927—The Colour out of Space * §
1928—The Dunwich Horror * §
1930—The Whisperer in Darkness *
1931—At the Mountains of Madness * <
1931—The Shadow over Innsmouth ■ <
1932—The Dreams in the Witch House *
1933—The Thing on the Doorstep *
1935—The Shadow out of Time *
1935—The Haunter of the Dark *

| | | | | | |
|---|---|---|---|---|---|
| 1917—3 | 1923—3 | 1929—0 | 1935—2 | 1941— | 1947— |
| 1918—1 | 1924—1 | 1930—1 | 1936—0 | 1942— | 1948— |
| 1919—4 | 1925—3 | 1931—2 | 1937— | 1943— | |
| 1920—8 | 1926—5 | 1932—1 | 1938— | 1944— | |
| 1921—7 | 1927—1 | 1933—1 | 1939— | 1945— | |
| 1922—3 | 1928—1 | 1934—0 | 1940— | 1946— | |

*Notes*

1. The 4 stories marked with this symbol presumably are those that HPL, in the text of the letter, states WC has already seen.

[18]   [ANS]

[Postmarked Providence, RI,
9 March 1937]

Names outlined in pencil are of my invention. I can't recall any more.
    Am very ill & likely to be so for a long time.[1]

*Notes*

1. These comments are written faintly on WC's postcard to HPL dated 8 March 1937, querying about which of the entities and characters WC had listed were HPL's creations. The note about HPL's health was written on the address side of the card. HPL circled the names (represented here by underlining): "Please let me know, as soon as possible, just which of the following are your own inventions: Nyarlathotep, Shub-Nigurath, Yuggoth, Leng, Cthulhu, Yog-Sothoth, and Outside myths. Also the following: Klarkash-Ton (CAS), Comte D'Erlette (AWD), Khut-N'hah (HK), Bho Blok (alias Ludvig Prinn (RB)." To WC's query "hope you can decipher this" HPL replied "Yes." The postcard, mailed in an envelope with the return address of "Mrs. Phillips Gamwell", was addressed by HPL's aunt Annie.

# Appendix

## *Robert Bloch*

### A Visit with H. P. Lovecraft

I don't know why I did it. I swear I don't. I must have been crazy, I guess. Every time I shave I foam at the mouth.

Yes, I'll admit it. I *am* crazy. Everybody is crazy here at the asylum. Even the cockroaches are bugs.

If I had only known! But how could I know? "You are cordially invited to dinner at H. P. Lovecraft's," the invitation read. And I, like a fool, accepted.

It was dark that night as I walked along the streets of Arkham. Clouds pierced the jaws of a crescent moon. The wind whistled through the trees in a demon's dirge. I was afraid of the old houses that stood like silent sentinels along the crooked streets. I had heard talk of witches. Witches—what was that?

*Somebody was following me—a little bent figure with a broom.* Witches! Was this a witch? That broom . . .

I stopped and let the figure pass me, then sighed with relief. The figure with the broom was not a witch—merely a street-cleaner.

Somewhat reassured, I hurried on. Lovecraft's house stood on Leprous Street. I didn't like its looks, nor the graves in the front yard. And I don't think that his idea of using a corpse for a door-mat was so funny, either. Nevertheless I rang the bell and waited.

I was wondering what my host would look like. I had never met the man before, although I'd heard vague rumors. Evil, disturbing ones. Some said that he was a vampire, eight feet tall. Vampire? That sounded batty to me. Others described him as a werewolf in sheep's clothing. Still others claimed that H. P. Lovecraft was an invisible solid, with eight heads, like an octopus.

The door swung open.

"Come in," said a voice. Its owner stood in shadow.

I entered. The door closed as I turned and faced my host.

H. P. Lovecraft was a little old man with a long white beard. As a matter of fact, all I could see was the beard, which caused me to guess that he was old. And since the beard was not so very big yet hid him completely, I judged him to be little.

It was quite an imposing sight, that beard. You have heard of beards so vast that their owners were able to go without neckties? Well, some idea of this beard's size may be gained by the knowledge that Lovecraft didn't even need to wear trousers. I stood gazing at it for some moments.

"What a nice flowing beard," I observed, at last.

"Is it flowing again? Dear me," said Mr. Lovecraft, "I'll have to turn it off."

"You mean 'cut if off', don't you?" I inquired.

"Meant what I said," snapped the voice behind the beard. "I can't cut it off. When I was a baby I promised my mother that I would never cut this beard."

"You don't mean to say that you were born with that hirsute appurtenance?" I gasped.

"Yes," said Mr. Lovecraft. "That is my big secret. I was born with this beard. For seventy years I have never seen my face. I've lived here all alone in my beard; eaten in it, slept in it, mumbled in it."

"Incredulous!" I exclaimed. (As a matter of fact, I really gasped again; but I can't use the same verb twice in row, can I?)

"Well," said Mr. Lovecraft, "you may believe it or not, because it really isn't true, but I'm afraid to cut off my beard. You see, I have never looked at myself, and of late I've been terribly afraid."

"Afraid?" I echoed.

"Yes. I have never looked at myself, you see; and the thought recently struck me—suppose I were to cut off my beard and not find *anything* underneath?"

"Sounds like a good plot for a story," I mused.

"A hair-raising one," he agreed. We both sighed over the barber-ous pun.

"You must be hungry," he said. "Let's eat."

"Which way is the dining-room?" I asked.

"Just go straight north," he directed.

"But how can I tell what direction north is in?"

"Just look at my beard—there's moss on the north side," he explained.

We went down the north corridor. The sight of that beard bobbing whitely in the dusk behind me was very unnerving. Consequently I walked faster, and almost bumped into a grinning skeleton in my efforts to escape the sight of that beard. In other words, I went from beard to worse.

I gazed at the skeleton with horrified eyes. "What's this?" I cried.

"Don't worry," said Lovecraft. "That's just a little something left over from lunch."

"Ought to have closets for those things," I grumbled.

We entered the dining-room. It was a quaint little place, done in the architectural manner of a tomb in the Catacombs. There were nice little coffins to sit on, and a huge floral bouquet in the form of a horseshoe graced the table. "Rest in peace," it read.

"Lovely sentiment for a meal," Lovecraft observed. "One should never quarrel or behave violently at the table. Disturbs the blood."

We sat down. For a long moment there was silence. Suddenly I noticed something peculiar. The table was bare!

"What's all this?" I asked my host. "There's nothing on this table. I thought you invited me for a meal."

"I did," said he. "You're the meal."

So saying, he threw back his beard, revealing several sets of long, glistening fangs. I sat paralyzed as he crept towards me, closer and closer, and closer . . .

H. P. Lovecraft, cackling insanely, seized me in his monstrous paws and ate me up.

Now I ask you, wasn't that a dirty trick to play on a guy?

## Lilies

*Presented in lieu of Mr. Bloch's scheduled yarn— "The Madness of Lucian Gray"—as a result of a mix-up in manuscripts, this weird tale is well worth a second reading.*

The Colorado Apartments is a substantial building, its red-brick walls rising to a four-story eminence that sets it definitely apart from the squalid sordidness of the surrounding neighborhood. Its tenants are likewise removed from the general wretched run of tenement scum that dwells in the ramshackle pest-holes adjoining the dignified brick edifice.

Most of these tenants have been in the building since its construction twenty-three years ago; they are solid, middle-aged and infinitely respectable—the men white collar clerks or accountants, the women plump, comfortable and childless, filling lonely hours with parental ministration to pet canaries. There are widowers, too—grey old men, and widows—grey old women; a very solid, conservative group of tenants indeed. They are a clannish group, the women exchanging gossip and recipes across the back porch of a morning; the men greeting each other from behind their evening papers on the front porch. They would visit one another perhaps, were it not for the unseen barrier of an apartment, the alien sense of espionage that is implied in the phrase, "across the hall." Apartment dwellers love privacy. Still, they do exchange foods—a cut of pie or pudding or perhaps a cool drink in the spring or summer.

There was, for example. Mrs. Hahn and her flowers.

Mrs Hahn was an elderly widow who dwelt directly below our 3rd floor apartment in number 13. She was German, a motherly soul much given to puttering around in her kitchen. She never left her house save on a Saturday afternoon when her married son called for her in his car and they spent the rest of the afternoon in the country. Invariably on Saturday evening she would laboriously mount the stairs to our apartment and present my mother with an armful of wild flowers gathered in the country by "me and my son Willie."

Her pathetic pleasure in this humble task and her reward in our thanks she enjoyed with wistful pride. She was grateful for this, her one weekly rite, the one chance she still had to be giving and doing in a world that had passed her by.

This weekly incident was repeated regularly for nearly a year. Every Saturday the old woman and her flowers came in the midnight dust—the floral tributes varying with the season; violets, sweet peas, marigolds, gladiolas, nasturtiums, poppies, roses.

Finally there came a Saturday late in October when the expected visitor did not materialize. Night deepened, and still no familiar ring upon our doorbell. We had not seen the old woman all week, and my mother was greatly relieved when at eight o'clock the bell finally rang and she opened the door to find the bent, familiar figure of the old woman standing outside in the darkness of the shadowed hall.

"Good evening." The usual greeting, cheerful yet hesitant.

"Why, good evening, Mrs. Hahn. Been out in the country again this week?"

"Well, no, not exactly. Anyway, my son Willie come and bring me these flowers—what a thoughtful boy he is, my son! and I thought if you might like a few——"

She proffered the bouquet. My mother thanked her; she turned and slowly descended the stairs once more. We heard the door of her apartment close softly, and closed our own.

My Mother snapped on the light. Then she gasped—for the flowers in her arms were white calla lilies. She held them, staring oddly at the waxen blooms; was still holding them, in fact, when she looked through the window. A big car pulled up—black it was and shiny, with a closed back, and very long—and two men stepped out. One of them was Willie Hahn, and he was crying. Mother stepped over to the window. Hahn and the stranger were coming up the steps. They were outside our door now, on the way upstairs, and I heard a flash of their conversation.

"Yes, I brought some flowers—lilies, of course. Left them here about an hour ago on the——"

Mother looked out of the window at the funeral car. Then she glanced down at the flowers again, and for the first time noticed the tag around the stems.

"In memory of my dear mother, Mrs. Ludwig Hahn."

Upstairs they were moving the coffin, and nobody noticed that the flowers on her breast were gone.

THE END

# The Black Lotus

*Since we published "Lilies" back in '34, Mr. Bloch's work has won recognition in a wider field, where he is being hailed as one of the "finds" of the year.—You'll like "The Black Lotus."*

This is the story of Genghir the Dreamer, and of the curious fate that overtook him in his dreams; a story old men whisper in the souks of Ispahan as other old men once whispered it in fabled Teraz, five thousand years ago. What portion of it is truth and what portion only fantasy, I leave unto your judgement. There are strange sayings in the banned books, and Alhazred had reasons for his madness; but as I have said, the judgement rests with you. I but relate the tale.

Know then that Genghir was lord over a distant kingdom in the days of the griffin and the fleet-winged unicorn. Rich and powerful was his domain, and peaceful and well-ruled withal, so that its sovereign need occupy himself only with his pleasures.

Handsome was Genghir, but formed as a woman is formed, so that he cared not for the chase or manly combat. His days were spent in rest and study, and his nights in revelry amongst the women. The functions of government rested upon the shoulders of Hassim el Wadir, the Vizier, whilst the true sultan dallied at his pleasures.

Grievous was the life he led, and soon the land was torn by dissension and corruption. But this Genghir heeded not at all, and Hassim he ordered flayed for misuse of his office. And there was revolution and killing throughout the land; and then a fearful plague arose; but all this Genghir minded not, even though two-thirds of his people died. For his thoughts were alien and far away, and the weight of his rule he felt as but a feather. His eyes knew only the musty pages of ensorcelled books and the soft white flesh of women. The witchery of words and wine and wenches cast a spell upon his senses. There was dark magic in the black-bound books his father had brought from ancient conquered realms, and there was enchantment in the old wines and the young bodies that his desires knew; so that he lived in a land of unreality and dreams. Surely he would have died were it not that those left in the land after the plague had fled to other kingdoms, leaving him in an empty city. The report of their going never reached his ears, for well his courtiers knew that those who brought displeasing news were beheaded. But one by one they slipped away, taking with them gold and precious jewels, until the palace lay deserted under a sun that shone upon a barren land.

No longer did the women rest within the zenana, or disport as nymphs beside the amber pools. The sultan turned to other pleasures from the realms of Cathay, and in robes of velvet black he lay and toyed with the juices of the poppy. Then did life become indeed but a dream, and the opium-visioned nightmares took on the semblances of events and places mentioned in the eldritch volumes that he read by day. Time became but as the lengthening of a monstrous dream. Genghir ventured forth into his gardens no more, and less and less did he partake of food or wine. Even his books he forgot, and lay for all time in a drugged sleep, nor heeded the coming and going of the few followers that remained within his retinue. And a silence of desolation fell upon the land.

Now it came to pass that opium and other drugs were not enough, so that Genghir was forced to seek recourse in other and more potent distillations. And in one of the curious evil books he read of a subtle potion brewed from the juices of the Black Lotus that grows beneath the waning moon. Dire and dreadful were the warnings of the scribe regarding the concoction of this forbidden preparation, for its genesis was deemed unholy, and the dangers surrounding its use by a novice were couched in trenchant terms. But Genghir thirsted for the lurid magic of its dreams and for the promise of its delight, nor would he be content until he should taste of its forbidden ecstasy.

His palace stood dim and deserted, for in the latter days the remnant of his sycophants and houris had departed from the dusky halls whose cheap material splendours had long since been nurtured for the true delights found only in the land of opiate dreams. There now remained but three faithful servitors to guard Genghir on his couch of visions, and these he called unto his side and commanded them to journey forth and seek the venom-distilled beauty of the Black Lotus, in the hidden swamps afar of which the cryptic book had told. And they were much afraid, both for him and for themselves, because they had heard curious legends; with one accord they beseeched him to recall his words. But he grew angered, and his eyes were seen to flame like opals, whereat they departed

A fortnight passed ere one of them returned—a fortnight during which the dreamer tried in vain to beguile his satiated senses with the common reek of the white flower. Overjoyed was he when the slave returned with his precious burden and brewed from it the blissful juices of nepenthe, following the injunctions set forth in the curious book. But he did not speak of his journey, or venture aught concerning the fate of his two companions; and even the dazed dreamer wondered why he kept his features veiled. In his eagerness he did not inquire, but was content to see the philter carefully compounded and the pearly-hued liquor inserted in the nargileh. Immediately upon the completion of this task, the servitor departed, and no man knows the manner of his going, save that he lashed his camel far across the desert, riding as though possessed by demons. Genghir did not note his genii-beset progress, for already he was enraptured at the thought of what was to come. Indeed he had not stirred from his divan in the palace chambers, and in his brain was naught but the thirsty dement of desire for the strange new thrill foretold in the elder lore. Queer dreams were promised to him who durst inhale the fumes, dreams of which the old book dare not even hint—"Dreams which surpass Reality, or blend with it in new and unhallowed ways." So spake the scribes, but Genghir was not afraid, and heeded only the promise of delights it was said to hold.

And so it was that he lay on his couch that evening and smoked his hookah alone in the deepening darkness, a dream-king in a land where all but dreams was dead. His divan overlooked the balcony high above the empty city, and as the moon rose, its crescent-given rays glistened upon the irides-cent bubblings of the white fluid in the great bowl through which the smoke was drawn. Sweet indeed was the essence's taste, sweeter than the honey-combs of Kashmir or the kisses of the chosen brides of Paradise. Slowly there came stealing over his senses a new and delightful languor—it was as if he were a creature free-born, a being of the boundless air. He gazed half-seeing at the bubbles, and suddenly they bubbled up, up, up, until they bathed the room in a veil of shimmering beauty, and he felt all identity vanish in their crystalline depths.

Now ensued a period of profound and mystic sadness. He seemed to lie with-in the graven walls of a tomb, upon a slab of pale-white marble. Shrill funere-al pipings seemed to echo from afar, and his nostrils were titillated by the distilled aromatic incense of the sepulchral lily. He knew himself to be dead, and yet he yet he retained the consciousness that was his own in life. The timelessness of common dreams was not his lot; centuries passed on leadenly, and he knew every second of their length as he lay within the tomb of his fa-thers; enmausoleumed upon a slab covered with stone that was carven with demon-given basilisks.

Long after the odors and the music had faded from the darkness in which he lay came the advent of corruption. He felt his body grow bloatedly purulent; felt his features coagulate and his limbs slough off into charnel, ooz-ing slime. And even that was as an instant in the weary, dragging hours of his eternity there. So much longer did he lie bodiless that he lost all conscious recollection of ever having possessed one, and even the dust that had been his bones lost all significance to him. The past, present and future were as naught; and thus; unconsciously Genghir had revealed unto him the basic mystery of life.

Years later the crumbling walls clove thunderously asunder, and shards of debris covered over the decaying slab that now housed naught but an un-dying consciousness. And even they were overcast by dust and earth, until there was nothingness to mark the sight of the proud tomb where once lay the lords of the house of Genghir. And the soul of Genghir was as nothing-ness along amongst nothingness.

Such was the substance of the first dream. As the flicker of his soul ex-pired into everlasting darkness within the earth, Genghir awoke, and he was sweat-bathed, trembling with fear, and as pale as the death he feared. And anon he turned the pages of his book to where it spoke of the Lotus and its prophecies thereof and this he read:

"The first dream shall foretell that which is to come."

Whereat Genghir grew much afraid, and closed the book in the ensilvered moonlight, they lay back upon his couch and tried to sleep, and to forget. But then there came stealing upon his senses the subtly sweet odor of the essence, and its magic englamoured and engulfed, till he grew frantic with the insidious craving for its sinister soothing. Forgotten was fear and prophetic warning; all dissolved into desire. His fumbling fingers found the hookah, his feverish lips closed upon the stem, his being knew peace.

But not for long. Once again the opaque mists of roseate, sweet voluptuousness parted and dissolved, and the enchantment of rapturous, ineffable bliss faded as a new vision supervened.

He saw himself awaken and rise from the couch in the light of dawn, to gaze haggardly upon a new day. He saw the wretched agony of his being as the drug wore off its potency and left his body racked with spasms of exquisite pain. His head seemed to swell as if about to burst; his rotting, benightmared brain seemed to grow inside his skull and split his head asunder. He beheld his frantic gropings about the deserted chamber, the mad capers of grotesque agony that made him tear his hair and foam epileptically at the mouth and gibber terribly as he clawed with twitching fingers at his temples. A white-hot mist of searing anguish sent him reeling to the floor, and then it seemed as though in his dream-consciousness there came to him a horrible longing to be rid of his torment at any cost, and to escape from a living hell to a dead one. In his madness he cursed the book and the warning; cursed the ghastly lotus flower and its essence; cursed himself and his pain. And as the stark biting teeth of his torture bored still closer to the roots of his sanity, he saw himself drag his rigid, paralytic body to the outer balcony of his deserted palace, and with a grimace of agony greater than can be sensed by sanity, he raised himself slowly to the rail. Meanwhile, as he stood there, his head swelled and bloated to monstrous, unbelievable proportions, then burst rottenly asunder in a ghastly blob of grey and scarlet putrefaction, from which arose the stupefying scent of black lotuses. Then, with a single inarticulate cry of horror and despair, he crumpled and toppled from the balcony, to spatter himself in red madness upon the court below.

At this instant he awoke, and his teeth shook inside his mouth as he gagged and retched in terrible repulsion. He felt old and decrepit, and the tide of life ebbed in his veins. He would have fainted were it not for the revivifying fumes of the nargileh that still smoldered beside him. Then unto himself he swore a mighty oath to abandon the ways of the dreamer forever, and rose to his feet and took unto himself the book and turned the pages to the passage of warning, wherein he read this rune:

"The second dream shall show what might have been."

Then there descended upon him a resignation and a black despair. All of his life unrolled before him once again and he knew himself for what he was—a deluded fool. And he knew also that, if he did not go back to his drugged slumber there would come to pass the horror of his second dream, as it foretold. So, wearily, and with queer wonder in his heart, he clasped the book to his bosom and betook himself once again to his couch in the moonlight. And his pale fingers lifted the hookah to his ashen lips once again and he once more knew the bliss of Nirvana. He was under the compulsion of a sorcerous thrall.

. . . . Oh night-black lotus flower, growth beneath the River Nile! Oh poisoned perfumer of all darkness, waving and weaving in the spells of moonlight! Oh cryptic magic that worketh only evil! . . . .

Genghir the Dreamer slept. But there was brooding ecstasy and mystic wonder in his dreams, and he knew the beauty that lies in twilight grottoes on the dark side of the moon, and his brow was fanned and his slumbers lulled by the pale wind that is the little gods who dance in paradise. And he stood alone in a sea of endless infinity, before a monstrous flower that beckoned great, hypnotic petals before his dream-dazed eyes, and whispered unto him a command, In his vision he glanced down to where a dagger hung by his side, in his jeweled stomacher of sultanship.

And there came to him a sudden gleam of understanding. This before him was the Black Lotus, symbol of the evil that waits for men in sleep. It was casting a spell upon him that would lure him to death. He knew now the way of atonement for the past and the release of his enchantment—he must strike!

But even as he moved, the great flower shot out one velvet petal steeped in the cloying scent that was a wind from the gate of heaven. And the black petal entwined itself about his neck like a loathsome and beautiful serpent, and with its succubi-like embrace sought to drown his senses in a sea of scented bliss.

But Genghir would not be frustrated. The allurement of delight left him cold, but his numbing brain commanded him. He raised the silver dagger from his side and with a single blow, slashed off the twining coiler from his neck . . . .

Then Genghir saw the flowers and the petals vanish, and he was left alone in a universe of mocking laughter; a dim world that rocked with leering mirth of idiotic gods. For an instant he awoke to see a ruby necklace encircling his bare throat; to realize monstrously that in his dream he had cut his own throat. Then, on a bed of moonlight, he died, and there was silence in the deserted room, while from the dead throat of Genghir the Dreamer little drops of blood fell upon an open page of a curious book; upon a curious sentence in oddly underlined letters:

"The third dream brings reality."

Nothing more remained, save the all-pervading scent of lotus-flowers that filled the nighted room.

## How I Get My Inspiration

by A Weird Tales Author

There is a vague, unfounded rumor current that in order to indite a story for *Weird Tales*, it is necessary to write with a pen dipped in human blood. That is a lie. I know, because I once wrote a story with a pen dipped in chimpanzee blood, and the editor accepted it. He never knew the difference.

A fundamental requisite, however, is the possession of some antique book. At present the ancient manuscripts used are these: *The Book of Eibon*, *The Necronomicon*, *The Mysteries of the Worm*, *Unaussprechlichen Kulten*, *Cultes des Goules*, and the *Black Book*. All these may be purchased from Panurge Press for $1.49, prepaid. They will be sent to you in a plain sealed wrapper.

Other references are indispensable. Suppose you are writing a story about talismans and prophecies. You will need to refer to such magazines as *Signs and Invention* or *The Omen's Home Companion*.*

Then, too, you must exercise a vocabulary. Practice using such words as *anthropolith, vivisepulture, nacrocosmic, teratological, anthropomorphosis, noctambulist, nyctaphobia, nyctaloptic,* etc. Fifteen minutes a day devoted to writing down such words will not only provide you with a vocabulary, but will also give you writer's cramp.

Always write your stories at midnight, preferably in a pitch-dark room. Stories should be written on the skin of a gander. That usually gives the readers goose flesh.

Follow the above rules and you can't go wrong. If, however, for some strange reason these hints fail you, always remember there is one infallible way to break into the pages of *Weird Tales*.

Write a letter to "The Eyrie."

## Milwaukee Youth Writes Horror Tales, Sells 'Em

### Started at 16, Saves to Become Comedian, Also Draws and Molds Statues

Voodooism and vampires, cabalistic charms and demons—of these materials Robert Bloch weaves strange fantastic tales that have made him at 18 a sought after contributor to magazines dealing with black magic and necromancy.

At an age when most boys are interested only in the literal world about them, in football scores or in getting a job, this amazing young man, who aspires to be a comedian, has sold nine stories dealing with the black arts. He is the son of Mr. and Mrs. R. M. Bloch and lives with his parents at 620 E. Knapp st.

[Stories?] with evil, diabolic characters, have been read by this six-foot youth since he was a child. Now he himself pours out equally monstrous pieces for others. Since his graduation last year from Lincoln High school, he has turned to writing these strange yarns as a profession.

---

*RB's parodies of *Science and Invention* and *Woman's Home Companion*.

## Out of the Fog

He sold his first story when he was 16, and his second, "The Secret of the Tomb," a few weeks after he finished school. To hear him tell of the experience that led to the writing of the second story is to hear a log of an eerie adventure.

The idea for that story was conceived on a fog ridden night in June, the night the street cars were called in because of the Electric Co. strike.

"The fog on that night," he reminds you, "was so thick that it was impossible to see a foot ahead of you. For some reason I wanted to do something unusual that night and the weirdest thing I could think of was to spend the night in a cemetery. So I walked from my home on E. Knapp st. to soldiers' home cemetery, and spent the night sitting on a tombstone staring into the fog.*

"Occasionally the wind would shift the heavy mist and then I would see the gravestones quite clearly and to me they looked like the fingernails of a corpse. I wouldn't let myself get frightened and I kept reminding myself that I had deliberately undertaken an experiment to discover how I would react to such a situation."

## The Grinning Ghoul

As he sat there, fragments of ghost stories flitted through his mind. Gradually vague ideas began to take shape. He created characters, a plot.

He outlined the details of his story as he walked home in the early dawn. Once in the house he sat down immediately and in longhand wrote "The Secret of the Tomb," a yarn dealing with ghouls.

Since then "The Feast in the Abbey," a tale of a grisly banquet, has been published; "The Suicide in the Study," a story of hypnotism and dual personality, and "The Black Lotus."

Among the stories purchased during the last few weeks is "The Grinning Ghoul." Bloch has been asked to illustrate this tale, for this young man can use his pencil with equal ease for writing or drawing his grotesqueries.

Six different pieces of horror writing are claiming his attention at the present time. One of them is a story of 10,000 words and another a novelette of 15,000 words. The latter deals with witchcraft in the New England states in the colonial days and is based on an excerpt from Cotton Mather.

Important as terror tales are to him, Robert views them only as an interlude to help him realize his ambition—to become a comedian. He has wanted to be a comedian as long back as he can remember and meanwhile, scarcely a day goes by that he does not write four or five "gags" and tuck them away in a drawer for the time he will be able to use them. He wants to act in sketches that he writes.

To Robert there is nothing strange in being interested at the same time in horror and humor.

---

*In his autobiography (p. 72), RB says he did not in fact spend a night in the cemetery.

"There is such a slight line of differentiation between what is horrible and what is ludicrous that I think they come from the same thought pattern," he explains. "As an example, the grotesque masks worn in mardi gras parades are ludicrous and horrible at the same time."

He is also writing a humor novel based on the adventures of a man who can shape his dreams and live in them just as he would in real life. The novel is entirely outlined and one-fourth written.

"I think it wise to work on several stories at one time—at least two or three," says the young man gravely. "Jumping from one to the other is recreation if you write constantly and at the same time it helps to develop a uniform style.

### Also Sculpts

Black magic has had a strange fascination on Robert since he was 10 years old and saw Lon Chaney in "The Phantom of the Opera." It was his first visit to a movie alone and the horrible visage of the phantom made so profound an impression upon him that for a long time after he would wake at night and see the terrible skull-like face leering at him. He remembered the face of the phantom so well that he has since drawn a crayon sketch of it. The drawing hangs on one wall of the Bloch living room and on another wall is a drawing of a ghoul. On the piano are a statue of a huge ape and a grinning skull, both of which he modeled.

"If I were to allow it, every inch of wall space in the room would be hung with those terrible drawings," Mrs. Bloch says.

Robert has ruled out college as a step toward higher education. His interests are psychology, philosophy, and the history of literature and knowledge of these, he is confident, he can acquire by reading. He is an individualist and feels that rules and regulations of college would "cramp his style."

### Afraid of Death

Robert is a voracious reader and has read every type of horror story imaginable. He likes biography, history of all kinds—oriental, Hindu, Chinese and Japanese history have been of particular interest to him lately—and humor tales.

And still this unusual young man who can write impersonally and rationally of demons, who can calmly spend a night in a graveyard, who, with words, can conjure up frightful scenes and who can talk with astonishing maturity of literature and economic and social trends—this same young man confesses to an inexplicable, profound fear of death.

"I can write horror tales very impersonally, but I can't view death impersonally," he said. "The more I read of it the more I fear it. I guess it's my imagination, but right now there doesn't seem to be much I can do about it."

From the *Milwaukee Journal,* "The Green Sheet,"
Saturday, 6 April 1935, pp. 1, 3.

# Natalie H. Wooley

## Admonition

I would walk soberly by you forever,
    Never gaze seaward where argosies wait.
But hold me close, and cease loving me never,
    For once I was wanderer . . . and love came late.

## Dream Fantasy

(Laureateship Entry)

In dreams I walked a dim, white road that led on through a night
Where mistlike trees on either hand were touched with pale starlight.
And somewhere in the unreal dusk a bird sang wild and sweet . .
I moved toward some mysterious goal on dream-enchanted feet.
The warm winds that caressed my face were sweet with clover bloom—
Then, suddenly, you were beside me, moving through the gloom.
Wearied, we paused awhile to rest, then, when I sought to rise,
The wild dark face of you came near, and blotted out the skies.

## Antares

Aloof Antares, high in the midnight sky,
    Wearied with aeons, filled with ageless hate,
Stares down with cold, unwinking, ancient eye,
    Contemptuous of mankind and of its fate.

What monstrous shapes have known its crimson cheer,
    And on its planets snatched a vital breath,
None reckons, for its ruin-littered sphere
    Reels on through space in universal death.

Our young-gold sun stares back with puzzled rays,
    Heedless of cycles yawning grim ahead,
When on still unborn star-streams it will blaze,
    Itself as old, as bitter, and as dead.

## Avatar

Strange longings stir deep in my heart tonight.
    The moon on me a magic spell has cast.
The stars are blazing down and by their light
    I travel back in memory, till at last.

I waited by a pagan temple wall.
> A virgin moon's slim sickle cut the sky,
And then as though in answer to my call
> The nightingale sent forth its passioned cry.

You came to me on silver-sandaled feet;
> Through the warm dusk, unerringly you came
To nestle close . . . Your lips were warm and sweet.
> Together we touched life's eternal flame.

Strange jewels clasped your wrists and held your hair.
> Your hands were pale as lotus buds at dawn.
The gods were kind, the hour was ours to share.
> But . . . the pattern changes . . . you are gone. . . .

Your name is on my lips when I awaken,
> Bringing the aching loss of you again.
The ashes of my heart again are shaken
> By piercing winds of unforgetting pain.

## The Alien

She is like living golden flame.
She knows not whence or why she came
> Into this world . . . and yet at times
I hear her call strange gods by name.

There is no warmth in her embrace,
Of human passions not a trace
> She seems remote, a thing attuned
To summonings from outer space.

And on each starry, moonlit night
She gazes long in rapt delight
> Toward the skies . . . while I weep
Lest the message come, and she take flight.

## Flight

The world says you are dead, but they are wrong
I will not listen to the things they say.
How could they know you've merely gone before
To blaze the trail that I must take some day?

You fled into the sunset after-glow
You who loved the sky, its changing light.

(Remember how one summer night you cried
At the sheer poignant beauty of the night?)

And somehow I am sure that you await me
Until the time comes when I too shall rise
To find you wrapped in star-dust, crowned with glory
Beyond the farflung mystery of the skies.

## A Heavenly Tragedy

The little Bear is weeping there on high,
For he has spilled his milk across the sky;
And left a Milky Way . . . The Dipper lies
Empty, forgotten, while in sad surprise
The Great Bear stands and scolds her wayward son,
"You naughty little Bear, see what you've done."

## Lines to Cleopatra

Frail flesh and blood upon enduring stone;
A voice upon the wind that soon is gone—
        The gods have given you your little day,
And now they laugh above an empty throne.

Those stars that shone so cold and far above,
What did they know or care of human love?
        To them, your little dream of pomp and power
Were meaningless, as yonder worn out glove.

Drained is the wine, flung down the empty glass,
Your little hour of love and life. Alas,
        You and your dream are one, and both are gone,
But the Nile flows, the centuries still pass.

## Coward

I would yield myself to life,
        Let it have its way.
Say, "Life, have your will with me,"
        Ah, but not today!

Tomorrow will do just as well.
        Today I've much to do.
It's better to be cautious,
        Than to make haste, and rue.

So my days are gray, and boast
    Of neither joy nor sorrow,
But sometime I will taste of life.
    Perhaps—tomorrow!

## Sailor's Child

(Laureateship Entry)

Through the long day he sits upon the cliff, his childish eyes
Fixed on horizons where the gulls careen down cloudswept skies.
The sharp and salty tang of spray is flung against his lips—
The rock beneath his feet becomes in turn the decks of ships
From Mandalay or Portugal. The wind against his face
Brings half-remembered dreams of one who, going, left no trace
Save this strange passion for the sea—this longing without name.
So first the father, now the son, his heritage must claim.
And words nor tears can hold him—when the time comes he will go—
Already in his young veins mystic oceans ebb and flow.

## Western Night

Night . . . and a chill wind blowing,
    Stars hang low in a velvet sky.
Then from out the vast dark spaces
    Quavers a coyote's lonely cry.

Night . . . and the sagebrush rustling,
    Softly the wind drifts down the plain;
High in the sky a new moon rocks gently
    Lulling the earth to sleep again.

## Mountain Trail

Are you feeling tired and disillusioned,
    Everything seems futile, life gone stale?
Then come with me in fancy, I will take you
    Up a silver-moonlit mountain trail.

An autumn moon above us in the heavens
    Lends her light to guide us on our way,
Stars bend low to twinkle us a greeting,
    "Home at last," their message seems to say.

The mountains stretch away to far horizons,
    Tall pines around us pierce the midnight sky;
And carried on the breeze across the ridges
    The mystic cadence of a coyote's cry.

At last we reach the crest, and pause in silence,
    Transfixed by beauty we can see unrolled,
There below us, Lake and wood and valley
    In wondrous panorama we behold.

Through the night there comes in benediction,
    Heralding the mystery of it all,
A message of the wild throughout the ages—
    The eerie music of the coyote's call.

## End of the Trail

(Suggested by The Scout, a Statue)

Into the setting sun on lagging feet,
Conceding victory, gallant in retreat,
Seeing your virgin plain become acres of golden wheat.

Yet once this land was yours . . . in moons gone by
You pitched your tents beneath this starry sky,
And drifted dreamward on the coyote's cry.

What lies before you now—what destiny?
There beyond the sunset, do you see
The beckoning lands of vast eternity?

LINOLEUM BLOCK CARVING, AFTER AUTHOR'S PEN SKETCH

## Mountain Pool

It mirrors the blue of the sky by day.
And at night the stars within it play.
Upon its face pale lilies gleam
Like fairy faces in a dream.
Tall willows lean above its brink,
Where wild things come and pause to drink.
A sanctuary, dim and cool—
The crystal depths of a mountain pool.

## Sanctuary

Ah, there are dreams that all the world of dreamers understands,
　　We all have dreamed of strange dim lands beyond horizons' bars,
Where purple peaks lift to the sky, and shining silver sands,
　　Lie in a drowsy quietude beneath the swinging stars.

And here is sanctuary for the dreamer, where the gleam
　　Of white stars burn, and night drifts down on sable velvet wing,
Where time and space are but a thought, tomorrow but a dream,
　　And life a strange dim echo of the song the ages sing.

## Dream Tryst

In dreams I walked a dim white road that led on through a night
Where mistlike trees on either hand were touched with pale starlight.
And somewhere in the unreal dusk a bird sang wild and sweet . . .
I moved toward some mysterious goal, on dream-enchanted feet.
The warm winds that caressed my face were sweet with clover bloom—
Then, suddenly, you were beside me, moving through the gloom.
Wearied, we paused awhile to rest, then, when I sought to rise,
The wild dark face of you came near and blotted out the skies.

## The Adventure Story

　　"Velannus shuddered. Turning, he walked to a casement and stared silently out over the river, black and shiny under the glint of the stars. Beyond the river the jungle rose like an ebony wall. The distant screech of a panther broke the stillness. The night pressed in, blurring the sounds of the soldiers outside the blockhouse, dimming the fires. A wind whispered through the black branches, rippling the dusky water. On its wings came a low, rhythmic pulsing, sinister as the pad of a leopard's foot."
　　—Excerpt from "Beyond the Black River," by Robert E Howard.

There, my friends, is writing. A paragraph of less than a hundred words, yet combining description, menace, and a hint of action to come. Each word is carefully chosen. Note the artfully worded last sentence, with its intimation of impending conflict; sustaining the reader's interest through what otherwise might be a rather colorless bit of description. Mr. Howard, well known adventure-fiction story writer, is one of a few who do not sacrifice beautiful narrative style for the action demanded in such stories, but combines the two masterfully.

The formula for the adventure story is simple. A brave superbly-physiqued hero, preferably American; A hitherto unexplored country, A white goddess ruling over: (a) natives, (b) apes, (c) your imagination is the limit here. Follow with conflict, capture, escape, more conflict, and then victory, clinch, fadeout. No clever, intricately worked out plots, such as the mystery and detective magazines demand, is necessary. But, good writing is essential. The author must keep his action from lagging, at the same time injecting necessary bits of description here and there, as a background, or tapestry, against which the drama is played. The day is past when a writer could begin his story with a half-column of information. Today, the writer must jump into action with the first hundred words, preferably dialog, to catch the reader's interest and intrigue him into reading further.

While the adventure field is not as large as others, for the writer who would combine good writing with imagination, it offers a highly paying market. Besides the better known magazines using adventure tales, such as *Adventure, Top-Notch, Argosy,* and *Blue Book,* there are many smaller markets using this type of fiction, and should a story fall sort of the former, it may rate a check from the latter.

Comment from the *1935 Writers' [and Artists'] Year Book:*

"Good adventure stoires are in brisk demand . . . prefer that stories be laid in foreign countries, although American heroes are desired. Out-of-the-way places like Borneo, Tasmania, Afghanistan, Burma, haven't been written about much, and good stories laid in those countries will be bought eagerly. Good character work is essential in adventure stories."

## Is Criticism Necessary?

*Amateurs Quick to Detect Insincerity*

Criticism is necessary to the amateur writer, but it should be sincere, encouraging and reasonably intelligent; constructive, not destructive. One wonders how many really worthwhile writers may have been lost to the world because of some thoughtless, half-intelligent criticism that destroyed the confidence of the embryo writer in his ability.

It is next to impossible for the amateur to criticize his own work. He cannot get the necessary perspective for he is too close to it and it is too much a part of him. Its faults are his and, being such, escape notice. I can vouch for that, as I had such an experience. In a story I wrote some time ago, I had created a certain character named Uncle Charles. The story came back, needless to say. I rechecked it for faults and imagine my horror to discover a few pages back in the story Charles, for no apparent reason at all became James. I am still at sea as to how it happened. Had I had an impersonal criticism of my story, such an obvious mistake would certainly have been noticed and corrected.

The average amateur writer is very quick to detect insincerity in criticism, and quick to see his fault when they are intelligently pointed out to him. But he has one fault. Being shyly proud of his "brain children," he sometimes rushes in where an angel would hesitate and requests comment or criticism from someone who is totally unfitted to help him. For example, there is the half-sincere careless criticism of friends, if it can be called criticism, which is very flattering, but which offers very little help.

But there is another kind. The real criticism comes from a friend who intelligently studies your effort, gives sincere praise when earned, criticizes when necessary and who tells you sincerely, "It's good. I like it, but I think you can do better still. You have the talent and the vision. Try again, won't you?"

If you have such a priceless friend, bless him and offer incense at his shrine, for he is a friend indeed.

## Have You a Hobby?

What are you, and you, and you, going to do with all these extra leisure hours now allotted you by shortened hours of labor? Or are you going to do anything?

Perhaps you intend merely lying around, resting and sleeping. At first this will seem very pleasant, but after a while it will pall, and you will find yourself wondering what to do to fill these empty hours. And this is where hobbies come into the picture. I don't necessarily mean collecting stamps, first editions, or old china. Mr. Webster's little book defines hobbies as "a favorite pursuit or object." So it may encompass anything; range from the study of our universe to finding a restaurant that serves good pies. It holds endless possibilities. And if you have more than one pursuit, so much the better. Your horizon is correspondingly widened.

Your scribe has many, ranging from the making of all types of needlework to hiking in all sorts of weather, and embracing movies, reading, (everything from fiction to fact), writing, amateur painting, music, and so on. Perhaps my favorite is an intense love of outdoors, a sort of carryover from a childhood spent in the Pacific Northwest.

So choose a hobby. Whatever you like best; are most interested in. Life will take on new interest, new meaning. And whether it is collecting butterflies or studying social economics, go to it! The world is yours!

Get yourself a hobby!

## "Tillicum"

The new school teacher was from the east, and had the average easterner's credulity, at least that of those hailing from east of the Mississippi River.

'Old Tom' Horn, driver of the decrepit Ford which made the weekly trip from Sagebrush, the nearest railway point, with mail and supplies for the ranchers, was holding him spellbound with his stories. Old Tom was an ex-cowboy—age and the passing of the old west had left him stranded high and dry, here in this western community. He was weather beaten to a dull leather color, bow-legged from a lifetime spent in the saddle, and addicted to tobacco chewing and the telling of tall stories when he could find a listener. Those who knew him well had long since found him out, but the new teacher, unaware of his Baron Munchausen tendencies, listened eagerly, while blood-thirsty Indians of old, vicious cattle rustlers and treacherous, knife toting Mexicans were resurrected and disposed of as the miles slipped by. With such an admiring audience Old Tom rose to still greater heights, always with a wary eye turned to catch the first flicker or incredulity or disbelief on the other's part. But he met only awed, respectful glances and at last, temporarily exhausted of ideas, he paused and reached for his ever-present 'plug'.

The teacher drew a long breath, and began to look about him. The tall pines along the canyon road, the dwarfed clumps of sagebrush on the levels, and the clear heady air all combined to stir a queer excitement in him. Then he thought of something.

"And hunting? I suppose there is wild game too?" he asked, eagerly. "I heard some men on the train talking about something called tillicum. I thought perhaps it was some sort of wild animal. I remember one of the men said they were sure scarce, but fine when you did find one." He paused in dismay. Old Tom seemed to be having a seizure of some sort. He gasped and strangled, gave voice to strange noises, and only after an interval did he seem to recover. A wicked gleam came into his eyes then, and what followed made history for him.

In the first place, he said, a tillicum is very shy. It sometimes takes weeks or even months to catch sight of one. Then you have to be careful, because they have such keen ears. Very few people have ever seen one, let alone got one. But if you were so lucky, your name would go down in history. And so on, till at the end of the trip, and he deposited the other at the Double O ranch, which was to be his home during the coming term of school.

The Double O ranch was typical of that part of the country at that time. It had no traditional bunk house, no regular cowboys. During branding time the ranchers helped each other. The Double O was luckier than many, in that there were four grown boys to help run it, and even eighteen-year-old Jane Carey was as good as a man at roping and riding. Yet she was feminine enough to enjoy the routine or housework, and cooking.

The arrival of the new teacher brought forth her second best pink and white checked apron, and later, a faint blush to her cheeks when she met his admiring eyes across the supper table.

Mr. Cary passed him the enormous platter of meat. "Have some venison?" he inquired, genially.

"Venison?" startled at the unfamiliar word.

"Why, yes. Deer meat. John, here, went out and brought in a buck yesterday."

The teacher's face lit up eagerly.

"I'd like to go hunting," he exclaimed. "I'd like to shoot a tillicum."

A gasp went up from around the table.

"A what?" asked Mr. Cary, puzzled.

"A tillicum," began the teacher, eager to explain. But he got no farther. The entire family seemed on the verge of insanity. The boys bent double in strange convulsions, while emitting strange spluttering sounds. Mr. Cary seemed to be strangling, and even Jane's face was purpling with suppressed mirth. When she met his bewildered gaze it was the last straw. Between gusts of laughter she tried to explain.

"Old Tom was just stringing you. He's a terrible liar. In the Indian language, 'tillicum' means friend."

## The Dance

It was the harvest dance, held in the school house in the valley. Anticipated for months, it was an event in the lives of the ranchers. The desks were pushed back against the walls, forming beds in which the younger generation were tucked away to sleep, when one by one, they lost the battle with old man Morpheus. Pine branches and ripened sprays of wheat decorated the rough pine walls.

Outside, in the shadows of the pines behind the building, wagons and other farm vehicles loomed in the darkness. Saddle horses nickered softly and moved restlessly by the hitching rack. The eerie wailing of a coyote drifted faintly from a distant ridge.

Men clustered by a great bonfire outside. Scraps of conversation drifted from a group of the older men, anent the hay crop, cattle prices, and the newer menace of the sheep. A bottle passed guardedly among a few of the younger men, and brought forth loud laughter and rough chaffing.

From the open door of the schoolhouse drifted the rhythmic shuffle of dancing feet and threaded over and through it, the musical calling of the "square dance." Suddenly from somewhere in the ever-changing, ever-shifting crowd around the fire came the clear sweet strains of a harmonica, muted, plaintive, playing an old cow camp melody. Slowly silence fell, as the song caught the attention. Some of the younger men joined in, singing the words. Other songs followed, songs handed down by word of mouth from father to son, songs that brought memories to the older men, of almost forgotten trails down which other men had carried these melodies. The fire flickered in the chilly night wind, casting mysterious shadows on the trees. From the building drifted the music of the supper waltz.

Supper intermission. The fire deserted while the inner man is satisfied. Coffee, hot and strong, from a great boiler. Sandwiches, home-made cakes and pies. Mince pies, made with venison. And last but by no means least, fried chicken, great golden-brown platters of it.

Much, much later, the familiar strains of "Home, Sweet Home", preceding the long ride homeward in the cold gray dawn. The sun rises in splendor over the mountains. And the harvest dance is over for another year.

## Reminiscense

A soft haze veils the land; Indian summer is here. The cottonwoods are a blaze of glory, and the tamarack's needles have turned to gold. Each day is a perfect thing, from the glorious sunrise over the far peaks, to the cool and tranquil dusk. At night, a golden, enormous moon rides majestically across the heavens, while from every ridge the coyote serenades the night with poignant, lonely cry. Stars hang huge and low.

Come with me on this golden September afternoon. We will climb Lost River Mountain, to its bare and lofty peak. Our feet sink into the fallen leaves, which form as colorful and glorious a carpet as a queen could ever own. From yonder grove of wild chokecherry bushes, heavy with frost-ripened fruit, startled wild pheasants take slow, unhurried flight, flying low over the trees. Crows and blue jays, perched in the branches, scream raucously at us, resenting our intrusion, and perhaps a frightened rabbit bounds away into the brush.

We climb higher, and now the leafy trees have given way to pine and fir and tamarack. The scarlet berried kinnickkinnick vine covers the forest floor, here where the sun slants through the trees; and chipmunk and squirrel break into angry chatter as we pass. We cross a small canyon, pausing to gather a spray of fragrant wild snapdragon, whose great purple flowers hang from the rocky sides. Higher, steeper, grow the slopes, and then we emerge into the open. Now we are above timberline, and here the air is like wine, heady and sharp, freighted with the wild pungent tang of sage-brush, which, although stunted with the high altitude, persists even here, clinging to the steep and rocky slopes. Rocks, loosened by our passing, go bounding down the slopes, and crash among the trees. We climb higher, and now our goal is in sight. Panting, we gain the top, and drop exhausted on the great flat rock that juts from the broken rim of what strangely resembles the crater or an extinct volcano, part of which has fallen. And now for the first time we look back over our route.

Can one wonder that once the Indian desperately contested every foot of this land, to them an earthly Happy Hunting Grounds, with its heaven-flung peaks, its great forests teeming with game, and its crystal-clear lakes and streams?

Mountains, mountains, that march away and melt into a far blue horizon; valleys that sparkle here and there with the flashing silver-blue of lake or stream. Far to the northwest, the snow-capped Cascades thrust against the skyline their eternally white peaks.

The world and its petty cares are forgotten. Here we seem to catch a fleeting glimpse of the meaning of life, the ultimate purpose of the great eternal plan. A strange peace and contentment flows into our soul, and like Whittier, we

> "feel the earth move sunward,
>
> join the great march forward—"

## Spurs of Death

The warden leaned back in his chair as he watched the door close, then turned to the man who stood looking out of the window.

"Well, Jim?" he queried. The other came slowly back to the desk and re-seated himself. His face was puzzled.

"Who was that, Tom? He seems strangely familiar, and yet I can't seem to place him."

"That man was Cliff Williams, the cowboy murderer," said the warden. "You may have seen his picture in the papers. He gets the chair next month for the three murders he has committed."

Jim Kelton registered surprise.

"He doesn't look like the sort of person to do such a thing like that. He seems almost a kid."

The warden smiled grimly. "His looks are deceiving. He has killed three men in the last ten years, and as far as anyone knows, without any reason. I'll tell you the story if you care to hear it."

The other assented.

"Well, the first one was a cow hand down in Texas about ten years ago. He was working on a ranch down there and he and this fellow got in an argument over something. He shot him. Then he raked his face open with his spurs. That was the thing that trapped him in the end. Every time he killed, he marked his victim's face. Horrible, I grant you. Well, he disappeared, and finally the case was forgotten. He was a kid of nineteen or twenty then. Five years later he turned up in Oregon. Worked on the Lazy T ranch there. All the men liked him, too. He was quiet, knew his business, and never talked much. Then one day, he came in from line camp and the foreman gave him his pay. There seemed to be some mistake in it, and he went to the ranch house to see Danby, the owner. None of the boys noticed him come out, but when the cook went to call him to dinner, he found Danby dead. Choked to death, his face ripped open, and the cowboy gone. When they went to look for Williams, he was gone. When they next heard of him, the police got a call to investigate a brawl in a Laredo saloon. When they arrived and broke through the circle, they saw two men struggling. Suddenly, one fell, and then before they could reach Williams, he lifted his spurred foot, and slashed the face of the fallen man. Then they got him. Then the police started for him. They got him after a terrible fight. The other fellow died in the hospital short-ly after." The Warden shook his head. "He's a tough one. Never [moved] a muscle when they sentenced him."

"Too bad." Jim Kelton rose and picked up his hat. "Well, guess I'd better run along. Come out for a game of bridge some night, Tom. Ellen was saying the other day that we never see you anymore."

The warden opened the door for his friend. "I'll be out some night soon," he promised, smiling.

As Williams stood waiting for the trusty to unlock the door of his cell, his eyes met those of Lawrie, the man in the next cell. Between the two had grown up an active dislike, the more threatening because unspoken. At least, so far. It remained for Claffin, across the way, to bring the thing out into the open. They were all discussing an expected arrival.

Said Claffin, "I guess this new bird is plenty tough. He murdered his wife and two kids. That's even worse than 'cowboy' there."

Lawrie cut in sneeringly. "I don't agree with you. He didn't carve 'em up afterwards like Williams did. Nobody in their right mind could do a thing like that. I couldn't, and neither could any of the rest of you fellows," he charged. No one answered. The others knew of the enmity between the two, and a strained silence filled the place. Then at last, Williams spoke, his voice hoarse, fairly quivering with rage.

"All right, Lawrie, you've said plenty. I'll remember it. And don't forget this; you'll be next! You'll be next!" he repeated harshly. Lawrie laughed, mockingly. The guard coming down the hall put a stop to further conversa-tion for the time being. But now the quarrel between the two was out in the open, and through the following days and weeks, Lawrie seemed possessed of some imp of perversity and taunted and gibed at Williams continuously. Much of the time, the 'cowboy murderer' lay on his back on the cot and stared sullenly at the ceiling, only turning at times to throw Lawrie a venom-ous glance. At times, Lawrie grew ashamed for taunting a doomed man, but something inside of him, stronger than he, urged him on implacably. Once in a while, he shuddered at the looks given him by the other, and silently he blessed the bars that kept them apart.

Then came Williams' last morning. The prison chaplain came to adminis-ter the last rites, but fled before the storm of curses that met him. After his departure, a long silence fell that lasted till they came for him. Even Lawrie was silent and sat soberly watching. As they brought him out, and he passed Lawrie, he stopped and looked in. His eyes, filled with immeasurable hatred, met those of Lawrie. On his face was a malignant sneer."

"Remember, you're next," he said slowly, and passed on down the corridor. Lawrie watched his retreating form till it passed from sight. Claffin called across in a hoarse whisper. "What do you make of this; Williams asked them to bury him with his spurs on. Funny, isn't it?"

Lawrie did not answer for the reason that at the word 'spurs,' a queerly premonitory chill passed over him. Uneasily, he recalled the other's parting word and the cold, evil hatred of the other's glance. He tried to shake off the cold, chilly feeling that was settling over him, but without success. There seemed to be an indefinable change in the atmosphere, a sense of something horrible about to happen. They all felt it, in a lesser degree. The gray day dragged along, and conversation lagged. By common consent, they all avoided glancing at the empty cell. It seemed too potent a reminder of the thing that waited for them all. Dusk settled down and shadows began to fill the corners. And then Lawrie glancing idly out of the door of his cell, gave a startled cry. There in the shadows before his cell door, he saw something. A shadow that formed, that seemed to pause and linger before him. Then, as he cried out, it melted into nothing and was gone.

"His heart was beating fast, pounding with the nameless fear that held him in an ever-tightening grip. The sense of impending calamity drew closer. He began to shake.

"What's wrong?" called Claffin, curiously, his voice low.

Lawrie, eyes fastened on the empty cell next to him, did not answer. He could not. He was watching something—something that formed before his eyes into a man, a shadowy figure that smiled horribly and wore gleaming spurs. He saw it form, growing clearer and drawing nearer the bars. The shadowy eyes gazed back into his terrified ones, and then he screamed at the thing he read in them. A scream that died in his throat in a gurgle as he fell heavily.

The guard came running. "What's going on here?" he demanded, angrily. He peered in suspiciously at the fallen figure. At last they entered the silent cell and raised him to his cot. He was dead. And across the horror that death had stamped indelibly on his face, there ran the livid gash of a spur!

# Robert Nelson

## Night of Unrest

I tore a mask from off a trull
    And plucked a lotus drenched with blood;
I threw them to the wrathful flood,
    And kissed and wooed a lonely skull.

## Fragment

With the red bewitchment of the moon canines collect
And feast and howl o'er carrion and orts and bones
In green and putrid grots that echo shrill sea-moans;
And huge and hoary phantigrades on crags most high,
Hearing together on the topmost frozen mounds
To hurl immense boulders on them until all die.

## The Unremembered Realm

Nameless: that unremembered realm of the temporal universe
Which the sundry gods have slighted to complete:
These azure ice-peaks thrive and wane in wild exult,
And shift their freezing heights in tremulous tumult;
The wan ice-forms are vanished creatures lost in time.

Nameless: that unremembered realm of the temporal universe
Which the sundry gods have slighted to complete:
There the youthful moon is like a fount of living flame;
The eldern sun moves in a clique of pallid, dying mist;
Dark birds flow endlessly to turn the dawn to amethyst;
When moon and sun and birds are gone the dead make fires
In reeking, foul-swept skies above the great ice-spires,
And view the cold-fraught land with last and mad proclaim.

## Below the Phosphor

The swaying corpse upon the wall
Grows rotten with the waning light;
And crawling shadows of the night
Lie on the body like a pall.

Dead spirits dance upon the slope;
Blatant are bat-things overhead;

But now the revenants have fled,
The glad fantasias yet grope.

Only the ghouls are gently stirred
By tainted gusts lost from the gale;
And in the faun-infested vale
Wild screeches of a fiend are heard.

Impending o'er the noisome spawn,
In glaucous haze the Phosphor steals—
Thence to Azrael's eyes reveals
The wrestling wraiths on death's dark lawn—

Fast scaling up the ebon sky
To cull and slay the gnawing blight,
All cool of the corpse's mute delight
Or if the baneful field should die.

## Dream-Stair

What naked, bald and drunken child
Leads me to some mad, topless stair
And keeps me toiling upward there,
A withered thing, forlorn and wild?
About me swarm Satanic goats,
The seas below are frothing red,
And harsh winds sting my seething head
As steel on stone drops down in moats
Where drown and rot accursed swains—
Dismembered thralls of some mad king—
Whose bloated heads arise and sing.
But, lo! whence all these hellish rains
That seem to linger for an age
And pour upon my harried life
Such airs, with loathsome larvae rife,
As whisper o'er a wizard's page?
Then, mounting with white moons, I see
The frenzied flight of huge man-birds,
And hear the cold and lethal words
Babbled behind the drapery
Whose swelling folds lean forth and sway,
Shrouding a handed Shape, that grasps
And throttles all the Gorgon's asps,
And braves the Gorgon's eyes to slay!

The child brings ardent wine to me,
And still I climb the dream-built stair;
And in fell silence spreading there
Great shadows eat the sphered sea.
False child! false child! O traitor child!
What image meets my frozen eyes?
Is it what Satan sanctifies—
Full-fraught with bale but pleasing mild?
But the stair crumbles, clean destroyed,
The circling mists and phantoms flee,
The child pursues them mad with glee,
And leaves me in the falling void.

## Jorgas

With sighs the potioned flowers stooped to kiss
Pale Jorgas just awaking from his dream
Of olent wine and swirling-shadowed bliss,
And as the blue mist crawled upon the glade
The flowers talked and sang to him, and swayed
In shades with his, but all at once did scream,
"O Jorgas, why art thou a saddened man?"
"My thoughts are wildly blown with lunar dust,
   My lips, wine-steeped, are sore from evil prongs,
   I cannot break the thousand dream-wrought thongs
That trammel me with dreadful death and must."
"O, Jorgas, wine . . . perfumes . . . no courtezan? . . ."
"Oh, cease, and leave me to my misery.
   What poisoned hand is this that smooths a face
   Of bronze and plucks thy bitter petals free?"
"O Jorgas, wine and shadows all embrace
   Themselves with us and thee in ecstasy."
"No! No! I see . . . I hear . . . my eyes . . . that glare . . ."
"Pale one, look up . . . Her palm . . . Her heart . . . laid bare . . .
   Take it, and she an orb will give to thee . . ."
"No! No! It is accurst! I know . . . I know
   The vipers three who kissed and nuzzled it . . ."
"You dream as One who dreams below the Pit."
"I would let the flames to wrestle with the snow—"
"No, stay—take thou this knife and cut in twain
   The throat of Him who offered thee domain
   Within the realm where Specters laugh and dwell."
"On, do not say—what is there I can gain?

No! No! I would rather dream in silent hell . . ."
"He tramps on skulls and gluts on matted hair.
He comes—the Thing, whose noisome cerements shed,
Reveal the storm, the dead, in tortured tread.
O Jorgas, fare thee well! We die in prayer."
"Jorgas, I am He who comes in burning sod."
"My mind betrayed! Oh, do not slay me now!
Remove thy long-dead face and burnt-off brow—"
"Jorgas! Beat thy evil breast and cry for God!"

## Sable Revelry

(Written to music)

Black roses sprout across the sky,
Pipes sing insensate 'neath the sea,
The clamant heads of madmen fly
And shatter with a dark outcry,
As tones transpose to deeper dye
And leaves whirl wild with jubilee
Through the mad organist's rambling brain;
In the disordered sepulcher
A lady's dead eyes strive to stir,
She dares to laugh, but all in vain;
Three-fingered hands paint a far frieze
With the black blood of vanquished devils,
Who sway and slay the music-breeze
In their daft and dying revels.

Now ebon fluids 'gin to flow
And drip with waxen candle-men;
Black disks of stone are trundling low;
From the organ's bosom fuming slow,
Fouler and sadder perfumes blow
To drown the bourns of demon ken;
Skulls flown from swarthy corpses kiss
And feed upon the organist's soul,
Which ne'er doth cease to toll and toll
Bell-like within this dark abyss;
Fell plants and flowers writhe in wombs
Of blighted worlds remote from morn,
And musty myrrh exhales from tombs
Whirling in utmost stars forlorn.

Swart suns on sounding waters swell
The turgid notes to direr din,
And murky spirits soar from hell
To flap their cerements palpable
In the wild player's face, and tell
Jet jewels into his mouth, and spin
Mad gossamers amid his hair;
Swift raven locks entwine his throat,
His eyes no longer glare and gloat;
As from a tower high in air,
The console wakes a weirder fear;
His flaming, fitful fingers chill;
One tear he weeps, a dead man's tear;
The sable revery is still.

## Under the Tomb

Dread beings grope and sport in gory lakes,
A foul mist creeps and feeds on swollen slugs;
From beds of perfumed plants squirm fetid snakes,
And like a flower grown from sable drugs,
A moon of steel drips blood upon a sky
Darkened by what mad phantoms prophesy.

But this hath ceased and passed, and now in that
Mephitic, crumbling woodland 'neath the tomb
The dead sup with the dead o'er flowing vat,
And searing candles cleanse the rotting gloom;
And they who stood in sorrow's joy and pain,
Tread now through hell's ecstatical refrain.

Far still beneath, where bloated babes are kept
In glacial rooms, and skulls are lit as lamps
To guide through the life beyond, and where are swept
Green veils of oozing slime and deadly damps,
There is an everlasting resonance
Pealed by the tomb in glad deliverance.

# Lost Excerpts

## I. In Living Darkness

In dreams agone I walked aimlessly and long in far and distant realms.

I have seen wretched and depressed women feed with their milk the famished spirits that swelter and moulder amid the rank noisomeness of charnel hells. By blue and rotting trees I have seen colossal and cankered white worms fawning to their young and devouring themselves.

I have seen evil and demented dwarfs fling flaring torches into the faces of maids who were playing sad violins and dying with nameless sins and melody. And I have stood on red rocks overlooking a black and ever-surging sea wherein dread things stabbed and slew and shrieked in exaltation to the molten dripping skies.

## II. The Feast of the Centaurs

The enormous chamber was aflare with a myriad lamps. There were long tables covered with seemingly endless varieties of meats, wines, cheeses, birds, and other viands and edibles. Drunken centaurs carried other intoxicated centaurs across the tables trampling everything that came their way, causing both wrath and mirth to others. Wine was spilled heavily all about; and centaurs fell and grappled with one another on the lubricious earth. Two there were who fought for the possession of a fried grasshopper; and three belabored each other's heads with weighty stools. Some threw great platters of food from the tables and demanded more wine. And the exaltation that arose from the food and creatures became heavier; and the rejoicing and the swearing and debating of tongues increased.

There were huge mirrors of multiplied convexity in the vast room and these seemed to enhance and sharpen the ebbing and flowing luminosity from the immense wax lights and bright vases. The mirrors caused much confusion among the inebriated and over-gorged creatures, for they crashed and careened with one another against the mirrors and cut themselves, and laughed and cursed at their own grotesque and misshapen likenesses.

## III. The Flinging of the Rocks

He stood upon the precipice of the world, laughing wildly and flinging golden rocks of happiness upon the mountains, valleys, and seas below. The hoary mountains were crowned with gold and quaked in glee; the manifold valleys shook their bosoms and babbled in joyousness; the heaving seas shone with the golden blood of the bursting rocks.

The laughing winds screamed about him and perished in the golden mist far beneath. He stood on golden feet; and golden blood sped through his veins. In endless perpetuation he hurled the rocks of golden happiness until they all flowed in one mighty stream, and men knew not where it began nor where it ceased. And he defied both heaven and hell to halt him. His words were almighty cannons of universe-splitting bombardment, crashing levin-flashes that turned the eye to stone, the soul to everlasting darkness. His curses mingled with the golden torrent, and the rocks became happier.

They made the sun to dribble hot tears of golden gladness, and spattered upon the silken moon a flushed gold, so that it turned more swiftly, letting men see its other side for the first time. Then they slew each other in city and on plain in mad jubilation. And the dead rose to die again with grim laughter stamped on their skulls. Blue flowers were sprinkled with the powder of the dead, and drank the blood of the dying and turned golden. On and on came the rocks. They whirled in the cosmic dust and burned in a million worlds.

## Trilogy of Death

Death is a wheel . . .

Death is a wheel, grinding, rending, crushing. The little boy skipped gayly to the grocery store for his mother. Crossing the street, he did not see an on-coming truck. It was too late and—Death is a wheel, grinding, rending, crushing. Death is a wheel . . .

Death is a dollar bill . . .

Death is a dollar bill. A gust of wind swept a vagrant dollar bill into the gutter. It sped onward thru the streets. Onward to a jutting pier. Onward it went. A man espied it. He ran for it. Stumbled. Ran on. He came to the end of the pier. Fell into the water. But he grasped the dollar bill. "I've got it!" he cried. And then he sank beneath the waves. Death is a dollar bill . . .

Death is a dream . . .

Death is a dream. "Death, too, must be a dream," said the man in his dream. "Pretty hills. Endless. Light all about. Light . . . gladness . . . music . . . voices of women. But my throat. How tight. I am choking . . . Breath, breath. My breath. Pretty hills. Endless. My breath. God, my breath. Light . . . breath . . . hills . . . music . . . voices of women. Breath . . ." Death is a dream . . .

## The Weird Tale (A Dialogue)

Gerald: So you say that science fiction has fallen into decay?

Sidney: Precisely. By its own outlandish and inflated ridiculousness it has been reduced to the tedium and monotony of everyday life.

Gerald: Oh, but you make me laugh, Sidney! What of weird fiction? How can anyone endure these everlastingly infernal vampire stories with their boorish waving of crosses to defy and fight off the vampire! I dare say that if I should fling a putrid tomato at one of the accursed things it would run helter-skelter!

Sidney: It is very true. Vampire stories are a bit worn, and deserve to have gone out of existence long ago. But it is the weird tale, Gerald, the sort of tale as produced by Lovecraft and Smith, that truly makes weird literature something far more noble and beautiful than most modern fiction, with its silly tea-lady romances, modern love, and high society twaddle.

For an illustration of weird fiction, Gerald, let us take Clark Ashton Smith's most superb tale, "The Double Shadow." Here we have one of the most beautiful weird tales in the English language. When we read it we experience the sensation of a sweeping and stirring symphony. We read of Pharpetron, "the last and most forward pupil of the wise Avyctes," and how he and his master live in the marble house above the "loud, every-ravening sea." We see the wind-swept sea, the white towers, the eerie demonisms and necromancies, the Double Shadow. It creates for us a life which we would wish to live, and fills us with a sense of external, majestic beauty of which we have been ignorant. All of this is so beautifully weird. Is not this more appealing than science fiction?

Gerald: Of course it all depends upon the individual. But I suppose the weird and macabre is more appealing, and rightfully, perhaps, it is. But you mentioned and inferred that the weird tale, as executed by Lovecraft and Smith, is the most worthwhile of the whole. Personally, I like Robert E. Howard the best of them all

Sidney: My dear boy, all three are great writers. We know that, but it cannot be denied that Smith is a truer artist, and that makes him the greatest. Oh, Gerald, if more people could only appreciate and understand the significance of the weird tale! And if scribes could only emulate Smith or Lovecraft or Howard! If they would only strive for originality and beauty! But no! we poor and insignificant readers of the weird tale must continue to be plagued with time-worn vampires, witches, rituals, and other weird senilities!

Gerald: Well, why don't you try to write a weird tale, Sidney? You seem to know all its merits and demerits.

Sidney: Well, because I— er— well, I just haven't the time.

# William F. Anger

## Fantastic Bread & Butter; or, the Mystery of the Missing Authors

Gentle reader, at my bequest, please take the nearest copy of *Weird Tales* magazine from your library shelf and look at it! What do you see? Answer: "Why, nothing special, just the same old periodical!" Immediately I differ with you despite the *unnamability* of the subject, which, like halitosis and "B.O.", should be at once remedied.

As a starter, we find a gaudy cover which would be fine for a bedroom story magazine. Two (usually two) figures, monsters of misproportion are

placed here as a sort of opening riddle or teaser; the purpose doubtlessly being to warm the reader up for that nasty let-down just inside, frustration, I
calls it! Back to the aforementioned riddle we find the main question to be,
*"Is that a woman?"* Answer: "Well, maybe!" (This sort of half-heartedly). The
second question which is of less importance: "Is that a vampire or the editor
with his arms around that unknown quantity we just discussed?" Answer:
"From what your correspondent is able to glean, it must be two other fellows."

Half the cover is devoted to blurbs which are promises unfulfilled, more
frustration; nevertheless we have the other half to account for and this is
briefly done. The cover illustration could well be supplanted by a chapter
from the Koran in Arabic and none of the weirdness or eldritchness missed!
Does this cover remind you of the days when Hugh Rankin, J. Allan St. John,
and others endeavored to make the illustrations at least hint of weirdness?
Answer: "Hell no!"

Now, down to the real marrow of my bone of contention: the contents.
We search valiantly and vainly, what do we find, any new plots or suggestions
of originality? Ideas seem to be lacking, color and setting is re-incarnated, any
plots that even suggest that the author originated them are smothered by a
mushroom sauce (should I say apple sauce?) of dictionary dredging.

Imitations of Poe, Lovecraft and any other great hero who had intestinal
fortitude in sufficient quantity to think for his own ideas are given howls of
applause and appreciation. The question is: WHY? The answer is because the
readers are so hypnotized by ballyhoo and punch-drunk from trying to understand stories that are quite beyond their comprehension (unless they pack a
pocket-Webster) that they wouldn't recognize a *real* weird tale if it hurled its
eldritch self down their outré necks!

Why don't we have the old time, dazzling array of writers to greet us each
month! Why are half the old faithfuls of five years ago writing adventure, western, and detective stories instead of weird fiction? My suspicion is that it's because the payment on publication policy consistently maintained by the magazine
of the bizarre and unusual, *during booms as well as depressions,* final got them peeved.
They gotta eat during the months in which an accepted story lies unpublished. I
picked up and verified a rumor about a tale by a popular writer being buried in
the demon-haunted vaults for 17 months before it reached print.

Contributors to phantasy soon find out that cash on the barrel head
awaits them in other fields and who would be "bizarre and unusual" enough
to refuse it? Should they go out and sip the nectar of the hibiscus by moonlight and write for WT, or should they sit down and write realistic stories for
real money? To profusely illustrate my point, let us whip up a few examples.

1.—Eli Colter used to write for WT's serials. But now we find Miss
Coulter doing bits for *Lariat,* novels of the rip-roaring west; penning away for
*Liberty,* and such like slicks. This does not suggest that her fertile brain has
failed and that she is unable to turn out those creamy tales of ten years ago!

2.—And Victor Rousseau—'member him from 'way back, with his oc-cult serials? These days he consistently makes *Five Novels,* the Dell magazine which gives even a beginner $250 for a romance, adventure, mystery, or a sport novelette.

3.—Otis A. Kline has lately appeared in the *Thrilling* books.

4.—Kirk Mashburn no longer writes fascinating phantasies of Louisiana and Yucatan. But he has not quit writing. Far from it. His westerns are selling, and they are good.

5.—Edmond Hamilton has less and less time to save a few worlds or galaxies. But he has not retired. On the contrary, one sees more and more de-tective magazines with Hamilton stories. Last year, one of his detective nov-elettes appeared not only in this country but in Sweden.

6.—Frank Belknap Long, Jr., is becoming more and more a stranger in the phantastic fiction field. And oddly enough, his appearances in detective and mystery magazines become increasingly frequent. In a word, this sensa-tional writer has not forgotten his stuff.

7.—Why the long absences of Seabury Quinn? The fans are still yelling for Jules de Grandin. Though it has been persistently whispered that Quinn no longer has time to grind out fiction as he used to.

8.—But when I saw an advance announcement of "Cyclops of Xotal", by Otis Adelbert Kline and E. Hoffmann Price I welcomed the latter writer back from an absence of a whole year; and to ask him, how come his remedying his neglect? After a moment of inscrutable oriental pondering, he said that "Cyclops" was something which had been accepted over two years ago, and that, moreover, he probably was losing his phantasy touch, as most of his 1933 and 1934 offerings had been rejected, and thus he had sort of passed from. the picture. Moreover, he had not the least idea why some of the other phantasy writers also were missing.

But this inscrutable and cryptic stuff doesn't always succeed. He did ad-mit when I confronted him with the facts, that he had sold 17 weird stories to *Spicy Mystery* since March, 1935, and in the midst of it all came a check, via airmail, for number 18, which he had sent out just 8 days previous. And I read "Hasheesh Wisdom" in that same magazine—probably the best orien-tale he has ever written. I saw, in his office, stacks of mystery, adventure, and detective magazines, dated 1934–1935–1936, containing his cover-featured novelettes. Moreover, he had sold 8 novelettes in Sweden.

Maybe WT did reject so many of his offerings he lost heart, though it's a cinch he hasn't forgotten how to write phantastic fiction. But I wonder if WT consistently rejected all the offerings of all the writers I've picked as exam-ples? They've not ALL lost their punch.

Maybe personal interviews with other ex-phantasy writers would be more illuminating, but I couldn't tour the country to visit them. And it is tough try-ing to get the truth out of the evasive and cryptic creator of Ismeddin the

Dervish, so all I can do is let you draw your own conclusions from my deductions on 7 authors and my interviews with one. Despite oriental indirectness, I still figure that pay on publication and indefinite burial of scripts has shoved a lot of old timers out of the phantasy field.

There are others whose names are too holy, rather *unnamable,* don't you know. Still and all, I'm wondering that H. P. Lovecraft is finally appearing again, after a siege of reprints; I'm wondering how long C. L. Moore will be an active phantasy writer. I'm wondering who will take Robert E. Howard's place, or whether we'll just get Howard reprints, which are cheaper than new material by living authors.

All of it boils down to this: would you rather see the old timers appear in reprints, or would you like to see the old gang break loose again? And if that's what you want, why aren't you getting it?

## An Answer to Mr. Anger

By Farnsworth Wright, Editor of *Weird Tales*

I am somewhat astonished at the criticism of *Weird Tales* made by Fred Anger.

In his criticism he asks: "Why don't we have the old time, dazzling array of writers to greet us each month?" The answer is simple: *Weird Tales* marches on. This magazine buys stories and not names. We are consistently uncovering new authors, with fresh viewpoints. *Weird Tales* would be derelict indeed in its duty to its readers if it printed nothing but the old plots by the old authors and offered them nothing new. The old authors are always welcome in *Weird Tales* when they submit stories that are new, fresh and unusual.

If all contributors were as meticulously careful with their work as is Seabury Quinn, for example, there would be little chance of their work being rejected. Mr. Quinn has frequently torn up manuscripts of his stories because they did not quite suit him. When a story leaves his hands, it is as good a piece of work as he can possibly write, and he does not rest on his previous laurels, nor rely upon his fame to get his stories across. We have rejected but one story by Mr. Quinn; that was not rejected because of its quality, but because it was not really weird. We have printed eighty-three stories from his pen, and all of them have been popular with our readers.

A group of new authors with real imagination is gradually taking the place of those whose offerings no longer come up to their previous standards. Among these new writers are Henry Kuttner, who is gaining skill with each passing week; Earl Pierce, Jr., whose "Doom of the House of Duryea" gave a new twist to the old vampire theme, and whose forthcoming story "The Last Archer," will be talked about for a long time, we prophesy; Thorp McCluskey, whose story in the January issue, "The Woman in Room 607," is a veritable tour de force of the imagination; Harry Hasse, whose "Guardian of the Book" is certain to be very popular; Robert Bloch, who has developed into a master of phantasy; J. R. Speer, a sailor, whose utterly strange and weird novelette, "Symphony of the Damned," will be published soon. And there are others.

It is my opinion that *Weird Tales* today is a better magazine than it ever was. We have lost some of our best writers by death—notably Robert E. Howard, Henry S. Whitehead, and Arlton Eadie. Serious losses, these; but in spite of them *Weird Tales* is getting better and better.

As to the covers—Mr. Anger says: "Half the cover is devoted to blurbs which are promises unfulfilled, more frustration." Candidly, we think he is wrong. The stories in the magazine do live up to the ballyhoo on the cover—barring an occasional bit of poor judgement by the editor. Of course, we do not claim to be infallible in our judgement.

Much as we like Margaret Brundage's covers, we have already begun to vary our cover designs by alternating her work with St. John's and other artists'. Seabury Quinn's fine story "The Globe of Memories will have a superb cover illustration by Virgil Finlay.

Just a word as to the one case with which Mr. Anger claims personal knowledge—"Cyclops of Xotal" by Otis Adelbert Kline and E. Hoffmann Price, which was "accepted over two years ago." (I take Mr. Anger's figure on that, as it is probably true.) What Mr. Anger does *not* say (because he did not know it) is that Mr. Kline had withdrawn the story from *Weird Tales,* and except for that withdrawal it would have been published long before it finally appeared.

Mr. Anger ends his criticism with the question: "Would you rather see the old-timers appear in reprints, or would you like to see the old gang break loose again? And if that's what you want, why aren't you getting it?" In answer to this, we can only say that the gang is always welcome in *Weird Tales* every time they offer something as good as the stories which first established their fame. Many of our old stand-bys appear quite regularly in *Weird Tales* because they have progressed with the magazine. Others write for slick paper magazines. We do not blame them for this, but take pride in the number of our authors writing for big-time magazines.

## A Writer Comments on the Anger–Wright Controversy

A *Weird Tales* writer, who does not desire us to use his name, writes in part: "The practice of payment on publication is indefensible. But Gernsback did the same thing with his *Wonder;* and *Amazing Stories* does likewise. Farnsworth Wright is extremely courteous in this regard and never holds a script for months before letting the author know the verdict. I've sold a number of articles to *Weird Tales* and do not complain of my treatment, although in the manner of payment I've been treated the same as any other contributor. It may seem odd to Mr. Anger, but the stories I've written for WT have been done for the sheer pleasure of it and  the expectation of payment was a purely secondary consideration. I'm not wealthy, and because I can't afford to make it writing, I also turn out material for more "formula" magazines—which pay on acceptance. But even if there were no chance of selling my weird stuff at all, I would still write it—for my own pleasure. It seems to me that the writers who sell their work consistently to the pulps and slicks can, if they wish, take time to turn out a few stories a year for *Weird Tales;* if they do not it's because they do not want to, and I don't really blame them. Personally, I'm just screwy enough to prefer making a little less dough, and occasionally write the kind of stories I like to write.

I don't blame Colter or Hamilton or Wandrei for writing for other magazines; but neither is Wright to be censured for his policy. If Wright were not at all concerned with the quality of his material he'd change his book into a second *Terror Tales,* buy hack stuff, reduce the price, and clean up. But he prefers to cater to genuine lovers of the weird, although this limits his circulation. Thus payment on publication, I think, is a necessity rather than anything else. Farnsworth Wright has had, ever since he first ventured into the editorial field, a reputation for integrity which is far superior to certain other editors who have had the bad habit of leaving their contributors to hold the sack! I know a select group of weird writers who continue to turn out work for *Weird Tales*, despite the payment-on-publication basis, simply because they enjoy the work, and would not be happy if they bottled up their creative impulse and ground out hack stuff for formula markets.

## An Interview with E. Hoffmann Price

With Louis C Smith

Author, linguist, world-traveller, automobile mechanic and cook—that, fantasy fans, is a fairly representative picture of E. Hoffmann Price! The Syrian quarters of Chicago and New York and the Old French Quarter of New Orleans are no strange places to this prolific author of weird stories and detective yarns; he is equally at home in the Philippines and in certain little-known sections of France. Hs is—but wait!—let's go about this in an orderly manner.

Contrary to popular belief, E. Hoffmann Price did *not* have his first story published in *Weird Tales;* his first was sold to *Droll Stories,* and brought him the magnificent sum of twenty-four dollars (he chuckles over it now). His first story in Weird Tales was "The Rajah's Gift" which appeared in January 1925; and from this time on, until his job as manager of an acetylene plant petered out, Price wrote exclusively for *Weird Tales* and *Oriental Stories*. Since the spring of 1932 he has devoted all his time to fictioneering.

"The Sultan's Jest" his third story in the "Unique Magazine" was later reprinted in *The Sovereign Magazine* published in London.

"The Lord of the Fourth Axis," in *Weird Tales* last year was revised three times before Farnsworth Wright accepted it. The strange, unique design for

462 ❀ *Letters to Robert Bloch and Others*

the rug which played so prominent part in this latter tale was suggested by a Turkestan prayer rug of unusual shape now hanging in the Chicago home of Editor Wright.

The locale of the Pierre D'artois stories is authentic: there is a city of Bayonne, France, and there Price lived for some time, visiting the underground chambers, soaking in the atmosphere of the place. Also in France, he visited the city of Lourdes where he obtained from several old legends, material for "Tarbis of the Lake."

To *Strange Detective Stories* Price sold one of the Pierre D'artois stories, which he considers the wildest story he has ever written.

Material for "The Prophet's Grandchildren" (W. T. October 1925) was picked up in the Philippines.

Having sold every story in which a peacock was mentioned, Price quite naturally considers this beautiful bird the best of good luck emblems. But enough for the writings of E. Hoffmann Price! For the man himself:

His favorite smoke is the *nargileh* or water pipe; though on occasions he does relish a cigar or a cigarette rolled from Bull Durham tobacco.

He speaks German, mangles French and Spanish, and gargles a smattering of Arabic.

While in Oklahoma this spring, he salvaged sheet metal from an abandoned smokestack—welded the pieces together to make an automatic feed acetylene generator for a friend who owned a repair shop.

He lived several years in "Le Vieux Carre"—that's creole for "Old French Quarter"—of New Orleans, which accounts for his frequent use of Crescent City atmosphere. He has been in the Philippines, Japan, Hawaii, Mexico, has covered France from end to end, and is at home in most parts of the States.

Favorite dishes: Chili con Carne, East Indian Curry, and on state occasions, a capon stuffed with pistachios and basted with sherry until, when completely roasted, the fowl is coated with a high glaze of deep walnut color: the result being called "Varnished Vulture" by the crew of fictioneers who make Weird Tales Editorial Rooms their headquarters. And a close second to the foregoing is turtle stew, prepared according to an old creole recipe.

And, there, in a fragmentary, woefully incomplete way, you have E. Hoffmann Price: swell spinner of tall yarns, linguist, mechanic, cook par excellence—and in general a hell of a good fellow.

Selah!

# Donald A. Wollheim

## Allalieor

Far world, that once 'round brilliant Altair whirled
Upon whose green islets fair cities stood
From whose golden ports with emerald sails unfurled
Sailed marvel caravels of crimson wood.
Where art thou now? Whence fled thy worldly soul?
For surely so beauteous a sphere as thou
Must have that mystic essence true of all
Beloved things that with life God did endow.
Alas, that sad time when came the scourge of
Lost spheres of lightless void to burn and sear
Forever they know bleak plains that know love
No more, but only phantom's shriek and leer
Oh world that was, oh land of wondrous love,
Somewhere still though liveth, Allalieor!

## [Review]

THE NECRONOMICON as *Translated and Abridged from the original Arabic of Abdul Alhazred,* by W. T. Faraday. Privately printed by the author.

In the early days of the Middle Ages, shortly before the advent of Mohammed, a half-mad Arab, Abdul Alhazred by name, compiled this odd book. According to the foreword this is the first English translation ever made, and the only other translation ever prepared for publication is the extremely rare Latin work of the so-called black magician Olaus Wormius; who was burned at the stake several hundred years ago for heresy. This version is a compilation from the original.

This book was not intended for sale to the public. It was printed chiefly for purchase by those students of the Occult who found it necessary to consult this work in their researches. It purports to be the account of the Spheres of the Occult and their dealings with mankind from the dawn of history. It shows very clearly the deranged mind of the writer, who was so convinced he received these facts from supernatural sources. Curiously enough, it does leave a feeling of some truth in this reviewer's mind.

If we are to judge from the foreword, this book is very much abridged. The original ran to nine hundred pages of manuscript. This edition contains three hundred pages. Dr. Faraday admits to having omitted whole chapters for safety's sake. . . . On the whole, this publication will live as an outstanding contribution to Occult lore. It is also the introduction to the element of Elder Gods who according to the ideas of mystics came before the Modern Demons set in. It is claimed that the late Robert W. Chambers and Ambrose Bierce both consulted the work on writing some of their earlier and more fantastic works. This is a volume that will prove invaluable to certain individuals.

Under the "Book Chats" column of the *Branford Review and East Haven News* 8, No. 24 (Thursday, 12 September 1935): 7.*

## Umbriel

*A Short Short Story*

*Form letter from the files of the Oberon Government Department of Interlunar Navigation:*—In answer to the oft-repeated query of space-minded citizens as to why our vessels always avoid the second satellite of our Uranian system, the following document is in evidence. It is a condensation of the report of K'yaldiu, pioneer astronaut of several generations ago.—

My craft slipped through the atmosphere of Umbriel without much trouble. It was much thicker and warmer than any previously experienced. After landing my instruments registered as high as 60 degrees below zero Fahrenheit (Earth translation)!

I grounded the ship upon a flat surface of soft greenish sod (or so it seemed first glance through the ice windows). After shutting the rockets off, I made ready to go ashore and claim the territory for Oberon providing there were no natives.

Stepping out, my nostrils were greeted by a most foul stench. The air was thick, heavy, warm, and very bad of odour. It was barely breathable, and an excessive heat poured up from the ground itself, which soon sapped my energy very much.

As soon as I set out to walk about, my feet sunk into the soil and it was necessary to keep pulling them out, which was accompanied by a most discomforting sucking noise. The ground seemed more like some of the semi-liquids that our scientists produce in their laboratories when they get temperatures high enough to almost melt ice!

For a while I squished my way along. Then a section of the ground before me swelled while I watched into a large hemispherical dome and snapped. A cloud of noxious vapour was released and swirled past me. It was most peculiarly like a bubble.

Coming upon a large pitted yellowish rock, towering isolated out of the ground, I stopped and examined it. It was composed of some porous hard shiny substance unlike anything nature produces. There was a most unnatural feeling about the thing.

There was a movement behind me and turning I saw one of the beings na-

---

*Discovered by Donovan K. Loucks.

tive to Umbriel. Oozing from a hole in the ground, came a large shapeless white object having neither arms, legs, eyes, ears, nor other external appendages. It had a mouth and a tubular several foot long slimy body. And something else.

I stared at it to see what it was doing. And when I saw and recognized, I knew then what sort of sphere I was on. For the thing was eating the soil. It was devouring the greenish ground with considerable voracity! It was a worm, a grave worm of enormous proportions. And it could only be eating the flesh of a dead creature!

Fleeing back to my Ovoid, I found it already half sunk in the rotting terrain. Leaping into it, I slammed the door and took off with a crash of my gunpowder rockets that lit the scene.

Never will any sane creature go to Umbriel again. For it is not a natural globe—it is the curled up carcass of a dead animal, a great monster from some colossal world out of far space. Somehow it had been hurled through the void and captured by Uranus. And now that it has been warmed a little by the heat of the far off sun and near Uranus, it has started its rotting and the worms have come out of the depths of its body to feed.

Forever let it fester in isolation, for they are not the only beings that dwell there. About the worm's surface was a metal belt with strange glyphs on it. Somewhere in the depths, in the very bowels of that rotten corpse world, lives intelligence, a race of unutterable horror feeding off the bodies of the worms, even as the worms feed off the rotten planet-being. A race of unspeakable foulness and revoltingness dwelling therein. So far they know naught of other worlds. Grant then never do learn.

## Pure Fantasy

The average reader is inclined to regard adult fantasy as belonging to only two general classifications, science fiction and weird fiction. These classifications may be roughly defined as follows: science-fiction is that branch of fantasy, which, while not true of known present day knowledge, is rendered plausible by the reader's recognition of the scientific possibilities of it being possible at some future date or at some uncertain period in the past. Weird fiction is that branch of fantasy dealing with supernatural or occult subjects, which is rendered plausible by the reader's recognition of the fact that there are people somewhere who at present or in the past, did believe, or do believe in the truth of the ideas therein and is therefore willing to concede the truth of these things for the period in which he is reading the story

There is however a third class of fantasy which cannot come under either of these headings and therefore must of necessity be classed separately. This I will term Pure Fantasy. It is known to everyone in its juvenile version as fairy tales. But it does not stop at the juvenile. Unknown apparently to most people, it extends into adult fiction in an almost pure form in a few unfrequent books and authors. While it is true that science fiction and weird fiction are also derived from the juvenile fairy tale, it is equally true that their form and style have changed greatly. This is not so with pure fantasy. When reading it, one becomes clearly conscious of the fairy tale origin immediately. Nevertheless this does not detract from the story since it is obvious that the book would not be enjoyed by children and is distinctly adult reading.

I will define this third class of fantasy as follows: pure fantasy is that branch of fantasy which, dealing with subjects recognizable as non-existent and entirely imaginary, is rendered plausible by the reader's desire to consider it as such during the period of reading. As you will notice, this definition holds true for fairy tales in the mind of a child as well as for pure fantasy in the mind of an adult.

There are only a few writers of pure fantasy but they are well appreciated in their circles. Practically all work of that type must be published in books. There is no professional magazine in the world that uses pure fantasy although the writers of such are well known and appreciated in the world of literature. I may mention here that probably the finest author of pure fantasy is Lord Dunsany. Walter de la Mare is another author of this type. H. P. Lovecraft has written several stories that may be classed under this type. His earlier works in particular, such as "The Silver Kay," "The Quest of Iranon," and "Celephaïs," are some. James Branch Cabell, Clark Ashton Smith, and R. H. Barlow are writers who have strong tendencies towards this field.

The pure fantasy story deals in general with imaginary lands and places. There is a strong current of the dream running all through them. The reader is seized with a longing and inward desire to be away to these far off wonder lands. There is the desire in them to escape to an unapproachable childhood. In them one is lost and wanders off to wander among ivory cities and gem-studded castle, to sit on the edge of the world looking into the star strewn chasm beyond, or perhaps gaze curiously at the strange land on the opposite bank beyond World's End. Perhaps the reader may find himself traversing the mystic forest of Mluna or lolling on a caravel floating down the river Yann watching the dreamy cities go by. Or perhaps he finds himself in some quaint town in a sleepy little country bordering on the Debatable Mountains across which lies forbidden Fairyland. There are many delightful places in the Lands of Fancy and many ways to enter them. We might walk into a little dimestore in a forgotten London side street and walk out the back door straight into the dream lands. Or merely wander into a meadow and find our ways into these hidden places. Yet these are not fairy tales.

Some good books of short stories of pure fantasy are Lord Dunsany's *Tales of Three Hemispheres*, *The Sword of Welleran*, and *A Dreamer's Tales;* among the novels *Lud-in-the-Mist* by Hope Mirrlees is outstanding.

In closing I recommend to the reader who has not made the acquaintance of this field of Fantasy, by all means to hasten to his nearest library and find a copy of something by Dunsany. I am sure he will never regret it. He will have found something that on occasions will delight him perhaps more than any other book he ever read.

## Howard Phillips Lovecraft

Doubtless by this time the news of the death of H. P. Lovecraft will have been published in all the important amateur papers. It would be needless for us to go into details of his death, and superfluous for us to attempt to sketch his life. There are so many who could and probably will do that so much better than the writer.

I had the pleasure of meeting Mr. Lovecraft and of corresponding with him for a period of about two years. At first I had been attracted to him by my admiration for his excellent stories in *Weird Tales*. My acquaintance with him served but to raise my already high opinion immeasurably and gave me a hint of the really wide and brilliant scope his mental sphere encompassed.

In the writer's brief span of existence, but twenty-two years, H. P. Lovecraft ranks as the most brilliant mind I have ever met. One can go a long time before meeting another so fair, as capably learned, and as *intelligent* as was he. Yet he was never aloof, never vain. His was a spirit that sought the best in every man. He never rebuffed a correspondent, never failed to help when requested or to volunteer help even when it was not expected of him.

In a way, *The Phantagraph* was always edited with him in mind. When selecting material for an issue, I always thought "would HPL approve of this?" For he had become the freely acknowledged leader of the phantasy group to which virtually all the amateur phantasists catered. When he passed away, it was a severe blow to all.

His writings were multifold yet never received the recognition they deserved from the literary world. His friends have determined now to see that they get that recognition. August W. Derleth, aided by Donald Wandrei, R. H. Barlow, Farnsworth Wright and all of the HPL circle, is preparing for publication an omnibus volume of his best works—fiction, poetry and articles. Plans are being made for additional volumes, including one for his letters. It is hoped eventually to publish everything he wrote. Such volumes will merit publication by professional firms.

H. P. Lovecraft has not died. He has been born. The years to come will find him steadily climbing upwards to his true place in American literature: the American Machen, the Edgar Allen Poe of the twentieth century.

## Editor's Preface [to "The Shadow out of Time"]

Lack of recognition, the ancient curse of the creative writer and artist that brought despair and introverted fury to so many, has been mainly alleviated in these days of alert and prolific publishing. But for Howard Phillips Lovecraft this was not so. Born in 1890 in the city of Providence, Rhode Island, he was to die in that city in 1937 with but two small books to his credit, both volumes privately published by his admirers, both of very limited circulation. They were *The Shunned House* (1928), and *The Shadow over Innsmouth* (1936).

Unlike those who had suffered from publishers' oversight, Lovecraft never permitted this to affect his mood or his writings. For he was, at heart, not interested in the things of this twentieth-century world. His heart preferred the past ages, specifically the eighteenth century. As a result of this, as a result of his careful and scholarly erudition and the style he sought, if ever the title of the Edgar Allan Poe of this century is granted, it will rest most easily on the brow of H. P. Lovecraft. Lovecraft saw the terror of the aeons. To him past and future were dim and shadowy abysses, filled with the nameless horror of the unknown powers of nature and alien intelligence. Because he was remarkably erudite, a master of languages, well versed in sciences such as astronomy, psychology, physics, architecture, biology, archeology and others, he did not need to draw upon occultism for the background of his literary terrors. He drew upon science and its problematic possibilities for the skeletons upon which he pegged Poesque tales of cosmic dread. It is that factor which brought him towering above the other writers in magazines where appeared his occasional creations.

"The Shadow Out of Time" is a perfect example of the use of science-fiction to create terror. Its speculative pasts and futures are sound. To Lovecraft the millions of years gone by and the millions of years to come are sources of dread, because of his knowledge of the cold cruelty of nature. Contrast this with the detached view of John Taine, and with the faith in futurity of Olaf Stapledon and H. G. Wells. Yet Lovecraft, himself, was anything but a morbid man.

Since his death, his writings have gained steady recognition. Three original collections have won him the place in literature he deserved: *The Outsider Others* (1939), *Beyond the Wall of Sleep* (1943), and *Marginalia* (1944). Resulting from these have come *The Best Supernatural Stories of H . P. Lovecraft* (1945), *Supernatural Horror in Literature* (1945), *The Lurker at the Threshold* (1945), inclusion in numerous anthologies, and a critical study of his life and writings by August Derleth entitled *H.P.L.: A Memoir* (1945). "The Shadow out of Time" first appeared in print in 1936.

## The Future of Publishing

Not much thought has been given to the question of the development of publishing in the future. Yet certainly we have a right to believe that this field of enterprise, a vitally important one so far as the continuance of civilized society is concerned, will see advances comparable to the great changes that have taken place in other fields of work. Essentially there have been no great changes in the publishing business for decades.

Books, magazines, and newspapers are still the form that printed matter takes—paper printed and bound copies of the literary item, distributed about by various more or less haphazard methods over a small percentage of the population. Efficiency of production and distribution have been increased, but the method of conveyance—the book form—remains.

Already we are beginning to understand that one form of publishing is facing grave and far-reaching changes—journalism. The radio is rapidly overtaking and replacing the distributed daily sheet. Methods of reproducing a newspaper via automatic radio reception are fast being made more practical and already a number of papers in this country have radio editions. But what about books and magazines?

A book is considered a successful product if it sells 25,000 copies. Basically that is absurd. A pulp magazine which sells 70,000 copies is a tremendous hit; that is also absurd. A slick magazine that distributes a million copies is a wow. That is still silly. For there are 135,000,000 persons in this country. 25,000 books among one million is an absurdity. Yet that is a successful book! Even a million copies of a magazine are not touching the surface of what a literate American should demand.

Let us consider that in the future, which, if civilization is to continue must be one of peace, full free play for scientific enterprise and mass production (with no bars concerning scarcity necessities and profit requirements; with no unemployment and universal free education and high living conditions), literature and the desires of the people for literary recreation and endeavor will have found its real base, its real mass appeal, and will begin to fulfill its potentialities.

To do so it will be necessary to place at the disposal of everyone who desires it cheap, efficient and free (from censorship of any kind) means of publication and distribution for any of the literary creations of individuals— whether it is poetry, fiction, essays, polemics, scientific theses, criticisms (political, literary, social) or just blowing off wind. To guarantee that their works may be publishable at means within the expense of each individual, thus removing the tyranny of a select group of moneyed publishers such as the present setup requires (consciously or otherwise) Professional publishers must be done away with if absolute freedom of the press is to be obtained. This can only be done if the need for expensive, ponderous, and complicated presses, paper plants, and distribution centers is done away with. They can only be done away with by the introduction of new methods in publishing.

The key to these new methods lies in the work known as "microfilm" reproduction. Already the bigger city and college libraries are equipped with apparatus for microfilm publishing and reading. The method is simple and inexpensive. A page of book or manuscript is simply photographed on a roll of 16 mm film. Page (double-page, that is) by page a book can be recorded on microfilm. This film, when complete, can be run off page by page on a simple cheap reading machine which enlarges the film to full size (or any size convenient to the reader) and can be read at leisure.

By the method of microfilm, only one master copy is made of the original work—which may be a copy of an already published book or magazine, or may be a new manuscript filmed from typed or hand-drawn sheets. Anyone desiring a copy of this has but to order it, and a copy is run off from the master film—in similar manner to mass production of motion picture reels.

It is possible, for instance, today to obtain a complete file of every science-fiction magazine in existence by simply writing to the Library of Congress for microfilm copies of those magazines. They charge something like a penny or two a page—it would be expensive today, for, after all, the process is new and the demand is low. But, if one could afford it, one could amass a collection of any type of literature that would make any existing private collection look sick.

But what of the future of microfilm publishing? Therein lies the key to future literature. With mass education and well-being, publish publishing offices could be set up in every town and district. Those who wish to get something of their published take their manuscript to that office, pay a small fee, and receive in a short while a copy of their work in microfilm. The publishing office sends a master negative to the state of national publishing center for filing. Lists and critical analysis of every published work are issued periodically from this central office (perhaps weekly or daily). Persons wishing copies put in a request for a copy of such and such work at their local office. In a day or so, they receive, via the central office, their copy in microfilm. Cost of that book at that rate will be very low, perhaps a few cents. Author will be credited with a sale, and, at the end of a set period, total sales of each author's work listed and paid.

Such may well be the free press of the future—free of editors, commercial requirements, slavery to newspaper reviewers; free of distribution, costs of paper, advertising strangleholds, etc. such a press would bring literature to every person able to read (and, in the future, all people will be able to read and appreciate one or another type of literature). Not 25,000 copies of a good book—more likely 5 million. Not the seven or eight concerns dominating the popular fiction magazine field, as today, but a hundred million persons dominating their own fiction or other publishing houses.

*Editors' note:* Donald Wollheim became a prominent figure in the publishing of science fiction, as author, editor, and publisher, for more than four decades. He may have missed in his prediction of the spread of microfilm for the mass distribution of published material, but the Kindle and other means of electronic publishing have virtually fulfilled his prediction.

# Kenneth Sterling

## The Horror Element in Poe

*Dedicated with admiration to the memory of H. P. Lovecraft*

Fear is among the strongest of human emotions. Springing from primitive man's deep-seated dread of the enemies that lurked in the dark, primeval jungle, it has always been a basic factor in conditioning human behavior and reactions.

This is particularly evident in the superstitions and religious cults of savage peoples. Fear is one of the most powerful emotions of the Old Testament—indeed, it is fundamentally integral with the early conception of an anthropomorphic god. It is evident that the evolution of more advanced ideas of religion, such as the substitution of a god of love for a god of fear, parallels the development of the knowledge of the facts and laws of the cosmos. The most potent fear is the fear of the unknown, so it follows that where ignorance is greatest, fear is greatest. Understanding illumines the dim and mysterious caverns of the awful unknown and shows that these aboriginal terrors are mere illusions. Therefore, stark horror is seldom experienced by the normal, educated adult of modern times.

The very young child, like early Man, lives in a world of monsters, demons, and all manner of hostile supernatural creatures. These fears are not superficial, but are grounded in the animal instinct of self-preservation. Hideous creatures in dreams (which appear very real to the ignorant child or savage), unexplained natural phenomena (lightning, thunder, etc.), together with an utter lack of comprehension of life and nature in general make deep, indelible impressions in the mind that is acute enough to be curious and afraid, but untutored and thus incapable of understanding.

That there is no terror in the commonplace is axiomatic. The danger of being killed by an automobile may arouse strong emotion but never genuine horror. As a child grows older, his familiarity with his surroundings increases, and the frontiers of his knowledge are extended. With the mental reorientation caused by these acquisitions, his infantile phobias seem to wither away gradually as his total environment assumes the aspect of the commonplace.

The normal adult has a feeling of security regarding cosmic forces—only the demented retain the extravagant fears of childhood. Even the world of dreams, the shadow-land of the supernatural, has less of the fantastic and the grotesque. In short, the power of the weird imagination, which is a prerequisite to the feeling of horror, seems lulled into a dull numbness beneath the heavy cloak of somber, matter-of-fact materialism.

That even dreams tend to be marshalled into coherent patterns with the advent of maturity shows how thoroughly the system of logic has saturated the brain. However, the infrequent occurrence of nightmares and the still rarer occasions of awesome shocks in waking life indicate that the emotion of horror is not entirely absent. The inborn fears are still lingering deep in the subconscious.

*The successful weird tale must tear aside the veneer of conscious realism and probe into the dormant senses of horror in the remotest, most inaccessible recesses of the mind.* That is the keynote of the horror story as developed by Edgar Allan Poe.

Although there were some notable contributions to the weird field before Poe's time, such as the Gothic romances (e.g., Mrs. Radcliffe's work), Mrs. Shelley's "Frankenstein," "The Dybbuk," and others, it is safe to say that the bulk of pre-Poe writers were working largely in the dark. The terror theme is quite common in the great writings of the past from the Scylla and Charybdis of Greek mythology to the hideous witches of Shakespeare's "Macbeth." But, in most of the great classics the supernatural theme, notwithstanding its effectiveness, is often merely incidental, and thus consigned to a position of minor importance. At best it is used as a device to advance the main theme of the work (as in "Hamlet" and "Macbeth"), but is rarely an end in itself.

Edgar Allan Poe is chiefly responsible for the development and perfection of the horror story as an individual literary form. Poe realized that all aspects of life—the dismal and morbid as well as the brighter side—are equally acceptable as subject matter for creative expression. Being melancholy by nature, and addicted to the strange and macabre by predilection, it is quite logical that Poe should become an exponent of weird literature.

The squalor, misery, and tragedy of his life had a great effect on his sensitive, esthetic temperament as reflected in most of his major works. The wasting away and sad death of his young wife and cousin, Virginia Clemm, had considerable influence on his writings—this theme is seen throughout both poetry and prose.

Gifted with great powers of imagination, Poe had the fire of genius which produced eerie and fantastic conceptions. His habitual heavy drinking and occasional use of opium doubtless stimulated his normally fertile brain to produce the awful demons that leer at us from his pages.

Nevertheless, contrary to the popular belief, Poe's works are not wild, rhapsodical flights of fancy dashed off during a moment of emotional intensity, induced perhaps by the use of a drug or liquor. They are carefully planned, methodically constructed pieces, and show the hand of the painstaking craftsman as well as the inspired artist. This is demonstrated by his constant experimentation with a given idea which in many cases extends over a period of several years and is evident in numerous stories.

Besides the emotional, poetic side of Poe which is readily apparent, he had coldly methodical and analytical capacities such as are rarely seen in imaginative or artistic persons. His tales of ratiocination, such as "The Purloined Letter" and "The Gold Bug," which were precursors of the modern detective story, illustrate his acute logic. These are, however, purely stories of scientific deduction, and having no horror element other than the brutal murders which are merely part of the framework for the detective theme, they will not be considered in this study. However, it is this systematic type of thinking which enabled Poe to express graphically his eldritch dreams and to resolve them into coherent and effective patterns.

Poe used the short story as a vehicle for terror, and his narratives virtually, all of which are in this form, have been of monumental importance not only in the weird field, but also in that of short fiction as a whole.

The short story is ideal as a medium for the strange or supernatural. The advantage that it can be read at one sitting can not be overestimated, for in the terror tale the maintenance of a certain dreary frame of mind in the reader which will be receptive to fear is of prime importance. Indeed, it is next to impossible to sustain such a sensation for an extended length of time.

A weird novel, read at intervals between periods of hum-drum daily work, is much more likely to fall short of its mark. I do not claim that successful novels of this sort have never been written, but I contend that the short story is the more satisfactory form. Such a novel must, by its very nature, be a series of eerie episodes with stretches of lessened intensity, emotional "letdowns," so to speak, in between. The short story can convey a more compact, unified impression than the novel even if the latter could be read without interruption.

Short stories are generally classified according to their emphasis on either plot, character, or atmosphere. On this basis literally all of Poe's horror tales would fall in the last division. But I prefer to term them stories of *mood* inasmuch as each is fundamentally the interpretation of an emotion of dread rather than the depiction of a setting.

All incident, characterization, and other elements are subdued except insofar as they build up the unified impression of fear which is the sole object of the work.

The unknown and mysterious is essential to true horror. But it is also necessary that the tale win the reader's credence in the plausibility of the material presented during the time of perusal. This constitutes the principal problem of the weird tale and involves the temporary suspension of the reader's sense of logic and realism which is antagonistic to supernatural horror.

It is a general rule that the more horrible conceptions (as, for example, a super-dreadful monster out of space) are the more fantastic, and thus correspondingly harder to convey in a convincing manner. The most effective method of overcoming this obstacle is by bringing the horror into a close relation to the actual gruesomeness of reality. A subtle distortion or perversion of the true to life can be much more realistic than any abrupt departure. By the effective use of this technique, Poe renders alive and gripping the dread horrors that stalk through the weird realm conjured up by his vivid imagination.

## The Horror of Abnormal Psychology

In several of Poe's tales, horror is produced by means of the telling of a strange crime by a deranged narrator. In this class the abnormal mind serves as a stage on which a gruesome drama is enacted. The supernatural is generally absent from this group; the bizarre effects can be ascribed to the madness of the recorder of the narrative.

"The Imp of the Perverse" is a typical story of this type. It should be observed that before telling how constant pondering on his state of complete safety ultimately drives him to impassioned confession of a carefully prepared "perfect" crime, the murderer explains the operation of the queer sense of the perverse that caused his disclosure.

In this explanatory material, Poe endeavors to have the demented relator gain the momentary sympathy of the reader. There is an uncanny rational thread running through the mad cogitation that gives it the aspect of logic. When one gazes down from a high precipice or building, it is not unusual to experience an odd impulse to jump. This species of feeling, magnified to the nth degree, is the cause of the killer's damning acknowledgment of guilt. Under the spell of Poe's penetrating psychology the motivation of this paradoxical action can be comprehended and believed by the reader. That is the distinctive feature of these tales. Mere insane ravings would be of no interest *per se,* and would not be literature. By a clever exaggeration or caricature of the peculiarities of the normal mind, Poe presents a picture of abnormal thinking which is amazingly convincing.

The basic idea of all the stories in this class is essentially the same; they differ in the placement of emphasis. In "The Tell-Tale Heart" the hideous murder of the old man, whose vulture-like eye torments the relator to the core, is descried in all its shocking details. On the other hand, the actual killing of the preceding tale is limited to a single paragraph. The same feeling of absolute security is seen in each—in "The Tell-Tale Heart" the assassin gives himself up to the investigators with him when his fortitude is shattered by the imagined audible beating of his victim's heart.

There is no frenzied confession in "The Black Cat," but, as before, the madman is undone by his overconfidence and fancied invulnerability: as the authorities are about to depart, satisfied of his innocence, he raps on the brick partition behind which he has concealed his wife's body, and the howls of the black cat which was accidentally walled in, brings about the denouement.

"The Cask of Amontillado" stresses the accomplishment of terrible vengeance by playing on the vanity of the enemy. The narrator is coldly diabolical rather than insane. In contract to the previous stories, the apprehension of the culprit is omitted entirely here, and the force is concentrated on the achievement of the awful deed—the entombing of the victim, alive, in the wine cellar.

While in "The Tell-Tale Heart" madness is vigorously and repeatedly denied (which, of course, emphasizes it), the relator of "Berenice" realizes, indeed gives a detailed description of, his mental affection. He explains how his strange monomania becomes fixed on the pearly teeth of his dying wife. The molesting of her tomb to gain possession of these objects of his obsession corresponds to the crazed acts of the previous narratives.

Coordinate with this horror of monomania is the theme of the malady and languishing of Berenice, which recalls the torment Poe suffered at the bedside of his tubercular wife. It should be observed that the narrator of this story is wedded to a cousin, as was Poe in real life. The revelation that the woman has been interred alive adds to the loathsomeness of the relator's deed, and brings in an auxiliary idea, that of premature burial, which is also employed in other stories.

"Berenice" was written many years earlier than any of the other stories mentioned, and before their formula as such was developed. Consequently, it is rather different from them. Because of the presence of the other two weird elements noted above, its placement in this category must be made with reservation.

All these tales have much in common. The types of derangement are varied: perverse, suicidally irrational action, abhorrence of a friend's eye and hallucinations of the audible heart-beat of a corpse, abhorrence of a cat, passion for revenge, and monomania. This divergence shows experimentation on one fundamental theme. Revolting physical brutality (such as the cutting out of the black cat's eye and the dismembering of a corpse) is present to a greater or lesser degree in each piece.

"William Wilson" is a fascinating psychological study which differs markedly from the above stories—it is an allegorical portrayal of the mental agonies of a criminal wherein the conscience is represented as a person exactly like the narrator and bearing the identical appellation. Though nervous, perhaps neurotic, Wilson is not demented; the treatment of his mental processes is unique. The revelation of Wilson's cheating in the card game by the double may be likened to the confession in "The Imp of the Perverse," but here the emotions causing the action are *objectified* in the person of the second William Wilson. This allegorical device sets the tale apart from all others.

The final horror of the murder of that hellish twin which dares to oppose his unscrupulous lust brings Wilson into *physical* rather than verbal or mental conflict with his foil for the first time. In this act of violence against the presumably actual *alter ego* the narrator's utter moral downfall is consummated. The preceding stories depict a single form of derangement which, as expressed in the madness of the narrative, constitutes the horror element; it is devoid of the more subtle *conflict* of this tale. Here the horror of the inner turmoil, the clash of opposing forces, is seen as a moving drama, outside the mind, in stark, corporeal reality!

With the possible exception of "William Wilson," none of the stories of this group can be considered truly supernatural since anything can be envisioned by a madman. So, excluding "Wilson" whose psychic horror is in a class by itself, these tales show the most hideous, morbid aspects of reality. Since they involve no basic contradiction of fact, the task of making them realistic is simplified. The more penetrating terror of the unknown is absent; instead there is the most awful phase of the known.

A more devastating mode of inspiring horror is the supernatural which involves the repudiation of accepted facts with some consequent fearful reorientation of fundamental conceptions. If successful, such a rebellion against reality can unseat the sense of security and strike at the dormant fears of the subconscious.

It is significant that while the narrator of the story is the motive force in the studies of abnormal psychology, he is usually much less conspicuous in the supernatural fiction. In general, little about his character is revealed, for he is commonly merely an interpreter of the events and setting, often taking a relatively minor part in the action

## The Horror of the Return of the Dead

Everyone has pondered on the inscrutable mysteries of death, and most people have, at one time or another, entertained some notion that death is not the utter end of being, and that it may be possible to overcome mortality. The source of such a theory may be religious conviction, superstition, vivid dreams of deceased friends, or the unbelief which attends the passing of someone who seems so lofty of stature, so permanent, that his ceasing to exist seems inconceivable.

The latter idea is used in "Ligeia" whose theme finds a thread of credulity in every reader, and in its negation of the accepted conception arouses the manifold fears which center on the strangeness of death. That Poe was deeply fascinated by this subject is shown by his constant treatment of it in both poetry and prose. Despite the tone of "nevermore" in "The Raven," Poe was a believer in personal immortality, and this view is expounded by "Ligeia," which Poe considered his finest prose work.

The first part of the story, which is preparatory in the supernatural horror, is a description of Ligeia of lofty and mysterious origin, showing her as a figure of heroic proportions. Her physical appearance—tall, slender stature, raven-black hair, and large, luminous eyes—has an air of profound strangeness. Her supreme powers of intellect and strength of will set her aside as a unique being. Despite the vividness of the delineation, one never seems to *know* her familiarly. It is necessary that she have the aloofness of a Greek goddess, for closer contact would destroy the illusion of preternatural powers. The relator's statements that he cannot recall when and where he first met Ligeia and that he has never known her surname add to her air of alienage. This is further augmented by the quaint, poetic style of the tale. The cast of the sentences, such as, "In the classical tongues was she deeply proficient," and "If this I saw—not so Rowena" have a melodious, lyrical quality that lends a dreamy, exotic tone to the narrative and more particularly to the person of Ligeia. Thus one is made to feel the immense psychic power of this superior being. This impression is sustained by the forceful ghastliness of "The Conqueror Worm," the poem composed shortly before her death, and her dying words expressing the conviction that Man is not utterly conquered by death "save only through the weakness of his feeble will."

The horror of the story is achieved in the scene where the narrator is sitting alone in the weird bridal chamber with the body of the detested second wife who he had the misfortune to marry after the decease of the adored Ligeia. Innumerable times after his reminiscent visions of Ligeia the breath of life seems to return to the corpse, and his repeated vain and frenzied efforts to revive it inspire the most potent dread. *Reiteration* of an abhorred act (which is usually frustrated) commonly constitutes the source of terror of a nightmare, and Poe has realistically translated this dream-fear into the action of waking life.

The awful climax occurs when the enshrouded figure arises, the cerements fall off, and the eye-lids open to reveal the black eyes of Ligeia. The abrupt ending does not disclose whether the astounding reanimation of the body by Ligeia's spirit, accompanied as it is by the acquiring of her physical aspect, is but momentary or whether it is a permanent return from the grave. It is probably more in keeping with the trend of the story to assume that the latter is not the case. Moreover, any subsequent explanation would be superfluous and anticlimactic since the entire weird effect of the tale is consummated in the amazing denouement.

"Morella," which is the prototype of "Ligeia," is a much briefer and less arresting piece. In dying, Morella gives birth to a daughter who is her reincarnation—thus the theme of the return from the dead is more or less diffused throughout the account of the maturing child, rather than being contained in one compact climax (as in "Ligeia") and is consequently attenuated. In a sense, the mystic element of the father's inadvertently naming the daughter Morella forms a climax—but this is essentially a reiteration and reinforcement of the idea of reincarnation, not an original disclosure of it, as is the culmination of the later piece.

The musical qualities of style are also evident here, and likewise the occurrence of biblical phraseology, as "How knowest thou this?", in moments of intense emotion; the use of "lustra" as units of time is a quaint peculiarity. The general plan of the tale (excepting the difference in the conclusion mentioned above) is quite like that of the later story. Even the device of including a significant poem by the main character is present, although in this case the selection is not written during the fatal sickness.

The sad melancholy of "Morella" is more prominent than the fear element, which can seldom reach its apex within the limits of a very short tale. It has been postulated that a single weird effect cannot be prolonged to an undue extent. On the other hand, it is also true that there must be sufficient material leading up to this element. A gradual approach will convince the reader much more readily than if he is precipitated headlong into a series of fantastic events. "Ligeia" has a more lengthy, thorough preliminary development which affords adequate emotional preparation for the supernatural horror of the conclusion. Although "Morella" does not fall short of its mark, it is not aimed at the level of intensity achieved in the later version.

As in the series on abnormal psychology, the author has tried a variation of the same subject, with considerable improvement in this instance. Poe displays the same capacity for experimentation and revision seen in Pope's rehashing of "The Rape of the Lock." This exemplifies aptly that his works are not wholly spontaneous emotional effusions, such as those of Byron.

"Metzengerstein" is one of the few Poe stories told in the third person; although the pronoun "I" appears in the two initial paragraphs containing introductory material, it is not found in the narrative proper. It would be impossible to have Metzengerstein tell the story, as he is killed in the end, and there seems to be no convenient place to insert a narrator.

The present story can be likened to the two tales just discussed in that it also involves reincarnation—Berlifitzing's soul lives on after his corporeal decease in the body of a strange horse. However, it will be readily observed that otherwise "Metzengerstein" has little in common with the preceding narratives.

The first hint of the reincarnation is skillfully achieved in the scene where the eccentric young Baron Metzengerstein sees that the strange, fiery-colored horse of the hostile Berlifitzing family in the tapestry has moved and wears an oddly human expression in its eyes. This evidently occurs at the same time as Berlifitzing is killed in the holocaust of his castle and the metempsychosis is accomplished. The appearance of a real, uncannily intelligent, fiery-colored steed, which Metzengerstein is to ride with fiendish delight, coincides with the vanishing of the piece of tapestry containing the horse. In this material Poe employs incident and circumstance to create and reinforce his supernatural conception. The approach is gradual at first, and then the pace accelerates so that the successive omens keep building up the horror in crescendo fashion. The final scene where the uncontrollable horse plunges with his unwilling rider into the flames of the Metzengerstein castle and a cloud of smoke settles over the battlements in the shape of a gigantic horse is an impressive if unexpected climax.

It is difficult to correlate this ending with the obscure and cryptic prophecy that "as the rider over his horse, the mortality of Metzengerstein shall triumph over the immortality of Berlifitzing. It seems at the same time significant and meaningless. Merged with the terror of reincarnation of this tale is the element of dread in fatality—for it is fatality, however recondite. The inexorable nemesis is always a source of horror. The fulfillment of some curse or prophecy of doom is quite common as a theme in great literature—

excellent examples are to be found in the Greek tragedies and in Shake-speare's "Macbeth." As in the plot of the latter play, a series of significant oc-currences leads up to the inevitable fate of Metzengerstein.

"The Case of M. Valdemar" should be mentioned here, for although it does not concern a return from the dead, it involves the suspension of the putrefaction of a corpse and the retention of its soul by means of mesmerism. It is built on the pattern of the earlier "Mesmeric Revelation," but the philo-sophical discourse of the latter is sacrificed in order to create an atmosphere of horror rather than one of academic investigation. The maintenance of Val-demar in a trance with body intact, decay arrested, for seven months after his death, and his immediate degeneration into detestable putrescence on the breaking of the hypnotic spell have loathsome physical horror in addition to the terrifying psychical phenomena involving death.

## The Horror of Decay and Doom

"The Fall of the House of Usher," which his commonly considered Poe's greatest prose work, has a brooding atmosphere of dread which seems more fascinating with each additional reading. Its excellence cannot be exaggerated. Indeed, I believe it represents the ultimate acme that can be achieved through the medium of the short story—in all fields as well as the weird.

The subject is the decay of the House of Usher, that is, the last two members of the family line, Roderick and his twin sister, Madeline, and the ancient mansion with which their destiny is weirdly linked. This *motif* is deftly and subtly woven into each detail of the narrative from the physical descrip-tion of the sullen, lurid waters of the tarn by the decrepit abode to the awful spiritual wasting away of Roderick Usher. That is the superlative feature of this tale—every sentence, every word has been carefully selected and consid-ered to see whether or not it will contribute to the mood of decay and im-pending doom. The piece was virtually as painstakingly composed as Gray's "Elegy." Yet, curiously enough, the style does not seem heavy or labored, but flows along—the reader is not conscious of the extreme care and precision the author used to achieve so striking an effect.

Roderick Usher, with his fine features, cadaverous complexion, and "large, liquid, and luminous" eye, is a perfect portrait of Poe at the age of thirty, according to Hervey Allen. Usher has the same ethereal strangeness that clings to the person of Ligeia, but he is characterized by weakness and fear rather than strength and fortitude. The abject terror of his death throes is the direct antithesis of the courage of Ligeia, whose dying poem, "The Con-queror Worm," may express a gruesome grimness, but never the awful des-pair and futility of Usher's "The Haunted Palace." Indeed, Ligeia's last words expressed the belief that death is not the absolute end of being, while this note is entirely absent from Usher's morbid fatalism.

I contend that the subject matter of "Usher" is superior to that of "Ligeia." The terror of the return of the dead can never vie with the stark horror of utter doom. There is not only the death of the individual but the dissolution of his whole family line as symbolized by the collapse of the hereditary mansion. Although the treatment of "Usher" is more polished and forceful, the technique of both stories is superb. The maximum degree of fear inherent in the horror element of each is exploited, but "Usher" excels by virtue of the greater potentiality of its theme.

Furthermore, "Ligeia" is based on a more complex plot; the author first builds up the character of Ligeia, and then turns to the resurrection idea. From the first to the last "Usher" is a concentrated, unified picture of decay, and every minutest detail of the story is directed toward this sole object. The terror of premature burial (in its effects on the languishing Roderick Usher) is made to blend rather than clash with the central theme. The fungus spreading over the masonry, the ghastly pallor of Usher's skin, the cavernous halls kept in dimness because of Usher's antipathy to the faintest glare, his superstitious attachment to the family mansion which he never leaves, his morbid state of mind as reflected in his weird painting, music, and verses, as well as his conversation and actions in general, the storm and the eerie natural phenomena, the strange character of the malady of Lady Madeline, her interment alive and the horror of the sounds of her return from the vault hideously coinciding with the noises depicted in the book being read to Usher, and the final death of the Ushers and the collapse of the house—all these pictures show the house and family, closely linked, moving inexorably toward the doom.

It should be observed that "Berenice," which was considered earlier, is somewhat similar to "Usher," but this tale is told by the character corresponding to Roderick. Both involve a languid decline, both are reminiscent of Poe's actual distress at his wife's sickness, and both have a premature burial. However, in "Berenice," which is also the prototype for the tale of abnormal psychology, the element of decay does not predominate as it does in "Usher," and the style is not nearly so relentlessly powerful.

The sprawling cumbrousness of Hawthorne's "The House of the Seven Gables" forms an interesting and significant contrast with Poe's opus. The few brief snatches of the truly weird are interrupted by long stretches of such varied topics as love, philosophy, and humor, which mar, if not destroy, the illusion of horror. This demonstrates that the weird is most successfully achieved in the brief, simple, compact narrative where there is no diversification of interest.

## The Horror of Mystery

"The Narrative of A. Gordon Pym," which is almost of novel length, would seem to refute the above inference as it is certainly a work of distinction. However, closer scrutiny reveals that the terror element of the narrative is limited to the latter portion, which is itself only of novelette length. The first part, which constitutes the bulk of the story, relates some lengthy, and at times rather tedious maritime adventures—there are a few scattered bits of the weird such as the strange ship of the dead. This beginning, which has the air of authentic fact, establishes a sober materialistic groundwork on which the fantastic superstructure rests firmly. The realistic tone paves the way for the more uncanny occurrences described later. Nevertheless, granting that the unprecedented revolutionary character of the discoveries of the latter part of the tale necessitates a more gradual approach then the ordinary horror story, I maintain that a comparatively brief weird element never merits such a prolonged preamble, and that the same effect could have been achieved in a small fraction of this material.

Notwithstanding, the tale is quite powerful—it contains ghastly, veiled hints of profound secrets of the unknown and the unknowable. Ostensibly the true chronicle of Arthur Gordon Pym prepared with Poe's assistance, the mystery is built up slowly and deliberately and climaxed in the concluding note which tells of the sudden death of Pym and the irrevocable loss of the final chapters of the unusual narrative.

The utter strangeness, which is merely suggested by vague and cryptic inklings, is gradually and subtly brought into the focus of the reader's conscious attention. Thus one is first shown that the waters near Tsalal are murky, then that the savages are ebon-hued, and all their animal skins and other possessions are of a sombre shade. By degrees, one notices that everything on the island is black, and the final touch is the discovery that Nu-Nu's teeth are black—hitherto the teeth of the natives were concealed beneath their thick lips.

Equally deft is the step by step correlation of this dark land with the whiteness of the realm to the south with its gigantic birds of snowy plumage issuing from the vapory white curtain. Pym's diagrams of the shape of the chasms in the cliff spell the root "to be shady" in the Ethiopian language, and the indentures in the rock wall of the fissures read "to be white" and "the region of the south" in Arabic and Egyptian respectively. The black savages of Tsalal have some queer antipathy to white—this is evidently connected with their unprovoked massacre of the party of white men. Their affrighted cry of "Tekeli-li" on seeing white objects is duplicated by the shrieks of the huge white birds of the south. The abrupt ending of the narrative because of Pym's death and the loss of the closing chapters precludes any full explanation and renders the tale the more puzzling. Such a conclusion is indeed effective, as the secret is gone forever. Perhaps some would prefer a further elucidation, but no possible explanation would be adequate, and would ruin the sense of the occult.

In one incident of the tale the motivation seems questionable. The narrator, exploring a fissure in a cliff with two comrades, is startled by an avalanche which almost covers him and cuts off the means of egress. He and one of his companions make a successful search for another exit which evidently consumes at least five minutes, and then they suddenly remember that the third friend is missing; at length his corpse is found buried in the landslide. In my opinion, it is quite improbable that the two could completely forget their friend for so long. However, this oversight, if such it be, is of minor importance.

On the whole, despite the tardiness in getting started, the tale achieves a note of the unwholesomely curious and the fear of unfathomable mystery that more than counterbalances its defects.

"MS. Found in a Bottle" is in some respects similar to "The Narrative of A. Gordon Pym" which was written several years later. It likewise involves maritime vicissitudes and occurs in the unexplored southern seas.

As in "Pym," the perplexing mystery is the essence of the horror element. The sinister vessel on which the terror theme centers resembles somewhat the awful ship of the dead seen by the drifting seamen in the earlier part of "Pym," and also reminds one of the scenes of the walking corpses in "The Ancient Mariner." The strange crew of the dreadful craft seem to move as if in dream, and their failure to take the slightest notice of the narrator inspires the greatest amazement and awe. The inexplicable actions of the aged-looking seamen, their odd mutterings in an utterly alien tongue, the queer instruments and other objects bespeaking the remote antiquity of the ship, and the final terror of the impending plunge into the vortex of the whirlpool make a picture of infinite strangeness and the horror of the unknown. As in "Pym" the tale is not completed, for the manuscript is cast adrift in a bottle as the apparent destruction of the writer draws near—this heightens the effect of mystification.

The story is more compact than the rambling "Pym," and the realistic approach is limited to a minute fraction of the length of that in the latter narrative, while it is just as successful. I consider "MS. Found in a Bottle" the equal of "Pym" in every way; this is one case where Poe's treatment of a mode of terror did not improve with the passage of time. Nevertheless, both items are excellent illustrations of the development of horror through mystery.

"The Man of the Crowd" strikes a note of the occult in the queer action of a stranger who constantly mingles with the populace and shuns lonesome streets. There is an inference of some awful secret he keeps hidden deep in his soul. It is remarkable that this effect can be so successfully attained with so commonplace a locale as the center of London. Nevertheless, the setting precludes the attainment of the level of the *outré* achieved by the preceding two stories.

A few other tales which do not fall into groupings readily are worthy of cursory mention. "Hop-Frog," a narrative of the grotesque—the revenge of a weird dwarf—recalls the plot of "The Cask of Amontillado" which also involves the wreaking of vengeance. However, the present piece is utterly unlike the psychological study in being quite objective—indeed, it is virtually a narration of the third person as the pronoun "I" occurs only in parenthetical remarks. The jauntiness of the style sometimes adds to the air of the bizarre, but is often out of harmony with an atmosphere of weirdness as in this specimen: "wine . . . excited the poor cripple almost to madness; and madness is no comfortable feeling." The theme has further possibilities that would doubtless have been exploited by Poe later, had it not been for his early death. The proper approach to horror through the medium of the grotesque should have more of the somber and less of the whimsical.

Without underestimating its considerable merit, I feel it is fair to assert that "The Pit and the Pendulum" has received an undue measure of attention and praise while some of Poe's more deserving works have remained in relative obscurity. Here the feeling of fear is inspired by the threat of hideous devices of torture. The suspense of the gradually descending pendulum blade, and of the moving walls forcing the victim closer and closer to the pit is not readily forgotten. This feeling of terror is marred by a happy ending—a rescue in the nick of time. This may be the classic torture story, but the fear of mere physical harm is not nearly so penetrating as the psychic horrors evoked by the supernatural.

"The Premature Burial" is the most disappointing in view of the effectiveness with which its theme is used in both "Berenice" and "The Fall of the House of Usher." The present story is spoiled by a poor trick ending which besides being anticipated by the reader, destroys the illusion of horror entirely—the apparent victim finds his supposed coffin turns out to be the berth of a sloop. The most impressive part of the story is the friend's revelation of the graves of all mankind, where it is seen that most bodies are struggling feebly, interred alive. It is unfortunate that this vein is not continued throughout the story.

The use of such a surprise ending to explain the supernatural occurrences of a weird tale is virtually repudiated by modern authors. This device is also employed in "The Sphinx," and here with even less success. The optical illusion by which a small insect could appear to be a huge monster is a trifle far-fetched. Some of Poe's more obvious hackwork is on a still lower level, but this must be forgiven as his financial status necessitated mechanical productions.

## Pure Fantasy

The field which I term "pure fantasy" can not be dwelt on at length, as it does not fall directly within the province of horror. However, its close relationship to horror, and the heights to which it soars on the pinions of Poe's artistry make at least some mention of it mandatory.

By "pure fantasy" I mean the free unrestrained flights of imagination, the sylph-like wonder dreams of "the wild, weird clime that lieth, sublime, out of Space—out of Time." This never-never realm of the golden twilight is reached in some of the poems, notably "Ulalume," "The City in the Sea," and "Dreamland," and also to a lesser degree in "The Raven," "Annabel Lee," and "The Bells." Some of Poe's poetic tales catch this same wraithlike splendor by virtue of their melodious, lyrical style and radiant sensory imagery—such are "the Masque of the Red Death," "Eleanora," "Silence—A Fable," and

"Shadow—A Parable." A musical tone identical with that of Poe's rarest poetry is attained in the transcendent beauty of these prose pieces with their quaint, rhythmic, quasi-oriental style (not unlike that of the King James Bible) which savors of remote antiquity and utter alienage.

The element of horror is generally subordinate to the fantasy, for esthetic rather than emotional values are emphasized. The most conspicuous specimen or intensity of feeling in pure fantasy is "The Raven," which has a profoundly somber mood attained in no other poem. Consequently, atmospheric sublimity must be sacrificed, and "The Raven" is surpassed in this quality by "Ulalume" and "Dreamland," while it is unquestionably supreme in emotional depth.

A detailed analysis of the methods used to achieve these effects is beyond the scope of this study. Comparison of a passage from "Fairyland" with one from the much later "Dreamland"—which is as superb a poem as it is obscure—will suffice as an illustration of Poe's revision.

> "Dim vales—and shadowy flood—
> And cloudy-looking woods,
> Whose forms we can't discover
> For the tears that drip all over"
> —Fairyland

> "Bottomless vales and boundless floods,
> And chasms, and caves, and Titan woods,
> With forms that no man can discover
> For the dews that drip all over;"
> —Dreamland

Even in the sphere of pure fantasy, Poe is, as ever, systematic and analytical.

The scenes of the majority of the horror tales discussed earlier are laid in unknown or at least highly unusual places in an indefinite age. This uncertainty of time and place provides a setting of exotic "outsideness" most conducive to the weird, as it permits an effective escape from the commonplace. Frequently the author has even omitted mechanical devices or other objects which might identify the period of the story and thus beget the air of the prosaic attending familiarity. Poe is perhaps unique among great writers in that he seldom if ever reflects the background of his times, but conceals it to achieve the timelessness essential to the weird.

Thus, it is apparent that the dream-world of the pure fantasy (often in a more realistic version) is likewise present to a lesser degree in Poe's horror tales (being most evident in "Ligeia"), but here the attention is focused on the fear element with the *outré* scene serving as background material. On the other hand, in the pure fantasy the fanciful realm is the cynosure while eerie effects are secondary. Thus, we may consider the weird mood to be based on the emotion of fear and on imaginative atmosphere, the former being stresses in the horror story and the latter in the pure fantasy.

In my opinion, Poe's main contribution to the horror field is his scientific method, his clear understanding of the psychological sources of horror. Before his advent the horror element was found as a central theme only in relatively obscure writings, or was relegated to a position of minor importance in the great classics. Poe's epoch-making works have established the weird as an independent branch of literature with his principles as criteria. Therefore, Edgar Allan Poe is assured a permanent place as the preeminent exponent of horror.

# *Wilson Shepherd*

## "Death"

<In printing this, you had better *indent* the *second* & *fourth* lines of each stanza.>*

I <opened the door> one night<,> ~~turned on the light~~
> No rhyme in original
> *light* & *night* conflict

<Having turned up the lamp erewhile,>
~~And opened the door so wide~~
And in walked Death with his sable cloak,
And ~~he~~ said to me with a smile:
> Never use rhyming words except where the rhyme scheme calls for them

"Your life ~~the~~ on <the> earth is ~~ended~~ <past>—
"Your <bodily>>~~terrestrial~~< race is run—
"So gather your dreams about you,
"And come with me, my son."
> *terrestrial* is not a very good word for poetry

I looked in~~to the~~ <his> deep, dead eyes<,> >illegible<
And <strange> ~~many~~ were the thoughts that ran
> line too long
> *squirming worms* has conflict of sound
> *brain-pan* too technical for poetic use

Like <wriggling> ~~squirming~~ worms through my fevered brain ~~pan~~
"I want to come—*and I can!*"

He stretched <~~forth~~> out his hand<s> to~~ward~~ me,
> watch the rhythm
> *to´ward* doesn't fit the line as well as *to*
> syllable cannot rhyme *with itself*

And gathered mine in his own;

Through the dim, dread door he led me forth

---

*Note:* HPL tagged each of these lines with a dash to indicate which to indent. HPL's revisions are indicated by <>, his deletions by strikeout text. HPL crossed out lines 19–20 so throroughly the underlying text cannot be read. Lines 19–20 here are HPL's.

~~And claimed me for his own~~                     better image was
To the dark that is his alone.                     needed

The light flickered out behind<,> ~~me~~           Better end with a regu-
And the door <in the dead, black air>              lar stanza
          >         illegible          <
<Slammed shut and was gone—as the blessed void
Closed round me from everywhere.>

# Willis Conover, Jr.

## Observations and Otherwise

"The oldest and strongest emotion of mankind is fear, and the oldest and strongest fear is fear of the unknown. These facts few psychologists will dispute, and their admitted truth must establish for all time the genuineness and dignity of the weirdly horrible tale as a literary form."

In his scholarly treatise "Supernatural Horror in Literature," H. P. Lovecraft began with these words in an attempt to defend, clarify and popularize the more classical eerie works of masters living and dead. Lovecraft, a recluse of Providence, Rhode Island, died on March 15th, this year. He had established himself, not only as the modern master of the macabre, worthy of a literary position beside Poe, Machen, and Blackwood, but as a learned student of many sciences and branches of philosophy. His essays on the latter saw print in nonprofessionally published books and amateur magazines, for he seldom wrote such on a commercial basis. But his fictional output, whose leisurely development and intricately detailed description combined to produce a spectral atmosphere of cosmic horror, was obtained and read by a larger audience of fantaisistes.

Obviously it is impossible because of the technical difficulties involved to acquaint you with even the more brief units of his weird prose. His verse, however, possesses that same uncanny atmosphere and breath of supernatural feat which is predominant in all his prose work, and naturally can be reproduced with greater facility.

Following are a few representative sonnets from Lovecraft's unpublished series entitled *Fungi from Yuggoth.*

> [*Here "The Pigeon-Flyers," "Homecoming,"*
> *"A Memory," and "Night-Gaunts" are printed.*]

"It is a narrow though essential branch of human expression, and will chiefly appeal as always to a limited audience with keen special sensibilities. Whatever universal masterpiece of tomorrow may be wrought from phantasm or terror will owe its acceptance rather to a supreme workmanship than to a sympathetic theme. Yet who shall declare the dark theme a positive handicap? Radiant with beauty, the Cup of the Ptolemies was carven of onyx."

H. P. Lovecraft was only forty-six years of age, yet had built up a following such as few authors ever had. He was a titan of weird and fantastic literature, whose literary achievement and impeccable craftsmanship were acclaimed throughout the English-speaking world. With all his studies, his capabilities, his wide knowledge, and his vast intelligence, H. P. Lovecraft was a kindly, generous human being, modest as to his work, and ever ready to lend a helping hand to others. Peace be to his shade!

## The Lost Chord

*A Story of Atmosphere, a Tale of Strange Music*
By Joseph Allan Ryan

The Wanderer paused at the steps of the massive cathedral. It loomed there before him, dark, silent. He climbed the broad steps with a firm tread, the sound of his metal-soled boots ringing in his ears. At the huge, open arch, leading to the interior of the cathedral, the Wanderer paused again and looked in.

He saw dark recesses and shadowy, indiscernible objects with faintly revealed parts presenting themselves in the dim light which filtered through the high, stained-glass windows. And all about him was an atmosphere of enormity and of unawakened power.

Crossing the threshold, he entered and, with long, steady strides, walked down the wide center aisle toward a colossal organ, the keyboard of which glistened and reflected into his eyes the dim light, and the thousand pipes of which extended far into the concealing shadows of the upper cathedral. He became conscious of a certain attraction which it held for him; he felt drawn toward it and had neither the power nor the will to resist.

Sitting himself at the keyboard, he played a few chords, then broke into the strains of the prelude to some mighty, unwritten sonata. The music crescendoed into a tremendous climax in vox humana, then subsided into a slow, rhythmic rambling up and down the octaves, resembling the faint, low beat of a savage's tom-tom amid the dying moan of a stormy wind which has expended its fury.

Suddenly it stopped. The Wanderer's fingers remained in the same position on the keys; he seemed paralyzed. What was that chord he had just played? He brought the keys down again. That chord—it struck a sympathetic chord somewhere within him. It was the Lost Chord, which man had never before heard!

He did not lift his fingers from the keys; the Chord reached every corner of the great cathedral. The Wanderer's soul drank it in, thrilling at the sweet but excruciating pain it produced within him. It lifted him into a noumenal world of ethereal, painful beauty, utterly foreign, yet utterly appealing.

The Wanderer lifted his fingers from the keys. He felt that hearing the Lost Chord had brought him into momentary contact with some great power, had somehow changed him immeasurably. The music had ceased, but the Chord was indelibly burned into his memory. He knew it would never escape him.

The Wanderer rose and turned from the keyboard of the mighty console. The sound of his boots, as he strode back toward the massive arch, echoed and reverberated through the cathedral and then died away, leaving it silent once more.

## The Spirits Mourn

Macabre ghosts join hands and dance
    Around the grave of one departed—
A lunatic, forlorn, downhearted.
    To searing flame his soul does prance.

The spirits cease. One kneels and pants:
    "Return! Return!" But he has started;
To endless pain his soul has darted.
    The spirits mourn in silent trance.

# Chronology

| | | |
|---|---|---|
| Robert Bloch | RB 1 | April 22, 1933 |
| Robert Bloch | RB 2 | April 27, 1933 |
| Robert Bloch | RB 3 | May 9, 1933 |
| Robert Bloch | RB 4 | late May 1933 |
| Robert Bloch | RB 5 | June 1, 1933 |
| Robert Bloch | RB 6 | June 9, 1933 |
| Robert Bloch | RB 7 | June 21, 1933 |
| Robert Bloch | RB 8 | Late June 1933 |
| Natalie H. Wooley | NHW 1 | July 7, 1933 |
| Robert Bloch | RB 9 | early to mid-July 1933 |
| Natalie H. Wooley | NHW 2 | July 18, 1933 |
| Robert Bloch | RB 10 | July 22, 1933 |
| Robert Bloch | RB 11 | Late July 1933 |
| Natalie H. Wooley | NHW 3 | August 6, 1933 |
| Robert Bloch | RB 12 | August 22, 1933 |
| Natalie H. Wooley | NHW 4 | August 30, 1933 |
| Robert Bloch | RB 13 | September 3, 1933 |
| Robert Bloch | RB 14 | September 15, 1933 |
| Robert Bloch | RB 15 | September 25, 1933 |
| Natalie H. Wooley | NHW 5 | October 24, 1933 |
| Robert Bloch | RB 16 | late October 1933 |
| Robert Bloch | RB 17 | November, 1933 |
| Natalie H. Wooley | NHW 6 | November 27, 1933 |
| Robert Bloch | RB 18 | c. December 6, 1933 |
| Robert Bloch | RB 19 | December 15, 1933 |
| Robert Bloch | RB 20 | Christmas 1933 |
| Natalie H. Wooley | NHW 7 | January 3, 1934 |
| Robert Bloch | RB 21 | February 2, 1934 |
| Natalie H. Wooley | NHW 8 | February 19, 1934 |
| Natalie H. Wooley | NHW 9 | February 22, 1934 |
| Robert Bloch | RB 22 | late March 1934 |

| Robert Bloch | RB 23 | April 9, 1934 |
| Robert Bloch | RB 24 | April 28, 1934 |
| Robert Bloch | RB 25 | June 1, 1934 |
| Robert Bloch | RB 26 | June 8, 1934 |
| Robert Bloch | RB 27 | June 24, 1934 |
| Robert Bloch | RB 28 | July 14, 1934 |
| Robert Bloch | RB 29 | July 21, 1934 |
| Robert Bloch | RB 30 | mid- to late July 1934 |
| Robert Bloch | RB 31 | August 11, 1934 |
| William F. Anger | WFA 1 | August 14, 1934 |
| Robert Bloch | RB 32 | August 22, 1934 |
| Robert Bloch | RB 33 | August 30, 1934 |
| William F. Anger | WFA 2 | August 31, 1934 |
| Robert Bloch | RB 34 | mid-September 1934 |
| Robert Bloch | RB 35 | Early October 1934 |
| Robert Bloch | RB 36 | October 18, 1934 |
| Robert Nelson | RB 1 | October 19, 1934 |
| Robert Nelson | RB 2 | October 27, 1934 |
| Robert Bloch | RB 37 | Late October 1934 |
| Robert Bloch | RB 38 | early to mid-November 1934 |
| Robert Bloch | RB 39 | December 22, 1934 |
| William F. Anger | WFA 3 | December 29, 1934 |
| Robert Nelson | RB 3 | January 16, 1935 |
| Robert Nelson | RB 4 | January 17, 1935 |
| Natalie H. Wooley | NHW 10 | January 26, 1935 |
| William F. Anger | WFA 4 | January 28, 1935 |
| Robert Bloch | RB 40 | late January 1935 |
| Robert Bloch | RB 41 | early February 1935 |
| William F. Anger | WFA 5 | February 16, 1935 |
| Robert Bloch | RB 42 | late Feb./early March 1935 |
| Robert Bloch | RB 43 | Mid-march 1935 |
| William F. Anger | WFA 6 | March 27, 1935 |
| Natalie H. Wooley | NHW 11 | March 28, 1935 |
| Robert Bloch | RB 44 | late March–early April 1935 |

| | | |
|---|---|---|
| Robert Bloch | RB 45 | mid-April 1935 |
| Robert Bloch | RB 46 | April 30, 1935 |
| William F. Anger | WFA 7 | April 24, 1935 |
| William F. Anger | WFA 8 | April 28, 1935 |
| Donald A. Wollheim | DAW 1 | May 1935 |
| William F. Anger | WFA 9 | May 19, 1935 |
| Robert Bloch | RB 47 | early June 1935 |
| William F. Anger | WFA 10 | June 1, 1935 |
| Robert Bloch | RB 48 | mid- to late June 1935 |
| William F. Anger | WFA 11 | June 20, 1935 |
| Natalie H. Wooley | NHW 12 | June 28, 1935 |
| Kenneth Sterling | KS 1 | July 1, 1935 |
| Donald A. Wollheim | DAW 2 | July 9, 1935 |
| Robert Bloch | RB 49 | mid-July 1935 |
| William F. Anger | WFA 12 | July 22, 1935 |
| Kenneth Sterling | KS 2 | August 3, 1935 |
| Robert Bloch | RB 50 | August 7, 1935 |
| William F. Anger | WFA 13 | August 14, 1935 |
| Robert Bloch | RB 51 | August 25, 1935 |
| Robert Bloch | RB 52 | September 19, 1935 |
| Mrs. Elmer Nelson | RB 5 | September 19, 1935 |
| Donald A. Wollheim | DAW 3 | September 20, 1935 |
| Donald A. Wollheim | DAW 4 | October 1, 1935 |
| William F. Anger | WFA 14 | October 1, 1935 |
| Robert Bloch | RB 53 | early October 1935 |
| Kenneth Sterling | KS 3 | October 6, 1935 |
| Donald A. Wollheim | DAW 5 | October 7, 1935 |
| Kenneth Sterling | KS 4 | October 23, 1935 |
| Robert Bloch | RB 54 | November 2, 1935 |
| Donald A. Wollheim | DAW 6 | November 13, 1935 |
| Kenneth Sterling | KS 5 | November 20, 1935 |
| Robert Bloch | RB 55 | December 4, 1935 |
| Kenneth Sterling | KS 6 | December 14, 1935 |
| Robert Bloch | RB 56 | December 28, 1935 |

| | | |
|---|---|---|
| Natalie H. Wooley | NHW 13 | December 30, 1935 |
| Kenneth Sterling | KS 7 | January 15, 1936 |
| William F. Anger | WFA 15 | January 16, 1936 |
| Kenneth Sterling | KS 8 | January 21, 1936 |
| Donald A. Wollheim | DAW 7 | February 7, 1936 |
| William F. Anger | WFA 16 | February 17, 1936 |
| Robert Bloch | RB 57 | March 14, 1936 |
| Robert Bloch | RB 58 | April 1, 1936 |
| Donald A. Wollheim | DAW 8 | April 19, 1936 |
| Wilson Shepherd | WS 1 | April 29, 1936 |
| Natalie H. Wooley | NHW 14 | May 2, 1936 |
| Wilson Shepherd | WS 2 | May 10, 1936 |
| Robert Bloch | RB 59 | Mid-may 1936 |
| Kenneth Sterling | KS 9 | May 25, 1936 |
| Wilson Shepherd | WS 3 | May 29, 1936 |
| Kenneth Sterling | KS 10 | June 20, 1936 |
| Wilson Shepherd | WS 4 | June 20, 1936 |
| Robert Bloch | RB 60 | late June 1936 |
| Donald A. Wollheim | DAW 9 | July 6, 1936 |
| Donald A. Wollheim | DAW 10 | July 9, 1936 |
| Willis Conover | WC 1 | July 9, 1936 |
| Wilson Shepherd | WS 5 | July 14, 1936 |
| Willis Conover | WC 2 | July 21, 1936 |
| Willis Conover | WC 3 | July 29, 1936 |
| Willis Conover | WC 4 | August 2, 1936 |
| Wilson Shepherd | WS 6 | August 11, 1936 |
| Robert Bloch | RB 61 | August 12, 1936 |
| Willis Conover | WC 5 | August 14, 1936 |
| Willis Conover | WC 6 | August 17, 1936 |
| Donald A. Wollheim | DAW 11 | August 23, 1936 |
| Willis Conover | WC 7 | August 29, 1936 |
| Donald A. Wollheim | DAW 12 | August 30, 1936 |
| Robert Bloch | RB 62 | August 31, 1936 |
| Willis Conover | WC 8 | September 1, 1936 |

| | | |
|---|---|---|
| William F. Anger | WFA 17 | September 2, 1936 |
| Wilson Shepherd | WS 7 | September 5, 1936 |
| Kenneth Sterling | KS 11 | September 16, 1936 |
| Willis Conover | WC 9 | September 23, 1936 |
| Kenneth Sterling | KS 12 | September 26, 1936 |
| Wilson Shepherd | WS 8 | October 1, 1936 |
| Kenneth Sterling | KS 13 | October 18, 1936 |
| Willis Conover | WC 10 | October 24, 1936 |
| Wilson Shepherd | WS 9 | November 3, 1936 |
| Willis Conover | WC 11 | November 18, 1936 |
| Natalie H. Wooley | NHW 15 | November 21, 1936 |
| Robert Bloch | RB 64 | December 3, 1936 |
| Willis Conover | WC 12 | December 4, 1936 |
| Kenneth Sterling | KS 14 | December 9, 1936 |
| Wilson Shepherd | WS 10 | December 15, 1936 |
| Willis Conover | WC 13 | December 24, 1936 |
| Robert Bloch | RB 63 | October 15, 1936 |
| Robert Bloch | RB 65 | January 7, 1937 |
| Kenneth Sterling | KS 15 | January 10, 1937 |
| Willis Conover | WC 14 | January 10, 1937 |
| Willis Conover | WC 15 | January 11, 1937 |
| Willis Conover | WC 16 | January 12, 1937 |
| Wilson Shepherd | WS 11 | January 21, 1937 |
| Robert Bloch | RB 66 | January 25, 1937 |
| Kenneth Sterling | KS 16 | January 27, 1937 |
| Willis Conover | WC 17 | January 31, 1937 |
| Wilson Shepherd | WS 12 | February 17, 1937 |
| Willis Conover | WC 18 | March 9, 1937 |

# Glossary of
# Frequently Mentioned Names

**Ackerman, Forrest J** (1916–2008), American agent, author, editor. Ackerman had been a science fiction fan since the late '20s; he corresponded sporadically with HPL from around 1931 onward.

**Baird, Edwin** (1886–1957), first editor of *WT* (March 1923–April 1924), who accepted HPL's first submissions to the magazine. Also editor of *Real Detective Stories*.

**Baldwin, F[ranklin] Lee** (1913–1987), weird fiction fan and late associate of HPL. He had intended to publish "The Colour out of Space" as a booklet, but never did so. He wrote an early biography, "H. P. Lovecraft: A Biographical Sketch" (*Fantasy Magazine*, April 1935).

**Barlow, R[obert] H[ayward]** (1918–1951), author and collector. As a teenager he corresponded with HPL and acted as his host during two long visits in the summers of 1934 and 1935. In the 1930s he wrote several works of weird and fantasy fiction, some in collaboration with HPL. HPL appointed him his literary executor. He assisted August Derleth and Donald Wandrei in preparing the early HPL volumes for Arkham House. In the 1940s he went to Mexico and became a distinguished anthropologist. He died by suicide. HPL's letters to Barlow have been published as *O Fortunate Floridian* (2007).

**Bates, Harry** (1900–1981), editor of *Strange Tales* and *Astounding Stories*.

**Bishop, Zealia Brown (Reed)** (1897–1968), HPL's revision client. HPL ghostwrote "The Curse of Yig" (1928), "The Mound" (1929–30), and "Medusa's Coil" (1930) for her based on her slim plot synopses.

**Blackwood, Algernon** (1869–1951), leading British writer of weird fiction who gained celebrity with *John Silence—Physician Extraordinary* (1908), *Incredible Adventures* (1914), and other volumes. HPL considered his novella "The Willows" (1907) the greatest weird tale in literature.

**Blish, James** (1921–1975), pioneering American science fiction writer who corresponded briefly with HPL (1936). He planned to issue the *Planeteer*, with work by HPL, but never did so.

**Boland, Stuart M[orton]** (1909–1973), librarian in San Francisco who corresponded with HPL in the 1930s, as recounted in his memoir, "Interlude with Lovecraft" (1945).

**Bradofsky, Hyman** (1906–2002), correspondent of HPL (1934–37). He was president of the NAPA (1935–36) and edited the *Californian* (1933f.), one of the most distinguished and voluminous amateur journals of the period.

**Brobst, Harry K[ern]** (1909–2010), late associate of HPL who moved to Providence in 1932 and saw HPL regularly thereafter.

**Brosnatch, Andrew** (1896–1965), *WT* artist.

**Brundage, Margaret** (1900–1976), *WT* cover artist, known for her scandalous nudes.

**Burks, Arthur J.** (1898–1974), voluminous contributor to *WT* and other pulp magazines.

**Coates, Walter J[ohn]** (1880–1941), correspondent of HPL, friend of W. Paul Cook, and editor of *Driftwind*.

**Cole, Edward H[arold]** (1892–1966), longtime amateur associate of HPL, living in the Boston area. He edited the amateur journal, the *Olympian*.

**Cook, W. Paul** (1880–1948), publisher of the *Monadnock Monthly*, the *Vagrant*, and other amateur journals; a longtime amateur journalist, printer, and lifelong friend of HPL. He first visited HPL in 1917, and it was he who urged HPL to resume writing fiction after a hiatus of nine years. In 1927 Cook published the *Recluse*, containing HPL's "Supernatural Horror in Literature."

**Crawford, William L[evy]** (1911–1984), editor of *Marvel Tales* and *Unusual Stories* and publisher of the Visionary Publishing Company, which issued HPL's *The Shadow over Innsmouth* (1936).

**Cummings, Ray** (1897–1957), prolific science fiction writer who gained celebrity with the story "The Girl in the Golden Atom" (*All-Story*, 15 March 1919).

**Daas, Edward F.** (1879–1962), amateur journalist who recruited HPL into the movement in 1914.

**Davis, Edgar J.** (1908–1949), young amateur journalist with whom HPL explored Newburyport and other locales in New England.

**de Castro, Adolphe (Danziger)** (1859–1959), author, co-translator with Ambrose Bierce of Richard Voss's *The Monk and the Hangman's Daughter*, and correspondent of HPL. HPL revised his "The Last Test" and "The Electric Executioner."

**de la Mare, Walter** (1873–1956), British author and poet who wrote occasional weird tales much admired by HPL for their subtlety and allusiveness.

**Derleth, August W[illiam]** (1909–1971), author of weird tales and also a long series of regional and historical works set in his native Wisconsin. After HPL's death, he and Donald Wandrei founded the publishing firm of Arkham House to preserve HPL's work in book form.

**Dunsany, Lord (Edward John Moreton Drax Plunkett)** (1878–1957), Irish writer of fantasy tales whose work notably influenced HPL after HPL read it in 1919.

**Dwyer, Bernard Austin** (1897–1943), weird fiction fan and would-be writer and artist, living in West Shokan, NY; correspondent of HPL.

**Edkins, Ernest A[rthur]** (1867–1946), amateur journalist associated with the "halcyon days" of the National Amateur Press Association (1885–95). He came in touch with HPL in 1932.

**Eshbach, Lloyd Arthur** (1910–2003), science fiction writer and publisher who edited the *Galleon* and published some of HPL's poems and stories in the magazine.

**Farnese, Harold S.** (1885–1945), musical composer and sporadic correspondent of HPL. It was he who provided August Derleth with the spurious "Black Magic" quotation attributed to HPL.

**Finlay, Virgil** (1914–1971), one of the great weird artists of his time and a prolific contributor of artwork to the pulps; late correspondent of HPL.

**Frome, Nils** (1918–1962), late correspondent of HPL (1936–37) and editor of the fanzine *Supramundane Stories*.

**Gamwell, Annie E[meline] P[hillips]** (1866–1941), HPL's younger aunt, living with him at 66 College Street (1933–37). She had been married (1897–1936) to Edward F[rancis] Gamwell (1869–1936).

**Gernsback, Hugo** (1884–1967), editor of *Amazing Stories, Wonder Stories,* and other pioneering science fiction pulps.

**Goodenough, Arthur H[enry]** (1871–1936), amateur poet who resided in Brattleboro, VT. HPL visited him there on several occasions.

**Harré, T[homas] Everett** (1884–1948), American journalist who edited the horror anthology *Beware After Dark!* (1929), containing HPL's "The Call of Cthulhu." HPL met him on a few occasions in New York in the 1930s.

**Henneberger, J[acob] C[lark]** (1890–1969), founder of *College Humor* (1922f.) and the original publisher of *WT*.

**Hersey, Harold** (1893–1956), science fiction editor and publisher. He edited the *Thrill Book* (1919) and took over the editorship of *Ghost Stories* during its final years (1930–31).

**Hodgson, William Hope** (1877–1918), British author of weird fiction whose work had fallen into obscurity until it was rediscovered in the 1930s, largely through the efforts of H. C. Koenig.

**Hornig, Charles D[erwin]** (1916–1999), editor of the *Fantasy Fan* (1933–35) and associate editor of *Wonder Stories*.

**Howard, Robert E[rvin]** (1906–1936), prolific Texas author of weird and adventure tales for *Weird Tales* and other pulp magazines; creator of the adventure hero Conan the Barbarian. He and HPL corresponded voluminously from 1930 to 1936. He committed suicide when he heard of his mother's impending death.

**Jacobi, Carl** (1908–1997), prolific author of weird, weird menace, and science fiction stories for the pulp magazines. He published three collections of tales with Arkham House.

**Keller, David H[enry]** (1880–1966), physician, psychiatrist, and popular science fiction author.

**Kleiner, Rheinhart** (1882–1949), amateur poet and longtime friend of HPL. He visited HPL in Providence in 1918, 1919, and 1920, and met him frequently during the heyday of the Kalem Club (1924–26).

**Koenig, H[erman] C[harles]** (1893–1959), late associate of HPL who spearheaded the rediscovery of the work of William Hope Hodgson.

**Kuttner, Henry** (1915–1958), prolific author of science fiction and horror tales for the pulp magazines and a late correspondent of HPL (1936–37). HPL introduced Kuttner to C. L. Moore, whom he would later marry.

**La Spina, Greye** (1880–1969), American weird fiction writer who contributed several tales to *WT* and other pulp magazines. Arkham House published her novella *Invaders from the Dark* (1960; orig. *WT,* April, May, and June 1925).

**Leeds, Arthur** (1882–1952?), an associate of HPL in New York and member of the Kalem Club. He was the author (with J. Berg Esenwein) of *Writing the Photoplay* (1913; rev. ed. 1919).

**Lenniger, August,** pulp author and literary agent.

**Long, Frank Belknap** (1901–1994), fiction writer and poet and one of HPL's closest friends and correspondents. Late in life he wrote the memoir *Howard Phillips Lovecraft: Dreamer on the Nightside* (1975).

**Loveman, Samuel** (1887–1976), poet and longtime friend of HPL and Hart Crane, and associate of Ambrose Bierce, George Sterling, and Clark Ashton Smith. He wrote *The Hermaphrodite* (1926) and other poems.

**Lumley, William** (1880–1960), eccentric late associate of HPL for whom HPL ghostwrote "The Diary of Alonzo Typer" (1935).

**Machen, Arthur** (1863–1947), Welsh author of weird fiction whose work influenced HPL significantly after he read it in 1923.

**Martin, Margaret Nickerson,** president of the NAPA in 1936–37, succeeding Hyman Bradofsky. She was a poet and literary critic based in Jackson MI, and editor of the *Literary Record.*

**Merritt, A[braham]** (1884–1943), writer of fantasy and horror tales for the pulps. His work was much admired by HPL in spite of its concessions to pulp formulae. His late novel *Dwellers in the Mirage* (1932) may have been influenced by HPL.

**Miniter, Edith** (1867–1934), amateur author who also professionally published a novel, *Our Natupski Neighbors* (1916), and many short stories. HPL was guest at her home in Wilbraham, MA, in the summer of 1928.

**Moe, Maurice W[inter]** (1882–1940), amateur journalist, English teacher, and longtime friend and correspondent of HPL, living in Appleton and Milwaukee, WI.

**Moe, Robert Ellis** (1912–1992), one of Maurice W. Moe's two sons (the other was Donald), who began corresponding with HPL in 1934 and met him on several occasions.

**Moore, C[atherine] L[ucile]** (1911–1987), late associate of HPL who later married Henry Kuttner and became a leading figure in science fiction and fantasy.

**Morse, Richard Ely** (1909–1986), poet, librarian at Princeton University, and correspondent of HPL.

**Morton, James F[erdinand]** (1870–1941), amateur journalist, member of the Kalem Club, author of many tracts on race prejudice, freethought, taxation, and other topics, and longtime friend of HPL. See *Letters to James F. Morton* (Hippocampus Press, 2011).

**Munn, H[arold] Warner** (1903–1981), contributor to the pulp magazines, living near W. Paul Cook in Athol, MA.

**Nelson, Robert** (1912–1935), young poet and weird fiction writer who committed suicide shortly after coming into correspondence with HPL.

**Olinick, George O.** (1888–1957), early *WT* illustrator.

**Peirce, Earl, Jr.** (1917–1983), weird fiction writer who published a few stories in *WT* and other pulps, and corresponded with HPL in the 1930s.

**Petaja, Emil** (1915–2000), science fiction fan and late associate of HPL; later a prolific author and editor.

**Price, E[dgar] Hoffmann** (1898–1988), prolific pulp writer of weird and adventure tales. HPL met him in New Orleans in 1932 and corresponded extensively with him thereafter.

**Quinn, Seabury** (1889–1969), prolific author of weird and detective tales to the pulps, notably tales involving the psychic detective Jules de Grandin.

**Rankin, Hugh Doak** (1878–1956), illustrator for *WT*.

**Rimel, Duane W[eldon]** (1915–1996), weird fiction fan and late associate of HPL, who revised some of his early tales.

**Ruppert, Conrad** (1912–1997), publisher of the *Fantasy Fan* (1933–35).

**Schwartz, Julius** (1915–2004), editor of *Fantasy Magazine* who acted as HPL's agent in marketing *At the Mountains of Madness* to *Astounding Stories*.

**Senf, C[onstantine] C.** (1873–1949), illustrator for *WT*.

**Shiel, M[atthew] P[hipps]** (1865–1947), British author of weird fiction. HPL thought highly of his "The House of Sounds" and *The Purple Cloud* (1901).

**Smith, Clark Ashton** (1893–1961), prolific California poet and writer of fantasy tales. He received a fan letter from HPL in 1922 and corresponded with him until HPL's death.

**Stickney, Corwin F.** (1921–1998), copublisher with Willis Conover, Jr., of *Science-Fantasy Correspondent* (1936–37), later titled *Amateur Correspondent* (1937f.), edited by Stickney alone.

**Strauch, Carl Ferdinand** (1908–1989), friend of Harry Brobst and correspondent of HPL. He later became a distinguished professor and critic.

**Sully, Helen V.** (1904–1997), friend of CAS who corresponded with HPL (1933–37). She visited HPL in Providence in 1933, then saw Donald Wandrei and others in New York.

**Talman, Wilfred B[lanch]** (1904–1986), correspondent of HPL and late member of the Kalem Club. HPL assisted Talman on his story "Two Black Bottles" (1926) and wrote "Some Dutch Footprints in New England" for Talman to publish in *De Halve Maen,* the journal of the Holland Society of New York. Late in life Talman wrote the memoir *The Normal Lovecraft* (1973).

**Utpatel, Frank** (1905–1980), artist friend of August Derleth who illustrated some of Derleth's work for *WT* and later did many jackets and interiors (primarily woodcuts) for Arkham House; late correspondent of HPL.

**Wandrei, Donald** (1908–1987), poet and author of weird fiction, science fiction, and detective tales. He corresponded with HPL from 1926 to 1937, visited HPL in Providence in 1927 and 1932, and met HPL occasionally in New York in the 1930s. He helped HPL get "The Shadow out of Time" published in *Astounding Stories*. After HPL's death he and August Derleth founded the publishing firm Arkham House to preserve HPL's work. For their joint correspondence, see *Mysteries of Time and Spirit* (2002).

**Wandrei, Howard** (1909–1956), younger brother of Donald Wandrei, premier weird artist and prolific author of weird fiction, science fiction, and detective stories; correspondent of HPL.

**Weir, John. J.** (1922–1977), late correspondent of HPL and editor of the fanzine *Fantasmagoria*.

**Whitehead, Henry S[t. Clair]** (1882–1932), author of weird and adventure tales, many of them set in the Virgin Islands. HPL corresponded with him and visited him in Florida in 1931. HPL wrote a brief eulogy of Whitehead for *WT*.

**Wright, Farnsworth** (1888–1940), editor of *Weird Tales* (1924–40). He rejected some of HPL's best work of the 1930s, only to publish it after HPL's death upon submittal by August Derleth.

# Bibliography

## A. Works by H. P. Lovecraft

*Books*

*The Ancient Track: Complete Poetical Works.* Edited by S. T. Joshi. 2nd ed. New York: Hippocampus Press, 2013.

*The Annotated Supernatural Horror in Literature.* Edited by S. T. Joshi. 2nd ed. New York: Hippocampus Press, 2012.

*The Battle That Ended the Century* (with R. H. Barlow). [De Land, FL: R. H. Barlow, 1934.]

*The Cats of Ulthar.* Cassia, FL: The Dragon-Fly Press, Christmas 1935. (*LL* 547)

*Charleston.* [New York: H. C. Koenig, 1936.]

*Collected Essays.* Edited by S. T. Joshi. New York: Hippocampus Press, 2004–06. 5 vols. [*CE*]

*Collected Fiction—A Variorum Edition.* Edited by S. T. Joshi. New York: Hippocampus Press, 2015 (Volumes 1–3), 2016 (Volume 4). [*CF*]

*Commonplace Book.* Edited by David E. Schultz. West Warwick, RI: Necronomicon Press, 1987. [*CB*]

*Essential Solitude: The Letters of H. P. Lovecraft and August Derleth.* Edited by David E. Schultz and S. T. Joshi. New York: Hippocampus Press, 2008. 2 vols.

*From the Pest Zone: The New York Stories.* Edited by S. T. Joshi and David E. Schultz. New York: Hippocampus Press, 2003.

*Further Criticism of Poetry.* [Louisville, KY: Printed on the Press of George G. Fetter Co, 1932.] In *CE* 2.

*History of the Necronomicon.* Oakman, AL: Wilson H. Shepherd (The Rebel Press), [November 1937].

*Letters to Robert Bloch.* Edited by David E. Schultz and S. T. Joshi. West Warwick, RI: Necronomicon Press, 1993.

*Letters to Robert Bloch: Supplement.* Edited by David E. Schultz and S. T. Joshi. West Warwick, RI: Necronomicon Press, 1993.

*Lovecraft at Last* (with Willis Conover). Arlington, VA: Carrollton-Clark, 1975. New York: Cooper Square Press, 2002.

*Mysteries of Time and Spirit: The Letters of H. P. Lovecraft and Donald Wandrei.* Edited by S. T. Joshi and David E. Schultz. San Francisco: Night Shade Books, 2002.

*O Fortunate Floridian: H. P. Lovecraft's Letters to R. H. Barlow.* Edited by S. T. Joshi and David E. Schultz. Tampa: University of Tampa Press, 2007.

*Selected Letters*. Edited by August Derleth, Donald Wandrei, and James Turner. Sauk City, WI: Arkham House, 1965–76. 5 vols. [*SL*]

*The Shadow over Innsmouth*. Everett, PA: Visionary Publishing Co., 1936.

*The Shunned House*. Athol, MA: Recluse Press, 1928 (printed but not bound or distributed until 1959–61).

*Uncollected Letters*. Ed. S. T. Joshi. West Warwick, RI: Necronomicon Press, 1986.

*Stories*

"The Alchemist." *United Amateur* 16, No. 4 (November 1916): 53–57. In *CF* 1.

"Arthur Jermyn." See "Facts concerning the Late Arthur Jermyn and His Family."

*At the Mountains of Madness*. *Astounding Stories* 16, No. 6 (February 1936): 8–32; 17, No. 1 (March 1936): 125–55; 17, No. 2 (April 1936): 132–50. In *CF* 3.

"The Beast in the Cave." *Vagrant* No. 7 (June 1918): 113–20. In *CF* 1.

"Beyond the Wall of Sleep." *Pine Cones* 1, No. 6 (October 1919): 2–10. *Fantasy Fan*, 2, No. 2 (October 1934): 25–32. In *CF* 1.

"The Call of Cthulhu." *WT* 11, No. 2 (February 1928): 159–78, 287. In *Beware After Dark! The World's Most Stupendous Tales of Mystery, Horror, Thrills and Terror*, ed. T. Everett Harré. New York: Macaulay, 1929. 223–59. In *CF* 2.

*The Case of Charles Dexter Ward*. In *CF* 2.

"The Cats of Ulthar." *Tryout* 6, No. 11 (November 1920): [3–9]. *WT* 7, No. 2 (February 1926): 252–54. *WT* 21, No. 2 (February 1933): 259–61. Cassia, FL: Dragonfly Press, 1935. In *CF* 1.

"Celephaïs." *Rainbow* No. 2 (May 1922): 10–12. *Marvel Tales* 1, No. 1 (May 1934): 26, 28–32. In *CF* 1.

"The Colour out of Space." *Amazing Stories* 2, No. 6 (September 1927): 557–67. In *CF* 2.

"Cool Air." *Tales of Magic and Mystery* 1, No. 4 (March 1928): 29–34. In *CF* 2.

"Dagon." *Vagrant* No. 11 (November 1919): 23–29. *WT* 2, No. 3 (October 1923): 23–25. In *CF* 1.

"The Doom That Came to Sarnath." *Scot* No. 44 (June 1920): 90–98. *Marvel Tales of Science and Fantasy* 1, No. 4 (March–April 1935): 157–63. In *CF* 1.

*The Dream-Quest of Unknown Kadath*. In *CF* 2.

"The Dreams in the Witch House."' *WT* 22, No. 1 (July 1933): 86–111. In *CF* 3.

"The Dunwich Horror." *WT* 13, No. 4 (April 1929): 481–508. In *CF* 2.

"Ex Oblivione." *United Amateur* 20, No. 4 (March 1921): 59–60 (as by "Ward Phillips"). In *CF* 1.

"Facts concerning the Late Arthur Jermyn and His Family." *Wolverine* No. 9 (March 1921): 3–11. *WT* 3, No. 4 (April 1924): 15–18 (as "The White Ape"). *WT* 25, No. 5 (May 1935): 642–48 (as "Arthur Jermyn"). In *CF* 1.

"The Festival." *WT* 5, No. 1 (January 1925): 169–74. *WT* 22, No. 4 (October 1933): 519–20, 522–28. In *CF* 1.

"From Beyond." *Fantasy Fan* 1, No. 10 (June 1934): 147–51, 160. In *CF* 1.

"The Haunter of the Dark." *WT* 28, No. 5 (December 1936): 538–53. In *CF* 2.

"He." *WT* 8, No. 3 (September 1926): 373–80. In *CF* 1.

"Herbert West—Reanimator." (as "Grewsome Tales"). *Home Brew:* 1, No. 1 (February 1922): 84–88 ("From the Dark"); 1, No. 2 (March 1922): 45–50 ("The Plague Demon"); 1, No. 3 (April 1922): 21–26 ("Six Shots by Moonlight"); 1, No. 4 (May 1922): 53–58 ("The Scream of the Dead"); 1, No. 5 (June 1922): 45–50 ("The Horror from the Shadows,"); 1, No. 6 (July 1922): 57–62 ("The Tomb-Legions"). In *CF* 1.

"History of the 'Necronomicon.'" In *CF* 2.

"The Horror at Red Hook." *WT* 9, No. 1 (January 1927): 59–73. In *You'll Need a Night Light*, ed. Christine Campbell Thomson. London: Selwyn & Blount, 1927. 228–54. In *CF* 1.

"The Hound." *WT* 3, No. 2 (February 1924): 50–52, 78. *WT* 14, No. 3 (September 1929): 421–25, 432. In *CF* 1.

"Hypnos." *National Amateur* 45, No. 5 (May 1923): 1–3. *Weird Tales* 4, No. 2 (May–June–July 1924): 33–35. In *CF* 1.

"In the Vault." *Tryout* 10, No. 6 (November 1925): [3–17]. *WT* 19, No. 4 (April 1932): 459–65. In *CF* 1.

"The Lurking Fear." *Home Brew* 2, No. 6 (January 1923): 4–10; 3, No. 1 (February 1923): 18–23; 3, No. 2 (March 1923): 31–37, 44, 48; 3, No. 3 (April 1923): 35–42. *WT* 11, No. 6 (June 1928): 791–804. In *CF* 1.

"The Moon-Bog." *WT* 7, No. 6 (June 1926): 805–10. In *CF* 1.

"The Music of Erich Zann." *National Amateur* 44, No. 4 (March 1922): 38–40. *WT* 5, No. 5 (May 1925): 219–34. In *Creeps by Night: Chills and Thrills*, ed. Dashiell Hammett. New York: John Day Co., 1931. 347–63. In *Modern Tales of Horror*, ed. Dashiell Hammett. London: Victor Gollancz, 1932. 301–17. *Evening Standard* (London) (24 October 1932): 20–21. *WT* 24, No. 5 (November 1934): 644–48, 655–56. In *CF* 1.

"The Nameless City." *Wolverine* No. 11 (November 1921): 3–15. *Fanciful Tales* 1, No. 1 (Fall 1936): 5–18. In *CF* 1.

"Nyarlathotep." *United Amateur* 20, No. 2 (November 1920): 19–21. *National Amateur* 48, No. 6 (July 1926): 53–54. *Supramundane Stories* 1, No. 2 (Spring 1938): 1–2, 4. In *CF* 1.

"The Other Gods." *Fantasy Fan* 1, No. 3 (November 1933): 35–38. In *CF* 1.

"The Outsider." *WT* 7, No. 4 (April 1926): 449–53. *WT* 17, No. 4 (June–July 1931): 566–71. In *CF* 1.

"Pickman's Model." *WT* 10, No. 4 (October 1927): 505–14. In *By Daylight Only*, ed. Christine Campbell Thomson. London: Selwyn & Blount, 1929. 37–52. *WT* 28, No. 4 (November 1936): 495–505. In *The "Not at Night" Omnibus*, ed. Christine Campbell Thomson. London: Selwyn & Blount, [1937]. 279–307. In *CF* 2.

"The Picture." Nonextant.

"The Picture in the House." *National Amateur* 41, No. 6 (July 1919 [*sic*]): 246–49. *WT* 3, No. 1 (January 1924): 40–42. *WT* 29, No. 3 (March 1937): 370–73. In *CF* 1.

"Polaris." *Philosopher* 1, No. 1 (December 1920): 3–5. *National Amateur* 48, No. 5 (May 1926): 48–49. *Fantasy Fan* 1, No. 6 (February 1934): 83–85. In *CF* 1.

"The Quest of Iranon." *Galleon* 1, No. 5 (July–August 1935): 12–20. In *CF* 1.

"The Rats in the Walls." *WT* 3, No. 3 (March 1924): 25–31. *WT* 15, No. 6 (June 1930): 841–53. In *Switch On the Light*, ed. Christine Campbell Thomson. London: Selwyn & Blount, 1931. 141–65. In *CF* 1.

"The Shadow out of Time."*Astounding Stories* 17, No. 4 (June 1936): 110–54. In *CF* 3.

"The Shadow over Innsmouth." In *CF* 3.

"The Shunned House." In *CF* 1.

"The Silver Key." *WT* 13, No. 1 (January 1929): 41–49, 144. In *CF* 2.

"The Statement of Randolph Carter." *Vagrant* No. 13 (May 1920): 41–48. *WT* 5, No. 2 (February 1925): 149–53. In *CF* 1.

"Strange High House in the Mist." *WT* 18, No. 3 (October 1931): 394–400. In *CF* 2.

"The Temple." *WT* 6, No. 3 (September 1925): 329–36, 429–31; rpt. *WT* 27, No. 2 (February 1936): 239–44, 246–49. In *CF* 1.

"The Terrible Old Man." *Tryout* 7, No. 4 (July 1921): [10–14]. *WT* 8, No. 2 (August 1926): 191–92. In *CF* 1.

"The Thing on the Doorstep." *WT* 29, No. 1 (January 1937): 52–70. In *CF* 3.

"The Tomb." *Vagrant* No. 14 (March 1922): 50–64. *WT* 7, No. 1 (January 1926): 117–23. In *CF* 1.

"The Tree." *Tryout* 7, No. 7 (October 1921): [3–10]. In *CF* 1.

"The Unnamable." *WT* 6, No. 1 (July 1925): 78–82. In *CF* 1.

"The Whisperer in Darkness." *WT* 18, No. 1 (August 1931): 32–73. In *CF* 2.

"What the Moon Brings" (1922). *National Amateur* 45, No. 5 (May 1923): 9. In *CF* 1.

"The White Ape." See "Facts concerning the Late Arthur Jermyn and His Family."

"The White Ship." *United Amateur* 19, No. 2 (November 1919): 30–33. *WT* 9, No. 3 (March 1927): 386–89. In *CF* 1.

*Revisions and Collaborations*

"The Battle That Ended the Century" (with R. H. Barlow). In *CF* 4.

"The Challenge from Beyond" (with C. L. Moore, A. Merritt, Robert E. Howard, and Frank Belknap Long). *Fantasy Magazine* 5, No. 4 (September 1935): 221–29 (Lovecraft portion 223–27). In *CF* 4.

"The Curse of Yig" (with Zealia Bishop). *WT* 14, No. 5 (November 1929): 625–36. In *Switch On the Light*, ed. Christine Campbell Thomson. London:

Selwyn & Blount, 1931. 9–31. In *The "Not at Night" Omnibus,* ed. Christine Campbell Thomson. London: Selwyn & Blount, [1937]. 13–29. In *CF* 4.

"The Diary of Alonzo Typer" (with William Lumley). *WT* 31, No. 2 (February 1938): 152–66. In *CF* 4.

"The Disinterment" (with Duane W. Rimel). *WT* 29, No. .1 (January 1937): 95–102.

"The Electric Executioner" (with Adolphe de Castro). *WT* 16, No. 2 (August 1930): 223–36; *CF* 4.

"In the Walls of Eryx" (with Kenneth Sterling). *WT* 34, No. 4 (October 1939): 60–58. In *CF* 4.

"The Last Test" (with Adolphe de Castro). *WT* 12, No. 5 (November 1928): 625–56. In *CF* 4.

"The Loved Dead" (with C. M. Eddy, Jr.). *WT* 4, No. 2 (May–June–July 1924): 54–57. In *CF* 4.

"The Night Ocean" (with R. H. Barlow). *Californian* 4, No. 3 (Winter 1936): 41–56. (The final two paragraphs had appeared as "A Fragment," *Californian* 3, No. 3 [Winter 1935]: 43.)

"Out of the Aeons" (with Hazel Heald). *WT* 25, No. 4 (April 1935): 478–96. In *CF* 4.

"Through the Gates of the Silver Key" (with E. Hoffmann Price). *WT* 24, No. 1 (July 1934): 60–85. In *CF* 3.

"Winged Death" (with Hazel Heald). *WT* 23, No. 3 (March 1934): 299–315. In *CF* 4.

*Essays*

"An Account of a Trip to the Antient Fairbanks House, in Dedham, and to the Red Horse Tavern in Sudbury, in the Province of the Massachusetts-Bay." In *CE* 4.

"Bureau of Critics Comment on Verse, Typography, Prose." *National Amateur* 56, No. 2 (December 1933): 1–2. In *CE* 1.

"Can the Moon Be Reached by Man? Showing That the Trip to Our Satellite, Heretofore Attempted Only in Fiction, May Be a Scientific Possibility." *Pawtuxet Valley Gleaner,* 31, No. 41 (12 October 1906): 2. In *CE* 3.

"Commonplace Book." In *CE* 5.

"Correspondence between R. H. Barlow and Wilson Shepherd of Oakman, Alabama—September–November 1932." *Lovecraft Studies* No. 13 (Fall 1986): 68–71. In *CE* 5.

"In Memoriam: Henry St. Clair Whitehead." *WT* 21, N. 3 (March 1933): 391 (unsigned). In *CE* 5.

"In Memoriam: Robert Ervin Howard." *Fantasy Magazine* No. 38 (September 1936): 29–31. In *CE* 5.

"A List of Certain Basic Underlying Horrors Effectively Used in Weird Fiction." In *CE* 5.

"[List of Correspondents to Whom Postcards Have Been Sent]." In *CE* 5.

"List of Primary Ideas Motivating Possible Weird Tales." In *CE* 5.

"Robert Ervin Howard: 1906–1936." *Phantagraph* 4, No. 5 (August 1936): 4–5 (unsigned). In *CE* 5.

"Some Notes on Interplanetary Fiction." *Californian* 3, No. 3 (Winter 1935): 39–42. In *CE* 2.

"Suggestions for Writing Story" (later "Notes on Writing Weird Fiction"). In *CE* 5.

"Supernatural Horror in Literature." *Recluse* No. 1 (1927): 23–59. Rev. ed. in *Fantasy Fan* (October 1933–February 1935). In *CE* 2.

"Supernatural Horror in Literature" [summary of chs. I–VIII]. In *Supernatural Horror in Literature as Revised in 1936*. Arlington, VA: Carrollton-Clark, 1974. In *CE* 2.

"The Unknown City in the Ocean." *Perspective Review* (Winter 1934): 7–8. In *CE* 4.

"Weird Story Plots." In *CE* 5.

"The Weird Work of William Hope Hodgson." *Phantagraph* 5, No. 5 (February 1937): 5–7. Incorporated into "Supernatural Horror in Literature."

"What's the Trouble with Weird Fiction?" [unsigned.] *Phantagraph* 5, No. 5 (February 1937): 4, 8.

*Poems* [all poems are in *The Ancient Track*]

"The City." *Vagrant* No. 10 (October 1919): 6–7 (as by "Ward Phillips").

"Clouds." *See* "A Cycle of Verse."

"A Cycle of Verse." *Tryout* 5, No. 7 (July 1919): [19–22] (as by "Ward Phillips"). [Includes "Oceanus," "Clouds," and "Mother Earth."]

"Edith Miniter: Born on Wilbraham Mountain, Massachusetts, May 5, 1869. Died at North Wilbraham, Massachusetts, June 8, 1934." *Tryout* 16, No. 8 (August 1934): [5–6].

*Fungi from Yuggoth.*

    I. "The Book." *Fantasy Fan* 2, No. 2 (October 1934): 24.

    II. "Pursuit." *Fantasy Fan* 2, No. 2 (October 1934): 24.

    III. "The Key." *Fantasy Fan* 2, No. 5 (January 1935): 72.

    V. "Homecoming." *Fantasy Fan* 2, No. 5 (January 1935): 72. *Science-Fantasy Correspondent* 1, No. 1 (November–December 1936): 24.

    XX. "Night-Gaunts." *Providence Journal* (26 March 1930): 15. *Interesting Items* No. 605 (November 1934): [6] (as "Night Gaunts"). *Phantagraph* 4, No. 3 ([June] 1936): 8. *The Science Fiction Bard* 1, No. 1 (May 1937): 2–3.

    XXIII. "Mirage." *WT* 17, No. 2 (February–March 1931): 175.

    XXVII. "The Elder Pharos." *WT* 17, No. 2 (February–March 1931): 175.

    XXIX. "Nostalgia." *Providence Journal* (12 March 1930): 15. *Phantagraph* 4, No. 4 (July 1936): 1.

XXX. "Background." *Providence Journal* (16 April 1930): 13. *Interesting Items* No. 592 (September 1932): [1]. *Galleon* 1, No. 4 (May–June 1935): 8. *The Lovecrafter* 47, No. 1 (20 August 1936): 1 (as "A Sonnet").

XXXI. "The Dweller." *Providence Journal* (7 May 1930): 15. *Phantagraph* 4, No. 2 (November–December 1935): 1935: [3].

XXXIII. "Harbour Whistles." *Silver Fern* 1, No. 5 (May 1930): [1]. *L'Alouette* 3, No. 6 (September–October 1930): 161. *Phantagraph* 5, No. 2 (November 1936): 1.

XXXIV. "Recapture." *WT* 15, No. 5 (May 1930): 693.

"Hallowe'en in a Suburb." *National Amateur* 48, No. 4 (March 1926): 33 (as "In a Suburb"). *Phantagraph* 6, No. 2 (June 1937): 3–4.

"The House." *National Enquirer* 9, No. 11 (11 December 1919): 3. *Philosopher* 1, No. 1 (December 1920): 6 (as by "Ward Phillips").

"In a Sequester'd Providence Churchyard Where Once Poe Walk'd." *Science-Fantasy Correspondent* 1, No. 3 (March–April 1937): 16–17 (as "In a Sequestered Churchyard Where Once Poe Walked").

"Mother Earth." *See* "A Cycle of Verse."

"Nemesis." *The Vagrant*, No. 7 (June 1918). *Weird Tales* 3, No. 4 (April 1924): 78.

"The Nightmare Lake." *Vagrant* No. 12 (December 1919): 13–14.

"Oceanus." *See* "A Cycle of Verse."

"October." *Tryout* 6, No. 10 (October 1920): [17] (as by "Henry Paget-Lowe").

"Psychopompos: A Tale in Rhyme." *Vagrant*. No. 10 (October 1919). *WT* 30, No. 3 (September 1937): 341–48 (without subtitle).

"The Wood." *Tryout* 11, No. 2 (January 1929): [16] (as by "L. Theobald, Jun.").

*Letters*

To Donald A. Wollheim [May 1935]. *Cosmic Tales* 1, No. 4 (January–February 1938): 33.

To Donald A. Wollheim [c. September 1935]. In Robert E. Howard. *The Hyborian Age. And A Probable Outline of Conan's Career* by P. Schuyler Miller and John D. Clark, Ph.D. Los Angeles: LANY Coöperative Publications, 1938, p. v (as "Introduction"); In Robert E. Howard. *The Coming of Conan*. New York: Gnome Press, 1953. 13–14 (as "Introduction" to *The Hyborian Age*).

To [Donald A. Wollheim], [October? 1935]. *Phantagraph* 4, No. 2 (November–December 1935): [1].

To Willis Conover, Jr., 14 August 1936. Selections, under "Odds and Ends: H. P. Lovecraft." *Science Fantasy Correspondent* 1, No. 1 (November–December 1936): 28.

To Willis Conover, Jr., 14 August 1936 and 18 November 1936. Selections, under "Odds and Ends: H. P. Lovecraft." *Science Fantasy Correspondent* 1, No. 2 (January–February 1937): 28.

# B. Works by Lovecraft's Correspondents

## William F. Anger

With Louis C. Smith. "An Interview with E. Hoffman [*sic*] Price." *Fantasy Fan* 2, No. 4 (December 1934): 60–61.

"Phantastic Bread & Butter; or, the Mystery of the Missing Authors." As by Fred Anger. *Phantagraph* 5, No. 2 (November 1936): 4–8.

## Robert Bloch

*Books*

*Mysteries of the Worm.* Edited by Robert M. Price. 2nd ed. Oakland: Chaosium, 1993. [*MW*]

*Once Around the Bloch: An Unauthorized Autobiography.* New York: Tor, 1993.

*The Opener of the Way.* Sauk City, WI: Arkham House, 1945.

*Strange Eons.* Chapel Hill, NC: Whispers Press, 1978.

*Fiction*

"The Black Kiss" (with Henry Kuttner). *WT* (June 1937).

"Black Lotus." *Unusual Stories* 1, No. 2 (Winter 1935): 76–85.

"The Blasphemy Beneath." Nonextant.

"The Brood of Bubastis." *WT* (March 1937). In *MW*.

"The Dark Demon." *WT* (November 1936). In *OW, MW*.

"Dr. Lichorn." Nonextant.

"The Druidic Doom." *WT* (April 1936).

"Evil Genius." Nonextant.

"The Faceless God." *WT* (May 1936). In *OW, MW*.

"The Feast in the Abbey." *WT* (January 1935). In *OW*.

"The Fountain of Youth." Nonextant.

"The Fog." Nonextant.

"The Gallows." Nonextant.

"Glass Eye." Nonextant.

"The Grave." Nonextant.

"The Grinning Ghoul." *WT* (June 1936). In *MW*.

"The Keeper in the Crypt." *WT* (July 1937).

"The Laughter of a Ghoul." *Fantasy Fan* 2, No. 4 (December 1934): 62–63.

"Lilies." *Marvel Tales* 1, No. 3 (Winter 1934): 78–80.

"The Madness of Lucian Grey." Nonextant.

"Mother of Serpents." *WT* (December 1936). In *OW*.

"Nocturne Macabre." Nonextant.

"The Opener of the Way." *WT* (October 1936). In *OW*.

"Satan's Servants." In H. P. Lovecraft et al. *Something about Cats and Other Pieces.* Edited by August Derleth. Sauk City, WI: Arkham House, 1949. 117–45 (including assorted comments by HPL, 146–47).

"The Secret in the Tomb." *WT* (May 1935). In *MW.*

"The Shadow from the Steeple." *WT* (September 1950). In *MW.*

"The Shambler from the Stars," *WT* (September 1935). In *OW, MW.*

"Sons of the Serpent." Nonextant.

"The Soul." Nonextant.

"Spawn of the Elder Pits." Nonextant

"The Sorcerer's Tale." Nonextant.

'The Suicide in the Study." *WT* (June 1935). In *MW.*

"The Torture-Master." Nonextant.

"The Touch of a Corpse." Nonextant.

"A Visit with H. P. Lovecraft." *Science-Fantasy Correspondent* (January–February 1937). Rpt. *LAL* 52–54.

"Wine of the Sabbat." *WT* (November 1940).

*Verse*

"Delirium." Nonextant.

"Dinner at Eight." Nonextant.

"Dreams." Nonextant.

"Finis." Nonextant.

"Necrophile." Nonextant.

"Nightmare." Nonextant.

"Spectators." Nonextant.

"Weird Wood." Nonextant.

*Nonfiction*

"Funtasy" (column). *Fantasy Magazine* No. 38 (September 1936); No. 39 (January 1937).

"How I Get My Inspiration." *Phantagraph* 4, No. 2 (November–December 1935): 11. Rpt. *Operation Phantasy,* ed. Donald A. Wollheim. Rego Park, NY: Phantagraph Press, 1967. 29–30.

## Willis Conover, Jr.

"Artjay's Dilemma." *Science Fiction Critic* (1938); *Science Fiction Digest* (September 1952).

"The Call of Lovecraft." *Xenophile* 2, No. 6 (October 1975): 15–16.

"Hit 'n' Run." As by "Joseph Allan Ryan." *Science-Fantasy Correspondent* 1, No. 1 (November–December 1936): 30–32; 1, No. 2 (January–February 1937): 30–31.

"The Lost Chord." As by "Joseph Allan Ryan." *Science-Fantasy Correspondent* 1, No. 1 (November–December 1936): 25–26.

"Mother Goose Crimes." *Science Fiction Critic.* 2. No. 1. Ed. Claire P. Beck and Groo Beck. Lakeport, CA: The Futile Press, January 1938.

[Untitled piece on Arthur J. Forrester and amateur journalism, including a letter from Forrester.] *Science Fiction Critic.* 2. No. 14. Ed. Groo Beck. July 1938.

"Observations." *Helios* 1, No. 3 (August–September 1937).

"Observations and Otherwise." *Democrat and News* (Cambridge, MD) (8 July 1937).

"The Spirits Mourn." *Amateur Correspondent* 2, No. 1 (May–June 1937): 15.

"The Terrible Parchment" [letter to "The Eyrie"]. *WT* 30, No. 4 (October 1937): 509. In *A Weird Writer in Our Midst: Early Criticism of H. P. Lovecraft,* ed. S. T. Joshi. New York: Hippocampus Press, 2010. 93.

## Robert Nelson

*Sable Revery.* Ed. Douglas A. Anderson. n.p.: Nodens Books, 2012. Contains all the following items.

*Verse*

"Below the Phosphor." *Fantasy Fan* 1, No. 10 (June 1934): 158.

"Dream-Stair." *WT* 25, No. 4 (April 1935): 465.

"Fragment." *Fantasy Fan* 2, No. 5 (January 1935): 75

"Jorgas." *WT* 27, No. 2 (February 1936): 187. In *The Eighth Green Man & Other Strange Folk* ed. Robert E. Weinberg. Mercer Island, WA: Starmont House 1989. 169.

"Night of Unrest." *WT* 30, No. 3 (September 1937): 281.

"Sable Reverie." *WT* 24, No. 3 (September 1934): 351.

"Under the Tomb." *WT* 25, No. 5 (May 1935): 581. In *Far Below and Other Horrors from the Pulps,* ed. Robert E. Weinberg. FAX Collector's Editions, 1974.; Wildside Press, 2003: 151.

"The Unremembered Realm." *Fantasy Fan* 1, No. 12 (August 1934): 188.

*Sketches*

"Lost Excerpts": "I. In Living Darkness," *Fantasy Fan* 2, No. 3 (November 1934): 45; "II. The Feast of the Centaurs," *Fantasy Fan* 2, No. 4 (December 1934): 63; "III. The Flinging of the Rocks," *Phantagraph* 4, No. 4 (July 1936): 2.

"Trilogy of Death." *Fantasy Fan,* 2 No. 5 (January 1935): 78.

"The Weird Tale (A Dialogue)." *Fantasy Fan* 2, No. 8 (May 1934): 141.

## Wilson Shepherd

"Death." Unpublished; ms., JHL.

"A Few Words from the General Manager." *Bulletin of the Terrestrial Fantascience Guild* (April 1935).

"He Waits—For What." *Astonishing Stories* (May 1935).

"Wanderer's Return." First published as "Wander's Return" in *Literary Quarterly* 1, No. 1 (Winter 1937). In *The Ancient Track*.

## Kenneth Sterling

"The Bipeds of Bjulhu." *Wonder Stories* 7, No. 7 (January–February 1936): 817–19.

"The Brain-Eaters of Pluto." *Wonder Stories* 5, No. 8 (March 1934): 822–25.

"Caverns Measureless to Man." *Science-Fantasy Correspondent* No. 1 (1975): 36–43. In *Caverns Measureless to Man: 18 Memoirs of H. P. Lovecraft*, ed. S. T. Joshi. West Warwick, RI: Necronomicon Press, 1996. 46–54. In *Lovecraft Remembered*, ed. Peter Cannon. Sauk City, WI: Arkham House, 1998. 370–84.

"Death of H. P. Lovecraft" [letter to "The Eyrie"]. *WT* 30, No. 1 (July 1937): 122. In *A Weird Writer in Our Midst: Early Criticism of H. P. Lovecraft*, ed. S. T. Joshi. New York: Hippocampus Press, 2010. 84–85.

"The Horror Element in Poe." *Californian*, 5, No. 3 (Winter 1937): 33–45.

"Lovecraft and Science." In H. P. Lovecraft et al. *Marginalia*. Sauk City, WI: Arkham House, 1944. 351–54. In *Lovecraft Remembered*, ed. Peter Cannon. Sauk City, WI: Arkham House, 1998. 423–25.

"Red Moon." *Wonder Stories* 7, No. 6 (December 1935): 678–82.

## Donald A. Wollheim

"Allaileor." *Unusual Stories* 1, No. 1 (May–June 1935): 34.

"The Astronomer." *International Observer* (April 1935).

"Cartoonvents." *International Observer* (November 1935).

"Editor's Preface" to "The Shadow out of Time." In *The Viking Portable Novels of Science*. New York: Viking, 1945. 391–93.

"Fanfarade." *Science Fiction Fan* (July 1936 etc.).

"The Future of Publishing." *Phantagraph* 8, No. 2 (June 1940): 13–16.

"The Gravity Globe." *Astonishing Stories* (May 1935).

"Howard Phillips Lovecraft." *Phantagraph* 6, No. 1 (May 1937): 2–3. In *Operation Phantasy*, ed. Donald A. Wollheim. Rego Park, NY: Phantagraph Press, 1967. 32–33.

"H. P. Lovecraft: *The Outsider and Others*." In *Horror: 100 Best Books*, ed. Stephen Jones and Kim Newman. London: Xanadu, 1988; New York: Carroll & Graf, 1988. 96–98.

"The Large Moons of Jupiter." *International Observer* (November 1935).

"The Man from Ariel." *Wonder Stories* (January 1934). In Wollheim's *The Man from Ariel*. Boston: NESFA Press, 1982.

"My Experiences with *Wonder Stories*." *Bulletin of the Terrestrial Fantascience Guild* (April 1935).

"THE NECRONOMICON as *Translated and Abridged from the original Arabic of Abdul Alhazred*, by W. T. Faraday. Privately printed by the author." Under "Book Chats." *Branford Review and East Haven News* 8, No. 24 (12 September 1935): 7.

"Phantascope." *Phantagraph* 5, No. 2 (November 1936): 2–4; 5, No. 5 (February 1937): 2

"Pure Fantasy." *Fantasy Magazine* 4, No. 5 (April 1935): 128–9. *Californian* 4, No. 1 (Summer 1936): 55–56.

"Sun-Spots." *International Observer* (April 1935); *Phantagraph* (November–December 1935, July 1936).

"True Thought Variants." *Science Fiction Fan* (September 1936).

## Natalie H. Wooley

*Verse*

"Admonition." *Kaleidograph,* 6, No. 9 (December 1934): 10.

"The Alien." *Literati* 1, No. 1 (Autumn 1934): 3; *Fantasy Fan* 2, No. 5 (January 1935): 74.

"Antares." *Marvel Tales* 1, No. 1 (May 1934): 20. *Arkham Sampler* 1, No. 4 (1984): 29.

"Avatar." *Literati* 1, No. 4 (Summer 1935): [1].

"Coward." *Manettism* 8, No. 12 (24 November 1934): n.p.

"Dream Fantasy." *Manettism.* 8, No. 23 (11 May 1935): n.p.

"Dream Tryst." *Goldenrod* 7, No. 2 (December 1956): 9.

"End of the Trail." *Goldenrod* 8, No. 1 (July 1957): [1].

"Flight." *Sea Gull.* No. 41(October 1933): [9].

"A Heavenly Tragedy." *Tryout* 16, No. 7 (August 1934): 11.

"Lines to Cleopatra." *Tryout* 16, No. 10 (December 1934): 18.

"Mountain Pool." *Goldenrod* 4, No. 1 (Winter 1934): 5.

"Mountain Trail." *Goldenrod* 3, No. 4 (Fall 1933): 6.

"The Path." *Arkham Sampler* 1, No. 4 (1984): 5.

"Release." *Arkham Sampler* 1, No. 4 (1984): 32.

"Sailor's Child." *Manettism* 8, No. 23 (11 May 1935): n.p. In *Threads in Tapestry,* ed. Charles A. A. Parker, Rachel Hall, and Marcia A. Taylor. Medford, MA: C. A. A. Parker, 1935. 109.

"Sanctuary." *Sea Gull* No. 46 (March 1934): [14]; *Marvel Tales* 1, No. 4 (March–April 1935): 170.

"Sphinx." *Arkham Sampler* 1, No. 4 (1984): 32.

"Western Night." *Goldenrod* 3, No. 3 (Summer 1933): 7.

*Fiction*

"The Dance." *Goldenrod* 3, No. 4 (Fall 1933): 8–9.

"Reminiscence." *Goldenrod* 5, No. 2 (Winter 1938): 14–15.

"Spurs of Death." *Fantasy Fan* 1, No. 4 (December 1933): 59–61.

"The Tale of a Shirt." *Star Journal* 2, No. 4. (n.d.): [1], 3.

"'Tillicum.'" *Goldenrod* 4, No. 1 (Winter 1934): 2–4.

*Nonfiction*

"The Adventure Story." *Californian* 3, No. 2 (Fall 1935): 9. In *West Is West and Others,* ed. Rob Roehm and Alex Runions. n.p.: Lulu.com, 2006. n.p.: Roehm's Room Press, 2007. 134–36.

"Have You a Hobby?" *Californian,* 2, No. 2 [i.e., 3] (Winter 1934): 3.

"Intimations—The Hand in the Dark." Unpublished?

"Is Criticism Necessary?" *Sea Gull* No. 44 (January 1934): 3–4.

## C. Works by Others

*Dates in angular brackets indicate first publication.*

Allen, Hervey (1889–1949). *Anthony Adverse.* New York: Holt, Rinehart & Winston, 1933.

Andreyev, Leonid Nikolaevich (1871–1919). *The Seven That Were Hanged.* New York: Boni & Liveright (Modern Library), [1918] or [1925]. Also includes *The Red Laugh.* (*LL* 29)

*The Arabian Nights Entertainments.* Selected and Edited by Andrew Lang. New York: Longmans, Green, 1898. (*LL* 38)

Arlen, Michael (1895–1936). *Ghost Stories.* London: Collins, [1927]. (*LL* 41)

Asbury, Herbert (1891–1963), ed. *Not at Night!* New York: Macy-Masius (The Vanguard Press), 1928. (*LL* 44)

Asquith, Cynthia (1887–1960), ed. *The Ghost Book.* London: Hutchinson, 1927. New York: Charles Scribner's Sons, 1927.

Astor, John Jacob (1864–1912). *A Journey in Other Worlds: A Romance of the Future.* New York: D. Appleton & Co., 1894. 476 pp. (*LL* 46)

Austin, F. Britten (1885–1941). *On the Borderland.* Garden City, NY: Doubleday, Page, 1923. (*LL* 51)

Baldwin, F. Lee. "H. P. Lovecraft: A Biographical Sketch." *Fantasy Magazine* 4, No. 5 (April 1935): 108–10, 132. In *LAL* 60–63.

Barbey d'Aurevilly, Jules (1808–1889). *The Story without a Name.* Tr. Edgar Saltus. New York: Bedford & Co., 1891; *or* New York: Brentano's, 1919. (*LL* 65)

Baring-Gould, S[abine] (1834–1924). *Curious Myths of the Middle Ages.* <1866> (*LL* 66)

Barlow, R. H. (1918–1951). "A Dim-Remembered Story." *Californian* 4, No. 1 (Summer 1936): 72–87.

———. *Eyes of the God: The Weird Fiction and Poetry of R. H. Barlow.* Ed. S. T. Joshi, David E. Schultz, and Douglas A. Anderson. New York: Hippocampus Press, 2002.

———. "R. E. H." *WT* 28, No. 3 (October 1936): 353.

Barrett, Francis. *The Magus; or, Celestial Intelligencer.* London: Printed for Lackington, Allen & Co., 1801. London: W. W. Harmon, 1896 (as *The Book of the Magi*).

Baudelaire, Charles Pierre (1821–1867). *Baudelaire: His Prose and Poetry.* Ed. T. R. Smith. New York: Boni & Liveright (Modern Library), [1919]. (*LL* 69)

Beckford, William (1759–1844). *The Episodes of Vathek.* <1912> Translated from the Original French by Sir Frank T. Marzials. Boston: Small, Maynard & Co., [1922?] or [1924?]. (*LL* 73)

———. *Vathek.* <1786> Illustrated by Mahlon Blaine. New York: John Day Co., 1928. (*LL* 75)

Bennett, Arnold (1867–1931). *The Old Wives' Tale.* London: Chapman & Hall, 1908.

Benson, E[dward] F[rederic] (1867–1940). *Spook Stories.* London: Hutchinson, 1928.

———. *Visible and Invisible.* New York, George H. Doran, 1923. (*LL* 79)

———, and Brander Matthews. *Two Masterly Ghost Stories.* Girard, KS: Haldeman-Julius, n.d. (*LL* 80) [Contains "The Man Who Went Too Far."]

Béraud, Henri (1885–1958). *Lazarus.* Tr. Eric Sutton. New York: Macmillan, 1925. (*LL* 81) Rpt. New York: Hippocampus Press, 2007.

Besant, Annie (1847–1933). *The Pedigree of Man.* London: Theosophical Publishing Society, 1904.

Bierce, Ambrose (1842–1914?). *Can Such Things Be?* <1893> New York: Boni & Liveright (Modern Library), 1918. (*LL* 87)

———. *In the Midst of Life: Tales of Soldiers and Civilians.* <1891> New York: Modern Library, [1927]. (*LL* 88)

———. *The Monk and the Hangman's Daughter; Fantastic Fables;* [etc.]. New York: A. & C. Boni, 1925. 383 pp. (*LL* 90)

Birch, A. G. *The Moon Terror.* And Stories by Anthony M. Rud, Vincent Starrett, and Farnsworth Wright. Indianapolis: Popular Fiction Publishing Co., [1927]. (*LL* 93)

[Birkin, Charles (1907–1985), ed.] *Creeps: A Collection of Uneasy Tales.* London: Philip Allan, 1932. (*LL* 209)

———. *Shudders: A Collection of Uneasy Tales.* London: Philip Allan, 1932. (*LL* 802)

Birkhead, Edith. *The Tale of Terror: A Study of the Gothic Romance.* New York: E. P. Dutton, 1921. (*LL* 94)

Blackwood, Algernon (1869–1951). *Incredible Adventures.* London: Macmillan, 1914. New York: Macmillan, 1914. [Contains "A Descent into Egypt."]

———. *Jimbo: A Fantasy.* New York: Macmillan, 1909. (*LL* 95)

———. *John Silence—Physician Extraordinary.* London: Eveleigh Nash, 1908. Boston: John W. Luce, 1909. London: Macmillan, 1912. New York: Vaughan & Gomme, 1914. New York: Knopf, 1917. New York, E. P. Dutton, [1920]. (*LL* 96, 97) [Contains "Ancient Sorceries" and "The Nemesis of Fire."]

Blakeborough, Richard (d. 1918). *The Hand of Glory and Further Grandfather's Tales and Legends of Highwaymen and Others.* Edited by J. Fairfax Blakeborough. London: Grant Richards, [1924]. (*LL* 105)

Blavatsky, Madame Helena Petrovana (1831–1891). *The Secret Doctrine.* London: Theosophical Publishing Co., 1888.

Bond, Mary Bligh. *Avernus.* Oxford: Basil Blackwell, 1924. (*LL* 107)

Boswell, James (1740–1795). *The Life of Samuel Johnson, LL.D.* <1791> London: J. M. Dent; New York: E. P. Dutton (Everyman's Library), December 1910. 2 vols. (*LL* 113)

Buchan, John (1875–1940). *The Runagates Club.* Boston: Houghton Mifflin, 1928. (*LL* 129)

———. *Witch Wood.* Boston: Houghton Mifflin, 1927.

Bulfinch, Thomas (1796–1867). *The Age of Fable; or, Beauties of Mythology.* <1855> Edited by J. Loughran Scott. Rev. ed. Philadelphia: D. McKay, [1898]. (*LL* 130)

Bulwer-Lytton, Edward (1803–1873). *A Strange Story; The Haunted House [sic]; Zanoni.* <1862; 1859; 1842> Boston: Desmond Publishing Co., [18—?]. (*LL* 132). [The second story is "The Haunted and the Haunters; or, The House and the Brain."]

Burke, Thomas (1886–1945). *Limehouse Nights.* New York: McBride, 1917.

Busson, Paul (1873–1924). *Die Wiedergeburt des Melchior Dronte.* <1924> Tr. by Prince Mirski and Thomas Moult as *The Man Who Was Born Again.* New York: John Day Co., 1927. (*LL* 141)

Cabell, James Branch (1879–1958). *Jurgen: A Comedy of Justice.* New York: McBride, 1919.

———. *Smirt: An Urbane Nightmare.* New York: McBride, 1934.

*Chambers's Encyclopædia: A Dictionary of Universal Knowledge.* London: W. & R. Chambers, 1860–68. 10 vols. Philadelphia: J. B. Lippincott Co., 1860–69. [Rev eds. up to 1935.] (*LL* 986)

Chambers, Robert W. (1865–1933). *In Search of the Unknown.* New York: Harper & Brothers, 1904. (*LL* 166)

———. *The King in Yellow.* Chicago: F. Tennyson Neely, 1895. (*LL* 167) [Contains "The Yellow Sign."]

Cline, Leonard (1893–1929). *The Dark Chamber.* New York: Viking Press, 1927. (*LL* 183)

Cowan, Frank (1844–1905). *Revi-Lona: A Romance of Love in a Marvellous Land.* [Greensburg, PA: Tribune Press Publishing Co., 188-?]. (*LL* 198)

de la Mare, Walter (1873–1956). *The Connoisseur and Other Stories.* London: Collins, 1926. New York: Alfred A. Knopf, 1926. (*LL* 228) [Contains "All Hallows" and "Mr. Kempe."]

———. *The Riddle and Other Stories.* <1923> New York: Alfred A. Knopf, 1930. (*LL* 229) [Contains "Seaton's Aunt" and "The Tree."]

De Mille, James (1837–1880). *A Strange Manuscript Found in a Copper Cylinder.* <1888> New York: Harper & Brothers, 1900. (*LL* 230)

Derleth, August (1909–1971). *Evening in Spring.* New York: Charles Scribner's Sons, 1941.

————. *The Man on All Fours: A Judge Peck Mystery Story.* New York: Loring & Mussey, [1934]. (*LL* 234)

————. *Place of Hawks.* Illustrated with wood engravings by George Barford. New York: Loring & Mussey, 1935. (*LL* 235).

————. *Sign of Fear: A Judge Peck Mystery.* New York, Loring & Mussey, [1935]. (*LL* 236)

————*Three Who Died: A Judge Peck Mystery* (New York: Loring & Mussey, [1935]; *LL* 237).

Derleth, August, and Raymond E. F. Larsson, ed. *Poetry out of Wisconsin.* New York: Henry Harrison, 1937.

Disraeli, Benjamin (1804–1881). *Alroy.* <1833> (*LL* 252)

Doyle, Sir Arthur Conan (1859–1930). *Tales of Long Ago.* London: John Murray, [1922]. (*LL* 261)

————. *Tales of Twilight and the Unseen.* London: John Murray, 1922. (*LL* 262)

Drake, H[enry] B[urgess] (1894–1963). *The Shadowy Thing.* <1925> New York: Macy-Masius, 1928. Rpt. New York: Hippocampus Press, 2010.

Dunsany, Lord (Edward John Moreton Drax Plunkett, 18th baron) (1878–1957). *The Book of Wonder* <1912> [and *Time and the Gods* <1906>]. New York: Boni & Liveright (Modern Library), [1918]. (*LL* 271)

————. *The Curse of the Wise Woman.* London: William Heinemann; New York: Longmans, Green, 1933.

————. *Don Rodriguez: Chronicles of Shadow Valley.* London & New York: G. P. Putnam's Sons, 1922. (*LL* 273). [Originally published as *The Chronicles of Rodriguez* (London, 1922).]

————. *A Dreamer's Tales and Other Stories* [*A Dreamer's Tales* <1910> and *The Sword of Welleran* <1908>]. New York: Boni & Liveright (Modern Library), [1917], [1919], or [1921]. (*LL* 273)

————. *Fifty-one Tales.* <1915> (*LL* 274)

————. *Five Plays: The Gods of the Mountain; The Golden Doom; King Argimēnēs and the Unknown Warrior; The Glittering Gate; The Lost Silk Hat.* <1914> Boston: Little, Brown, 1923. (*LL* 275)

————. *The Gods of Pegāna.* <1905>. (*LL* 276)

————. *The King of Elfland's Daughter.* London: G. P. Putnam's Sons, 1924. (*LL* 277)

————. *The Last Book of Wonder.* Boston: J. W. Luce, 1916. (*LL* 278)

————. *A Night at an Inn.* New York: The Sunwise Turn, 1916.

————. *Plays of Gods and Men.* Boston: J. W. Luce, [1917]. (*LL* 279)

————. *Plays of Near and Far.* New York: G. P. Putnam's Sons, 1923. (*LL* 280)

————. *Tales of Three Hemispheres*. <1919>. (*LL* 281)

Durant, Will (1885–1981). *The Story of Philosophy: The Lives and Opinions of the Greater Philosophers*. Garden City, NY: Garden City Publishing Co., 1927. (*LL* 284)

*The Encyclopaedia Britannica: A Dictionary of Arts, Sciences, and General Literature* . . . With . . . Revisions and Additions by W. H. De Puy. 9th Ed. Chicago: Werner Co., 1896. 24 vols. (*LL* 299)

Eddison, E. R. (1882–1945). *The Worm Ouroboros: A Romance*. Illustrated by Keith Henderson. New York: A. & C. Boni, 1926. (*LL* 291)

Endore, Guy (1900–1970). *The Werewolf of Paris*. New York: Farrar & Rinehart, 1933.

England, George Allan (1877–1936). "The Elixir of Hate." *Cavalier* (August–November 1911).

Esenwein, J. Berg (1867–1946), and Arthur Leeds (1882–1952). *Writing the Photoplay*. [Springfield, MA: The Home Correspondence School, c. 1913.]

Everett, Mrs. H[enrietta] D. (1851–1923). *The Death-Mask and Other Ghosts*. London: Philip Allan, 1920.

Fiske, John (1842–1901). *Myths and Myth-Makers: Old Tales and Superstitions Interpreted by Comparative Mythology*. <1872> Boston: Houghton Mifflin, 1900. (*LL* 317)

Flammarion, Camille (1842–1925). *Haunted Houses*. London: T. Fisher Unwin, [1924]. (*LL* 319)

Flaubert, Gustave (1821–1880). *Salammbô: A Romance of Ancient Carthage*. <1862> (*LL* 320)

————. *The Temptation of St. Anthony*. <1874> Translated by Lafcadio Hearn <1910>. New York: Boni & Liveright (Modern Library), [1920]. (*LL* 321)

Forbes, Esther (1891–1967). *A Mirror for Witches*. London: William Heinemann, 1928. Boston: Houghton, Mifflin, 1928.

Frazer, Sir James George (1854–1941). *The Golden Bough*. <1890–1915>

French, Joseph Lewis (1858–1936), ed. *The Best Psychic Stories*. Introduction by Dorothy Scarborough. New York: Boni & Liveright (Modern Library), [1920]. (*LL* 334)

————. *Ghosts, Grim and Gentle*. New York: Dodd, Mead, 1926.

————. *Masterpieces of Mystery*. Garden City, NY, Doubleday, Page, 1920. 4 vols. (*LL* 335)

Gautier, Théophile (1811–1872). *Clarimonde*. <1836> New York: Brentano's, 1899. 81 pp. *or Clarimonde and Other Stories*. London: T. C. & E. C. Jack, 1908. (*LL* 344) ["Le Morte Amoreuse" was translated as "Clarimonde."]

————. *One of Cleopatra's Nights and Other Fantastic Romances*. Translated by Lafcadio Hearn. <1882> (*LL* 346)

————, and Prosper Mérimée (1803–1870). *Tales Before Supper*. Told in English by Myndart Verelst [i.e., Edgar Saltus] and Delayed with a Poem by

Edgar Saltus. New York: Brentano's, 1887. (*LL* 347) [Includes Gautier's "Avatar" and Mérimée's "The Venus of Ille."]

Gawsworth, John [pseud. of Terence Ian Fytton Armstrong] (1912–1970), ed. *Strange Assembly.* London: Unicorn Press, 1932. (*LL* 42)

Gorman, Herbert (1893–1954). *The Place Called Dagon.* New York: George H. Doran, 1927. Rpt. New York: Hippocampus Press, 2003.

Graves, Robert (1895–1985). *I, Claudius.* London, A. Barker, 1934.

———. *Claudius, the God, and His Wife Messalina.* New York: H. Smith & R. Haas, 1935.

Gummere, Francis B. (1855–1919). *A Handbook of Poetics, for Students of English Verse.* Boston: Ginn & Co., 1885.

Haeckel, Ernst (1834–1919). *Die Welträthsel.* <1899> Tr. Joseph McCabe as *The Riddle of the Universe.* New York: Harpr & Brothers, 1900.

Haggard, H. Rider (1856–1925). *She: A History of Adventure.* <1887> (*LL* 385)

Hall, Leland (1883–1957). *Sinister House.* Boston: Houghton Mifflin, 1919. Rpt. New York: Hippocampus Press, 2008.

Hamilton, Anne. *How to Revise Your Own Poems: A Primer for Poets.* Los Angeles: Abbey San Encino Press, 1936.

Hammett, Dashiell (1894–1961), ed. *Creeps by Night: Chills and Thrills.* New York: John Day Co., 1931. (*LL* 394)

Harré, T. Everett (1884–1948), ed. *Beware After Dark! The World's Most Stupendous Tales of Mystery, Horror, Thrills and Terror,* New York: Macaulay, 1929. (*LL* 397)

Hawthorne, Julian (1846–1934), ed. *The Lock and Key Library: Classic Mystery and Detective Stories.* New York: Review of Reviews Co., 1909. 10 vols. (*LL* 400)

Hawthorne, Nathaniel (1804–1864). *Grandfather's Chair: A History for Youth.* <1841> Philadelphia: H. Altemus, 1898. (*LL* 401)

———. *The House of the Seven Gables, and The Snow-Image and Other Twice-Told Tales.* <1851; 1852> Boston: Houghton Mifflin, 1886. (*LL* 402)

Hearn, Lafcadio (1850–1904). *Kwaidan: Stories and Stodies of Strange Things.* <1904> Boston: Houghton Mifflin, 1930. (*LL* 412)

Hecht, Ben (1894–1964). *Erik Dorn.* New York: G. P. Putnam's Sons, 1921. New York: Modern Library, 1924.

———. *Fantazius Mallare: A Mysterious Oath.* Chicago: Covici-McGee, 1922.

Houdini, Harry [*pseud.*] (1874–1926). *A Magician among the Spirits.* New York: Harper & Brothers, 1924. (*LL* 443)

Hugo, Victor (1802–1885). *Hans of Iceland.* <1823> (*LL* 448)

Howard, Robert E. *The Collected Poetry of Robert E. Howard.* Sugar Land, TX: Robert E. Howard Foundation, 2009.

———. *The Hyborian Age.* Los Angeles: LANY Cooperative Publications, 1938.

Huysmans, Joris-Karl (1848–1907). *A Rebours*. 1884. Tr. John Howard as *Against the Grain*. New York: A. & C. Boni, 1930. (*LL* 454)

———. *Là-Bas*. Tr. Keene Wallis as *Down There*. New York: A. & C. Boni, 1924.

Ingram, John H. (1842–1916). *The Haunted Homes and Family Traditions of Great Britain*. London: Gibbings, 1901. (*LL* 458)

Irving, Washington (1783–1859). *A History of New-York, from the Beginning of the World to the End of the Dutch Dynasty*. <1809> (*LL* 462)

Jackson, Charles Loring (1847–1935). *The Gold Point and Other Strange Stories*. Boston: Stratford Co., 1926. (*LL* 466)

James, Henry (1843–1916). *The Two Magics: The Turn of the Screw; Covering End*. <1898> New York: Macmillan, 1911. (*LL* 467)

James, M[ontague] R[hodes] (1862–1936). *The Collected Ghost Stories of M. R. James*. London: Edward Arnold, 1931.

———. *Ghost-Stories of an Antiquary*. London: Edward Arnold, 1904. (*LL* 468) [Contains "Count Magnus" and "The Treasure of Abbot Thomas."]

———. *More Ghost Stories of an Antiquary*. London: Edward Arnold, 1911. (*LL* 469) [Contains "The Tractate Middoth" and "Casting the Runes."]

———. *A Thin Ghost and Others*. London: Edward Arnold, 1919. (*LL* 470) [Contains "An Episode of Cathedral History."]

———. *A Warning to the Curious*. London: Edward Arnold, 1925. (*LL* 471) [Contains "A View from a Hill."]

Joshi, S. T. "A Literary Tutelage: Robert Bloch and H. P. Lovecraft." *Studies in Weird Fiction* No. 16 (Winter 1995): 13–25. In Joshi's *Lovecraft and a World in Transition: Collected Essays on H. P. Lovecraft*. New York: Hippocampus Press, 2014. 548–65.

Joshi, S. T., ed. *Caverns Measureless to Man: 18 Memoirs of H. P. Lovecraft*. West Warwick, RI: Necronomicon Press, 1996.

———. *A Weird Writer in Our Midst: Early Criticism of H. P. Lovecraft*. New York: Hippocampus Press, 2010.

Jung-Stilling, Johann Heinrich (1740–1817). *Theory of Pneumatology, in Reply to the Question, What Ought to Be Believed or Disbelieved concerning Presentiments, Visions, and Apparitions, According to Nature, Reason, and Scripture*. Tr. from the German, with Copious Notes, by Samuel Jackson. London: Longman, Rees, Orme, Brown, Green & Longman, 1834. (*LL* 488)

King, Basil (1859–1928). *The Spreading Dawn: Stories of the Great Transition*. New York: Harper & Brothers, 1927. (*LL* 495)

Kipling, Rudyard (1865–1936). *The Mark of the Beast, and The Head of the District*. Girard, KS: Haldeman-Julius Co., [19—]. (*LL* 501)

———. *The Phantom 'Rickshaw and Other Tales*. <1888> (*LL* 502)

Kuttner, Henry (1914–1958). "Hydra." *WT* (April 1939). In *The Book of Iod*. Ed. Robert M. Price. Oakland, CA: Chaosium, 1995.

———. "It Walks by Night." *WT* (December 1936).

————. "The Salem Horror." *WT* (May 1937). In *The Book of Iod* (q.v.).

La Motte Fouqué, Friedrich Heinrich Karl, baron de (1777–1843). *Undine and Sintram.* <1811; 1815> Boston: Estes & Lauriat, [18—]. (*LL* 513)

Larson, Randall. *The Complete Robert Bloch: An Illustrated, Comprehensive Bibliography.* Sunnyvale, CA: Fandom Unlimited, 1986.

————. *Robert Bloch.* (Starmont Reader's Guide 37.) Mercer Island, WA: Starmont House, 1986.

Le Fanu, J[oseph] Sheridan (1814–1873). *The House by the Churchyard.* <1863> London: Macmillan, 1899. (*LL* 523)

Leadbeater, C. W. (1847–1934). *The Inner Life.* Chicago: Rajput Press, 1911–12. 2 vols.

Leeds, Arthur. "The Return of the Undead." *WT* (November 1925).

Level, Maurice (1875–1926). *Tales of Mystery and Horror.* Tr. Alys Eyre Macklin. New York: McBride, 1920. (*LL* 529)

————. *Those Who Return [L'Ombre].* Tr. B. Drillien. New York: McBride, 1923. (*LL* 530)

Lévi, Eliphas. *The History of Magic: Including a Clear and Precise Exposition of Its Procedure, Its Rites and Its Mysteries.* Tr. A. E. Waite. London: W. Rider & Son, 1913.

Lewis, Matthew Gregory (1775–1818). *The Monk: A Romance.* <1796> London: Brentano's, [1924]. 3 vols. in 1. (*LL* 531).

Lewis, Sinclair (1885–1951). *It Can't Happen Here.* Garden City, N.Y., Doubleday, Doran, 1935.

Liddell, Henry George (1811–1898), and Robert Scott (1811–1887). *A Greek-English Lexicon.* <1843>. (*LL* 532)

London, Jack (1876–1916). *The Star Rover.* <1915> (*LL* 543)

Long, Frank Belknap, Jr. (1901–1994). *The Goblin Tower.* Cassia, FL.: Dragon-Fly Press, 1935. (*LL*)

————. *The Man from Genoa and Other Poems.* Athol, MA: Recluse Press, 1926. (*LL*)

————. "The Space-Eaters." *WT* (July 1928).

Loveman, Samuel (1887–1976). *The Hermaphrodite and Other Poems.* Caldwell, ID: Caxton Printers, 1936. (*LL* 550)

Lynch, John Gilbert Bohun (1884–1928), ed. *The Best Ghost Stories.* Boston: Small, Maynard & Co., [1924]. (*LL* 558)

McConaughy, John. *From Cain to Capone: Racketeering Down the Ages.* New York: Coward-McCann, 1931.

MacDonald, George (1824–1905). *Lilith: A Romance.* New York: Dodd, Mead, 1895. (*LL* 567)

Machen, Arthur (1863–1947). "The Coming of the Terror." *Century* 94, No. 6 (October 1917): 801–25. (*LL* 157) [An abridged version of *The Terror.*]

————. *The Green Round.* London: Ernest Benn, 1933.

————. *The Hill of Dreams.* <1907> (*LL* 572)

———. *The House of Souls.* <1906> New York: Alfred A. Knopf, 1923. (*LL* 573) [Contains "The White People."]

———. *The Shining Pyramid.* London: Martin Secker, 1925. (*LL* 576)

———. *The Three Impostors.* <1895> New York: Alfred A. Knopf, 1930. (*LL* 578)

McKenna, Stephen (1888–1967). *The Oldest God: A Novel.* Boston: Little, Brown, 1926.

MacLeish, Archibald (1892–1982). *Conquistador.* Boston: Houghton Mifflin, 1932.

MacPhilpin, John, ed. *The Apparitions and Miracles at Knock: Also the Official Depositions of the Eyewitnesses.* New York: D. & J. Sadlier & Co., 1880. (*LL* 583)

McSpadden, J. Walker (1874–1960), ed. *Famous Psychic Stories.* New York: Thomas Y. Crowell Co., 1920. (*LL* 584)

Marryat, Capt. Frederick (1792–1848). *The Phantom Ship.* <1839> (*LL* 593)

Marsh, Richard (1857–1915). *The Beetle.* London: Skeffington, 1897. (*LL* 595)

Mather, Cotton (1663–1728). *Magnalia Christi Americana; or, The Ecclesiastical History of New-England, from Its First Planting in the Year 1620, unto the Year of Our Lord, 1698.* London: Printed for T. Parkhurst, 1702. (*LL* 598)

Matthews, Brander (1852–1929). *A Study of Versification.* Boston: Houghton Mifflin, 1911.

Maturin, Charles Robert (1782?–1824). *Melmoth the Wanderer.* <1820> London: Richard Bentley & Son, 1892. 3 vols. (*LL* 599)

Maurice, Michael [pseud. of Conrad Arthur Skinner (1889–)]. *Not in Our Stars.* Philadelphia: J. B. Lippincott Co., [1923]. 288 pp. (*LL* 808)

Mencken, H. L. (1880–1956). *Treatise on the Gods.* New York: Knopf, 1930.

Mérimée, Prosper (1803–1870). *The Venus of Ille.* <1837> [See Gautier, *Tales Before Supper.*]

Merritt, A. (1882–1943). "The Moon Pool." *All-Story Weekly* (24 November 1917). (*LL* 17)

———. *Seven Footprints to Satan. Argosy* (2 July–1 August 1927). New York: Boni & Liveright, 1928.

———. *The Ship of Ishtar. Argosy* (8 November–13 December 1924). New York: G. P. Putnam's Sons, 1926.

Meyrink, Gustav (1868–1932). *The Golem.* Tr. Madge Pemberton. London: Gollancz; Boston: Houghton Mifflin, 1928.

Morse, Richard Ely (1909–1986). "Dark Garden." *Phantagraph* 4, No. 6 (September 1936): [1]. *Californian* 4, No. 2 (Fall 1936): 27.

———. "Mad Dream." *Phantagraph* 5, No. 1 (October 1936): [1]. *Californian* 4, No. 2 (Fall 1936): 39.

Murray, Margaret A. *The Witch-Cult in Western Europe.* Oxford: Clarendon Press, 1921.

Neale, Arthur, ed. *The Great Weird Stories.* New York: Duffield, 1929. (*LL* 637)

Nietzsche, Friedrich Wilhelm (1844–1900). *Zur Genealogie der Moral: Eine Streitschrift.* <1887> Tr. as *On the Genealogy of Morals: A Polemic.*

Onions, Oliver (1873–1961). *Ghosts in Daylight.* London: Chapman & Hall, 1924. (*LL* 654)

Ovid (P. Ovidius Naso) (43 B.C.E.–17 C.E.). *The Metamorphoses of Ovid.* Literally Translated, with Notes and Explanations, by Henry T. Riley. New York: Hinds, Noble & Eldridge, [190-?]. 2 vols. (*LL* 662)

Owen, Frank (pseud. of Roswell Williams, 1893–1968). *The Wind That Tramps the World: Splashes of Chinese Color.* New York: Lantern Press, 1929. (*LL* 962)

Oxenford, John (1812–1877), and C. A. Feiling, ed. & tr. *Tales from the German: Comprising Specimens from the Most Celebrated Authors.* London: Chapman & Hall, 1844. (*LL* 666)

Pain, Barry (1865–1928). *An Exchange of Souls.* London: Eveleigh Nash, 1911. (*LL* 670) New York: Hippocampus Press, 2007.

Palgrave, Francis T. (1814–1897), ed. *The Golden Treasury: Selected from the Best Songs and Lyrical Poems in the English Language.* <1861> (*LL* 671)

Pattee, Fred Lewis (1863–1950). *The House of the Black Ring.* Harrisburg, PA: Mount Pleasant Press, 1916. (*LL* 679)

Perutz, Leo (1884–1957). *Der Meister des Jüngsten Tages.* <1923> Tr. by Hedwig Singer as *The Master of the Day of Judgment.* London: Elkin Mathews & Marrot, 1929. New York: Charles Boni, 1930. (*LL* 687)

Pitkin, Walter B. (1878–1953). *A Short Introduction to the History of Human Stupidity.* New York: Simon & Schuster, 1932.

Poe, Edgar Allan (1809–1849). *The Works of Edgar Allan Poe.* The Raven Edition. New York: P. F. Collier & Son, 1903. 5 vols. (*LL* 702)

———. *The Narrative of Arthur Gordon Pym.* <1837–38> In *Works* (Raven Edition), Vol. 3.

Quiller-Couch, Sir Arthur (1863–1944). *Noughts and Crosses: Stories, Studies, and Sketches.* By "Q." London: Cassell, 1893. (*LL* 715)

———. *Old Fires and Profitable Ghosts: A Book of Stories.* New York: Charles Scribner's Sons, 1900. (*LL* 716)

———. *Wandering Heath: Stories, Studies, and Sketches.* By "Q." New York: Charles Scribner's Sons, 1896. 276 pp. (*LL* 717)

Quiller-Couch, Sir Arthur, ed. *The Oxford Book of English Verse, 1250–1900.* Oxford: Clarendon Press, 1901.

Radcliffe, Ann (1764–1823). *The Mysteries of Udolpho.* <1794> London: George Routledge & Sons, [1882]–[192-]. (*LL* 718)

Railo, Eino (1884–1948). *The Haunted Castle: A Study of the Elements of English Romanticism.* New York: E. P. Dutton, 1927.

Ransome, Arthur (1884–1967). *The Elixir of Life.* London: Methuen, 1915. New York: Hippocampus Press, 2009.

Reeve, Clara (1729–1807). *Old English Baron: A Gothic Story.* <1777/1778> (*LL* 724)

Renshaw, Anne Tillery. *Well Bred Speech: A Brief, Intensive Aid for English Students.* [Washington, DC: Standard Press, 1936.] (*LL* 726)

Reynolds, George W. M. (1814–1879). *Wagner, the Wehr-Wolf.* London: J. Dicks, 1848, 1857, 1872.

Rohmer, Sax [pseud. of Arthur Sarsfield Ward] (1883–1959). *Brood of the Witch-Queen.* New York: A. L. Burt, 1926. (*LL* 920)

———. *The Day the World Ended.* Garden City, NY: Doubleday, Doran, 1930.

———. *The Romance of Sorcery.* London: Methuen, 1914.

Rudwin, Maximilian J. (1885–1946?), ed. *Devil Stories: An Anthology.* New York: Alfred A. Knopf, 1921. (*LL* 747)

Russell, W. Clark (1844–1911). *The Flying Dutchman; or, The Death Ship.* <1888> New York: Hurst, n.d. (*LL* 751)

———. *The Frozen Pirate.* <1887> (*LL* 752)

Saintsbury, George (1843–1933), ed. *Tales of Mystery.* New York: Macmillan, 1891. [Containing extracts of Ann Radcliffe, *The Mysteries of Udolpho;* Matthew Gregory Lewis, *The Monk;* and Charles Robert Maturin, *Melmoth the Wanderer.*] (*LL* 755)

Savile, Frank Mackenzie. *Beyond the Great South Wall: The Secret of the Antarctic.* <1899> New York: Grosset & Dunlap, 1901. (*LL* 759)

Sayers, Dorothy L[eigh] (1893–1957), ed. *The Omnibus of Crime.* <1928> Garden City, NY: Garden City Publishing Co., 1931. (*LL* 761)

———, ed. *The Second Omnibus of Crime.* <1931> New York: Coward-McCann, 1932.

Scarborough, Dorothy (1878–1935). *The Supernatural in Modern English Fiction.* New York: G. P. Putnam's Sons, 1917.

Scott, Sir Walter (1771–1832). *Letters on Demonology and Witchcraft.* <1830> London: George Routledge & Sons, 1884. (*LL* 770)

Scott-Elliot, W[illiam] (d. 1930). *The Story of Atlantis and The Lost Lemuria.* London: Theosophical Publishing Society, 1925.

Seabrook, William B. (1887–1945). *The Magic Island.* New York: Harcourt, Brace, 1929, 1936.

Shelley, Mary (1797–1851). *Frankenstein; or, The Modern Prometheus.* <1818> New-York: H. G. Daggers, 1845. (*LL* 793)

Shiel, M. P. (1865–1947). *Dr. Krasinski's Secret.* New York: Vanguard, 1929.

———. *Prince Zaleski.* Boston: Roberts Brothers, 1895. (*LL* 799)

———. *The Pale Ape and Other Pulses.* London: T. Werner Laurie, 1911.

———. *The Purple Cloud.* London: Chatto & Windus, 1901; rev. ed. New York: Vanguard, 1930. (*LL* 800)

Sinnett, A. P. (1840–1921). *Esoteric Buddhism.* Boston: Houghton, Mifflin, 1898.

Sitwell, Sir Osbert (1892–1969). *The Man Who Lost Himself.* London: Duckworth, 1929. (*LL* 805)

Smith, Clark Ashton (1893–1961). *The Double Shadow and Other Fantasies*. [Auburn, CA:] Auburn Journal, 1933. (*LL* 810)

———. *Ebony and Crystal*. Introduction by George Sterling. Auburn, CA: [Auburn Journal,] 1922. (*LL* 811)

———. *Odes and Sonnets*. San Francisco: Book Club of California, 1918. (*LL* 812)

———. *Sandalwood*. Auburn, CA: Auburn Journal, 1925. (*LL* 813)

———. *The Star-Treader and Other Poems*. San Francisco: A. M. Robertson, 1912. (*LL* 814)

———. "The Weird Work of M. R. James." *Fantasy Fan* 1, No. 6 (February 1934): 89–90.

Spence, Lewis (1874–1955). *An Encyclopaedia of Occultism: A Compendium of Information on the Occult Sciences, Occult Personalities, Psychic Science, Magic, Demonology, Spiritism and Mysticism*. New York: Dodd, Mead, 1920. (*LL* 827)

Spengler, Oswald (1880–1936). *The Hour of Decision*. Tr. Charles Francis Atkinson. New York: Knopf, 1934.

———. *Der Untergang des Abendlandes*. <1918–22> Tr. Charles Francis Atkinson as *The Decline of the West*. London: George Allen & Unwin, 1922–26. 2 vols.

Stapledon, [William] Olaf (1886–1950). *Last and First Men*. London: Methuen, 1930.

Stevenson, Robert Louis (1850–1894). *Dr. Jekyll and Mr. Hyde and The Merry Men and Other Tales*. <1886; 1887> London: J. M. Dent; New York: E. P. Dutton (Everyman's Library), [1914]–[1932]. (*LL* 846)

Stoker, Bram (1847–1912). *Dracula*. <1897> [*LL* 848]

Stormonth, James (1824–1882). *A Dictionary of the English Language*. <1871> New York: Harper & Brothers, 1885. (*LL* 850)

Symmes, Mrs. William B. [Cassie Doty]. *Old World Footprints*. Athol, MA: W. Paul Cook [Recluse Press], 1928.

Talman, Wilfred Blanche (1904–1986). *Cloisonné and Other Verses*. Providence, RI: Brown University, 1925.

*Terrible Tales: Italian*. New York: Brentano's, [1891?]. (*LL* 867)

Teter, George E. (1877–1940) *An Introduction to Some Elements of Poetry*. Wauwatosa, WI: Kenyon Press, 1927.

Thomson, Christine Campbell (1897–1985), ed. *By Daylight Only*. London: Selwyn & Blount, 1929. (*LL* 876)

———. *Grim Death*. London: Selwyn & Blount, 1932. (*LL* 877)

———. *Gruesome Cargoes*. London: Selwyn & Blount, 1928. (*LL* 878)

———. *Not at Night*. London: Selwyn & Blount, 1925. (*LL* 879)

———. *Switch On the Light*. London: Selwyn & Blount, 1931. (*LL* 881)

———. *You'll Need a Night Light*. London: Selwyn & Blount, 1927. (*LL* 882)

Toksvig, Signe [Kristine] (1891–1983). *The Last Devil*. New York: John Day Co., 1927. (*LL* 887)

[Unsigned.] "A Writer Comments on the Anger–Wright Controversy." *Phantagraph Phantagraph* 5, No. 3 (January 1937): 7–8.

Untermeyer, Louis (1885–1977), ed. *Modern American Poetry: A Critical Anthology*. 5th rev. ed. New York: Harcourt, Brace, 1936.

Verne, Jules (1828–1905). *From the Earth to the Moon.* <1865> (*LL* 908)

———. *20,000 Leagues under the Sea.* <1869> (*LL* 909)

Viereck, George Sylvester (1884–1962), and Paul Eldridge (1888–1982). *My First Two Thousand Years: The Autobiography of the Wandering Jew.* New York: Macaulay, 1928.

Villars, Abbé de (Nicolas-Pierre-Henri) (1635–1673). *Le Comte de Gabalis, ou Entretiens sur les sciences secrètes.* Cologne: Chez Pierre Marteau, 1675.

Waite, Arthur Edward (1857–1942). *The Book of Black Magic and of Pacts: including the Rites and Mysteries of Goëtic Theury, Sorcery, and Infernal Necromancy.* London: G. Redway, 1898.

Wakefield, H[erbert] Russell (1890–1964). *Others Who Returned: Fifteen Disturbing Tales.* New York: D. Appleton, 1929. (*LL* 912) [Contains "The Cairn."]

———. *They Return at Evening.* New York: D. Appleton, 1928. (*LL* 913)

Walpole, Horace (1717–1797). *The Castle of Otranto.* <1764> (*LL* 916)

Walpole, Hugh (1884–1941). *Portrait of a Man with Red Hair: A Romantic Macabre.* New York: George H. Doran, 1925.

Wandrei, Donald (1908–1987). "Colossus." *Astounding Stories* 12, No. 5 (January 1934): 41–72.

———. "The Corpse Speaks." *Midwest Student* (May 1927) (as "In the Grave"). *Recluse* No. 1 (1927): 76 (as "In the Grave").

———. *Dark Odyssey.* St. Paul, MN: Webb Publishing Co., [1931]. (*LL* 917)

———. *Dead Titans, Waken! Invisible Sun—Two Novels by Donald Wandrei.* Ed. S. T. Joshi. Lakewood, CO: Centipede Press, 2011.

———. *Ecstasy and Other Poems.* Athol, MA: Recluse Press, 1928. (*LL* 918)

———. "The Red Brain." *WT* (October 1927). In *Creeps by Night: Chills and Thrills.* New York: John Day Co., 1931. 423–40. (*LL* 394)

Webster, J. Provand. *The Oracle of Baal: A Narrative of Some Curious Events in the Life of Professor Horatio Charmichael, M.A.* Philadelphia: J. B. Lippincott Co., 1896. (*LL* 928)

Weigall, Arthur (1880–1934). *Wanderings in Roman Britain.* London: T. Butterworth, [1926]. (*LL* 933)

Weinbaum, Stanley G. (1902–1935). *Dawn of Flame: The Stanley G. Weinbaum Memorial Volume.* Milwaukee: WI, Milwaukee Fictioneers and Milwaukee Chapter of the American Fiction Guild, 1936.

Wells, H[erbert] G[eorge] (1866–1946). *The First Men in the Moon.* London: Newnes, 1901. (*LL* 935)

———. *The Outline of History.* <1921> Garden City, NY: Garden City Publishing Co., 1929.

—————. *The Island of Dr. Moreau*. London: Heinemann, 1896. New York: Stone & Kimball, 1896. Rpt. in *Amazing Stories* (October–November 1926). (*LL* 22)

—————. *The War of the Worlds*. New York: Harper & Brothers, 1898. Rpt. in *Amazing Stories* (August 1927). (*LL* 22)

Wells, H. G.; Huxley, Julian; and Wells, G. P. *The Science of Life: A Summary of Contemporary Knowledge about Life and Its Possibilities*. London: Amalgamated Press, 1930 (2 vols.). Garden City, NY: Doubleday, Doran, 1931 (4 vols.).

White, Edward Lucas (1866–1934). *Lukundoo and Other Stories*. New York: George H. Doran, 1927. (*LL* 943)

—————. *The Song of the Sirens and Other Stories*. New York: E. P. Dutton, 1919. (*LL* 944)

Wiggam, Albert Edward (1871–1957). *The Fruit of the Family Tree*. Indianapolis: Bobbs-Merrill, 1924.

Wilde, Oscar (1854–1900). *Fairy Tales and Poems in Prose*. New York: Boni & Liveright (Modern Library), [1918]. (*LL* 954).

—————. *The Picture of Dorian Gray*. <1890> New York: Boni & Liveright (Modern Library), 1918. (*LL* 956)

Winsor G. MacLeod (1856–1939). *Station X*. London: Herbert Jenkins, 1919. Rpt. in *Amazing Stories* (July–September 1926). (*LL* 22)

Wright, Farnsworth. "An Answer to Mr. Anger." *Phantagraph* 5, No. 2 (December 1936): 4–6.

Wright, S. Fowler (1874–1965). *The World Below*. New York: Longmans, Green, 1930. (*LL* 974)

Wylie, Philip (1902–1971). *Finnley Wren: His Notions and Opinions*. New York: Farrar & Reinhart, 1934.

Wyllarde, Dolf (d. 1950). *Stories of Strange Happenings*. London: Mills & Boon, 1930. (*LL* 975)

## C. Items Published in *Weird Tales*

Stories mentioned by HPL in the correspondence.

21, No. 1 (January 1933)

| | |
|---|---|
| The Night Wire | H. F. Arnold |

21, No. 2 (February 1933)

| | |
|---|---|
| The Cats of Ulthar | H. P. Lovecraft |

21, No. 3 (March 1933)

| | |
|---|---|
| In Memoriam: Henry St. Clair Whitehead | [H. P. Lovecraft] |

21, No. 6 (June 1933)

| | |
|---|---|
| The Floor Above (rpt.) | H. L. Humphries |
| Genius Loci | Clark Ashton Smith |

| The Iron Man | Paul Ernst |
| The Last Drive | Carl Jacobi |

22, No. 1 (July 1933)

| The Dreams in the Witch-House | H. P. Lovecraft |
| The Horror in the Museum | Hazel Heald [Lovecraft] |
| Ubbo-Sathla | Clark Ashton Smith |

22, No. 2 (August 1933)

| The Chosen of Vishnu | Seabury Quinn |
| An Elegy for Mr. Danielson | August W. Derleth |
| The Superior Judge | J. Paul Suter |

22, No. 3 (September 1933)

| The Horror on the Asteroid | Edmond Hamilton |

22, No. 4 (October 1933)

| The Black, Dead Thing | Frank Belknap Long |
| The Festival (rpt.) | H. P. Lovecraft |
| The House of the Worm | Mearle Prout |
| The Pool of the Black One | Robert E. Howard |
| The Seed of the Sepulchre | Clark Ashton Smith |

22, No. 5 (November 1933)

| Shambleau | C. L. Moore |

23, No. 1 (January 1934)

| In the Triangle | Howard Wandrei |
| Rogues in the House | Robert E. Howard |
| The Weaver in the Vault | Clark Ashton Smith |
| The Woman of the Wood | A. Merritt |

23, No. 2 (February 1934)

| The Man Who Returned | Edmond Hamilton |
| The Place of Hairy Death | Anthony Rud |
| The Sapphire Goddess | Nictzin Dyalhis |
| Tarbis of the Lake | E. Hoffmann Price |
| The Valley of the Worm | Robert E. Howard |
| The Virus of Hell | William H. Pope |
| The Witchcraft of Ulua | Clark Ashton Smith |

23, No. 3 (March 1934)

| The Charnel God | Clark Ashton Smith |
| Winged Death | Hazel Heald [H. P. Lovecraft] |

23, No. 4 (April 1934)
The Bells of Oceana (rpt)   Arthur Burks
Black Thirst   C. L. Moore
The Death of Malygris   Clark Ashton Smith
Shadows in the Moonlight   Robert E. Howard

23, No. 5 (May 1934)
Queen of the Black Coast   Robert E. Howard

23, No. 6 (June 1934)
The Colossus of Ylourgne   Clark Ashton Smith

24, No. 1 (July 1934)
Through the Gates of the Silver Key   H. P. Lovecraft & E. Hoffmann Price

24, No. 2 (August 1934)
The Devil in Iron   Robert E. Howard
Dust of the Gods   C. L. Moore

24, No. 3 (September 1934)
The People of the Black Circle [1/3]   Robert E. Howard

24, No. 4 (October 1934)
The Black God's Kiss   C. L. Moore
Old Sledge   Paul Ernst
The People of the Black Circle [2/3]   Robert E. Howard
The Seven Geases   Clark Ashton Smith

24, No. 5 (November 1934)
The People of the Black Circle [3/3]   Robert E. Howard
The Music of Erich Zann (rpt.)   H. P. Lovecraft

24, No. 6 (December 1934)
Black God's Shadow   C. L. Moore
Xeethra   Clark Ashton Smith

25, No. 1 (January 1935)
The Dark Eidolon   Clark Ashton Smith
The Feast in the Abbey   Robert Bloch

25, No. 2 (February 1935)
The Fireplace (rpt.)   Henry S. Whitehead
Murder in the Grave   Edmond Hamilton

25, No. 4 (April 1935)

| | |
|---|---|
| The Canal | Everil Worrell |
| The Hand of the O'Mecca | Howard Wandrei |
| The Last Hieroglyph | Clark Ashton Smith |
| The Man Who Was Two Men | A. W. Bernal |
| Out of the Eons | Hazel Heald [H. P. Lovecraft] |
| Shadows of Blood | Eando Binder |

25, No. 5 (May 1935)

| | |
|---|---|
| Arthur Jermyn (rpt.) | H. P. Lovecraft |
| The Secret of the Tomb | Robert Bloch |

25, No. 6 (June 1935)

| | |
|---|---|
| The Suicide in the Study | Robert Bloch |

26, No. 2 (August 1935)

| | |
|---|---|
| Doctor Satan | Paul Ernst |
| In Amundsen's Tent | John Martin Leahy |
| The Treader in the Dust | Clark Ashton Smith |

26, No. 3 (September 1935)

| | |
|---|---|
| The Monster God of Mamurth | Edmond Hamilton |
| The Shambler from the Stars | Robert Bloch |
| Vulthoom | Clark Ashton Smith |

26, No. 4 (October1935)

| | |
|---|---|
| In a Graveyard | Eando Binder |

26, No. 5 (November 1935)

| | |
|---|---|
| The Hand of Wrath | E. Hoffmann Price |
| Shadows in Zamboula | Robert E. Howard |
| The Way Home | Paul Frederick Stern |

26, No. 6 (December 1935)

| | |
|---|---|
| The Hour of the Dragon [1/5] | Robert E. Howard |

27, No. 1 (January 1936)

| | |
|---|---|
| Dagon (rpt.) | H. P. Lovecraft |
| The Dark Land | C. L. Moore |
| The Hour of the Dragon [2/5] | Robert E. Howard |

27, No. 2 (February 1936)

| | |
|---|---|
| The Hour of the Dragon [3/5] | Robert E. Howard |
| Norn | Everil Worrell [as Lireve Monet] |
| The Temple (rpt.) | H. P. Lovecraft |
| Yvala | C. L. Moore |

27, No. 3 (March 1936)
The Black Abbott of Puthuum — Clark Ashton Smith
The Crystal Curse — Eando Binder
The Hour of the Dragon [4/5] — Robert E. Howard
In the World's Dusk — Edmond Hamilton

27, No. 4 (April 1936)
The Druidic Doom — Robert Bloch
The Face in the Wind — Carl Jacobi
The Hour of the Dragon [5/5] — Robert E. Howard
Rajah's Gift — E. Hoffmann Price
They Shall Rise — August W. Derleth and Mark Schorer

27, No. 5 (May 1936)
Child of the Winds — Edmond Hamilton
The Faceless God — Robert Bloch
The Red Brain (rpt) — Robert Wandrei
The Room of Shadows — Arthur J. Burks

27, No. 6 (June 1936)
The Brain in the Jar — R. F. Searight and Norman E. Hammerstrom
Black Canaan — Robert E. Howard
The Grinning Ghoul — Robert Bloch
The Harbor of Ghosts — M. J. Bardine
Lethe — Harold G. Shane
Loot of the Vampire [1/2] — Thorp McClusky
The Telephone in the Library — August W. Derleth

28, No. 1 (July 1936)
Loot of the Vampire [2/2] — Thorp McClusky
Lost Paradise — C. L. Moore
Necromancy in Naat — Clark Ashton Smith
Red Nails [1/3] — Robert E. Howard
When the World Slept — Edmond Hamilton

28, No. 2 (August/September 1936)
Red Nails [2/3] — Robert E. Howard

28, No. 3 (October 1936)
Doom of the House of Duryea — Earl Peirce, Jr.
The Lost Door — Dorothy Quick
The Opener of the Way — Robert Bloch
R.E.H. [v] — R. H. Barlow
Red Nails [3/3] — Robert E. Howard

| | |
|---|---|
| The Secret of Kralitz | Henry Kuttner |
| The Tree of Life | C. L. Moore |

**28, No. 4 (November 1936)**

| | |
|---|---|
| Black Hound of Death | Robert E. Howard |
| Brother Lucifer | Chandler H. Whipple |
| The Crawling Horror | Thorp McClusky |
| The Dark Demon | Robert Bloch |
| Pickman's Model (rpt.) | H. P. Lovecraft |

**28, No. 5 (December 1936)**

| | |
|---|---|
| The Album | Amelia Reynolds Long |
| The Haunter of the Dark | H. P. Lovecraft |
| It Walks by Night | Henry Kuttner |
| Mother of Serpents | Robert Bloch |

**29 No. 1 (January 1937)**

| | |
|---|---|
| The Disinterment | Duane W. Rimel |
| The Thing on the Doorstep | H. P. Lovecraft |

**29, No. 3 (March 1937)**

| | |
|---|---|
| The Brood of Bubastis | Robert Bloch |
| The Guardian of the Book | Henry Hasse |
| The Picture in the House (rpt.) | H. P. Lovecraft |

**29, No. 5 (May 1937)**

| | |
|---|---|
| Edgar Allan Poe | Adophe de Castro |

# Index

Ackerman, Forrest J 13, 154, 174, 205, 371, 388, 391, 397, 410–11

Adams, Franklin Pierce 274

Adams, John 10

*Adventure* 119

*Against the Grain* (Huysmans) 149

*Ah, Wilderness!* (film) 275

Albertus Magnus 377–78

*Albertus Magnus* (attrib. Albertus Magnus) 381

Albigenses 267

"Album, The" (Long) 418

"Alchemist, The" (Lovecraft) 43n4, 413

*Alciphron; or, The Minute Philosopher* (Berkeley) 69, 141

Alexander the Great 134

Alhazred, Abdul 29, 59, 142, 223, 369, 372, 377, 382, 395

*All Our Yesterdays* (Warner) 11

Allen, Hervey 100n2

*Amateur Correspondent* 16

*Amazing Stories* 13, 333, 355, 384

American Amateur Press Association 16, 339n2

American Fiction Guild 170, 176, 178, 205, 244

"American Way of Life, The" (Davis) 300

"Ancient Sorceries" (Blackwood) 129, 130

"'And He Shall Sing . . .'" (Wakefield)

Anger, William F. 11–12, 145, 182, 184, 312–13, 315

*Anthony Adverse* (Allen) 100

Aquinas, Thomas 377

*Arabian Nights* 303, 369, 372

*Argosy* 13, 170, 362, 364

Aristotle 377

Arkham, MA 24, 56, 71, 108, 168, 170, 174, 176, 385, 394, 407; HPL's map of, 169

Arkham House 26n8

Arnold, Benedict 252

"Arthur Jermyn" (Lovecraft). *See* "Facts concerning the Late Arthur Jermyn and His Family"

Ashburn, Bill 10

*Asia* 196

*Astonishing Stories* 320

*Astounding Stories* 13, 15, 69–70, 80, 93, 126, 155, 159, 162, 173, 207, 245, 326, 383, 396, 411

*At the Mountains of Madness* (Lovecraft) 27, 48, 145, 155, 159, 166, 171, 182, 225, 245, 246, 322, 325–26, 332, 362, 383, 384, 419

Atlantis 359, 379

Averonius, Petrus 108

*Avon Fantasy Reader, The* (Wollheim) 14

Azathoth 103, 249

*Azif, Al* (Alhazred) 54, 223, 395

Babcock, Ralph W. 329, 344, 347

Bacon, Roger 377

"Baby's Playmate" [drawing] (Bloch) 96

"Background" (Lovecraft) 16, 137n4, 361

Bacon, Sir Francis 120

Baird, Edwin 137n2, 420n1

Baldwin, F. Lee 185, 225, 235, 380

Baldwin, Robert B. 146n1

Baldwin, Stanley 298

Balzac, Honoré de 248

Bardine, M. J. 172

Barlow, E. D. 146

Barlow, R. H.: and amateur journalism, 63, 65, 159, 329, 332, 337; as artist, 108, 110; and Robert Bloch, 112, 114, 122; and *Fungi from Yuggoth,* 241, 242, 244, 245, 320; literary tastes of, 143, 160; and Lovecraft, 8, 15, 22n4, 54, 94n1, 100, 124, 183, 234n3, 331, 343, 385, 401, 406, 413; Lovecraft's visits with, 102, 103, 104, 144, 145–46, 148, 149, 150, 236, 238–39, 247–48, 276, 313; and C. L. Moore, 205, 413; and Robert Nelson, 221–22, 314; in New York City, 227, 342, 392, 395; and photography, 105, 106, 225, 416; politics of, 300; as publisher, 26n8, 206–7, 413; and Wilson Shepherd, 335; and Clark Ashton Smith, 168, 206–7; vis-

its with Lovecraft in New England, 173–74, 176–77, 213–14, 246, 340, 381, 387, 388, 390; and *Weird Tales,* 235; as writer, 7, 202–3, 204, 337, 420
Barlow, Wayne 146, 148, 247
*Baroque* 351, 353
Barrett, Francis 379
*Barretts of Wimpole Street, The* (film) 120
Barrie, J. M. 120
Bartel, Jacques. *See* Kaplan, Maurice M.
"Battle That Ended the Century, The" (Lovecraft-Barlow) 13, 116n1
Baum, L. Frank 249n1
"Beast in the Cave, The" (Lovecraft) 43n4, 413
Beauchasne, Bernard de 167
Beebe, Evanore 318n9
Benda, W. T. 197
Bergson, Henri 257
Berkeley, George 69, 141
*Berkeley Square* (film) 95
Bernal, A. W. 138, 229
*Best Short Stories* (O'Brien) 26n2, 43n6
"Bethmoora" (Dunsany) 407
*Beware After Dark!* (Harré) 19
"Beyond the Wall of Sleep" (Lovecraft) 70n4, 201n1, 217
Bierce, Ambrose 93, 100n1, 174, 175, 187, 190, 213, 340, 343, 385
Binder, Eando 145, 147, 168, 178, 244, 274, 332, 387, 392
Binder, Jack 232n2
"Bipeds of Bjulhu, The" (Sterling) 13
Birkhead, Edith 24
Bishop, Zealia Brown Reed 205
Bivonae 256, 257
Black, B. C. 54, 246
*Black Book* (Junzt) 29, 187
"Black Canaan" (Howard) 171, 173, 279–80, 359, 400
"Black God's Kiss, The" (Moore) 215, 230
"Black God's Shadow" (Moore) 227, 230
"Black Kiss, The" (Bloch-Kuttner) 178, 184, 229
"Black Lotus, The" (Bloch) 118, 124, 150
*Black Rites* (Luveh-Keraph) 9
*Black Spell of Saboth* (Mazonides) 108
"Black Thirst" (Moore) 102, 227, 230

Blackwood, Algernon 129, 130, 189, 371, 381, 407, 418
"Blasphemy Beneath, The" (Bloch) 53
"Blind Man's Buff" (Wakefield) 62
Blish, James 172n1, 367–68
Bloch, Robert: art by, 50, 56, 59, 61–62, 65, 72–73, 75, 78, 87, 94–95, 96, 99, 111, 138, 202, 403; career of, 9; fiction by, 7, 9, 25, 35–37, 48, 49–50, 53–54, 58–59, 64–65, 66–67, 71–72, 74–75, 87–88, 107–8, 109, 112, 113, 116, 118, 124, 128–31, 132–33, 135–36, 139, 142–43, 149, 171, 179–80, 202, 203, 205, 231, 303, 315–16, 332, 362, 395, 405, 411; and forbidden books, 108, 139, 142, 377, 382; and Lovecraft, 207, 313, 362, 381, 394, 418; poetry by, 97, 103, 106, 126–27; travels by, 73, 77, 104, 106, 145; on weird music, 412
*Blue Book* 13
Blum, Léon 283
Boland, Stuart M. 178, 402n3
*Book of Black Magic and of Pacts, The* (Waite) 379
*Book of Eibon* 29, 59, 187, 223, 377, 378
*Book of Wonder, The* (Dunsany) 251
Bordley, Kemp 411, 413, 419
Boston, MA 26–27, 7, 111, 152, 157, 164, 253, 310, 322
"Bowmen, The" (Machen) 395
Boyce, Dwight A. 316
Bradley, Chester P. 329
Bradofsky, Hyman 338
"Brain-Eaters of Pluto, The" (Sterling) 12, 250n1
Briffault, Robert 289, 295
Brobst, Harry 54, 55, 57
"Brood of Bubastis, The" (Bloch) 177, 185
*Brood of the Witch-Queen* (Rohmer) 35
Brosnatch, Andrew 231, 316, 386n2
Browder, Earl 300
Brown, Howard V. 167n3, 332
Brown University 29, 31, 44, 88, 174, 241, 242, 280, 343, 395–96, 401
Brundage, Margaret 216n1, 386n2, 392, 397, 401
Buchan, John 24, 130
Buckingham, George Villiers, Duke of 88

Bukharin, Nikolai 300
*Bulletin* (Terrestrial Fantascience Guild) 14, 234n4
"Bureau of Critics Comment on Verse, Typography, Prose" (Lovecraft) 77n6
"Buried Moon" (Gallun) 326
Burke, Thomas 94
Burks, Arthur J. 102, 172, 236, 244
Burroughs, George 129
*By Daylight Only* (Thomson) 19
Byrd, Richard E. 325

*Cabala of Saboth, The* 9, 109n2
Caballero, Francisco Largo 301
Cabell, James Branch 143, 149, 160, 182, 254
"Cairn, The" (Wakefield) 62
Caldwell, Erskine 240
Calhoun, John C. 252
*Californian* 213, 335, 336, 337, 420
Caligula (Emperor of Rome) 138, 146n1, 233
"Call of Cthulhu, The" (Lovecraft) 19, 47, 60
"Can the Moon Be Reached by Man?" (Lovecraft) 254
Cantor, Eddie 121
Cape Cod, MA 63, 65–66, 155, 258
"Cassius" (Whitehead) 234n3
*Catiline* (Jonson) 120
"Cats of Ulthar, The" (Lovecraft) 48
*Cats of Ulthar, The* (Lovecraft) 246
*Causerie* 329, 336, 337
Cave, Hugh B. 23
"Caverns Measureless to Man" (Sterling) 12n11, 14, 17
"Celephaïs" (Lovecraft) 34, 87n2, 95, 103
Century of Progress Exposition (Chicago) 63, 71, 77
"Challenge from Beyond, The" (Lovecraft et al.) 163n6
Chambers, Robert W. 20, 187, 190
*Charles W. Morgan* (ship) 141, 176, 344
Charleston, SC 102, 145, 151, 247
"Charnel God, The" (Smith) 94n8
"Charon" (Cahill) 231
Chase, Stuart 260–61
Chaugnar Faugn 65, 105
Chesterton, G. K. 115
"Child of the Winds" (Hamilton) 172

Christianity 98, 210, 251, 265–71, 380–81
*Chu Chin Chow* (film) 128
Churchward, Col. James 379
"City, The" (Lovecraft) 337
Clark, Lillian D. 49n1
Clarke, Harry 231
Clemence, Thomas 87n5, 193
*Cleopatra* (film) 134
*Clive of India* (film) 128
*Cloisonnè and Other Verses* (Talman) 51
"Clouds" (Lovecraft) 337
Coates, Walter J. 26n8, 35, 62
Coblentz, Stanton A. 275
Cole, Edward H. 117n3, 138, 141, 152, 157, 329
Coleman, Carroll D. 351
"Colossus" (Wandrei) 387
"Colossus of Ylourgne, The" (Smith) 103
"Colour out of Space, The" (Lovecraft) 25, 27, 47, 218, 221, 223, 384, 407, 419
*Comet* 88
commonplace book (Lovecraft) 70n1
*Communist Manifesto, The* (Marx-Engels) 281
*Compendium Daemonum* (Averonius) 108
*Comte de Gobalis, Le* (Villars) 381
Conover, Howard R. 390
Conover, Willis 7, 16–17, 173, 178, 179, 183, 338, 341, 342, 365–66, 368, 369, 371
*Conquistador* (MacLeish) 134
Constant, Alphonse-Louis. *See* Levi, Eliphas
Cook, W. Paul 26n8, 34, 57, 108, 110, 111, 138, 361–62, 363, 399
"Cool Air" (Lovecraft) 34, 238
Copernicus, Nicolaus 277–78
"Coronation of Mr. Thomas Shap, The" (Dunsany) 47
"Corpse Speaks, The" (Wandrei) 43n5
"Correspondence between R. H. Barlow and Wilson Shepherd" (Lovecraft) 15
Corwin, Jonathan 176, 390
Coryciani 10
Coughlin, Charles E. 270, 294n1, 296
"Count Magnus" (James) 24, 312, 407
Crane, Verner W. 138
Crawford, William L. 74, 87, 92, 97–98, 133, 143–44, 145, 150, 153, 168, 180,

225–26, 227, 232, 241, 245, 312, 316, 324, 332, 335, 338, 341, 348, 351, 352, 364, 366, 368, 371
*Creep, Shadow!* (Merritt)  138
"Creeper in the Crypt, The" (Bloch)  168
*Creeps* (Birkin)  315
*Creeps by Night* (Hammett)  19
*Crime and Punishment* (Dostoevsky)  151, 162
*Crime and Punishment* (film)  162
Crowley, Aleister  62
*Cry Horror!* (Lovecraft)  14
Cthulhu  29, 56, 105, 106, 146, 164, 388–89, 390
"Cthulhu" [carving] (Smith)  321
*Cultes des Goules* (d'Erlette)  9, 133, 382
Cummings, Ray  387
*Curious Stories*  365
Curley, James Michael  170, 171
*Curse of the Wise Woman, The* (Dunsany)  100, 251
"Curse of Yig, The" (Lovecraft-Bishop)  205

Daas, Edward F.  336
*Daemonolatreia* (Remigius)  190
"Dagon" (Lovecraft)  34, 48, 60
"Dagon" [carving] (Smith)  321
Daniels, David R.  356n
"Dark Beasts, The" (Long)  109–10
"Dark Demon, The" (Bloch)  179
"Dark Eidolon, The" (Smith)  202, 227, 231
*Dark Odyssey* (Wandrei)  34
Darrow, Jack  13, 147, 388, 391, 397
Darwin, Charles  248, 281
*David Copperfield* (film)  128
Davis, Elmer  300
Davis, Robert H.  362
*Day the World Ended, The* (Rohmer)  35
de Camp, L. Sprague  17
de Castro, Adolphe  130, 174–75, 176, 205, 213–14, 246, 340, 343, 385
de la Mare, Walter  20, 190
De Lay, Harold  386n2
*De Rebus Metallicis et Minerabilibus* (Albertus)  378
*De Secretis Mulierum* (Albertus)  378
de Sitter, Willem  185, 195
*De Vermis Mysteriis* (Prinn)  9, 139, 142, 171, 178, 183–84, 377

"Death" (Shepherd)  16, 358
*Death-Mask and Other Ghosts, The* (Everett)  43n2
"Death of Malygris, The" (Smith)  47
"Death Shower, The" (Freeman)  386n2
*Decline of the West, The* (Spengler)  194, 196
"Delirium" (Bloch)  126
Democritus  220
Derleth, August, 20, 384, 389, 395; and Robert Bloch, 37, 48, 50, 54, 67, 75, 77, 106, 113, 127, 137, 150, 151, 155, 161, 162, 168, 182; as editor, 214; and forbidden books, 380, 382, 391; and Carl Jacobi, 28; and Lovecraft, 9, 24, 46, 64, 86, 101, 105, 107, 108, 133, 136, 138, 143, 172, 226n2, 293; as publisher, 14; and pulp fiction, 69, 125, 235; and Frank Utpatel, 316, 332; and Donald Wandrei, 412; and weird fiction, 115; as writer, 22, 35, 50–51, 55, 62, 71 72, 92, 112, 128, 145, 147, 159, 171, 231, 332, 352n3, 366, 368, 386n2
d'Erlette, Comte  9, 137, 382
Detrick, Charles L.  329
"Diary of Alonzo Typer, The" (Lovecraft-Lumley)  338
Dickens, Charles  128
"Dim-Remembered Story, A" (Barlow)  213
*Dime Mystery*  107, 233
d'Indy, Vincent  23
"Dine and Dance" [drawing] (Bloch)  72, 75
"Dinner at Eight" (Bloch)  112
Dinocrates  134
"Disinterment, The" (Lovecraft-Rimel)  184n2
Doak. *See* Rankin, Hugh
*Doctor Death*  136
*Don Quixote* (film)  128
Donne, John  356
Donnelly, Ignatius  379
Doolin, Joseph  231
"Doom That Came to Sarnath, The" (Lovecraft)  87n2, 95, 136, 225, 232
Doty, Cassie  159n2
"Double Shadow, The" (Smith)  47
*Double Shadow and Other Fantasies, The* (Smith)  26n4, 47, 56, 188n1
Doubleday Doran  178

Dowe, Jennie E. T. 153n6, 154
*Down There* (Huysmans). *See Là-Bas*
*Dr. Krasinski's Secret* (Shiel) 242
"Dr. Lichorn" (Bloch) 50
"Dr. Satan" stories (Ernst) 315
*Dracula* (Stoker) 188
*Dragon-Fly* 159, 320, 336, 337
*Dreamer's Tales, A* (Dunsany) 251, 407
"Dreams" (Bloch) 97
"Dreams in the Witch House, The"
   (Lovecraft) 19, 51, 59, 73n2, 130,
   193, 342, 401
"Drone Man, The" (Merritt) 340n6
"Druidic Doom, The" (Bloch) 144, 145,
   168, 170, 171
Dunne, James E. 290
Dunsany, Lord 20, 27, 29, 32, 34, 47,
   49n8, 50, 100, 110, 136, 170, 187, 189,
   204, 225, 232, 251, 254, 304, 320, 332,
   396, 404, 407
Dunwich, MA 152, 154–55, 243, 313,
   317
"Dunwich Horror, The" (Lovecraft) 53,
   223, 240, 391
Durant, Will 258
Durante, Jimmy 65
Dutt, R. Palme 297, 298
"Dweller, The" (Lovecraft) 324
Dwyer, Bernard Austin 46, 51, 54–55, 62,
   64, 66n3, 77, 78, 92, 94, 98, 100, 104,
   106, 110, 114, 117, 127, 185, 313, 349
Dyalhis, Nictzin 49n4, 97

Eastman, Max 300
*Ebony and Crystal* (Smith) 187, 206
*Ecstasy and Other Poems* (Wandrei) 34
Eddington, Arthur S. 277
Eddy, C. M., Jr. 132, 170
Eden, Anthony 159
"Edith Miniter" (Lovecraft) 113n3
Edkins, Ernest A. 285, 328, 342
Edwards, John 91n5
*Egyptian Secrets. See Albertus Magnus*
Einstein, Albert 185, 195, 277
"Elder Pharos, The" (Lovecraft) 114–
   15, 183
"Electric Executioner, The" (Lovecraft-
   de Castro) 175, 343
"Elixir of Hate, The" (England) 135
Ellsworth, Lincoln 325
*Encyclopaedia Britannica* 415

*Encyclopedia of Occultism, An* (Spence) 377
Endore, Guy 57n10, 304
Engels, Friedrich 281
England, George Allan 135, 172, 356
Epicurus 211
"Episode of Cathedral History, An"
   (James) 312
Erford, J. F. Roy 32n1, 336, 344
*Erik Dorn* (Hecht) 176
Ernst, Paul Frederick 47, 163, 243, 322
Esenwein, J. Berg 274
Eshbach, Lloyd Arthur 133, 136, 304,
   321
*Esoteric Buddhism* (Sinnett) 379
*Evening in Spring* (Derleth) 35
"Evil Genius, The" (Bloch) 114
"Ex Oblivione" (Lovecraft) 368
"Expectancy" (Lovecraft) 314n6

"Faceless God, The" (Bloch) 149n1,
   168, 171, 175
"Facts concerning the Late Arthur
   Jermyn and His Family" (Lovecraft)
   34, 48, 93, 103, 119, 238
"Fading Ghost, The" (Jones) 386n2
Faig, Kenneth W., Jr. 9
"Fall of Babbulkund, The" (Dunsany)
   404
"Fall of the House of Usher, The" (Poe)
   407
*Fanciful Tales* 14, 16, 80, 181, 183, 327,
   338, 347, 348, 351, 352, 353, 355, 356,
   357, 362, 363, 366, 368, 370, 371
Fantasy Amateur Press Association 14
*Fantasy Fan:* and Robert Bloch, 87, 89,
   97, 112, 113–14, 124, 202; contents
   of, 68, 121, 203, 218, 225, 233, 313,
   320; demise of, 13, 133, 136, 143, 153,
   232, 243, 375; founding of, 66n4; and
   Charles D. Hornig, 144, 146, 222,
   238, 349–50, 368, 403; Lovecraft in,
   16, 74, 94, 95, 100, 101, 117, 196, 316,
   338, 364, 389, 402, 408; Lovecraft's
   copies of, 108, 109, 111, 128, 224,
   384; and Robert Nelson, 11, 150, 221;
   and Farnsworth Wright, 398
*Fantasy Fiction Telegram* 367
*Fantasy Magazine* 126, 133, 151, 152, 163,
   71, 178–79, 180, 183, 184, 185, 218,
   224, 232, 240, 315–16, 351, 358, 364,

368, 375, 376, 380, 381, 384, 387, 388, 395, 398, 408, 409, 413, 414, 418
*Fantazius Mallare* (Hecht) 176
Farley, Ralph Milne 143, 149
Farnese, Harold S. 115, 116–17, 182–83
Fearn, John Russell 410
"Feast, The" (Bloch) 50
"Feast in the Abbey, The" (Bloch) 76n4, 114, 116, 117, 118, 124, 127, 133, 231
*Fen River* (Farnese) 116n2
Ferguson, Clay, Jr. 318n1, 348, 349, 358
"Festival, The" (Lovecraft) 19, 34, 79, 193
Fictioneers. *See* Milwaukee Fictioneers
Field, John 277–78
"Finis" (Bloch) 126
Finlay, Virgil 16, 175–76, 178, 180, 182, 184, 355, 360, 362, 366, 367, 384, 386n2, 397, 403, 405, 412, 414, 416
*Finnley Wren* (Wylie) 182
"Five Alone" (Derleth) 43n6
*Flabbergasting Stories* 233, 312
"Flight" (Wooley) 10
"Fog, The" (Bloch) 113, 114
Fort, Charles 379
Fossils 338
"Fountain of Youth, The" (Bloch) 135–36
France, Anatole 143
Franco, Franciso 297
*Frankenstein* (film) 92
Frankfurter, Felix 292
Franklin, Benjamin 138
Freeman, Tom 386n2
Freud, Sigmund 68, 281
"From Beyond" (Lovecraft) 34, 108
*From Cain to Capone* (McConaughty) 140
Frome, Nils H. 184, 367
*Fruit of the Family Tree, The* (Wiggam) 197
*Fungi from Yuggoth* (Lovecraft) 11, 14, 16, 114–15, 117, 133, 136, 145, 152, 154, 182–83, 238, 240, 241, 242, 243–44, 245, 312–13, 315, 316, 318, 320, 324, 326, 413
*Further Criticism of Poetry* (Lovecraft) 339n1
Futurians 14

*Galleon* 136, 304, 321, 377
"Gallows, The" (Bloch) 25
Gallun, Raymond Z. 178
Galpin, Alfred 22–23, 46, 60, 77
Galsworthy, John 204

Galton, Sir Francis 305
Gamwell, Annie E. P. 13, 30n7, 37, 44, 51–52, 56, 57, 59, 63, 66, 72, 76, 77, 87, 104, 112, 117, 165, 167, 168–69, 247, 328, 397
Ganesha 66n2
"Garden of Fear, The" (Howard) 108
Gaspard du Nord 142
Gauer, Harold 148n5, 167n2
Gawsworth, John 108
"Genius Loci" (Smith) 46
Gernsback, Hugo 12, 13, 153, 160, 233, 249, 312, 336
*Ghorl Nigral* (Mülder) 385, 395, 399, 412
*Ghost Stories* 312
"Ghoul, The" [drawing] (Bloch) 50, 136
Gibbon, Edward 88
Giesy, J. U. 386n2
Glanvill, Joseph 190
"Glass Eye, The" (Bloch) 48
*Goblin Tower, The* (Long) 159n3, 166, 246, 320, 322
Goddard, Robert H. 257
*Gods of Pegāna, The* (Dunsany) 251
*Gods of the Mountain, The* (Dunsany) 204
*Golden Bough, The* (Frazer) 92
"Golden Bough, The" (Keller) 225
*Golden Treasury, The* (Palgrave) 213
Goldsmith, Oliver 229
"Golem, The" [drawing] (Bloch) 92, 94–95
*Golem, The* (Meyrink) 92, 415
*Golem, The* (film) 92, 415
Gorman, Herbert 24
*Grandfather's Chair* (Hawthorne) 129
"Grave, The" (Bloch) 28, 31, 36–37
Graves, Robert 144n1
"Graveyard Rats, The" (Kuttner) 386n2
Gray, Robert 141
"Great Illusion, The" (Binder et al.) 409
Green, E. H. R. 141, 176, 344
Green, Hetty 141
Green, Theodore Francis 116n3, 170
*Green Round, The* (Machen) 101
"Grinning Ghoul, The" (Bloch) 118, 127, 132, 171
"Grip of Death, The" (Bloch-Kuttner) 172
"Guardian of the Book, The" (Hasse) 373n1

Gummere, Francis B. 413

"H. P. Lovecraft: Viewed by E. Hoffmann Price" (Price) 406

Haeckel, Ernst 208

Haggerty, Vincent B. 336, 362, 363

Haldane, J. B. S. 197

Hall, Desmond 70, 80, 112, 126

"Hallowe'en in a Suburb" (Lovecraft) 368

Hamilton, Anne 213, 404

Hamilton, Edmond 13, 47, 72, 97, 128, 147, 168, 172, 176, 178, 195, 229, 242, 243, 315, 326, 327, 386n2, 388, 394, 397, 411, 412

Hammett, Dashiell 19

Hammond, H. R. 231

"Hand of the O'Mecca, The" (Wandrei) 138, 160, 232, 233

*Handbook of Poetics, A* (Gummere) 413

"Harbor of Ghosts, The" (Bardine) 172

"Harbour Whistles" (Lovecraft) 137n4

*Harper's Magazine* 211, 300, 413

Harré, T. Everett 19, 126, 127, 227, 312

Harris, John Beynon 136

*Hashish-Eater; or, The Apocalypse of Evil, The* (Smith) 187

Hasse, Henry 372

*Haunted Castle, The* (Railo) 24

"Haunter of the Dark, The" (Lovecraft) 30n8, 159–60, 161, 162, 174, 175, 176, 178, 180, 182, 207, 323n2, 324, 330, 338, 365n2, 397, 399, 402–3, 407, 411

Hawthorne, Nathaniel 129, 176

Hayward, Barzillai 343, 395

"He" (Lovecraft) 24

"'He Cometh and He Passeth By!'" (Wakefield) 62

Heald, Hazel 130, 205

Hearn, Lafcadio 93

"Heavens for August, The" (Loveraft) 204n2

Hecht, Ben 176

Henley, Samuel 54, 395

Henneberger, J. C. 416

*Hermaphrodite and Other Poems, The* (Loveman) 167n4

Hermes Trismegistus 378, 381, 383–84

*Hill of Dreams, The* (Machen) 407

*History of Magic, The* (Levi) 379

*History of New-York, A* (Irving) 212n1

"History of the 'Necronomicon'" (Lovecraft) 224n3, 370n2, 399

*History of the Necronomicon, A* (Lovecraft) 16

Hitler, Adolf 12, 80–84, 98–99

Hoare, Samuel 159

Hodgson, William Hope 111, 114, 347, 350

Hohman, John George 381

Holt, Rush D., Sr. 276

*Home Brew* 51

"Homecoming" (Lovecraft) 16, 375, 402

Hoover, Herbert 140, 262, 291

Hopkins, Mr. 350

Hornig, Charles D. 68, 92, 133, 144, 146, 17, 222, 233, 238, 243, 249, 312, 331, 338, 368, 389, 403

"Horror at Red Hook, The" (Lovecraft) 19, 27, 115, 116

*Horror from the Hills, The* (Long) 66n3

"Horror in the Museum, The" (Lovecraft-Heald) 59

"Horror on the Links, The" (Quinn) 386n2

*Horror Stories* 121, 132, 136, 226, 316, 367, 401

"Hound, The" (Lovecraft) 48

*Hour of Decision, The* (Spengler) 196

"Hour of the Dragon, The" (Howard) 279

"House, The" (Lovecraft) 337

"House of Horror, The" (Quinn) 410

"House of Sounds, The" (Shiel) 242, 407

*House of the Seven Gables, The* (Hawthorne) 176

"House of the Worm, The" (Prout) 79

*How to Revise Your Own Poems* (Hamilton) 213, 404

Howard, I. M. 172, 173, 334, 339, 356, 360, 367, 376

Howard, Robert E.: and F. Lee Baldwin, 235; and R. H. Barlow, 337; Robert Bloch on, 119, 121n2, 133, 381; character of, 23, 28, 56, 101, 205, 256–57, 394; death of, 172, 173, 181, 278–80, 334, 335, 338–39, 354, 356, 358, 375, 389, 393; essays by, 324, 346, 353; fiction by, 79–80, 97, 108, 109, 119, 122,

163, 171, 205, 319, 321, 322, 381, 382–83, 386n2, 400; and forbidden books, 29, 54, 187, 223, 377, 380, 391; and Lovecraft, 69, 313, 394, 399; poetry by, 205, 321, 366, 368; possible book by, 342, 359–60, 362, 364, 365, 367, 370; and E. Hoffmann Price, 102, 104, 321, 341, 376, 384, 412

Howard Payne College 173, 376

Hubbard, L. Ron 178

Hughes, Charles Evans 290

Huxley, Julian 153

Huysmans, Joris-Karl 149, 356, 357

*Hyborian Age, The* (Howard) 280, 319n1, 321, 324, 334, 338, 339, 353, 358, 383

"Hydra" (Kuttner) 181, 182

"Hyperborean Snake-Eater" [carving] (Smith) 161, 207

Iamblichus 206

*Immortal Storm, The* (Moskowitz) 11

"In a Sequester'd Providence Churchyard Where Poe Once Walk'd" (Lovecraft) 16

"In Amundsen's Tent" (Leahy) 242

"In Memoriam: Robert Ervin Howard" (Lovecraft) 175n3

"In the Grave" (Wandrei) 43n5, 399

"In the Vault" (Lovecraft) 132

"In the Walls of Eryx" (Lovecraft-Sterling) 13, 234n4

*Incantations* (Smith) 207, 320

*Incredible Adventures* (Blackwood) 407, 418

*Informer, The* (film) 275

"Inn[, The?]" (Bloch) 132

"Intimations—The Hand in the Dark" (Wooley) 10, 211

*Introduction to Some Elements of Poetry, An* (Teter) 213, 359, 404

*Invisible Man, The* (film) 95

*Iron Duke, The* (film) 128

Irving, Washington 212

*It Can't Happen Here* (Lewis) 282

"It Walks by Night" (Kuttner) 179

Jacobi, Carl 28, 47, 116, 168, 170, 332

James, M. R. 20, 23–24, 101, 172, 190, 312, 356, 407

Jammy, Pierre 377, 380

Jay Publishing Co. 69

*John Silence—Physician Extraordinary* (Blackwood) 130, 418

Johnson, Samuel 88, 95, 160

Jonson, Ben 120

Jones, William Knapp 386n2

"Julhi" (Moore) 230

Junzt, Friedrich von 29, 54, 59, 142, 187, 223, 377, 380, 412

*Jurgen* (Cabell) 143

Justinian (Emperor of Rome) 134–35

Kadath 32

"Kadath" [drawing] (Bloch) 96

Kalem Club 123n1

Kaplan, Maurice M. 244

Keller, David H. 225, 227, 366, 384, 388, 402

*King John* (Shakespeare) 120

*King Lear* (Shakespeare) 120

King Philip's War 129, 141, 158, 310

Kingsport, MA 24, 71, 144, 176

Kipling, Rudyard 398

Kleiner, Rheinhart 122, 274, 326, 328, 332

Kline, Otis Adelbert 178, 339

Knopf, Alfred A. 68, 72, 73, 191, 192

Koenig, H. C. 114, 124, 136, 177, 203, 228, 312, 332, 335, 347, 350, 354, 377, 395, 411

Koresh. *See* Teed, Cyrus

Kuttner, Henry 148n1, 165, 167, 170, 171, 173, 175n7, 176, 178, 179, 181, 182, 214, 332, 353, 359, 362, 368, 371, 372, 386n2, 398, 405, 411

Kyansita 112

*Là-Bas* (Huysmans) 149, 178, 180, 356

La Mettrie, Julien Offray de 209

La Motte Fouqué, Friedrich Heinrich Karl, baron de 381

La Spina, Greye 197

Lamb, Charles 274, 327

Landon, Alf 294n1

*Last and First Men* (Stapledon) 319, 348

*Last Days of Pompeii, The* (film) 253

*Last Gentleman, The* (film) 128

"Last Test, The" (Lovecraft-de Castro) 175, 343

"Laughter of a Ghoul, The" (Bloch) 48, 124

"Layman Looks at the Government, A" (Lovecraft) 92n7

Le Gallienne, Eva 163
Le Plongeon, Augustus 379, 381
Leahy, John Martin 242–43
*Leaves* 175n6
Leeds, Arthur 122, 273n5, 274, 326, 332
Leiber, Fritz, Sr. 120
Leiharder, Mr. 149
Lemke, William 294n1
Leng 32, 394
Leroux, Gaston 92
Lescarbault, Edmond Modeste 255
"Lethe" (Shane) 172
*Letters on Demonology and Witchcraft* (Scott) 190
Leuba, James H. 211
Level, Maurice 28
Levi, Eliphas 190, 372, 379
Lewis, M. G. 20, 124
Lewis, Sinclair 282
*Liber Ivonis* 142
*Life* 413
"Ligeia" (Poe) 407
"Lilies" (Bloch) 71–72
*Limehouse Nights* (Burke) 92
Lindbergh, Charles 257, 341
*Literary Quarterly* 16
*Livre d'Eibon* 142
Lobo, Jéronimo 160–61
*Logada* (ship) 176
Long, Huey P. 296
Long, Frank Belknap, Jr.: and amateur journalism, 332; appearance of, 45, 326; and R. H. Barlow, 177; and Willis Conover, 388, 392, 395; as correspondent, 393; and Adolphe de Castro, 175, 213, 343, 385; family of, 159, 298, 320–21; fiction by, 56, 64, 65, 108, 109–10, 139, 233, 242, 251–52, 315, 326, 349; and Lovecraft, 20, 23, 35, 56, 122, 139, 178, 238, 255, 256, 257, 274, 276–77, 389; Lovecraft's visits with, 63, 76, 86, 94, 102, 105, 123, 151, 165, 166, 227, 244, 258; poetry by, 320; politics of, 80, 276, 279, 295, 300; and Duane W. Rimel, 412; and Kenneth Sterling, 249n2; and Donald A. Wollheim, 312, 323, 328, 342
Long, Frank Belknap, Sr. 45
Long, Julius 227

Lonsdell, C. W. 153, 318, 324, 346n
"'Look Up There!'" (Wakefield) 62
"Loot of the Vampire" (McClusky) 394
*Lord of the Rings, The* (Tolkien) 14
Loring & Mussey 133, 143, 145
"Lost Chord, The" (Conover) 402
"Lost Excerpts" (Nelson) 11, 150, 218, 221, 314
Lovecraft, H. P.: and amateur journalism, 28, 31, 63, 65, 76, 89, 328–30, 332, 336, 338, 344, 353, 357, 376–77; on his ancestry, 343, 384–85, 395–96; appearance of, 35, 45, 235, 415–16; art by, 56; and astronomy, 88, 174, 249–50, 255, 277–78, 318, 401; on cabbalism, 414–15; and cats, 63, 65, 66, 67, 108, 115, 134, 280, 293–94; and chain letters, 236–37; on collaboration, 13, 130, 404–5; as correspondent, 7–17, 316, 344, 383, 392–93, 394, 405, 416–17; on the crucifix, 251–52; on debating, 78–79; and dreams, 67–68, 124, 399, 404, 413, 429–20; on economics, 258–64, 281–89, 290–92, 306–7; on elementals, 381; on ethics, 264–72; on eugenics, 197–201, 258–59; on fanzines, 133, 153, 171, 173, 183, 184, 223–24, 313, 320, 335, 367–68, 370–71, 375–76, 409–10; fiction by, 19–20, 21–22, 24, 25, 26–27, 31–32, 34, 47–48, 74, 93–94, 99, 101, 103, 127–28, 133, 152, 159–60, 161, 162, 204, 207, 217–18, 245, 322, 338, 407–8, 411, 419, 420–22; on films, 95, 120, 128, 134, 152, 275; finances of, 59, 393–94; and forbidden books, 29, 108, 139, 142, 187, 223, 369, 372, 377–79, 380–81, 385, 391, 395; on Greek, 181–82; on handwriting, 248, 324–25, 330–32; health of, 51, 114, 179, 373, 415, 422; on intelligence, 255–57, 305–6; library of, 38–43, 115, 190, 354; move to 66 College St., 29, 30–31, 44–45; on music, 182–83; on nostalgia, 275–76; and pens, 127; on the plot genie, 257–58; poetry by, 154, 249, 337; on poetry, 195, 207, 212–13, 354, 358, 359, 413; on politics, 289–90, 292; possible book publications by, 68, 72, 133, 143–44, 145,

174; on printing and typography, 345–47, 348, 351, 355–56, 361–62, 363, 365, 417–18; on religion, 208–12, 218–19, 264–71, 276–77, 303, 305; revision work by, 16, 69, 153, 160, 376–77, 393; on rockets, 254, 247; on science fiction, 47, 319, 326, 347–48, 350, 387, 390, 396; on the supernatural, 303, 304–5; travels of, 24, 58, 63, 69, 70–71, 76, 86, 89, 102–3, 104–5, 110, 111, 112, 117, 123–24, 125–26, 141, 144, 145–46, 148, 149, 150–51, 152, 154–55, 157, 165, 166, 173–74, 176, 224, 227–28, 238–39, 240, 243, 244, 246, 247, 252–53, 293–94, 313–14, 317, 322, 340, 388, 401; and weather, 44, 51, 60–61, 68–69, 99, 108, 122, 126, 131, 136, 138, 148, 152, 153, 163, 166, 167, 172, 183, 193, 280, 317; weight of, 45–46; on weird fiction, 20, 23–24, 28–29, 33–34, 38–43, 46–47, 52, 60, 62–63, 72, 100, 109–10, 119, 156–57, 188–90, 191, 196–97, 215–16, 217, 222, 229, 233, 251, 254, 303, 312, 345, 350, 372–73, 391, 407, 418–19; on words, 193–94; on world affairs, 80–86, 90–91, 93, 98–99, 140, 157–59, 160, 185, 294–98, 299–301
Lovecraft, Joseph 384
"Lovecraft and Science" (Sterling) 14
*Lovecraft: A Biography* (de Camp) 17
*Lovecraft at Last* (Lovecraft–Conover) 16–17
*Lovecrafter* 16, 340, 342, 363
"Loved Dead, The" (Lovecraft-Eddy) 132, 170
Loveman, Samuel 27, 28, 47, 62, 93, 120, 122, 125, 157, 166, 168, 206, 228, 245, 253, 322, 326, 333
"Lukundoo" (White) 113
*Lukundoo and Other Stories* (White) 52, 72
Lumley, William 52n8, 55, 59, 255–56, 313, 338
"Lurking Fear, The" (Lovecraft) 36, 48, 51
*Lurking Fear and Other Stories, The* (Lovecraft) 14

*Macbeth* (Shakespeare) 120
McCabe, Joseph 211

McClusky, Thorpe 386n2, 399
Machen, Arthur 32, 55, 100n1, 101, 108, 187, 189, 354, 395, 407
MacLeish, Archibald 134
McNeil, Everett 123n2, 274
MacSparren, James 58
*Mad Love* (film) 152
Madle, Robert A. 341
"Madness of Lucien Grey, The" (Bloch) 37, 47, 53–54, 107
*Magic Island, The* (Seabrook) 119, 203
*Magnalia Christi Americana* (Mather) 129
*Magus, The* (Barrett) 379
Maier, Michael 378
*Malleus Maleficarum* (Sprenger-Kramer) 125, 203
"Man from Ariel, The" (Wollheim) 14
*Man from Genoa, The* (Long) 322
*Man on All Fours, The* (Derleth) 128
"Man Who Played with Time, The" (Bernal) 229
"Man Who Was Two Men, The" (Bernal) 233
*Manettism* 336
Mantell, Robert 120
Marblehead, MA 24
Margulies, Leo 336, 348–49
"Martian Odyssey, A" (Weinbaum) 147
Martin, Margaret Nickerson 338
*Marvel Tales* 43n7, 96n1, 108, 109, 124, 133, 136, 143, 218, 224, 225, 232, 241, 244, 316, 320, 335, 338, 341, 351, 364, 368, 384
Marx, Karl 281, 283
Marxism 140, 199, 255, 261, 276, 281, 284
Mashburn, W. Kirk 19, 133, 326, 327, 335
"Masque of the Red Death, The" (Poe) 37
*Masses* 300
"Mathematica" (Fearn) 326
Mather, Cotton 129
Mather, Increase 164
Matthews, Brander 213, 337, 359, 404, 413
Maturin, Charles Robert
Mazonides 108
*Melmoth the Wanderer* (Maturin) 20, 347

"Memnons of the Night, The" (Smith) 328n1
"Men of Avalon" (Keller) 226, 227
Mencken, H. L. 211
*Merchant of Venice, The* (Shakespeare) 120
"Merman, The" (Bloch) 87–88, 92
Merritt, A. 100, 110, 126, 138, 156–57, 171, 227, 326, 327, 338, 387
*Metal Monster, The* (Merritt) 100
*Metamorphoses* (Ovid) 206
Michelson-Morley experiment 169, 277
*Mid Atlantic Amateur* 344
*Midsummer Night's Dream, A* (Shakespeare) 122
Miller, Dayton C. 277
Miller, P. Schuyler 341–42, 360, 362, 383, 394–95
Miller, Richard 275
Miller, William, Jr. 172n1
Milton, John 168n1
Milwaukee Fictioneers 143, 147, 149, 150, 154, 162, 168
*Milwaukee Journal* 101, 137
"Mind in Shadow, A" (Swinges) 386n2
Miniter, Edith 318n9
"Mirage" (Lovecraft) 114–15, 183
Moe, Maurice W. 10, 20, 22, 23, 27, 28, 46, 60, 88, 137, 140–41, 173, 175n7, 185, 213, 214, 342–43, 359, 404
Moe, Robert Ellis 140–41, 173, 235n5, 342
Mohammad 206, 305, 395
Mola y Vidal, Don Emilio 297
*Monk, The* (Lewis) 20, 124
*Monk and the Hangman's Daughter* (Voss [tr. Bierce-de Castro]) 175
Monroe, James 343
"Monster-God of Mamurth, The" (Hamilton) 13, 47, 178, 315, 397
"Moon Pool, The" (Merritt) 110, 126
Mooney, Jim 178
Moore, C. L. 109, 171, 172n3, 177, 205, 214, 227, 229, 230, 278, 327, 344, 388, 389, 412, 418–19
Morley, Christopher 274
Morse, Richard Ely 207, 327, 338
Morton, James F. 66, 69, 76, 110, 122, 177–78, 185, 298, 329, 343
Moskowitz, Sam 11
Mosley, Oswald 296

"Mother Earth" (Lovecraft) 337
"Mother of Serpents" (Bloch) 179
Mülder 385, 412
Muller, P. 355, 357
Munn, H. Warner 20, 49–50
Murray, Margaret A. 190
"Music of Chaos, The" [drawing] (Bloch) 96
"Music of Erich Zann, The" (Lovecraft) 19, 25, 47, 48, 51, 115, 116, 119, 218, 221
*My First Two Thousand Years* (Viereck-Eldridge) 122
*Mysteries of the Worm* (Bloch) 9
*Mysteries of the Worm* (Prinn) 9, 108, 112
*Mysteries of Udolpho, The* (Radcliffe) 20
*Mystery Novels Magazine* 121, 226
NRA (National Recovery Administration) 85
"Nameless City, The" (Lovecraft) 14, 16, 34, 118, 137n4, 181, 183, 320n, 324, 330, 355, 357, 358, 366, 369
*Nameless Cults* (Junzt) 380, 391
"Nameless Offspring, The" (Smith) 48
Nantucket, MA 111, 112, 224
Narragansett Country, RI 58, 117
*Narrative of Arthur Gordon Pym, The* (Poe) 326
*National Amateur* 76
National Amateur Press Association 10, 31, 63, 65, 76, 89, 113, 120, 166, 211, 274, 320, 327, 329, 330, 332, 336, 338, 346–47, 348, 351, 353, 357, 369, 377
Nazism 80–84, 140, 198, 270, 296, 301
Nearing, Scott 292, 295
*Necronomicon* (Alhazred) 7, 9, 29, 53–54, 55, 59, 107, 138, 173, 187, 221, 223, 224, 369, 372, 377, 378, 380, 382, 395, 399
"Necronomicon, The" (Shea) 182
"Necrophile" (Bloch) 143
Nelson, Mrs. Elmer 314
Nelson, Robert 11, 150, 203, 243, 313, 314
"Nemesis" (Lovecraft) 248, 249
"Nemesis of Fire, The" (Blackwood) 381
New Bedford, MA 141
New Haven, CT 157, 252–53, 322

New York City, NY 76, 102, 122, 123–24, 125–26, 151, 166, 227–28, 243, 244, 307–11
*New York Herald Tribune* 12
*New York Times* 295
Newburyport, MA 27
Newport, RI 110, 141, 173, 176, 340
Nietzsche, Friedrich 211, 264
*Night at an Inn, A* (Dunsany) 204
night-gaunts 317
"Night in Malnéant, A" (Smith) 47
"Night Ocean, The" (Lovecraft-Barlow) 213, 420
"Nightmare" (Bloch) 48
"Nightmare Lake, The" (Lovecraft) 337
"Nocturne Macabre" (Bloch) 48, 49, 50, 54
Noel, Clyde F. 330, 336, 344
*Not at Night* series (Thomson) 19, 112, 366, 406
*"Not at Night" Omnibus, The* (Thomson) 366, 406
Nug 391, 397
*Nuggets* 57n6, 246
Nyarlathotep 103, 147, 149, 249
"Nyarlathotep" [drawing] (Bloch) 50

*O. Henry Memorial Award Prize Stories* 23
O'Brien, Edward J. 23, 35, 223
"Oceanus" (Lovecraft) 337
"October" (Lovecraft) 334
*Odyssey* (Homer) 206
"Ol' Black Sarah" (Dwyer) 51
"Old Ladies" (Derleth) 43n6
"Old Sledge" (Ernst) 215
*Old Wives' Tale, The* (Bennett) 114
*Old World Footprints* (Symmes) 322
Olinick, G. O. 231, 232
*On the Genealogy of Morals* (Nietzsche) 211, 264
*Once Around the Bloch* (Bloch) 9
"Opener of the Way, The" (Bloch) 171, 173, 179
Ostrow, Alexander 121n5
*Othello* (Shakespeare) 120
"Other Gods, The" (Lovecraft) 94, 95
"Out of the Aeons" (Lovecraft-Heald) 138, 234
*Outline of History, The* (Wells) 212
"Outsider, The" (Lovecraft) 48, 207

"Outsider, The" [carving] (Smith) 161, 207, 321
Ovid (P. Ovidius Naso) 206
Owen, Frank 197
*Oxford Book of English Verse, The* (Quiller-Couch) 213

Pabodie, Elizabeth Alden 141
*Pale Ape and Other Pulses, The* (Shiel) 242
Paracelsus 378, 381
Parker, Charles A. A. 351
*Pawtuxet Valley Gleaner* 88
Peirce, Earl 143, 154
"People of the Black Circle, The" (Howard) 215
Pericles 194
*Perspective Review* 329, 336
Petaja, Emil 150, 170, 203, 222, 313, 315, 323, 324, 346, 352, 355, 405
*Phantagraph* 14, 16, 153, 157, 171, 182, 184, 243, 257, 312, 314, 316, 318, 319, 320, 322, 323, 327, 330, 334, 336, 338, 341, 344, 345–47, 348, 349, 350, 351, 353, 354, 355, 356, 357, 358, 363, 364, 370, 371, 375, 383, 384, 412
"Phantastic Bread & Butter" (Anger) 11
"Phantom Farmhouse, The" (Quinn) 28, 409–10
Philetas, Theodorus 223
Phillips, Dean P. 113
*Philosopher* 337
Phips, William 129
"Pickman's Model" (Lovecraft) 19, 26–27, 43n7, 99, 112, 157, 164, 303, 366, 402, 406, 407, 413
"Picture, The" (Lovecraft) 37
"Picture in the House, The" (Lovecraft) 19, 24
Pitkin, Walter B. 124
*Place Called Dagon, The* (Gorman) 24
*Place of Hawks* (Derleth) 321
*Planeteer* 171, 173, 335, 365
Pnakotic Manuscripts 29, 187
Poe, Edgar Allan 32, 37, 50, 100n1, 105, 174, 180, 184n4, 187, 189, 214, 246, 326, 340, 343, 385, 396, 407, 415
*Poetry out of Wisconsin* (Derleth-Larsson) 214n3
Pohl, Frederik 323n1
"Polaris" (Lovecraft) 34, 100, 101

"Pool of the Black One, The" (Howard) 79

Pope, William H. 97

Popular Publications 69

*Portable Novels of Science, The* (Wollheim) 15

*Portrait of a Man with Red Hair* (Walpole) 125

*Pow-Wows, or the Long Lost Friend* (Hohman) 381

Price, E. Hoffmann: and W. F. Anger, 11, 226, 228, 234, 239, 240, 245, 246; and Robert Bloch, 26; in California, 131, 224, 327, 335, 362; character of, 23, 227; collaboration with Lovecraft, 19, 72, 74, 89, 93, 130; and Willis Conover, 399, 403, 418; and Adolphe de Castro, 175; fiction by, 63, 97, 322, 386n2, 409; and Edmond Hamilton, 397; and Robert E. Howard, 102, 319, 334, 338, 341, 358, 359, 365, 375, 376, 384; and Lovecraft, 64, 237, 242, 258, 379, 406, 411–12; and pulp writing, 47, 54, 192, 205, 244; travels of, 73, 76, 104, 159, 322; visits with Lovecraft, 57–58, 69, 117, 225, 236; and Donald A. Wollheim, 326, 332

"Primal City, The" (Smith) 196

Prinn, Ludvig 9, 108, 112, 137, 142, 178, 183, 377, 395

*Printer's Helper* 347

Pritchard, Kenneth B. 305, 314, 366, 368

*Private Life of Henry VIII, The* (film) 95

*Proof Sheet* 329

"Prophet's Grandchildren, The" (Price) 386n2

Proust, Marcel 35, 204

Prout, Mearle 79

Providence, RI 60–61, 72, 115, 146, 162, 207

[Providence] *Evening Bulletin* 162, 282, 300

*Providence Gazette and Country-Journal* 162

*Providence Journal* 312, 316, 317, 324

[Providence] *Tribune* 88

"Psychopompos" (Lovecraft) 252, 337

*Purple Cloud, The* (Shiel) 242

Putnam's Sons, G. P. 25, 68, 192

Quebec, Canada 70–71

"Queen of the Black Coast, The" (Howard) 119

*Queer* 336, 353

"Querida, a Spanish Serenade" (Wooley) 10

"Quest of Iranon, The" (Lovecraft) 31, 137n4, 321, 380n1

*Quill* 88, 93, 95, 353

Quillman, Norman 329

Quinn, Seabury 23, 28, 47, 62, 119, 166, 197, 216n1, 231, 257, 327, 386n2, 387, 388, 409–10

Quintero, brothers 163

Radcliffe, Ann 20

Railo, Eino 24

Randolph, John 200

Rankin, Hugh 176, 182, 230, 231, 232, 316, 386n2, 397

Rathbone, John 246, 343, 385

"Rats in the Walls, The" (Lovecraft) 19, 77n5, 112, 362, 411, 419

*Real America* 136

"Recapture" (Lovecraft) 241

*Recluse* 34, 363, 388, 392, 399, 403, 408, 414, 415

"Red Brain, The" (Wandrei) 28, 170

"Red Lodge, The" (Wakefield) 62

Reed, John 283

Reed, Zealia B. *See* Bishop, Zealia Brown Reed

*Rehearsal, The* (Buckingham) 88

"Religious Beliefs of American Scientists" (Leuba) 211

Remigius (Nicholas Remi) 190

Renshaw, Anne Tillery 179n1, 289n1, 398n1

"Return of the Sorcerer, The" (Smith) 54

"Return of the Undead, The" (Leeds) 274, 326

"Revelations in Black" (Jacobi) 30n5

Revere, Paul 27, 164

Reynolds, B. M. 161n1

Reynolds, George W. M. 124

Rhine, Joseph Banks 410

*Rhode Island Journal of Astronomy* 88, 89, 92, 239, 338, 370

Rhode Island School of Design 169

*Riddle of the Universe, The* (Haeckel) 208

Rimel, Duane W. 8, 14, 110, 156n2, 182, 203, 235, 313, 323, 324, 330, 332, 346,

349, 352, 355, 366, 368, 389, 395, 405, 412
"Robert Ervin Howard: 1906–1936" (Lovecraft) 14, 175n3
Robinson, Hannah 58
Rockefeller, John D. 294
Rogers, Mr. 342
Rogers, Will 121
"Rogues in the House" (Howard) 97
Rohmer, Sax 35, 379
*Romance of Sorcery, The* (Rohmer) 380n2
"Room of Shadows, The" (Burks) 172
Roosevelt, Franklin D. 286, 290, 293, 296
Roosevelt, Theodore, Jr. 296
*Rosmersholm* (Ibsen) 163
Rud, Anthony M. 97
Ruppert, Conrad 324, 349–50, 408–9
Ryan, Joseph Allen [pseud. of Willis Conover] 383, 394, 399

Saari, Oliver A. 412
"Sabbat[, The?]" (Bloch) 133
*Saducismus Triumphatus* (Glanvill) 190
St. Augustine, FL 24, 104, 105, 150
St. John, J. Allen 231, 397
Salem, MA 24
"Salem Horror, The" (Kuttner) 178
Samples, John Milton 104n1
"Satan's Servants" (Bloch) 7, 128–31, 133
Savery, William Briggs 162–63
Scarborough, Dorothy 24
Schwartz, Julius 12, 155, 159, 174, 176, 276, 322, 338, 351, 358, 368
*Science-Fantasy Correspondent* 16, 17, 173, 183, 184, 214, 338, 364, 367, 368, 370, 371, 375–76, 383, 384, 387–88, 389, 398, 399, 401, 402, 403, 405, 408, 409, 412, 414, 418, 420
*Science Fiction Bard* 14
*Science Fiction Digest* 126, 409
*Science Fiction Fan* 370
Science Fiction League 12, 13, 136–37, 153, 233, 235, 319n3
*Science of Life, The* (Wells-Huxley-Wells) 153
Scott, Sir Walter 190
Scott-Elliott, W. 379
*Sea-Gull* 329
Seabrook, William B. 94, 121n3, 203

Searight, Richard F. 160, 328
"Secret in the Tomb, The" (Bloch) 9, 106, 107–8, 114, 139, 142
Segal, Harold 329
*Sejanus* (Jonson) 120
*Sensations* 125
"Sentient Clay" (Anger) 224
Service, Robert W. 354
"Seven Geases, The" (Smith) 215
*Seven Footprints to Satan* (Merritt) 234
"Seventeenth Hole at Duncaster, The" (Wakefield) 62
"Shadow from the Steeple, The" (Bloch) 9, 181n2
"Shadow in the Steeple, The" (Bloch) 180, 182
"Shadow out of Time, The" (Lovecraft) 15, 123n6, 127–28, 133, 136, 143, 152, 159, 166, 171, 182, 203n1, 234n3, 322, 362, 411, 419
"Shadow over Innsmouth, The" (Lovecraft) 27, 32, 48, 56, 107, 108, 128, 129, 225, 384
*Shadow over Innsmouth, The* (Lovecraft) 145, 168, 180, 181, 245, 341, 348, 352, 360, 364, 366, 367
"Shadows of Blood" (Binder) 138, 146n1, 233
Shakespeare, William 120, 150, 418
"Shambleau" (Moore) 227, 230
"Shambler from the Stars, The" (Bloch) 9, 120n1, 139, 142, 144, 151, 161n1, 180, 315–16
"Shambler in the Night, The" (Bloch) 118
Shane, Harold G. 172
"Shapes, The" (Miller) 326
*She* (film) 152
Shea, J. Vernon 26n7, 52n4, 55, 59, 62, 64, 65, 70n2, 74, 80, 85, 93, 95, 127, 136, 182, 332
Shepherd, Wilson 14, 15–16, 280, 321, 324, 333, 334, 335, 340, 341, 342
Shiel, M. P. 190, 242, 407
*Ship of Ishtar, The* (Merritt) 234
*Short Introduction to the History of Human Stupidity, A* (Pitkin) 124
*Shudders* (Birkin) 315
Shub-Niggurath 87, 391
"Shunned House, The" (Lovecraft) 20, 24, 31, 35, 48, 62, 408, 419

*Sign of Fear, The* (Derleth) 159, 321
"Silver Key, The" (Lovecraft) 19, 223, 379
Sime, S. H. 231
Sinnett, A. P. 379, 381
*Six Novels of the Supernatural* (Wagenknecht) 15
*Skylark of Space, The* (Smith) 390
*Smirt* (Cabell) 182
Smith, Adam 283
Smith, Charles W. ("Tryout") 337
Smith, Clark Ashton: and W. F. Anger, 11, 225, 228–29, 232, 239, 240, 242; as artist, 50, 72–73, 74, 76, 78, 93, 97, 125, 148, 161, 168, 174, 231, 249, 321, 322–23, 333, 358, 386; and Robert Bloch, 37, 48, 50–51, 61, 110, 137; in California, 224, 384, 389–90, 413; essays by, 101; family of, 155, 237, 243, 342; and *Fantasy Fan,* 66, 68, 80, 196; fiction by, 28, 34–35, 46, 47, 48, 54, 79, 97, 100, 138, 157, 192, 196, 202, 205, 226, 227, 315, 332, 411; and forbidden books, 29, 43, 187, 223, 377; and Hugo Gernsback, 233; on Robert E. Howard, 28, 381; library of, 372–73; and Lovecraft, 17, 23, 105, 106, 115, 148, 245, 342; and *Phantagraph,* 335; poetry by, 206–7, 313, 321; and E. Hoffmann Price, 102, 104; and Helen Sully, 63, 65
Smith, Edwin Hadley 344
Smith, Louis C. 11, 145, 238, 241, 242, 244, 245, 312, 315, 342
"Snout, The" (White) 52, 72
"Snouted Thing, The" (Shea) 70n2
"Some Notes on a Nonentity" (Lovecraft) 96n2
"Some Notes on Interplanetary Fiction" (Lovecraft) 335
"Some Repetitions on the Times" (Lovecraft) 92n7
*Something about Cats and Other Pieces* (Lovecraft et al.) 9
"Sons of the Serpent" (Bloch) 48, 50, 51, 54, 62
"Sorcerer's Tale, The" (Bloch) 50
"Soul, The" (Bloch) 50
"Space-Eaters, The" (Long) 56, 142n1, 242, 253n1, 315

"Spawn of the Elder Pits" (Bloch) 109
"Spectators" (Bloch) 97
Spence, Lewis 377, 379
Spengler, Oswald 194, 196
Spink, Helm C. 347
Sprenger, William R. 106
Stalin, Josef 300
Stapledon, Olaf 15, 319, 396
*Star-Treader and Other Poems, The* (Smith) 206
"Statement of Randolph Carter, The" (Lovecraft) 27, 31, 62, 93, 413
Sterling, Kenneth 12–14, 17, 136–37, 139–40, 156n3, 164, 168, 173, 176, 177, 214, 232, 233, 238, 246, 314, 323n5, 324, 327, 332–33, 335, 340, 342, 356n, 385, 387, 388, 390, 396
Stern, Paul Frederick. *See* Ernst, Paul Frederick
Stickney, Corwin F. 16, 365–66, 368, 371, 390, 393, 399, 415
*Story* 170
*Story of Atlantis and The Lost Lemuria, The* (Scott-Elliot) 379
*Story of Philosophy, The* (Durant) 258
*Strange Assembly* (Gawsworth) 108
*Strange Eons* (Bloch) 9
"Strange High House in the Mist, The" (Lovecraft) 23, 27
*Strange Tales* 48, 112, 384
"Stranger from Kurdistan, The" (Price) 63
Strauch, Carl Ferdinand 55, 64
Street & Smith 69–70, 112, 232, 362
Stuart, Gilbert 117
*Study of Versification, A* (Matthews) 213, 337, 359, 404
Stugatche, Dr. 147, 183
"[Suggestions for a Reading Guide]" (Lovecraft) 144n1
"Suicide in the Study, The" (Bloch) 132, 136, 142, 144
Sully, Helen V. 64n6, 65–66
Summers, Montague 143, 190, 380
"Supernatural Horror in Literature" (Lovecraft) 16, 32, 179, 191n1, 316, 364, 388, 389, 392, 398–99, 403–4, 406, 408–9, 414–15
*Supernatural Horror in Literature as Revised in 1936* (Lovecraft) 16, 22n3

*Supernatural in Modern English Fiction, The* (Scarborough) 24
*Supramundane Stories* 184, 367
Suter, J. Paul 68
Swanson, Carl 236
Swinburne, Algernon Charles 193
Swinges, Tessida 386n2
*Switch On the Light* (Thomson) 19
*Sword of Welleran, The* (Dunsany) 251, 407
Sykora, William S. 366, 368
Sylvester, Margaret 332
Symons, Arthur 193

Tacitus (P. Cornelius Tacitus) 85
Taine, John 15
*Tale of Terror, The* (Birkhead) 24
"Tales by H. P. Lovecraft" 21–22
*Tales of Magic and Mystery* 43n3, 238
Talman, Wilfred Blanch 26n9, 46, 51, 94, 122, 180
Tcho-Tcho Lama of Leng 142
Teed, Cyrus 414n4
"Telephone in the Library, The" (Derleth) 171–72
television 86
"Temple, The" (Lovecraft) 60
Terrestrial Fantascience Guild 14, 153, 234n4, 319n3
Terrill, Rogers 69, 365
*Terror Tales* 107, 110, 112, 113, 114, 116, 121, 132, 136, 173, 233, 316, 351, 367, 401
Teter, Georg E. 213, 359, 404
*They Return at Evening* (Wakefield) 24
*Things to Come* (film) 172, 410
"Thing on the Doorstep, The" (Lovecraft) 49n2, 74, 99, 101, 103–4, 123, 152, 162, 174, 176, 182, 224, 338, 366, 405, 407, 411
"Thirsty Blades" (Kline-Price) 234
Thomas, Norman 262
*Three Who Died* (Derleth) 231
*Thrilling Mystery* 176, 177, 371, 418
"Through the Gates of the Silver Key" (Lovecraft-Price) 19, 69, 70, 72, 74, 76, 89, 93, 130, 133, 223, 379
"'Till A' the Seas'" (Barlow) 7
*Time and the Gods* (Dunsany) 251, 407
"To Mr. Finlay . . ." (Lovecraft) 170n2
*Tobacco Road* (Kirkland) 238, 240
Tolkien, J. R. R. 14

"Tomb, The" (Lovecraft) 34
"Torture-Master, The" (Bloch) 362
"Touch of a Corpse, The" (Bloch) 109, 112, 113, 114
Townsend, Clyde G. 344
Townsend, Francis E. 294n1
"Treasure of Abbot Thomas, The" (James) 24, 312
*Treatise on the Gods* (Mencken) 211
"Tree, The" (Lovecraft) 31, 34, 419
Tremaine, F. Orlin 70, 171, 318, 322, 387
Trotsky, Leon 300
*Tryout* 337, 344
Tsathoggua 29, 142, 223, 228
Tucker, Bob 13
Tugwell, Rexford G. 292
"Two Bottles of Relish, The" (Dunsany) 170
"Ultimate Ultimatum, The" (Bloch) 153n2
"Umbriel" (Wollheim) 363
*Unaussprechlichen Kulten* (Junzt) 187, 223, 377, 380, 391
*Undine* (La Motte Fouqué) 381
Unitarians 272
*United Amateur* 336
United Amateur Press Association 77, 329–30, 332, 336, 353, 369, 390
United Amateur Press Association of America 10, 329–30, 336, 344, 353, 357
"Unknown City in the Ocean, The" (Lovecraft) 111n2, 225n2
"Unnamable, The" (Lovecraft) 342, 388
Untermeyer, Louis 213
*Unusual Stories* 74, 80, 87, 89, 95, 97, 126, 233, 384
Utpatel, Frank 245, 316, 332, 349, 352, 355, 360

*Vagrant* 337
"Vampires of the Moon" (Bernal) 233
Vanguard (publisher) 68, 192
*Vathek* (Beckford) 54, 395
Viereck, George Sylvester 122
Viking Portable Library 15
Villars, abbé de 381
"Visit with H. P. Lovecraft, A" (Bloch) 175n2
Vulcan 255

"Vulthoom" (Smith) 315

Wagenknecht, Edward 15

*Wagner the Wehr-Wolf* (Reynolds) 124

Waite, A. E. 190, 372, 379

Wakefield, H. Russell 24, 62

Walpole, Horace 220

Walpole, Hugh 125

"Wanderer's Return" (Shepherd) 16

*Wandering Jew, The* (film) 152

*Wanderings in Roman Britain* (Weigall) 126

Wandrei, Donald 20, 23, 26–27, 28, 34, 46, 47, 55, 66n3, 70, 94, 113, 122, 124, 144, 146, 151, 155, 159, 170, 225, 227, 229, 238, 243, 258, 314, 316, 322, 342, 384, 388, 399, 412

Wandrei, Howard 96, 97, 101, 113, 124, 125, 138, 151, 155, 160, 227, 232, 233, 316, 326

Warner, Harry, Jr. 11

Washington, George 44, 240, 313

"Way Home, The" (Stern) 322

"Weaver in the Vault, The" (Smith) 78, 93, 97

Weigall, Arthur 126

Weinbaum, Stanley G. 147, 151–52, 164, 166, 207, 278, 396

Weir, John J. 367, 419

"Weird &c. Items in Library of H. P. Lovecraft" 26n6, 38–43

*Weird Tales,* 54, 55, 315, 371; art in, 166, 232, 355, 366, 391–92, 397, 405, 412; and R. H. Barlow, 173, 202–3; and Robert Bloch, 9, 51, 53, 116, 124, 127, 142, 143, 144, 149, 151, 168, 171, 303; and Adolphe de Castro, 214, 343; and August Derleth, 352; and Robert E. Howard, 334, 342, 353, 383; index to, 145, 238, 239, 241, 242, 243, 342; and Henry Kuttner, 165, 178; and Lovecraft, 9, 10, 19, 25, 48, 51, 73–74, 93, 103, 117, 133, 145, 174, 175, 187, 205, 240, 339, 349, 416; Lovecraft rejected by, 27, 89; Lovecraft's copies of, 56, 62, 235, 384; Lovecraft's opinions of, 68, 72, 79, 97, 100, 102, 106, 109, 122, 128, 138, 146, 155, 163, 170, 177, 180, 188, 226, 229, 244, 245, 278–79, 312, 332, 351, 362, 364, 394, 396, 400–401, 419; and Robert Nelson, 11, 221; as pulp mag-

azine, 112, 156, 160, 182, 184, 215–16, 222, 230, 322; and Clark Ashton Smith, 23, 196, 202, 227; and Kenneth Sterling, 13; stories in, 28, 236, 372, 388, 418; writers in, 29, 46, 119, 179, 274, 326, 404, 407

"Weird-Wood" (Bloch) 48

"Weird Work of William Hope Hodgson, The" (Lovecraft) 14, 111n2, 352n2

Weisinger, Mort 176

*Well Bred Speech* (Renshaw) 179n1, 289n1, 398n1

Wellman, Manly Wade 386n2

Wells, G. P. 153

Wells, H. G. 15, 153, 212, 396, 410

*Werewolf of London* (film) 143, 241

*Werewolf of Paris, The* (Endore) 56, 304

"Werewolf of Ponkert, The" (Munn) 50

West Townsend, MA 117

"Western Night" (Wooley) 10

*What Every Woman Knows* (Barrie) 120

"What's the Trouble with Weird Fiction?" (Lovecraft) 14, 156n2

"Whisperer in Darkness, The" (Lovecraft) 226n2

White, Edward Lucas 52, 68

White, Lee, Jr. 353, 356

"White Ape, The" [statue] (Bloch) 105

"White People, The" (Machen) 215, 407

"White Sibyl, The" (Smith) 226, 227

"White Ship, The" (Lovecraft) 27

Whitehead, Henry S. 23, 46, 54, 119, 128, 172, 197, 234n3, 236, 278, 280, 334, 354, 379

Whittemore, Thomas 134

"Wicked Flea, The" (Giesy) 386n2

Widner, A. L. 185

Wiggam, Albert Edward 197

Wilbraham, MA 154–55, 317

Wilcox, Ella Wheeler 197

Wilkes, Charles 325

William (King of Holland) 378

Williams, Charles 114, 115

Williams, Herb 148n5

Williams, Roger 170

Williamson, Jack 402, 411

"Willows, The" (Blackwood) 215, 407, 418

Wilson, Edmund 15

Wilson, Woodrow 290
"Winged Death" (Lovecraft-Heald) 103
Winthrop, Deane 71
*Witch-Cult in Western Europe, The* (Murray)
 190
*Witch's Tales* 180, 364, 365, 367, 401
*Witch Wood* (Buchan) 24, 130
Wollheim, Donald A. 14–15, 16, 153,
 233, 244, 250, 255, 273n2, 280, 299,
 348, 351, 353, 357, 358, 360, 362, 363,
 366, 368, 370, 371, 391, 395
*Wonder Stories* 12, 13, 14, 15, 144, 222,
 233, 249, 336, 338, 348–49
"Wood, The" (Lovecraft) 368
Wooley, George 9
Wooley, Natalie Hartley 9–10, 332
Woolworth, F. W. 123
Wright, Farnsworth: appearance of, 46;
 and R. H. Barlow, 214; and Robert
 Bloch, 48, 72, 73, 107, 109n1, 112,
 121, 126, 132, 136, 139, 145, 147, 153,
 175; and Willis Conover, 405; as edi-
 tor, 56, 68, 97, 108, 110, 118, 133,
137, 143, 156, 160, 170, 173, 182, 184,
 227, 230, 232, 233, 236, 316, 322, 337,
 350, 351, 352, 371, 392; and Robert
 E. Howard, 280, 342, 383, 395; and
 Henry Kuttner, 167; and Lovecraft,
 13, 69, 93, 101, 119, 128, 162, 332,
 384, 395, 398, 403, 411; rejections of
 Lovecraft's stories by, 27, 34, 70, 89,
 225, 245, 332; and Clark Ashton
 Smith, 56, 78
Wright, Wilfred D. [pseud. of Robert
 Nelson] 215, 216n1
Wylie, Philip 184n3
"Xeethra" (Smith) 226
Yaddith 87
Yeb 391, 397
Yog-Sothoth 29, 223, 388, 390–91, 397,
 412
*You'll Need a Night Light* (Thomson) 19
Yuggoth 59, 62, 138
Zothique 99

www.ingramcontent.com/pod-product-compliance
Lightning Source LLC
Chambersburg PA
CBHW070354030726
47504CB00001B/175